# Professional ebXML Foundations

David A. Chappell
Vivek Chopra
Jean-Jacques Dubray
Pim van der Eijk
Colleen Evans
Betty Harvey
Tim McGrath
Duane Nickull
Marcel Noordzij
Bruce Peat
Jan Vegt

*Wrox Press Ltd.* ®

# Professional ebXML Foundations

Published by Wrox Press Ltd,
Arden House, 1102 Warwick Road, Acocks Green,
Birmingham, B27 6BH, UK
Printed in the United States
ISBN 1-861005-90-3

## Trademark Acknowledgements



## Credits

**Authors**
David A. Chappell
Vivek Chopra
Jean-Jacques Dubray
Pim van der Eijk
Colleen Evans
Betty Harvey
Tim McGrath
Duane Nickull
Marcel Noordzij
Bruce Peat
Jan Vegt

**Category Managers**
Simon Cox
Dave Galloway

**Technical Architect**
Dianne Arrow

**Technical Editors**
Chris Mills
Ian Nutt

**Author Agent**
Trish Weir

**Project Manager**
Beckie Stones

**Indexing**
Andrew Criddle

**Technical Reviewers**
Terry Allen
Danny Ayers
Martin Beaulieu
James Britt
Chris Crane
Kevin Farnham
Paul Houle
William Kammerer
Jim MacIntosh
Jonathan Pinnock
Phil Powers-DeGeorge
Andrew Stopford
Dominic Tramontana
Adwait Ullal
Dmitry E. Voytenko

**Production Coordinator**
Pip Wonson

**Production Manager**
Liz Toy

**Figures**
Matt Clark
Emma Eato
Abbie Forletta
Natalie O'Donnell
Pip Wonson

**Cover**
Dawn Chellingworth

**Proof Reader**
Agnes Wiggers

# About the Authors

## David A. Chappell

David is vice president and SonicMQ chief technology evangelist at Progress Software Corp. He has over 18 years' industry experience building software tools and infrastructure for application developers, spanning all aspects of R&D, sales, marketing, and support services. He is co-author of *The Java Message Service*, published by O'Reilly & Associates, and his work has also been published in Network World magazine, XML Journal. He is currently writing a series of contributed articles for the Java Developers Journal. David has presented technical topics at numerous speaking engagements including JavaOne, XMLOne, and XMLDevCon.

As director of engineering for SonicMQ, Progress Software's award-winning JMS Internet Commerce Messaging System, David oversaw the design and development of the fastest and most scalable, reliable, and robust implementation of JMS in the marketplace.

David has under his belt a broad cross-platform background in designing and developing Internet-based middleware and distributed object systems across a wide range of technologies including C++, Java, DCOM, CORBA, and EJB. His experience also includes development of client/server infrastructure, graphical user interfaces, language interpreters, and various utility libraries.

## Vivek Chopra

Vivek has seven years' experience in software design and development, the last two years of which have been in Web Services and various XML technologies. He is the co-author of *Professional XML Web Services* (Wrox Press) and works for Insight Solutions Inc., Cupertino as a senior consultant to HP. He is also the technical lead at HP for the UDDI V2 version of UDDI4J – an open-source Java API for UDDI.

His previous areas of experience and interests include compilers, middleware, clustering and GNU/Linux. In addition, he operates a resource site for Web Services (http://www.soaprpc.com).

Vivek holds a Bachelors' degree in Electronics and a Masters' in Computer Science, both from Pune University, India. He can be reached at vivek@soaprpc.com.

## Jean-Jacques Dubray

"JJ" is Chief Architect at Eigner, Corp. He has contributed to the work of several standard organizations: ebXML BPSS, BPML and the Open Applications Group. He is also the Chief Architect of the STAR/XML (Standard for Technology in the Automotive Retail) project. He has been a member of the Research Staff at Hughes Research Laboratories, and founder of IFE Technologies.

His interests include playing with this two kids, Marie and Matthieu, and traveling to the hamlet of Aquadilici, Corsica, where his family originated. He graduated with a BSc from Ecole Centrale de Lyon and holds a PhD from the University of Marseilles at Luminy. He can be reached at jjd@ep-ag.com.

## *Pim van der Eijk*

Pim has been working with SGML and XML for over a decade, initially while working as a researcher in computational linguistics and later as a technology consultant and project leader with Cap Gemini Ernst and Young. Over the years, his interests and activities have followed the evolution of SGML, historically a standard for document processing, into XML, the universal basis for e-business integration and (mobile) Internet technology. Pim currently has his own consulting company, Sonnenglanz, and works from his home in Maarn, Netherlands, or with customers across Europe.

Aside from his consulting work, Pim serves as European Representative for OASIS, working to increase the active participation of European organizations in the development of XML-based interoperability specifications. He is also an active member of the Netherlands SGML/XML User Group. You can contact him at pvde@sonnenglanz.net.

Pim would like to thank the people who created and contributed to the ebXML specifications; the co-authors of this book; current and previous colleagues, customers and employers, for the opportunity to learn about the topics discussed in this book; the people at Wrox Press, for their enthusiasm and editorial assistance; and Angela, for patience and support.

## *Colleen Evans*

Colleen has over 13 years' industry experience, primarily in areas related to distributed computing and Message-Oriented Middleware (MOM). Her experience includes applications development, architecture, marketing, and product management. Prior to joining Sonic Software, she worked for over 11 years in the travel industry for Covia Corporation, Galileo International, and The Sabre Group, focusing on linking disparate business enterprises and systems.

She has been involved in EDIFACT and XML standards development since 1993. Colleen chaired the International Air Transport Association (IATA) PADIS RES EDIFACT committee and co-chaired the UN/EDIFACT I-EDI working group. She currently participates in the OASIS ebXML Messaging Services Technical Committee, and also participated in the ebXML Transport, Routing, and Packaging Working Group under OASIS and UN/CEFACT sponsorship.

## *Betty Harvey*

As President of Electronic Commerce Connection, Inc., Betty has participated with many Government and commercial enterprises in planning and executing their migration to structured information. Over the past seven years she has developed many SGML and XML solutions for a wide range of clients. Prior to starting ECC, Inc., Betty worked in Scientific and Engineering Computing at David Taylor Model Basin, Navy Systems Weapon Center. At David Taylor, Betty participated in the development of US DoD CALS standards, including IETMs, SGML and Internet protocols. In 1994, she was awarded *Employee of the Year (Engineer/Scientist)*. Betty is the founder and coordinator of the current Washington, DC Area SGML/XML Users Group.

Betty would like to thank her children, Jennifer, John and Meredith for enduring the time she was engrossed in the computer. She would especially like to thank her husband, John, for supporting her goals, keeping her focused and always keeping her humble!

## Tim McGrath

Tim is recognised as a leader in the introduction of Internet technologies to the e-commerce marketplace in Australia. He brings to the field a strong foundation in data analysis and information system design. His qualifications include a Bachelor of Business degree with a major in Information Processing systems.

Most recently, Tim was Quality Review Team Leader for the ebXML initiative, reporting to the Executive Committee, and a member of the ebXML Steering Committee. Before his involvement with ebXML, Tim's exposure was as a user of various e-commerce standards. Taking these specifications and turning them into workable solutions has given him a valuable insight into the appropriateness, relevance and practicality of this work.

Tim sold his software company in May 2001, and he is now concentrating on a career in fiction writing. To keep himself amused he also lectures on e-commerce and is still trying to learn the piano.

Tim would like to acknowledge the many hundreds of quiet achievers (and some of the noisy ones as well) who made the ebXML project a milestone in standards development. Specifically, he must thank the heterogeneous band of mavericks that comprised the Quality Review team.

## Duane Nickull

Duane is a co-founder of XML Global Technologies, Inc. and shares responsibility for the company's overall technology direction. He is a co-inventor of the first context-sensitive XML Search Engine, GoXML, and the first web-based XML e-Commerce ASP.

In addition to his work with XML Global Technologies, Inc., he is also the Technical Director for XSLT.com and participates in a number of standards bodies including UDDI and OAG. Duane was the co-leader/editor of the Technical Architecture team for ebXML, and is currently Chair of the UN/CEFACT ebTWG eBusiness Architecture group. Duane is well known as a regular contributor of technical articles to a wide variety of established industry publications.

## Marcel Noordzij

Marcel is a management consultant who currently works for Software AG. He has a solid technical background both as an architect and developer in several settings, from client-server to multi-tier applications, using several languages and on a multitude of platforms. His passion and main area of expertise is with enterprise application integration – both from the technical and business sides.

For the last couple of years, Marcel has been focussing on the application of XML in almost every XML application scenario you can think of. He, and his team at Software AG, support their customers throughout their projects with both expertise and advice, as with hands-on tooling and coding.

Marcel enjoys and is involved in sport in the same way that he involves himself in all other activities: his definition of sport is "if you're not completely exhausted afterwards, then it's not a sport but a hobby". In the same manner, Marcel is both admired and feared for his views on all sorts of issues: you may not like his answers, but he will always give you 200% worth of effort and output.

## Bruce Peat

Bruce assisted the ebXML initiative in several areas, sharing his implementation experiences and the vision of the XML/EDI Group, an organization which he co-founded in 1997 and which brought XML to the e-business industry. Bruce is also co-author of the popular Wrox title *Professional XML.*

When he's not working as Director of Consulting at XML Global Technologies, a company foremost known for implementing successful ebXML solutions, Bruce can be found on the beach with his wife, Susan and three children; Jennifer, Caroline, and Isaac.

Bruce can be reached at Bruce.Peat@xmlglobal.com.

## Jan Vegt

Jan works as an XML consultant for a leading XML vendor. Analysis and problem-solving are his favourite activities and there are several application areas he uses as an outlet for this interest. He prefers to be found at the interface of customer problems and software solutions, where he is constantly amazed by the scope and breadth of problems solved daily by customers.

Jan has a broad and deep interest in several subjects in computer science and beyond. He is a big fan of *Miffy*, the children's book character of Dick Bruna, and hopes that one day the clearness of his analysis can match this "less is more" approach. When Jan isn't travelling to experience the creations of his favourite Spanish architect, Santiago Calatrava, you will almost certainly find him near a computer. Perhaps he'll be at home surrounded by his collection of vintage Apple Macs, playing his favourite game, *Civilization.* Or he may be checking out the life and activities of computer pioneers he admires, like Peter Luhn, Douglas Englebart or Alan Kay.

Jan has a background in information retrieval and is passionately interested in digital preservation. This is how he found out about SGML, the precursor of XML, and which started his interest in markup languages in the early 1990s. He is one of the few XML consultants around who has worked practically with STEP/EXPRESS, the markup language for product data used in the automotive and aerospace industry. Within XML there are only a few subjects he is not interested in, although he always hopes for new ways and technologies that actually make things simpler.

# Table of Contents

## SECTION 3: REPOSITORY AND REGISTRY

MLFoundationsProfessionalebXMLFoundations

# Introduction

The ebXML initiative was an 18-month project, concluded in May 2001, to develop a set of specifications for electronic business interoperability. It is one of the most ambitious and important specification development efforts in its field in recent times, and it has arguably been a key project for the two organizations that started and managed it: **OASIS**, a member-based organization comprised of companies working in the area of XML and interoperability specifications, and **UN/CEFACT**, an organization that has been driving the development of international standards in the area of Electronic Data Interchange (EDI).

Several hundreds of people have been actively involved in ebXML as contributors to the distributed, multinational development teams that worked on the specifications, and several thousands of people were subscribed to one or more of the mailing lists through which the teams communicated and obtained feedback on their drafts. These developers collectively represent many decades of experience in a variety of disciplines, and this experience is visible in the e-business framework the project has produced.

At the time of publication of this book, several software implementations of (parts of) the ebXML framework are already available, and more will follow as activities progress. These implementations allow you to start developing ebXML solutions, and this book is here to help you build up the background knowledge you need to get up to speed with ebXML. At the same time, work on ebXML continues within working groups at OASIS and within UN/CEFACT, both on improving existing specifications and on providing additional, complementary e-business interoperability specifications. As authors of this book, we believe that ebXML is a major step forward and will have a significant impact on the e-business industry. We've written this book to help accelerate that process, and are inviting you to join.

## What Does This Book Cover?

This is a book for programmers and other developers interested in learning about ebXML and who want to be able to apply ebXML technology in practical projects. It covers all of the initial ebXML specifications, provides additional background information and illustration, and covers some additional topics that extend or complement ebXML.

While the ebXML specification documents are the only official reference for ebXML, this book offers a complete, self-contained overview of all the approved specifications of the ebXML project and some of the work that resulted in technical reports. We also provide introductory, background, or contextual information without which some of these specifications would be hard to follow: for example an introduction to business process modeling helps in the understanding of the business process specification schema, and a discussion of SOAP is necessary for ebXML messaging. Some related relevant work done outside the ebXML framework, either complementary or competing, is discussed too. This is the case with, for example, UDDI, WSFL, and XLANG.

We've also highlighted the interrelations between the various components that make up ebXML, information that isn't always easy to find in the specifications themselves. We've also added our own commentary where the specifications seem incomplete or unfinished. In some sections, we provide references to, or use examples from, a realistic case study that shows how you could use the various parts of ebXML in a practical situation. There is also one additional, self-contained chapter dedicated to a real-life application of ebXML.

While the book touches on them, it does not attempt to provide full coverage of Web Services, vertical XML applications, specific vendor solutions, implementation strategies, ebXML project management, and the broader area of e-business systems modeling, analysis, and design.

## Who Is This Book for?

This book is of interest to anyone professionally involved at a technical level in designing and developing ebXML-based systems, solutions, and implementations. This includes programmers, designers, and software architects. Our emphasis has been to provide programmers with all the detailed knowledge needed to understand and apply the ebXML specifications.

Currently, ebXML is still a fairly new topic, and it is likely to be of interest to quite a broad audience, including analysts, (technology) consultants, and IT managers, many of whom are or will be assessing the relevance or importance of ebXML for their (customers') business or technical requirements.

This is not an introductory book on XML, so if you are new to XML and surrounding standards like XSLT and XML Schemas, you should consider reading an introductory or advanced XML title first, such as the *Beginning XML* or *Professional XML* titles in this series (ISBN 1-861005-59-8 and 1-861005-05-9 respectively). We also assume that you are familiar with general web and e-business technology, concepts, and jargon.

We will provide basic introductions to some technologies that form the basis of the ebXML specifications, such as XML schema languages, SOAP, UML notation, and modeling methodologies, to the extent that they are needed or useful when you are working with ebXML technology.

## What You Need To Use This Book

The different chapters of the book require you to download several free programs and accessories, depending on which client language you're dealing with at the time. It would be unhelpful to mention all of these downloads at this point, as they are detailed in their respective chapters.

The code included in this book can be downloaded from http://www.wrox.com/. More details are given in the *Customer Support* section.

## How Is This Book Structured?

This book is organized into seven sections, containing chapters that discuss related topics. The order of these is such that if you read the book sequentially from cover to cover, the introductory chapters largely precede the more advanced topics that build on them. In some cases, such as CPP/CPA and BPSS, the specifications are strongly interrelated, with cross-references that you may want to follow to fully understand the subject.

The sections are:

- Section 1 (Chapters 1–4) covers foundation material, introducing the **ebXML framework**. It provides a historical introduction to ebXML, discusses the context in which it was started, and covers the larger landscape of XML-based e-business standards and e-business integration technology. This section also contains three introductory chapters on pre-requisite topics. One discusses UMM, an object-oriented methodology for modeling and structuring e-business projects that will help you understand the business process specifications chapters. That chapter also introduces a sample case used in several chapters of the book. Another provides an introduction to modeling business document structure, and the third describes SOAP, upon which ebXML messaging is based.
- Section 2 (Chapters 5–6) discusses **business processes** and collaborations. It covers the ebXML Business Process Specification Schema, as well as the wider field of business process management systems, and the standards developed to support them.
- Section 3 (Chapters 7–9) is concerned with **registries, repositories, and protocol agreements**. This section covers the process of discovering business partners and setting up trading agreements. This section also contains a chapter on UDDI, a related initiative.
- Section 4 (Chapters 10–12) discusses the actual content of **business messages**, with chapters on Core Components, reusable XML vocabularies, and XML representations of EDIFACT messages.
- Section 5 (Chapters 13–14) is dedicated to **messaging services**. This section shows how ebXML messaging builds on top of SOAP. It also provides a chapter on advanced implementations using ebXML with the Java Message Service and the Java API for XML Messaging.
- Section 6 (Chapter 15) focuses on **security**, a critical and complex subject matter that any e-business infrastructure needs to take into consideration.
- Section 7 (Chapter 16) is a self-contained discussion of a real-life application of ebXML to a permit application system.

The book includes appendices that explain some of the UML diagramming techniques, and provide bibliographic information.

# Section 1: Foundations

**Chapter 1: Introduction to ebXML**
**Pim van der Eijk**
Chapter 1 introduces the ebXML framework, describing the history of the project and the organizations involved, the components making up ebXML and their current status. We review the topics of application integration and middleware, and show how ebXML fits into e-business architecture patterns.

**Chapter 2: e-Business Methodology and Process Modeling**
**Pim van der Eijk**
In Chapter 2 we look at modeling business processes and developing business process descriptions such that ebXML-compliant tools can be used for implementation. This includes an introduction to UML and UMM (modeling language and methodology). Both are demonstrated using a sample use case (preparing for export in an international purchase and supply scenario), which is used for illustration purposes in several subsequent chapters.

**Chapter 3: e-Business Document Modeling**
**Betty Harvey**
A well-designed data model can increase the effectiveness of business activities. Chapter 3 discusses best practices for modeling business documents, including issues to be considered at the analysis and design stages. We also consider the advantages and disadvantages of using DTDs and XML Schemas for representing the model.

**Chapter 4: SOAP**
**Marcel Noordzij and Jan Vegt**
Messaging in ebXML is based on SOAP (Simple Object Access Protocol). For readers with little or no previous SOAP knowledge, this chapter provides a thorough introduction to messaging with SOAP. We look at the history of SOAP, the format of SOAP messages, SOAP Messages With Attachments, and transporting SOAP over HTTP. To demonstrate its use, we build a simple SOAP client and server application.

# Section 2: Business Processes

**Chapter 5: The ebXML Business Process Specification Schema (BPSS)**
**JJ Dubray**
ebXML includes a specification, BPSS, for defining shared views of the messages which are to be exchanged between trading partners. In Chapter 5 we introduce the core concepts of business transactions/collaborations, and show how to use BPSS to capture and communicate business processes in a machine-readable and unambiguous way. We also look at the role of a business service interface, which sits between the messaging service and the application, enforcing the process specifications.

**Chapter 6: Implementing BPSS**
**JJ Dubray**
Chapter 6 provides further details of implementing BPSS, focusing on the architecture of business process management systems for communicating in a distributed computing scenario. We also look at how BPSS relates to other existing business process standards such as BPML, XLANG, and WSFL.

## Section 3: Repository and Registry

**Chapter 7: ebXML Registry/Repository**
**Bruce Peat**
A core part of any electronic trading system involves discovery of potential business partners. ebXML provides a repository where business information can be stored, and registry services for accessing and using the repository. Chapter 7 describes the purpose of both registry and repository, discusses hosting your own, and shows how to implement or interface with a registry/repository system.

**Chapter 8: Collaboration Protocol Profiles and Agreements**
**Pim van der Eijk**
Any organization or department wishing to take part in electronic trading and wanting to find new partners needs a means of specifying what services they offer – this is implemented in ebXML using collaboration protocol profiles (CPPs). When two bodies agree to trade, a collaboration protocol agreement (CPA) is created. This chapter covers both aspects, showing how to structure CPPs and form CPAs, and various adoption strategies for making the transition to a CPP/CPA-based implementation.

**Chapter 9: UDDI**
**Vivek Chopra**
ebXML is a relatively immature technology but one which can be implemented as a series of modules – meaning that investments in earlier standards can be incorporated into the overall solution. UDDI is an alternative initiative to the ebXML registry/repository, and the subject of Chapter 9. We look at UDDI data structures, APIs, and current implementations, and demonstrate publishing and searching information in a UDDI registry. We also compare UDDI to an ebXML registry/repository and discuss how both approaches can be integrated.

## Section 4: Core Components and Payload Standards

**Chapter 10: ebXML Core Components**
**Duane Nickull**
Core components are reusable pieces of business information from which business document schemas can be assembled, according to context rules. Although the work on core components is still at a very early stage, this chapter discusses how to build reusable core components and demonstrates building a business document template from a core component fragment and a context rules message.

**Chapter 11: Other Standards for Payload**
**Tim McGrath**
Core components require further work, and it is very likely that other payloads will continue to be used for some time. Chapter 11 describes several of these alternative, non-ebXML, payload standards, both XML-based (OAGI, RosettaNet, xCBL, UBL) and EDI-based (UN/EDIFACT, ANSI ASC X12). We consider the integrity and interoperability of messages written in these standards and discuss how a solution can be implemented using a mixture of these payloads.

**Chapter 12: Using XML/EDI Message Payload Content**
**Pim van der Eijk**
Following on from the previous chapter, Chapter 12 takes a closer look at EDIFACT message syntax and discusses approaches to take if you are moving towards an ebXML system. ebXML messaging services support transport of EDI messages – alternatively an XML encoding can be used, and in this chapter we look at XEDI and an alternative approach developed by the European XML/EDI project. The main focus of the chapter is an example of creating DTD and XML instance documents based on an existing EDIFACT message.

## Section 5: Messaging

**Chapter 13: ebXML Messaging**
**Marcel Noordzij and Jan Vegt**
ebXML Messaging Services (ebXML MS) provides all of the services needed for business document exchange. As this chapter explains, ebXML MS builds upon SOAP, adding reliability and security. Chapter 13 is a comprehensive study of the message service handler, message structure, and the interfaces and services provided. We also build an application to demonstrate the implementation of one of the services.

**Chapter 14: Java Messaging Protocols**
**David A. Chappell and Colleen Evans**
In Chapter 14 we describe and demonstrate two other standards for messaging – Java Message Service (JMS) and Java API for XML Messaging (JAXM). We discuss how they can be used to support and enhance ebXML Messaging Services.

## Section 6: Security

**Chapter 15: e-Business Security**
**Marcel Noordzij and Jan Vegt**
Security is an important concern in any system, and in Chapter 15 we look at the security risks and counter-measures pertinent to electronic business applications. We start by discussing general security technologies such as encryption, integrity checksums, digital certificates, and certification. Then we look at XML technologies such as SAML, XACML, XML Digital Signatures, and XKMS. Finally we consider each aspect of an ebXML solution and demonstrate specific security measures which can be taken to protect the organization and its data.

## Section 7: Case Study

**Chapter 16: Implementing ebXML**
**Duane Nickull**
In this case study we look at a real-world implementation of ebXML, discussing how ebXML was used and how gaps in the ebXML specifications at the time were and could have been filled. The case study proves that it is possible to develop a functioning, interoperable, and flexible ebXML implementation and provides plenty of advice for implementing your own solution.

## The Appendices

**Appendix A: UML Diagram Reference**
Gives examples of each type of UML diagram, many of which are used throughout the book.

**Appendix B: Resources**
Lists suggested further reading, provides details of references made throughout the book, briefly describes each of the ebXML specifications, technical documents, and whitepapers available from the ebXML project, and identifies where they can be downloaded from.

# Conventions

To help you get the most from the text and keep track of what's happening, we've used a number of conventions throughout the book.

For instance:

> **These boxes hold important, not-to-be forgotten information, which is directly relevant to the surrounding text.**

*By contrast, this indented italicized style is used for asides to the current discussion.*

As for styles in the text:

- When we introduce them, we **highlight** important words
- We show keyboard strokes like this: *Ctrl-A*
- We show filenames, and code within the text, like this: `sample.xml`
- Text on user interfaces is shown like this: File | Save
- URLs are shown in a similar font for example: http://www.wrox.com/
- Namespace URIs, however, are shown like this: `http://www.w3.org/2001/XMLSchema`
- When referring to a chapter section or title, like the *Introduction*, we italicize it

We present code in two different ways. Code that is new or important is shown as so:

```
In our code examples, the code foreground style shows
new, important, and pertinent code
```

Code that is an aside, or has been seen before is shown as so:

```
Code background shows code that's less important in the present context,
or that has been seen before.
```

In addition, when something is to be typed at a command line interface (for example, a DOS/Command prompt), then we use the following style to show what is typed:

**> set WSTK_HOME=c:\wstk-2.3**

# Customer Support

We always value hearing from our readers, and we want to know what you think about this book: what you liked, what you didn't like, and what you think we can do better next time. You can send us your comments, either by returning the reply card in the back of the book, or by e-mail to feedback@wrox.com. Please be sure to mention the book title in your message.

## How To Download the Sample Code for the Book

When you log on to the Wrox site http://www.wrox.com/, simply locate the title through our Search facility or by using one of the title lists. Click on Download in the Code column, or on Download Code on the book's detail page.

The files that are available for download from our site have been archived using WinZip. When you have saved the attachments to a folder on your hard-drive, you need to extract the files using a de-compression program such as WinZip or PKUnzip. When you extract the files, the code is usually extracted into chapter folders. When you start the extraction process, ensure your software (WinZip, PKUnzip, etc.) is set to extract to Use Folder Names.

## Errata

We've made every effort to make sure that there are no errors in the text or in the code. However, no one is perfect and mistakes do occur. If you find an error in one of our books, like a spelling mistake or a faulty piece of code, we would be very grateful for feedback. By sending in errata you may save another reader hours of frustration, and of course, you will be helping us provide even higher quality information. Simply e-mail the information to support@wrox.com, your information will be checked and if correct, posted to the errata page for that title, or used in subsequent editions of the book.

To find errata on the web site, log on to http://www.wrox.com/, and simply locate the title through our Advanced Search or title list. Click on the Book Errata link, which is below the cover graphic on the book's detail page.

## E-mail Support

If you wish to directly query a problem in the book page with an expert who knows the book in detail then e-mail support@wrox.com, with the title of the book and the last four numbers of the ISBN in the subject field of the e-mail. A typical e-mail should include the following things:

- The **name**, **last four digits of the ISBN**, and **page number** of the problem in the Subject field.
- Your **name**, **contact information**, and the **problem** in the body of the message.

We **won't** send you junk mail. We need the details to save your time and ours. When you send an e-mail message, it will go through the following chain of support:

- Customer Support – Your message is delivered to one of our customer support staff, who are the first people to read it. They have files on most frequently asked questions and will answer anything general about the book or the web site immediately.
- Editorial – Deeper queries are forwarded to the technical editor responsible for that book. They have experience with the programming language or particular product, and are able to answer detailed technical questions on the subject. Once an issue has been resolved, the editor can post the errata to the web site.
- The Authors – Finally, in the unlikely event that the editor cannot answer your problem, he or she will forward the request to the author. We do try to protect the author from any distractions to their writing, however, we are quite happy to forward specific requests to them. All Wrox authors help with the support on their books. They will mail the customer and the editor with their response, and again all readers should benefit.

The Wrox Support process can only offer support to issues that are directly pertinent to the content of our published title. Support for questions that fall outside the scope of normal book support, is provided via the community lists of our http://p2p.wrox.com/ forum.

## p2p.wrox.com

For author and peer discussion join the P2P mailing lists. Our unique system provides **programmer to programmer™** contact on mailing lists, forums, and newsgroups, all **in addition** to our one-to-one e-mail support system. Be confident that your query is being examined by the many Wrox authors and other industry experts who are present on our mailing lists. At p2p.wrox.com you will find a number of different lists that will help you, not only while you read this book, but also as you develop your own applications.

To subscribe to a mailing list just follow these steps:

1. Go to http://p2p.wrox.com/.
2. Choose the appropriate category from the left menu bar.
3. Click on the mailing list you wish to join.
4. Follow the instructions to subscribe and fill in your e-mail address and password.
5. Reply to the confirmation e-mail you receive.
6. Use the subscription manager to join more lists and set your mail preferences.

# 1

# Introduction To ebXML

In various presentations and reports, analysts such as the Gartner group have described the evolution in e-business as a movement from tactical applications with limited scope towards increasingly strategic e-business initiatives. Up to around 1995, information technology in most organizations was only used to support internal business applications, often at departmental level. Network connectivity in general was limited to being used within the enterprise. From the mid-1990s until the end of that decade, with the arrival of widespread Internet use, the focus broadened to include direct web-based business-to-consumer (B2C) applications.

At the same time, companies increasingly started supporting external electronic commerce transactions with traditional business partners in their value chains. They invested heavily in **Enterprise Resource Planning** (**ERP**) software solutions (from vendors like BAAN, PeopleSoft and SAP) to replace legacy departmental systems. These systems now provide the backbone for most (if not all) of their enterprise applications in use in larger companies, and increasingly include extended facilities for electronic commerce, customer relationship management, and supply chain management.

The challenge for this next century is to open up these enterprise systems, and the business applications used in small and medium-size enterprises, and to integrate them into a multi-enterprise **collaborative commerce** framework, based on interactions between businesses operating within "a single global electronic marketplace where enterprises of any size and in any geographical location can meet and conduct business with each other" (in the words of the ebXML executive white paper, found at http://www.ebxml.org/white_papers/whitepaper.htm).

The **ebXML framework** fits very well in this vision of collaborative commerce and can be viewed as a set of specifications that (again quoting the ebXML white paper) "together enable a modular, yet complete electronic business framework" for collaborative commerce. As ebXML is further developed, adopted in the market, and supported by compliant e-business middleware software, off-the-shelf software for vertical (industry-specific) or horizontal (cross-industry) applications, systems integration services, as well as complementary specifications, it will enable such a global marketplace to be built.

In this chapter we'll provide an introduction to the ebXML framework, both by example and in relation to the more general topic of business-to-business (B2B) integration. This chapter includes the following sections:

- We'll start with a brief description of the project in which the ebXML specifications were developed: its structure, the organizations that were involved, and the status of ebXML-related activities now that the project has been completed.
- Then we'll discuss a typical complete e-business scenario that ebXML supports, and use this scenario to provide a brief introduction to the main components that make up ebXML.
- Next, we'll position ebXML in the context of the state-of-the-art in e-business application architectures, showing how it supports high-level e-business application integration applications and modern e-business architecture "patterns". We'll provide plenty of background to application integration and middleware technology for the benefit of readers who are (relatively) new to the topic.
- The next section will show that ebXML is more than just a state-of-the-art framework of e-business interoperability specifications, but that it provides support for developing lower-cost, more flexible e-business systems that may increase the applicability of ebXML to small and medium-sized organizations.
- The final section provides a summary, some additional scenarios, and a forward reference to some of the other chapters in this book.

# The ebXML Project

The ebXML framework, as delivered in the summer of 2001, is the result of a specific project that has been completed; there is no ebXML organization, not even a virtual organization. Instead, ebXML represents a collaborative effort of two organizations, their members and supporters:

- The **United Nations Center for Trade Facilitation and Electronic Business** (**UN/CEFACT**, http://www.uncefact.org/) – a global organization responsible for worldwide policy and technical development in the area of trade facilitation and electronic business for trade facilitation. It is well known for delivering the UN/EDIFACT framework for **Electronic Data Interchange** (**EDI**).
- **OASIS** (http://www.oasis-open.org/) – a not-for-profit, member-based consortium that identifies, builds, and maintains industry-standard specifications for interoperability. OASIS has a strong background in providing a forum for developers and vendors to identify and resolve interoperability issues regarding SGML/XML software products. OASIS is also home to the XML.org portal (http://www.xml.org/), a registry for XML Schemas and XML news source geared toward industry, and to Robin Cover's *Cover Pages*, the authoritative web-based bibliography for SGML/XML related matters (http://xml.coverpages.org/).

Background, purpose, and scope of the ebXML project are described in the invitation letter sent out in 1999 to potential participants in the ebXML project, (which can be viewed by checking out http://www.ebxml.org/documents/199909/ebXML_invitation.htm), and in the ebXML terms of reference document (http://www.ebxml.org/documents/199909/terms_of_reference.htm). These documents identify two main issues that ebXML set out to address as it was initiated:

- At the time, XML was emerging as the technology of choice for the exchange of structured information over the Web, including business transaction related information. As a Web-based technology, XML was felt to offer opportunities for small and medium-size enterprises (SMEs), developing countries, and economies in transition, which had been unable to benefit from the traditional EDI frameworks.
- The downside of the successful adoption of XML was a proliferation of XML-based specifications, many of which are overlapping, thus causing confusion and unnecessary duplication of efforts among users.

In this context, ebXML was intended to offer (to quote from the terms of reference document) an "open technical framework to enable XML to be utilized in a consistent and uniform manner for the exchange of electronic business data in application-to-application, application-to-person and person-to-application environments". In addition to developing a framework for XML-based e-business, the project was chartered to analyze current e-business and data interchange processes and issues, and to provide an assessment of the advantages and disadvantages of utilizing XML.

The ebXML project was organized as an executive committee, a steering committee, and a number of project teams working on specific topics:

- Requirements
- Registry/repository
- Business process
- Core components
- Trading partner agreements
- Quality review
- Technical architecture
- Proof of concept
- Transport, routing and packaging
- Marketing, awareness and education
- Security

Leaving aside the more general project-related topics (such as quality and marketing), these working groups cover specific functional parts of the ebXML framework, or aspects (such as architecture and security) that relate to the framework as a whole. We'll touch upon the results of these groups in this chapter, with further chapters dedicated to them later in the book.

The ebXML project involved over 300 active participants working in the various teams, and over 4000 subscribers to mailing lists. The project had its first meeting in November 1999; this was followed by a series of quarterly meetings. The final meeting took place in May 2001 in Vienna, Austria. At this meeting, the project delivered some 25 documents, all of which are available for download from the project's web site, http://www.ebxml.org/.

At the project completion stage it was clear that, although an impressive amount of work had been delivered, additional work would be needed in all areas. The two founding organizations agreed on a Memorandum of Understanding regarding future work on ebXML. Organizationally, OASIS and UN/CEFACT decided to maintain joint committees for coordination, architecture, and marketing activities, and to divide the technical work areas between them. OASIS Technical Committees have since focused on infrastructure-related activities. These include messaging, protocol collaboration, registry and repository, interoperability, implementation, and conformance. Business content-related work has continued within UN/CEFACT, with business collaborations and core components as ongoing work items.

The ebXML project has managed to obtain endorsements from some of the major e-business initiatives. These endorsements indicate that ebXML has indeed become a credible core e-business framework on top of which other (horizontal or vertical) initiatives can build:

- **RosettaNet** is an e-business standardization initiative in the high tech industry. As an early adopter of XML and in the absence of horizontal frameworks, RosettaNet had to develop its own messaging framework as part of its **RosettaNet Implementation Framework** (**RNIF**). RosettaNet has decided to incorporate the ebXML messaging specification into future versions of RNIF and acknowledges that ebXML offers significant complementary functionality in the areas of registries and trading partner agreements. (You can read the full story by following a link to the press release news page at http://www.rosettanet.org/).

- The **Open Applications Group (OAG)** is the largest XML-based horizontal e-business framework. The OAG has decided to integrate the ebXML specifications into the 182 business transaction standards currently published by the organization (http://www.openapplications.org/news/010730.htm).

- The **Open Travel Alliance (OTA)** is an initiative to develop standards for the travel industry. Applications standardized by the OTA include those in airline and car rental industries, for example for requesting availability or booking reservations, as well as for booking holiday tours. The OTA has endorsed ebXML in the most recent versions of its specifications (http://www.ebxml.org/news/pr_20010801.htm).

- **Covisint** is one of the best-known and successful digital marketplaces in the world. Founded by some of the world's major automotive companies, Covisint supports very large-scale procurement processes in the automotive industry (http://www.covisint.com/). Covisint is currently expanding its services to become an application service provider for supply chain management services. Covisint has announced public support for ebXML (http://www.covisint.com/about/pressroom/pr/ebxml.shtml).

- The **Global Commerce Initiative (GCI)** is an international standardization consortium for companies in the consumer goods industry, supported by the major players in this industry (go to http://www.globalcommerceinitiative.org/ for more information). The GCI announced plans to use ebXML as the backbone for its new data exchange standard for B2B trade in the consumer goods industry (http://www.ebxml.org/news/pr_20000911.htm).

Announcements like these are evidence that ebXML has achieved its objective of helping vertical or horizontal e-business initiatives by providing functionality that is common to all such initiatives, such as messaging, partner agreements, registries and repositories, and business processes. With ebXML this is standard functionality that more specialized initiatives can build upon, and for which there is no longer any need to develop proprietary mechanisms.

Various vendors, many of whom are OASIS members, are currently working on products that support parts of ebXML, and some have released (beta) versions in late 2001. We'll refrain from mentioning any of these, as this is an area where developments are particularly subject to change. The ebXML project site, http://www.ebxml.org/, is dedicated to maintaining an up-to-date listing of ebXML-related software.

# Overview of the ebXML Framework

Now that we've discussed the background to the project that resulted in the ebXML framework, we'll look at the components that make up the framework. We'll achieve this by working through a typical situation that will become one of multiple ways of using ebXML-compliant solutions as the ebXML framework gets more widely adopted. This situation has the virtue of including all components in a single scenario, and has been used in various presentations by the ebXML project team.

After we've presented the scenario we'll summarize the main components of ebXML.

## A Sample Scenario for ebXML

Consider the case depicted in the following figure. We will discuss each numbered step in turn:

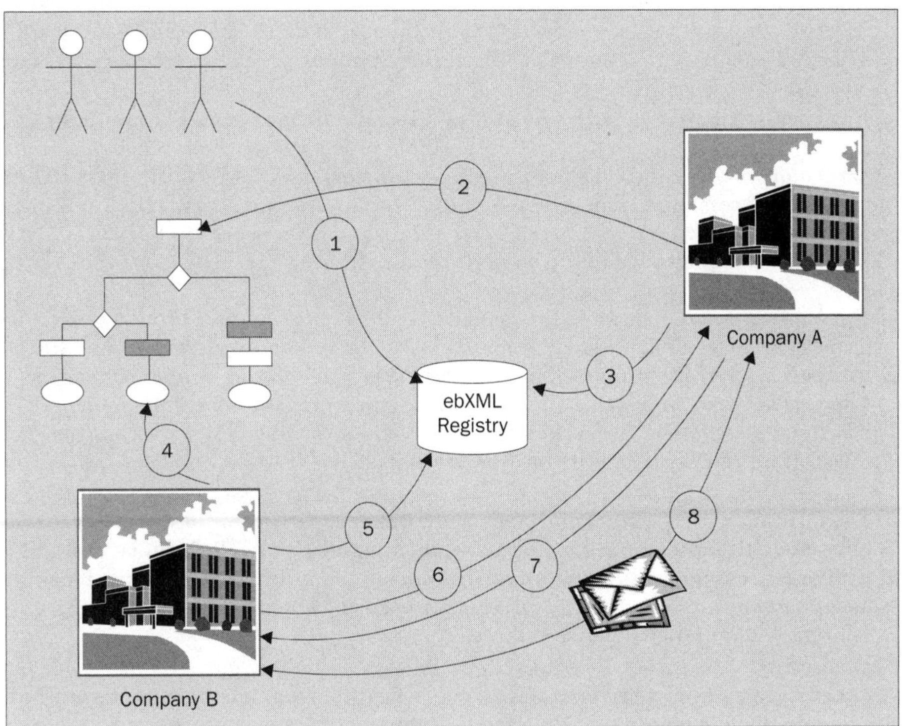

1. As a first step, a project team will analyze a particular B2B process in order to enable organizations to engage in e-business interactions that implement this process. This project team may be a vertical industry standardization initiative, or a project initiated by one or several business partners. The project team may adopt an e-business methodology, such as the **UN/CEFACT Modeling Methodology** (**UMM**; see Chapter 2), to structure this analysis, but this is not essential.

   In any case, the results of their work will be a formal description of the process encoded according to the **ebXML Business Process Specification Schema** (**BPSS**; see Chapter 5 for more on this). This description will reference certain **roles** that partners may fulfill and will consist of a number of choreographed business transaction **activities**. For instance, in the business of international shipping, there will be a company that acts as an 'Exporter', a 'Freight Forwarder', and 'Customs', and they will perform activities such as 'Make Shipment Reservation', 'Obtain Export License', etc. See Chapter 2 for a more detailed example.

   As part of this work, the project team will look at the types of business information that need to be exchanged in these activities. The **ebXML Core Components** framework (see Chapter 10) may be used for this purpose, or other types of "payload" content can be adopted (see Chapters 11 and 12).

   Once completed, the project team can store this BPSS representation, its documentation, and any core components needed to implement it in an **ebXML-compliant repository**, and make it available through an **ebXML registry** (both of which are covered in Chapter 7).

2. A particular company that wants to expand its electronic business can use the ebXML registry's search functionality to find business processes in which it can perform a particular role. For instance, an insurance company may find the international shipping business process (modeled at Step 1 of this scenario) and determine that it wants to sell its shipping insurance services here. To do so, it should see what kind of ebXML message interactions it needs to support to perform the 'Insurer' role in this process.

   Once this is done, it also needs to make sure it can support this process, which will probably require development of interfaces to its backend systems, or modification of the backend systems themselves. The company can provide such support in various ways, for example using its in-house staff, contracting an external systems integrator, or investigating whether the backend systems vendor or other software company has an off-the-shelf e-business "adaptor" for this process.

3. The insurance company can formally state its capability to fulfill its role in the international shipping business in a document known as a **collaboration protocol profile** (**CPP**; see Chapter 8). In addition to referencing the business process document, this document encodes much more information – such as message payload packing information, and digital signatures.

4. Other companies can browse the registry to find relevant business processes. For example, the diagram might illustrate a company that wants to export and to have its goods insured during transport. This is similar to Step 2.

5. Once this company has found the same business process, it can start a search for business partners that offer complementary services (in this case, insurance). It will then find the CPP registered in Step 3 and find the insurance company that registered it.

6. The exporting company now needs to make sure its B2B integration product supports the ebXML framework and that its back-end system can be integrated with it to fulfill its role. This process will yield information similar to the one encoded by the insurance company in its CPP. The exporter can create a proposal for a trading partner agreement, called a **collaboration protocol agreement** (**CPA**, also discussed in Chapter 8) and propose this to the insurer directly.

   It can also create and register a CPP of its own, but this is not strictly necessary. If it did, you could imagine third party "match-making" agents that would assist in the business partner discovery process.

   A CPA does not cover all aspects the companies may want to agree on, and there will probably be some additional paperwork to be settled. The CPA may reference such a mutually agreed contract.

7. The insurance company can agree with this proposal or reply to it with a counter-proposal. There may be several iterations of Steps 6 and 7.

   Once there is an agreement, companies can configure their systems and make other internal preparations needed to support the business interactions controlled by the CPA.

8. Instances of the business collaboration agreed upon in the CPA can now be started as long as the CPA remains valid. The messages exchanged here and in the other interactions can use the facilities of the **ebXML messaging services** (discussed in Chapter 13.)

This completes the sample scenario. To further whet your appetite, here are some additional scenarios and enhancements:

- Software engineering tools or business modeling tools could support ebXML and offer an integrated development environment, including graphical process modeling tools that support the creation of BPSS, CPP, and CPA documents.
- Other development tools, perhaps integrated with the modeling tools just mentioned or with an application server, could offer code generation based on CPA and BPSS documents.
- Some software products that interact with information servers on the Internet may build on top of the ebXML infrastructure. For example, consider a home banking product distributed by a bank to its customers. This product could use an implicit CPA, which is created when the user fills out a set of forms as part of the installation process and finally presses the "OK" button that both signals agreement with the license terms and conditions of use, and completes the configuration information. This would then cause the software to send an initial message to the bank that results in the service being activated.

Hopefully this book will provide you with enough information and inspiration to start designing and implementing e-business scenarios that are at least as exciting as the ones we could think of at the time we wrote this book, when ebXML was still a very new technology and when the developer community had just started to explore its possibilities.

## Overview of ebXML Framework Components

We've already discussed the main components of the ebXML framework, in the scenario section above. They are summarized here for convenience:

- **Business Process Specification Schema**: BPSS is an XML-based specification language that formally defines "public" business processes. It focuses on the collaboration of trading partners, the binary collaborations that these trading partners are engaged in bilaterally (that is, in pairs), and the business transaction activities they perform in the context of those collaborations (see Chapter 5 for discussion). The BPSS is strongly influenced by UMM, a modeling methodology developed by UN/CEFACT (discussed in Chapter 2), but does not require it.
- **Core Components**: these provide the business information that is encoded in business documents that are exchanged between business partners. As components, you should be able to assemble these core components from public or private registries into structures, thus re-using common business structures and eliminating overlap. Core components are tagged with universal identifiers and facilitate multilingual environments. The work on core components did not obtain the formal label of "ebXML specification", and is currently being worked on as part of the follow-on activities (see Chapter 10 for discussion).
- **Registry/Repository**: the ebXML registry/repository deliverables specify a general-purpose repository that is useful for more than merely conducting business searches. Some scenarios, including our example scenario, depend heavily on registries to support setting up business relationships (see Chapter 7 for discussion).
- **Collaboration Protocol Profiles and Agreement**: these are XML documents that encode a party's e-business capabilities or two parties' e-business agreements, respectively. They are closely related to BPSS. With the messaging service, they provide configuration information to generic, high-level ebXML-compliant B2B integration products. With the registry, they support business discovery and the process of setting up new e-business relations (see Chapter 8 for discussion).
- **Transport, Routing, and Packaging**: the ebXML messaging services provide an elegant general-purpose messaging mechanism. It is quite a mature specification that is required implicitly by many other components, for instance to access the registry (see Chapter 13 for discussion). The ebXML messaging service is layered over SOAP with Attachments (see Chapter 4), and can transport arbitrary types of business content.
- **Security**: this is a topic that is pervasive to all the components and is critical for a production e-business system. In this book we've included a dedicated chapter (Chapter 15) on security, which discusses ebXML security issues and related initiatives in W3C and OASIS.
- **Architecture**: the ebXML architecture is discussed in the next section.

# e-Business Architecture

As stated in the ebXML white paper, the ebXML framework is evolutionary rather than revolutionary. It represents the state-of-the-art in e-business architecture, addresses the issue of integration at a high level, namely the level of public process interfaces, and supports the public process management application pattern – concepts which you'll find explained in more detail later in this chapter.

In this section we'll provide an overview of e-business integration and some common approaches and technological solutions that will allow you to appreciate the kind of architectural options that ebXML supports. Keep in mind that, in isolation, the ebXML specifications are not a functional description of an e-business integration product. They are *specifications* that enable interoperability of software products (especially at the messaging level) and provide high-level systems configuration information (especially the protocol agreement and business process layers). This means that developers can use a variety of middleware products to implement an ebXML-compliant system.

We'll address the following topics in this section:

- Types of integration: enterprise integration and B2B integration.
- Integration and a multi-tier application model.
- Integration middleware technology.
- E-business integration patterns.

While the first three of these subsections contain preparatory material that provides no original or innovative content, they introduce concepts that you'll find useful, when attempting to understand ebXML and e-business integration at a high level. The fourth subsection is also important, as we'll use it to position ebXML in relation to other common approaches to B2B interaction, including the Web Services integration model.

## Types of Integration

Application integration is concerned with the issue of connecting two or more applications that were not initially designed to be connected, in order to have them interoperate and/or share data. Application integration in itself is not a new problem. In fact, it predates the Internet and even client/server architecture; systems integration accounts for a significant percentage of the IT budget in many companies.

When discussing application integration, it is useful to distinguish two major classes of application integration:

- **Enterprise Application Integration (EAI)** is concerned with integrating applications within an enterprise. It is concerned with "internal" processes that are typically not visible to the outside world and the software applications used to implement them.
- **Business-to-business Integration (B2Bi)** is concerned with the application integration to automate interactions of "external" business processes across enterprises. B2Bi is sometimes referred to as the "extended enterprise" model.

In practice, the differences between these two types of integration are not always as clear-cut as they are presented here, but the distinction is nevertheless important and useful to make. Some technologies or approaches that work well in one area are less appropriate for, or perhaps just less commonly used in, the other area. Typically, B2Bi is more high-level than EAI, although EAI products are increasingly incorporating B2Bi functionality. You are most likely to encounter ebXML in B2Bi projects, or in large-scale EAI projects in large companies.

You will often need to address both B2Bi and EAI in a single project, because the external processes that B2Bi is concerned with, viewed in isolation, do not constitute an end-to-end business system but need to be associated with back-end systems and processes. Another way of thinking about this is to view external interactions between two parties as process synchronization signals for their internal processes, where the overall business state is maintained by the backend applications at the two sides. This is an idea that is developed further in Chapter 6.

You can further classify and compare the various approaches to application integration (whether EAI or B2Bi), as well as the software that implements those approaches, along a number of dimensions. Two common dimensions are:

- The application **tiers** at which the integration is achieved.
- The type of **middleware** technology that is used.

A third dimension is to consider common e-business application architectural **patterns** for solving business-to-business integration issues. These B2Bi e-business patterns are more easily understood in reference to the first two classifications, which is why we'll look at them first. The discussion in this chapter is partly based on overviews of application integration – examples include *Building B2B Applications with XML*, by M. Fitzgerald (Wiley, 2001, ISBN 0-471404-01-2), and *B2B Application Integration. e-Business-Enable your Enterprise*, by D. Linthicum (Addison-Wesley, 2001, ISBN 0-201709-36-8).

## Application Tiers

Applications can be integrated at multiple levels, and the choice depends on the situation. The classic three-tier client/server model is a common reference model for application layers. For our purposes, we've extended it with a fourth, business service/process level, following recent proposals (for example, see http://eai.ebizq.net/bpm/white_1.html), as it is particularly useful in the B2Bi context. These tiers are:

- The **database** tier deals with data integrity and consistency, maintained using mechanisms such as SQL triggers, stored procedures, keys, and data types.
- The **application** tier is where the core program business logic is encoded.
- The **presentation** tier is used to separate the (graphical) user interface from the application code.
- The **service** or **business process** tier is concerned with higher-level, business process-oriented interfaces. Business processes may be composite entities, involving multiple service invocations, organized in orchestration flow models.

The fourth layer is the non-standard tier in this system, and it is an alternative or replacement for the presentation tier, rather than a higher-level tier. You can think of it as a control layer for the application layer, as a kind of meta application layer, or (traditionally) as design documentation only. We'll talk about business process management systems that can be configured using executable process models later in this chapter, as well as in Chapters 5 and 6.

The following diagram visualizes these layers and their relations. The diagram shows how access to the database layer from both the presentation layer and the business service/process layer passes through the application layer. We've displayed presentation and services as alternative layers that access application functionality. The presentation layer provides this access (synchronously) to humans. The service and process layers provide this access (quite often asynchronously) to external applications. We draw the business process interface as a box to show that it can encapsulate multiple services and application interfaces.

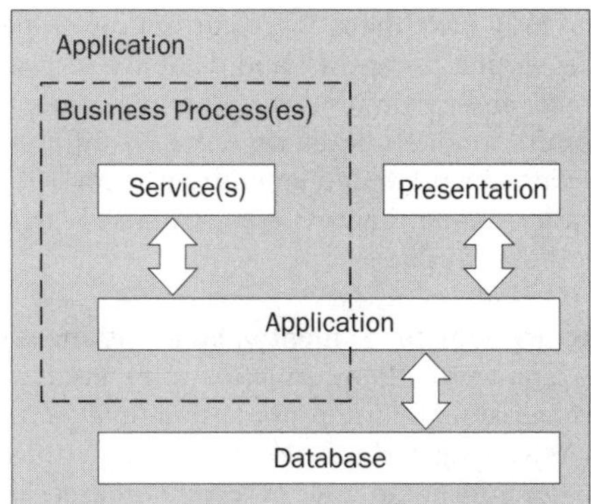


This diagram opens up many issues and questions (such as the relation between business service interfaces and business process interfaces) that we will get into later in this chapter, when we discuss e-business patterns. One thing to note here is that in this diagram we've assumed (for expository reasons) that there is only one application and that (business) service and business process interactions are part of this application. We'll later refine this, and view business services and business process interfaces as a layer that can actually provide access to multiple applications and may have its own mechanisms to maintain state information.

In an e-business context, distinguishing a business service and process layer makes it easier to define processes that involve multiple business partners, as in a B2B supply chain. It is often a first step for organizations that are planning to outsource part of their business; the IT systems that manage that part of the business would then move out of the outsourcer's control but could still be interfaced with their IT systems.

When you look at two arbitrary applications, you can in principle use any of these four application tiers as starting points for integration. In fact, the number of possible combinations is sixteen rather than four, because the integration can attach to the two applications at different levels. For instance, if your only access to an application is by running a Perl script to extract information from the HTML generated by its web interface, you are accessing that application's *presentation* layer from your system's *application* layer. Similarly, in EAI applications you sometimes have to bypass an application layer and access the data layer directly. In practice, only a few of these combinations make sense, and we'll concentrate on integration at a single level.

At the *database* layer, one application could directly manipulate information managed by another application's database layer or obtain information via calls to an intermediate data access layer. The application layer and higher levels of the receiving application don't even need to be aware of the fact that part of its information is obtained from an external source. In general, this approach is limited to EAI scenarios where you cannot (easily) modify the application layer, but are able to bypass it to (safely, hopefully) access the database layer directly. You'll rarely encounter this scenario in a B2B context.

Access at the *application* layer is the preferred type of application integration within the enterprise. You can integrate with an application in a variety of ways, for instance by calling its API or by using a batch file format interface. It's easier to integrate with larger applications if you break them down into components that each perform more specialized functionality, and use a component framework to build new, integrated enterprise applications using these components. System integrators often use the term "legacy wrapping" to refer to the process of encapsulating the functionality of existing enterprise systems (some of which may represent millions of lines of COBOL code and hundreds of programmer-years of development) within a component to open up its functionality to develop the new applications.

Larger enterprises typically not only have many large custom-developed applications, they also use package-based applications, developed using ERP and database software packages. While offering similar functionality (for instance, enterprise resource planning), the products in a particular category (such as SAP, Baan, or Peoplesoft) are often based on radically different approaches. The need to integrate package-based applications has created an entire category of integration software called EAI **adaptors** (or **connectors**) that offer standard access components for the various products, and for the various releases or versions of those products.

**Enterprise Information Portals** are sometimes mentioned as instances of *presentation*-level integration, although strictly speaking they don't provide information to external applications but rather to externally-based users. Portals occasionally use presentation-level access. This happens when they need to obtain their information by retrieving and transforming applications via their web interface, or when "screen scraping" is needed to get information out of terminal-based legacy mainframe applications.

In a B2B context, the number of enterprise applications involved is multiplied by the number of partners involved, and rapidly becomes unmanageable. There are also other complicating issues, both technical and business-related. Companies may not allow direct access to enterprise applications for security reasons and may be committed to different, incompatible middleware (perhaps even to different EAI middleware!), which none of them can enforce upon their business partners. There may also be business-level (procedural) mismatches between the internal business processes of various companies.

In the discussion of patterns, we'll see that it is often useful to make a distinction between exposing the "raw" *application* interface and exposing a *service* interface, where a service is a lightweight business-to-business interface component that can provide a higher-level interface. It may even interface intelligently with multiple applications. The service interfaces are still defined by the exposing organization, and will typically be limited to synchronous interactions.

The very reason that companies become interested in collaborative commerce also makes any tight coupling of applications undesirable. Companies outsource activities to reduce their dependence on a single (formerly internal) supplier of those services, so the IT systems integration needs to be flexible to support other partner systems quickly. In this case, the approach to take is to integrate at the *business process* level. This means that companies need to define high-level, generic interfaces that expose their e-business capabilities. These business process interfaces will have a many-to-many relationship with back-end enterprise systems. Preferably, you will organize those external interfaces according to industry-standard business interface models to reduce the cost of development and to increase the number of potential partners that this allows you to do e-business with.

## Integration Middleware

We've seen two ways of looking at integration solutions so far: one based on whether the integration is within the enterprise or between connecting businesses, and the other based on the application level at which integration is addressed. A third way of classifying approaches to integration is to look at the specific integration middleware technology used in a solution. In this section we'll provide a high-level summary of the main features of, and requirements for, integration middleware, and briefly review some of the more common types of middleware. We'll adopt a broad definition of "technology" here, which includes product categories, programming interfaces, and communication protocols. Clearly, a detailed discussion of middleware frameworks that can be used with ebXML would constitute a book in itself. The purpose of this overview is to introduce some of the technologies you're likely to encounter in a practical ebXML project, and to provide a reference for the discussion of e-business integration patterns.

### Features and Requirements

The middleware we'll discuss in this section serves as the run-time framework that allows applications to exchange information with each other, and to jointly implement an (intra-enterprise) internal or (inter-enterprise) external business process. Minimally, it serves as the transport mechanism that moves the data to be processed between the applications or components. In practice, middleware systems also provide some or all of the following features:

- Supporting distribution of processing over multiple computer nodes, hiding the complexity of various network protocols and operating systems from the developer.
- Providing availability; preventing loss of data and allowing systems to function in spite of network, hardware, or software failures ("failover").
- System administration and management.
- Tracking and tracing.
- Data representation, translation, and transformation.
- Intelligent routing.
- High-level, graphical development tools.
- Adaptors (or connectors) for commonly used applications packages.
- Security features such as encryption and digital signatures.

### Component Frameworks

As we mentioned, component frameworks are important enablers for application integration. You can design (or re-design) an application as a collection of collaborating components to facilitate the construction of new applications and integration with other applications. You can "wrap" a legacy system in a component to hide its complexity from other developers who need to access its services. A component should be modular, hide its internal structure and implementation, and present itself to the outside world using a well-defined interface. In many frameworks, that interface is programming language independent.

A component middleware framework allows components to access each other's functionality by offering a communication bus through which the components can communicate. A distributed framework makes accessing a component that runs on a completely different platform as easy as connecting to a component running on the same computer, and hides this complexity from the developer. Three widely-supported component middleware frameworks are:

- Microsoft **COM+** and the (upcoming) **.NET Framework**.
- **Java 2 Platform, Enterprise Edition** (**J2EE**).
- The Object Management Group's **Common Object Request Broker Architecture** (OMG **CORBA**). The **Internet Inter-ORB Protocol** (**IIOP**) interface is the CORBA standard interface to connect component buses over the Internet. CORBA is widely used in some industries, particularly in the telecom industry.

Component frameworks have been adopted in many enterprises as the basis for new applications and to open up functionality in legacy applications. In the mid-1990s, component frameworks also received much attention as a potential future implementation platform for business-to-business integration. Various initiatives were exploring the possibilities they offered in this space, including the following:

- The Open Applications Group (OAG, http://www.openapplications.org/) was formed in 1995 to address the interoperability of business software, with some of the major ERP vendors as founders.
- The United Nations Center for Trade Facilitation and Electronic Business (UN/CEFACT), aside from being responsible for maintaining and extending the UN/EDIFACT framework, was carrying out work on an object-oriented EDI successor to the EDIFACT framework, to operate over component frameworks like IIOP.

The OAG officially adopted XML as a business message notation in 1997, finding it a better fit for the loosely coupled, asynchronous business interaction model it felt to be appropriate for business-to-business e-business. Part of UN/CEFACT's work on object-oriented models for e-business is still visible in the UN/CEFACT modeling methodology (UMM) that we'll discuss in Chapter 2. Like OAG and other organizations, UN/CEFACT gradually adopted XML as the business message format of choice and, in late 1999, became one of the founding organizations of the ebXML project.

It is commonly felt that the component frameworks we've discussed are best positioned within the enterprise, rather than as a business-to-business integration technology. This is partly due to the complexity of these frameworks, the fact that you normally can't deploy them across firewalls, and the fact that there isn't a single component framework, as each of the three main frameworks is widely supported. Recently, this problem has been addressed by defining an interoperability layer that effectively hides these frameworks under an XML interface. This is the field of Web Services, with **SOAP** (**Simple Object Access Interface**) as the most important standard. SOAP is discussed in detail in Chapter 4 of this book.

## *Message Queuing*

Message queuing has been used to integrate applications in production systems for over a decade. It is based on an idea that is both simple and powerful. Instead of invoking a service by performing a synchronous (remote) procedure call, the sending application asynchronously puts a request in a message queue. The processing application reads requests from that queue and processes them. This may occur a few milliseconds after the request is put on the queue, or hours later, for example if the receiving application is a legacy mainframe application that is scheduled to do a batch run overnight. Once processing has completed, the processing application puts a reply in the receive queue of the sending application, again using asynchronous communication.

Message queuing products support distributed processing by using a store-and-forward mechanism to transport messages from one machine to another. This process is very robust; if there are temporary network or software failures, the queuing software can just wait until the connection is re-established. It is also scalable, as it doesn't overload applications at peak load time. The messaging framework can also take care of multiple protocol support, perform encryption and authentication, and may offer functionality such as load balancing or priority-based handling. The downside of using message queuing is that existing applications need to be modified if they assume a synchronous (remote) procedure call style of interaction.

The **Java Messaging Service** (**JMS**) API of the Java 2 platform is a product-independent API that allows developers to use message queuing in their applications without being tied to a particular implementation. Many vendors of message queuing products support JMS. This subject is covered further in Chapter 14.

Message queuing is the prevailing middleware used to implement application level EAI. This is because of the need to access batch applications distributed across multiple computers, its support for reliable, asynchronous messaging, and because you may have to support a variety of hardware platforms, network protocols, and operating systems to interact with enterprise systems. If the message queuing product supports raw TCP/IP or Internet protocols like HTTP and especially SMTP, you can also use it for business-to-business integration. However, this often requires software from the same vendor both at the sending and receiving ends.

## EAI Platforms

Several vendors have developed specialized solutions for EAI. These products are typically built on top of some of the other middleware solutions we've mentioned so far, message queuing software in particular, and provide numerous adapters to common applications and database systems. They have built-in management tools and development tools.

You can use such an EAI platform as a bridge between an application server or B2Bi server, and packaged or legacy applications.

## Application Servers

Application servers have emerged as the integration and development tools of choice for web-based transactional systems. They provide a standard middle-tier environment for application developers and offer efficient support for scalability and high availability. Most application servers support the Java 2 platform for enterprise computing, which means support for various APIs, including:

- **Enterprise JavaBeans (EJB)**: a generic component model that provides a standard framework for transaction management, security, and other issues such as persistence and resource pooling, thus allowing the programmer to focus purely on implementing business logic.
- **Java Interface Definition Language (IDL)**, a standard interface between Java programs and distributed services and objects built using the CORBA component model.
- **RMI (Remote Method Invocation)**, an approach to distributed computing based on remote invocation of Java methods.
- **Java Database Connectivity (JDBC)**, a vendor-independent API for accessing relational database systems.
- **Java Servlets**, a mechanism for web client interaction control and page construction.
- **Java Naming and Directory Interface (JNDI)**, an API for accessing naming and directory services.
- **Java Messaging Service (JMS)**, the generic API for invoking message services, including queue-based messaging.
- **Java Connector Architecture (JCA)**, a work-in-progress standard API for developing connectors to legacy enterprise applications.

An application server can access enterprise systems using custom code components, components developed using JCA, or via a specialized EAI infrastructure product.

The most common way of integrating two component-based applications using an application server results in a tightly coupled solution, requiring synchronous application invocation. As a result, application servers are more suited for integration within a company, rather than for business-to-business integration. In a business-to-business context, you can use the application server's facilities to interface with web servers to manage the message traffic with external business partners, and to provide scalability for the application components that implement the e-business interaction.

## *Electronic Data Interchange (EDI)*

**Electronic Data Interchange** (**EDI**) is a technology that has supported a large-scale business-to-business e-business infrastructure for many years. EDI predates XML and even the Web. EDI is successfully used in production systems that support large-scale e-business, both in terms of transaction volumes and in economic value. Nevertheless, EDI has not managed to extend its reach outside a limited number of application areas; in particular, it hasn't extended its reach to **small and medium-size enterprises** (**SMEs**). This is commonly attributed to a number of factors:

- The EDI message syntax is cryptic and hard to understand.
- EDI relies on expensive private **value added networks** (**VANs**).
- Software and services for EDI are very expensive.
- EDI is tied to batch applications.
- The EDI world is fragmented in multiple communities.

EDI uses its own syntax to encode messages. For illustration, the following example is a piece of EDIFACT (copied from M. Bryan's article *Using XML for Electronic Data Interchange: ISIS European XML/EDI Pilot Project Deliverable D9*, found at http://palvelut.tieke.fi/edi/isis-xmledi/deliver/d9.doc) that encodes an ORDERS message:

```
UNH+1857+ORDERS:D:99A:UN:FI0084'BGM+220+1999B2734:9'DTM+137:19991105:102'
RFF+CT:652744'NAD+BY+5012345678900::9'NAD+SU+6012345678900::9'
NAD+CA+7012345678900::9'NAD+CZ+7012345678950::9'
NAD+CN+++THE VILLAGE STORE+2 THE REDDINGS:CHELTENHAM+GLOS++GL51 2UP'
LIN++1+37534656:EN'IMD+F+8+:::SUPER PARTY POPPERS'QTY+21:100'
DTM+2:1999121:102'UNT+13+1857''
```

The EDI message format uses short alphanumeric codes and has various ways to omit unused message sections to reduce the overall message size. You need external code tables and knowledge of the message structure to interpret the message. Message size was certainly an important issue at the time EDI was designed, as bandwidth was expensive. This issue is less relevant nowadays because Internet bandwidth is much less expensive, and because compression technology can reduce message size at transport (rather than application) level.

The EDI syntax is undeniably terse, and already SGML, the ancestor of XML, offered advantages over the EDI format because of support for validation using standard parsers, availability of more and better conversion tools to translate EDI messages in SGML format to other formats, and SGML's superior support for character sets – see *Practical SGML*, by E. van Herwijnen (Kluwer, 1994, ISBN 0-792394-34-8), Chapter 21. This argument has only gained in strength now that XML has become the ubiquitous Internet content encoding language, and now that software facilities for XML, such as DOM or XSLT, are widespread.

XML documents, in a sense, include their own meta data, in the form of element and attribute names that label information. This allows you to find information in a document using the meta data, rather than using positional information, which offers increased flexibility to extend the XML document with additional information without breaking existing applications. Various people in the EDI community have acknowledged these advantages and agree that, with XML, the EDI syntax has become obsolete.

Perhaps most significantly of all, EDI suffers from being unfashionable, from being associated with an expensive pre-Internet infrastructure, and from being viewed as fax or paper document replacement rather than as a business application integration technology. The main (and often underestimated) value of EDI for the broader e-business developer community is represented by the standard directories of message definitions, which incorporate a tremendous amount of business knowledge and are based on detailed analysis of inter-enterprise business processes. We'll elaborate on this in Chapter 12.

EDI syntax obsolescence is probably more important than its reliance on VANs, the cost of EDI software, or its traditional batch orientation. This is because some EDI software vendors actually support the Internet as an alternative transport channel; sometimes VANs are preferred, for example because of security or because changing the interface to use the Internet would cost more than it would save. The EDI format, while less easy to process than XML, is not exceedingly complex, and there is even a free `XML::Edifact` Perl module that facilitates EDI message processing (see http://www.xml-edifact.org/). EDI is not by nature restricted to batch applications, and there are "interactive" EDIFACT message sets designed for use in, for instance, travel reservation systems. Finally, the XML vocabulary space is much more fragmented than the EDI world, however, this hasn't stopped it from becoming the open Internet data format of choice.

As argued by the ISO **Open-edi** project (http://www.iso.ch/cate/d25154.html), which we'll discuss later in this chapter, the main reason why EDI has proved to be too expensive may well be a different one from those we've discussed so far, namely the absence of support for "common business scenarios" that causes the process of setting up partner agreements to be too expensive. This issue is really independent of interchange format syntax and needs other solutions, which we'll come back to later in this chapter.

## XML Vocabularies

There is every reason to consider interoperability specifications as an e-business integration technology, like the other technologies we've grouped under this heading. XML-based initiatives and standards, often referred to as "vocabularies", have grown considerably, both in importance and in diversity, and are relevant at various architectural levels. Often, messages combine elements from multiple vocabularies and use XML Namespaces to manage this. There are some common ways to classify XML vocabularies as relevant to e-business, and we'll mention a few of these here.

Some XML vocabularies are not used (directly) to encode e-business messages, but serve to configure an e-business system or otherwise specify its behavior. In ebXML, the XML-based specification languages for business collaborations (BPSS) and trading protocols (CPP/CPA) fall into this category.

When looking at e-business as an exchange of business messages, it is common to distinguish messaging *framework*-related content from *payload*-related content, typically transported in a message body or attachment. (See Chapter 11 for more discussion on the relationship between these two).

Framework-related content determines the message "envelope" and handles lower-level information typically included in headers – such as identification of sender and intended recipient, what request the message is a response to (if the message is a response message), references to external protocol agreements, timing, routing or priority information, etc. Various e-business frameworks (including ebXML, RosettaNet, and BizTalk) actually use the MIME general-purpose format to provide an ability to transport both XML and non-XML content. Frameworks are application-neutral and can be used both across and within a particular industry.

Security-related standards for issues like digital signing, encryption, and authorization are an important class of supporting vocabularies. Security can sometimes be addressed at multiple protocol levels, and may affect either the framework-dependent message structure or the payload. The payload-related content reflects the diversity of the e-business application space. A coarse distinction is used to separate functions and verticals, as seen in *Even More Extensible; An Updated Survey of XML Business Vocabularies* by A. Kotok (http://www.xml.com/pub/a/2000/08/02/ebiz/extensible.html). These are defined as follows:

- **Functions**: guidelines for specific business operations that cut across industry boundaries.
- **Verticals**: messages for exchanges within a specific industry.

The RosettaNet consortium (http://www.rosettanet.org) makes a more refined distinction between standards concerned with universal business processes, standards that are concerned with specific business models, and standards concerned with specific supply chains. They also identify the need to standardize dictionary structure and content, at both the "universal" and supply chain levels.

In this book we'll discuss the XML vocabularies that are defined by the ebXML framework in the relevant chapters. With respect to payload, ebXML is designed to be independent of a particular payload format, and is even compatible with non-XML formats, including EDI and multimedia payloads. We'll discuss EDI and XML-based payload standards in Chapter 11.

XML has traditionally been more important for B2Bi than for EAI, as the need for open standards is more pressing in communication *between* businesses than *within* an enterprise. However, XML is increasingly being adopted in EAI projects too, and many adopters are offering XML interfaces to enterprise systems. Enterprise software products are often adopting direct XML interfaces, allowing them to be plugged into B2Bi products without the need for intermediate EAI adapter technology. These developments further narrow the gap between EAI and B2Bi.

## B2B Integration Products

A specialized category of products has emerged that is designed to support development of B2B e-commerce applications. A B2Bi product is responsible for managing the e-business interactions of an enterprise and its external partners. The precise capabilities of a B2Bi product vary depending on the specific integration pattern the product implements, but will include some of the following features:

- Partner management, including management of bilateral (technical or business) agreements and support for the process of setting up such agreements.
- Management of external business processes/collaborations.
- Encryption, authentication, authorization, and non-repudiation.
- Interfaces with external and internal registries and repositories.
- Support for Internet communication protocols.
- Support for XML and XML-related standards, such as DOM, XSLT, and SOAP.
- Support for non-Internet communication channels like VANs and fax.
- Support for common business-to-business protocols such as EDI and XML-based frameworks such as RosettaNet.

- Data translation from external (possibly partner-specific) formats to internal formats, XML-based or other.
- Integration with back-end enterprise systems.

A J2EE-compliant B2B integration product can use the facilities of an application server for scalability and failover. A B2Bi product can use a specialized EAI product to integrate with enterprise systems, or use other components or interfaces to integrate with internal processes. It can access a workflow management system to interface with non-automated internal processes that require human intervention.

As we've outlined in this chapter (and will elaborate in the remainder of this book), ebXML is a framework of interoperability specifications that standardizes some of these functional requirements. This means that different implementations of those specifications in ebXML-compliant B2Bi products will interoperate. Currently, some B2Bi products require that all partners engaged in an e-business collaboration managed by the product use the run-time version of that product. As a result of ebXML and related standards, companies will be less tied to the proprietary features of a product and will be able to migrate more easily from one implementation to a competing product that supports the same ebXML interfaces. Furthermore, members in a trading community do not need to standardize on a particular product to engage in collaborative e-business.

## e-Business Integration Patterns

So far, we've looked at three ways of classifying application integration scenarios, being focused on: enterprise level integration or integration of multiple enterprises; the level at which integration is applied in a three-plus-one tier model of application logic; and the specific middleware technology used to perform the integration. Theoretically, this yields a three-dimensional classification matrix with an enormous variety of potential approaches to integration. If you were to fill this matrix with references to actually-deployed solutions, you would find this to be a rather sparse matrix. This is because some combinations are much more common than others, typically because they represent common solutions to common problems that have proven themselves repeatedly in practical projects.

Such common approaches to common problems, and the application architecture and technology selection that go with them, are often called **patterns**. Patterns also reflect progress in the e-business industry, either because new middleware technology becomes available that makes more advanced approaches possible or affordable, or because specifications are developed that improve their interoperability, or simply because of "best practices": lessons learned, often the hard way, by software developers and systems integrators developing e-business solutions for their users or customers.

The ebXML project is a framework of interoperability specifications for e-business, and it is very instructive to position the ebXML specifications in a reference framework for e-business patterns. In this section we'll review a leading overview of e-business patterns, developed by IBM Corporation. IBM's patterns for e-business are documented at the IBM DeveloperWorks web site (http://www.ibm.com/developerworks/patterns/). We'll focus on the subset of business-to-business integration patterns, referred to as "extended enterprise patterns" in their classification. After this, we'll position the ebXML specifications in relation to these patterns.

In their overview, the authors of the extended enterprise site distinguish five application patterns:

- The **document exchange** application pattern.
- The **exposed applications** application pattern.

- The **exposed business services** application pattern.
- The **managed public processes** application.
- The **managed public and private processes** application.

We'll look at each of these five application patterns. We've simplified the pattern diagrams here; for more detail please refer to http://www-106.ibm.com/developerworks/patterns/b2bi/select-application-topology.html.

## The Document Exchange Pattern

The document exchange pattern is suited for business partners who replace paper document-based communication by electronic batched data interchange. The overall architecture is displayed in the following diagram:

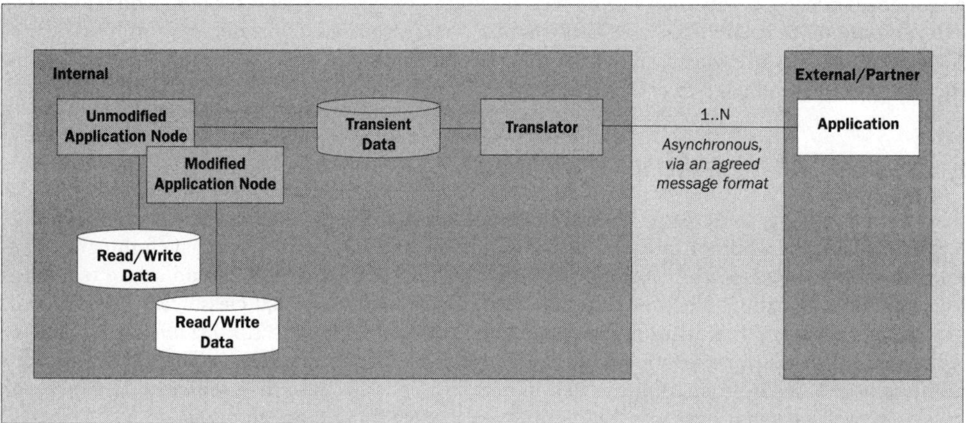


This diagram essentially describes classic EDI implementation scenarios. The parties that exchange information need to have detailed agreements on document format and the communication channel used to transport those messages, typically a particular VAN. In practice, such agreements are often biased towards the requirements of the dominant partner, such as a large manufacturer or retailer who can impose these agreements on its smaller suppliers. In such a situation, the internal, private business applications serve to support specific, fixed public processes. The integration of the various layers in this model reflects this. The EDI translator is directly integrated in the enterprise application and maps the internal data structures of that application to EDI message formats.

This setup has several drawbacks that limit its suitability for more general e-business interactions. The direct association of external and internal processes reduces the overall flexibility of the architecture, as internal applications may need to be changed if external business processes change, and vice versa. The document exchange paradigm is also typically limited to batch applications.

## The Exposed Applications Application Pattern

The exposed application pattern is one where an application's application tier is exposed directly to the outside world, rather than via an intermediate presentation layer. The integration can use either message queuing or a component framework to communicate with partners, depending on the need for such communication to be asynchronous or synchronous. Typically, asynchronous communication is preferred to manage application load and to make the business-to-business connection less vulnerable to network or system failures. Usually, this also means that all partners need to standardize on a common middleware platform. For network connectivity you can use the public Internet instead of private networks, with security addressed by installing a **virtual private network** (**VPN**).

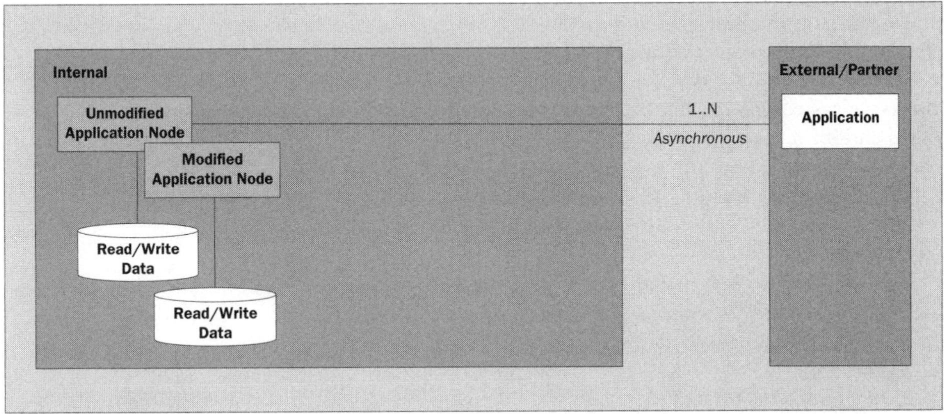


Due to the direct association of external processes and internal applications, this architecture is quite inflexible. If you directly access a partner application, you will need to accommodate any changes to that application in your own application, depending on how well the partner API hides its internal complexity from you. More complex interactions, which may involve multiple applications, essentially require you to familiarize yourself in detail with the application infrastructure of all partners you integrate with. This quickly becomes unmanageable and very expensive. If this is the case, direct application integration is actually far worse than using EDI, as EDI message sets are at least defined to express interactions at business process level, a process that emphasizes the commonality of business-level interactions over the uncontrollable variation of arbitrary applications.

## The Exposed Business Services Application Pattern

You can mitigate the complexity and high cost that the exposed application pattern potentially brings with it, by putting a layer between the backend enterprise applications and the partner tier. This layer exposes an interface that is much more oriented towards e-business interactions and manages the interaction with the backend applications. Such an interface is called a **business service** interface.

The complexity of a business service interface can vary from being a straightforward delegation component to a more intelligent component that performs data translation and invokes multiple applications. These applications may be invoked in a fixed or variable order, and the order and structure of the application invocations can perhaps be guided by the content of the request and/or the return values of invoked components. The core business logic and state information would still remain within the enterprise applications.

The main advantage of having a separate business service interface is that an enterprise remains in control of its internal systems and is not tied to partner agreements. As long as the service interface remains constant, they can improve their internal systems independently (perhaps replacing multiple legacy systems by a single modern ERP system). Multiple companies can offer the same business interface but implement it in radically different ways.

The interface exposed by a business layer can be determined (or dictated) by a single organization, or it can be agreed bilaterally between the organization that exposes the service and the organization that uses it. In this sense, there is no logical distinction between internal (private) and external (public) business processes. A single business service interface also cannot be parameterized for different business partners. This means that you cannot easily separate the "generic" aspects of a business service interface (common to all parties that invoke it) from aspects of a business service interface that are specific to (the requirements of) a particular party.

Business services can be implemented both in closed trading communities, which mutually agree which protocols and infrastructure products they use, and in open environments that use open Internet standards. In closed environments, organizations would typically use a message queuing product to benefit from advanced features such as support for asynchronous and reliable communication.

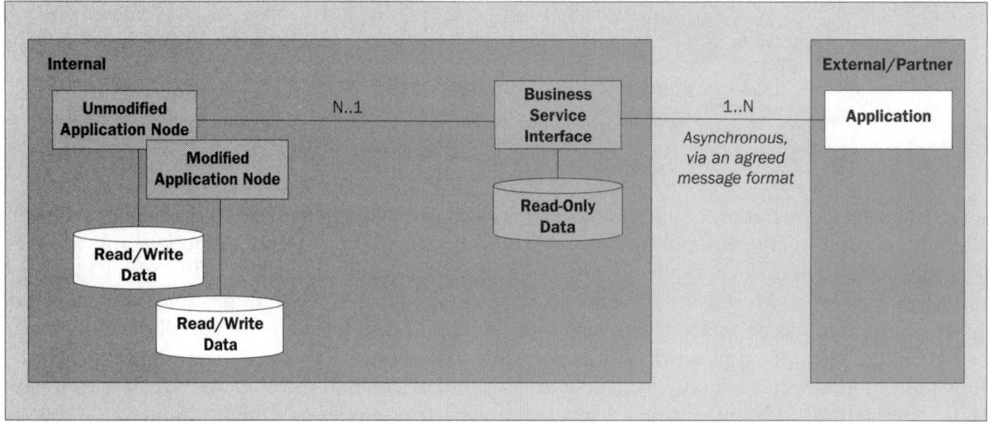


Much work has been done recently to make it easier to develop such service interfaces using the public Internet and web infrastructure. Collectively, this technology is referenced as **Web Services**. The Web Services area is organized around a number of interoperability specifications, including the Simple Object Access Protocol (SOAP), the Web Services Description Language (WSDL), and the Universal Description, Discovery and Integration (UDDI) initiative. We won't discuss any of these here, as we will look at them in more detail later in this book where they intersect with or complement parts of ebXML (see Chapter 9). A thorough coverage of Web Services is provided by *Professional XML Web Services* by Patrick Cauldwell *et al* (Wrox, ISBN 1-861005-09-1).

## The Managed Public Processes Application Pattern

When we move to consider larger e-business communities, the sheer increase in the number of organizations, backend enterprise systems, and internal and external processes involved makes a straightforward application of the exposed services pattern very difficult to manage. Each new organization will introduce its own, possibly unique set of services, which it may need to expose in different ways to accommodate interactions with different (kinds of) business partners. With this model, inter-enterprise e-business becomes unmanageable and unaffordable for all but a limited set of very high-volume or high-value business transactions.

The managed public processes application pattern addresses integration at a higher level than the business service level, namely at the public process level. It focuses on open standards, for transport protocols (Internet protocols such as HTTP, SMTP), for business message encoding (Internet standards like MIME and XML), and for external business process descriptions.

To organize such larger e-business interactions, a cleaner organization of the business services interfaces is needed. In particular, a stricter separation of internal (private) processes and external public processes, or collaboration interactions, is needed. If a trading community identifies, analyzes, and formally describes its public processes, its members can align their business interfaces with standardized descriptions of these processes. This idea already underlies the efforts in the EDI standardization bodies to develop standard EDI message sets, which reflect (interactions in) common business processes.

The RosettaNet consortium is perhaps one of the best-known, successful initiatives to develop an XML-based e-business framework focused on business process analysis (see http://www.rosettanet.org/). The RosettaNet consortium is made up of companies in the electronic components, information technology, and semiconductor manufacturing industries, dedicated to developing e-business interoperability specifications for supply chain management applications in its member industry base.

Among other results, the RosettaNet consortium delivered and maintains a set of process specifications, called **partner interface processes** (**PIPs**), for application in its target industry supply chains. Individual PIPs (for instance, PIP 3A4, 'Manage Purchase Order') are organized in **segments** (such as Segment A, 'Quote and Order Entry'), which in turn are grouped in **clusters** (for example, Cluster 3, 'Order Management'). A PIP includes role-based references to the partner business roles, activities performed by each partner, the sequence in which those activities occur, structure and content of documents exchanged, as well as requirements for timing, security, and performance constraints.

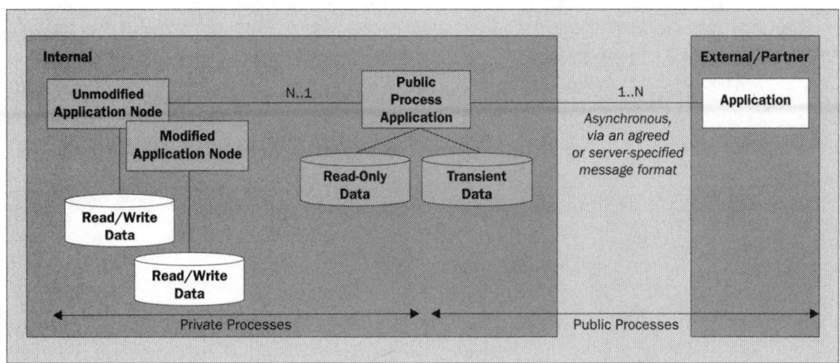

To manage a public business process, you need a software middleware layer that interfaces between enterprise applications and external partner systems. Note that a single PIP, or (more generally) business process description, may involve multiple interrelated message exchanges. Therefore, the managed public process pattern is a higher-level concept than an exposed service. The middleware layer extends the functionality of a business service interface layer in its ability to orchestrate and interrelate the various service invocations that jointly constitute the business process interaction. You could use a Web Services infrastructure as an implementation framework for a business process integration framework.

Aligning external business processes with industry standards, and grouping services that together implement a composite business process, are two ways of organizing business processes and thus of managing the complexity of the services that implement them. A third way is to separate partner-specific agreements from partner-independent aspects of an e-business interaction. To interact, two partners must make agreements on a number of issues, some of which are about business collaboration aspects (roles, message choreography, formats) and others about technical infrastructure issues (security, transport protocols) or service level agreements (such as agreed response times). Together, agreements on these are referred to as business of **trading partner agreements** (**TPA**). A modular design of the process management layer would separate those aspects, thus allowing you to sign up additional business partners, and support additional business processes or additional transport protocols, all independently of one another.

## The Managed Public and Private Processes

In the previous pattern, the process management interface only covers public processes. A major part of the actual application logic is still handled by backend enterprise systems, which are also responsible for managing state information. For instance, an enterprise ERP system may have numerous status fields to encode the internal states a particular business interaction may be in. The B2Bi layer can interface with those systems in a variety ways, including use of a specialized EAI product or by invoking wrapper components for those legacy systems. Some of the business processes may require more or less manual intervention, which could be managed by a traditional **workflow management** (**WfM**) application. Taken together, internal and external business processes are long running processes, which may take anything from hours to months to complete.

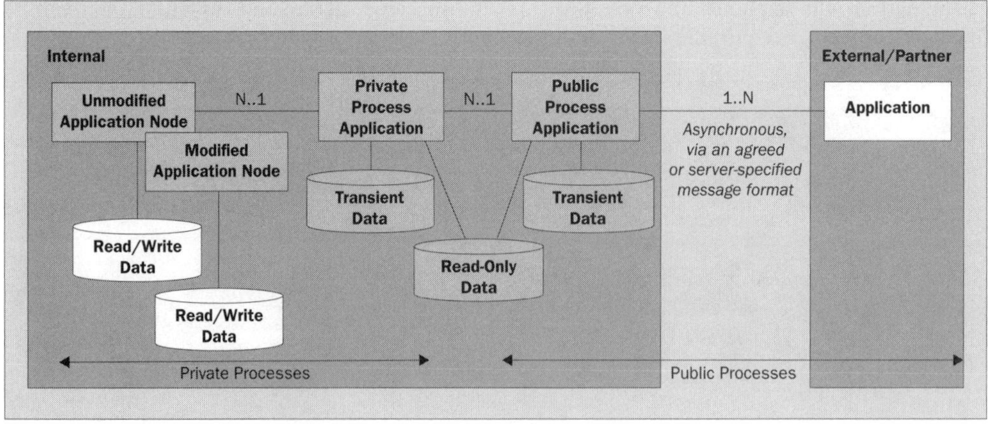

The managed public and private processes pattern is an extension of the previous pattern that intends to provide a unified management environment for internal and external processes. In this scenario, the B2Bi product does not interface with internal applications directly, but rather provides an interface to an enterprise business process management system. Such a business process management system is configured by unified specifications of business processes, and can be thought of as "next generation EAI", extending the external process management layer into the enterprise.

This pattern is much more ambitious than the previous one, as in practice it will mean that you have to redesign your applications to externalize the business process state and the process flow logic that specifies the conditions that govern navigation among business states. Such a redesign is likely to be very expensive and complex, especially for complex, non-modular legacy systems. The upside of this is that it does result in a very flexible IT infrastructure, where you can easily redesign business processes (say, in response to business challenges like increased competition, changing regulation, etc.) at a very high level, and rely on the process management middleware to percolate those changes down to the information systems that support those processes.

# e-Business Integration and ebXML

So far we've provided an overview of:

- The application *tier* at which you can implement e-business integration.
- The *middleware* commonly used to integrate systems.
- The five application *patterns* for business-to-business integration.

We are now ready to position ebXML in relation to this categorization system. The most important dimensions are the first and the third, and these determine which middleware is appropriate for implementing ebXML. In principle, an ebXML platform developer can build the ebXML messaging service on top of various middleware technologies, including a Web Services framework and an existing message queuing product. An ebXML project or derived product can use an ebXML infrastructure platform or implement (parts of) ebXML itself.

The ebXML framework is an advanced framework for e-business, rather than for application integration. It is clearly focused on providing a flexible, business process tier oriented approach to B2B interactions. As we've remarked earlier, business processes are composite and long running, and therefore constitute an even higher-level concept than pure service-based integration architectures, that focus on relatively simple interactions and in practice don't go beyond simple, synchronous, request/response-based interactions.

The ebXML framework is designed to support development of the managed public processes pattern. It does so, not by specifying the precise functionality of an ebXML middleware product or an application programming interface that such products should make available, but by providing a number of declarative, XML-based specifications that can be used as ways to configure or integrate an ebXML product with other (ebXML-based) products.

It offers a declarative, XML-based language for the specification of public processes, or business collaborations – the ebXML BPSS. Similarly, the ebXML CPA is an XML-based specification language that allows partners to formally define partner protocol agreements at a bilateral level. BPSS, CPA, and the ebXML messaging service together specify precisely the business services that implement the business collaborations agreed in the CPA. Together, these three specifications can be used as input to configure an ebXML-compliant software platform.

Standardization of such specification languages greatly simplifies development of B2Bi projects, as you can develop such a business collaboration using generic ebXML middleware and XML-based configuration documents, instead of having to program *ad hoc* business process interfaces.

The ebXML framework does not offer direct support for implementing the managed public and private processes pattern (apart, of course, from functionality shared with it). This is because BPSS is actually more a specification of business collaborations (public business process interfaces), and leaves the internal processes unspecified. Some other specifications, not in the scope of ebXML, actually go beyond BPSS in this respect and offer a more complete framework; in particular the **Business Process Management Initiative** (**BPMI**, see http://www.bpmi.org/) is addressing this field. BPMI and its unified process management markup language are discussed in Chapter 15.

# Flexible and Dynamic e-Business

The previous discussion has focused on positioning ebXML as a set of e-business interoperability specifications for state-of-the-art XML-based business-to-business integration solutions based on the "managed public process pattern". As such, it obviates the needs for industry initiatives to develop specifications for the more generic platform interoperability issues. Announcements such as the support expressed by RosettaNet, OAG, OTA, and GCI for ebXML in future versions of their specifications confirm that ebXML has managed to fulfill this part of its charter: unifying the disparity in XML-based initiatives, and providing a standard framework on top of which additional specifications, horizontal or vertical, or ad hoc solutions can be developed. However, this is only part of the motivation for ebXML.

The other main concern the organizations that founded ebXML wanted to address was the problem that e-business, prior to ebXML, had not managed to extend its reach beyond a limited set of scenarios, involving large companies and fixed, high business transaction volumes. The challenge for an e-business framework is to enable solutions that are affordable for SMEs, or in economically less developed parts of the world.

A significant number of production e-business systems are based on EDI. Earlier in this chapter we looked at EDI and have pointed out some of its problems, including its proprietary syntax, use of expensive private networks, and the non-modular application designs often associated with EDI implementations. However, many of these problems could have been addressed and, to some extent, have indeed been addressed, in the period from 1995 onwards, by re-deploying the EDI infrastructure on the public Internet.

The main problem with re-deploying EDI over the Internet is that this only results in lowering the operational costs of a deployed e-business system, but not in lowering its initial and maintenance costs, as discussed in the introduction to Open-edi, one of the more recent and interesting EDI-related ISO standards (ISO/IEC 14662: *Open-edi reference model).* As this document points out, two organizations need to establish and implement detailed bilateral business and technical agreements before they can actually exchange EDI messages. The initial costs of setting up such trading agreements are very high, as are the costs to modify them if business arrangements need to be modified. Second, these costs increase non-linearly with an increasing number of business partners. As a result, successful EDI implementations have been restricted to long-term partnerships between a limited number of partners, which automate high-volume (and/or high revenue) transaction volumes.

## Standard Business Scenarios

The solution envisaged in the Open-edi document is to identify "standard business scenarios", which essentially are pre-defined specifications of very common business processes and of the business information that needs to be exchanged to support these processes. These scenarios are to be defined sufficiently rigorously to enable conformance testing of compliant applications. If two business partners recognize that there is a standard scenario that describes their intended interaction, they would be able to go out and purchase an off-the-shelf compliant application, or a relevant B2B "adaptor" that allows their enterprise system to support this scenario. In doing this, they would avoid the initial cost of setting up the business relation and e-business would become affordable for shorter-term relationships or lower volume (or lower margin) applications.

The concept of standard business scenarios is supported by ebXML in the following way:

- The Business Process Specification Schema (see the *ebXML Business Process Specification Schema* at http://www.ebxml.org/specs/ebBPSS.pdf, and Chapter 5) provides a way to define business collaborations in terms of the roles that business partners fulfill in them. Industry standards bodies can use it to express common processes in their industry, in the same way the RosettaNet consortium has done for its industry.

- Standardized descriptions of those collaborations can be published using the ebXML registry/repository mechanism (see the *ebXML Registry Services Specification* and the *ebXML Registry Information Model* at http://www.ebxml.org/specs/ebRS.pdf and http://www.ebxml.org/specs/ebRIM.pdf, respectively, and Chapter 7).

- Organizations can reference their capability to perform a role in such collaborations by referring to it from a CPP (collaboration protocol profile) document that describes its e-business capabilities. They can publish this document on the web site or using the same registry mechanism. Two organizations can formally specify protocol agreements in a similar CPA (collaboration protocol **agreement**) document (see the *Collaboration Protocol Profile and Agreement Specification* at http://www.ebxml.org/specs/ebCCP.pdf (sic), and Chapter 8).

- Independent software vendors can develop software components that automate the e-business interaction for a particular role in a business scenario. Vendors of software products targeted at SMEs (such as finance or administration) could incorporate those components in their products to open these up for e-business interactions, and could offer support for CPA formation from this application as well.

Note that the preceding paragraphs include a lot of "coulds" and "ifs". At this point, we're assuming a lot of development to have been completed that, at the time of writing, has just started. At present, all ebXML has to offer is an infrastructure framework that supports the concept of standard scenarios. The task of defining the actual scenarios is to be taken up by standards bodies or industry associations. The development of ebXML compliant commercial-off-the-shelf software is also beyond the scope of the specifications and is to be taken up by developers of such products.

## Modular and Flexible e-Business Systems

As mentioned in the discussion of EDI, many EDI system implementations provide a limited separation of internal business processes and external business processes. As a result, these systems are difficult to adapt when the organization needs to support new or modified business interactions, or when the internal IT systems change. This inflexibility is another reason that many potential applications found EDI to be too expensive a solution.

The Open-edi specification proposes an architectural distinction in two levels in an e-business interaction that increases the flexibility of e-business systems. This model is adopted in both the RosettaNet implementation framework and in the ebXML technical architecture. These levels are referred to as the **Business Operational View** (**BOV**) and the **Functional Service View** (**FSV**), respectively. They address different aspects of e-business transactions, and different people are involved with them:

- The BOV is concerned with the semantics of business data in business transactions and associated message exchange. It is also concerned with business rules for business transactions, including operational conventions, agreements and mutual obligations.
- The FSV addresses the supporting services of the information systems that implement the information exchange. It focuses on functional capabilities, service interfaces and communication protocols. These capabilities include initiating, operating and tracking the progress of transactions, security, protocols and data or message translation.

The people involved in creating and maintaining the business layers of an e-business system are likely to be different from the people involved in the information systems implementation (with some people operating at both levels to provide the interface). Developments at FSV level should be able to have their own life cycle independent of the BOV lifecycle.

When working at the BOV level and interacting with business people, you should be able to use methods and tools that are appropriate for and commonly used at that level, such as graphical process modeling tools. Fortunately, the modeling tools used at business level are increasingly based on the same modeling language as is used for modeling software: the **Unified Modeling Language** (**UML**). We'll discuss this issue in more detail in Chapter 2. Ideally, at BOV level the entire issue of what notation is used to transport the data over the network (XML, EDIFACT, or perhaps even something like CORBA IIOP) should be irrelevant.

By contrast, at FSV level, document format and message encoding will be important considerations, as will be issues like security, message compression, or application interfaces and data translation layers (for example, from XML to a legacy EDIFACT interface).

The following figure is from the ISO/IEC 14662: *Open-edi reference model*, and illustrates these two layers and their interrelationship. It also indicates that each layer will be governed by its own set of (interrelated) standards:

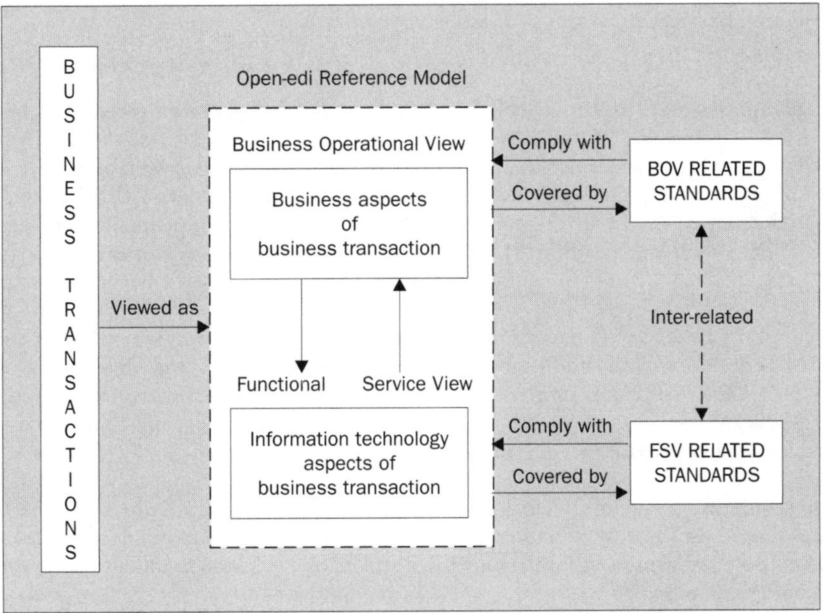


The UN/CEFACT Modeling Methodology (UMM) distinguishes various abstraction levels, workflows, and project phases and supports an e-business process complementary to the Open-edi specification. We'll discuss UMM and illustrate its application to a use case in Chapter 2. UMM is formally defined in the UN/CEFACT Technology and Methodology Working Group *UN/CEFACT Modelling Methodology* document (CEFACT/TMWG/N090R9.1). You can find this at http://www.unece.org/cefact/docum/download/91-1.zip.

# Summary

In this chapter we provided an introduction to the ebXML project, the main constituent parts of the ebXML framework, and its architecture in relation to the more general topic of e-business integration. We've seen that e-business integration can be addressed at several application **tiers** in a multi-tier architecture model for software application, and can build on a variety of existing **middleware** technology. We've also seen that practical business-to-business integration projects tend to cluster themselves around a limited number of **patterns**, or common solutions to common problems. These patterns show a progress towards increasingly flexible architectures, facilitated by increasingly capable middleware technology and configured by declarative configuration languages rather than procedural programming interfaces.

The ebXML framework is a set of specifications that is focused on supporting solutions that adopt the **managed public processes** pattern for e-business integration at the **business process tier**. This pattern is a state-of-the-art integration pattern that addresses e-business integration at the level of public processes (also referred to as collaborations). It reduces the operational complexity of having to manage a multitude of business services interfaces to multiple business partners by:

- Aligning business processes with industry standards
- Grouping **services** that together implement a composite business **process**
- Separating generic aspects of collaboration from **trading partner agreements**

The ebXML framework includes declarative, executable languages to express e-business collaborations (BPSS) and protocol profiles and agreements (CPP/CPA) in a non-proprietary, XML-based format. These specification documents can be shared and ported between compliant implementations. The ebXML messaging services complements these by offering a very capable standards-based e-business messaging system. Jointly, these can be used to configure and manage ebXML-based e-business message exchange.

As a collection of e-business infrastructure interoperability specifications, the ebXML framework allows horizontal or vertical standards bodies to focus on their specific needs, and obviates the need for them to develop proprietary solutions for generic e-business infrastructure issues. Initial announcements by leading organizations developing such horizontal or vertical standards seems to indicate that ebXML is indeed successful, and provides a generic framework to support them.

In addition to offering a state-of-the-art framework for e-business, ebXML also incorporates some mechanisms that lower the cost of setting up and maintaining e-business relations, an issue that has restricted the use of e-business to large companies and stable, (semi-)permanent business relations. These mechanisms are:

- Facilitation of registering standard business scenarios and collaboration protocols of organizations
- Facilitation of partially automating the process of negotiating and setting up trading partner agreements dynamically
- Separation of business aspects from implementation aspects of e-business, thus making it easier for business people to concentrate on defining (and refining) the business aspects of e-business collaboration

While it is widely acknowledged that we still have a long way to go here, many people feel that these are important initial attempts to increase ebXML's utility for small and medium-size enterprises or enterprises in parts of the world other than the highly developed countries.

MLFoundationsProfessionalebXMLFoundatio
nsProfessionalebXMLFoundationsProfessio

# 2

# e-Business Methodology and Process Modeling

In the previous chapter, we looked at ebXML in the context of the evolution of e-business integration technology and in relation to a classification of e-business patterns. We've seen that ebXML is a framework of specifications based on state-of-the-art software architecture concepts and on experience in production e-business systems:

- The ebXML specifications constitute a framework of specifications to support the **managed public processes** e-business pattern, where the e-business interactions between organizations are modeled, standardized and published via e-business registries.
- The use of executable, XML-based, **declarative specification languages** achieves configurability and interoperability of software implementations of the ebXML framework, and can act as a (partial) replacement for procedural programming interfaces.
- Architectural separation of **business** and **information technology** aspects of e-business systems is important, allowing business people and technical people independently to concentrate on (and optimize) the aspects of the systems that are their responsibility.

The managed public processes model is based on the idea that the majority of business interactions of most organizations can be reduced to a small number of common business processes. These business processes are either generic or particular to a vertical industry, supply chain, or business model.

If the business interactions that make up a business process are standardized and described in a sufficiently formal way, you can use standard business messages to automate the execution of that business process. This allows companies to do electronic business with all (current and potential) partners that support those e-business processes, rather than just the ones with whom they have existing business agreements. Various organizations can create public e-business process descriptions: national or international standards bodies, branch organizations, digital market places and application service providers (ASPs), or *ad hoc* consortia. Large companies can specify these processes for (mandatory) use by their suppliers and business partners – in the same way that, in the past, some large companies have imposed the use of EDI upon their suppliers.

For large companies that have in-house software development, adherence to public business processes means they can spread the cost of creating e-business interfaces to their enterprise systems to support those business interactions over many business relations, thus improving return on investment in e-business solutions. Small and medium-sized enterprises often use off-the-shelf software packages, either generic small business administration packages or packages specific to their industry. The providers of those packages can build support for such standard business processes into these products, thus allowing their SME customers to engage in e-business at relatively low cost.

In this chapter, we'll look at how you can develop such business process descriptions and how you can model processes in a way that makes it easy to use ebXML-compliant tools to implement those processes. To do this, we'll introduce a standard modeling language, the **Unified Modeling Language** (**UML**), and an accompanying standard process, the **UN/CEFACT Modeling Methodology** (**UMM**), and show how you would apply them to a realistic case study.

Note that the application of UML and UMM is not restricted to process descriptions that aspire to become standard descriptions; you can also adopt them purely for company-internal, project-specific use. Also note that neither UML nor UMM are parts of ebXML. They are useful tools in an ebXML context, but you can use (parts of) ebXML without having to adopt UMM or UML, and you can use UMM or UML without adopting an ebXML implementation framework.

Business process models in ebXML are more than documentation. Descriptions of e-business collaborations specified using the Business Process Specification Schema (ebBPSS – see the specifcation document at http://www.ebxml.org and Chapter 5) are declarative, machine-interpretable specification documents. In combination with protocol agreements (documents that formally define bilateral e-business agreements between partners; see the ebCPP specification and Chapter 8), they can be used to configure ebXML-compliant e-business middleware tools, and obviate the need to program *ad hoc* e-business interfaces. It is therefore useful to have a methodology to organize the creation of such formal descriptions in a project. That methodology is provided by UMM.

This chapter also introduces a case study, which we'll meet again during the course of the book (particularly in Chapters 6 and 8). The case study is taken from comprehensive analysis of the international supply chain, or purchasing and supplying internationally (P&SI), and focuses on the 'Prepare for Export' phase.

In this chapter, we'll apply UMM techniques to the case study, and we'll see how UMM allows us to address a real-life e-business problem using an iterative, model-based, use case-driven, component-based process methodology. In subsequent chapters, we'll show how the results of this study transfer seamlessly to the relevant components of the ebXML framework, and hence allow us directly to implement the e-business system using (a collection of) software that supports the ebXML framework.

This chapter consists of the following sections:

- The section on **e-business and process modeling** will provide a definition of e-business as automation of business processes, give examples of e-business applications, and will introduce the issue of business modeling in relation to modeling, methodology, and process in software engineering.
- The section on the **UN/CEFACT Modelling Methodology** will provide an overview of the structure of UMM-based e-business projects along three dimensions: workflows, phases, and iterations.
- The section on **workflows and worksheets in UMM and ebXML** discusses the activities performed in the various workflows in UMM and the artifacts (results) produced by each workflow. The ebXML project team has designed worksheets that assist in these phases. The ebXML business process specification can be viewed as an additional view that combines information from the various UMM views.
- The next section will introduce our case study, **Purchase and Supply Internationally** (**P&SI**), of which we will use parts in this book to illustrate the various components of ebXML. In this section, we will apply a UMM-style approach to this case.
- Before summarizing, we provide a section on **workflow management,** which introduces administrative workflow and workflow automation and shows the application of process modeling in this area. The main purpose of this section is to explain how workflow management relates to e-business process modeling and application integration.
- We conclude the chapter with a brief summary of the main points of the chapter.

After reading this chapter, you'll have an understanding of how e-business relates to the use of information technology to automate the execution of business processes; and appreciation of the role of business process modeling in an e-business project. Specifically, you'll be familiar with the structure of UMM and will understand its relation to ebXML, and why it is useful in an ebXML-based e-business integration project.

In addition to modeling and methodology, you'll be familiar with our main case study, Purchase and Supply Internationally, and the subset (the export preparation phase) we will focus on in later chapters. You'll also have seen what an application of UMM to this subset might look like.

# e-Business and Process Modeling

In our quest to understand why ebXML and process modeling are going to be useful to us, let's begin by getting a high-level picture of the concepts and relationships between e-business applications, business processes, (languages for) visual process modeling, and (ultimately) UMM, an e-business modeling methodology.

First of all, here are some definitions. A **business process** consists of a structured series of activities and exchanges of **business information** among business partners to achieve a particular business goal. Of course, all business processes are not the same – they vary greatly in complexity and in character. They also vary in that some business processes are more easily modeled or formalized than others.

Some business processes are very simple; they involve just two organizations, and can be implemented as a single request message and a single response message. In the discussion of e-business patterns in the previous chapter, we've referred to this as a exposing **business services**. By contrast, other business processes are very complex; they involve many organizations and many activities. Some of these activities can take place multiple times, in sequence or in parallel, are subject to conditions, etc. The coordination of such activities is commonly referred to as business process **orchestration** or **choreography**.

An **e-business application** is an application that is intended to automate some or all of the tasks in the execution of a business process. For illustration, the following is a diverse collection of business processes. Each of them might be automated, to a lesser or greater degree, through the development of an e-business application:

- A sales transaction in a business-to-consumer electronic commerce application (such as a retail web site that sells books or electronic equipment over the Internet).
- An exchange of sales forecasts and inventory reports between a company and its suppliers in a business-to-business value chain.
- Submission of tax reports, from individuals and businesses to government tax agencies.
- Customs declarations, between businesses and customs authorities.
- Case handling in the legal system, involving information exchange between attorneys, courts, law firms, and police departments.

The diversity of these e-business applications, and of the business information that is exchanged in the execution of these processes, is a reflection of the diversity of the business processes automated by these systems. Some of these processes involve economic transactions whereas others are only about exchanging information. Some are short running (completed in seconds or minutes), whereas others may take up to several months or longer to complete.

Importantly, these e-business applications also share common requirements, such as the need for security, generic messaging functionality, and the ability to set up (bilateral or multilateral) agreements. This is shared functionality that is provided by a generic framework like ebXML.

The sheer diversity of these applications shows that you need to take quite a few steps to get from a high-level problem description into something that's sufficiently specific to start any real technical implementation work, even if you have a complete set of ebXML-compliant middleware tools at your disposal. The following items are useful tools to take these steps:

- A **modeling language** to precisely model the business process that the e-business system automates and the activities that are performed in the process.
- A standard **process** to organize the project activities needed to develop these models.
- **Schema languages** to model the business information that is exchanged in e-business messaging.

The topic of schema languages is discussed in detail in Chapter 3, so we'll focus on the modeling language and process here.

## The Modeling Language

A modeling language needs to satisfy a number of requirements to be useful in an e-business context:

- e-Business projects often involve multidisciplinary teams and iterative development, with regular shifts of emphasis back and forth between requirements specification (or adjustment), design, and implementation. This means that you need the language to be a visual language to allow the IT-minded project workers to exchange information with subject matter experts and business people.
- It should be a standard language, not one specific to ebXML (or, more generally, to e-business applications). This allows you to benefit from common modeling tools that support the language and makes sure the necessary skills are commonly available among developers.
- It should make it easy to subsequently implement those process models using the facilities offered by ebXML – in particular, the ebXML Business Process Specification Language (see Chapter 5), the ebXML standard for encoding public business processes.

Only a few years ago, anyone looking for standards in the area of modeling languages would be confronted with an impenetrable acronym jungle of competing modeling languages and standards. Fortunately, the e-business community is rapidly following the software engineering community in standardizing on the **Unified Modeling Language (UML)** for these purposes (see Robin Cover's overview article at http://xml.coverpages.org/conceptualModeling.html for discussion of modeling and XML).

UML is a visual language that includes several diagram techniques used in the ebXML specifications and in this book. We've provided a summary of these diagrams in Appendix A, and will introduce some of these in this chapter. UML was designed by some of the leading experts in object-oriented modeling and is currently maintained by the OMG (see http://www.uml.org/). It is a general modeling language and is widely used for designing software systems. This means that it satisfies the requirement of not being proprietary to ebXML, because knowledge of UML is a generic, independently useful, software development skill. UML is quite flexible and compatible with many approaches to software development. The creators of UML have written a UML reference manual (*The Unified Modelling Language Reference Manual*, Addison-Wesley, ISBN 0-201309-98-X) and a more approachable UML user guide (*The Unified Modelling Language User Guide,* Addison-Wesley, ISBN 0-201571-68-4).

## The Development Process

Complementary to the UML visual modeling language, the designers of UML also developed a **Unified Software Development Process** that builds on UML and is complementary to it. It is described in Jacobson *et al*'s *The Unified Software Development Process* (Addison-Wesley, ISBN 0-201571-69-2). Like UML, the Unified Process is generic, which means that it can be specialized for specific types of software development projects. These specializations retain the general characteristics of the Unified Process, which are:

- **Iterative development**: e-business systems should be developed and delivered incrementally, to be able to validate assumptions on architecture and requirements early on, and to adapt the system architecture as requirements evolve and as complications and risks are better understood.
- **Use-case driven**: the project should take the desired functionality of the system that is to be delivered as a starting point for requirements specification, analysis, design, and construction. A use case is a specification of the behavior of a system or part of a system, and a use case diagram (see Appendix A) is a way to visualize a use case. We will discuss and illustrate the concepts of "use cases" and "use case diagrams" later in this chapter.
- **Requirements and change management**: in your project, you should constantly check that assumptions made at an earlier stage remain valid throughout the project, and have a process in place to manage requests for changes or functionality extensions.

- **Model-based**: visual models facilitate communication in multi-disciplinary e-business project teams, and are easier to maintain than other forms of documentation. Visual tools that help you express models using UML or using the ebBPSS notation can support configuration of operational systems that implement a business scenario from graphical descriptions.
- **Component-based**: the very architecture of a distributed Internet-based e-business system, with its loosely-coupled, asynchronously communicating, independent units is very naturally suited for **component-based development** (**CBD**).

## UMM, RUP, and the Unified Software Development Process

As mentioned, these are characteristics of the Unified Process that are inherited by all specializations of the process for specific application areas, such as UMM – which we'll start talking about a few paragraphs from here. The Unified Process is a generic standard that needs to be tuned to fit the requirements for a specific application area. In the present context, we're obviously most interested in specializations of the Unified Process for e-business applications, in particular ebXML-based applications. Fortunately, there has been much work in this particular area. The following diagram references a few important proposals in this area and uses an arrow notation to visualize how these approaches build on each other:

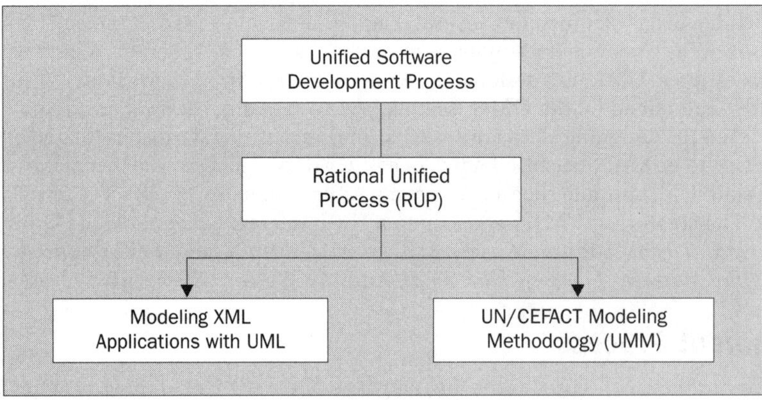


The first main specialization is the **Rational Unified Process** (**RUP**). RUP is a software engineering framework, originally developed by the Rational Corporation. e-Business projects have been an important application area for RUP, and one of the extensions of RUP over the normal Unified Process is a set of "business modeling" activities. UMM in turn inherits these from RUP. The Rational Unified Process is described in P. Kruchten's book *The Rational Unified Process: An Introduction* (Addison-Wesley, ISBN 0-201707-10-1).

Two applications of RUP to e-business are the approach discussed in a recent book by David Carlson (*Modeling XML Applications with UML,* Addison-Wesley, ISBN 0-201709-15-5), and the **UN/CEFACT's Unified Modeling Methodology** (**UMM**). In this chapter, we'll focus on UMM, because in the context of this book we're interested in modeling and process issues to support ebXML-based e-business projects. The ebXML architecture is strongly based on UMM, which is not surprising given that UN/CEFACT was one of the two founding organizations behind ebXML. UMM is described in a document by UN/CEFACT's Technology and Methodology Working Group (http://www.unece.org/cefact/docum/download/01bp_n090.zip).

UMM has been developed as a specialization of a modified subset of the RUP. It is intended as a framework for modeling business processes using UML for application in e-business projects. The subset covers the first two "phases" recognized by the RUP and four "workflows" relevant in those phases. We'll discuss what "phase" and "workflow" mean in RUP and UMM in the next section.

The influence of UMM on ebXML is clearly expressed in the ebXML architecture document (ebTA – see http://www.ebxml.org/specs/index.htm). The ebBPSS specification is strongly influenced by UMM, and shares much of its terminology. Further on in this chapter we will provide precise mappings between UMM views and the ebBPSS. An encoding in ebBPSS of a business process model contains information from models created in various UMM workflows.

At the time of writing, development of modeling tools for UMM and ebXML had just started, so it is premature for us to discuss the details of how UMM information would be transferred to ebBPSS or other executable process notations. Apart from the visual notation, the OMG has also developed an XML encoding of UML models, the OMG XMI (XML Metadata Initiative – http://www.omg.org/technology/documents/formal/xmi.htm). That XML notation could be used as input for (semi-)automatic creation of the corresponding ebBPSS encoding.

In case you're curious as to how UMM relates to other methodologies (such as the one described in David Carlson's book), the main distinctive feature of UMM is its emphasis on modeling business processes as the core of the e-business system. These processes are viewed in isolation from the business information exchanged in the course of executing a business process, and are even more strongly separated from the syntax used to encode that information. The designers of UMM, like other working groups in UN/CEFACT, focus on syntax-neutral models that could be implemented using several (XML or non-XML) encodings of that information in a runtime system. The approach proposed in David Carlson's book is more centrally focused on defining a core business vocabulary as starting point.

## The UN/CEFACT Modelling Methodology (UMM)

So far, we've seen that e-business applications are applications that automate business processes. Business processes can differ greatly in complexity, and may involve just two or many business partners. They may just involve a simple request/response interaction or consist of a complex set of choreographed interactions. A project team that works on the implementation of more complex business processes, usually consists of both technical and business people.

To facilitate communication in such a team, it is useful to adopt a visual modeling language that integrates well with tools for e-business software development. UML is the *de facto* standard in that area. You will also benefit from a standard process to provide structure for the modelling activities. UMM is an instance of a more general modern software development process and is particularly well suited for ebXML projects.

Now that we've seen how UMM fits in the broader e-business integration context, let's look at how UMM structures the modeling activities in a project and what the results of these activities are. UMM, like the more general methodologies it is based on (RUP, and the Unified Software Development Process) classifies activities in an e-business software development project along three dimensions:

- A **workflow** is a logical grouping of activities in the project. UMM focuses on four workflows, which are a modified subset of the nine workflows defined by RUP. We'll provide a listing of what these workflows are and what kind of activities take place in each of them, a few paragraphs down from here.

- A **phase** is an interval between two major milestones in a project. UMM and RUP distinguish four major phases in a project. Within a single phase you may work on multiple workflows.
- An **iteration** is a development cycle within the project. It starts with a request for functionality enhancement or a change request and covers implementation and testing of a modified version of the operational or prototype system. That modified version may give cause to change requests that are the basis for the next iteration. You can have multiple iterations in a single phase.

We'll discuss these three dimensions in turn.

# UMM Workflows

UMM recognizes four workflows, dedicated to business modeling, establishing high-level requirements, analysis, and design of a business case. The following is a listing of these four workflows, and the main result of each:

- The **business modeling** workflow focuses on the description of business processes. It produces a **business operations map** (**BOM**).
- The **requirements** workflow focuses on the description of business collaborations. It produces a **business requirements view** (**BRV**).
- The **analysis** workflow focuses on the description of business transactions. It produces a **business transaction view** (**BTV**).
- The **design** workflow focuses on the dynamics of the e-business collaboration and on the design of the data exchanged between business partners. It produces a **business service view** (**BSV**).

Each of these workflows produces a set of modeling **artifacts**, which, taken together, provide a description of the business case at various levels of detail and from various perspectives. (The term *artifact* is a typical UML/UMM term that refers to any result produced in the project – including models, documentation, prototypes, test reports etc. A subset of the artifacts, known as the **deliverables**, are those artifacts that must be formally accepted or are contractually agreed between the project team and the customer or user organization.)

Separating out an analysis view and a design view is a specialization of UMM with respect to the RUP, which has a single workflow covering both analysis *and* design. We will discuss these workflows in more detail in the next section of this chapter.

The four workflows discussed so far are workflows for which UMM provides *specific* guidelines that are not in the standard RUP or Unified Software Development Process. In a project that uses UMM and/or ebXML, there are obviously other activities that are standard for software development projects and not specific to e-business integration projects. UMM and ebXML have no special additions or modifications to these phases, so the remaining six workflows listed here are taken from RUP:

- The **implementation** workflow covers software development of the various components in the overall system and covers programming, unit testing, and integration. In general, use of ebXML greatly reduces the amount of programming as it moves a lot of business logic from programming language code to declarative specifications of business processes and partner protocol agreements. Implementations will make significant reuse of core ebXML framework functionality provided by implementations of the ebXML framework.

- The **test** workflow covers activities needed to verify the correct interaction and integration of the various components and subsystems, and the correct implementation of all requirements. In the early stages in a project you will specify some representative set of scenarios for each of the main ways in which the system is intended to be used. Those scenarios will serve as test cases for the various prototypes, as well as for the final production system.
- The **deployment** workflow addresses operational rollout of the functional production system delivered in your project.
- The **configuration and change management** workflow is concerned with maintaining the integrity of the system under development and handling of change requests.
- The **project management** workflow covers activities to manage the activities covered by other workflows: planning, staffing, and monitoring, as well as risk management. UMM and ebXML are compatible with iterative e-business development methods.
- The **environment** workflow is about setting up and maintaining the infrastructure needed to carry out an e-business development project, including technical services and configuration and management of security services.

In Chapter 1, we noted that ebXML also represents an evolution towards the use of declarative, XML-based specification documents to configure generic middleware systems, thus reducing the amount of custom programming needed. This means a shift in emphasis in the project from activities in the implementation workflow towards creating (thorough, formal, executable) designs.

## UMM Phases

UMM inherits a standard model from the Unified Process, which takes the view that each software engineering or e-business project broadly goes through the following four phases:

- In the **inception** phase, the project focuses on the requirements specification and determining the scope and vision of the overall project. An early prototype may be developed, as proof of concept or simply as a showcase.
- In the **elaboration** phase, requirements are analyzed in detail and an "architectural prototype" is delivered. The architectural prototype acts as a baseline for the overall system.
- In the **construction** phase, we're mostly concerned with the implementation and testing workflows.
- In the **transition** phase, the important workflows are testing and deployment.

The activities in the four workflows that are particularly relevant for UMM are concentrated into the first two of these phases. The shift in emphasis towards declarative, executable specifications noted in the discussion of workflows also has an impact on the overall distribution of effort over these phases. While individual projects may obviously differ greatly, Kruchten (in his book – see Appendix B) estimates that in general these four phases take 10%, 30%, 50%, and 10% respectively of the overall effort of a software engineering project.

In the context of an ebXML-based e-business integration project, these numbers are likely to differ:

- The **inception** phase is likely to require above average efforts, if only because there are (probably) a number of partners who all need to agree jointly on the scope.

- By contrast, ebXML is designed to reduce the amount of effort required in the **construction** phase, by specifying frameworks that supporting software implementations will implement.

The design of standard ebXML specification languages is aimed at allowing you to use ebXML middleware to generate, or configure, the "core" of an operational e-business integration system from a BPSS-compliant business process specification (which you can look at as a notation for the information collected by application of UMM), and collaboration protocol agreements (CPAs, see Chapter 8) between the business partners involved, using the ebXML messaging service on all network endpoints.

## Workflows and Phases

The following figure provides an overview of how the various workflows and phases in the Unified Process relate. The waveforms in the diagram show how the effort spent in a particular workflow is distributed over the timeline of a project:

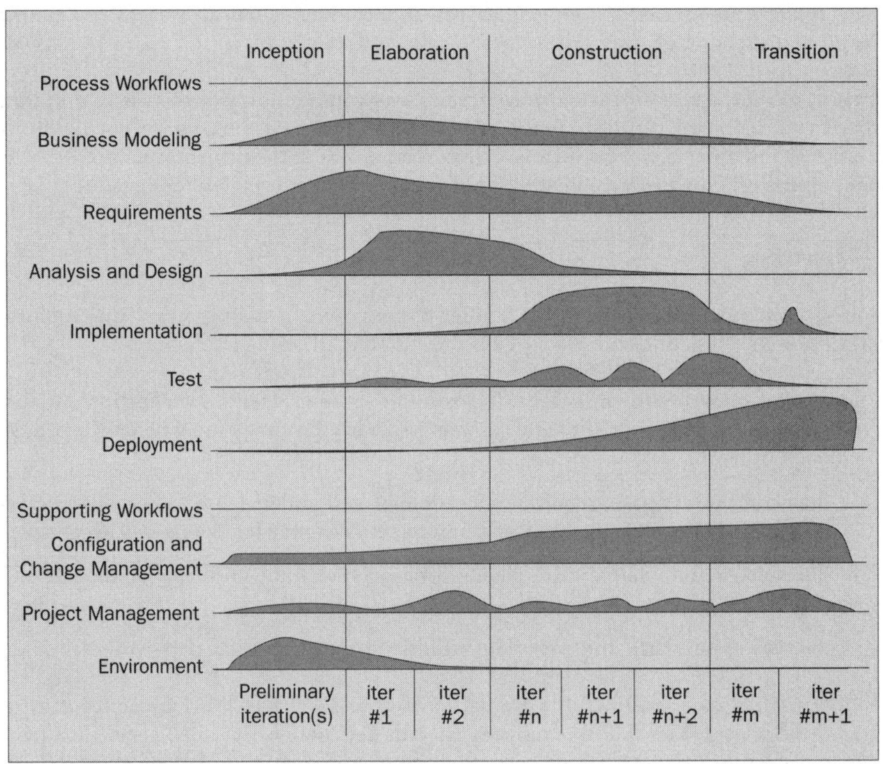


As noted previously, UMM is a specialization of the Unified Process and provides detailed guidelines for the business modeling, requirements, analysis and design workflows and the inception and elaboration phases. The other workflows and other phases are similar to other software development and implementation projects.

## Iterations

The third dimension by which you can classify activities in the Unified Process, and derivatives like UMM, is the **iteration** dimension. The idea of iterations is to break (long, complex) projects up into a series of mini-projects, that each go through a series of analysis, design, coding, integration and testing activities. This results in more robust projects, because flaws can be detected and handled early in the project and integration is not postponed until the very end of the project, but is addressed progressively. An iterative project can also adapt to changes more quickly and is easier to manage.

Unlike workflows and phases, there is no predefined set of iterations for UMM, so this is something you would decide upon for each individual project, based upon the nature of that project.

# Workflows and Worksheets in UMM and ebXML

We can use the four main workflows in UMM to approach the design of an e-business application from a variety of angles. The artifacts that result from these workflows are formal models of:

- The application's business processes
- The business information that's exchanged in the course of application's business interactions

The artifacts need to be sufficiently detailed to allow us to begin to implement the application – but they must be independent of a specific implementation framework.

A **worksheet** is an alternative way of encoding the results of a workflow. Worksheets are especially useful at this time, since the market for ebXML-based development tools is still in an early stage. A worksheet is a template that provides a predefined structure to organize the results of a workflow.

As noted before, UMM has strongly influenced the design of the ebBPSS. Consequently, there is a straightforward mapping between aspects of a UMM model of an application, and elements of information as expressed in the BPSS document. Therefore, UMM provides a process to create such documents, which (in turn) you can use in the implementation phase of your project as machine-interpretable specifications of the relevant business processes, as configuration information for an ebXML-compliant e-business collaboration management system.

In UMM, the various phases produce models and descriptions expressed as constructs, terminology, and diagrams from UML. Apart from the ebBPSS technical specification (which provides an XML notation for the specification of business processes), the ebXML BPSS team has delivered two other technical reports:

- The *Business Process and Information Analysis Overview* provides an overview of methodological issues related to business process and business information analysis (see http://www.ebxml.org/specs/bpOVER.pdf).
- The *Business Process Analysis Worksheets and Guidelines* discusses the use of worksheets and tools as analysis aids to support the four workflows in the scope of UMM. You can also use these worksheets independently from UMM models (see http://www.ebxml.org/specs/bpWS.pdf).

We'll discuss UML notations and the worksheets throughout this chapter as they are introduced in the context of the appropriate workflow. A summary overview of all UML diagrams and notations used in this book is provided in Appendix A.

As you apply the various workflows to real examples, you will obviously find common problems and will benefit from, or help develop, common solutions, or **patterns**, to address them. The designers of UMM intend to provide patterns for each of the workflows; indeed, they have already delivered results for some workflows, in particular for the analysis workflow.

*The workflows in the UMM model do not directly correspond to phases in an e-business project; for example, it is not necessarily the case that your business modeling activities are completed before you start the activities in the requirements workflow. In particular, this will not be the case if you work iteratively. However, for illustrative reasons we will assume a top-down, time-linear scenario, which starts out with business modeling and moves down towards design.*

In practice, other scenarios are also conceivable. For instance, assume you are developing a system for a company who wants to join an existing electronic trading network used by that company's business partners. In that case, you are developing a system that needs to accommodate the existing messaging framework of the trading network. This means that you are likely to work bottom-up from the low-level message descriptions to the business entities that they encode, and will design your business process to accommodate the message schemas specified in the messaging framework.

In the remainder of this section, we will discuss the business modeling, requirements and analysis workflows. We won't go into the design workflow here, because our current focus is on process modeling. The UMM design workflow is concerned with the detailed organization of message interactions that correspond to business transactions and with business information design. We will discuss the former in the context of the ebXML messaging service and the latter in the chapters on core components and message payload.

After this section, we provide a case study of the application of UMM, which provides a practical illustration of how the three workflows work out in practice.

## The Business Modeling Workflow

The business modeling workflow in the UMM model provides the general business context for the project. Its purpose, to paraphrase the UMM documentation (http://www.unece.org/cefact/docum/download/01bp_n090.zip), is to enable developers and other members in the project team to have a good understanding of the relevant business processes, the business context (business area and process area) of these processes, and the requirements, business issues, and business justification for the e-business system. In this section, we will discuss the workers (people in the project team performing a particular role) involved in this workflow, and the artifacts produced as a result of this workflow, both as worksheets and as UML diagrams.

*The terms business context, business area and process area are UMM terms. A* ***process area*** *is a category of business processes and business transactions that together constitute a complete value chain. A* ***business area*** *is a group of process areas in a particular context. A* ***value chain*** *consists of all the activities and processes needed to provide a particular product with a service of value to its consumer, including preparatory and supporting activities and activities performed by third parties like suppliers and partners.*

As we mentioned earlier, the artifacts produced in this workflow are referred to as the **business operations map** (or **BOM**). The information modeled here is subsequently refined in the business requirements, analysis, and design workflows. Ultimately, those three workflows will produce a more precise specification, which is directly transportable to machine-interpretable ebXML business process specifications.

*This section is largely based on titles already mentioned in this chapter, and listed in Appendix B: Booch et al's* UML User Guide, *Jacobson et al's* The Unified Software Development Process, *Kruchten's* The Rational Unified Process, *plus Chapters 2 and 9 of the TMWG's UMM document* (http://www.unece.org/cefact/docum/download/01bp_n090.zip) *and Section 7 of the ebXML bpWS document* (http://www.ebxml.org/specs/).

## Workers in the Business Modeling Workflow

Let's identify the main **workers** involved in the business modeling workflow:

- The **business process analyst**'s responsibility is to coordinate and facilitate business use case modeling, and to define the scope for the project (both in terms of the organizations involved and the business processes to be modeled, and subsequently automated, by the e-business system). In many projects, the person performing this role will also act as the **system analyst** in the requirements workflow (see later).
- The **business domain expert** provides relevant business knowledge for the application.
- The **technical modeler** (or **business designer**) records the information provided by the business domain expert as business use cases, identifying the various partners involved in the e-business process, and specifying the division of labor and responsibilities among the various partners. In many projects, the person performing this role will also act as the **use case specifier** in the requirements workflow, and as the designer of the BPSS schema for the implementation in an ebXML framework.

## Artifacts of the Business Modeling Workflow

The main artifact of the business modeling workflow is the BOM (see above). The BOM provides the following:

- The context of the e-business system, and the project to develop it, will be specified using a reference process area and general business area. The business area and process areas organize the business processes involved in the project logically and hierarchically.
- Descriptions of business processes, described using use case diagrams and scenario descriptions. (The BOM may also contain preliminary versions of activity diagrams, which would subsequently be further developed during the requirements workflow, and which we'll discuss later as part of the description of that workflow.)
- Identification of **business information objects**. Business information objects relate to the information that is exchanged during the lifetime of a business process instance. We'll defer discussion of these objects until we meet **core components**, in Chapters 10 and 11.

### Worksheets in the Business Modeling Workflow

The ebXML bpWS document proposes a number of worksheets that can help in this workflow. Later in the chapter, we'll provide completed example worksheets for our case study. For now, let's just identify these worksheets:

- The **business reference model form** is designed to specify a frame of reference for the business processes being described. Standard classification schemes and terminology exist in some industries; where they are available, it useful to adopt them because they facilitate cross-referencing with other projects. This form positions the project within a specific industry segment, provides a domain scope that encompasses all business areas, and provides a listing of the main business areas. The project will also need to reference its **business justification**.
- A **business area form** contains a listed collection of process areas. It specifies the scope of the various process areas within the business area and draws the boundary of the business area around a set of process areas that involve the same set of stakeholders and actors (the term *actor* is defined in the next subsection, when we discuss use cases). It also provides references and identify constraints shared by all process areas. Finally, it will specify the main business opportunity given the objective of the business area.
- A **process area form** contains a collection of business processes. Together, these form a complete value chain in the business area. For the process area, we should try to be as specific as possible on scope, objective, boundary, and constraints. The stakeholders involved are likely to be a subset of the stakeholders of the business area. Finally, specifying the business opportunity will later help specify verifiable requirements.
- The **identify business process form** allows us to identify each business process and to position it within a particular process area and business area. During the requirements workflow, or after the inception phase, we are likely to further decompose any business processes identified at this stage.

### Models and Diagrams in the Business Modeling Workflow

The central UML modeling construct used in business modeling is **use case modeling**. A **use case** is a specification of the behavior of a system or part of a system. A use case provides a high-level view of the behavior of a system as a series of actions performed to yield an observable result of value. A use case description normally provides the following information:

- A unique use case name, used for identification purposes.
- A listing of the various actors associated with the use case. An **actor** (which is not necessarily a human, but anything that can "act") represents a coherent set of roles that users of use cases play when interacting with these use cases. In an e-business system, actors correspond one-to-one with various business partners and other organizations involved in the execution of a particular business process (or the automated information systems that act on behalf of those partners).
- A short description of the use case.
- A more complete description of the use case as a set of sequences of events and actions. This description often generalizes over many alternative realizations of the use case. In any case, you should describe the typical flow of events and a set of common alternative or exceptional flows of events. The "base" case and variants are collectively called **scenarios**.

Use case descriptions can be represented diagrammatically. In such a diagram, a use case is represented as an ellipse, associated with the textual string encoding its name. An actor is rendered as a stick figure. We'll see some examples later in this chapter, and in Appendix A.

A use case diagram only shows *what* a system does, but not *how* the system does it. A use case description is a natural language description of the main flow of events over the lifetime of a business process. The complete set of scenarios for a use case may be very large or, theoretically (if there are loops in the business process), even infinite. You can identify common or important scenarios as test scenarios and treat them with special attention in the test workflow.

From the point of view of UMM, the concept of the use case is the most important UML concept – because UMM is a use case-driven methodology. Development of any (e-business) system is based on a thorough understanding of how the delivered system will be used. The notions of use cases and scenarios are used to align the process flow from requirements capture through testing, and to provide traceable threads through development to the delivered system.

Examples of use cases, both in natural language and using use case diagrams, are given later in the chapter. There's a summary of the different types of UML diagrams in Appendix A.

### *Organizing Use Cases*

In real-life e-business applications there may be a huge variety and complexity of business processes and business partners involved in them. It is important to capture the similarity and differences between these to enable efficient organization of use cases, for instance to facilitate retrieval of information about a use case from a repository (see Chapter 7). You can organize use cases in a number of ways:

- **Generalization**: you can organize use cases and actors in generalization hierarchies like object-oriented class hierarchies.
- **Include**: one use case can include another use case. This allows you to reuse common "subprocesses".
- **Extend**: a use case can provide "extension points" at which specific additional functionality is provided. This allows you to express that one use case is like another, except that it has some extra steps at specific points.

The description of the P&SI case study, provided later in this chapter, provides examples for each of these.

## The Requirements Workflow

The requirements workflow focuses on modeling the **business processes** of a UMM or ebXML project. In this workflow, we elaborate the use cases identified in the business modeling workflow to obtain an understanding of the requirements of each use case. As in the case of the business modeling workflow, this section provides an overview of the workers involved in this workflow, and the artifacts produced in the course of its execution as worksheets and as UML models.

> *Again, more information on these topics is provided in the references already mentioned in this chapter, and listed in Appendix B: Booch et al's* UML User Guide, *Jacobson et al's* The Unified Software Development Process, *Chapter 9 of Kruchten's* The Rational Unified Process, *plus Chapters 3 and 9 of the TMWG's UMM document (http://www.unece.org/cefact/docum/download/01bp_n090.zip) and Sections 8–10 of the ebXML bpWS document (http://www.ebxml.org/specs/).*

## Workers in the Requirements Workflow

The main workers involved in the requirements workflow are similar to those involved in the business modeling workflow. At this stage, the business process analyst is sometimes referred to as **system analyst** – this worker coordinates and facilitates requirements elicitation and use-case modeling.

## Artifacts of the Requirements Workflow

The main artifacts produced in the workflow are models for:

- **Business collaborations** that associate business partners in a choreography of business transactions. Business processes may involve multiple business collaborations. You can model these as use cases to record functionality and as activity diagrams to capture choreography.
- **Business transactions** are modeled functionally only.
- **Economic elements**. These are elements that express the economic meaning of transactions, (for example, creating a *commitment* to perform an *economic event* at some point in time, in exchange for particular *economic resources*). We won't discuss these further as they are still very much work in progress and have not been carried over to ebXML.

*Note that the term* ***business transaction*** *is used ambiguously to cover two concepts – message request/response pairs that serve a business transaction purpose in the "legally binding" business sense, and general message exchanges that may also serve interactions, such as notifications, confirmations, etc.*

Collectively, these three artifacts make up the business requirements view or BRV (see earlier). Apart from models, we may produce a glossary to precisely define key concepts. In terms of what the BRV delivers in the context of an e-business project, note that the focus for requirements specification is in the inception and elaboration phases of the project. By the end of these phases, we need to be able to get a precise estimate of the effort needed for implementation and testing in a project plan or commercial proposal. The requirements view should be sufficiently precise to enable you to make such estimates with confidence.

### Business Collaborations

The business modeling workflow may identify business processes which are essentially **composite processes** – that is, they involve other constituent business processes as part of their execution. As part of the requirements workflow, we can refine these use cases down to the level of "atomic" business processes – these are called **business collaborations**. A business collaboration associates a number of partners involved in a number of business transaction activities performed in some order.

For an ebXML project, we need to decompose any business collaborations that involve more than two partners into a set of interrelated pairwise **binary collaborations** (each binary collaboration involves two parties). We can then provide choreography for the binary collaborations that jointly implement a **multi-party collaboration**, and also for the business transactions within a binary collaboration.

Later, in the analysis workflow, we'll model the business transactions of the application. Here in the requirements workflow, the only information we need to record in relation to any business transaction is to classify the two business partners involved in the transaction and to indicate whether they play a requesting role or a responding role.

In addition to completing worksheets and drawing activity diagrams, it is often worthwhile to create a glossary of precise definitions of concepts relevant to the business case, and to update higher-level use cases to reflect any important new insights you've gained in this workflow.

### Worksheets in the Requirements Workflow

The ebXML bpWS document proposes that the following worksheets are used to specify requirements for the application's business processes.

- A **business process use case worksheet** provides an overview of the actors involved in the use case. It should describe the main actions performed in the use case, any conditions which must be met before it starts, any events that activate it, what condition or event causes its normal or exceptional termination, and what conditions hold true of the business state after normal completion. It also describes any non-functional goals (for example, performance goals) that the process needs to satisfy.
- A **business collaboration worksheet** provides a description of the collaboration, lists the roles that business partners play within it, legal or economic consequences of any of the steps in the collaboration, events that trigger or terminate it, events occurring in the collaboration, boundaries, and constraints.
- A **business collaboration protocol table worksheet** specifies transitions between the business transactions that make up the collaboration.

### Models and Diagrams in the Requirements Workflow

In requirements modeling, a main focus is on modeling the dynamic aspects of the e-business system. **Activity diagrams** are a central UML construct used in the modeling of dynamic systems. An activity diagram is essentially a flowchart that emphasizes the flow of business activities that take place over time (see the *UML User Guide*). An activity diagram contains:

- **Action states**, represented graphically by lozenge shapes, which collectively make up the business process.
- Special symbols for **start** and **completion states**. The completion states are **success** and (several kinds of) **failure**.
- **Parallelism** is expressed using horizontal bars for **forking** (with multiple arrows leaving from the bar) and **joining** (with multiple arrows arriving at the bar).
- **Transitions** are the flows that connect the activities. They are represented as directed lines. A transition can have **guard conditions**, which means that the transition will only apply if the specified condition applies. We'll provide sample diagrams later that conditionally transition to success or failure states.
- **Objects** can be involved in activities. They are represented using (simplified) class diagrams and connected to the transition that impacts them using **dependency symbols**, which are dotted directed lines.

See Appendix A for examples. You can use activity diagrams to express the choreography both of collaborations in a process and of transaction activities in a collaboration.

A practical example of an application of the activities of the requirements workflow to our case is provided in the P&SI section of this chapter.

#### *The ebBPSS Specification and the BRV*

Various entities in the BRV have direct counterparts in the ebBPSS, as summarized in the following mapping:

- Business process packages correspond to the root `<ProcessSpecification>` element of a BPSS document.
- Each main business process use case for the package corresponds to a `<MultiPartyCollaboration>`.
- Collaborations that together constitute a business process correspond to `<BinaryCollaboration>s`.
- The choreography of the `<BinaryCollaboration>s` within a `<MultiPartyCollaboration>` is expressed as `<Transition>s` associated with each `<BusinessPartnerRole>`.

Economic modeling elements are not represented in ebXML business process models.

## The Analysis Workflow

The requirements workflow yields a complete set of business requirements, including models of business processes and collaborations, with references to business transaction activities within those collaborations. The purpose of the **analysis workflow** is to further develop the business transactions within the various business collaborations, with sufficient detail that we can start the implementation workflow and the construction phase.

> *Again, more information on these topics is provided in Booch et al's* UML User Guide, *Jacobson et al's* The Unified Software Development Process, *Chapter 10 of Kruchten's* The Rational Unified Process, *plus Chapters 4, 8 and 9 of the TMWG's UMM document (http://www.unece.org/cefact/docum/download/01bp_n090.zip) and Section 11 of the ebXML bpWS document (http://www.ebxml.org/specs/).*

The main focus for the analysis workflow is the descripton of the application's business transactions (where we use the word *transaction* in the general sense of activities involving formal exchange of business documents). The artifacts produced in the analysis workflow collectively make up the business transaction view or BTV (see earlier); these artifacts can be encoded directly as XML specifications for business process and collaboration protocols.

The main workers involved in analysis are the business process analyst (acting as architect of the detailed system design), and the technical modeler. Usually, the domain expert does not need to be involved in this workflow.

The main result of this workflow is a BTV that includes the following artifacts:

- **Business collaborations**: these are refinements of the requirements activity diagrams. You should in particular look at opportunities to design (or redesign) the collaboration using parallel activities where possible, as this is an area where e-business systems can deliver time savings, which are a potential (business) justification for your project.

- **Business transactions**: you will now specify the actual activities and activity flow of the transactions and set a number of timing, authorization, and non-repudiation parameters. Ideally, you will identify a UMM analysis pattern that suits your needs, if not you can set values for the individual properties. (An analysis pattern is a combination of parameter settings appropriate for a particular type of transaction; see below.)
- **Business documents**: Up to now, the focus has been on obtaining detailed requirements about business processes. In UMM, the analysis workflow is the first workflow to cover an initial analysis of **business information** encoded in business messages exchanged between business partners.

As mentioned earlier, we will postpone discussion of business document and business information modeling to Chapters 3, 10 and 11 of this book.

## Business Transactions

Each business transaction involves a **requesting business activity** and a **responding business activity**. The requesting business activity is associated with a single business document. The responding business activity may be associated with any number (zero or more) of business documents. There is no responding business document if the business transaction follows the notification or information distribution patterns (see below). Responses that carry no documents are called **business signals**. You can specify multiple allowed responding business documents to signal different result states. We will illustrate this for the 'Perform pre-shipment inspection' transaction of the P&SI case, later in this chapter.

For requesting and responding business activities in a transaction, we need to specify values for seven interaction parameters, if we're not using an analysis pattern. These parameters are:

- **Time to acknowledge receipt**: this means more than simply a requirement to provide a receipt acknowledgment signal for a message within a specified time interval; it also implies that the message is syntactically correct, meets transaction choreography requirements, and is valid according to business document schema agreements.
- **Time to acknowledge acceptance**: this refers to business acceptance within a specified time interval, which includes everything covered by "receipt" (as defined in the previous point) but also means the message does not violate any business rules. It only applies to requesting business transaction activities.

*These first two parameters provide requirements on response messages that are "business signals" and do not involve response documents. UMM refers to "substantive acceptance" if the transaction delivers a responding business document and is not just a signal that acknowledges acceptance.*

- **Time to perform**: this assumes receipt and acceptance acknowledgment as well as all activities required to produce a response business document within a specified time interval, which, in a business transaction, will have the status of an electronic contract.
- **Authorization required**: this requires the sending party to digitally sign the business document being exchanged. Parties must throw an exception if asked (or asking) to perform an activity that the performer is not authorized to perform.
- **Non-repudiation of origin and content**: this means the business activity must store the business document in its original form for an agreed duration to be able to verify that the document has not been tampered with.

- **Non-repudiation of receipt**: this requires the receiving party to return a signed receipt, and the original sender to save a copy of the receipt.
- **Recurrence**: this is a retry count to recover for any potential temporary communication or other failures.

Some of these properties are discussed in more detail in Chapter 5.

Note that there are different properties for receipt acknowledgment and acceptance acknowledgment, and that a transaction activity may or may not be associated with a business document. This means that there is no one-to-one correspondence between a `<RespondingBusinessActivity>` and a return message, as there may be several such return messages. Similar remarks apply to the `<RequestingBusinessActivity>`, as the messaging system may perform retries. This is covered in the UMM design workflow and in the ebXML messaging specification (see the ebXML ebMS Specification).

## *Analysis Patterns*

A **pattern** is a software engineering term for a common solution to a common problem in a given context. A business transaction design pattern is a named category of business transactions with parameter values that are reasonable for those parameters for the category. UMM provides us with six such design patterns (see Chapter 8 of the UMM documentation, at http://www.unece.org/cefact/docum/download/01bp_n090.zip):

- **Business transaction**: this pattern is used for interactions that result in economic commitments among business partners. Therefore, non-repudiation and authentication are essential.
- **Request/confirm**: this pattern is for obtaining status information and involves business documents for request and response. There are no economic commitments after this interaction and no business acceptance or receipt confirmation.
- **Request/response**: this pattern is for exchange of dynamic information, such as requests for quote or availability checks. There is no need for receipt or acceptance acknowledgments.
- **Query/response**: this pattern is for exchange of static information, such as catalogs. Query and response are business documents. There is no receipt acknowledgment or business acceptance acknowledgment.
- **Notification**: this pattern specifies the exchange of a notifying business document and a receipt acknowledgment business signal. This pattern models a formal information exchange and therefore has non-repudiation requirements.
- **Information distribution**: this is similar to notification, except that it is about informal information exchange, and therefore has no non-repudiation requirements.

In UMM, these patterns prescribe specific values for the business transaction activities, as specified in the following table (taken from http://www.unece.org/cefact/docum/download/01bp_n090.zip). For each pattern, the first row provides values for the requesting business activity and the second row for the responding business activity. The value "`null`" means the value is not specified in the pattern and can be specified for each conforming business pattern:

| | Time to Acknowledge Receipt | Time to Acknowledge Acceptance | Time to Perform | Authorization Required | Non-repudiation of Origin and Content | Non-repudiation of Receipt | Recurrence |
|---|---|---|---|---|---|---|---|
| **Business Transaction** | 2hrs | 6hr | 24hr | true | true | true | 3 |
| | 2hrs | 6hr | 24hr | true | true | | |
| **Request/Confirm** | null | null | 24hr | false | false | true | 3 |
| | 2hrs | null | 24hr | true | false | | |
| **Request/Response** | null | null | 4hrs | false | false | null | 3 |
| | null | null | 4hrs | false | false | | |
| **Query/Response** | null | null | 4hrs | false | false | null | 3 |
| | null | null | 4hrs | false | false | | |
| **Notification** | 24hrs | null | 24hrs | false | true | true | 3 |
| | 24hrs | null | 24hrs | false | false | | |
| **Information Distribution** | 24hrs | null | 24hrs | false | false | false | 3 |
| | 24hrs | null | 24hrs | false | false | | |

## *Worksheets in the Analysis Workflow*

In the ebXML bpWS document, information corresponding to UMM analysis workflow artifacts is encoded using the following worksheets:

- A **business transaction worksheet** allows you to specify a description of a transaction, the business activities that make up the transaction, and the business partners (authorized to play a particular role) that perform those activities. A transaction involves a request and (optionally) a response, and for both of these you can specify role and associated documents. We can (and, wherever possible, should) also associate the transaction with a **business transaction pattern**. This will make sure the transaction will be associated with reasonable default values for a number of transaction-related properties.
- In the (unusual) case where none of the business transaction patterns is applicable, we can specify a transaction-specific property value in a **business transaction property value table**.
- We can specify the allowable transitions between states in a transaction in a **business transaction transition table**.

## *Models and Diagrams in the Analysis Workflow*

You can use activity diagrams to specify business collaborations and business transactions, as we discussed for the requirements workflow, and as illustrated later in this chapter for the P&SI case study. UML provides additional diagrams to model dynamic systems. Although we won't need these in this chapter, we will briefly mention them and examples of both are provided in Appendix A:

- **State machines** model the behavior of an individual business partner engaged in an e-business interaction as transitions of the object between states.
- **Interaction diagrams** show business partners and their interaction using messages (*interaction diagram* is a general term that covers sequence diagrams and collaboration diagrams). A **sequence diagram** visualizes temporal order of messages. A **collaboration diagram** visualizes the structural organization of the collaborating business partners.

To model business information, you can use **class** diagrams. A practical example of applying the activities of the analysis workflow to our case is provided in a section of the case study description, later in the chapter.

### The ebBPSS Specification and the BTV

Various entities in the BTV have direct counterparts in the ebBPSS Specification, as summarized in the following mapping:

- UMM and ebXML share a `<BusinessTransaction>` element. It has a `pattern` attribute that we can use to specify an applicable analysis pattern. If specified, this allows us (or a UMM-aware, ebXML BPSS compliant e-business collaboration management system) to infer values for the interaction parameters discussed.
- The UMM activity graph that expresses choreography of transaction activities in a collaboration is explicit in BPSS `BusinessState` elements, which includes `<Start>`, `<Success>`, `<Fork>`, and `<Join>` elements, and `<Transition>`s between these.
- The requesting and responding activities that together form a business transaction are represented as `<RequestingBusinessActivity>` and `<RespondingBusinessActivity>`.
- Complex transactions can be built from basic transaction activities using the BPSS `<CollaborationActivity>` element.
- UMM and BPSS share a `<DocumentEnvelope>` element that combines all document data exchanged in a transaction activity. UMM distinguishes `StructuredDocument` and `UnstructuredDocument` business documents. In BPSS, the latter roughly correspond to `<Attachment>` elements.

### Summary

This concludes our discussion of the three main workflows of UMM: business modeling, requirements and analysis. For each workflow, we've discussed its purpose and the aspects of e-business that are addressed by the modeling activities in the scope of the particular workflow.

The following section is structured analogously to this section, and will illustrate how you can apply UMM to a realistic case study.

## Introducing the Case Study

We'll use the remainder of this chapter to introduce a case study. The case appears regularly thoughout the book, and is used to illustrate how the various specifications complement each other and how they address some of the aspects and requirements of e-business systems.

The case study is taken from a description of the international supply chain domain, with a special reference to **purchasing and supplying internationally** (**P&SI**). In the following pages, we'll give a high-level introduction to the case; and we'll analyse part of the case, concerned with the 'Prepare for Export' stage of the case, using UMM.

The case description is based on the **UN/CEFACT International Trade Transaction** (**ITT**) **model**, which is a reference model for international trade. According to the ITT documentation, the main objective of the ITT framework is to provide a common reference case for all of UN/CEFACT's relevant future activities, including appropriate liaison with outside agencies. The ITT framework is described in a series of documents posted on the UN/CEFACT web site (http://www.unece.org/trade/itt/itt_tip.htm). These documents provide references to an EDIFACT implementation that we shall examine in Chapters 10 and 11 of this book.

We have adopted this particular case in this book for a number of reasons:

- By adopting the same business application used by the UN/CEFACT working groups, we will hopefully make it easier for you to appreciate the results of those working groups (as and when those results become available).
- The case is well-described. It's also representative of real-life e-business applications in terms of complexity – witness the sheer number of actors and use cases involved. Thus it provides a good opportunity to address the importance and application of iteration and other techniques provided by a standard process for e-business projects like UMM.
- The case focuses on the field of international trade – a field which often requires special arrangements for financing and insurance, and which is subject to control by regulatory authorities. As such, it addresses real-life complications that production e-business systems need to take into account.

The ITT model predates both UMM and ebXML. However, the **UN/CEFACT Business Process Analysis Working Group** (**BPAWG**) has begun a reworking of ITT as a UMM-compliant model. The work of BPAWG is focused on business process analysis, and complements the **Techniques and Methodologies Working Group** (**TMWG**), which is responsible for UMM. The preliminary results of this work are described in a working draft document (see http://www.unece.org/cefact/docum/download/00bp024.pdf). The document aims to follow UMM and to provide a reference model to support activities of other working groups in UN/CEFACT.

*Note that the BPAWG document describing the P&SI case is an* ***incomplete*** *working draft. It covers the BOM and BRV at a highlevel, but does not cover the BTV (see the workflow section earlier in this chapter). While it provides some information on mapping from the models to UN/EDIFACT messages and to an XML syntax, it does not cover the mapping to ebXML. Also note that, at the time of writing, the working group structure within UN/CEFACT is being revised.*

*The mapping to these more specific workflows, and the interpretation of the case needed to provide these mappings, are provided by (and the responsibility of) the authors of this book. Furthermore, our presentation of the case and subsequent ebXML implementation does not strictly follow the outline provided in the BPAWG document. The description given here serves as a case and does not claim to cover the business of international trade in its full scope or with 100% accuracy.*

In the following sections, we will provide an application of the three main UMM modeling workflows: business modeling, requirements and analysis to the P&SI application. As you'll see, we illustrate the discussion using both the ebXML business modeling worksheets and the UML diagrams used in UMM.

# The International Trade Business Modeling Workflow

The purpose of the business modeling workflow is to capture the structure of the business domain from the point of view of the main stakeholders involved. The ITT model essentially provides a time-based view of the overall domain. This is a useful and very natural way of structuring the overall case, so we'll provide a description of the overall P&SI case along these lines. Like any other methodology, UMM represents best practices rather than exact science, so you need to be pragmatic and creative when applying it to a real life application like P&SI.

At the business process level, the main issue is how supply chains are organized in the particular industry. (In particular, we're not so interested in identifying the specific industry segment in which the exporter/seller or importer/buyer is active.) Let's make it easier to discuss the issue of trading partner agreements, by assuming the following specific instantiation of the exporter/seller and importer/buyer roles:

- The **exporter/seller** is a small Italian company producing high-quality professional food and beverage equipment. This company ships its products worldwide.
- The **importer/buyer** is a coffee shop in a densely programmer-populated US East Coast neighborhood. Its customers only want the very best.

We will assume a scenario in which the buyer performs a survey of the state-of-the-art in the field of espresso machine technology, and decides to purchase some equipment from the seller directly. In this scenario, the seller has no re-seller in the US. Therefore, since transportation of the equipment involves overseas shipment, it must be imported.

## *A Description of the P&SI Case*

The business modeling workflow is concerned with providing descriptions of the overall functionality of the main use cases for the e-business system under development. These use cases can be described using use case diagrams (as we'll provide shortly), possibly other diagrams (such as state charts or activity diagrams) and natural language descriptions. We'll start out with the latter, based on existing descriptions of the overall P&SI case (see http://www.unece.org/trade/itt/itt_tip.htm and http://www.unece.org/cefact/docum/download/01bp015r3.doc), and using a tabular format for the use case description similar to one used in the UN/CEFACT documents. In this description, we've identified the main (categories of) actors, a main scenario and some alternative scenarios.

| Name | Purchase and Supply Internationally (P&SI) |
|---|---|
| Short description | Importer purchases goods from Exporter.<br><br>Exporter arranges transport and handles all administrative documents. |
| Actors | There are four broad *classes* of actor involved in P&SI:<br><br>**Exporter**: a company that sells goods internationally.<br><br>**Importer**: the company that buys goods from the exporter.<br><br>**Intermediary**: assists the process of delivering goods commercially internationally. A variety of intermediary organizations are involved: banks (of both exporter and importer), insurance companies, solvency checking agencies, freight inspection companies, freight forwarders, and carriers.<br><br>**Authority**: legal trade is subject to the national and international frameworks of trade regulations. Export and Import Control authorities, Customs, Consulate, Health Authorities, Chamber of Commerce, and Consulates play their roles in this.<br><br>*During the initial iterations in the business modeling workflow, you can generalize over various actors – using broad categories like "intermediary" and "authority". Use case descriptions for the various phases will more precisely specify the involvement of individual actors.* |
| Precondition | Importer and exporter are aware of each other and have identified means of exchanging information. |
| Postcondition | Goods purchased are transported and delivered at importer; exporter has received payment. |
| Main scenario | At the top level, you can distinguish the following seven major phases:<br><br>**Contract negotiations**: covers all work done by importer and exporter to agree on a business contract. It covers request for quotation, preparation of quotation, quotation, and creation of a contract.<br><br>**Payment negotiations**: covers the agreement on payments of the goods purchased and sold internationally; this typically involves banks of both parties and requires a Letter of Credit.<br><br>**Preparation for export**: covers insurance, transport reservation, and arrangement of export and import documents.<br>We will elaborate on this phase in detail in this chapter.<br><br>**Exportation**: covers preparation of goods for shipment, exchange of shipment documents, release of goods to the carrier, obtaining of customs clearance and loading of goods.<br><br>**Transport**: covers transportation of the goods by the carrier from the exporting country to the importing country.<br><br>**Importation**: covers customs inspection and delivery to the buyer.<br><br>**Payment final phase**: covers completion of all outstanding financial transactions. |

*Table continued on following page*

| Name | Purchase and Supply Internationally (P&SI) |
|---|---|
| **Exceptional scenarios** | Permissions may be refused, credit arrangements may fail, etc. Detail is not included here. We work out these exceptions iteratively when we look in more detail at use cases for the individual phases. |
| **Alternative scenarios** | Administrative handling differs in detail depending on choice between air and sea transport.<br><br>Various licenses may be required, depending on destination and nature of goods shipped. |

As you can see, the initial phase of trading partner search and identification is not included in the ITT description. To exchange information electronically, the various business partners need to **discover** each other and to mutually **agree** protocol agreements. These topics are addressed in this book in Chapters 7–9.

## Identifying Business Areas, Process Areas, and Business Processes

We could view the seven phases identified in the description as constituent use cases of the overall system, that we would later work out as sets of more refined (sets of) business processes. Then, we could iteratively work our way down, taking each phase as a starting point.

But there's a drawback to the technique of equating phases and business process use cases, and this quickly becomes clear when you look at the overall case. The problem is that most actors are involved in most (or all) of the seven phases of the ITT model. Consequently, use case diagrams would be fairly uninformative – because they would essentially link all actors with all phases.

So let's consider an alternative way of providing structure, as recommended in UMM: namely, by trying to distinguish **business areas** – collections of (groups of) business processes grouped according to the main business function of the business process. Each business area groups business processes that are primary business functions for at least some of the actors involved. In this view, the main business areas of P&SI are:

- **Contracting and ordering**: requesting and obtaining quotes (between seller and buyer, but also with insurers and transport agencies), solvency checks, orders, and order amendments.
- **Transport**: transport booking, packing and delivery options, shipping notifications.
- **Payment and insurance**: payment conditions, carrier insurance.
- **Legal/administrative document handling**: regulatory documents (we'll elaborate on these later). Also loading lists, permission to load, export manifest, airway bills, certificate of shipment, shipment confirmation. (We could have chosen to group these with the Transport business area, and split them off in a subsequent iteration.)

Now, the various actors involved in P&SI can be positioned with respect to these business areas using the following use case diagram (which is a bit more informative than one that simply associates actors with phases):

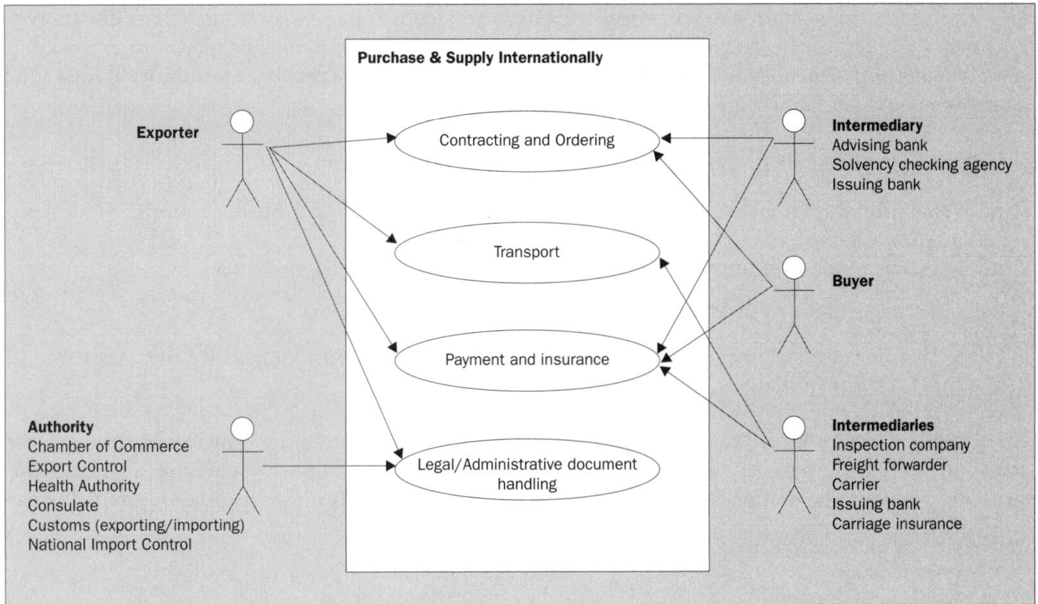


In UMM, a business area contains a group of **process areas**, and in turn, each process area is a group of individual **business processes**, performed in a particular sequence, to implement a complete value chain in the given business area. The P&SI case, broadly speaking, combines two main value chains: one is focused on change of ownership of goods in exchange for payment (order management) and the other on physical movement (order fulfillment). The international dimension introduces complications, which are handled by processes in the two supporting business areas (Payment and Insurance, and Legal/Administrative Document Handling).

In UMM, process areas are viewed as subcategories within business areas. Alternatively, you can think of process areas as a separate dimension used to classify processes, rather than as a subdivision within business area. For example, within the Payment and Insurance business area, the financial transactions between buyer and seller constitute a complete chain of processes. By contrast, the need for arrangement of transport insurance is a complication (due to the fact that the transaction involves transfer of ownership and movement of physical goods). Similarly, you can think of chronological position within more encompassing use cases as a third dimension in the classification of processes.

In subsequent iterations of the business modeling workflow, we would cover the various business areas, process areas, and phases in detail. We could adopt various strategies, such as:

- Start by looking at a business area; then analyze each of the process areas within that business area. This means that we'd look at all processes in the Contracting and Ordering business area, then move on to the Transport business area, and so on.
- Maintain the identification of business areas and process areas, but proceed using the original phase structure in mind. This strategy is particularly useful for very large supply chains, such as the P&SI model, because the number of activities and actors involved is more manageable within a particular phase than within the complete case.

In a real project you would have practical reasons for selecting a particular strategy. For illustrative reasons, we'll employ the second strategy for our case. The ITT case is a large case, and to work it out in detail would represent a significant amount of work. Therefore, for practical reasons, we'll focus on just *one* of the phases of P&SI – the 'Prepare for Export' phase.

## Case Description: the 'Prepare for Export' Phase

The 'Prepare for Export' phase involves processes from three of the four business areas:

- Finance- and insurance-related processes (obtaining transport insurance)
- Transport-related processes (reserving transport with a carrier)
- Document-handling processes (as international movement of goods legally requires certain documents)

To organize the various use cases, we can use the names of the business areas as names for packages (a **package** is a UML grouping construct). We've done just that in the following diagram. The diagram provides an overview of the actors and the business processes involved in this phase, grouped over three use case business areas:

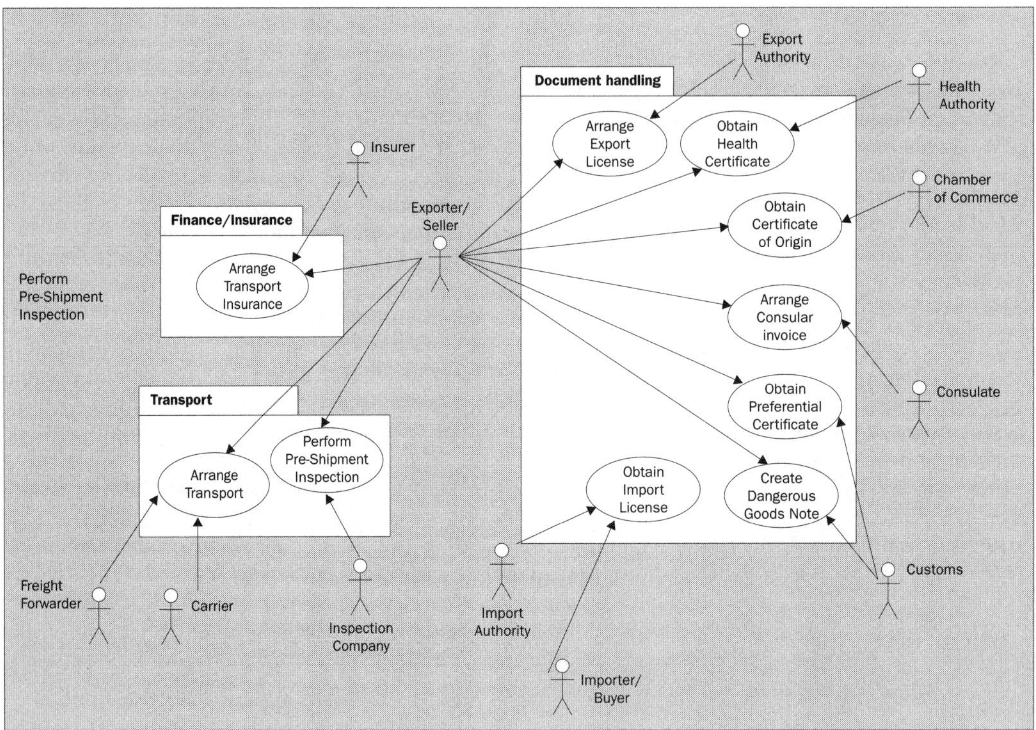


The diagram *only* shows business process use cases that are used in the 'Prepare for Export' phase. The following use case description provides information on what the various actions and actors mean in the context of the case:

| Name | Purchase and Supply Internationally: Prepare for Export |
|---|---|
| Short description | Exporter and importer take steps to make sure the purchased goods are ready for exportation and contact the relevant transportation intermediaries and authorities. |
| Actors | **Exporter**: Seller.<br><br>**Importer**: Buyer.<br><br>**Intermediaries**: Insurer, Freight forwarder, Carrier.<br><br>**Authorities**: Export Authority, Health Authority, Chamber of Commerce, Consulate, Customs, Import Authority, Inspection Company. |
| Preconditions | The Buyer has firmed his order with the Seller. |
| Postconditions | All documents required to proceed to export have been arranged. |
| Main scenario | The Seller submits an insurance request to the Insurer (an underwriter or insurance company). The scope of cover depends on type of cargo, transport route, and/or destination. The Insurer provides an insurance contract or an insurance certificate. Duration of insurance coverage is normally until the goods have been delivered properly with the Buyer.<br><br>The Seller subsequently makes arrangements for transport with a Freight Forwarder. These include preparations for shipping and preparations for delivery. Shipping requires information on where goods are located and where they need to be transported to. Delivery covers type/number of packages, gross weight and cube, and any special handling information for packing and delivery. The Freight Forwarder will arrange shipping notes, obtain a booking confirmation from the Carrier, and confirm transport with the Seller.<br><br>**Extension point**: an export license and/or import license may be required.<br><br>**Extension point**: a health certificate may be required.<br><br>The Chamber of Commerce can provide a certificate of origin. This can help the Buyer to obtain preferential rates of duty.<br><br>The Consulate can provide a consular invoice, which is a document that accompanies a commercial invoice and confirms details and origin of shipped goods.<br><br>A dangerous goods note needs to be drawn up by Seller, to specify the applicable Maritime Dangerous Goods Code (MDGC).<br><br>Customs can certify a preferential certificate that allows the seller to claim a (lower or zero) rate of duty, depending on trade tariff agreements between exporting and importing countries.<br><br>The Seller prepares a packing list to encode details on packaging, weights and measurements if not specified on the invoice.<br><br>The Buyer can request a specialized company to perform a Pre-Shipment Inspection (PSI). If the results of this are satisfactory, a Clean Report of Findings is issued. |

*Table continued on following page*

| Name | Purchase and Supply Internationally: Prepare for Export |
|---|---|
| **Exceptional scenarios** | Any number of the export documents may be refused for various reasons.<br>If the PSI finds any shortcomings, a non-negotiable failure report is issued. |
| **Alternative scenarios (to be covered by Use Case extensions)** | An export license is needed for controlled, sensitive or endangered goods, or when no diplomatic relations exist between two countries. The importing country may require similar licenses.<br>Plants, livestock, animal products and foodstuffs normally require certificates of health, issued by for example the veterinary service. |

*Note that our equipment exporting company doesn't need to worry about the alternative scenarios, as these cover special situations that are not relevant to them.*

## Re-organizing the 'Prepare for Export' Phase

As the P&SI case shows, real-life e-business scenarios can become very complex, with lots of actors and lots of business processes. We can employ **use case associations** to provide organization and to improve maintainability:

- **Include** relations. For example, we could split off the transport arrangement actions into a separate 'Arrange Shipping' use case. Then, we'd just include that use case from the base use case. Diagrams like this often signal business opportunities: an intermediary can offer (as a service) to manage all the administrative paperwork for exporting companies who can't (or don't want to) do this themselves.
- **Generalization** relations. For example, it's conceivable that 'Prepare for Air Transport' is structured differently from 'Prepare for Sea Transport', but both can be used interchangeably wherever a 'Prepare for Transport' is used. We could arrange use cases in generalization hierarchies. We could also arrange actors in such hierarchies, and thus identify properties common to, for instance, all authorities.
- **Extends** relations. We have listed a few alternative scenarios, mainly involving specific kinds of cargo or depending on specific source and target countries. We could view the main 'Prepare for Export' use case as a "base" use case. The **extension points** specified in the base scenario indicate where the base case can be extended. We could then specify a separate use case for the extended case, which references the base case and specifies the additional activity. Since these situations are not relevant for our exporter, we can ignore these.

## Business Processes in the 'Prepare for Export' Phase

In the remainder of this book, we will focus on the "base" use case for the 'Prepare for Export' phase, with extended scenarios omitted. This use case involves use cases for the following business processes:

- 'Arrange Transport Insurance'
- 'Arrange Transport'
- 'Obtain Certificate of Origin'
- 'Obtain Preferential Certificate'
- 'Perform Pre-Shipment Inspection'
- 'Prepare Dangerous Goods Note'

In the business modeling phase, the objective is to position these processes within business areas and to provide initial descriptions. In the ebXML bpWS document, worksheets are provided that allow us to specify the business reference model, business area, process area, and business process identification. The worksheet templates provide identification fields (for tracking purposes) – we have omitted them here.

The following is a (simplified) worksheet, which captures information about a business area:

| **Form: Describe Business Area** | |
|---|---|
| **Business Area Name** | **Transport** |
| **Description** | Provide international shipping and delivery |
| **Scope and boundaries** | Pick up goods at arranged time and location; pack and deliver according to goods; include all interactions with subcontracted carriers and relevant authorities; ability to provide tracking information |
| **References** | ITT reference model – http://www.unece.org/trade/itt/itt_tip.htm<br>UMM interpretation of ITT – http://www.unece.org/cefact/docum/download/01bp015r3.doc<br>UMM – http://www.unece.org/cefact/docum/download/01bp_n090.zip |
| **Constraints** | International shipping regulations;<br>service level agreements with customers |
| **Stakeholders** | Seller<br>Buyer<br>Freight Forwarder<br>Carrier<br>Inspection Company |
| **Process Areas** | Shipping and delivery<br>Deliver tracking information |
| **Optional for ebXML** | |
| **Objective** | To provide international pickup, shipping and delivery of products involved in international purchases |
| **Business Opportunity** | Integrate within an automated supply chain, thus improving customer relations with stakeholders involved by providing them with accurate information and saving cost by automating interactions of Seller and Buyer with the transport providers |

For space reasons, we will restrict our attention to (and only fill out the worksheets for) the following three business processes:

#### *Arrange Transport Insurance*

| Form: Identify Business Process | |
|---|---|
| **Business Process Name** | Arrange Transport Insurance |
| **Process Area** | Insurance |
| **Business Area** | Finance/Insurance |

#### *Arrange Transport*

| Form: Identify Business Process | |
|---|---|
| **Business Process Name** | Arrange Transport |
| **Process Area** | Shipping and Delivery |
| **Business Area** | Transport |

#### *Perform Pre-Shipment Inspection*

| Form: Identify Business Process | |
|---|---|
| **Business Process Name** | Perform Pre-Shipment Inspection |
| **Process Area** | Shipping and Delivery |
| **Business Area** | Transport |

We will track, and provide more detail for, these three processes as we move into the requirements and analysis workflows.

## *Overall Structure of the 'Prepare for Export' Phase*

The following diagrams provide an overall view of the P&SI *Prepare for Export* phase. These diagrams provide information about the various actors, activities, and documents exchanged. These diagrams use a non-UML process notation and provide the structure of the complete phase, and involve numerous business processes. We'll work out the individual business processes in the requirements workflow.

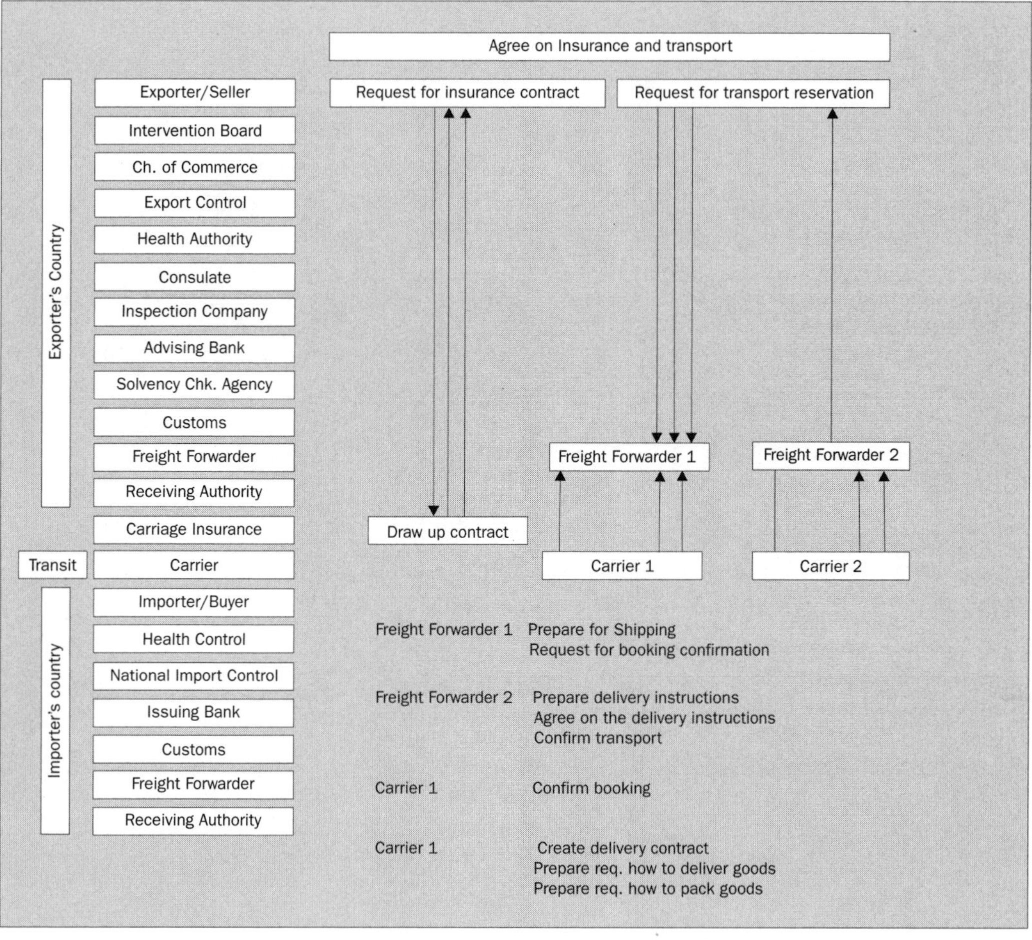
Agree on Insurance and transport
Exporter's Country
Exporter/Seller
Intervention Board
Ch. of Commerce
Export Control
Health Authority
Consulate
Inspection Company
Advising Bank
Solvency Chk. Agency
Customs
Freight Forwarder
Receiving Authority
Carriage Insurance
Transit
Carrier
Importer's country
Importer/Buyer
Health Control
National Import Control
Issuing Bank
Customs
Freight Forwarder
Receiving Authority
Request for insurance contract
Request for transport reservation
Draw up contract
Freight Forwarder 1
Freight Forwarder 2
Carrier 1
Carrier 2
Freight Forwarder 1 Prepare for Shipping
Request for booking confirmation
Freight Forwarder 2 Prepare delivery instructions
Agree on the delivery instructions
Confirm transport
Carrier 1 Confirm booking
Carrier 1 Create delivery contract
Prepare req. how to deliver goods
Prepare req. how to pack goods

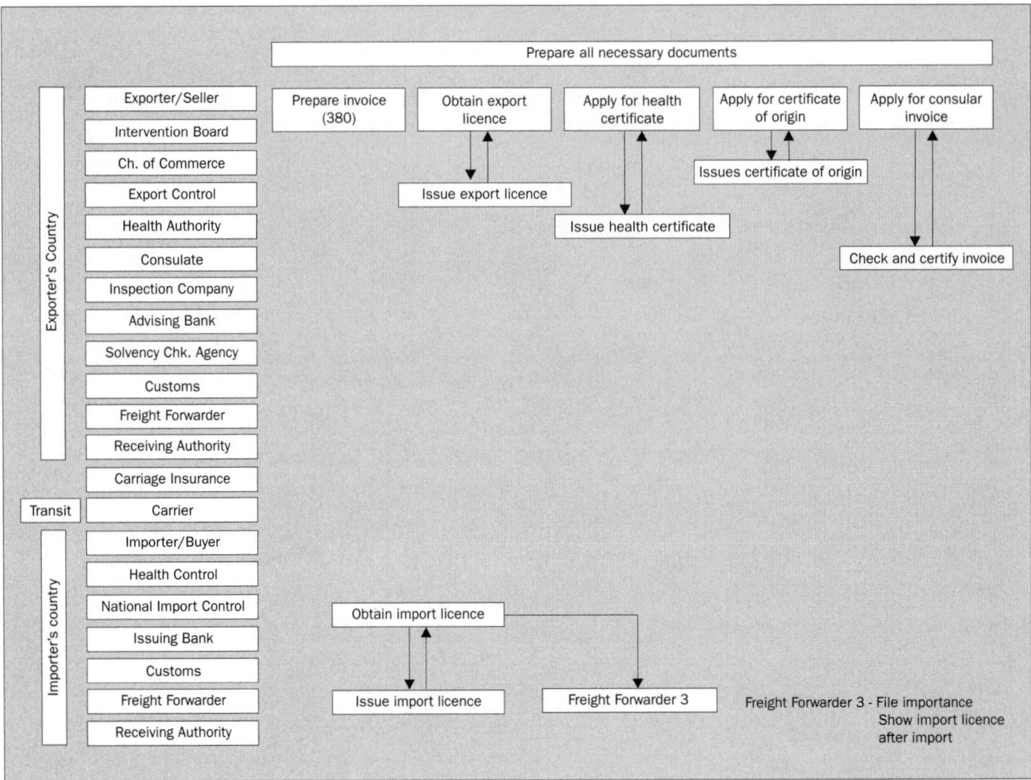
Prepare all necessary documents
Exporter's Country
Exporter/Seller
Intervention Board
Ch. of Commerce
Export Control
Health Authority
Consulate
Inspection Company
Advising Bank
Solvency Chk. Agency
Customs
Freight Forwarder
Receiving Authority
Carriage Insurance
Transit
Carrier
Importer's country
Importer/Buyer
Health Control
National Import Control
Issuing Bank
Customs
Freight Forwarder
Receiving Authority
Prepare invoice (380)
Obtain export licence
Apply for health certificate
Apply for certificate of origin
Apply for consular invoice
Issue export licence
Issues certificate of origin
Issue health certificate
Check and certify invoice
Obtain import licence
Issue import licence
Freight Forwarder 3
Freight Forwarder 3 - File importance
Show import licence
after import

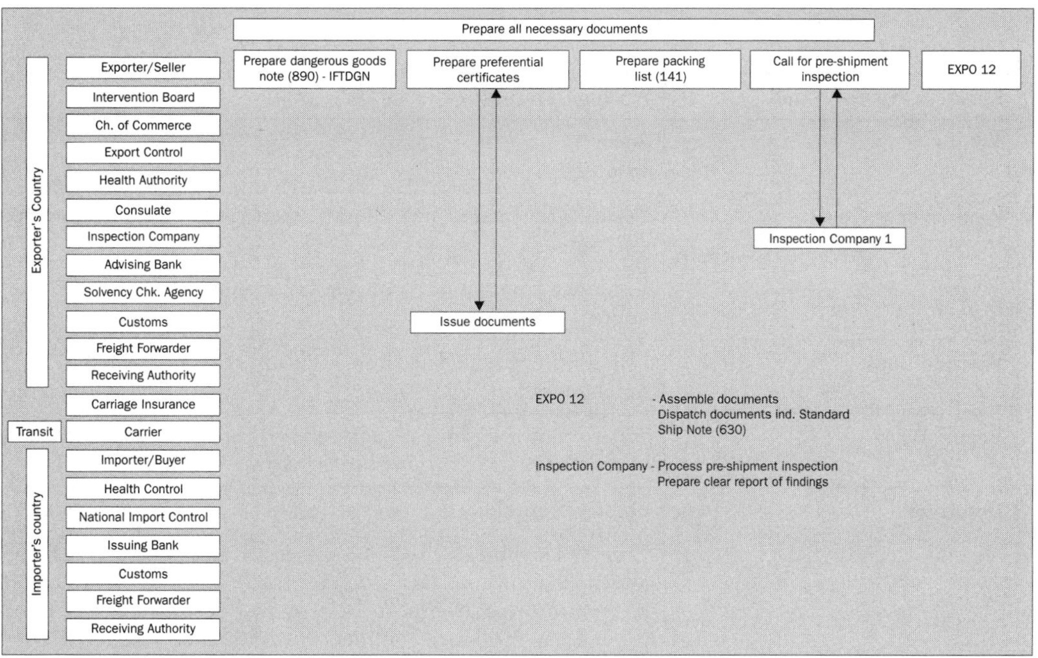


# The Requirements Workflow

In UMM, after completing the business modeling workflow we move on to the requirements workflow. So, let's apply the requirements workflow to the P&SI 'Prepare for Export' phase. We'll start by completing the bpWS business requirements worksheets; then we'll provide UML diagrams. For each business process, the ebXML bpWS document provides a business process use case worksheet. For reasons of space, we will provide worksheets for just the following three business processes:

- 'Arrange Transport Insurance'
- 'Arrange Transport'
- 'Perform Pre-Shipment Inspection'

We will also provide business collaboration worksheets and business collaboration protocol information for these three processes.

## Business Process Use Cases

We'll complete the business process use case worksheets for each of these business processes. We include the business process use case worksheets here, in order to illustrate the type of information that can be recorded in these worksheets. You could provide more or less detail in these worksheets (particularly in the area of exceptions), depending on the requirements of your project.

Here is the business process use case worksheet for the 'Arrange Transport Insurance' process:

| Form: Business Process Use Case | |
|---|---|
| **Business Process Name** | Arrange Transport Insurance |
| **Actors** | Seller<br>Insurer |
| **Performance Goals** | Business acceptance or exception message to be signaled within six hours.<br><br>Insurance contract or certificate to be returned to Seller within 36 hours. |
| **Preconditions** | Seller has negotiated an order with Buyer and obtained a purchase order. |
| **Begins When** | Seller sends insurance request to insurance company, with accompanying contract or order information from Buyer. |
| **Definition** | Quoted from the use case description (earlier in the chapter):<br><br>"The Seller submits an insurance request to the Insurer (an underwriter or insurance company). The scope of cover depends on type of cargo, transport route, and/or destination. The Insurer provides an insurance contract or an insurance certificate. Duration of insurance coverage is normally until the goods have been delivered properly with the Buyer." |
| **Ends When** | Insurance contract or insurance certificate is issued. |
| **Exceptions** | Insurer can refuse to insure for a variety of reasons. |
| **Postconditions** | Transport is insured. |

Now here's the business process use case worksheet for the 'Arrange Transport' process:

| Form: Business Process Use Case | |
|---|---|
| **Business Process Name** | Arrange Transport |
| **Actors** | Seller<br>Freight forwarder<br>Carrier |
| **Performance Goals** | Transport reservation to be confirmed within six hours.<br><br>Delivery contract to be confirmed within 24 hours. |
| **Preconditions** | Purchase order document provides volume, weight and special handling information, and delivery address. |
| **Begins When** | Exporter can provide required information electronically to Freight Forwarder. |

| Form: Business Process Use Case | |
|---|---|
| **Definition** | Quoted from use case description (earlier in the chapter):<br>"The Seller subsequently makes arrangements for transport with a Freight Forwarder. These include preparations for shipping and preparations for delivery. Shipping requires information on where goods are located and where they need to be transported to. Delivery covers type/number of packages, gross weight and cube, and any special handling information for packing and delivery. The Freight Forwarder will arrange shipping notes, obtain a booking confirmation from the Carrier, and confirm transport with the Seller." |
| **Ends When** | Booking confirmation and transport are confirmed with Seller. |
| **Exceptions** | Timeouts<br>Business rule violations (for example, unknown/incomplete delivery address etc.) |
| **Postconditions** | Transport reservation made. |

And finally for this section, the business process use case worksheet for the 'Perform Pre-Shipment Inspection' process:

| Form: Business Process Use Case | |
|---|---|
| **Business Process Name** | Perform Pre-Shipment Inspection |
| **Actors** | Buyer<br>Inspection Company |
| **Performance Goals** | Inspection date and location to be confirmed within six hours.<br>Inspection to be performed within three days. |
| **Preconditions** | Accurate description of goods<br>Indication of location of goods |
| **Begins When** | Seller provides required shipping documents. |
| **Definition** | Seller can request a specialized company to perform a Pre-Shipment Inspection (PSI). |
| **Ends When** | If the results of this are satisfactory, a Clean Report of Findings is issued. |
| **Exceptions** | If the PSI finds any shortcomings, a non-negotiable failure report is issued. |
| **Postconditions** | None |

## Business Collaborations and Business Collaboration Protocols

Business processes involve **collaboration** of business partners and a **dynamic exchange** of business messages. A single business process (at the business modeling level) can correspond to multiple collaborations (at the requirements level). A collaboration can involve two or more partners (in ebXML, there is an approach to unrestricted multi-party collaborations that models them as interrelated binary collaborations).

A collaboration is modeled using a **business collaboration form** and **collaboration protocol table** that encodes its dynamic structure. In the following subsections we'll present the form and the table for two of the three business processes (the *arrange transport insurance* and *arrange transport* processes).

### The 'Arrange Transport Insurance' Process

Here's the business collaboration form:

| **Form: Business Collaboration** | |
|---|---|
| **Description** | Arrange Transport Insurance |
| **Partner Types** | Seller<br>Insurer |
| **Authorized Roles** | Insurance Requestor<br>Insurance Provider |
| **Legal Steps/Requirements** | Seller legally owns exported goods |
| **Economic Consequences** | Seller is required to cover insurance cost<br>Insurer is bound by insurance terms and conditions |
| **Initial/Terminal Events** | Initial: goods are ready for shipping<br>Terminal: insurance is valid until delivery at destination |
| **Scope** | We assume a pre-existing framework contract between Seller and Insurer, so there is no need (for example) to negotiate terms or cost of insurance |
| **Boundary** | Systems include Exporter Order Management System and Insurer Contract Registration System |
| **Constraints** | Framework contract limits the kind of goods that can be insured, and limits the destination and carrier(s) that can be used |

The following UML activity diagram provides a graphical representation of this collaboration. It shows symbols for the start state (the black filled circle) and the end states (black ringed circles). The collaboration involves execution of a single transaction activity ('Insure Transport'), which is stereotyped as a business transaction activity. Note that this is a business **transaction** activity that implements a **collaboration.** The transaction activity may or may not have the same name as the collaboration. (The difference between collaborations and transaction activities will become clearer when we discuss collaborations that may involve multiple transactions, such as 'Arrange Transport'). The outgoing arrows are labeled with condition expressions or **guards**. These guards refer to the final state of execution of the invoked transaction:

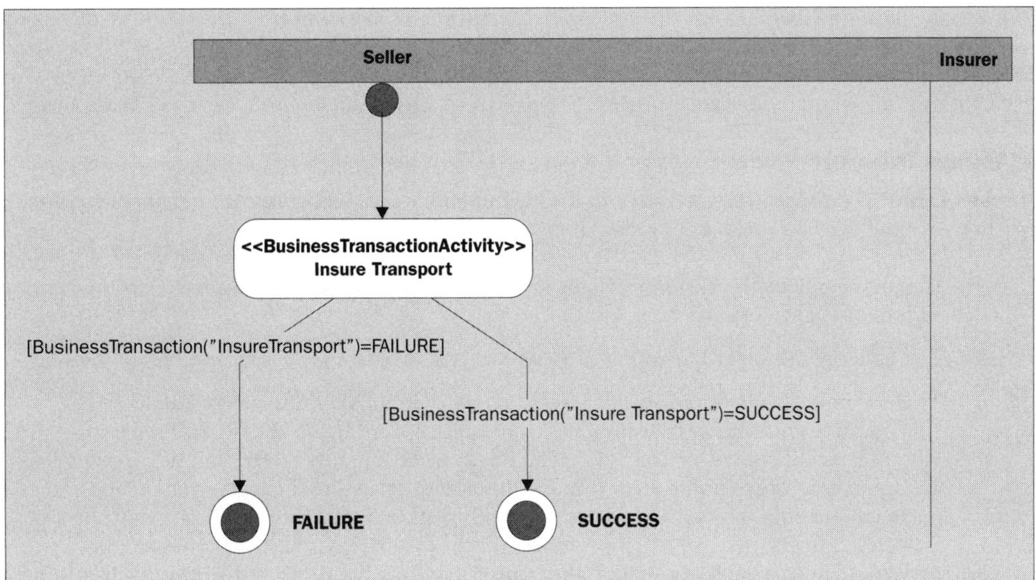


This relatively simple diagram can be rendered using a **business collaboration protocol table**. It provides identification information about the business collaboration, and one row for each transition allowed in the model. A transition has a **source** business activity and a **target** business activity and associates two business partners, one acting as initiator and another as responder. You can define conditions on transactions as conditions on the result state of the invoked transactions:

| **Form: Business Collaboration Protocol Table** | | | | |
|---|---|---|---|---|
| **Description** | Arrange Transport Insurance | | | |
| **From Business Activity** | **Initiating Partner Type** | **To Business Activity** | **Responding/ Receiving Partner Type** | **Transition Condition** |
| START | Insurance Requestor | Insure Transport | Insurance Provider | NONE |
| Insure Transport | N/A | SUCCESS | N/A | BusinessTransaction( "Insure Transport").State= SUCCESS |
| Insure Transport | N/A | FAILURE | N/A | BusinessTransaction( "Insure Transport").State= ANY-FAILURE |

Note that neither the diagram nor the table makes a distinction between business failures (such as when insurance cannot be provided because the insurer does not insure transport to the specified delivery address) and technical failures (such as when the network connection to the insurer's ebXML platform is down). You can set up the business process to perform alternative activities for each of these cases.

### The 'Arrange Transport' Process

In the 'Arrange Transport' case, we have to deal with a more complex collaboration between three parties – the Seller, the Freight Forwarder, and the Carrier:

- Having completed its business collaboration with Insurer, the Seller wants to obtain transport with the Freight Forwarder.
- The Seller and Freight Forwarder are associated in an 'Arrange Transport' collaboration.
- To perform this collaboration, the Freight Forwarder collaborates with a Carrier. The collaboration with the Carrier involves two separate transaction activities: 'Prepare for Shipping' and 'Prepare for Delivery'. The first transaction only covers shipping reservations, and invokes a transaction called 'Confirm Booking'. The second covers exchange of information about packaging and delivery and invokes a transaction called 'Confirm Delivery'. For the sake of this illustration, we will assume that these activities can be performed in parallel in a collaboration called 'Arrange Shipping and Delivery'. The following table elaborates on this collaboration.
- The Freight Forwarder can complete its obligations in 'Arrange Transport' once both booking and delivery are completed.
- After completion of the 'Arrange Transport' collaboration, the Seller moves to obtain its next business activity (which is to obtain a Certificate of Origin from the Chamber of Commerce).

This collaboration involves three actors. It can be modeled as a composition of two binary collaborations:

- One between the Seller and the Freight Forwarder
- One between the Freight Forwarder and the Carrier

The former collaboration requires the latter, which means that once the Seller has sent a request to the Freight Forwarder, the Freight Forwarder *in turn* becomes a requestor in a business collaboration with the Carrier. Only after this second collaboration completes, can the Freight Forwarder respond back to the Seller.

The collaboration between the Seller and Freight Forwarder is simple and similar to the collaboration between Seller and Insurer. The collaboration between the Freight Forwarder and Carrier is more complex, because it involves two separate transactions: a transport booking transaction and a delivery negotiation transaction. In our model, we have assumed that these two transactions can be done in parallel, but both need to be concluded successfully for the collaboration to be successful. We'll see this dependence in the activity diagram in a moment.

The following form provides information on the collaboration between the Freight Forwarder and the Carrier:

| Form: Business Collaboration | |
|---|---|
| **Description** | Arrange Shipping and Delivery |
| **Partner Types** | Freight Forwarder<br>Carrier |
| **Authorized Roles** | Shipping requestor<br>Shipping provider |
| **Legal Steps/Requirements** | Freight forwarder declares shipment with carrier<br>Freight forwarder agrees to be billed by carrier for shipping and delivery |
| **Economic Consequences** | Economic Contract for carrier to provide services to freight forwarder, in return for payment<br>Agreement commits carrier to specific shipping, delivery and packing instructions |
| **Initial/Terminal Events** | Initial: Freight Forwarder:<br>❑ performs booking request<br>❑ provides delivery instructions<br>Terminal: Carrier confirms transport and delivery |
| **Scope** | Transport and delivery |
| **Boundary** | Logistics management systems on both sides |
| **Constraints** | Requirements to notify Buyer of delivery |

The orchestration of business activities covered by this collaboration is provided in the following activity diagram. **Parallelism** is expressed using **forking** and **joining** symbols: the horizontal lines in the diagram with incoming and outgoing arrow symbols. The diagram is complicated by the fact that there are two `BusinessTransaction Activities` that each can succeed or fail. The overall collaboration fails if one of the two parallel collaborations fails. If both are successful, we conclude the overall collaboration is successful.

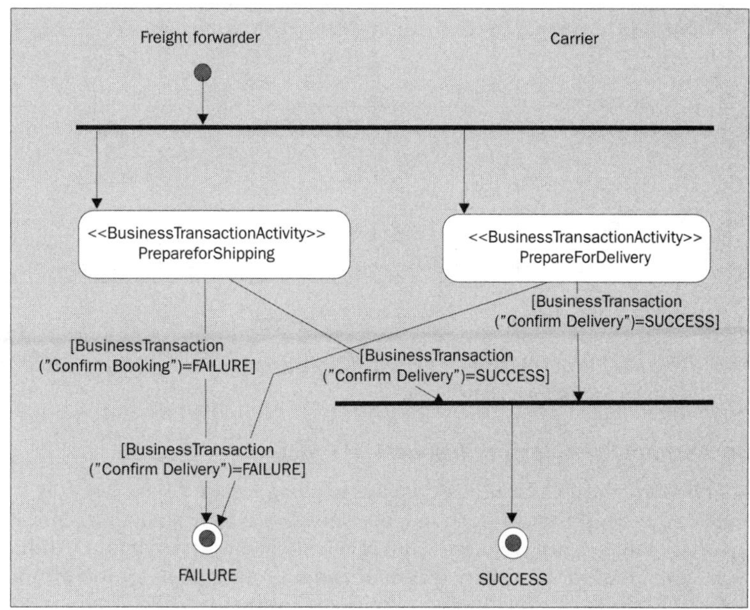

As before, we have a business collaboration protocol table, which provides another way of expressing this information:

| **Form: Business Collaboration Protocol Table** | | | | |
|---|---|---|---|---|
| **Description** | Arrange Shipping and Delivery | | | |
| **From Business Activity** | **Initiating Partner Type** | **To Business Activity** | **Responding / Receiving Partner Type** | **Transition Condition** |
| START | Shipping requestor | Arrange Shipping: Fork | Shipping Provider | NONE |
| ArrangeShipping: Fork | Shipping requestor | Confirm Booking | Shipping Provider | NONE |
| ArrangeShipping: Fork | Shipping requestor | Confirm Delivery | Shipping Provider | NONE |
| Confirm Booking | | Arrange Shipping: Join | | BusinessTransaction( "ConfirmBooking").State= SUCCESS |
| Conform Booking | N/A | FAILURE | N/A | BusinessTransaction( "ConfirmBooking").State= AnyFailure |
| Confirm Delivery | N/A | ArrangeShipping: Join | | BusinessTransaction( "ConfirmDelivery").State= SUCCESS |
| Confirm Delivery | N/A | FAILURE | N/A | BusinessTransaction( "ConfirmDelivery").State= AnyFailure |
| ArrangeShipping: Join | N/A | SUCCESS | N/A | NONE |

*Note that the* From Business Activity *and* To Business Activity *columns might more generally be called* From Business State *and* To Business State *– where states generalize over activities, start, end, and fork/join states.*

### The 'Perform Pre-shipment Inspection' Process

This is the third collaboration we are tracking in our discussion. It is a collaboration between the Seller and a Pre-Shipment Inspection Company. We'll have something interesting to say about this collaboration when we discuss the invoked business transaction. At this stage, we'll omit the collaboration form, activity diagram, and business collaboration protocol table for this collaboration as they are similar to the 'Arrange Transport Insurance' collaboration.

# The Analysis Workflow

In the business analysis workflow, the focus is on modeling **business transactions**. In the ebXML bpWS document, there are three worksheets produced by this workflow:

- The **business transaction form** provides the main description of a transaction, and the actors and documents involved.
- The **business transaction property values form** allows you to record values for business transaction properties, if not using or overriding values of an analysis pattern.
- The **business transaction transition table form** models the dynamic structure of the business transaction.

We will focus on the transactions associated with the collaborations we've looked at so far. The transaction for 'Arrange Transport' adds nothing to the 'Arrange Transport Insurance' transaction and is therefore omitted.

## *Business Transactions, Properties, and Transitions*

The analysis worksheets are concerned with identifying the business transactions, determining an applicable analysis pattern, setting values for business transaction property values (or selecting appropriate transaction patterns), and specifying a business transactions transition table.

In the state transition table, you should use BPSS terminology for terminal states to facilitate transition to an ebXML environment `Success`, `BusinessFailure`, `TechnicalFailure` and `AnyFailure`. The `AnyFailure` state is a way to generalize `BusinessFailure` and `TechnicalFailure`. Chapter 5 provides a detailed discussion of the topic of exceptions and business transaction modeling.

### *The 'Arrange Transport Insurance' Process*

Here's the business transaction form for this process:

| **Form: Business Transaction** | |
|---|---|
| **Description** | Insure Shipment |
| **Pattern** | Business Transaction |
| **Business Activities and associated authorized roles** | Shipment Insurance Request<br>Shipment Insurance Response |
| **Constraints** | |
| **Initiating/Requesting Partners Type** | Seller |
| **Initiating/Requesting Activity Role** | Insurance Requestor |
| **Initiating/Requesting Activity Document** | Shipment Insurance Request |
| **Responding Partner Type** | Insurer |
| **Responding Activity Role** | Insurance Provider |
| **Responding Activity Document** | Shipment Insurance Contract |

In the business transaction property values form, which follows, we would normally select just one of the UMM business transaction patterns. Since 'Insuring a Shipment' is a business transaction, this table just redundantly specifies the default values for the business transaction pattern specified in UMM (except for the Time to Perform field, which is set to 36 hours – a value we've taken from the example performance constraint we included in the encompassing business process use case). We could use the form if we needed to specify an altogether different set of property values:

| **Form: Business Transaction Property Values** | | | | | | | |
|---|---|---|---|---|---|---|---|
| **Form ID** | Insure Shipment | | | | | | |
| | **Time to acknowledge receipt** | **Time to acknowledge acceptance** | **Time to perform** | **Authorization Required** | **Non-repudiation of Origin and Content** | **Non-repudiation of Receipt** | **Recurrence** |
| **Requesting Business Activity** | 2hrs | 6hr | 36hr | true | true | true | 3 |
| **Responding Business Acitivity** | 2hrs | 6hr | 24hr | true | true | | |

In the business transaction transition table form, we specify the business transaction activity in terms of transitions between activities. As with transaction property values, transaction patterns are associated with default transition patterns that will cover in practice most business transactions.

| **Form: Business Transaction Transition Table** | | | | | |
|---|---|---|---|---|---|
| **Form ID:** | Insure Shipment | | | | |
| **From Activity** | **From Role** | **Document** | **To Activity** | **To Role** | **Guard Condition** |
| START | N/A | N/A | Shipment Insurance Request | Insurance requestor | NONE |
| Shipment Insurance Request | Insurance requestor | Shipment Insurance Request | Shipment Insurance Response | Insurance provider | NONE |
| Shipment Insurance Response | Insurance provider | Shipment Insurance Contract | SUCCESS | N/A | |
| Shipment Insurance Response | Insurance provider | NONE | FAILURE | N/A | |

### The 'Perform Pre-Shipment Inspection' Process

Here, the business transaction form and business transaction property values are similar to the previous case and are therefore omitted.

The business transaction transition table for this business transaction shows how you can associate different kinds of business documents with different results states. If inspection finds no errors, it issues a Clear Report of Findings and the transaction terminates successfully. Otherwise, it issues an inspection failure report and the transaction fails:

| **Form: Business Transaction Transition Table** | | | | | |
|---|---|---|---|---|---|
| **Form ID:** | Perform pre-shipment inspection | | | | |
| **From Activity** | **From Role** | **Document** | **To Activity** | **To Role** | **Guard Condition** |
| START | N/A | NONE | Shipment Inspection Request | Pre-shipment Inspection Requestor | |
| Shipment Inspection Request | Pre-shipment Inspection Requestor | Shipment Inspection Request | Response to Inspection Request | Pre-shipment Inspection Provider | |
| Response to Inspection Request | Pre-shipment Inspection Provider | Clear Report of Findings | SUCCESS | N/A | |
| Response to Inspection Request | Pre-shipment Inspection Provider | Inspection Failure Report | FAILURE | Pre-shipment Inspection Provider | |

As noted before, our focus in this chapter has been on modeling processes, collaborations and transactions, rather than business information. In Chapter 12, we will have a detailed look at encoding an 'Inspection Request' message in XML, based on an existing UN/EDIFACT message definition.

## Conclusion

This concludes our discussion of UMM and ebXML business process modeling worksheets. So far in this chapter, we've talked about business process analysis, the use of methods like UML developed for software engineering to model business processes, and the concept of workflows as a way to logically group particular sets of activities in a project. You may have heard these terms used to discuss another type of business applications: workflow management applications. The final section of this chapter is intended to clarify the relation between these applications and e-business applications.

# Process Modeling and Workflow Management

So far, we've talked about UMM as a methodology for modeling business processes, based on ideas originally developed for software development, and developed for use in e-business projects. The term *workflow* is central in UMM and serves to reference a logically-related group of modeling activities in an e-business development project.

Another application area where terms like *workflow* and *process modeling* are commonly used is the field of **workflow management (WfM)**, or **workflow automation**. Workflow management, like e-business process modeling, is another business application area that adopted formal process modeling methods. In fact, their use in this field actually predates their use for e-business processes and methodologies like UMM.

Unfortunately, key terms like *workflow* don't have the same meaning in the two fields, so to avoid confusion, it's useful to provide a brief review of how the two application areas relate to each other. We'll first give a brief introduction to functionality and benefits of workflow management systems and then discuss how they relate to e-business systems, in terms of the differences between the business processes that they automate.

## Workflow Management Systems

Workflow management systems are systems that are particularly concerned with administrative business processes whose activities are **document-intensive** and **require human involvement**. These processes are usually contained within a single organization or department. Insurance claims processing (or any administrative case-handling process) is a classic example of a business process that can be automated by workflow automation. Typically, a workflow process in an industry like the insurance industry is initiated by the arrival of some incoming paper document or fax, which becomes a first document in a dossier. This dossier is then routed through the organization: its employees, working in various capacities, create documents and fill out forms, and add them to the dossier.

Often, the first activity in an automated workflow system is to scan the document, so that the dossier exists in electronic format. This has two very obvious benefits:

- It improves the efficiency of the workflow process itself, by eliminating the hours or days required to move paper-based dossiers around in the organization.
- It also enables organizations to be more responsive to customers calling in to inquire about the status of their case, as the call center can have immediate access to status information associated with each dossier.

In addition to this, a workflow management system may also automate the process of assignment of activities to employees. For example, it might assign all written sales queries for a particular product to members of a sales team dedicated to that product (role-based assignment); it might also make sure that important (or time-critical) tasks are processed before less important tasks (priority-based assignment). Further, the routing functionality available in such systems can perform conditional branching (for instance, to handle special cases), parallel execution of tasks, load balancing among various workers, dynamic re-prioritization of cases, deadline management, and generation of management information.

> *A workflow automation product can provide an organization with a number of opportunities, for instance to take advantage of the parallelism inherent in many processes, and to reorganize and improve its process. Moreover, post-project the organization should expect an improvement in the amount and quality of management information – which may help in the discovery of bottlenecks in the process. Some products even offer simulation tools that perform execution of "what-if" scenarios – allowing an organization to evaluate process modifications without deploying them for real.*

Workflow automation projects are often compared to **business process re-engineering** projects, as both require formal analysis of business processes that prior to the project had only been described informally. Both employ formal modeling methodologies like UML. This use has inspired the more recent application of such modeling techniques to e-business scenarios.

## Comparing Workflow Management and e-Business

So what are the main similarities and differences between e-business processes, modeled using UMM for e-business integration, and business processes in a workflow management context? The main aspects to consider are:

- The difference of internal versus external processes;
- The level of human involvement;
- The organizational scope of the project;
- The degree of machine-processability of documents;
- The use of the term *workflow* to describe activities in the software development project, or to describe activities performed (or automated) by the software that the project is developing.

We'll explain each of these items in sequence.

First of all, in Chapter 1 we talked about **internal** and **external processes,** in our discussion of e-business integration patterns. There we noted that EAI (Enterprise Application Integration) is about integrating enterprise systems to automate internal processes and that business-to-business integration (B2Bi) is about integration across enterprises to automate external processes. Both EAI and B2Bi are essentially about application integration. Like EAI and unlike B2Bi, workflow management is concerned with internal processes.

However, it is important to note that many internal processes are not (or not completely) automated, and many require some amount of **human involvement**. Workflow management systems are software products that allow organizations to automate the management of internal processes where humans perform some (or all) activities. Where an EAI system routes data between applications, a workflow management system routes documents through an organization.

We also noted that internal and external processes are often related, because an incoming B2B request message may trigger an internal (potentially complex, and potentially manual) process that computes the information that is sent back in the reply message. The internal process is invisible to the external party and is not in the scope of UMM or ebXML. This means that the **organizational scope** of EAI and workflow automation is typically departmental or organization-bound, whereas e-business in a B2B context is associated with business among different organizations.

Documents and dossiers associated with workflow business processes are in an electronic format (or they have become electronic documents by scanning), but are in formats that still require human interpretation – such as faxes and word-processed documents. By contrast, both EAI and e-business are concerned with **machine-interpretable** documents, that is business messages in formats like EDI and XML that (informally speaking) include enough of their own meta data to support machine-interpretation.

Given this background, it will be clear that the term *workflow* as used in *workflow management systems* is not to be confused with the concept of *workflow* as used in UMM. An administrative workflow is an instance of a routine business process. A workflow automation project is a project that uses specialized workflow management software to automate these administrative workflows, to obtain some business benefits. In our discussion of UMM, we've used the term *workflow* as a logical grouping of activities in the e-business project. These workflows are *project workflows*, unrelated to the business process activity flows in the business processes that are modeled. To see the two concepts at work in a single context, you could imagine that a project team working on an insurance workflow automation project can adopt the Unified Process and organize its activities according to the workflows in the model.

## Technology Convergence of EAI, WFM and B2B

At an abstract level, business processes as automated by workflow management systems may not be fundamentally different from e-business processes, and they are also quite similar to processes automated by EAI systems. The differences between these areas are mostly due to the different application areas. Both for technical and business reasons, the differences between the various fields are becoming increasingly less apparent, and there are now hybrid systems operational that combine workflow management, EAI and e-business functionality:

- The designers of the ebXML messaging service and SOAP have recognized the need to transport non-XML data in business-to-business messages. For example, it might be necessary to transport digital photographs of items involved in a sale, or a scanned image of a signed delivery receipt confirmation form. This means that these messaging services could serve the needs of all three kinds of process automation. Further discussion of messaging is provided in Chapters 4, 13 and 14 of this book.
- A company may have business rules that identify implausible situations that may be signals for processing errors or attempts at fraud. An otherwise fully-automated business process should apply those rules as checks and provide appropriate routing of the relevant documents or messages to human supervisors. Some EAI and B2B products provide support for these scenarios, and provide mechanisms like XSLT stylesheets to transform the XML business message into an HTML page that includes an embedded form. This form allows the human to select the appropriate next action. The form generator and form handler thus integrate the human step within the overall automated business process execution environment.

In the workflow management application area, the **Workflow Management Coalition** (**WfMC** – http://www.wfmc.org/) is the main standards-setting body. The original focus of this organization has been on the specification of standard APIs to improve interoperability of workflow management systems. As long as organizations use these APIs in their own application, they will be able to port their applications to other supporting products.

More recently, the WfMC has addressed the issue of standard representations for workflow process specifications (see http://www.wfmc.org/standards/docs/Wf-XML-1.0.pdf). This would allow you to export a process definition from one product and re-import it into another product, and results in more opportunities for reuse and a higher degree of product independence. Like the OMG XMI we saw earlier in this chapter and process notations like BPSS we will discuss in Chapter 5, the WfMC uses an XML representation to express this interchange format.

# Summary

As we've attempted to demonstrate in this chapter, the ebXML framework is based on a history of the application of software engineering methods and processes to business modeling, and it recommends "best practices" in a number of areas, briefly summarized here:

- The use of the Unified Modeling Language (**UML**) as the standard language for specifying, constructing, visualizing, and documenting software-intensive systems such as e-business systems.
- The use of the UN/CEFACT Modeling Methodology (**UMM**) as a framework to structure e-business projects in terms of workflows, phases, and iterations.

We've looked in detail at three of the main workflows in UMM, which are:

- The **business modeling** workflow, which is focused on creating models for business **processes**.
- The **requirements** workflow, which is focused on models for e-business **collaborations**.
- The **analysis** workflow, which is focused on models for e-business **transactions**.

We've defined these concepts and discussed the activities that take place in these workflows and shown how you can record the results of those activities in worksheets or as UML models.

Although we've described these workflows sequentially, we've noted that it is not necessarily the case that the recommended order for performing these activities is to start with business modeling and to work down to the analysis workflow. A workflow is a logical grouping for activities. These activities may be performed in iterations and in project phases. Together, UML and UMM offer a methodology and a process by which to address system development and project management in e-business projects.

By way of illustration, we made a start in applying these to an actual realistic case – the 'Prepare for Export' phase of the ITT **Purchase and Supply Internationally** (**P&SI**) case. Throughout the chapter, there are forward references to other chapters in this book that discuss the various components of the ebXML framework – in particular, the business process specification schema. Those chapters will show that, with the artifacts produced in a UMM-based project, we have a specification that we can map directly to corresponding ebXML constructs, and which we in turn can use to configure ebXML-compliant e-business process management systems to operationally implement the specified business processes.

In the next chapter, we will give an overview of XML schema languages. These languages allow you to model the structure of XML documents. Understanding XML schemas (in DTD, W3C XML Schema or RELAX NG notation) is an important prerequisite for understanding the various components of the ebXML framework. XML schemas are also used by several standards for message "payload", to define the structure of business information exchanged by ebXML business transactions.

# 3

# e-Business Document Modeling

Many people think of electronic business documents as things like purchase orders and invoices. While these are valid examples, the term 'business document' represents a wider spectrum of information and document types, for example, insurance policies, contracts, medical records, bills of lading, financial reports, etc. Each industry and individual organization has a collection of document types that are unique to their line of business.

The ebXML family of specifications does not address modeling of information or documents. Even though modeling information is not part of the ebXML specification, it is important to the entire process and is included in this book.

> *Document modeling is the process of analysing and designing a data model for your organization, so that it enables your organization to perform its business activities effectively.*

Document modeling requires two distinct stages (each of which will be covered in more detail during the course of this chapter):

- **Analysis** of the information involved (both what is available from all sources of the information and what is required throughout the workflow) – this information can come from many different sources, including databases.
- **Creation** of the information model. This stage can in turn be broken down into two sub-stages:
    - Designing the model to meet those requirements, based on the constraints of available information.
    - Implementing the model as a DTD or XML Schema.

In this chapter we will discuss various issues that need to be considered when modeling and creating business documents or rule-based business information. For example, business documents are comprised of **information objects** – components that can be reusable or standalone. We will show you how to analyze your business information for both structural and content components. We will also show how to model the information and create a rule-based structure, using either a DTD or an XML Schema. There are currently several conflicting standards for XML Schemas, and we'll discuss some of these too.

# Information (Content) Analysis

The first stage in any document modelling process should be a thorough analysis of the information involved. This includes identifying what information is *available* from various sources, and identifying what information is *required* (and in what format) at each stage in the workflow, including consideration of other, secondary uses for the data.

# Information Availability

The first step is to identify what information is available and collect together all the relevant documents. Broadly speaking, there are two sources of business information that we will consider during the analysis process:

- **Internal data** – data that is maintained, controlled and/or created by an organization itself, such as employee records. All organizations have various types of information they keep internally. In many cases the information is located in different departments or offices, and the same information can be maintained, updated, and distributed by several offices within the organization. During the information analysis you should identify all sources and users of the information.

- **External data** – data that comes into the organization from an outside entity. For example, distributors of products normally receive catalog data from their suppliers. Organizations do not always have the opportunity to request external data in XML. Many times external data will be received in another format, such as EDI, PDF, faxes, etc.

Note that sometimes we'll need to consider **legacy data** – information that the organization maintains that is not in the current XML model. Legacy data can be data that has been created from internal and external data but has been published in a non-XML format. Legacy data could also consist of information contained in relational databases. In fact, as soon as information is created it becomes legacy data.

We will see later in the chapter that the source and nature of the information (internal or external, current or legacy) can impose constraints on the resulting design of the information model.

## *Analysis of Structure*

When determining what information is available, it is sometimes useful to look at the structure of current business documents. The names used to identify information objects (and their hierarchy) often give clues as to what content is available. In childhood, when we were just learning to read, we were taught to discern the structure of documents using the physical layout or style of the information – we gain an understanding of structure by observing how the information appears on the printed page. There are clues to the structure or hierarchy of information by the way it is presented on either a page or an electronic display. The format of information is useful to a human being but it not very useful for the exchange of information between computer systems or software. For example, we know a chapter generally starts with the word 'Chapter' and a number or letter. The title of the chapter is usually visually larger and bolder than the body of the chapter.

When analyzing information for an XML project, your primary concern shouldn't be the way it is formatted, because in XML, the format is separate from the content itself (unlike HTML – this is the main difference between XML and HTML). However, the form of the information (that is, the element names and their hierarchy) will provide clues about the content of the information, and suggest a structure (although you can give it whatever structure you wish using XSLT). You can therefore identify the available pieces of information based on both structure and actual content. We say that XML is **self-describing**.

For instance, remember that XML requires that you always have a 'root' or document element. For an invoice, it makes sense to call the document element `<invoice>`. So, by simply looking at a schema that describes such a document, we will be able to tell that it is supposed to be an invoice by its document element. We will probably be able to tell more as well – the schema will describe other contained elements, say, an `<invoiceType>` element that contains information on whether it is an invoice for services or goods.

## Information Requirements

Part of the analysis involves looking at how the information is used; how the information is maintained and updated in the various organizations; how the information flows through the organization; and how the information flows to outside sources. This is a good opportunity to look at internal processes and decide how your organization will supply information to both internal and external users of the information. In some cases, the information may be valuable enough that the organization may decide to charge external sources for access to the information.

While performing an information analysis, think about all of the information the organization would like to have access to. If you haven't recently looked at your business processes, this would be a good time to consider doing so, and to consider the possibilities of 're-engineering' and streamlining its processes. XML can play a vital role in re-engineering business processes. The flexibility of XML allows organizations to create more robust data than that contained within the original documents.

For example, an Electronic Data Interchange (EDI) message for an insurance claim is concise. XML too can be succinct and to the point, but it can also provide additional information internally or links to either internal or external information, for example pictures of the accident site, a police report, estimates, etc. XML Linking Language (http://www.w3.org/TR/xlink/) capability allows elements to be inserted into XML documents in order to create and describe links between resources.

As another example, a company in the shipping industry may think about including Material Safety Data Sheets (MSDSs) directly into the bill of ladings. MSDSs are informational sheets that provide information about hazardous materials. Linking to the MSDS will allow shipping companies that handle hazardous material the opportunity to access MSDS information quickly during abnormal situations, such as temperature changes in shipping containers or vehicle accidents where a product is spilled.

XML can provide increased value to business information. Providing value-added information can be difficult because it means looking at the entire business and thinking beyond the traditional business models. An example of how SGML/XML can benefit individuals is the prescription information sheets that are currently available to patients. Prescription information sheets are currently provided to patients with prescription drugs. The prescription information sheets are currently maintained by publishers of this information, in SGML. This information (before it was converted to SGML) was previously only available to the doctor and pharmacists in book format. This information is now available by pharmacists in electronic format. The application allows the prescription information sheets to be printed and provided to the patient with every prescription drug.

## Workflow Analysis

It is important to consider the workflow of the information. It is possible that you are receiving information from several external parties or departments internal to your organization, and the workflow can be quite complex. Decisions about how various pieces of information will be handled are necessary. The following figure illustrates a typical scenario:

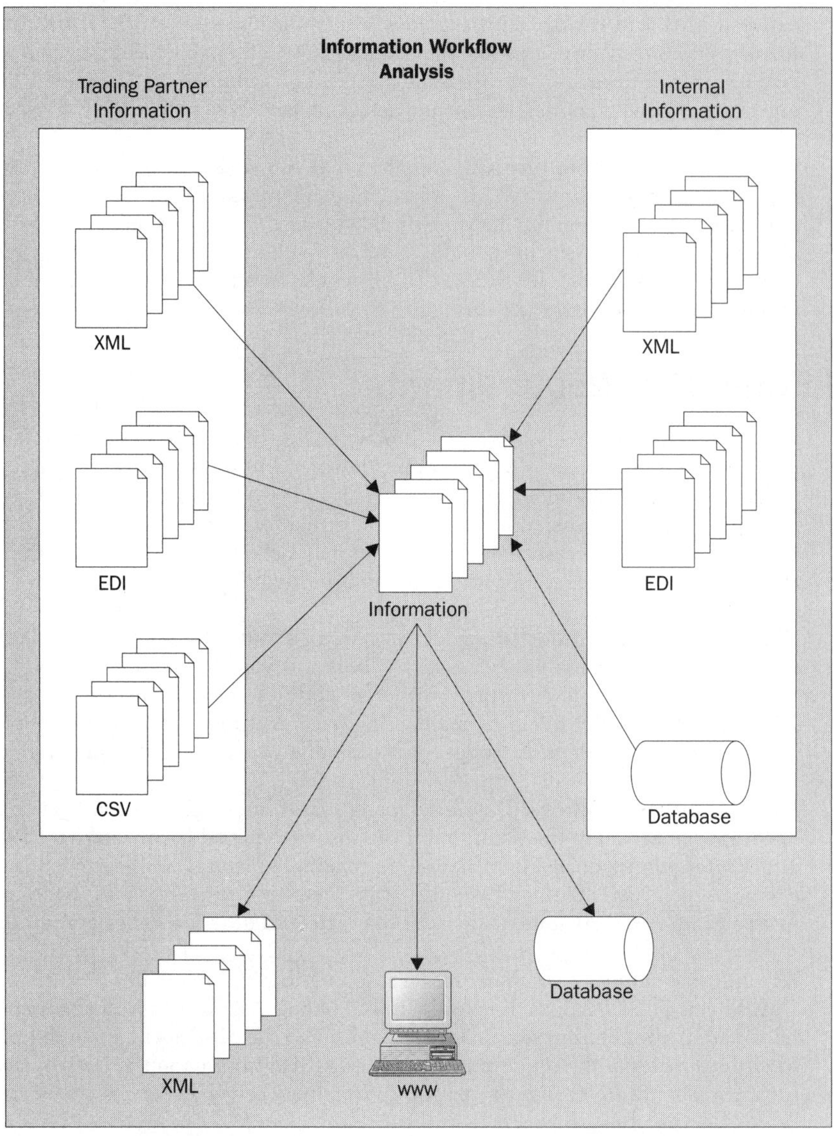


When a company is small and has limited resources, it can be difficult and costly for it to deal with the demands of their larger trading partners. For example, one small company sells *widgets* to a government agency. The government agency requires that the company receives purchases and sends invoices via the EDI X12 standard, but the small company has no IT specialists. They are forced to pay per transaction for each purchase order and invoice received and sent, although the cost of each transaction cutting into their profit margin is only one cost they incur.

In order to use a VAN system, they are doing double or triple manual entries of data to get this information from the VAN to their internal accounting and inventory systems. There isn't an automated process available to them. It requires a person to enter the same data into each system.

This problem is compounded when you have multiple 'bigger' trading partners that require different processes to interact with. XML provides the ability for these larger companies to streamline the processes not only for themselves but also for their trading partners. Standard commercial accounting and inventory software vendors are incorporating XML capability into their software packages.

Information that is received from outside your organization may require some transformation. For example, if you currently have trading partners with whom EDI messages are sent and received, you may want to look at the EDI messages and transform them into XML. Even though EDI data is not XML data, it has inherent structure, and is relatively easy to translate into XML. There are many software tools available to help with the translation. XSLT is a good way to transform data from XML to different markup structures, or other formats, such as EDI. However, XSLT only works if the input is valid XML. Omnimark (http://www.omnimark.com) is a very good tool for transforming XML data, as well as non-XML data, to XML. Omnimark is quite popular for both large and small conversion projects. Other tools worth checking out are Microsoft's Biztalk Mapper component (see http://www.microsoft.com/biztalk/default.asp for more information about Microsoft's Biztalk Server product).

The figure below shows how XML can be transformed to/from EDI.

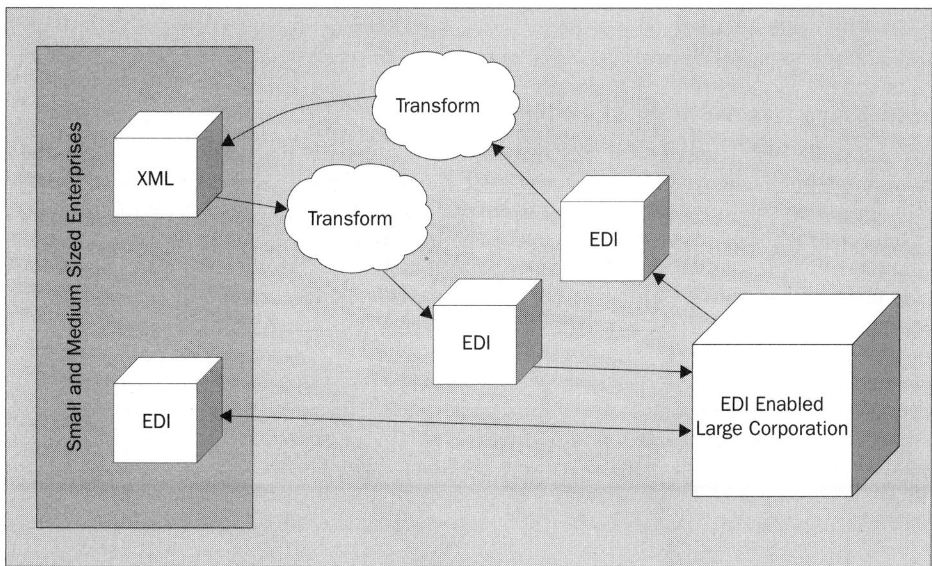


The most difficult information to deal with is word processing or unstructured information, because there isn't any semantic information about the structure of the document. Organizations that rely on word processing for their business documents usually develop standard templates or stylesheets. The stylesheets usually mimic structure and content, however, there aren't any enforcement rules within the word processor to ensure the creator of the information adheres to the styles. For example, the creator may use a designated style for *caption* in one instance and use *bold, italic, center* for another instance of a caption. Although format-wise they may look exactly the same, an automatic transformation engine will see them as being totally different.

Transformation also works in reverse – if you are a company dealing with a larger organization, you may have to send the information in the format they tell you to use. In these situations, XML is a good tool because you can create the data for your own internal purposes and translate it into whatever format your trading partners require.

## Output Requirements

As mentioned, a part of analyzing the workflow is to look at what information is required as output. However, we also need to consider what format the output should take, and any special requirements. We will look at a few different examples, where different information is to be included in each of the various output types.

### Multiple Media Types with Different Information

Traditional paper information often includes various types of graphics for special features, but companies moving to electronic information delivery will want a 'flashier' presentation. Color graphics in printed material result in a higher publishing cost, however, in electronic delivery there are no associated costs. Animation/video and sound may also be included in electronic delivery.

Suppliers of scientific journals and textbooks are taking this concept further. They are beginning to provide distance learning and interactive testing on-line. A DTD has been developed by IMS (IMS Global Learning Consortium, Inc.) to support "question and test" functionality (http://www.imsproject.org/question/). Online newspapers are also providing video news clips that aren't available with a traditional printed news article, with many using an XML Specification called News Markup Language (NewsML) – check out http://www.newsml.org/.

### Multiple Language Versions of the Same Information

The World Wide Web opens up a global marketplace. Companies who have traditionally sold in one country and in one language now have the opportunity to go 'global' with a single portal site. In some jurisdictions, local laws have been enacted so that information is distributed in multiple languages to make information accessible to everyone. Most manufacturers already market to an international customer base. Some manufacturers (for example automobile and heavy equipment) are required to provide their information in eight or more languages. Even manufacturers of household products are required to provide information in multiple languages.

Although there are automated services that provide language translations (such as the one provided at http://www.FreeTranslation.com) they are not accurate enough for reliable translation services to the corporate world, and will probably not be accurate enough in the foreseeable future. Many companies, for example automobile and airplane manufacturers, are using a simplified English Standard that is "both clear and unambiguous for English speakers and non-native English speakers alike". More information about the simplified English Standard can be obtained at http://www.aecma.org/Publications/SEnglish/senglish.htm.

Configuration management of multiple versions of information is very challenging. Traditional Standard Generalized Markup Language (SGML) has been a valuable tool in maintaining complex information. Because XML is a subset of SGML, we are seeing SGML projects that are moving towards XML. XML provides the same capability as SGML for providing functionality and configuration management of multiple languages.

Look at the DTD example below. The <description> element could be an example of a description of an item in a catalog. You will notice the <english-text> element is required since we will assume that the original format will be English. The other languages are optional. Once the English is completed, the document can be sent to a translation facility to be translated into the multiple languages. Some companies maintain their own translation personnel in-house, while other companies will outsource the translation of information. Outsourcing translations is popular in the automobile and airplane manufacturing industries. The configuration could also be done using attributes, but in this case elements are easier to work with.

You will also notice that we have included an optional <other-text> element with a required attribute of 'language' (bear in mind that XML also has a standard attribute, xml:lang, which allows for the standard language codes to be incorporated. This is an escape mechanism if another marketplace opens up with a different language. The DTD would not require modification.

```
<!ELEMENT description (picture?, sound?,
                      (english-text, french-text?,
                       spanish-text?,
                        other-text?))>

<!ELEMENT picture EMPTY>
<!ATTLIST picture
          alt-text CDATA #REQUIRED
          name ENTITY #REQUIRED>

<!ELEMENT sound EMPTY>
<!ATTLIST sound
          alt-text CDATA #REQUIRED
          name ENTITY #REQUIRED>

<!ELEMENT english-text (para)+>

<!ELEMENT french-text (para)+>

<!ELEMENT spanish-text (para+)>

<!ELEMENT other-text (para+)>
<!ATTLIST other-text
          language CDATA #REQUIRED>

<!ELEMENT para (#PCDATA)>
```

The following figure shows the resulting structure:

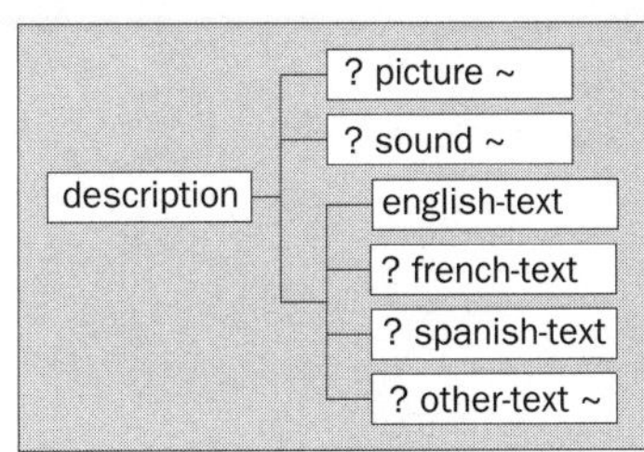


Note that in the above diagram, and the others like it that follow, there are many symbols, for example, the ? cardinality operator you can see above. The following table provides a key to the meaning of these symbols:

| SYMBOL | DEFINITION |
|---|---|
| + | One or more elements required |
| * | Zero or more elements required |
| ? | Optional but if present only 1 element can exist |
| ~ | Attributes associated with this element |
| | Parsed Character Data or #PCDATA |
| | One or more elements in any order |
| | Zero or more elements in any order |

### *Different Levels of Understanding*

Business documents are presented and used by many individuals. Regardless of the level of familiarity with a document displayed by the individuals who will be accessing and reading it (be it expert or novice), XML, because of its extensibility, has the ability to maintain information that will allow both the novice and the expert sufficient understanding for their needs. The presentation of the information can be based on personalization information maintained by the owner of the information. There are many ways to incorporate the personalization information. It can be maintained within the original XML. The personalization data can also be maintained in external XML source files and linked to via XML linking capabilities, see Xlink –(http://www.w3.org/XML/Linking). More information could also be presented on-demand. While the presentation of the information is an application decision, the XML document still contains all the information.

### *Different Levels of Access to Information for Internal Personnel and External Users*

XML data is commonly modeled to allow different levels of access to data. This approach is commonly used for the presentation of technical documentation. For example, if a company has a known problem with their product, they will include this information within the XML data but will only provide access to internal help desk personnel. There are many ways of accomplishing this using XML. Separate elements can be used or this information can be triggered by an attribute value. The example below shows how this can be accomplished through an element called `<internal-use>`. Individuals accessing this information from outside the organization would not have access to view the information.

```
<!DOCTYPE procedure [
<!--
=====================================
NOTE:  This is a fragment and not an
            entire DTD.
=====================================
-->
<!ELEMENT procedure (step+)>
<!ATTLIST procedure
          unique-id    ID      #REQUIRED>
<!ELEMENT step (action, result) >
<!ELEMENT action (#PCDATA | mnemonic)*>
<!ELEMENT mnemonic (#PCDATA)>
<!ELEMENT result (#PCDATA | internal-use)+>
```

```
<!ELEMENT internal-use (#PCDATA)>
]>
<!--
========================================
NOTE:  Tagged Fragment
========================================
-->
<procedure unique-id="fi122032">
   <step>
      <action>Open File
         <mnemonic>CNTRL O</mnemonic>
      </action>
      <result>
         File will appear in the editing window.
         <internal-use>
            This feature will cause the application to crash if the user
            is accessing data from the CD.  Tell the customer that this is
            a known bug and will be corrected in the next release.
         </internal-use>
      </result>
   </step>
   <step>
      ...
   </step>
</procedure>
```

### *Personalization Information*

Personalization information can also be maintained within the XML, in a number of ways. A separate DTD or XML Schema can be developed for the personalization information, which links to the data that is maintained within the parent DTD/Schema. Content management and Internet portal systems, such as those provided by TIBCO (http://www.tibco.com), Citrix (http://www.citrix.com) and Datachannel (http://www.datachannel.com) provide the integration of personalization information. Personalization allows companies such as Amazon.com and MyYahoo to push information based upon user preferences and profiles. Personalization information also allows for the aggregation of databases upon a user's profile.

For example, if an individual bought a Tom Clancy book from an on-line book store, the next time that individual logs into the site, the portal software would suggest that they purchase a book by another author who writes in the same genre.

XML personalization information is being used by software developers as a way of maintaining profile information about users' preferences, hardware/software environment, etc. Software configuration information (such as where files are being installed on the local machine, as well as information about the creators of the software) is also being maintained in XML.

Portal and B2B software is also using XML to maintain personalization information within their product.

Alternatively, the personalization DTD/Schema fragment can be included within the main e-business DTD. How an organization chooses to include personalization information depends on the application, and the workflow and purpose of the personalization information.

#### *Other Uses for the Data*

If your organization is in the business of selling information, this is a good opportunity to look at the information and see if it is possible to create new products from existing information using XML. Many publishers are currently repackaging old information in new products based upon the source XML. For example, several publishers of medical information have analyzed their data and classified it based upon particular specialties, such as cardiology. Special attributes are being included in the XML data that allow them to automatically create new products based upon a particular medical specialty. This practice increases revenue significantly without substantially increasing cost. It also enhances on-line subscription products that are provided by the publishers.

## Summary of Analysis Stage

The analysis stage of an XML project, if done correctly, comprises the largest part of the work. There aren't any viable shortcuts – only an in-depth information analysis will provide the required input to make informed decisions about how the information should be modeled and used in current and future business processes. Organizations who have tried to circumvent this process have ended up spending more money fixing data in the long run, and have in some cases ended up with a system that is cumbersome to use and not applicable in all situations. In most cases, after the analysis is completed a small pilot or proof-of-concept project is done to prove that the model and processes are completed.

Having analyzed the information (in terms of what is available, what format it is in, and how it is structured), and having identified the requirements of the resulting output, the next stage is to design and build the business document model. As well as the constraints related to information availability and requirements, there are other factors to take into account and we'll consider these next.

# Creating the Information Model

Most organizations that have made an informed and long-term commitment to XML understand that the analysis process may result in a redesign of their current methodologies. Companies who have exchanged information in a traditional EDI environment may look at migrating to an XML environment. They may look at initiatives such as ebXML or other initiatives to help create and maintain their trading partner environments.

In other cases, companies that have traditionally used VANs may look at using the Internet for their transactions and create and maintain the infrastructure in-house. VAN operators are also looking at how they can provide their customers with XML support.

In many cases, business process re-engineering and XML projects are accomplished during the same period and are married together. This redesign may, for example, result in a transition from the EDI environment to an XML environment. Or, if the organization is currently using EDI successfully with trading partners, new trading partners can be brought into the environment by plugging XML into appropriate processes. For example, NISO (http://www.niso.org) is currently creating an international standard for an XML architecture that allows library systems to exchange information (messages) that currently can't speak the same language. Software will be built that will allow messages from the various library systems to be translated into XML and sent to other library systems and translated into their native messaging format. This will allow the network of systems the opportunity to talk to each other.

This approach is also being done in the EDI community. The approach of translating to and from XML provides the opportunity to establish new trading partners at a significantly lower cost.

Moving into an e-business and e-content environment provides organizations the opportunity to reinvent and streamline their business processes. For example, instead of maintaining information in multiple formats and having one department control the web content and another department control the paper product (with each department having to communicate to keep the different versions in sync), organizations can now have one department handle the content and another to control the presentation and dissemination of that content. The savings involved in streamlining the process can be significant.

Redesign based on thorough analysis is a positive step forward. When the World Wide Web became a reality, most organizations haphazardly put information together quickly to get a presence on the Web. This was not necessarily a bad thing, however in most cases information was just converted from paper to HTML with a little programming put behind it. Real requirements and process analysis in the early days of the WWW was rare.

In the design stage we need to consider if there are any groups of information that could be modeled in a more useful and reusable way. We also need to take into account constraints on design, such as those imposed on us by the systems used by external partners or the inevitable legacy information that exists internally. We also need to make decisions about issues such as naming conventions, agreed vocabularies, and how granular the data needs to be.

## Identify Commonality in Content

During the analysis stage you will have looked at all current document types and identified what information is available in each. You should consider how the documents are related and, where there is overlap, it is advisable to try to create common, reusable **information objects** in your new document design. Information objects are chunks of information that can be reused over and over again in different contexts. An address, and a list of product items are both good examples of information objects. In some cases, organizations may call data by different names but they are all basically the same. For example, some organizations may select the element name `<contact>` while another uses `<contactInfo>`, and a third could use `<ContactInformation>`. Although the information is exactly the same, the element names are different. If these organizations wanted to share the information, transformation would be required. Having a single vocabulary among trading partners for the information would streamline the business processes.

You also need to think whether multiple outputs (products) are required or desired, as the aim is to create a model that will allow the information to be used in all of the company's data products. For example, organizations such as publishers that sell their information usually provide this information on multiple media. Multimedia cannot be used in paper publishing. However, the links to the multimedia can still be maintained within the XML but not published when the information is being published on paper.

Sometimes information objects can stand alone, with their own document type. For example, a specification sheet contains information about a manufactured product. A specification sheet can stand alone within its own document, or it can be included in other technical documentation, marketing information, etc.

As an example, if we look at the traditional EDI model, an organization may have a catalog, invoice, and purchase order document types. A separate DTD/Schema should be created for each type of document. However, during the analysis process, you want to look at all three documents together to see where the information intersects. In the following figure you can see the `Item` information component is reused in all three models, and `Send To` and `From` are used in both the invoice and purchase order.

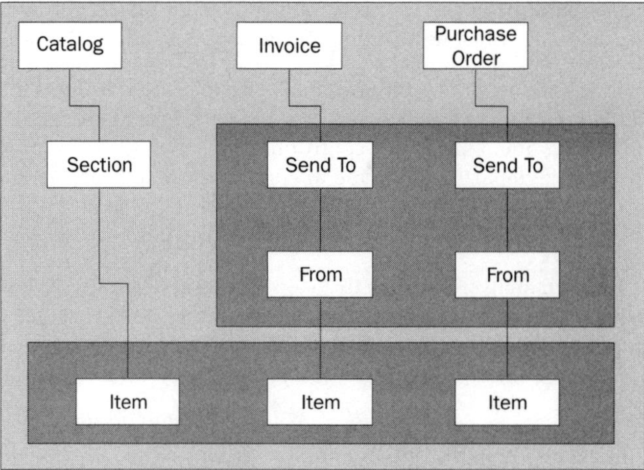


Let's consider the item in more detail – if we look at an invoice item, the following information may be needed for an individual item to support the invoice document:

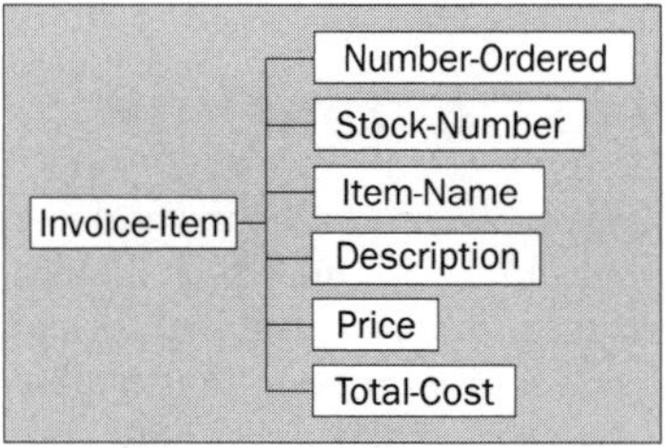


However, if the organization supplies products, they may also produce a catalog of information about these products. The organization will want to look at their catalogs, see where the item model intersects, and create a standard information object for items. Let's look at a fictitious example of an item for a catalog:

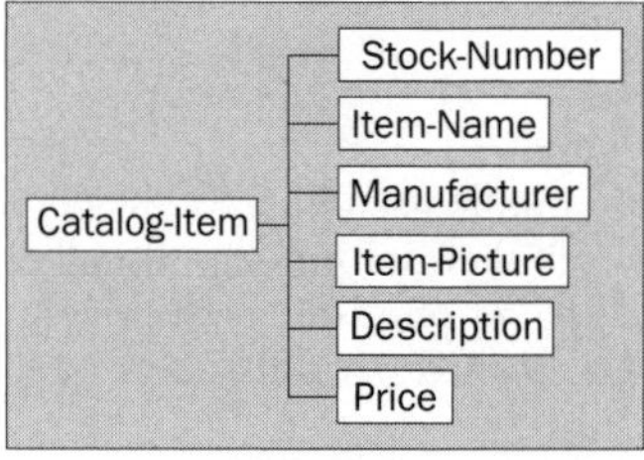


Looking at both the invoice and the catalog, the following information items are common to both models:

- Stock-Number
- Item-Name
- Description
- Price

There are several ways that we can create a common information object to support both the catalog and the invoice. One way would be to allow the catalog item to be the common information object. The resulting invoice model would look like this:

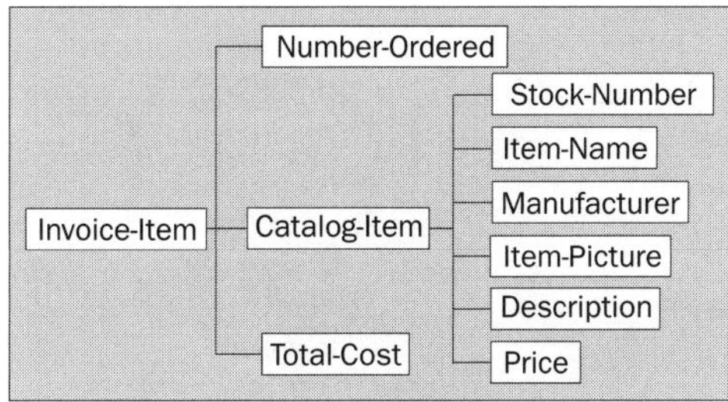


Note that the model above provides more information than the invoice actually requires. For example, if you compare this model for the invoice item with the one shown previously, you will see the elements <Manufacturer> and <Item-Picture> are not required for an invoice. These elements can be suppressed when the document is rendered for customers, or when sending EDI-type messages to trading partners. The model allows for the information object (<Catalog-Item>) to be created and stored once and to be reused in other business documents, such as invoices and purchase orders.

It is also possible for information objects to be included within other information objects. The following figure shows an element called <bill-to> that uses the information object <contact>. Embedded in the <contact> information object is an <address> information object. An <address> can be included in many contexts within a document model.

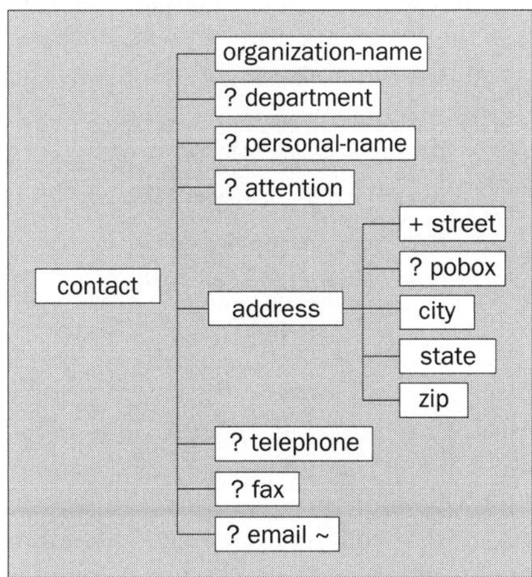


If you look at the figure below you can see that the <contact> information object is used in three models, <organization>, <bill-to> and <send-to>.

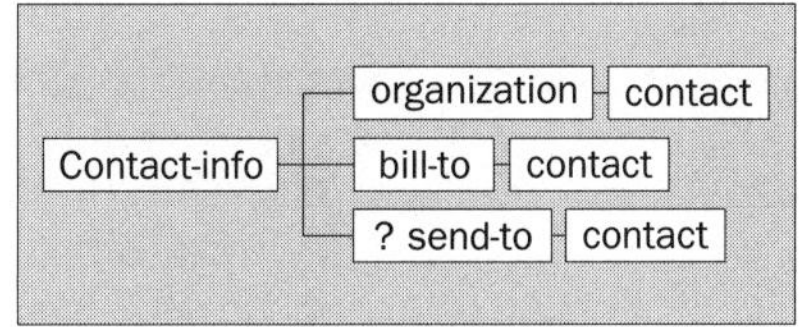

## Design of Information Objects

There are multiple ways for information objects to be defined. The graphic below shows the <bill-to> element that contains the <contact> information object:

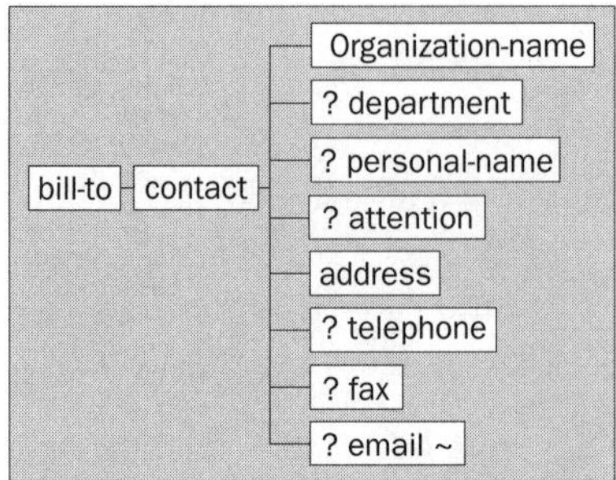


You can see that <contact> is a child element of <bill-to>. In order to process the <organization-name> element you are required to first walk the XML tree from <bill-to> to <contact>. The DTD fragment below shows the element declarations for <bill-to> and <contact>:

```
<!ELEMENT contact (organization-name, department?, personal-name?, attention?,
address, telephone?, fax?, email?)>
<!ELEMENT bill-to (contact)>
```

If we were only looking at the example above, the <contact> element doesn't really provide any extra value. If all instances of the <contact> information were just an unneeded container element, we could create an entity that would call in the information object without having the container element <contact>. The graphic below shows the model in this case:

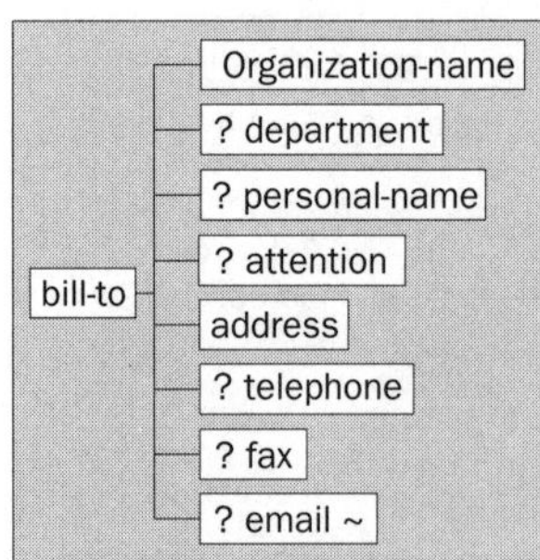


As you can see, there isn't a <contact> container element. Instead, the contents of <contact> are included as direct children elements of <bill-to>. This is accomplished through the use of a parameter entity. The parameter entity can be used wherever the information object contact is required throughout the DTD. The parameter entity declaration and the <bill-to> element declaration are as follows:

```
<!ENTITY % contact "organization-name, department?, personal-name?, attention?,
address, telephone?, fax?, email?">
<!ELEMENT bill-to (%contact;)>
```

# Constraints On Design

There are always constraints on a project during the development of any IT project. Some of the constraints can be helpful and some may not be. Determining how to work within these constraints can be difficult. The key is recognizing what these constraints are and being aware of the requirements at the beginning of the XML project. Dealing with potential constraints early in the project can save a great deal of time and money. Unless your organization is developing an internal application and will not be exchanging information with any outside sources, you will have constraints put upon your XML application by other organizations where you may not have control. There are also constraints resulting from the use of legacy data.

## *External Constraints*

Design constraints can be placed on the model based upon the source of information – information can be sent from many different sources. Some of the information may be in XML format, while others may be word processing files, databases, paper copies, etc. Organizations will want to control how information is received; however, it is not always possible for an organization to dictate where and how they receive their information.

If possible, you should attempt to get all external sources of information to supply their data in XML, conforming to the prescribed DTD or Schema you are using for data validation – this could be developed by your organization, or an industry standard). Depending upon the size and clout of the organization, this may not always be possible. However, if you can get them to supply the information in a structured format (EDI, XML, delimited data formats such as CSV, etc.), the information can be converted from the original format into an XML format that matches your DTD or XML Schema.

Let's look at an example – a medium-sized airplane manufacturer was a pioneer company in developing a repository of technical documentation in SGML. Technical documentation for airplanes is part of the deliverable of the airplane. Airplanes are each configured differently and the technical documentation is required to be customized for each airplane. The SGML information was created to help to automatically provide technical documentation based upon configuration of the airplane. The airplane manufacturer requested that their component and parts suppliers provide documentation for the parts or components they supplied to them in SGML using the ATA (Air Transport Association - http://www.air-transport.org), 2100 Standard. All of the suppliers complied, with the exception of one large engine manufacturer. Because the engine manufacturer was a larger company and supplying a main component of the airplane, the airplane manufacturer had two options: supply the information from the engine manufacture in another format (such as PDF), or convert the documentation to SGML themselves.

Having one supplier provide their information in a non-SGML format would have had a major impact on the overall project. Fortunately before their project was completed, another larger airplane manufacturer requested ATA 2100 from their component and parts suppliers as well, and the engine manufacturer complied (note that this is a simple case – it is not always this easy to resolve).

The smaller airplane manufacturer benefited from the larger company's clout. Before their project went live, the engine manufacturer came forward and provided documentation in SGML format.

The moral of this story is: if external information is a required component of your business model, you should get as many organizations involved as possible to ensure a successful project.

Many vertical industry organizations have come together to develop XML Standards for their particular marketplace. A few examples are:

- Health Care: **Health Level 7** (**HL7**), http://www.hl7.org/
- Telecommunications: **Alliance for Telecommunications Industry Solutions** (**ATIS**), http://www.atis.org/
- Financial: **Open financial Exchange** (**OFX**), http://www.ofx.net, and **Interactive financial Exchange** (**IFX**), http://www.ifxforum.org/
- Insurance: **Acord**, http://www.acord.org/
- Library Systems: **National Information Standards Organization** (**NISO**), http://www.niso.org/
- Shipping: **Information System Agreement** (**ISA**), http://www.isaweb.com/f_m_xml.htm
- Commercial Aviation: **ATA 2100 standard,** http://www.air-transport.org/
- And many more ...

Another good example of this problem is the US Patent and Trademark Office XML project (http://www.uspto.gov/ebc/index.html). The US Patent and Trademark Office has developed a DTD for submitting electronic patents. Patent examiners can review patents more quickly when the patent is received in XML, however, the Patent and Trademark Office cannot *dictate* to patent applicants the format for the submission of patent applications, they can only *suggest* a preferable format. In an effort to help applicants submit a patent application in XML, they have developed a customized patent authoring tool for writing patent applications using Microsoft Word and an XML toolkit – this tool is a customized XML editor developed only for the Patent Application DTD. Even though this tool is customized specifically for patent applications, it still involves training patent submitters and patent lawyers who do not understand XML. The challenge is getting all patent submitters to submit their patents in XML, but in the meantime, they are required to accept patent applications in any format. To download the tool, check out the above URL.

### *Trading Partner Requirements*

Trading partners sometimes place requirements on other organizations that they are required to meet. If there is a long-term established relationship between trading partners, they are probably already using some form of Electronic Data Interchange (EDI). In North America, industry experts have developed the X12 family of standards (http://www.x12.org/) through the umbrella organization Data Interchange Standards Association (DISA – http://www.disa.org/). In Europe, a working group under the umbrella of UN/CEFACT organization has developed EDIFACT (http://www.edifact-wg.org/).

Companies that do EDI transactions in both North America and Europe probably use several different formats to send transactions or business messages. When modeling business documents, it is necessary to perform an in-depth analysis of the transaction formats needed for use with trading partners.

EDI standardization efforts have accomplished an in-depth analysis of the transaction types. It is wise to take advantage of the analysis that has already been completed by EDI standardization efforts – use the EDI efforts as a foundation to help create your own models. You can enhance the models with information that EDI hasn't been able to accommodate, such as binary data. For example, insurance companies now have the opportunity to provide access to information that isn't usually available on-line, such as police reports, pictures of accidents, news reports, etc. Traditional EDI doesn't have the capability of linking to outside information or attaching binary information to the transaction. Organizations can also include information to be used internally within the model. When the information is sent to their trading partners the internal data can be stripped from the electronic message. XSLT is a very good tool to ensure that confidential information is not sent to trading partners.

Traditional EDI has a flat model, but there is an **implicit** hierarchy that can be used to help develop your model, as you can see in the example below (in XML, the hierarchy is explicit). Using the EDI as a basis for your own model will also help you to understand the transformation of the data required to get from EDI to XML and vice versa.

Below is an EDI name segment that includes an address:

```
N1*SH*ACE MANUFACTURING*1*987654321*N2*RECEIVING*N3*234 MARKET STREET*N4*SAN
FRANCISCO*CA*94103*US
```

As you can see, the example above is difficult to read. If we break the components down into their logical sequence according to the EDI specification (as you will see below), it is easy to understand the structure and content of the data. Notice that the asterisk (*) is used as a delimiter in the above example. Different EDI trading partners can use different delimiters. If an optional component is missing then it will be marked by two consecutive delimiters, so the interpreting software knows to go on and read the next component.

| EDI Component | EDI Semantics |
|---|---|
| N1 | Begin name sequence |
| SH | Shipper |
| ACE MANUFACTURING | Name |
| 1 | Type of identifier 1 equals D-U-N-S, 3 equals Federal Maritime Commission (Ocean) (FMC), 24 equals employer identification number. So, if there is a '1' in the transaction, the next number represents the D-U-N-S number. |
| 987654321 | D-U-N-S Number |
| N2 | Begin additional name information (optional) |
| RECEIVING | Division |
| N3 | Address Information |
| 234 MARKET STREET | Street |
| N4 | Geographic Information |
| SAN FRANCISCO | City |
| CA | State |
| 94103 | Postal Code or Zip |
| US | Country |

If we analyze the above information, we are able to develop XML data and derive our model. First we have the DTD fragment that models our data structure:

```
<!ELEMENT shipper (organization, address,
                  attention*)>
<!ATTLIST shipper
          DUNS CDATA #IMPLIED
          NAICS CDATA #IMPLIED>
<!ELEMENT organization (name, division*)>
<!ELEMENT name        (#PCDATA)>
<!ELEMENT division    (#PCDATA)>
<!ELEMENT address (street+, city, state?, country,
                  postalcode)>
<!ELEMENT street      (#PCDATA)>
<!ELEMENT city        (#PCDATA)>
<!ELEMENT state       (#PCDATA)>
<!ELEMENT country     (#PCDATA)>
<!ELEMENT postalcode (#PCDATA)>
```

Next, here is our data, in that structure:

```
<shipper duns="987654321">
   <organization unique-id="aceman">
   <name>ACE MANUFACTURING</name>
   <division>RECEIVING</division>
   <address>
      <street>234 MARKET STREET</street>
      <city>SAN FRANSISCO</city>
      <state>CA</state>
      <zip>94103</zip>
      <country>US</country>
   </address>
   </organization>
</shipper>
```

#### *Industry Standards*

As stated earlier in this chapter numerous groups are currently creating industry standards for XML. Some of the industries creating standards include financial, insurance, communications, transportation, publishing, education, manufacturing, health care, etc. When trading information within an industry, you may be required to share that data in an industry standard. Industry standards are a good thing because they require industries to come together and define their processes and develop a standardized way of doing business. This provides both the industry players and their trading partners with a standardized way to carry out the exchange of information.

We are seeing more global industry standards being developed. The reinsurance industry recently completed their global version 1 of the Joint Venture Reinsurance XML Standard (http://www.jvstandards.org/). NISO is also working on developing an international standard for exchange of information for library systems.

However, industry standards can be problematic for some organizations because industry standards tend to be unwieldy, as they deal with an entire industry. Some organizations may be required to conform to multiple industry standards. In other cases, conflicting standards are being developed, such as IFX and OFX in the financial sector.

As an example, in the aviation world, the Aviation Transportation Association (ATA) Standards creates and maintains commercial aviation standards. Many aviation manufacturers sell their products to both commercial and government aircraft manufacturers. Each government entity has its own SGML/XML Standard for technical data. The US **Department of Defense** (**DoD**) Standards are part of the **Continuous Acquisition and Lifecycle Support** (**CALS**) Standards (http://navycals.dt.navy.mil). CALS was a DoD initiative that attempted to improve weapon system acquisition and life-cycle support through the acquisition, creation, management, and use of digital product data and technical information.

Each branch of the US DoD has taken the CALS Standards and developed their own specific standard. The United Kingdom, Australia, Japan, NATO, etc. have also developed their own flavors of standards. Some of the governments have developed standards based on the CALS Standards, while others have developed standards around the **European Association of Aerospace Industries Standards** (**AECMA**) – see http://www.aecma.org/ for more details.

All of these standards pose a difficult problem for both large and small manufacturers. They must provide the data in the required format, in the ATA standard for commercial clients and in the CALS standard (various flavors) for government clients. Many organizations deal with this problem by having different technical writer teams to deal with each standard. Recently, however, organizations are beginning to understand the power and flexibility of using SGML/XML to handle this need for different information output. It is important to understand that currently all of these standards have both SGML (publishing) and EDI (purchasing) standards. In the future the SGML and EDI standards will evolve into XML.

One of the first areas that will converge is Interactive Electronic Technical Manuals (IETM). The current CALS standard for IETMs are SGML. However, XML is being considered because it will provide the mechanism for the technician to repair equipment and to order parts. The IETM can be integrated into back office supply systems to enable automatic ordering of parts when the supply is low.

These organizations are looking at the various standards and finding commonality within them. They are developing a common model based on the standards and their internal data and workflow processes. They maintain the data internally in an internal XML format. When they are required to send the data to a customer, they transform that data into the required standard, for example, ATA, CALS, AECMA, etc. XSLT or Omnimark, for example, can provide this kind of transformation. This harmonized model is shown below:

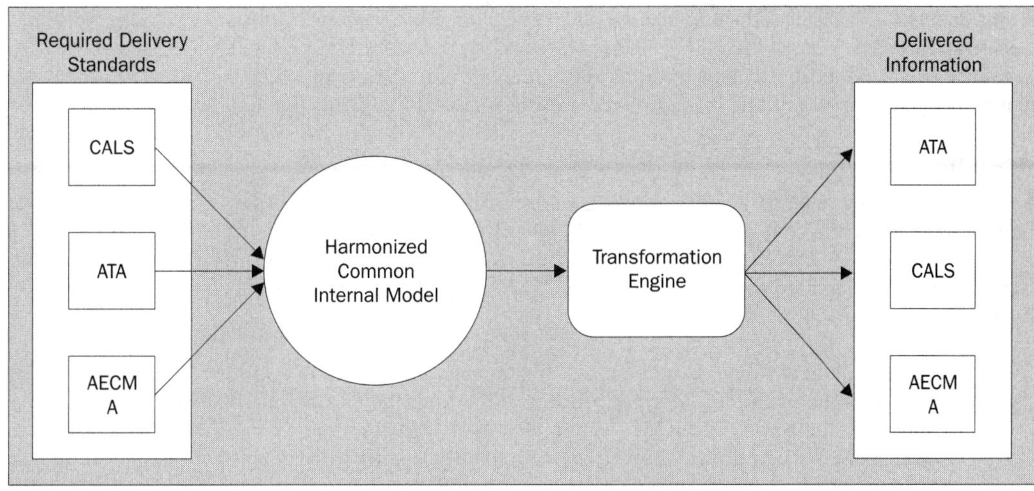

## Internal Constraints

Often there are internal constraints that may dictate how a DTD/Schema is modeled. Some of the internal constraints may be:

- Legacy data (covered in a later section).
- Data from internal relational databases. When data is being aggregated from various relational databases, this may affect how the DTD should be modeled because of the way information is stored within the database.
- Previous SGML/XML projects within an organization where a data dictionary has been developed and the models are dictated. This is common in government and large organizations. Your data may not align with the data dictionary your organization is required to use.
- DTD fragments from industry or commercial standards. Examples of DTD fragments that are often used are:
    - Table models. There are two common table models that are used: CALS or HTML. In many cases, neither of these table models are flexible enough to handle complex tables and require modifications. For example, both of the CALS and the HTML table models require modification in order to create statistical tables with source notes, end notes and table descriptions.
    - Mathematical Markup Language (MathML) – for more information on this see http://www.w3.org/TR/REC-MathML/.
    - Chemistry Markup Language (CML). For more information on this, see http://www.xml-cml.org/.
    - Various metadata models such as IMS Global Learning Consortium Inc http://www.imsproject.org/metadata/index.html, Resource Description Framework (RDF) – http://www.w3.org/RDF/, Agricultural XML Metadata (http://www.fao.org/agris/MagazineArchive/magazine/TaskForceonDCMI.htm), etc. Most industries are working on their own brand of metadata.

As time moves forward, more standard XML components will be developed, such as a standard address module. The ebXML Core Component Working Group was originally working on some Core Components for e-Business documents (see Chapter 10 for more on Core Components). This work has not been transferred to UN/CEFACT for further work. When this work is completed it will provide organizations the opportunity to use standard fragments within their own DTDs/Schemas. DTDs/Schemas can be built the way a building is constructed – using standard fragments like building blocks.

### Legacy Data

Legacy data is always an issue when moving an organization towards XML. How an organization will handle the conversion of legacy data should be decided at the time of the information analysis, as the conversion of legacy data can represent a significant cost in the XML project. How legacy data will be handled should be a major consideration in the XML project. Organizations basically have three options for dealing with legacy data:

- Convert all legacy data. Conversion of legacy data may result in a looser, less stringent DTD because of the unstructured model. When converting the legacy data to XML, you can convert the data in a tight XML model. However, depending upon the data to be converted, the cost can be significant when converting to a tight model. In most cases, it is necessary to model the data much more loosely than you would like.

- Convert no legacy data.
- Convert legacy data as needed.

Depending upon the type of legacy data, if the data hasn't been created in a structured manner, the cost of conversion can be significant. Usually the cost of conversion is priced at a cost per page or per keystroke. In some very rare cases, you can find conversion experts who will charge per element. Many companies will create a **conversion DTD**. The conversion DTD is a loose model of the more structured and stringent DTD. Legacy data is converted to the looser DTD in order to keep the cost of conversion at a reasonable level. The conversion DTD allows legacy data to be converted into an XML format and is more cost effective than converting the data to a more stringent DTD or Schema.

As an example, most publishers who currently provide their data for sale on-line have created a tight DTD that their current authors must comply with. However, pre-XML products have been created mostly in whatever manner the author wanted. There may have been some style guidelines, but probably not enough to provide for a stringent conversion to XML. These publishers have developed a relaxed DTD for the conversion of legacy products. A relaxed DTD is a DTD where the rules are very loose, and therefore accommodate conversion of information that has been created in the past, and so do not adhere to the restrictions of today's business documents.

In some cases, it may be even more cost-effective for companies to have the data re-keyed by companies specializing in XML conversion than converting the data programmatically themselves. In order to do a programmatic conversion the data must have been created in a consistent manner. If the individuals creating the data have adhered to defined rules, standard templates, defined styles, etc., the conversion can get partially converted programmatically. However, the manual clean-up requires more technical expertise than re-keying and could ultimately be more costly than re-keying.

However, organizations that have been dealing with structured data in the past (such as EDI) should seriously consider programmatically converting the data using **conversion scripts**. Traditional EDI involves the same processes as XML. In order for EDI to be successful it is stringent in its data structure design. Delimiters are used to differentiate the various components of an EDI message. Therefore, programmatic conversion of EDI to XML and XML to EDI are relatively easy. There are many tools available to assist the data conversion project. Omnimark has traditionally been the most popular tool for converting non-XML to XML. Commercial EDI software such as Sterling Commerce's GENTRAN (http://www.sterlingcommerce.com/solutions/products/index.asp) and Microsoft's BizTalk Server (http://www.microsoft.com/biztalk/default.asp) provide conversion tools to/from XML and EDI. Conversion tools are improving and becoming less costly with the advent of XML.

### *Working Vocabulary/Naming Conventions*

During development of the model, a working vocabulary should be determined. You will need to develop rules for naming elements and attributes. There are no naming guidelines established in XML, except for the naming rules defined in the W3C XML 1.0 Specification (http://www.w3.org/TR/REC-xml). Some of the things that you will want to consider before making decisions follow:

- **Use of abbreviations.** Will you allow abbreviations, or will the elements be verbose? If you allow abbreviations, common abbreviations should be identified. For example, decide whether the abbreviation 'nbr' or 'num' will be used for number. One of the defined design goals in the W3C XML Specification is: "Terseness in XML markup is of minimal importance". This is because using small element and attribute names will make negligible difference to document size and processing speed, except in the case of REALLY HUGE documents – human readability is a much more useful asset for your documents to have.

- **Definition of multiple words.** A decision about how multiple words used in an element will be strung together. You should make sure that you are consistent with your use of camel case and capitalization when naming elements and attributes. For example, you could name your elements `<FullName>`, `<AddressLines>`, and `<ZipCode>`, and you could name your attributes `<firstAddressLine>`, `<secondAddressLine>`, `<thirdAddressLine>`, etc.

- **Language of tags.** The language of the tags should be decided. If the organization is a French company and the data will only be used within France, then the element and attribute names should be in French. However, if it is a global project, then the language used should be global as well (English being the *de facto* global language at the moment).

## Meaningful Names

Naming the various elements and attributes in an XML project can be challenging. Individuals and organizations have their own naming conventions for various types of information, and sometimes they don't agree. If at all possible, it is good to provide a semantic or meaningful name for the structural components.

A good example of naming semantic structural components is the **Material Safety Data Sheets** (**MSDS**) for hazardous material. International and national law requires various sections be included in the MSDS. When creating a DTD or schema for the MSDS, it would have been logical to create a single, repeatable section; however, that wouldn't be the wisest approach. In the DTD below, the author created a semantic section for each required component.

Opposite is an example of three components from an actual MSDS sheet to show the sections are structured and identifiable:

| HAZARDOUS COMPONENTS | | | | |
|---|---|---|---|---|
| **Material or Component** | **%** | **CAS No.** | **TLV** | **PEL** |
| **Potassium nitrate**[1] | 70-76 | 007757-79-1 | NE | NE |
| **Sodium nitrate**[1] | 70-74 | 007631-99-4 | NE | NE |
| **Charcoal** | 8-18 | N/A | NE | NE |
| **Sulfur** | 9-20 | 007704-34-9 | NE | NE |
| **Graphite**[2] | Trace | 007782-42-5 | 15 mppcf (TWA) | 2.5 mg/m$^3$ |
| N/A = Not assigned    NE = Not established | | | | |

[1] Black Powder contains either potassium nitrate *or* sodium nitrate in the percentages indicated. Black powder ***does not contain both***.

[2] Not contained in all grades of black powder.

| PHYSICAL DATA | |
|---|---|
| **Boiling Point** | N/A |
| **Vapor Pressure** | N/A |
| **Vapor Density** | N/A |
| **Solubility in Water** | Good |
| **Specific Gravity** | 1.70 - 1.82 (mercury method) – 1.92 - 2.08 (pycnometer) |
| **PH** | 6.0 - 8.0 |
| **Evaporation Rate** | N/A |
| **Appearance and Odor** | Black granular powder. No odor detectable. |

| HAZARDOUS REACTIVITY | |
|---|---|
| **Instability** | Keep away from heat, sparks, and open flame. Avoid impact, friction, and static electricity. |
| **Incompatibility** | When dry, black powder is compatible with most metals; however, it is hygroscopic, and when wet, attracts all common metals except stainless steel.<br>Black powder must be tested for compatibility with any material not specified in the production/procurement package with which they may come in contact. Materials include other explosives, solvents, adhesives, metals, plastics, paints, cleaning compounds, floor and table coverings, packing materials, and other similar materials, situations, and equipment. |
| **Hazardous decomposition** | Detonation produces hazardous overpressures and fragments (if confined). Gases produced may be toxic if exposed in areas with inadequate ventilation. |
| **Polymerization** | Polymerization will not occur. |

The following example representation of an MSDS DTD shows how each section has been given its own semantic name based upon the government regulations:

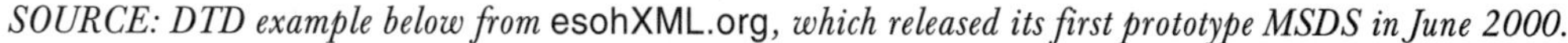

*SOURCE: DTD example below from* esohXML.org*, which released its first prototype MSDS in June 2000.*

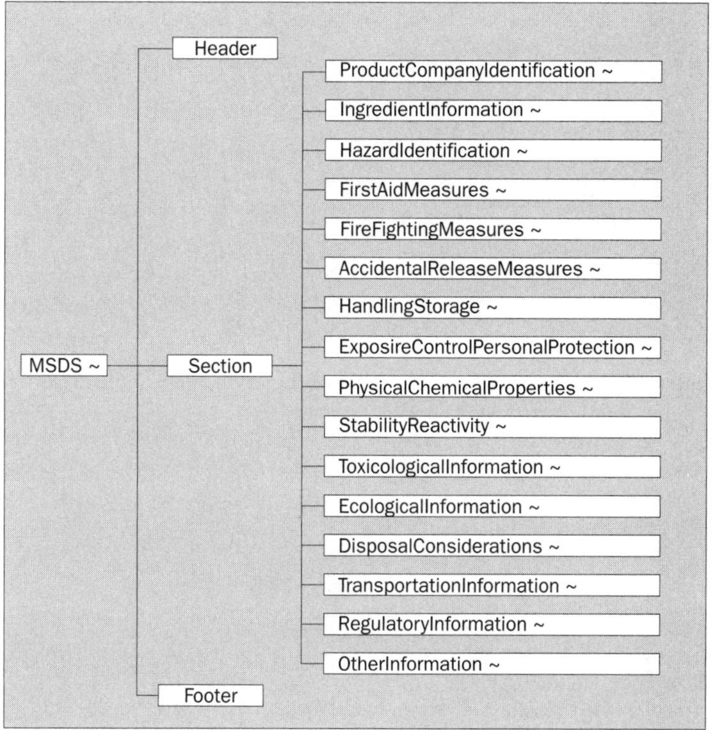


When developing a DTD or schema, it is important to give the structural components meaningful names. A structural component can be a chapter or section of a book, or an article in a magazine – in a catalog, it could be a product. Looking back to the invoice we mentioned earlier in the chapter, structurally, we can break the invoice into three components: header, item information, and summary.

> *We could alternatively break the information into these structural components: header, project information, and summary. Either would be correct. We would need to look further at how the information is used internally and externally within the organization to determine which model best defines our business processes.*

In the example overleaf we have created three structural components but opted to make project information a child of the `<header>` element. This will provide us wit the opportunity to easily capture the project information and perform business processes based on this information.

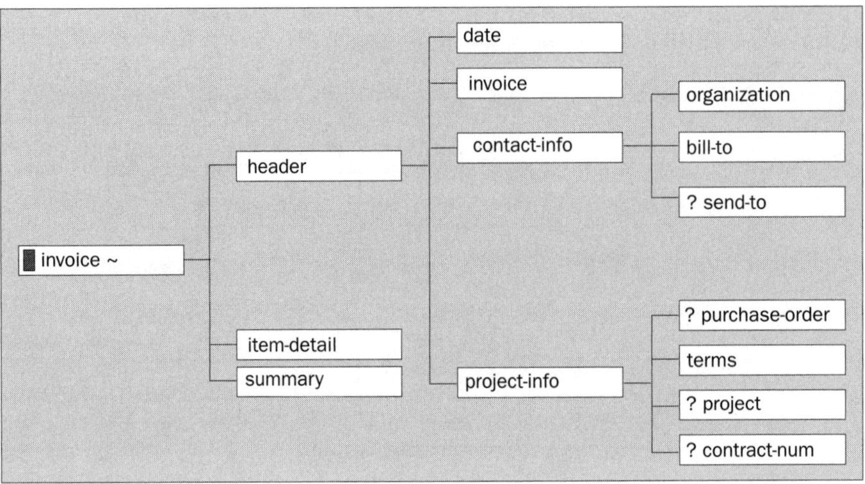


Below is an example XML invoice, which conforms to the invoice DTD illustrated graphically in the figure above:

```
<header>
   <date>20010827</date>
   <invoice-number>454</invoice-number>
   <contact-info>
      <organization>
      <organization-name>
         Electronic Commerce Connection, Inc.
      </organization-name>
      <address>
         <street>245 Hammarlee Road </street>
         <city>Glen Burnie</city>
         <state>MD</state>
         <zip>21060</zip>
      </address>
      <telephone>4107879200</telephone>
      </organization>
      <bill-to>
      <organization-name>ABC Company</organization-name>
      <department>Publications Department</department>
      <attention>
         <personal-name>Joe Smith</personal-name>
      </attention>
      <address>
         <street>2000 Pennsylvania Avenue</street>
         <city>Washington </city>
         <state>DC</state>
         <zip>20515-6601</zip>
      </address>
      </bill-to>
   </contact-info>
   <project-info> <purchase-order-number>OPR0101044</purchase-order-number>
```

```
        <terms>Net 30</terms>
        <contract-number>CCOM2001038</contract-number>
    </project-info>
</header>
```

*Notice in the XML example that the date is tagged as* `<date>20010827</date>` *yet in the printed invoice the date appears as '8/27/2001'. The transformation of the date field to a human-readable date can be accomplished through the output or transformation process. You will also notice that the qualifying words that you normally see on a printed invoice, such as 'DATE', 'INVOICE #' and BILL TO" do not appear in the XML example. These labels can be generated at the time of output based on the element names* `<date>`, `<invoice-number>`, *and* `<bill-to>`.

In this case we have attempted to give meaning to the structural components. We could have named the three components "top," "body," and "end," but those names would contain no contextual meaning about what those parts are. Semantic names or meaningful names are important because they will provide useful information to the users and programmers of the data.

## XML Component and Name Clashes

When using standard DTD fragments, there is always the possibility of name clashes, for example, the `<title>` element could refer to job title, book title, chapter title, etc. One way to deal with this problem is to rename the elements. Another way is to use XML Namespaces – make the similarly-named elements members of separate namespaces to distinguish them.

*For more on XML Namespaces, see on Namespaces chapter of* Beginning XML 2nd Edition, *by David Hunter et al (ISBN: 1-861005-59-8), published by Wrox Press. Alternatively, check out the W3C* Namespaces in XML *document at* http://www.w3.org/TR/1999/REC-xml-names-19990114/.

For example, let's say that we wanted to develop an online training class. We can choose to include the IMS Question and Test (Q&T) DTD fragment. The Q&T fragment uses some element names that are quite common in most DTDs. For an example, we will look at the Q&T `<item>` element. Below is the element declaration for that element, and a graphic representation showing its hierarchy.

```
<!ELEMENT item (qticomment?, duration?, itemmetadata,
               objectives*, itemcontrol*,
               itemprecondition*, itempostcondition*,
               (rubric |itemrubric)*, presentation?,
               resprocessing*, itemproc-extension?,
               itemfeedback*)>
<!ATTLIST item
          maxattempts CDATA #IMPLIED
          %I-Label;
          %I-Ident;
          %I-Title; >
```

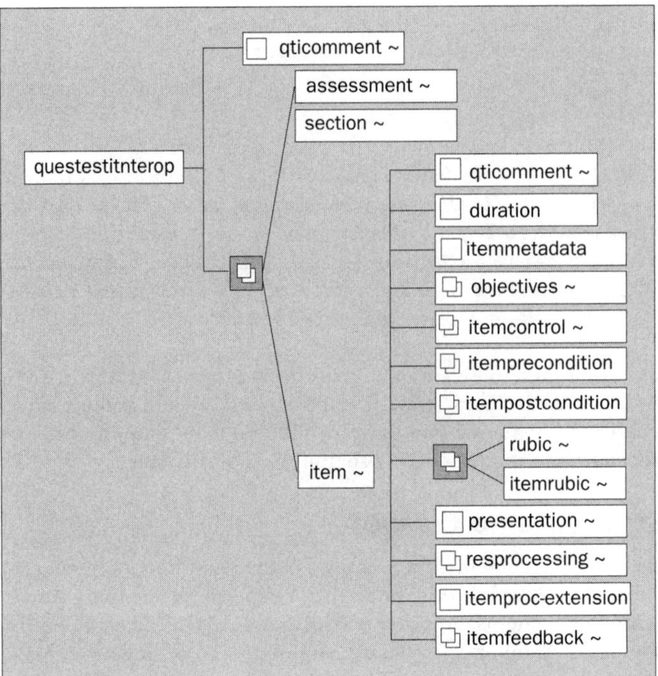


If we need a generic list in our DTD, we may use the following element declaration:

```
<!ELEMENT list (item+)>
<!ATTLIST list
          type (bullet | number |none) "bullet">

<!ELEMENT item (#PCDATA)>
```

This can be represented graphically as shown:

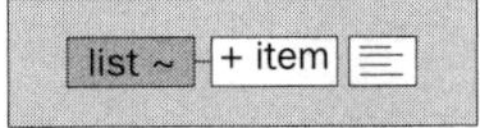


It is easy to see that the `<item>` from the IMS Q&T and the generic `<list><item>` have different structures. Therefore, we have a name clash. The two ways we can handle this are:

- Rename one of the elements. As a general rule, it is best to rename the element that would be used most infrequently. In the above case we would probably rename the IMS Q&T `<item>` to something like `<qt-item>`. Although this is a fairly quick easy solution, bear in mind that it will not be viable in a situation where the XML vocabulary we are looking at has already been used by an enterprise or company to create a large XML database.
- The second approach is to use XML Namespaces. The XML data would look like this:

```
<ims:item xmlns:ims="http://www.imsproject.org/question">
          ...
</ims:item>
```

In the above example, the attribute 'xmlns:ims' is used as a reference to a place where schema for the IMS specification can be found. The schema or DTD in this case can be found at the URL http://www.imsproject.org/question. Namespaces are highly controversial among XML developers and a good understanding of what they do and what they do not do would be valuable. A good resource for information about namespaces is available in the following Namespaces FAQ - http://www.rpbourret.com/xml/NamespacesFAQ.htm.

It is important to understand that DTDs do not support XML Namespaces as such (XML Schemas do), and you can only provide namespace support for DTDs using some very complex workarounds, involving the #FIXED attribute. This is demonstrated in the element declaration below:

```
<!ELEMENT ims:item (qticomment?, duration?, itemmetadata, objectives*,
                   itemcontrol*, itemprecondition*, itempostcondition*,
                   (rubric |itemrubric)*, presentation?, resprocessing*,
                   itemproc-extension?, itemfeedback*)>
<!ATTLIST ims:item
          xmlns:ims CDATA #FIXED "http://www.imsproject.org/question"
          maxattempts CDATA #IMPLIED
          %I-Label;
          %I-Ident;
          %I-Title;>
```

## Elements Versus Attributes

The *elements versus attributes* debate has been going on for as long as SGML has been around. There aren't any defined rules about when to make something an element and when to make something an attribute. In some cases, information is being transferred from database to database. In this case it is acceptable to use attributes. It is slightly easier to process elements. However, the ease of process isn't enough to determine the model.

For example, if we had the same content model in a purchase order for the 'send to' and 'buyer' roles, we could have a generic <contact> element with an attribute associated with it, in other words:

```
<contact role="buyer">...</contact>
```

This issue has been approached many times – for a good discussion of elements versus attributes, consult *Professional XML Databases*, by Kevin Williams et al (ISBN: 1-861003-58-7), published by Wrox Press.

## Information Granularity

Determining the appropriate level of granularity for your XML project can be difficult. In order to determine the granularity, you must decide during the analysis process how the data will be used. For example, let's look at a personal name. We could break the name down into its various components:

```
<name>
   <firstname>Betty</firstname>
   <middleInitial>L.</middleInitial>
   <lastname>Harvey</lastname>
</name>
```

compared to:

```
<name>Betty L. Harvey</name>
```

If your model includes `<firstname>`, `<middlename>`, and `<lastname>` and you are receiving data from another source that transmits the entire name "Betty L. Harvey", in order to validate your model, your transformation software would be required to parse the entire name and break it into the right components. The situation would get even more complicated if you add a prefix and degree, such as:

```
<name>
   <prefix>Dr.</prefix>
   <firstname>Benjamin</firstname>
   <lastname>Franklin</lastname>
   <degree>PhD</degree>
</name>
```

When developing your XML model, you want to provide enough granularity to support the functionality your application requires. At the same time, if the information doesn't need to be tagged to the *nth* degree then the data shouldn't be required to be so granular. Also bear in mind that the consequence of highly granular XML is large XML file sizes, so if you are using very large XML files, you may want to consider a less granular approach.

## DTD or XML Schema

Before making a decision about whether to use a DTD or XML Schema, you should understand the issues clearly. DTDs and XML Schemas provide the rules by which XML data is converted. DTDs are the traditional modeling language for SGML and XML. The DTD is an ISO Standard (ISO 8879) as well as being included in the W3C Extensible Markup Language (XML) 1.0 Recommendation. There are several XML schema specifications and flavors of schemas. The two schema specifications that are currently being implemented seriously are the W3C XML Schema language, **XSD** (see http://www.w3.org/XML/Schema), and the OASIS Open **RELAX NG** Specification (see http://www.oasis-open.org/committees/relax-ng/spec-20010811.html). OASIS Open is planning on submitting RELAX NG to ISO to become an international standard.

It is important to understand that software selection and computing environment may impact your decision to use a DTD or XML Schema for validation of the XML. In some projects, it may be necessary to have both a DTD and an XML Schema. For example, Microsoft's BizTalk Server currently uses a Schema specification called XML Data Reduced (XDR) based upon a simplified version of the first draft of the W3C Schema specification. If your project uses Microsoft's BizTalk Server, you may need to develop an XDR Schema in the interim until BizTalk server supports the complete W3C XML Schema language.

Also, most parsers only support a particular type of schema, for example DTDs. Therefore, if you choose a specific software platform, the software may dictate whether to use a DTD, or another kind of schema. All commercial-grade XML authoring software products, which are geared specifically towards authoring XML data only, support DTDs. However, this may change in the near future. Automated tools have been developed to help in converting from DTDs to schema and vice-versa. Two tools that provide this functionality are XMLSpy (http://www.xmlspy.com/) and Extensibility (http://www.tibco.com/products/extensibility/). However, some manual work will still be required, even with the specialized tools.

## Advantages of XML Schema

Now let's go through the advantages of using XML Schemas over DTDs.

### Written in XML Syntax

DTDs have their own syntax. Many people felt that the learning curve to learn a new syntax for DTDs was too complicated. Creating a rule-based modelling language for XML in XML syntax was one of the main rationales for developing XML schemas.

### Provides Strong datatyping

Datatyping is the number one reason for moving towards XML schemas. The original ISO SGML standard provided some limited datatyping. When the W3C developed XML, most of the limited datatyping from SGML was eliminated. After the XML specification was approved by the W3C, it became recognized as a major facilitator of business data. Most business data requires strong datatyping. Datatyping is important for ensuring that data is correct for internal use, as well as transporting it between business partners.

Because datatyping is so important, the W3C working group made datatyping its own specification. The datatyping specification is used by both the W3C XML Schema and the RELAX schema. The ebXML *Business Process Specification Schema* (BPSS) *v1.01* (see Chapter 5 of this book, or `ebBPSS.pdf` or `.doc` at http://www.ebxml.org/specs/ for more information) also identifies the W3C *XML Schema Part 2: Datatypes* (see http://www.w3.org/TR/xmlschema-2/) as the datatyping Specification.

DTDs do not have datatyping capability. However, as shown below you can specify datatypes within DTDs and have them programmatically validated externally using an externally-developed program. Below is a graphical representation of a DTD/Schema:

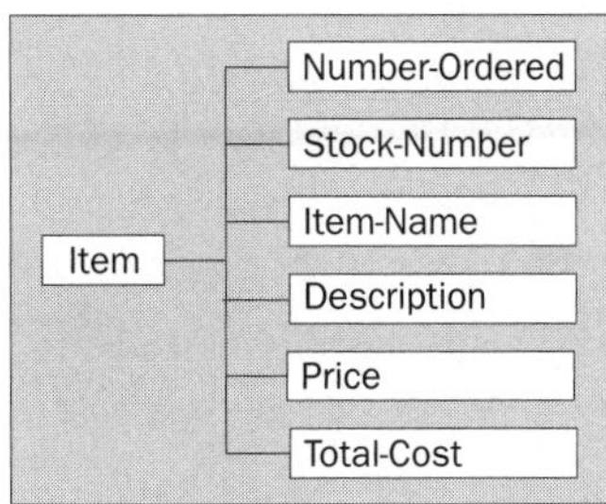


Let's look at the W3C and RELAX schema examples for the above element declaration. First the W3C XML Schema declaration for the `<item>` element:

```
<xs:element name="Item">
   <xs:complexType>
      <xs:sequence>
         <xs:element name="Number-Ordered" type="xs:positiveInteger"/>
         <xs:element name="Stock-Number" type="xs:string"/>
         <xs:element name="Item-Name" type="xs:string"/>
         <xs:element name="Description" type="xs:string"/>
         <xs:element name="Price" type="xs:decimal"/>
         <xs:element name="Total-Cost" type="xs:decimal"/>
      </xs:sequence>
   </xs:complexType>
</xs:element>
```

Next we have the RELAX NG Schema declaration:

```
<elementRule role = "Item">
   <sequence>
      <ref label = "Number-Ordered"/>
      <ref label = "Stock-Number"/>
      <ref label = "Item-Name"/>
      <ref label = "Description"/>
      <ref label = "Price"/>
      <ref label = "Total-Cost"/>
   </sequence>
</elementRule>
   <tag name = "Item"/>
      <elementRule role = "Number-Ordered" type = "positiveInteger"/>
   <tag name = "Number-Ordered"/>
      <elementRule role = "Stock-Number" type = "string"/>
   <tag name = "Stock-Number"/>
      <elementRule role = "Item-Name" type = "string"/>
   <tag name = "Item-Name"/>
      <elementRule role = "Description" type = "string"/>
   <tag name = "Description"/>
      <elementRule role = "Price" type = "decimal"/>
   <tag name = "Price"/>
      <elementRule role = "Total-Cost" type = "decimal"/>
   <tag name = "Total-Cost"/>
```

The DTD could be programmatically validated for the proper datatyping by using the following declarations:

```
<!ELEMENT Item (Number-Ordered, Stock-Number,
                Item-Name, Description, Price,
                 Total-Cost)>

<!ELEMENT Number-Ordered (#PCDATA)>
<!ATTLIST Number-Ordered
          datatype CDATA #FIXED "positiveInteger">

<!ELEMENT Stock-Number (#PCDATA)>
<!ATTLIST Stock-Number
          datatype CDATA #FIXED "string">

<!ELEMENT Item-Name (#PCDATA)>
<!ATTLIST Item-Name
          datatype CDATA #FIXED "string">
```

```
<!ELEMENT Description (#PCDATA)>
<!ATTLIST Description
          datatype CDATA #FIXED "string">

<!ELEMENT Price (#PCDATA)>
<!ATTLIST Price
          datatype CDATA #FIXED "decimal">

<!ELEMENT Total-Cost (#PCDATA)>
<!ATTLIST Total-Cost
          datatype CDATA #FIXED "decimal">
```

The above example shows how you can add datatyping using fixed attribute values within a DTD. The datatype values can be programmatically validated to insure they are correct by writing simple external programs. Also, both relational and XML databases will validate the datatype of the information when importing the data into a database.

### *Support for XML Namespaces*

XML schemas provide native support for XML namespaces. DTDs do not natively support namespaces, however you can still validate and use namespaces within a DTD by using a fixed attribute value for the namespace. We saw an example of this earlier in the chapter when we looked at overcoming name clashes.

### *Schema Provides Explicit Occurrence Values*

DTDs provide you only with the following options for the number of occurrences of an element:

- 0 or 1
- 0 or more
- 1
- 1 or more

Let's say that in an item list we want to have at least 3 items in the list – we can do that by explicitly declaring the element three times:

```
<!ELEMENT Item-List (Item, Item, Item+)>
```

The W3C schema specification has the ability to control the number of elements through attributes. The declaration above in a W3C schema would be:

```
<xs:element name="Item-List">
   <xs:complexType>
      <xs:sequence>
         <xs:element name="Item"
                     minOccurs="3"
                     maxOccurs="unbounded">
            <xs:complexType>
               <xs:sequence>
                  <xs:element name="Number-Ordered"
                              type="xs:positiveInteger"/>
```

```
                <xs:element name="Stock-Number"
                            type="xs:string"/>
                <xs:element name="Description"
                            type="xs:string"/>
                <xs:element name="Price"
                            type="xs:decimal"/>
                <xs:element name="TotalPrice"
                            type="xs:decimal"/>
              </xs:sequence>
            </xs:complexType>
          </xs:element>
        </xs:sequence>
      </xs:complexType>
    </xs:element>
```

The above example shows that `minOccurs` attribute is set to '3' and the `maxOccurs` attribute is set to 'unbounded' for the `<Item>` element in the context of the `<Item-List>`. This means that there must be at least three `<Item>` elements in an `<Item-List>`.

### Provides Constraints in Context

XSD allows elements to be extended or restricted within the context of the model. The element declaration "`extensionbase`" allows extension of an element in context, while the element declaration "`restriction`" puts restrictions on the model in context.

## Disadvantages of XML Schema

There are also some disadvantages to using XML Schema – some are listed below:

### New Specification

XML Schemas are relatively new. The DTD is a technology that has been successful for the last 15 years. The W3C Schema Specification became Full Recommendation on May 2, 2000. Therefore, not as much time has been invested into the use and development of Schemas as for DTDs.

### Limited Software

At the moment, the number of software is limited. Also, because the schema specification is relatively new, the parsers are inconsistent. There are currently no commercial XML authoring software tools suitable for editors that support XML Schema. The most commonly used XML authoring tools, SoftQuad's XMetal, Arbortext's Epic Editor, Word Perfect and Frame+SGML, and all 4 of these editors currently support DTD's. In the future, these products may be updated to support XML Schema as well, but they will continue to support DTD's.

### Complexity

The W3C Schema Specification is relatively complex. There have been a lot of complaints from the XML community that the Schema specification is overly complex – this led to the creation of simpler Schema specifications, such as the aforementioned RELAX NG.

## Summary

In summary, effective modeling of e-business documents requires the analysis of the entire business process. If you don't get the process model right, the model for the information will not be right. If you get the model wrong in the first instance, later it may need modification. Modifying the model will not result in much added expense; however, modifying the processes and systems built around the model will potentially result in a tremendous cost, especially after the system is deployed.

In this chapter we have learned:

- What constitutes a business document
- How to analyze the existing business documents to understand the structure and content
- How to find commonality within documents
- How to recognize information objects
- How to analyze workflow and trading partner requirements
- How to design a rules-based structured document

We saw that effective document modeling comprises two parts, analysis, and design and implementation. The "analyze" stage involves:

- Identifying what information is available from internal/external/legacy sources (it often helps to look at the structure for clues as to the content).
- Identifying workflows – what info is required at each stage and in what format (consider multimedia, different languages, selective access).
- Considering other, secondary, uses for the data.

The "design and implement" stage involves:

- Looking to see if there is any commonality that could be built into reusable information objects.
- Trying to get partners to agree on information models.
- Deciding what to do about legacy data.
- Considering constraints on design (industry/internal/partners/legacy/namespace issues/format).
- Deciding on vocabularies/naming conventions.
- Deciding whether to use elements or attributes.
- Deciding how granular the info needs to be.
- Deciding which schema type to use (take into account the features supported by each and the requirements of the project).

# 4

# SOAP

e-Business is dependent on some form of communication mechanism, and **messaging** is a fundamental communication strategy. Messaging involves agreement between the communicating parties on a common message structure or syntax, and the protocol or rules that are to be applied to that syntax.

Messages are data blocks. They're the fundamental building blocks of any computer network in which nodes send discrete blocks of data to one another. Consequently, we can find messages not only in e-mail, but in settings as diverse as object-oriented programming, inter-application communication, middleware and Electronic Data Interchange (EDI). At 'lower' protocol levels (like the physical, data link, or network levels) these messages are typically called **packets** or **frames**; while at the transport layer and up, the term **messages** is more common.

A message may consist of any kind of application data – commands, requests for services, event notifications, images, files, or a piece of e-mail. In fact, EDI (which deals with the exchange of business 'documents' such as purchase orders, invoices, or shipping notes) is based on a message-passing mechanism. And there are other familiar application areas which rely heavily on messaging – for example, object- and component-based middleware like CORBA and DCOM, and message-oriented middleware like MOM.

Enterprises have always been dependent on the ability to integrate (or couple) their vertical systems (ERP, CRM) – and this is increasingly the case. The oldest way to integrate systems is via remote procedure calls (RPCs). RPCs use a synchronous pattern of communication known as **request/reply** (sometimes referred to as **message transaction**): a client sends a request message to a server, and then blocks (that is, suspends execution) while it waits for the server to respond with a reply message. Consequently, RPCs are sometimes known as 'blocking middleware'. Blocking can be a problem, especially in distributed environments. RPCs are still very popular, and can also be seen as a mechanism for distributed computing.

A next phase in integration technology or middleware is MOM. MOM solved the blocking problem by employing a store-and-forward approach – it offers asynchronous services typically based on **message queuing**. Until recently, these solutions were proprietary in nature (such as IBM's MQ Series, Microsoft's MSMQ, Software AG's EntireX). However, the **Java Message Service** (**JMS**) has opened things up, in what can be considered a messaging reference architecture.

With respect to middleware and integration, Java adds an interesting dimension, since more thorough integration can be accomplished through its approach of employing a common virtual machine which executes platform-independent code. Java's impact on messaging is also quite exciting, and we'll look at JMS and **JAXM** (**Java API for XML Messaging**) in more detail in Chapter 14.

Given the pervasiveness of the Internet, emphasis on further levels of integration technology will typically lie outside the familiar and relatively secure borders of the enterprise. This is a great technical challenge given the scale and heterogeneity of this distributed environment – interoperability is the key issue. This demands flexible technology – scalable, loosely coupled, extensible – which is also easily adoptable. Arguably, only "open", non-proprietary solutions create the broad acceptance, and thus volume, to make this possible on a global scale – this is where SOAP and ebXML come in.

So in this chapter, we anticipate the *Messaging* section of this book (Chapters 13 and 14) by introducing SOAP. We will:

- Briefly discuss the purpose and history of SOAP, to provide a little perspective
- Explain SOAP's message structure, and discuss SOAP processing and message transfer
- Introduce SOAP With Attachments (SWA) – an extension of SOAP which allows us to send messages containing attachments
- Look at how the popular Apache SOAP toolkit can be used to build a sample application

Later in the book, in the *Messaging* section, we'll see how the ebXML Messaging Service extends the basic SOAP message constructs to provide a powerful messaging mechanism for ebXML systems.

# What Is SOAP?

Like COM and CORBA, **SOAP** (the **Simple Object Access Protocol**) is designed to facilitate the exchange of information in a distributed environment. Unlike COM and CORBA, SOAP is an **XML protocol** – that is, it can use XML to describe its message format. Moreover, it can use HTTP (or another transport protocol) to transport the messages. And this is a fundamental point: because SOAP can be implemented using such universal standards as XML and HTTP, it achieves a high level of interoperability – much higher than other such technologies. In other words, regardless of how a tool is implemented or where it is deployed, SOAP can allow that tool to make use of other services written in other languages and residing on other platforms.

> *This concept of interoperability is one that is becoming increasingly popular, and underlies movements in the area of Web Services. See Chapter 9, on UDDI, for more on Web Services.*

## What's in the Name?

SOAP is perceived by some to be a mechanism used mainly for invoking methods, services, components and objects on remote applications. It's certainly true that we can use a SOAP message body (or payload) to carry a method invocation, and this seems to be one of the more common applications of SOAP (although it's an area more commonly associated with distributed object architectures like CORBA, DCOM and EJB). However, that's not the whole story. For example, we can also use the SOAP message body to carry an order form or an invoice – indeed, within the context of ebXML, these are probably more appropriate examples of SOAP's capabilities. So, let's define SOAP in a much more general way – as a **message protocol**, designed to carry arbitrary payloads over a network.

The above paragraphs briefly outline the *Object Access Protocol* part of SOAP's expansion; but why does its name include the word *Simple*? Well, there may be more than one answer to this question. There are some folk that say, "simpleness is a familiarity index, not a complexity measure." These folk might interpret the word *Simple* as a reminder of the fact that SOAP can be run over the ubiquitous HTTP transport protocol, and that it uses XML for its main message structure. Others might argue it indicates that the SOAP protocol is designed to send and respond to RPCs in a specific way, and is thus related to Internet protocol cousins like Simple Mail Transfer Protocol (SMTP) and Simple Network Management Protocol (SNMP).

## SOAP As a Protocol

The purpose of a protocol is to provide a communication service, which can be used by higher-level objects (such as application processes or other higher-level protocols). Potentially, there could be many choices of protocol at any given level, each providing different communication services. And in the same way that SOAP can run on top of other transport protocols like HTTP and SMTP or mechanisms like JMS, protocol specifications like ebMS (the ebXML Messaging Service) extend SOAP to address more specialized communication needs.

In its relatively short life, SOAP has quickly become very popular. (Perhaps this is due to the fact that SOAP has a nice, versatile functionality mix, with coverage of both RPC-style communication and more general communication patterns.) It appeals to a broad audience of developers involved in anything from distributed component technology to Web Services and e-business. Thanks to the large and increasing number of SOAP tools available (such as the SOAP toolkits available from Microsoft and Apache), SOAP's popularity is still growing.

Since a SOAP message is encoded in XML, we can observe another advantage: that SOAP messages can be seen as **self-describing** documents. The term *self-describing* is frequently encountered in an XML context, and refers to the fact that the document uses XML tags which both organise *and* describe the data contained in the document. (We'll see some examples later, when we cover the SOAP main message structure.) This means that a SOAP message is not only more interoperable than a binary protocol or message frame message, but it's a lot easier to debug.

SOAP's message structure is a common one (using an **envelope**, a **header** and a **body**, as we shall see later) – a structure commonly employed by other Internet protocols. The relation between SOAP and other Internet protocols is significant, since SOAP builds on familiar Internet protocol concepts for reliable messaging functionality. We'll return to this subject in Chapter 13.

# A History of SOAP

SOAP was born in the second half of 1999 as an industry standard proposal by Microsoft for the exchange of data over the Web. In fact, SOAP built on an earlier XML-RPC proposal by Dave Winer of UserLand Software Inc. Microsoft's intention was to get away from their existing proprietary protocol, DCOM, by implementing a new, open and extensible protocol based on XML. At that time, it was perceived as a move that would give Microsoft a competitive edge, particularly because SOAP was being strongly associated with Microsoft's .NET (at that time, termed "next generation Windows services") Internet initiative.

In January 2000, Microsoft, UserLand and DevelopMentor submitted the SOAP specification to the **Internet Engineering Task Force** (**IETF**) as an Internet Draft. As IBM gave up its initial resistance to the proposal, SOAP gathered further momentum. The SOAP 1.1 specification, released in April 2000, carries a copyright notice, which includes IBM and Lotus as copyright holders. By that time, SOAP was increasingly being seen as the solution that could help the software industry find a way for businesses to link their disparate computer systems over the Internet. People were recognising that SOAP allows businesses to choose their own internal implementation technology (be it object brokers such as EJB, DCOM, or CORBA, or traditional languages such as COBOL) without fear of their choice creating a lock-in and preventing them from interfacing with other businesses. They were also beginning to see that SOAP allows integration and interfacing with heterogeneous (external) environments.

In May 2000, the SOAP 1.1 specification was submitted to and published by the World Wide Web Consortium (W3C), although still copyrighted (by Microsoft and IBM among others). The SOAP 1.1 version extended the asynchronous messaging capabilities and enabled support for SMTP, FTP and TCP/IP, although the SOAP specification itself only described HTTP.

Since then, proposals have been offered to the W3C concerning *SOAP Messages with Attachments* (http://www.w3.org/TR/SOAP-attachments, Dec 2000) and *SOAP Security Extensions* (http://www.w3.org/TR/SOAP-dsig, Feb 2001). Further technical development of SOAP is carried out under the auspices of the W3C XML Protocol Working Group. The SOAP version 1.2 Working Draft was published by the Working Group in July 2001 – this document is now copyrighted by W3C. For most observers, this particular detail signifies that SOAP is now indeed an *open standard*. Specifically, it goes some way to addressing the fears of some that concern dominant vendor influence on future directions of this open standard.

Adoption of SOAP is proving to be widespread. Several state-of-the-art initiatives – like UDDI, ebXML, Web Services, and Microsoft's .NET– are using SOAP in one form or another. Moreover, the Apache organization has released an open-source reference implementation of SOAP (based on the IBM SOAP4J implementation), which further affirms the spreading popularity of SOAP.

> *Don Box, one of the original proponents of the SOAP specification, provides a more complete history of SOAP in his aptly-titled article of March 2001,* A Brief History of SOAP *(http://www.develop.com/dbox/postsoap.html). The article offers some interesting insights into the political issues that surrounded the adoption of this standard.*

## The SOAP Specification

The SOAP 1.1 protocol specification covered here is found at http://www.w3.org/TR/SOAP. Among other things, it describes:

- The SOAP envelope (the message structure), and the rules to apply to that structure in order to process a SOAP message successfully
- The set of encoding rules used as the serialization mechanism
- The request/reply convention used within SOAP to represent RPCs

*We will return to serialization and RPCs later in the chapter.*

## The SOAP Versioning Model

SOAP uses its namespace as a versioning mechanism. So the namespace identifies the SOAP version, rather than a major and minor version number as in a more traditional versioning scheme. The namespaces are as follows:

- SOAP 1.1 uses the `http://schemas.xmlsoap.org/soap/envelope/` and `http://schemas.xmlsoap.org/soap/encoding/` namespaces
- The SOAP 1.2 Draft version is identified by the `http://www.w3.org/2001/06/soap-envelope` and `http://www.w3.org/2001/06/soap-encoding` namespaces.

*Recall that* namespaces *are a way to partition component names (for instance schema components such as type definitions, element declarations, attribute declarations) such that they do not conflict with each other. So namespaces uniquely identify the element and attribute names in XML documents, and distinguish between duplicate element names and attributes. A URI reference identifies a namespace. Note that the URI is just meant as a unique identifier and does not necessarily have a 'live' presence on the Internet, that is, it does not necessarily point to a location.*

We'll see these namespaces in action in a number of sample messages in this chapter.

## SOAP and XML Schemas

We use an XML Schema as a way of validating an XML document – that is, ensuring that the data in the XML document complies with a set of prescribed rules. The XML Schema defines these rules via descriptions of valid data types and element hierarchies, and other constraints.

Since a SOAP message is an XML document, we could use an XML Schema to describe the SOAP message structure. The complete schema for a SOAP message can be found at http://schemas.xmlsoap.org/soap/envelope/.

*This URL is, in fact, also used as a URI within SOAP. While URIs are just intended as unique identifiers and don't usually represent a "live" presence on the Internet, this one is an exception!*

Note that SOAP 1.1 (May 2000) predates XML Schema, which only became available as a W3C Recommendation in May 2001. Insofar as the SOAP specification references XML Schema, an older Draft version of XML Schema was used. This is one of the obvious things updated in SOAP 1.2. It also helps to explain why XML Schemas are not yet in common use for the description of SOAP payloads (message bodies), and especially not for "business document" message bodies. This is likely to change in time. When SOAP is used as an RPC system, the payload parameters may be based on XML Schema data types. Apart from that, SOAP offers its own compound data types for serialization purposes.

# SOAP Message Processing

SOAP messages are the basic unit of communication between peer SOAP-aware network nodes. From a SOAP node's perspective, the data that it receives from an application is just a piece of data. SOAP does not care whether the data represents a purchase order, an array of integers, an e-mail message or an image – it is simply charged with sending the data to its peer SOAP node. The sending SOAP node must of course communicate to its peer (receiving) SOAP node how to handle the message when it is received – this information is contained in the header section of the SOAP message. This will allow the receiving SOAP node to take appropriate action on receipt of the message. This process of wrapping additional housekeeping and utility data around the primary payload is called **encapsulation**. Encapsulation is essential to the operation of both high-level transport protocols like SOAP or SMTP and lower-level ones like TCP/IP.

In the following examples, we have a couple of SOAP messages run over HTTP, and we can see how HTTP added its own header information to the SOAP message.

## Some Example SOAP Messages

Let's first take a look at an example of a SOAP message to get a feeling for the ideas behind SOAP and the messages being transferred from one point to the other.

The two messages here describe a conversation between a SOAP client and a SOAP server. The client sends the first message. This is, in fact, a call to a procedure called `GetAddress()`, which is a method on an application hosted by the SOAP server. As you can probably guess from the sample, the `GetAddress()` method takes a single parameter, the `customerID` (that's the benefit of self-describing data!). The `<GetAddress>` element is defined by the `app` namespace, and the whole thing is embedded in an HTTP request:

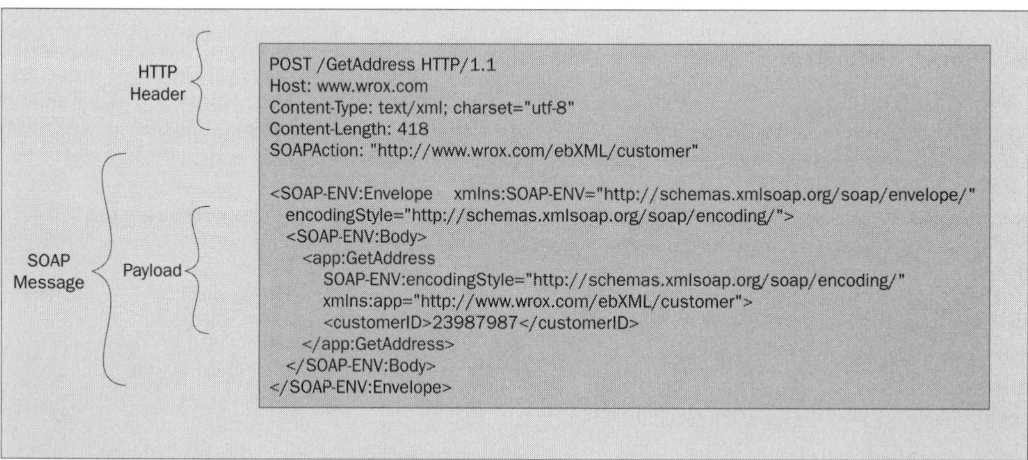


When the SOAP server receives this request, it examines it to see what type of message it is. In this case, it should recognise it as being a method call directed at a method of its application, so it should run that method and grab any result. Then it packs the result into a SOAP package and returns it in an HTTP response:

```
HTTP/1.1 200 OK
Content-Type: text/xml; charset="utf-8"
Content-Length: 715

<SOAP-ENV:Envelope
   xmlns:SOAP-ENV="http://schemas.xmlsoap.org/soap/envelope/"
   encodingStyle="http://schemas.xmlsoap.org/soap/encoding/">
   <SOAP-ENV:Body>
      <app:GetAddress
         SOAP-ENV:encodingStyle="http://schemas.xmlsoap.org/soap/encoding/"
         xmlns:app="http://www.wrox.com/ebXML/customer">
         <customer customerID="23987987">
            <name>
               <firstname>Jim</firstname>
               <surname>Hall</surname>
            </name>
            <address>
               <street nr="10">Belgrave Boulevard</street>
               <zip>2389</zip>
               <city>New York</city>
            </address>
         </customer>
      </app:GetAddress>
   </SOAP-ENV:Body>
</SOAP-ENV:Envelope>
```

We will look in more detail at the specifics of the structure and syntax of these messages later on, in the section entitled *The SOAP Message Structure.*

# SOAP Message Transfer

In fact, we can distinguish *three* types of SOAP node in the transfer of a SOAP message, namely, the **SOAP original sender**, the **SOAP intermediary** and the **SOAP ultimate receiver**. The SOAP original sender is the originator of the message. The SOAP ultimate receiver is the target node to which the message is ultimately intended. A SOAP intermediary is a node which receives a message and forwards it towards its final destination, in a similar fashion to that of an e-mail gateway; in that way it is both a receiver and a sender.

The following diagram illustrates these roles:

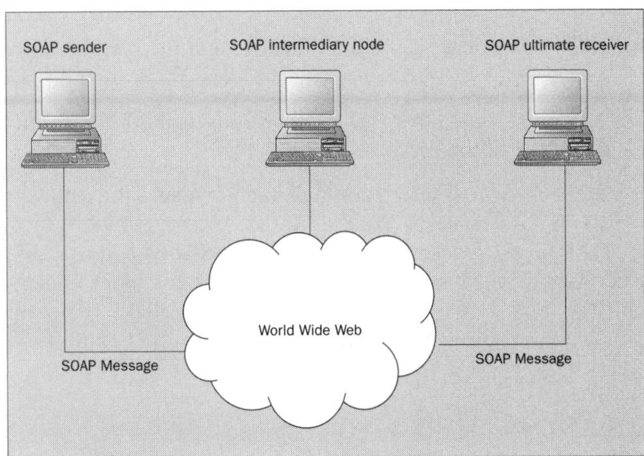

A SOAP message is sent from source to destination along a **message path**, a set of SOAP senders and receivers through which a single SOAP message passes, via potentially any number of SOAP intermediaries. We distinguish between two types of message transfer, as follows:

- Direct transmission between sender and receiver, in which no intermediaries are involved. This is called a **one-hop** message transfer
- Indirect transmission between sender and receiver, in which one-or-more intermediaries are involved. This is called a **multi-hop** message transfer.

When a message is received by a SOAP node, the node must parse the data in the header to establish what, if anything, it must do with the message. While this is a common encapsulation concept, SOAP has some specific terminology here, as we shall see below:

A SOAP node may assume a **SOAP actor** role. This is SOAP-speak for what the node has to do upon receipt of a message. This role, the **SOAP actor name,** is specified using a URI. To practice some SOAP jargon: a SOAP intermediary node will typically act in the SOAP actor role **next**, meaning that the node will "receive a message and forward it". In fact, any SOAP node must be able to act as the SOAP actor "next".

Also, the SOAP node may act in the additional role of an **anonymous** actor, meaning the node is the ultimate receiver and the action it needs to take is to pass on the message payload to the application. We'll return to the subject of SOAP actors briefly, when we examine the `<actor>` attribute within a SOAP message, later in the chapter.

An actor is not allowed to change its role during the processing of a message, though it can act in different roles for different messages. A SOAP node can assume additional actor roles, but only the roles mentioned before are prescribed. This means that we can add our own routines for, say, authentication and transaction services, but we need to handle them ourselves.

Let's now move on, to examine the elements and attributes that make up a SOAP message.

# The SOAP Message Structure

SOAP messages are XML documents that, like many other message protocol structures, consist of three parts:

- **The envelope** is the outermost part of the message, and the mandatory container for the other two parts.
- **The header** is an optional area designated for routing and other information, which allows processing and transfer of the message.
- **The body** is a mandatory area which contains the **payload** – the actual message content.

SOAP uses the term **SOAP block** to describe a block of data that is seen as a single computational unit of data by a node processing a SOAP message. A **header block** is a block encapsulated within the SOAP header, and a **body block** is a block encapsulated within a SOAP body. In its simplest form, a block would contain only one element, though typically they will be more complex.

*Note that in the SOAP 1.1 specification, these consitituents are called* **entries,** *not blocks; the term* ***SOAP block*** *used in this book comes from the SOAP version 1.2 specification. While the SOAP examples in this chapter use SOAP v1.1, and ebXML is also based on the SOAP v1.1, I've used the term SOAP block because it's more intuitive.*

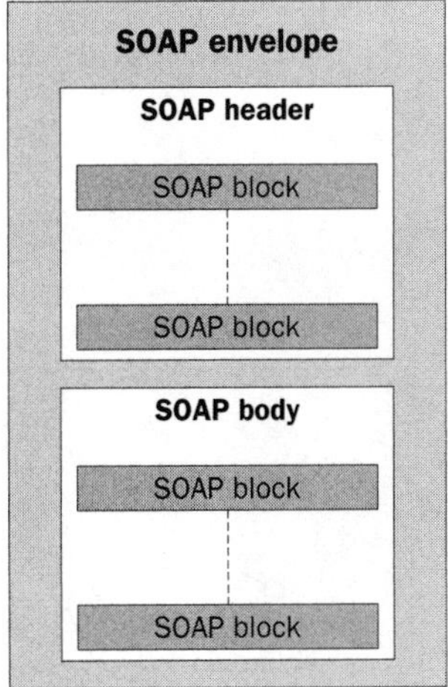


The next diagram expands the above block view to an overview of the main elements and attributes of a SOAP message:

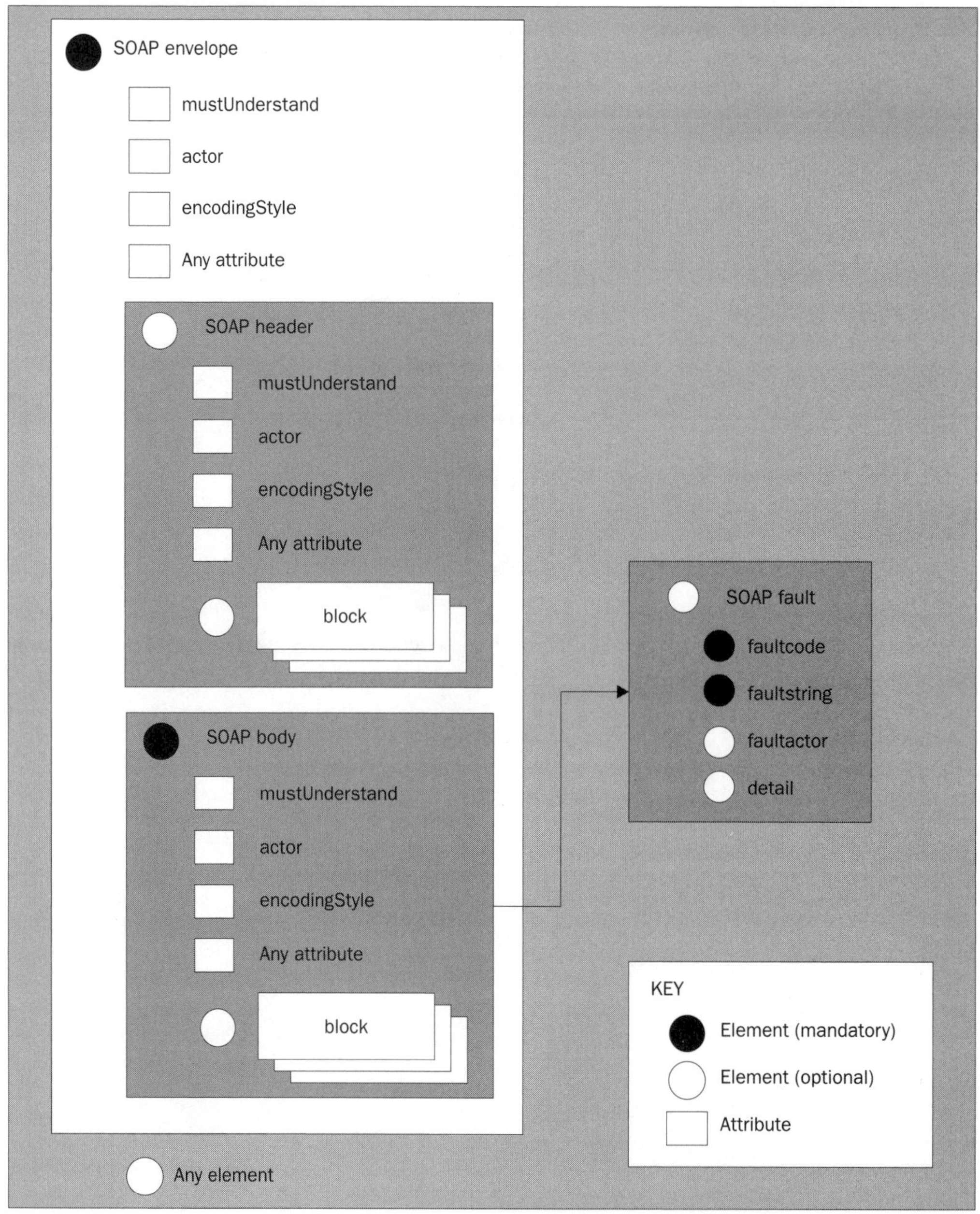


*Note that this diagram format is used in subsequent diagrams below, so you may wish to refer back to the key in this diagram.*

The mustUnderstand and actor attributes are global attributes – which means that they can occur in the envelope, header and body. However, they only have a (useful) defined behavior in the header, so we'll meet these attributes formally in our description of the SOAP header. We'll cover the encodingStyle attribute in our coverage of encoding and serialization. Let's take a look at the three parts of the SOAP message structure now.

## The SOAP Message Envelope

The term **envelope** is often used in a protocol context to describe the complete message frame, although (until XML protocols came along) it typically described complete binary or text message frames, where the envelope wasn't explicitly present. Thanks to the self-describing nature of XML in general, and of SOAP message tags in particular, the envelope has now literally become a visible XML element.

The <Envelope> element is used to carry general information (such as meta data) about the message, and is also the parent element of the <Header> and <Body> elements. In practice, this means that it's the area where general namespaces appear, as in the following sample:

```
<SOAP-ENV:Envelope
         xmlns:SOAP-ENV="http://schemas.xmlsoap.org/soap/envelope/"
         xmlns:xsi="http:/www.w3.org/1999/XMLSchema-instance"
         encodingStyle="http://schemas.xmlsoap.org/soap/encoding/">
   <SOAP-ENV:Header>
      <!-- The SOAP header is an optional element -->
   </SOAP-ENV:Header>
   <SOAP-ENV:Body>
      <!-- The SOAP body is a required element -->
   </SOAP-ENV:Body>
   <!-- Optional envelope elements here, after the body -->
</SOAP-ENV:Envelope>
```

The <Envelope> element is the document element of the XML document describing the SOAP message.

## The SOAP Message Header

As the name suggests, the header is usually attached to the front of the message. Generally speaking, it's a small data structure that is used to allow peer nodes to communicate with one another. In SOAP, the <Header> element is an optional element, into which we can add auxiliary information (relating to things like authentication and transactions) which is used by SOAP nodes. However, the implementation of both syntax to define, and functionality to deal with the header information is up to the developer. Any node along a SOAP message path can add items to (or delete items from) the header; nodes can also choose to ignore items if they are unrecognised. If a <Header> element is present, it must be the first child element of the <Envelope> element.

The SOAP node must explicitly report failure if so instructed (for header processing this is usually the case). We've already briefly come across the mustUnderstand and actor attributes – they play an important role here, as we will see now.

### The mustUnderstand Attribute

The SOAP mustUnderstand global attribute indicates whether a header entry is mandatory or optional for the recipient to process. The recipient of a header entry is defined by the SOAP <actor> attribute. The value of the mustUnderstand attribute is either 0 (the default) or 1. There are two important points to note about the effect of this attribute:

- If a message has `mustUnderstand="1"`, then it has to be "understood" completely before it may be processed. If the receiving SOAP node is not able to process the message successfully (that is, the message is not understood), then it must respond with a failure message, which must explicitly report the failure back via a `MustUnderstand faultcode`.
- A SOAP node may skip the processing of messages or parts of messages that are not explicitly defined as `mustUnderstand="1"` (that is, either empty or "0"). We will cover this later when discussing SOAP error messages.

#### *The actor Attribute*

The `actor` attribute is used to specify the intended role of the receiving node. Recall that we've already mentioned the different roles that an `actor` can assume, in the *SOAP Message Transfer* section of this chapter. As we said there, the role (or SOAP actor name) is specified using a URI:

- SOAP's only predefined role, `next`, is specified by the URI `http://schemas.xmlsoap.org/soap/actor/next` – this indicates that the recipient must play the role called `next`, and act on the message.
- If the `actor` attribute is omitted, it means the recipient is the ultimate destination of the SOAP message, and thus acts as we've seen before in the role of anonymous SOAP actor.

Remember that an actor can play many roles, but only plays one role per message.

## *A Sample Processing Scenario*

The SOAP document in the sample below will be sent from the sender (A) to a receiver (B). The SOAP message passes through several intermediate nodes during the transfer from the sender to the ultimate receiver. The `secure` actor (`http://www.wrox.com/secure`) performs all necessary steps to process the header block contained within the `<Authenticate>` element. Processing means the actor must understand the message, and for instance, perform an LDAP lookup using the supplied `<firstname>` and `<surname>`. It then sends the message to the next node in the chain. All nodes along the message path must understand the header (`mustUnderstand="1"`), but only the final node in the chain (the ultimate receiver, implicitly acting as the anonymous actor) must perform the necessary steps to process both the `<Transaction>` header block and the SOAP body.

```
<SOAP-ENV:Envelope
   xmlns:SOAP-ENV="http://schemas.xmlsoap.org/soap/envelope/"
   encodingStyle="http://schemas.xmlsoap.org/soap/encoding/">
   <SOAP-ENV:Header>
      <app:Authenticate xmlns:app="http://www.wrox.com/secure"
                        mustUnderstand="1"
                        actor="http://www.wrox.com/ebXML/authenticate">
         <name>
            <firstname>Jim</firstname>
            <surname>Hall</surname>
         </name>
      </app:Authenticate>
      <trx:Transaction xmlns:trx="http://www.wrox.com/ebXML/transaction"
                       mustUnderstand="1">
          <customerID>23987987</customerID>
      </trx:Transaction>
   </SOAP-ENV:Header>
```

```
    <SOAP-ENV:Body>
        <!-- The body -->
    </SOAP-ENV:Body>
</SOAP-ENV:Envelope>
```

In the above sample, the ultimate receiver node and all intermediary nodes have some processing to do. Each intermediate node removes any header information targeted specifically at that node, and it may add new information to the SOAP message header. There is no indication which node added what new information. This forces all nodes further along the SOAP message path to reinterpret the message header.

## The SOAP Message Body

The message body or payload is where we find the data being transmitted on behalf of the application. In specific SOAP terminology: the SOAP body is used for the exchange of the payload between the SOAP sender and SOAP ultimate receiver.

If a <Header> element is present, then the <Body> element must be its immediate sibling; otherwise, the <Body> element must be the first child element of the <Envelope> element. A SOAP body can consist of one or more blocks.

> *Logically speaking, this should mean that the payload of a SOAP message (the data passed on by the application) is always found in the <Body> element. However, as we will see shortly when we cover the **SOAP with Attachments** (SWA) proposal, this doesn't have to be the case.*

In the following sample, the SOAP <Body> carries a request for the execution of the `GetAddress()` method, and sends a `customerID`, needed to obtain the address information for the customer:

```
<SOAP-ENV:Envelope
    xmlns:SOAP-ENV="http://schemas.xmlsoap.org/soap/envelope/"
    encodingStyle="http://schemas.xmlsoap.org/soap/encoding/">
    <SOAP-ENV:Body>
        <app:GetAddress
            SOAP-ENV:encodingStyle="http://schemas.xmlsoap.org/soap/encoding/"
            xmlns:app="http://www.wrox.com/ebXML/customer">
            <customerID>23987987</customerID>
        </app:GetAddress>
    </SOAP-ENV:Body>
</SOAP-ENV:Envelope>
```

### The SOAP Fault

If an error is encountered during the processing of a SOAP message, then the fault is reported in a response that contains a body block consisting of a <SOAP-ENV:fault> element. This is the SOAP **fault block**. If present, it contains information on the error conditions encountered.

The fault block can contain four elements:

- The <faultcode> element is a required element that contains a qualified name, used to describe the type of error that has occurred. The SOAP 1.1 namespace defines four `faultcode` values (listed here, with their meanings):

- `VersionMismatch` – the processing party has received an invalid namespace for the SOAP `<Envelope>` element.
- `MustUnderstand` – indicates that the processing actor could not understand or process the SOAP `<Header>` element. (Note that we use an upper-case `M` here, while the SOAP `mustUnderstand` attribute uses a lower-case `m`.)
- `Client` – indicates that the message was incorrectly formed, or didn't contain the appropriate information required by the client.
- `Server` – indicates that the message could not be processed for reasons not directly related to the content, but rather to the processing of the message.

  Although the `SOAP-ENV` namespace is included in the element value above, it's not required – so custom `faultcode` values can easily be added.

- The `<faultstring>` element is a required element that provides a human-readable description of the fault.
- The `<faultactor>` element is an optional element that indicates the URI of the source of the fault.
- The `<detail>` element is an optional element used to add application-specific error information in case an error occurred while processing the SOAP `<Body>` element.

Let's have a look at another example. Here, the SOAP message replies with error information. The SOAP body contains a SOAP fault that consists of the required `<faultcode>` and `<faultstring>` elements. The additional `<detail>` element is used to carry application-specific information to the party that issued the SOAP request.

In this sample, the lookup of a customer failed since the specified customer (`customerID`) did not exist. An application could pass on this error information to the end-user.

```
<SOAP-ENV:Envelope
   xmlns:SOAP-ENV="http://schemas.xmlsoap.org/soap/envelope/"
   encodingStyle="http://schemas.xmlsoap.org/soap/encoding/">
   <SOAP-ENV:Body>
      <SOAP-ENV:Fault>
         <faultcode>SOAP-ENV:Client</faultcode>
         <faultstring>Client error</faultstring>
         <detail>
            <app:noSuchCustomer
                      xmlns:app="http://www.wrox.com/ebXML/customer">
               <app:message>No customer found with this ID</app:message>
               <app:field>customerID</app:field>
            </app:noSuchCustomer>
         </detail>
      </SOAP-ENV:Fault>
   </SOAP-ENV:Body>
</SOAP-ENV:Envelope>
```

*Note that, according to the XML Schema specification, the SOAP fault (a `complexType`) may also contain the "globally defined" attributes `actor`, `mustUnderstand` and `encodingStyle`. However, there is no useful associated behavior for these attributes in this context.*

mechanism is very similar in scope to **EDIINT** (EDI over the Internet) scenarios, in which e-mail attachments is used as a simple and cheap means to implement EDI. One of the organizational ıntages of such a scheme is that it allows smaller companies with limited IT resources to participate DI message chains because they can process the attachments by hand. In this case the attachments ld be human-readable business documents such as purchase orders, possibly with a corresponding payload (which is not human-readable) in the e-mail message itself.

in a particular supply chain, participants with various degrees of IT sophistication can be mixed, efiting overall flexibility and cutting costs.

SWA W3C Note is a proposal submitted by Hewlett Packard and Microsoft. Microsoft's lvement is interesting – they use a similar approach in their BizTalk solution. Technically, as saging solutions, BizTalk and the ebMS (the ebXML Messaging Service – see Chapter 13) are very lar. Both are based on SOAP, and both are intended primarily to support the exchange of electronic ness documents. It should be no surprise to learn that ebMS uses SWA.

L purists may consider SWA to be a crude approach (combining XML with MIME attachments), it does have some technical advantages:

- It implies that the SOAP message itself contains only message meta information, so processing a message is simpler.
- Given the technical difficulty of *complete* support for XML encoding of binary file attachments – think of underlying Unicode character encoding schemes – SWA may be a technically more robust approach, since MIME treatment is well-tested in similar SMTP based settings.

s diagram is a representation of the SWA message ıcture:

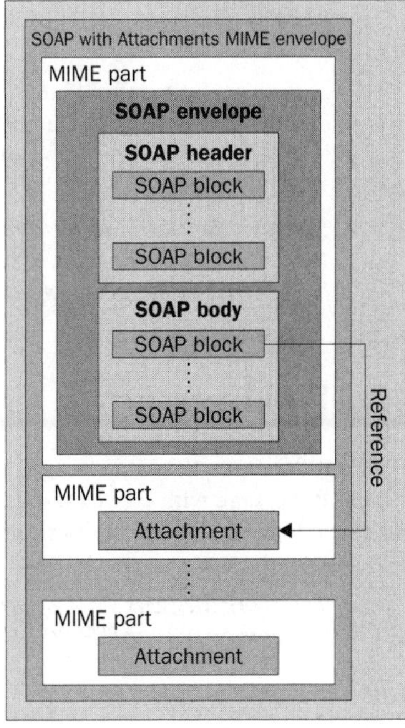

### SOAP and Multilingual Data

Since ebXML is about *global* e-commerce, let's look at an example that shows th capabilities of SOAP to handle **multilingual** payload entries in a SOAP message, `xml:lang` attribute:

```
<SOAP-ENV:Envelope
   xmlns:SOAP-ENV="http://schemas.xmlsoap.org/soap/envelope/"
   encodingStyle="http://schemas.xmlsoap.org/soap/encoding/">
   <SOAP-ENV:Body>
      <SOAP-ENV:Fault>
         <faultcode>SOAP-ENV:Client</faultcode>
         <faultstring>Client error</faultstring>
         <detail xmlns:app="http://www.wrox.com/ebXML/customer"
                 xml:lang="en">
            <app:message>
               No customer found with this ID
            </app:message>
            <app:message xml:lang="nl">
               De gevraagde klant is niet aanwezig in het systeem
            </app:message>
            <app:message xml:lang="ge">
               Es gibt keine Kunde unter diese Nummer.
            </app:message>
            <app:field>customerID</app:field>
         </detail>
      </SOAP-ENV:Fault>
   </SOAP-ENV:Body>
</SOAP-ENV:Envelope>
```

In this example, the default language for the detailed error description is set to `en` Detailed error messages in Dutch (`nl`) and German (`de`) are also supplied, and th decide locally which translation of the error message to employ.

> *Note that the codes used to denote the countries are the two-letter ISO 639-1 codes, a full list of which can be found at* *http://www.oasis-open.org/cover/iso639a.html.*

# SOAP Messages with Attachments

The W3C Note, **SOAP Messages With Attachments** (**SWA**), specifies a standard w SOAP message with one or more attachments in a multipart MIME structure for t the payload of a message does not necessarily have to be in the body part of a SO

> *The SOAP Messages With Attachments Note (December 2000) can be found at* *http://www.w3.org/TR/2000/NOTE-SOAP-attachments-20001211.*

The proposal is such that the processing rules for the SOAP 1.1 messages are prese SOAP parts are still present, although the envelope contains one or more **attachm** existing facilities in the SOAP and MIME mechanisms to carry and reference the a

A SOAP 1.1 message with attachments is called a **SOAP message package**. The primary SOAP message in a package may reference the attachments. The following example shows how a SOAP message is encapsulated with two attachments. The first attachment contains a GIF image of a contract, and the second attachment contains a manual in PDF format:

```
MIME-Version: 1.0
Content-Type: Multipart/Related; boundary="MIME_boundary"; type=text/xml;
              start="<contract8987665.xml@wrox.com>"
Content-Description: Writer information, including contract and
                     draft manual.

--MIME_boundary
Content-Type: text/xml; charset=UTF-8
Content-Transfer-Encoding: 8bit
Content-ID: <contract8987665.xml@wrox.com>

<?xml version='1.0' ?>
<SOAP-ENV:Envelope
   xmlns:SOAP-ENV="http://schemas.xmlsoap.org/soap/envelope/">
   <SOAP-ENV:Body>
      ...
      <contract href="cid:contract8987665.gif@wrox.com"/>
      <manual href="http://www.wrox.com/manual8987665.pdf"/>
      ...
   </SOAP-ENV:Body>
</SOAP-ENV:Envelope>

--MIME_boundary
Content-Type: image/gif
Content-Transfer-Encoding: base64
Content-ID: <contract8987665.gif@wrox.com>
Content-Location: http://www.wrox.com/contract8987665.gif

... the binary-encoded GIF image goes here ...
--MIME_boundary—

--MIME_boundary
Content-Type: application/pdf
Content-Transfer-Encoding: base64
Content-ID: <manual8987665.pdf@wrox.com>
Content-Location: http://www.wrox.com/manual8987665.pdf

... the binary-encoded PDF goes here ...
--MIME_boundary--
```

In the above sample, the `Content-Type` of the MIME header is `Multipart/Related`, and the `type` of the message is `text/xml`, both conforming to the specification for SWA. Following the advice in the specification, the (otherwise optional) `start` parameter points to the first element in the first MIME encapsulated body section. The optional `Content-Description` contains an explanation about the message.

The MIME parts must contain a `Content-ID` (in this case, it is `<contract8987665.xml@wrox.com>`) and/or a `Content-Location` (in this case, `http://www.wrox.com/contract8987665.gif`). In this sample, both are defined. The SOAP body references the carried attachments, using the `Content-Location` and the `Content-ID`.

The SOAP 1.1 message contains two elements in the body that reference an attachment. The `contract` references the GIF of the contract by using the `Content-ID`. The `manual` references the PDF of the manual by using the `Content-Location`.

Having looked at the definition of SOAP, and covered SOAP's origins, purpose, function, and message syntax, let's move on to look at the following more advanced aspects of SOAP: the set of encoding rules used as the serialization mechanism, and the request/reply convention used within SOAP to represent RPCs.

# SOAP and Distributed Object Architectures

Object- or component-based middleware (such as CORBA and COM) are popular models that allow the developer to construct (potentially distributed) applications using already available building blocks. These building blocks can reside on any location on the network and are called via location-transparent method invocation. The components and their interfaces and methods are defined using an **interface definition language** (**IDL**), and they can be implemented in any programming language. The components offer standardized interfaces for invocation via a particular RPC or **remote message invocation** (**RMI**) protocol discipline.

Although the idea of reuse behind CORBA and COM is the same, the implementation is not. Invocation of a CORBA object requires an **object request broker** (**ORB**) that acts differently from a (D)COM implementation. Different approaches have pros and cons, but the main point is that the interaction and interoperability between the different models is very hard. SOAP's intention is to solve this problem by offering a simple and open protocol to bridge the different technologies.

This means that component models should provide interaction possibilities based on the SOAP standard. Microsoft's COM was (for obvious reasons) the first component model offering mechanisms for SOAP via the Microsoft SOAP toolkit. The **Object Management Group** (**OMG**) is investigating a number of initiatives to provide a bridging facility between CORBA and SOAP.

## *SOAP Encoding*

Some view SOAP primarily as a wire protocol designed to serialize remote method invocations using its built-in extensible encoding rules. The problem addressed in **encoding** and **serialization** (the process of "flattening" data in order for it to be transmitted efficiently) is sometimes illustrated by trying to imagine how an application-specific data structure, like a pointer held in volatile memory, can be moved over a network and reconstructed on another machine. The challenge here is that we want to do this in an *interoperable* (for example, programming language-independent) and *efficient* way. So again, we need to agree on a common format, often called the **presentation format**, and rules to encode (that is, to marshal or serialize) this format for efficient transmission "over the wire". At the receiving end, the receiver node needs to decode (that is, unmarshal or deserialize) this message.

Since SOAP is an XML protocol, XML is the encoding used for its main message structure and, optionally, its payload. I say 'optionally' here, since SOAP can carry *arbitrary* payloads. This XML nature means that XML Schema data types and XML Schema instances can be used for SOAP encoding. However this would still allow for a lot of variation in encoding, especially for compound data types like arrays and structures important for RPCs (to be covered shortly). SOAP offers its own compound data types and constructs for serialization purposes (arrays, enumerations, arrays of bytes, generic compound types, polymorphic accessors, compound values, and references to values). The SOAP encoding rules can be seen as a further constraining of XML encoding in order to guarantee interoperable and efficient implementations.

### *The encodingStyle Attribute*

The global `encodingStyle` attribute – which we have already met in passing on several occasions in this chapter – is used to indicate the encoding rules for the SOAP message. The *global* encoding rules define the *default* serialization used in the SOAP message – these defaults can be overridden at any level or element in the message. The value of the `encodingStyle` attribute value is an ordered list of one or more URIs identifying the serialization rule or rules that can be used to deserialize the SOAP message, in the order of most-specific to least-specific.

The syntax for setting the `encodingStyle` to the serialization rules defined by SOAP, identified by a URI, is:

```
SOAP-ENV:encodingStyle="http://schemas.xmlsoap.org/soap/encoding/"
```

### *RPC*

In terms of serialization rules, RPCs are demanding since parameters can be complex, and are typically based on compound data types like arrays and structures. When using SOAP as an RPC system, the SOAP parameters can be **typed** or **untyped**. The default SOAP encoding scheme uses the `xsi:type` attribute to indicate an XML Schema instance. The XML Schema specification defines several basic types, including `int`, `byte`, `short`, `boolean`, `string`, `float`, `double`, `date`, `time` and `uriReference`. It also specifies a format for sending arrays and blocks of uninterpreted data.

We will not cover serialization and related issues in depth, but just to give you an idea, let's look at the `array` datatype. An `array` contains a combination of one or more defined simple types and is a datatype not directly supported in XML Schema. The following example is a serialization of an `array`:

```
<SOAP-ENC:Array xmlns:SOAP-ENC="http://schemas.xmlsoap.org/soap/encoding/"
                SOAP-ENC:arrayType="xsd:string[10,5] ">
   <item SOAP-ENC:position="[2,2]">Third row, third col</item>
   <item SOAP-ENC:position="[7,5]">Eighth row, sixth col</item>
</SOAP-ENC:Array>
```

In the above sample, the `array` is a sparse array of strings, in which only two elements of the `array` are specified.

### *SOAP and RPC*

One of the design goals of SOAP is to encapsulate remote procedure call functionality using the extensibility and flexibility of XML. To invoke an RPC, the following information is needed:

- The URI of the target SOAP node
- A procedure or method name
- An optional procedure or method signature
- The parameters to the procedure or method
- Optional header data

The RPC invocations and responses are carried in the SOAP `<Body>` element.

The example below shows an RPC invocation of the `GetAddress()` method, which has one parameter – `customerID`. The URI of the target SOAP node here is `http://www.wrox.com/ebXML/customer`:

```
<SOAP-ENV:Body>
   <app:GetAddress xmlns:app="http://www.wrox.com/ebXML/customer">
      <customerID>23987987</customerID>
   </app:GetAddress>
</SOAP-ENV:Body>
```

# SOAP and Transport

SOAP was originally designed to run on top of HTTP. Although other transport protocols and mechanisms can be used, the necessary interfaces (or bindings) are not described in the SOAP specification.

So, HTTP is the primary transport protocol for SOAP messages, and probably will be for the foreseeable future. Now that further development of SOAP is taking place under responsibility of the W3C Protocol Workgroup, the best indication for bindings to underlying protocols other than HTTP can be found in the W3C XML Protocol Abstract Model Working Draft, which can be found at http://www.w3.org/TR/2001/WD-xmlp-am-20010709/.

## SOAP and HTTP

SOAP supports both HTTP and the HTTP Extension Framework as a transport mechanism. Since SOAP was originally designed to run over HTTP, the binding of SOAP to HTTP is 'natural'. SOAP follows the HTTP request/response message model, providing the SOAP request within an HTTP request and the SOAP response within an HTTP response. The SOAP binding is only defined for the HTTP `POST` request, and not for the HTTP `GET`.

The `Content-Type` in the HTTP header for SOAP messages is `text/xml`. A SOAP message can add an additional field to the HTTP header – the `SOAPAction` field. The value is a URI that identifies the action requested by this request. Here is an example HTTP header for a SOAP message:

```
POST /GetAddress HTTP/1.1
Host: www.wrox.com
Content-Type: text/xml; charset="utf-8"
Content-Length: nnnn
SOAPAction: "http://www.wrox.com/ebXML/customer"
```

The content of the `SOAPAction` is intended for use by network infrastructure components, like firewalls and routers that are SOAP-aware. The `SOAPAction` can be used for filtering and routing purposes.

The SOAP HTTP binding follows the semantics of the **HTTP status codes** (for a full list of HTTP status codes, check out ftp://ftp.isi.edu/in-notes/rfc2616.txt). For example, a 2xx status code indicates that the client's request including the SOAP message was successfully received, understood and accepted.

This also means that in the case of a SOAP error, an HTTP response status code 500 (Internal Server Error) will be issued. However, it's important to note that this doesn't necessarily mean something went wrong during the transport or processing of the SOAP message. It could be that the underlying application raised an application-specific error (for example, Customer not found) and replied with a SOAP fault. This forces the application receiving an HTTP error to process the message for SOAP faults in order to find the cause.

The example below shows an application error returned via an HTTP reply:

```
HTTP/1.1 500 Internal Server Error
Content-Type: text/xml; charset="utf-8"
Content-Length: 619

<SOAP-ENV:Envelope
   xmlns:SOAP-ENV="http://schemas.xmlsoap.org/soap/envelope/"
   encodingStyle="http://schemas.xmlsoap.org/soap/encoding/">
   <SOAP-ENV:Body>
      <SOAP-ENV:Fault>
         <faultcode>SOAP-ENV:Client</faultcode>
         <faultstring>Client error</faultstring>
         <detail>
            <app:noSuchCustomer
               xmlns:app="http://www.wrox.com/ebXML/customer">
               <app:message>No customer found with this ID</app:message>
               <app:field>customerID</app:field>
            </app:noSuchCustomer>
         </detail>
      </SOAP-ENV:Fault>
   </SOAP-ENV:Body>
</SOAP-ENV:Envelope>
```

# SOAP and Security

Currently, neither the SOAP 1.1 Note (http://www.w3.org/TR/SOAP), nor the SOAP 1.2 Draft proposal (http://www.w3.org/TR/soap12), define any security-related measures to be taken – they merely note that this needs to be addressed in future versions.

Since SOAP "rides on top of" other transport protocols, it may make use of security mechanisms available at those lower levels. For example, SOAP using extended HTTP headers can make use of firewall security mechanisms, and if SOAP is layered on top of HTTP, it may use any standard HTTP security feature or any endpoint application-specific security feature. SOAP requests can use HTTP authentication mechanisms as well as **SSL** (**Secure Socket Layers**) for secure channel communications (using HTTPS).

However, at the SOAP level, we have to conclude that security is very much a work-in-progress. In fact, security is a work-in-progress in the XML community *as a whole*, with several proposals under consideration. See for instance, XML Key Management Specification (XKMS – http://www.w3.org/TR/2001/NOTE-xkms-20010330), and the work of the XML-Based Security Services Technical Committee (SSTC – http://www.oasis-open.org/committees/security/index.shtml).

IBM and Microsoft have proposed the **SOAP Security Extensions: Digital Signature** Specification to W3C, which is based on the W3C candidate Recommendation **XML-Signature Syntax and Processing**. This W3C Note can be found at http://www.w3.org/TR/SOAP-dsig/ – it proposes a standard way to use the XML Digital Signature syntax (XML-Signature) to digitally "sign" SOAP 1.1 messages. In fact, a specific SOAP header entry `<SOAP-SEC:Signature>` is defined for this purpose.

See Chapter 15 for a more in-depth analysis and overview of security issues.

# SOAP Toolkits

Several SOAP toolkits are available providing solutions for different programming languages and environments. Toolkits for Perl, Python, Java, JavaScript, C++ and Visual Basic are available for download on the Web. Currently, the two most popular toolkits are the Microsoft and Apache toolkits.

## *The Microsoft SOAP Toolkit*

Microsoft offers an implementation of SOAP version 1.1, which consists of several components that help to ease the development of SOAP clients and servers. The Microsoft SOAP toolkit focuses on integration of COM components by offering a server-side component that maps invoked service operations to COM object method calls. Necessary components that construct, transmit, read, and process SOAP messages (the marshalling and unmarshalling that we refered to earlier) are also provided.

You can download the Microsoft SOAP Toolkit, and obtain full documentation for it, from http://msdn.microsoft.com.

## *The Apache SOAP Toolkit*

The Apache Software Foundation offers an implementation of SOAP version 1.1. Apache SOAP is an implementation based on (but superseding) the IBM SOAP4J implementation.

Apache SOAP can be used as a client library to invoke SOAP services via HTTP, or as a server-side tool to implement SOAP-accessible services. As a client library it provides an API for invoking SOAP RPC services, as well as an API for sending and receiving SOAP messages. As a mechanism to write new RPC-accessible services or message-accessible services, it expects to be hosted by a servlet container.

The Apache SOAP Toolkit and its accompanying documentation can be obtained from http://xml.apache.org/soap.

# Implementing a SOAP Send-and-Response

To complete this chapter, we'll take a look at an example that illustrates the coding required for a SOAP client and a SOAP server. This is a fairly minimal code listing; we'll just focus on the essentials. The SOAP Toolkit used in this example is the Apache SOAP toolkit, version 2.2.

The implementation is based partly on the SOAP message samples shown earlier in this chapter, in which the SOAP client sends a SOAP request, asking for customer information associated with a specified `customerId`; and the SOAP server responds via a SOAP response message.

### The SOAP Client's Request Message

In order to find out the customer's details, the client application needs to interrogate the server application. This interrogation is in the form of a method call, and results in the execution of the getCustomerDetail() method on the server. The getCustomerDetail() method expects a single parameter – the customerId – and this value is passed as part of the request.

To invoke the method call on the server, the client wraps up the method call in a SOAP envelope:

```
<?xml version='1.0' encoding='UTF-8'?>
<SOAP-ENV:Envelope
   xmlns:SOAP-ENV="http://schemas.xmlsoap.org/soap/envelope/"
   xmlns:xsi="http://www.w3.org/1999/XMLSchema-instance"
   xmlns:xsd="http://www.w3.org/1999/XMLSchema">
   <SOAP-ENV:Body>
      <app:getCustomerDetail xmlns:app="urn:CustomerInfo"
               encodingStyle="http://schemas.xmlsoap.org/soap/encoding/">
         <customerId xsi:type="xsd:int">1</customerId>
      </app:getCustomerDetail>
   </SOAP-ENV:Body>
</SOAP-ENV:Envelope>
```

This SOAP message is then issued by the client across the network, to the server.

### Deploying the Service

The first step is to write the necessary code to act as a SOAP server and be able to execute the requested method. The SOAP server used here is the standard rpcrouter servlet (available with the Apache SOAP Toolkit) that acts as a SOAP server. The first step in configuring the rpcrouter is to specify the deployed services. The sample below shows the service definition that deploys a Java class, called Customers. This class has a method called getCustomerDetail(). The rpcrouter will pass the received getCustomerDetail() call to the Customers class. The service id is used as the namespace to guarantee name uniqueness of the getCustomerDetail() information.

To define the service, the Apache-SOAP Server Side Administration Tool uses a deployment descriptor of the SOAP service (the file DeploymentDescriptor.xml – see below). The deployment descriptor contains the information that the SOAP server needs to find the correct server application and the supported methods. It also defines mappings for marshalling the returned information:

```
<isd:service xmlns:isd="http://xml.apache.org/xml-soap/deployment"
             id="urn:CustomerInfo">
  <isd:provider type="java"
                scope="Application"
                methods="getCustomerDetail">
    <isd:java class="wrox.customer.Customers" static="false"/>
  </isd:provider>
  <isd:faultListener>
    org.apache.soap.server.DOMFaultListener
  </isd:faultListener>
  <isd:mappings>
    <isd:map
       encodingStyle="http://schemas.xmlsoap.org/soap/encoding/"
       xmlns:x="urn:wrox-customer"
```

```
          qname="x:customer"
          javaType="wrox.customer.Customer"
          java2XMLClassName="org.apache.soap.encoding.soapenc.BeanSerializer"
          xml2JavaClassName="org.apache.soap.encoding.soapenc.BeanSerializer"
       />
    </isd:mappings>
  </isd:service>
```

### *The Client Application*

The SOAP client application has to create the client SOAP message calling the `getCustomerDetail()` method.

The client `GetCustomerDetail` class, which creates and issues the SOAP request, is contained in the file `GetCustomerDetail.java`. After importing all the necessary packages required by Apache SOAP (not shown here), we set the URL of the SOAP server, `customerId`, and the uniform resource name (URN) for the service. The URN specifies an Internet resource, and provides enough significance for the receiver to locate the resource:

```
public class GetCustomerDetail
{
   public static void main(String[] args) throws Exception
   {
      URL url = new URL(args[0]);
      Integer customerId = new Integer(args[1]);
      String urn = "urn:CustomerInfo";
```

Now, since we're mapping an object (rather than a simple data type), we must define the mapping:

```
      SOAPMappingRegistry smr = new SOAPMappingRegistry();
      BeanSerializer beanSer = new BeanSerializer();
      // Map the types.
      smr.mapTypes(Constants.NS_URI_SOAP_ENC,
                      new QName("urn:wrox-customer", "customer"),
                      Customer.class, beanSer, beanSer);
```

Next, we prepare the service invocation by constructing a `Call` object and initializing all its necessary fields (the service's URN, the requested method, and the encoding and mapping). The method's single parameter is represented by a `Parameter` object, with the name, type and value of the argument, the used marshalling mapping, and the encoding style for the argument (`null` is the default SOAP encoding):

```
      Call call = new Call();
      call.setTargetObjectURI(urn);
      call.setMethodName("getCustomerDetail");
      call.setSOAPMappingRegistry(smr);
      call.setEncodingStyleURI(Constants.NS_URI_SOAP_ENC);
```

```
      Vector params = new Vector();
      params.addElement(new Parameter("customerId",
                                 Integer.class, customerId, null));
      call.setParams(params);
```

To send the message call, we use the `invoke()` method with the URL of the SOAP endpoint (the `rpcrouter`) and the `SOAPAction` (an empty string). The result is either returned with the primitives wrapped in their object equivalents, or an error situation (`SOAPException` or a SOAP fault) occurs.

```
      try
      {
         System.out.println( "Invoke service\nURL= " + url + "\nURN =" +
                             urn );
         Response response = call.invoke( url, "" );
         if(!response.generatedFault())
         {
            Parameter resp = response.getReturnValue();
            Object value = resp.getValue();
            if (value !=null)
            {
               System.out.println("\nCustomer details: " + value);
            } else {
               System.out.println("Customer details not found");
            }
         }
         else
         {
            Fault fault = response.getFault();
            System.err.println("Generated fault: " + fault.getFaultCode() +
                               " - " + fault.getFaultString() );
         }
      }
      catch(SOAPException e)
      {
         System.err.println("SOAPException:" + e.getFaultCode() + " - " +
            e.getMessage());
      }
   }
}
```

### The SOAP Server Application

Writing the SOAP server, using the provided `rpcrouter` servlet, is straightforward. We just need to create a class that offers the required method, and deploy this using the deployment service.

The `Customers` class provides all this. The source code for this class is contained in the file `Customers.java`. First, a small dataset containing details for two customers:

```
public class Customers
{
  private Hashtable customerTable = new Hashtable();
  public Customers()
```

```
    {
      addEntry(new Integer(1), new Customer(new Integer(1), "Jim", "Hall"));
      addEntry(new Integer(2), new Customer(new Integer(2), "Jan", "Bilk"));
    }
```

Next, a method for adding new entries:

```
    public void addEntry(Integer customerId, Customer customer)
    {
      customerTable.put(customerId, customer);
    }
```

Finally, the `getCustomerDetail()` method:

```
    public Customer getCustomerDetail(int customerId)
      throws IllegalArgumentException
    {
      if (customerId == 0)
      {
        throw new
               IllegalArgumentException("Please fillin a valid customerId");
      }
      Integer cid = new Integer(customerId);
      return (Customer)customerTable.get(cid);
    }
  }
```

The `Customer` class is little more than a data class, so I've omitted it here. It is available (in the file `Customer.java`), along with *all* the necessary code for this example, at http://www.wrox.com.

#### The SOAP Server's Response Message

The information returned by the SOAP server is shown below. The SOAP client example prints the received information (after unmarshalling) to the screen:

```
<SOAP-ENV:Envelope
   xmlns:SOAP-ENV="http://schemas.xmlsoap.org/soap/envelope/"
   xmlns:xsi="http://www.w3.org/1999/XMLSchema-instance"
   xmlns:xsd="http://www.w3.org/1999/XMLSchema">
   <SOAP-ENV:Body>
      <ns1:getCustomerDetailResponse
         xmlns:ns1="urn:CustomerInfo"
         SOAP-ENV:encodingStyle="http://schemas.xmlsoap.org/soap/encoding/">
         <return xmlns:app="urn:wrox-customer" xsi:type="app:customer">
            <surname xsi:type="xsd:string">Hall</surname>
            <firstname xsi:type="xsd:string">Jim</firstname>
            <customerId xsi:type="xsd:int">1</customerId>
         </return>
      </ns1:getCustomerDetailResponse>
   </SOAP-ENV:Body>
</SOAP-ENV:Envelope>
```

### *Execution and Debugging*

To execute the SOAP sample, run the `GetCustomerDetail` and provide the necessary parameters. The first parameter is the URL of the SOAP server and the second parameter is the `customerId` used to identify the customer. Thus, the call looks like this:

**> java GetCustomerDetail http://localhost:8080/soap/servlet/rpcrouter "1"**

The result printed to the screen is:

```
Invoke service
URL=http://localhost:8080/soap/servlet/rpcrouter
URN=urn:CustomerInfo

Customer details: Jim Hall (1)
```

Debugging of data transferred via a network protocol can be tricky. However, there is a tool included in the Apache SOAP toolkit to ease this problem – the **TCP Tunneler**. This tool shows the SOAP messages traveling back and forth between the client and the server.

The tool is started using the following:

**> java org.apache.soap.util.net.TcpTunnelGui *listenport tunnelhost tunnelport***

where *`listenport`* is the port that you want the tool to listen on, *`tunnelhost`* is the hostname of the SOAP server, and *`tunnelport`* is the port that the SOAP server is running on.

The screenshot below shows the SOAP messages sent by the client and server. The tunneler listens on port 2020 and tunnels the request to port 8080, the port the `rpcrouter` (SOAP server) is listening to:

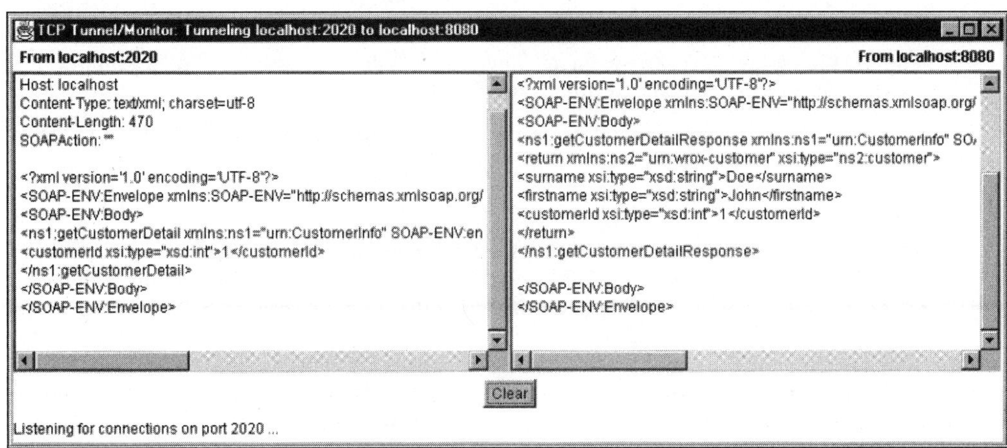


Now, to invoke the SOAP sample, you need to change the call to this:

**> java GetCustomerDetail http://localhost:2020/soap/servlet/rpcrouter "1"**

The result, however, stays the same.

# SOAP and the Future

Currently, the two main applications of SOAP are:

- RPC-style communication with a focus on solving integration problems in a component-based development style, which is synchronous in nature
- Asynchronous messaging: this is B2B business document exchange-oriented, as in BizTalk and ebXML.

So far, SOAP has appealed to a wide audience of developers because of its versatile functionality scope. I think it will be a challenge for the next version of SOAP, especially with the number of SOAP users increasing, to keep the RPC and messaging audiences in sync with each other. It's almost a Darwinian evolution branching issue, which hangs in a balance of further specialization or generalization.

When we look at the messaging in more detail, some predictions can safely be made:

- We will see more and better support of XML Schema for SOAP message payloads
- We may expect improved security schemes and measures to protect message content

# Summary

In this chapter, we discussed the SOAP message structure and SOAP processing. Specifically, we raised the following important points about SOAP:

- As a member of a new class of protocols using XML for their message structure, SOAP messages are self-describing, and offer better interoperability than previous binary-level approaches
- The SOAP message structure consists of `<Envelope>`, `<Header>` and `<Body>` elements, the latter including the `<Fault>` element. The SOAP With Attachments (SWA) proposal provides an alternative place for the payload
- SOAP messages are fundamentally one-way message transmissions between peer SOAP nodes
- SOAP messages travel down a message path, from SOAP sender, through zero-or-more SOAP intermediaries, finally reaching the SOAP receiver
- SOAP node actor roles, specified through a URI, determine the processing roles a SOAP node can assume. SOAP defines only "built-in" behavior for message forwarding through the actor roles `next` and `anonymous`. The latter indicates the ultimate receiver

In this chapter we've omitted to mention that SOAP messages are sent as unreliable transmissions, because SOAP offers no extra message reliability features. Given SOAP's fundamental role within ebXML Messaging Services as a core-messaging component for a B2B architecture, reliable messaging capability is quite essential.

This is exactly where ebMS, the ebXML Messaging Service, extends the SOAP message structure and defines additional behavior, as we shall see in the next chapter.

ebXMLFoundationsProfessional

# 5

# The ebXML Business Process Specification Schema (BPSS)

The **Business Process Specification Schema** (**BPSS**) is one of the most innovative sections of the ebXML Specification. At a high level, a BPSS instance specifies all the business messages that are exchanged between two business partner roles, their content, and their precise sequence and timing. As such it is the direct link between the business analysts or subject matter experts that defines the business processes, and the implementers that use these specifications to either configure their ebXML infrastructure, or write the appropriate code to enforce all aspects of the business process.

In particular, ebXML BPSS (or ebBPSS) could be used independently of the ebXML framework to capture and communicate business processes in a way that can be understood, without ambiguity, by both involved parties. It is also the first machine-readable specification of this kind that can be used to "configure" a B2B infrastructure implementing the ebXML Specification. The ebBPSS Specification is part of a general movement in the software engineering community to build declarative systems rather than procedural ones. Chapter 6 addresses this aspect of the specification, and its link with other business process standards, in more detail.

This specification is based upon prior UN/CEFACT work, specifically the meta model behind the UN/CEFACT Modeling Methodology (UMM) defined in the N090R9.1 specification (see Chapter 2 for more on UMM). In particular, it provides an additional view of the UMM meta model: "this subset is provided to support the direct specification of the nominal set of elements necessary to configure a runtime system in order to execute a set of ebXML business transactions". It forms a semantic subset of the UMM meta model.

The *ebXML Business Process Specification Schema* (`ebBPSS.pdf` or `.doc`), available from http://www.ebxml.org/specs/index.htm, is the only ebXML specification available in two stand-alone representations (a UML version and an XML version). The UML representation is intended to establish the necessary relationships with UMM. All the other ebXML specifications, which are not related to any other external UML-based specifications, are available as XML only. The XML version is intended to be interpretable by ebXML compliant software. For this reason, this chapter focuses mostly on the XML version.

In this chapter, we will:

- Introduce the fundamental concepts of BPSS
- Spend a fair amount of time looking at the core concepts of business transactions
- Define the object of the specification: binary and multiparty collaborations
- Take a look at the individual parts of the specification, which helps reusing process definitions and in particular the notion of substitution sets
- Round off the chapter by introducing the concept of a "business service interface" (BSI).

# BPSS Fundamentals

An instance of the BPSS (or a BPSS instance) defines a shared view of the messages that will be exchanged between two or more roles for the purpose of carrying out a business activity such as *Prepare for export* as a multiparty activity and *Insure shipment* as an activity between two parties. These business activities may often be non-repudiable and sometimes legally binding. Non-repudiation deals with providing the sender with receipts to prove that the recipient has effectively received their messages. This guarantee is always provided by the mode of transmission. In the paper world, a *facsimile*, a telex, and a "return receipt" from the post office are all non-repudiable. It is important to note that a transmission may be non-repudiable but not necessary legally binding.

A BPSS instance is composed of several definitions:

- **Business documents**
- **Business transactions**, which define a protocol to exchange business documents
- **Binary collaborations**, which represent a composition of business transactions
- **Multiparty collaborations**, which are synthesized with two or more binary collaborations
- **Substitution sets**, which replace or make more explicit document definition references and attribute values, for the purpose of specializing generic collaboration definitions for an industry or a particular business community

The ebBPSS technical specification points out that the BPSS provides "the semantics, elements, and properties necessary to define business collaborations" rather than business *processes.* This is also clear from the names of the elements. We will come back to the differences and relationships between collaboration and process in Chapter 6.

A collaboration definition can be viewed as a part of a contract between the parties involved, but not as the contract itself. The messages that the two parties exchange may correspond to specific commitments and exchange of economic resources – these semantics are not part of BPSS. Just like a traditional contract, the way each party implements the contract within their respective organization is hidden and most often irrelevant to the contract. The business processes deployed internally to fulfill this contract are not exposed to the other party by a BPSS instance. Contract formation is not explicitly addressed by ebBPSS and could potentially become another layer on top of this specification. The ebXML e-Commerce Patterns document (see `bpPATT.pdf`, found at http://www.ebxml.org/specs/index.htm) provides an excellent introduction to this topic.

ebBPSS does not specify a notation to represent the elements of a process specification. In this chapter, we will introduce the UMM notation for business transactions, binary collaborations and multiparty collaborations. It is important to note that this notation is not part of the BPSS specification (hence non-normative), and it is solely used for the purpose of guiding the reader. This notation does not capture all the semantics of the BPSS meta model. The XML document created as a process specification is the only definition that can be used to specify an agreement between parties.

## Business Transactions

The concept of **business transaction** is at the core of the specification since all message interchanges are defined as elements of a business transaction. As such, it is a protocol of message interchange. A message is also called a **business document flow** in the specification.

Business transactions are atomic and cannot be decomposed further into independent elements. For instance, if we want to specify that "Party A sends a message to Party B", it has to be part of a business transaction definition. As we will see in this section, the business transaction concept adds several and important "business semantics" to the exchange of a message from A to B. This is precisely what makes the ebBPSS approach different from other specifications, which view the exchange of messages merely as a middleware extension. Binary collaborations constitute choreography of business transactions, rather than choreography of messages. This distinction is very important, because business transactions define clear boundaries of what can fail, and what is non-repudiable, requires guaranteed delivery or yet is legally binding.

The ebBPSS Specification declares "A business transaction will always either succeed or fail". The failure of a business transaction is calculated from a variety of conditions that we will detail in the *Business Transaction Failures* section below. In case of failure, any commitment associated with the transaction is null and void, and partners must revert their respective state to the one prior to the start of the business transaction. In essence, this can be thought of as "rolling back" the business transaction.

At a high level, a transaction is a request message from a requesting role to a responding role and an optional response message chosen from several possibles. A **message** contains one or more business documents. The request message is specified as part of the `<RequestingBusinessActivity>` element, and the possible response messages are specified as part of the `<RespondingBusinessActivity>` element. These two elements inherit from an abstract class called **business action**. A business action cannot be defined or used outside of a business transaction. Only the business documents exchanged as part of a business transaction can be defined separately and reused across business transaction definitions.

Roles are not specified at the business transaction level because they are almost irrelevant. It is only the usage of a business transaction within a binary collaboration definition that clearly indicates the roles that initiate and respond to the business transaction. It may even be the case that the same business transaction definition is initiated by each role in different parts of the collaboration. A usage of a business transaction within a binary collaboration is called a **business transaction activity**, and points to a single business transaction definition.

There are two broad categories of transactions: **request/response** and **notification** (a request with no response). However, in the context of business transaction definitions, they are termed **solicit response** and **one-way**, because they are referenced with respect to the initiator of the collaboration. Note that this terminology is not part of BPSS – it is taken from WSDL (Web Service Definition Language).

The UMM Specification defines some patterns as business transaction definition templates – request/response, request/confirm, query/response, notification, and information distribution. They correspond to a specific combination of attributes and signals to achieve a given purpose. Further discussion can be found in Chapter 2. It is not mandatory that a given business transaction follows a UMM business pattern, but if it does, it can be specified with the `pattern` attribute, which has an `xsd:anyURI` data type.

In the sections that follow, we have divided the semantics of business transactions into the following groups:

- Message Payload Specification
- Message Reliability Specification
- Non-repudiation and legally binding transactions
- Message Security Specification
- Business Transaction Failure Specification

## Message Payload Specification

ebXML in general, and this specification in particular, were designed to be able to accommodate any kind of content as a message payload. A message (a.k.a. document flow) is used in two ways in the specification: of course, it contains the document that pertains to the business transaction, but in addition, response messages are also used to define some of the sequencing rules of the binary collaboration definition.

A message or document flow is modeled as a document envelope sent by one role and received by the other. The document envelopes are specified as part of the requesting activity, and responding activity definitions are specified as part of a business transaction definition.

*I often get asked the question "what is a requesting or responding activity?" They do not actually correspond to any physical entity like a message or a document. They rather mean that one of the parties is:*

*a. In the process of sending a request, waiting for an answer, or calculating the success of the transaction*

*b. In the process of sending a response.*

*We will see in the next section how a business transaction binds to an internal business process. As a general rule, the binding does not happen at the activity level but rather at the document flow or message level.*

A document envelope contains exactly one primary business document and any number of optional attachments, all related to the primary document. Attachments to the primary business document can potentially be of any type, however it is expected that the primary business document will be an XML document.

A responding document envelope has a property, which indicates the intent of the response from the responding role perspective (`isPositiveResponse`). This property is related to the business failure of a transaction. Ultimately, it is the responsibility of the requesting role to identify whether a transaction has been successful by looking at all the aspects (timeouts, signals, and so on). Consequently, the `isPositiveResponse` parameter alone is non-binding and cannot guarantee the success of the transaction (see also the section on *Business Transaction Failures* below). Let's take a look at the corresponding definition for the 'Insure shipment' business transaction (note that this example is deliberately incomplete, we will add to it as we develop the various semantics of the business transaction):

```
<BusinessTransaction name="BT:Insure shipment">
   <RequestingBusinessActivity name="ReqBA:Shipment insurance request">
      <DocumentEnvelope businessDocument="BD:Shipment insurance request">
         <Attachment businessDocument="BD:Equipment description"/>
      </DocumentEnvelope>
   </RequestingBusinessActivity>
   <RespondingBusinessActivity name="RspBA:Shipment insurance response">
      <DocumentEnvelope businessDocument="BD:Shipment insurance contract"
                        isPositiveResponse="true">
         <Attachment businessDocument="BD:Equipment description"/>
      </DocumentEnvelope>
      <DocumentEnvelope businessDocument="BD:Reject shipment insurance"
                        isPositiveResponse="false">
      </DocumentEnvelope>
   </RespondingBusinessActivity>
</BusinessTransaction>
```

A responding activity may have multiple document envelope definitions. One and exactly one document envelope will be sent back to the requesting activity. Of course, a document envelope may itself contain multiple documents. The ability to specify several possible responses is a fundamental aspect of the business transaction semantics and reflects the way business interactions are happening today. This property enables system implementers to develop sophisticated routing mechanisms based on the document envelope properties without necessarily looking at the content of the message. It also enables the designers of the collaboration to express the sequencing rules based on message intent rather than document format and content.

Document envelopes and attachments reference a single **business document** definition, in addition an envelope may contain multiple attachments. A BPSS business document is a logical entity, which is associated to a physical document format. Consequently, several BPSS business document definitions may share the same physical document format. BPSS gives us the ability to make the business document definition abstract when there is not a physical document associated to its definition. This is useful when the intent of the collaboration designer is to provide a collaboration definition that can be used in multiple contexts. The *Substitution Sets...* section will explain how to deal with this case. The document format is specified by:

- The `specificationLocation` attribute, which gives a reference to an external XML Schema or DTD
- The `specificationElement` attribute, which gives a reference to the element within the schema definition that defines this documents.

The `specificationLocation` data type is `xsd:anyURI`.

A condition expression can be associated with a business document. This is actually a way to distinguish two logical business documents associated to the same physical document format. In the example shown below, an Accept Purchase Order document and a Reject Purchase Order document differ just from a status code:

```
<BusinessDocument name="BD:Shipment insurance request"
                specificationLocation=
                "http://www.YeOldInsurer.com/Schemas/v1.1/shp_ins_req.dtd"
                   specificationElement="ShipmentInsuranceRequest">
</BusinessDocument>
<BusinessDocument name="BD:Shipment insurance contract"
                specificationLocation=
                "http://www.YeOldInsurer.com/Schemas/v1.1/shp_ins_ctc.dtd"
                   specificationElement="ShipmentInsuranceContract">
   <ConditionExpression expressionLanguage="XPath"
                        expression='//Status="Accept"'/>
</BusinessDocument>
<BusinessDocument name="BD:Reject shipment insurance"
                specificationLocation=
                "http://www.YeOldInsurer.com/Schemas/v1.1/shp_ins_ctc.dtd"
                   specificationElement="ShipmentInsuranceContract">
   <ConditionExpression expressionLanguage="XPath"
                        expression='//Status="Reject"'/>
</BusinessDocument>
```

This example above shows that two logical documents are derived from the same physical document. The only difference is in the `Status` of the document. The ebXML Specification does not provide any recommendation relative to the content of the expression language – in particular, `XPath`, `xpath`, or `XPATH` could all be used. It is unlikely that anyone would use something other than `XPATH` on an XML document, since it provides both a way to point to an element of the document and express the condition. However, nothing prevents the implementers from using TCL or Java expressions. Of course, both sides of the collaboration have to agree on the implementation model.

Logical documents are essential to the reuse of collaboration definitions across business partners or industries since they enable a clear decoupling between the collaboration sequencing rules and the document formats. Different industries may have specific documents associated with the same logical documents, while other groups may choose to use a given collaboration definition, in which logical documents are built from the same physical document but with slightly varying condition expressions. We will explore this aspect in the *Binary Collaborations* section, later in this chapter.

A document envelope attachment is an optional attachment to the primary `<BusinessDocument>`. Its properties include a `name`, a `mimeType`, an attachment `specification`, and a `version`. It must also include a reference to a `BusinessDocument` definition:

```
<DocumentEnvelope isPositiveResponse="true"
                  BusinessDocument="BD:Shipment insurance contract">
   <Attachment name="A:Fine prints"
               mimeType="text"
               BusinessDocument="BD:YeOld Fine Prints"
               specification=""
               version="78.0b"/>
   ...
</DocumentEnvelope>
```

Some of the properties of document envelopes and attachments (`isAuthenticated`, `isConfidential`, and `isTamperProof`) will be discussed in the paragraph relative to security – see below.

## Message Reliability

It would be hard to do business without the certainty that the intended recipient is receiving their messages, and that they can be processed. ebBPSS provides a **message reliability layer**, which is distinct from the ebXML Messaging Service layer (the ebMS Specification – see Chapter 13, *ebXML Messaging*, for more details). ebBPSS specifies what message reliability means at the business level.

At the messaging service level, guaranteed delivery means the recipient messaging service has received the message. At the business level, this is not enough: the receiving party is required to guarantee that the message has been archived and has passed some basic integrity checks to ensure that no matter what happens, it will be able to process them.

UMM and ebBPSS use business signals for that purpose. They are application-level documents that 'signal' the current state of the business transaction. These business signals have a specific business purpose and are separate from lower protocol and transport signals. Their structure does not vary from transaction to transaction; in particular, they do not contain any specific business elements relative to the current business transaction. Hence, they have been defined as part of the ebBPSS itself (see ebBPSS page 95 line 3017-3334).

The business transaction semantics specify two business signals, which are used to indicate that the business layers successfully received the request or the response. A receipt signal is used to indicate that the request or response was properly received and archived. In addition, the `isIntelligibleCheckRequired` property indicates that this signal should be sent only when the syntax and structure of the documents contained in the message have been validated:

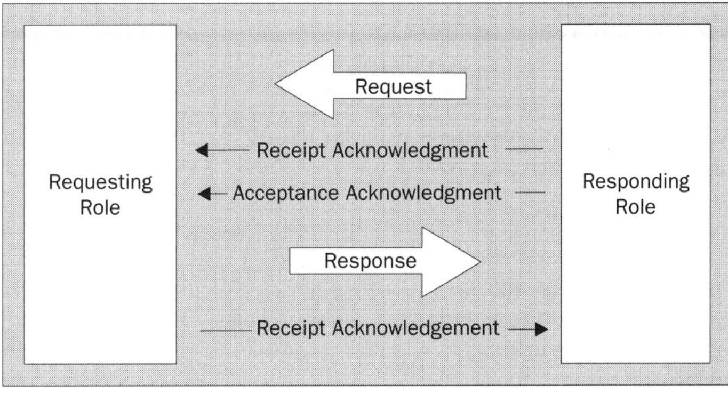

Once the syntax and structure has been validated, ebBPSS provides a second level of signals relative to the validity of the request: the acceptance signal. This signal indicates that the business document(s) passed business rule validity checks, and has been accepted for business processing. This signal is different from an "Accept Shipment Insurance" response. It simply means for instance that the equipment that needs to be insured meets the criteria of the insurer (size, price, etc). It is important to note that a positive acceptance signal does not imply a positive response message. For example, the insurer could still reject the request based on the credit rating of the requestor. Here's a summary of properties:

| Property {Possible Values} | Description |
|---|---|
| **BusinessTransaction/** *@isGuaranteedDeliveryRequired* *{true,false}* | Both partners must agree to use a transport that guarantees delivery. |
| **BusinessTransaction/ RequestingBusinessActivity/** *@timeToAcknowledgeReceipt* *{ISO 8601}* | A positive value indicates that a receipt is needed for the request – it also specifies the time given to the responder to send that signal. |
| **BusinessTransaction/ RequestingBusinessActivity/** *@timeToAcknowledgeAcceptance* *{ISO 8601}* | A positive value indicates that an acceptance is needed for the request – it also specifies the time given to the responder to send that signal. |
| **BusinessTransaction/ RequestingBusinessActivity/** *@isIntelligibleCheckRequired* *{true,false}* | A `true` value indicates that the responding activity has to verify that the document is not garbled (unreadable, unintelligible etc.) before sending of receipt. |
| **BusinessTransaction/ RespondingBusinessActivity/** *@ isIntelligibleCheckRequired* *{true,false}* | A `true` value indicates that the requesting activity has to verify that the document is not garbled (unreadable, unintelligible etc.) before sending of receipt. |
| **BusinessTransaction/ RespondingBusinessActivity/** *@TimetoAcknowledgeReceipt* *{ISO 8601}* | A positive value indicates that a receipt is needed for the response – it also specifies the time given to the requester to send that signal. |
| **BusinessTransactionActivity/** *@timeToPerform {ISO 8601}* | A positive value indicates that this transaction should be completed within a specific time frame. |

Time constraints are specified with the widely used ISO 8601 specification (for more information, check out http://www.w3.org/TR/NOTE-datetime).

If the time constraints specified for each signal are not respected (whether it be a request or response signal), the business transaction is considered null and void. It is important to keep these constrains within a reasonable range, otherwise the systems will generate exceptions simply when it is overloaded – signals are expected to return within seconds. It is recommended to keep this parameter in the 'hour' range unless there are some good business reasons for doing otherwise (for example, a user is waiting for the signal and response).

Here's an example:

```
<BusinessTransaction name="BT:Shipment insurance request"
                     isGuaranteedDeliveryRequired="true">
   <RequestingBusinessActivity name="ReqBA:Shipment insurance request"
                               isIntelligibleCheckRequired="true"
                               timeToAcknowledgeReceipt="P2H"
                               timeToAcknowledgeAcceptance="P4H">
      ...
   </RequestingBusinessActivity>
   <RespondingBusinessActivity name="ResBA:Shipment insurance response"
                               isIntelligibleCheckRequired="true"
                               timeToAcknowledgeReceipt="P2H">
      ...
   ...
   </RespondingBusinessActivity>
</BusinessTransaction>
   ...

   ...

<BusinessTransactionActivity
   businessTransaction="BT:Shipment insurance request"
   timeToPerform="P2D"/>
```

The `timeToPerform` attribute is defined at the business transaction activity level (that is, the usage of a business transaction in a collaboration definition) and not the business transaction level. Business transaction definitions can be reused in different contexts, which may require slightly different durations.

The complete sequence of messages and signals between the sending application and the receiving application is represented below:

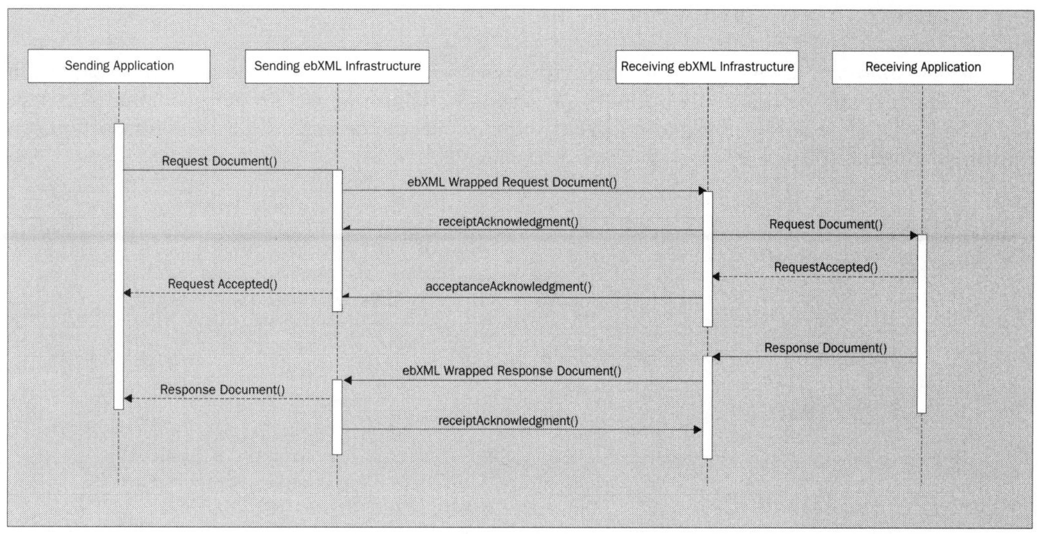

## Non-Repudiation and Legally Binding Transactions

In the "e-everything" world, we often forget the benefits we enjoyed with paper-based business transactions. A piece of paper acts as a universal "viewer". The content of a piece of paper can be agreed on, at the technical level, without ambiguities (no such a thing as an invisible font color). A piece of paper can be signed with any pen, and multiple people can sign different parts of the document. Signatures are often hard to duplicate without sophisticated means and can easily be opposed in the court of law. It is also fairly easy to distinguish between a copy and an original, as well as identify any attempt to tamper with the content of the document. All these attributes are actually fairly difficult to replicate in the electronic world, where files can be copied or edited without a trace. Electronic signatures require sophisticated methods to prove the identity of the author, while it is often hard to define the limits of what is being signed, and define boundaries for multiple signatures.

The ebBPSS does not claim to provide a complete legal framework to carry out business activities. This part of the specification is provided as a "best effort". The ebXML white paper on *Risk Assessment*, available from http://www.ebxml.org/specs/secRISK.doc, provides a very good introduction to this global issue.

**Non-repudiation** is based on digital signatures issued by the sender of a document (either a message or a receipt). The specification does not recommend the use of any particular signature technology, but simply indicates that the XML-DSIG Specification defined by the W3C (see http://www.w3.org/TR/xmldsig-core/) may be used for this purpose. The signed artifacts must be archived by both the sender and the recipient to form an audit trail, which can later be explored to reconstruct the occurrence of a disputed transaction. The specification provides two kinds of non-repudiation protocols:

- Messages only (`isNonRepudiationRequired`): indicated that you must save an audit trail of the messages. Optionally, document envelopes can be made tamperproof by digitally signing them as well (`isTamperProof`).
- Messages and receipts (`isNonRepudiationOfReceiptRequired`): must digitally sign receipt s.

The **legally binding** property of a transaction is defined at the business transaction activity level, which means that it is *only* the usage of a business transaction definition within a binary collaboration that is specified as either legally binding or not. The 'Shipment insurance request' business transaction can be further defined as follows:

```
<BusinessTransaction name="BT:Shipment insurance request"
                     isGuaranteedDeliveryRequired="true">
   <RequestingBusinessActivity name="ReqBA:Shipment insurance request"
                               isNonRepudiationOfReceiptRequired="true"
                               isNonRepudiationRequired="true">
      <DocumentEnvelope isTamperProof="true">
...
      </DocumentEnvelope>
   </RequestingBusinessActivity>
   <RespondingBusinessActivity name="RspBA:Shipment insurance response"
                               isNonRepudiationOfReceiptRequired="true"
                               isNonRepudiationRequired="true">
      <DocumentEnvelope isTamperProof="true">
         ...
```

```
            </DocumentEnvelope>
            ...
        </RespondingBusinessActivity>
    </BusinessTransaction>
    ...
```

```
    <BusinessTransactionActivity name="Shipment insurance request"
                        businessTransaction="BT:Shipment insurance request"
                        isLegallyBinding="true"/>
```

## *Message Security*

Security architecture should not be taken lightly for any web-based system, and even more so for a B2B infrastructure. If a security breach can be less noticeable than an attack on a B2C (business-to-consumer) system, its consequences could be dire for most enterprises. Several properties of the ebBPSS are related to the security of the transactions between parties. The main goals here are to guarantee the identity of the sender, and the integrity of the payload. Other security issues must be dealt with at the implementation level.

Both the requesting and responding activities can be configured to operate with `isAuthorizationRequired` set to `true`. In this case, the originator of the message must identify themselves (with a certificate for instance), and the receiving ebXML infrastructure software must validate the identity of originator against a list of authorized business partners. This option requires the ebXML Messaging Service to obtain the credentials of the message sender. The message payload in its entirety is associated with the originator of the message.

The specification also provides another authentication mechanism, this time at the document level (the `isAuthenticated` property). In this case, there is a digital certificate associated with the business document to prove the sender's identity.

These two mechanisms are often redundant. For instance, we could use a document-oriented authentication mechanism, when the messaging service layer does not support authentication at the message level. However, we might use a combination of both mechanisms, in cases where the document sender and the document author differ – for example, the sender of the message could be a market place acting as a pass through, delivering documents on behalf of another business.

In addition, a business document may be marked as confidential and tamper proof (via `isConfidential` and `isTamperProof`). When the content of a document is confidential, the ebXML infrastructure must encrypt the information entity so that unauthorized parties cannot view its content. When the content of a document should be made tamperproof, the information entity has an encrypted message digest that can be used to check if the message has been tampered with. This requires a digital signature (the sender's digital certificate and encrypted message digest) associated with the document entity. This parameter works both for non-repudiation purposes, and to prevent malicious attacks on the content of valid messages.

By default, the document envelope properties apply not only to the primary document, but also to the attachments (unless they are overridden):

```
...
<RespondingBusinessActivity name="ResBA:Shipment insurance request"
                            isAuthorizationRequired="false">
  <DocumentEnvelope isPositiveResponse="true"
                    isConfidential="false"
                    isTamperProof="true"
                    isAuthenticated="true"
                    BusinessDocument="BD:Shipment insurance request">
    <Attachment name="A:Delivery Notes"
                mimeType="text/xml"
                BusinessDocument="BD:Equipment description "
                specification=""
                isConfidential="false"
                isTamperProof="false"
                isAuthenticated="false"/>
  </DocumentEnvelope>
</RespondingBusinessActivity>
```

## *Business Transaction Failures*

The ebBPSS Specification states:

> *"A Business Transaction will always either succeed or fail. If it succeeds it may be designated as legally binding between the two partners, or otherwise govern their collaborative activity. If it fails it is null and void, and each partner must relinquish any mutual claim established by the transaction. This can be thought of as 'rolling back' the business transaction upon failure."*

Rolling back often means something different in the case of business transactions and database transactions. In general, a business state cannot be reverted back to, unlike a database state – businesses always want to keep track of what happened. Therefore, to return to the position of leaving the business in a coherent state, a business rollback is often, if not always, implemented as a set of compensating activities, rather than just reversing previous activities. This means that sometimes collaborations continue when a business transaction fails.

There is no assumption made about the relationship between a business transaction failure and the failure of the binary collaboration as a whole. In some cases, one entails the other, however in other cases, compensating transactions are executed. Take a case where someone orders some goods, and all the business transactions execute normally until the invoice is received. At this point, if the goods are not delivered for any reason we are not going to progress to successful business transactions. Instead, new transactions will be executed that will ultimately leave the general ledger of each company in the right state, despite failure. Note that the rollback is the responsibility of each role, as there is no two-phase commit mechanism specified by ebXML. The success of a business transaction might also entail the failure of its binary collaboration (for example, a successful 'Cancel Purchase Order' transaction will ultimately end its collaboration in a failure mode).

Condition guards may be defined on transitions between two business transaction or collaboration activities. There are four possible values: `Success`, `BusinessFailure`, `TechnicalFailure` and `AnyFailure`. `Success` obviously indicates that the first transaction must be successful for the transition to take place. `AnyFailure` indicates that the transition is to go ahead if any failure from the other two categories occurs. The other two categories, `BusinessFailure` and `TechnicalFailure`, indicate that only those types of failure will allow the transition to proceed – these failures are expanded on next.

#### Business Failure

Business failures are solely related to the agreed-upon intent of the response document envelope marked by the `isPositiveResponse` property. The first iterations of the BPSS specification had been designed with the possibility to define condition expressions at the business transaction level. Ultimately, this design introduced a strong coupling between the document format and the business collaboration definition, which would have entailed a lower level of reuse of collaboration definitions. Subsequently, it was decided that the condition expressions were to be defined at the business document level and to rather use 'logical documents', which can be related to a clear intent on the success or failure of the business transaction of which they are part.

Consequently, a `BusinessFailure` happens when the response document envelope (which is effectively coming back as part of the response message) has been defined with an `isPositiveResponse` attribute with a value of `false`.

#### Technical Failures: Timeouts

The first mode of technical failure is encountered when a **timeout** occurs for a business transaction activity, receipt , acceptance , or for the overall binary collaboration. All timers start when the initial requesting business document is sent.

A responding partner simply terminates if a timeout is thrown. This prevents responding business transactions from hanging indefinitely. A requesting partner terminates if a timeout is thrown and then sends a notification of failure to the responder as part of a separate transaction.

#### Technical Failures: Exceptions

The processing of the transaction payload by a business application could go wrong at either the responding or requesting activities based on a number of factors:

A **control exception** signals an error condition in the management of a business transaction. This exception is thrown each time the request cannot be processed, for whatever reason. This business signal is asynchronously returned to the requesting activity, and the exception must terminate the business transaction. The control exception errors detailed below deal with the mechanisms of message exchange and may occur up until message acceptance:

- Failure to verify the structure
- Unsuccessful validation of the syntax and message element values
- Unsuccessful authentication
- Unsuccessful authorization
- Sequence exceptions. The order or type of a business document or business signal is incorrect
- Business documents are not signed for non-repudiation when required

A **business protocol exception** (or **process exception**) signals a message acceptance error detected in the responding business activity after the control exception tests have been performed, and before the response document envelope is sent. In particular, this exception is used each time the response message cannot be prepared or computed by the core enterprise systems. This business signal is asynchronously returned to the initiating role that originated the request, and the exception must terminate the business transaction. For instance, in our 'Shipment insurance request' example, some business rules might be defined such that the insurer will only insure shipments below a certain value.

A violation of this business rule does not require any specific processing of the request (such as reviewing the request, calculating the insurance premium, etc.). These types of exception are signaled by a negative acceptance. The following are business protocol exceptions:

- One or more business rules are violated.
- The requested business action cannot be performed (systems could be down).

A process exception is not a substitute for a response but rather means that a response could not be computed based on the content of the request. For instance, if an item is out of stock, this information should be conveyed as part of the response message and not via a process exception since no business rules were violated from a request perspective. It is merely a set of circumstances based on the current set of the responder, which led to the business transaction failure via a negative response document envelope.

Here are the different sequence diagrams for syntax, business rule violation, transport, and application failure errors:

- **Syntax error:** The receiving ebXML infrastructure (Responder) detects parser level error and generates a negative acknowledgment of receipt exception:

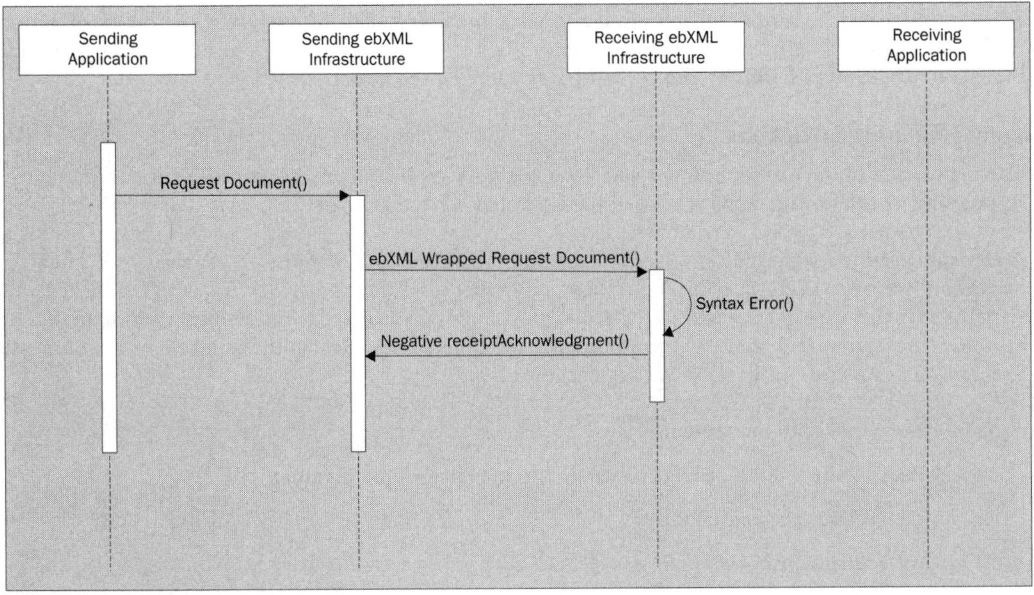


- **Business rule violations:** The receiving ebXML infrastructure (Responder) passes parser level validation but the application adapter or the application itself detects business rule violations. The ebXML infrastructure generates a negative acknowledgement of acceptance.

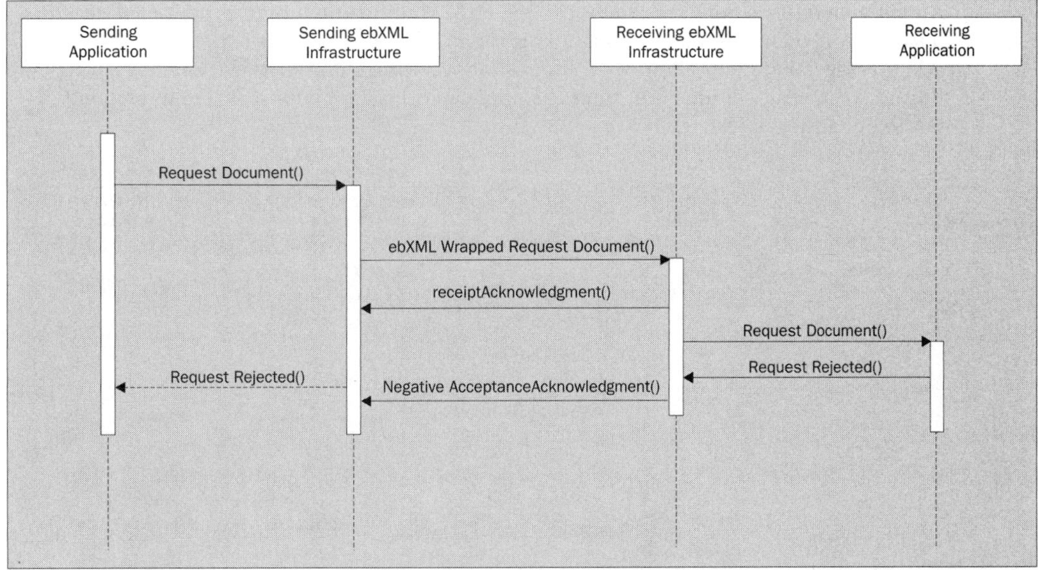


- **Delivery error:** The initiating ebXML infrastructure may never receive any kind of receipt associated with a request. It is expected that the initiating ebXML infrastructure will time out, since the receiving ebXML infrastructure is either unable to respond or has not received the message.

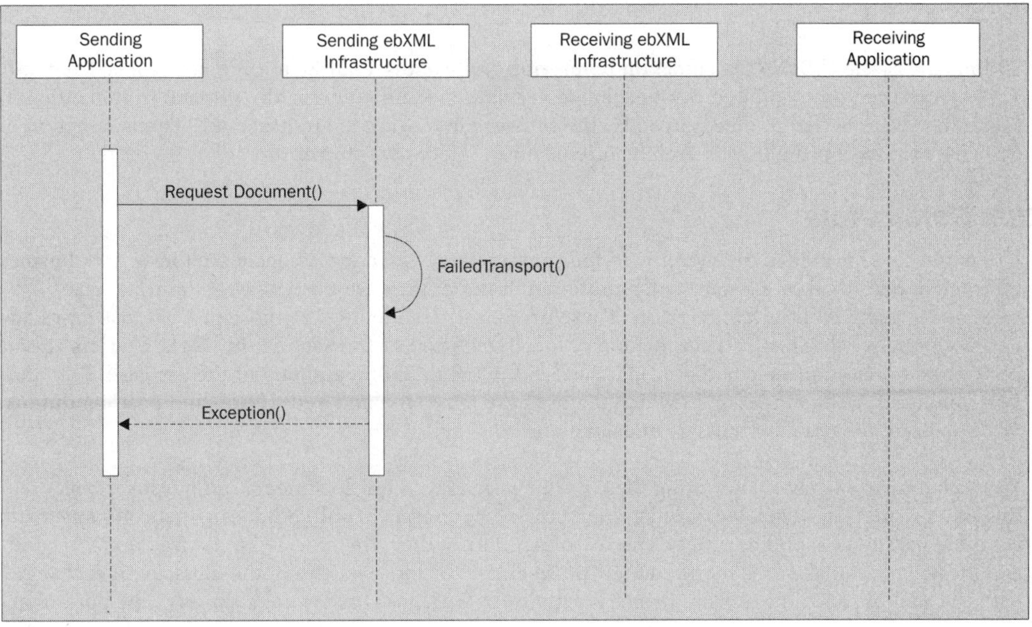

- **Application failure**: Similarly, the receiving ebXML infrastructure may fail to deliver the document envelope to the receiving application(s). In this case, it is expected that the acknowledgement of acceptance (or the response message if acknowledgement of acceptance was not required) will time out, since the application has not been solicited to respond positively or negatively.

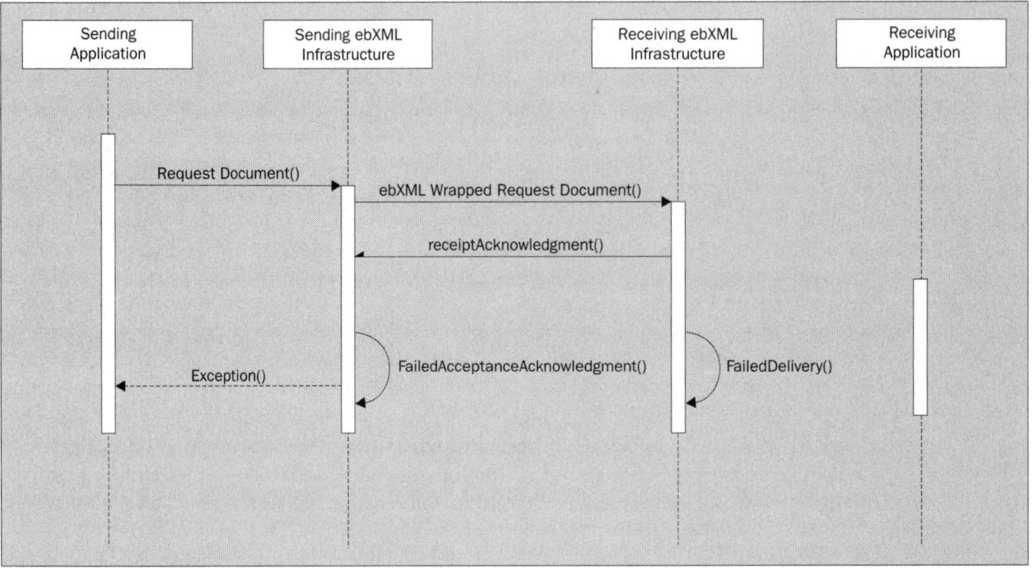


Ultimately, as the ebBPSS Specification points out, "a Business Transaction is a very specialized and very constrained protocol, in order to achieve very precise and enforceable transaction semantics. These semantics are expected to be enforced by the software managing the transaction". The last section of this chapter presents the logical architecture of such a piece of software.

## Other Parameters

Up to now, we have deliberately omitted four parameters, which are associated either with a business transaction definition or a binary collaboration definition: they are `beginsWhen`, `endsWhen`, `preCondition` and `postCondition`. These properties are identical to those of UML use cases and are here to formalize the start and completion of a collaboration or transaction. In UML, `beginsWhen` and `endsWhen` are used to specify the events that lead to the initiation and end of the use case. Pre- and Post-conditions define the state in which the use case must start and end. If pre- and post-conditions are not respected, the use case starts or ends in error.

We recommend in general not using these parameters except for documentation purposes because, first, they are not machine-readable. Unlike `ConditionExpression`, ebBPSS does not specify any syntax for these parameters; and as in UML use case definitions, they are expected to be free text. Second, a collaboration definition is a common view between two or more parties of the message interchanges with the goal of executing a given business activity. A UML use case is not a shared view but rather a system-centric view of the interactions with actors such as users or other systems. In addition, UML is hardly used (and not designed) to specify "contracts" between business parties.

To further the arguments, let us assume that we specified a condition as `beginsWhen`. (To be more concrete, let's say that this condition is "when my company receives an order from abroad, a `BC:Insure shipment` collaboration may begin".) This event should only be known to the party that initiates the collaboration. It is actually irrelevant to the responding party, which receives the request no matter what internal event triggered the collaboration. On the other hand, if this condition was required to be known by the responding party, the initiator would have to communicate the event ahead of time, which is equivalent to adding a business transaction activity at the beginning of the collaboration definition, which makes the `beginsWhen` property useless. A similar rationale is applicable to `endsWhen`.

In my opinion, it is not mandatory to collect this kind of information in the **shared view**, but it is of course very important for the developers that will implement the requesting party system. Some industries, which might need to follow regulation (such as the Aerospace industry), might want to use these attributes to document some of their internal processes. However, the mechanism provided here is not very generic and lacks a stable language to express the conditions.

In the case of a business transaction, we could say that a `BT:Process Invoice` begins when the `BP:Insure shipment request` has completed successfully. However, the correct way to specify this is to use `Transitions` between activities, and not conditions between transaction definitions. This method has the additional advantage that, in addition, the semantics of transitions are machine-readable.

The only one of these four parameters we recommend using is the `preCondition` on a business transaction definition. The corresponding usage is developed in the *Binary Collaboration Choreography* section of this chapter.

## Notation

This notation is not part of the ebBPSS Sspecification. It is provided here to help guide the documentation of business transaction definitions. The XML instance document that conforms to the BPSS is the only official record of the process specification or a business transaction definition.

Business transaction definitions may be represented as UML activity diagrams. The roles are represented as swim lanes. As we mentioned earlier, the roles of a business transaction definition are generic. It is only its usage as a business transaction activity that defines the specific document flows from one role to another. Document envelopes are represented as UML object flows from and to a generic requesting activity and responding activity. We do not represent either the business documents or the condition expressions associated with them. In my opinion, it is acceptable to represent these condition expressions as guards on the transition from `RequestingActivity` to the completion states (success or failure). It is also possible to use a stereotype of the object flow to distinguish between positive response and negative response. Signals are not represented or even hinted as part of this notation:

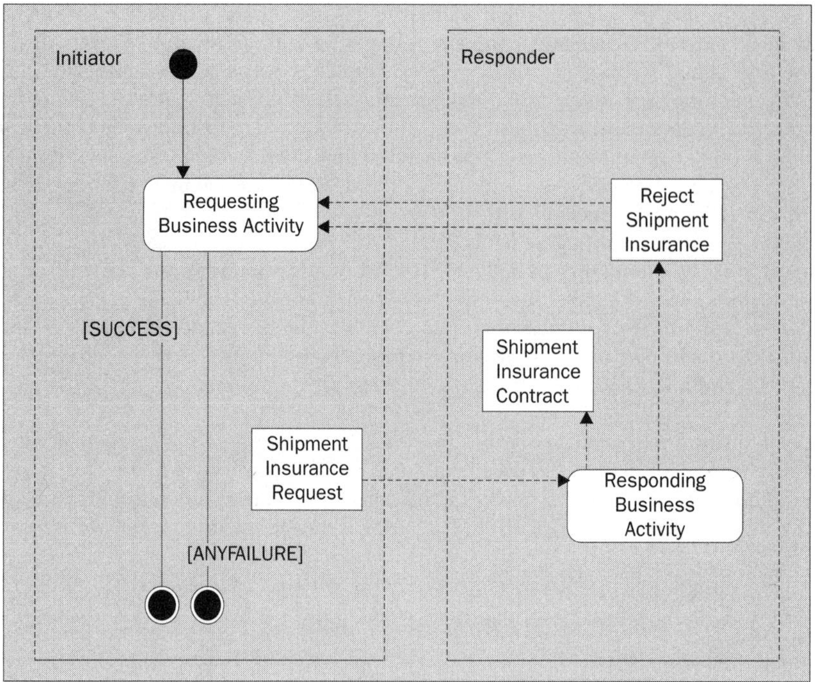


The requesting party computes the success of a business transaction, and based on this result, the transaction will reach a success state or a fail state.

The *Telematica Instituut* in the Netherlands has developed an alternative non-UML-based notation dedicated to ebXML BPSS, as part of the RDS project. Information can be found in the white paper at http://www.telin.nl/dscgi/ds.py/Get/File-17891/. They also provide a tool that supports this notation and the creation of ebXML BPSS XML documents.

# Binary Collaborations

A binary collaboration specifies the business process and the document formats as the protocol of interaction between two authorized roles (`InitiatingRole` and `RespondingRole`). Collaborations are often (if not always) constrained to be completed within a certain time frame (`timeToPerform` is based on the first message, which initiates the collaboration):

```
<BinaryCollaboration name="BC:Insure shipment"
                     timeToPerform="P7D">
   <InitiatingRole name="AR:Seller"/>
   <RespondingRole name="AR:Insurer"/>
   ...
</BinaryCollaboration>
```

A binary collaboration, as part of a process specification, is the main object of a CPP (and ultimately a CPA between two parties). A binary collaboration specifies when and why a message or a signal should be sent or received. This concept is fairly new, and allows us to carry out sophisticated and near real-time business activities over the Internet far beyond the traditional request/response model. It provides a model for end-to-end scenarios that includes negotiations, commitments, fulfillments, payments and all the necessary business, process or control exceptions.

If this specification could be used to formally document business requirements, it takes its entire dimension as a machine-readable specification of message and signal interchange protocol. Systems and applications can be configured automatically with a BPSS instance to perform a specific collaboration.

In the past, there was no formal framework available to achieve a direct transition from modeling to execution such as the one provided by BPSS in particular and ebXML overall. We will explore this concept further in Chapter 6.

## Business Transaction Activities and Collaboration Activities

A binary collaboration provides the context in which business transactions or other binary collaborations execute. When a collaboration definition is used within another collaboration definition, it may be called subcollaboration. Instances of business transaction or binary collaboration definitions are, respectively, called **business transaction activities** or **collaboration activities**. The choreography specified as part of the binary collaboration definition applies to activities. This means that the same definition can be used several times for different activities.

The main goal of an activity is to specify the direction of the transaction or collaboration usage. For that purpose we define the initiator and responder of the transaction or collaboration activities with respect to the parent binary collaboration `initiatingRole` and `respondingRole`. As mentioned earlier, a business transaction or collaboration definition can be used either way within a collaboration definition:

```
<BinaryCollaboration name="BC:Insure shipment"
                     timeToPerform="P7D">
   <InitiatingRole name="AR:Seller"/>
   <RespondingRole name="AR:Insurer"/>
   <BusinessTransactionActivity name="BTA:Request shipment insurance"
                           businessTransaction="BT:Insure shipment"
                           fromAuthorizedRole="AR:Seller"
                           toAuthorizedRole="AR:Insurer"/>

   <CollaborationActivity name="CA:Insurer:Modify shipment contract"
                           binaryCollaboration="BC:Modify shipment contract"
                           fromAuthorizedRole="AR:Insurer"
                           toAuthorizedRole="AR:Seller"/>
   <CollaborationActivity name="CA:Seller:Modify shipment contract"
                           binaryCollaboration="BC:Modify shipment contract"
                           fromAuthorizedRole="AR:Seller"
                           toAuthorizedRole="AR:Insurer"/>
   ...
</BinaryCollaboration>
```

Three more properties may be set to fully specify a business transaction activity: `isConcurrent`, `isLegallyBinding`, and `timeToPerform`. The `isConcurrent` property refers to the fact that the same business transaction activity may or may not be executed concurrently across several binary collaboration instances. The `isLegallyBinding` parameter has already been discussed earlier, in the *Non-repudiation and Legally Binding Transactions* section, and has no impact on the collaboration choreography.

Unlike business transaction activities, the `timeToPerform` of a binary collaboration activity is defined by the corresponding property in its binary collaboration definition.

Binary collaborations are also represented with a UML activity diagram, the two roles being represented as usual with swim lanes. The business transaction activities, which are initiated by a given role, are represented inside the corresponding swim lane. For instance, the `BTA:Insure shipment` is initiated by the `Seller` role as represented below:

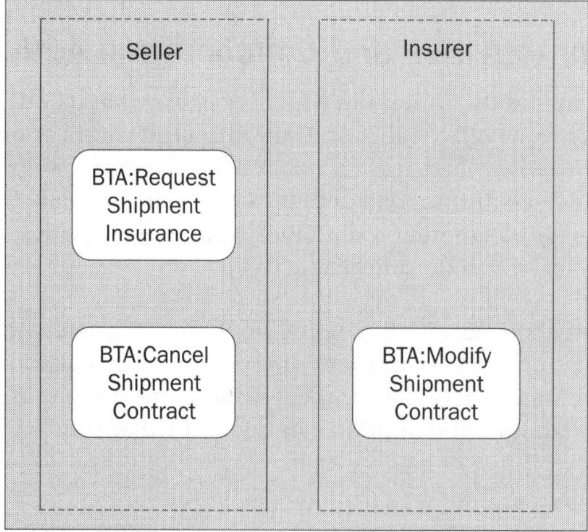


## Pseudo States

In order to specify the choreography of the collaboration, the BPSS specification defines five pseudo-states – `Start`, `Success`, `Failure`, `Fork` and `Join`, which can be interleaved with the business transaction or collaboration activities. These states are called pseudo-states in the sense that they have the same semantic as a state (transition from a state and transition to a state), but they do not correspond to any state in particular and are identical across collaboration definitions.

### Start

`Start` is (of course) the starting state for a binary collaboration. A binary collaboration should have at least one starting activity. If none is defined, then all activities are considered allowable entry points. This is particularly useful in defining subcollaborations that are used in a negotiation pattern. We will come back on this point in the next section, *Binary Collaboration Choreography*:

```
<BinaryCollaboration>
   ...
   <Start toBusinessState="BTA:Request shipment insurance"/>
   ...
</BinaryCollaboration>
```

A **completion state** denotes the end of the binary collaboration. There are two types of completion state: `Success` and `Failure`. A `conditionGuard` (which we met earlier in the context of transitions) may be specified for any of these states. The value of this guard will ultimately decide if the collaboration can transition from a business activity to a completion state. The possible values for the `conditionGuard` (as before) are `Success`, `BusinessFailure`, `TechnicalFailure`, and `AnyFailure`:

```
<BinaryCollaboration >
   ...
   <Success fromBusinessState="BTA:Request shipment insurance"
            conditionGuard="Success"/>
   <Failure fromBusinessState="BTA:Request shipment insurance"
            conditionGuard="AnyFailure"/>
   ...
</BinaryCollaboration>
```

### *Fork*

A `Fork` is a state with one inbound transition and multiple outbound transitions. All activities pointed to by the outbound transitions are assumed to happen in parallel. The specification does not provide any particular pseudo-state for an **XOR-Fork**. It is rather achieved by defining two or more guarded transitions coming out of the same business transaction activity. We will come back to this point in the next section, *Binary Collaboration Choreography*.

### *Join*

A `Join` is a business state where an activity is waiting for the completion of one or more other activities. It defines the point where previously forked activities join up again. `Join` has one optional attribute: `waitForAll`. If this is set to `true`, the join is commonly called an **AND-join**. Otherwise, it is technically an **OR-Join**, but practically an **XOR-Join** (exclusive-OR), since business transaction activities are unlikely to complete simultaneously.

When a business transaction activity completes on an OR-Join, there might be other business transaction activities open with the corresponding fork/join. These transactions may complete normally, however, the corresponding transition will not be executed as the state of the collaboration is now beyond the join element:

```
<BinaryCollaboration >
   ...
   <Fork name="Start:Modify shipment contract"/>
   <Join name="End:Modify shipment contract"
         waitForAll="false"/>
   ...
</BinaryCollaboration>
```

In the diagram below, we use the UML activity diagram notation with the `Fork` and `Join` pseudo-states to illustrate how the corresponding XML elements may be represented. Again, this notation is not official and its semantics are incomplete. It should only be used to guide the users of the binary collaboration definition, not to configure systems or as part of contracts between two parties.

This diagram shows how `Fork` and `Join` can be used to express that two business transaction activities may occur without a specific sequence: the insurer is free to change the contract at any time, while the seller may cancel the contract at any time:

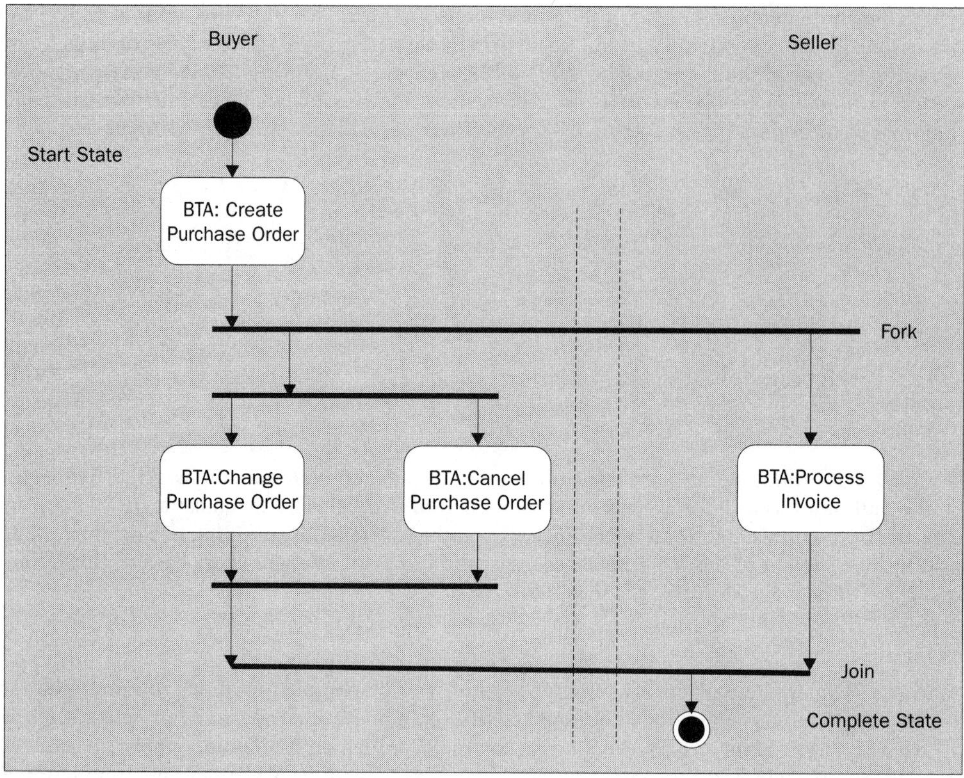


## Binary Collaboration Choreography

Choreography is expressed as transitions between business states (business transaction activities, collaboration activities and pseudo-states). The `beginsWhen`, `endsWhen`, `preCondition`, and `postCondition` attributes cannot be used effectively, since they apply to business transaction and binary collaboration definitions only, and not activities. In the discussion below, we only recommend to use the `preCondition` attribute in a very specific case.

### Transitions

A transition specifies that a given business transaction activity or collaboration activity (`from` activity) is followed by another business transaction activity or collaboration activity (`to` activity). When a given activity completes, the transition indicates what is expected to happen next. Only one transition may occur from any activity except for the Fork pseudo-state. However, multiple transitions may be defined from an activity. In this case, they have to be mutually exclusive. Transitions can be either **automatic** (when the `from` business transaction activity completes) or **conditional**. There are two ways to define a conditional transition. A transition may have a `conditionGuard` and/or a `ConditionExpression` associated with it. A `conditionGuard` makes reference to the `Success`, `BusinessFailure`, `TechnicalFailure` or `AnyFailure` condition of the `from` business transaction activity. This is the simplest way to express conditional choreographies and it should be used wherever possible.

The example opposite shows a sequence between the `Insure shipment request` business transaction activity, and a `Send Invoice` business transaction. In case any failure occurs (business or technical) during the business transaction activity, we have specified that the collaboration itself ends in failure:

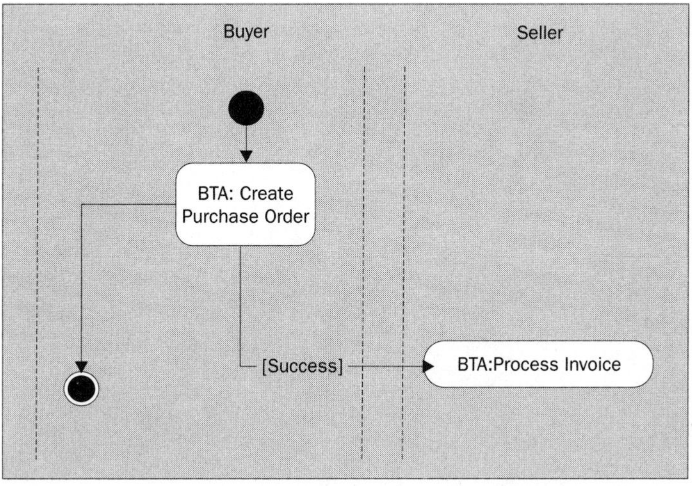


```
<BinaryCollaboration name="BC:Insure shipment"
                     timeToPerform="P7D">
   <InitiatingRole name="AR:Sellet"/>
   <RespondingRole name="AR:Insurer"/>

   <Start toBusinessState="BTA:Insure shipment request"/>
   <Transition conditionGuard="Success"
               fromBusinessState="BTA:Insure shipment request"
               toBusinessState="BTA:Send Invoice"/>
   <Failure fromBusinessState="BTA:Insure shipment request"
            conditionGuard="AnyFailure"/>
   ...
</BinaryCollaboration>
```

As you may have noticed, a `Failure` element is the combination of a transition and a completion state.

On the other hand, a `ConditionExpression` is a general expression, which can be evaluated to `true` or `false`. Often, the condition expression will consist of an XPath expression pointing to a business document that is part of the binary collaboration. For instance, the `BC:Insure shipment` collaboration above could take different paths based on the value of the equipment to insure, or the destination country.

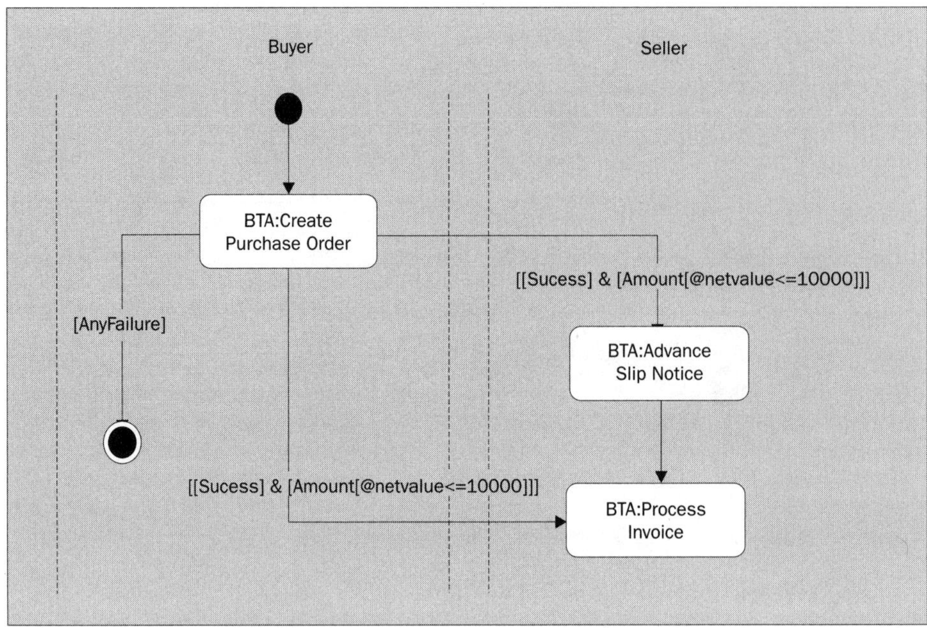


The corresponding XML is as follows:

```
<BinaryCollaboration name="BC:Insure shipment"
                     timeToPerform="P7D">
   <InitiatingRole name="AR:Seller"/>
   <RespondingRole name="AR:Insurer"/>
   <Start toBusinessState="BTA:Insure shipment request"/>
   <Transition fromBusinessState="BTA:Insure shipment request"
               toBusinessState="BTA:Send invoice">
      <ConditionExpression expressionLanguage="XPath"
                           expression="//Value[@insuredValue<10000]"/>
   </Transition>
   <Transition fromBusinessState="BTA:Insure shipment request"
               toBusinessState="BTA:Process down payment">
      <ConditionExpression expressionLanguage="XPath"
                           expression="//Value[@insuredValue>=10000]"/>
   </Transition>
   <Transition fromBusinessState="BTA:Process down payment"
               toBusinessState="BTA:Send invoice"
               conditionGuard="Success"/>
   <Failure fromBusinessState="BTA:Insure shipment request"
            conditionGuard="AnyFailure"/>
   ...
</BinaryCollaboration>
```

We also suggest using the event condition action (ECA) approach. This approach, like the XPath approach is not part of the ebBPSS Sspecification. In ECA, a Bbusiness transaction definition may be specified with several possible document envelope responses. Each document envelope represents an event, which can also be associated with a condition. For instance, the `BT:Insure shipment request` may be defined with two possible response document envelopes, one which contains the `BD:Insurance contract` business document, the other containing `BD:Reject insurance request`. Each response envelope corresponds to an event in the ECA model. We may optionally associate conditions to these events, which are the same as the `conditionGuard` conditions: `Success`, `BusinessFailure`, `TechnicalFailure`, or `AnyFailure`. The corresponding collaboration is represented below:

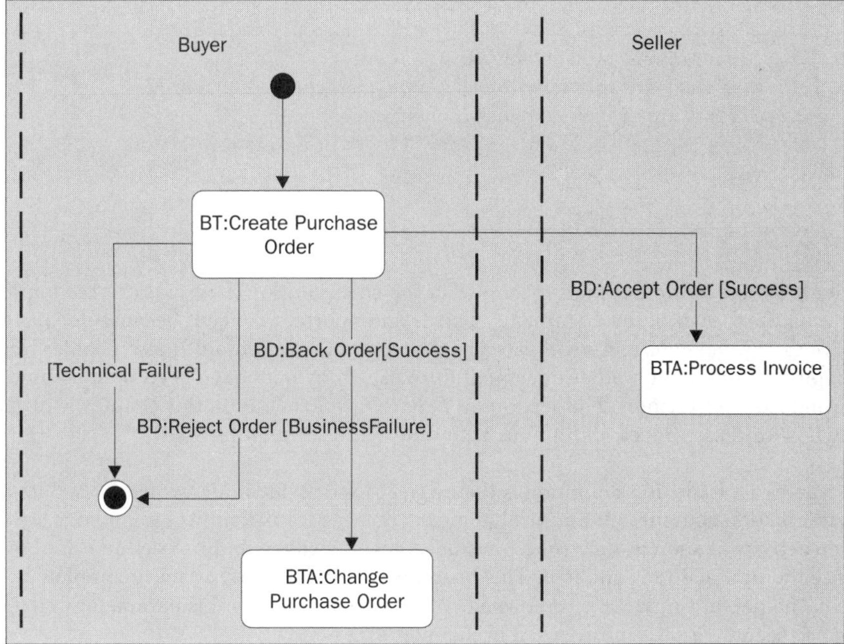


The condition expression `DE:Insurance contract[Success]` will be true when the insurance contract document envelope (DE prefix) is received by the seller and the business transaction activity is successful (meaning in this case, there is no technical failure). Note that each transition requires guarding by one of the four conditions, since otherwise two transitions might become valid. For instance, we could receive a positive Insurance contract response, but after a timeout has occurred. If this transition was not guarded by success, both transitions could potentially become valid.

The corresponding XML definition follows:

```
<BinaryCollaboration name="BC:Insure shipment"
                     timeToPerform="P7D">
   <InitiatingRole name="AR:Seller"/>
   <RespondingRole name="AR:Insurer"/>
   <!-- Business Transaction Activity definitions go here -->
   ...
```

```
    <Start toBusinessState="BTA:Insure shipment request"/>
    <Transition fromBusinessState="BTA:Insure shipment request"
                toBusinessState="BTA:Send invoice">
       <ConditionExpression expressionLanguage="ECA"
                            expression="DE:Insurance contract[Success]"/>
    </Transition>
    <Transition fromBusinessState="BTA:Insure shipment request"
                toBusinessState="BTA:Change insurance request">
       <ConditionExpression expressionLanguage="ECA"
                 expression="DE:Reject insurance request[Business Failure]"/>
    </Transition>
    <Failure fromBusinessState="BTA:Insure shipment request"
             conditionGuard="TechnicalFailure"/>
    <Failure fromBusinessState="BTA:Change insurance request">
       <ConditionExpression expressionLanguage="ECA"
                            expression="[AnyFailure]/>
    </Failure>
    ...
</BinaryCollaboration>
```

The main advantage of the ECA approach is that the collaboration definition choreography is not dependent on the format of the documents. This is an important concept because document formats may evolve to new versions and invalidate the choreography definition. It also enables reuse of the choreography definition with other document formats, which may have been defined by different parties or industry consortium. The section on *Substitution Sets* (later in this chapter) will give more details on how to reuse process definitions with different document formats.

The last aspect of a transition definition is the `onInitiation` attribute, which is used to create nested business transaction activities. A `true` value means that the transition fires to another business transaction activity as soon as the request has been acknowledged and before the response is returned, that is once the transaction is initiated. This business transaction activity must complete before the response of the parent transaction is returned. We will come back to this parameter in the *Multiparty Collaborations* section, as it is mostly used in that context.

### Negotiation Patterns

The choreography of binary collaborations often involves negotiation patterns. For instance, before the order could be placed, the two parties involved may decide to go over a **Request For (Insurance) Quote** (**RFQ**) business process. In this case, the seller of the equipment will issue an RFQ, and the insurer(s) will review the RFQ and respond with a quote. At the end of this negotiation, the seller may decide to proceed, and execute an Insure shipment request (as our example):

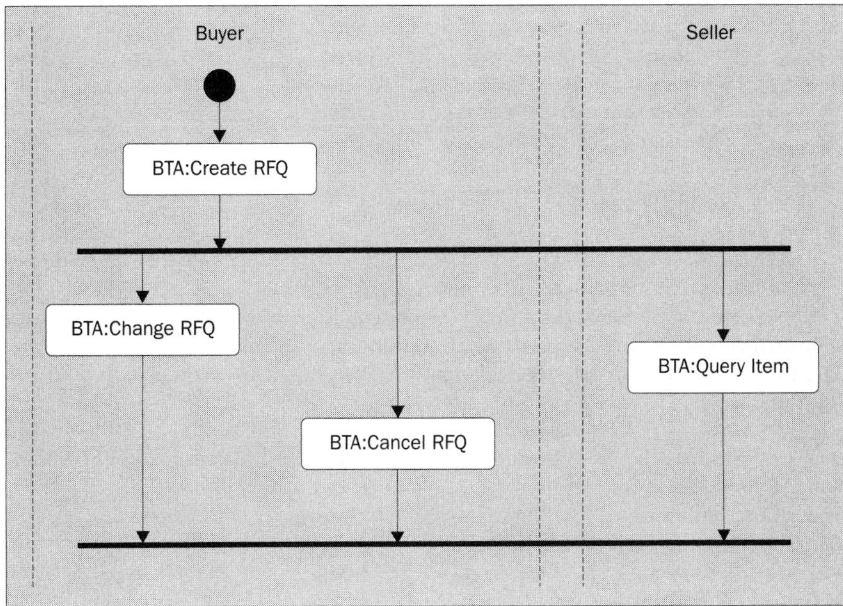


This negotiation pattern is very common. During this phase, the requester may change or cancel its RFQ and the "requestee" may ask questions about the RFQ as shown with the `BTA:Query item` transaction activity. In this type of pattern, there is often a business transaction activity that can be repeated any number of times (recurring activity), as long as the collaboration allows it. In the present case, it is `BTA:Query Item` or `BTA:Change RFQ`. `Query Item` represents a specific question about the RFQ, which will be followed by a response query document. With the UML notation, this type of business transaction activity is represented with a transition to self. It is also very common that during these open-ended sessions, one or both of the parties are allowed to cancel the current business activity (here `Cancel RFQ`). In this case, the Fail Completion State is defined after the join.

The corresponding XML definition is as follows:

```
<BinaryCollaboration name="BC:Insure shipment RFQ"
                     timeToPerform="P30D">
   <InitiatingRole name="AR:Seller"/>
   <RespondingRole name="AR:Insurer"/>
      ...
   <Start toBusinessState="BTA:Request for quote"/>
   <Fork name="Start:Review RFQ"/>
   <Transition fromBusinessState="BTA:Request for quote"
               toBusinessState="Start:Review RFQ"
               conditionGuard="Success"/>
   <Transition fromBusinessState="Start:Review RFQ"
               toBusinessState="BTA:Cancel RFQ" />

   <Transition fromBusinessState="Start:Review RFQ"
               toBusinessState="BTA:Change RFQ"/>
```

```
    <Transition fromBusinessState="Start:Review RFQ"
                toBusinessState="BTA:Query Item"/>
    <Transition fromBusinessState="BTA:Query Item"
                toBusinessState="BTA:Query Item"
                conditionGuard="Success"/>
    ...
</BinaryCollaboration>
```

However, there is an issue with our current design. As per BPSS, `Fork` and `Join` elements cannot be specified with a timeout. Since we want to enable `BTA:Change RFQ` and `BTA:Query item` to happen during a certain period of time, we must define the negotiation activities as a separate binary collaboration which will be used as a "subcollaboration", and assign it a `timeToPerform` attribute. We must also define a collaboration activity in the parent binary collaboration, which points to this new collaboration definition.

There is a second issue is relative to business transaction activities, which may happen with no specific sequence after a `Fork` (for example, `Change RFQ` and `Query Item`). Some business transaction activities may happen concurrently; however, others need to happen exclusively (such as `Cancel RFQ` with respect to `Change RFQ` and `Query Item`).

The ebBPSS does not address this issue very well. This is typically an instance where `preCondition` may be used throughout the specification and it does not recommend any specific semantics. In this case, a precondition means that the collaboration must be in a specific state, that is, no other business transaction activities are currently open. We propose a syntax for expressing this condition: in the business transaction definition, specify the content of the precondition attribute with the name of the transaction which must either be open or closed, separated by a semi-colon. If a transaction is required to be closed, use a "`!`"; otherwise, just specify the name:

```
<BusinessTransaction name="BT:Query Item"
                     precondition="!BT:Change
                     RFQ;!BT:Cancel RFQ">
    ...
</BusinessTransaction>
```

As you can see, it is a bit odd that this parameter is associated with a business transaction definition and not a business transaction activity – especially since it couples the business transaction definition and its usage in a particular binary collaboration. Clearly, this mechanism is not ideal, but there is no other mechanism in the specification available for the purpose of excluding business transactions while others are open.

We now define a new (sub)collaboration called `Review RFQ`:

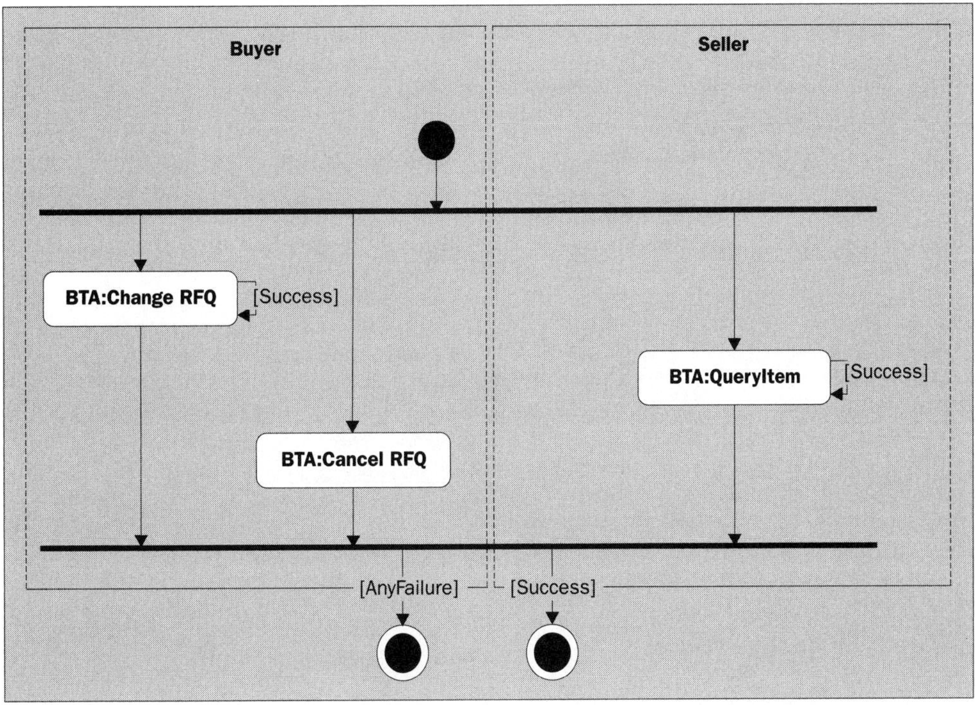


We can now define a new binary collaboration in lieu of the `BC:Insure shipment RFQ` that uses `BC:Review RFQ`, as well as `BC:Insure shipment request` as collaboration activities:

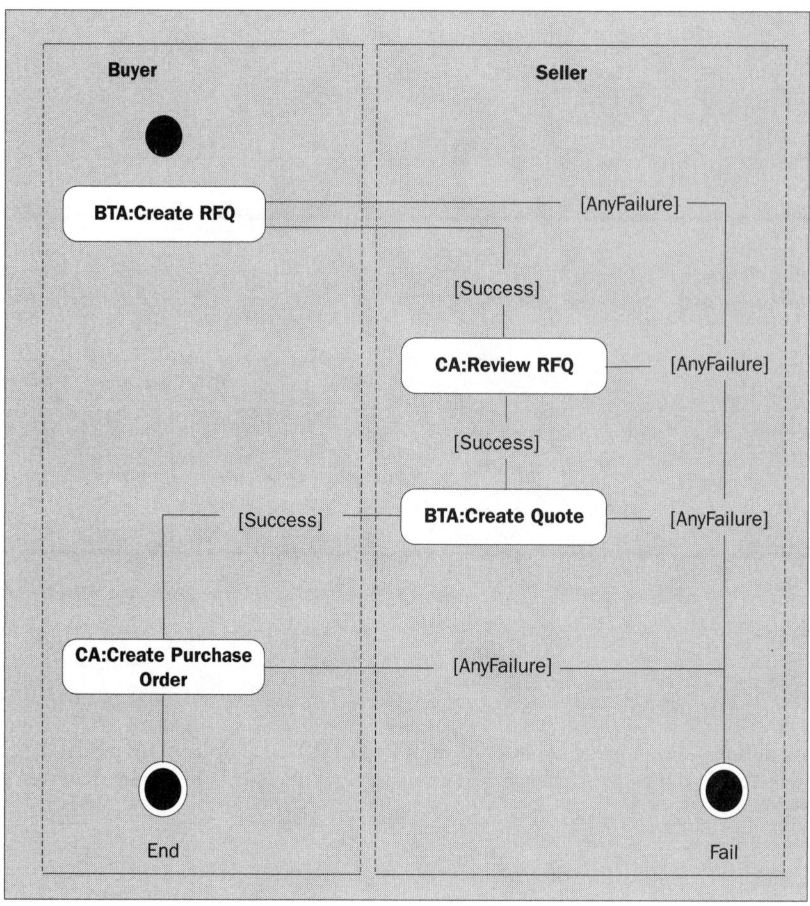


```
<BinaryCollaboration name="BC:Review RFQ"
                     timeToPerform="P10D">
   <InitiatingRole name="AR:Seller"/>
   <RespondingRole name="AR:Insurer"/>
      ...
   <Start toBusinessState="Star:Review RFQ"/>
   <Fork name="Start:Review RFQ"/>


   <Transition fromBusinessState="Start:Review RFQ"
               toBusinessState="BTA:Cancel RFQ" />

   <Transition fromBusinessState="Start:Review RFQ"
               toBusinessState="BTA:Change RFQ"/>

   <Transition fromBusinessState="Start:Review RFQ"
               toBusinessState="BTA:Query Item"/>

   <Transition fromBusinessState="BTA:Query Item"
```

```
                toBusinessState="BTA:Query Item"
                conditionGuard="Success"/>

    <Transition fromBusinessState="BTA:Change RFQ"
                toBusinessState="BTA:Change RFQ"
                conditionGuard="Success"/>

    <Transition fromBusinessState="BTA:Cancel RFQ"
                toBusinessState="BTA:Cancel RFQ"
                conditionGuard="AnyFailure"/>
  </BinaryCollaboration>
  <BinaryCollaboration name="BC:Insure shipment RFQ"
                       timeToPerform="P30D">
    <InitiatingRole name="AR:Seller"/>
    <RespondingRole name="AR:Insurer"/>
    <!-- Business transaction activity definitions go here -->
      ...
    <!-- normal flow of the collaboration -->
    <Start toBusinessState="BTA:Insure shipment RFQ"/>
    <Transition fromBusinessState="BTA:Insure shipment RFQ"
                toBusinessState="CA:Review RFQ"
                conditionGuard="Success"/>
    <Transition fromBusinessState="CA:Review RFQ"
                toBusinessState="BTA:Send Quote"
                conditionGuard="Success"/>
    <Transition fromBusinessState="BTA:Send Quote"
                toBusinessState="CA:Insure shipment"
                conditionGuard="Success" />
    <Success fromBusinessState="CA:Insure shipment"
             conditionGuard="Success" />

    <!-- collaboration exceptions -->
    <Failure fromBusinessState="BTA:Insure shipment RFQ"
             conditionGuard="AnyFailure"/>
    <Failure fromBusinessState="CA:Review RFQ"
             conditionGuard="AnyFailure"/>
    <Failure fromBusinessState="BTA:Send quote"
             conditionGuard="AnyFailure"/>
    <Failure fromBusinessState="CA:Insure shipment"
             conditionGuard="AnyFailure"/>
  </BinaryCollaboration>
```

As we have seen, collaboration definitions represent very precise protocol of message exchange, unmatched by any other specification today. The collaboration semantics require that its design be done by a combination of business analysts, subject matter experts and IT staff, who must work together to facilitate the discussion and capture all the details of the specification. In addition, the design of the collaboration and its business document formats is often done iteratively, since a collaboration may require a document or an element that would not necessarily have been used if the collaboration was not known in advance.

# Multiparty Collaborations

A **multiparty collaboration** is formed as a synthesis of two or more binary collaborations. Other approaches are possible, for instance assembling directly all the business transaction activities in a single multi-party collaboration with the corresponding roles. However, one major difficulty of this approach is that it is difficult to agree and enforce true multi-party agreements. Consequently, the authors of the specification have decided to remain closer to the way businesses operate: that is, that most business contracts involve two parties which are used by multi-party collaborations.

Hence, ebBPSS expresses dependencies between binary collaboration, rather than an overall collaboration amongst several parties. It is important to note that one needs to use multiparty collaboration definitions *only* when the dependencies need to be made explicit to all parties. Otherwise, using two independent binary collaborations is just fine.

A multiparty collaboration is defined from a business partner role perspective. A business partner role may **perform** one or more role (`fromAuthorizedRole` or `toAuthorizedRole` in a binary collaboration definition) in various binary collaboration definitions. This is how the specification links the binary collaborations to the multiparty collaboration.

If we take the example of a multiparty involving a buyer, a seller and a shipper as represented below:

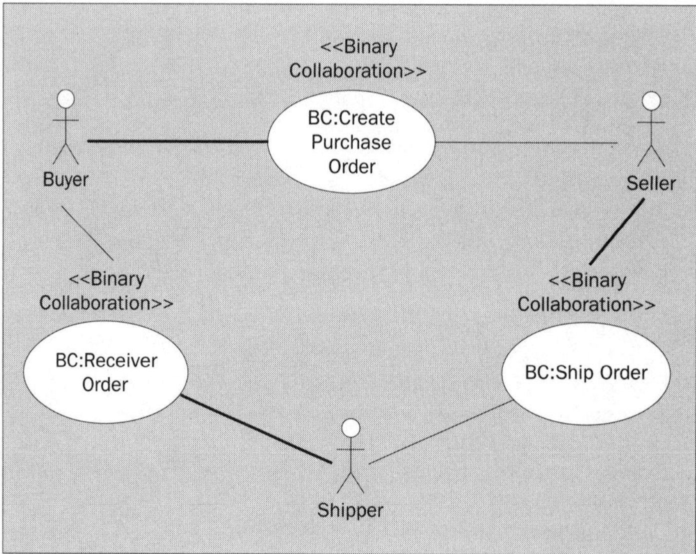


The `BC:Receive order` collaboration is of course an exchange of electronic messages. BPSS does not provide semantics associated with economic resources such as "goods" or "money". The designers of the collaboration have to always associate a message to the corresponding exchange of economic resources.

The multiparty collaboration is specified as follows:

```
<BinaryCollaboration name="BC:Create Purchase Order">
   <initiatingRole name="AR:Buyer" />
   <respondingRole name="AR:Seller"/>
```

```
      ...
</BinaryCollaboration>
<BinaryCollaboration name="BC:Ship Order">
   <initiatingRole name="AR:Seller" />
   <respondingRole name="AR:Shipper"/>
      ...
...
</BinaryCollaboration>
<BinaryCollaboration name="BC:Receive Order">
   <initiatingRole name="AR:Shipper" />
   <respondingRole name="AR:Buyer"/>
      ...
...
</BinaryCollaboration>

<MultipartyCollaboration name="MC:Create/Ship Purchase Order">
   <BusinessPartnerRole name="BPR:Buyer">
      <Performs initiatingRole="AR:Buyer"/>
      <Performs respondingRole="AR:Buyer" />
         ...
      ...
   </BusinessPartnerRole>
   <BusinessPartnerRole name="BPR:Seller">
      <Performs initiatingRole="AR:Seller"/>
      <Performs respondingRole="AR:Seller" />
         ...
      ...
   </BusinessPartnerRole>
   <BusinessPartnerRole name="BPR:Shipper">
      <Performs initiatingRole="AR:Shipper"/>
      <Performs respondingRole="AR:Shipper"/>
         ...
      ...
   </BusinessPartnerRole>
</MultipartyCollaboration>
```

Transitions may be added to a multiparty collaboration definition to indicate the dependencies between business transaction activities. In the present scenario, we could express a dependency that the business transaction activity `BTA:Process Invoice` in the `BC:Create Purchase Order` depends on the success of the `BTA:Receive Order` in the `BC:Receive Order`. We could also define that a product can be shipped once the `BTA:Create Purchase Transaction` is successful:

```
<BinaryCollaboration name="BC:Create Purchase Order">
   <initiatingRole name="AR:Buyer" />
   <respondingRole name="AR:Seller"/>
   <BusinessTransactionActivity name="BTA:Create Purchase Order" .../>
   <BusinessTransactionActivity name="BTA:Process Invoice" .../>
      ...
...
</BinaryCollaboration>
<BinaryCollaboration name="BC:Ship Order">
   <initiatingRole name="AR:Seller" />
   <respondingRole name="AR:Shipper"/>
```

```
   <BusinessTransactionActivity name="BTA:Ship Order" .../>
      ...
...
</BinaryCollaboration>
<BinaryCollaboration name="BC:Receive Order">
   <initiatingRole name="AR:Shipper" />
   <respondingRole name="AR:Buyer"/>
   <BusinessTransactionActivity name="BTA:Receive Order" .../>
      ...
...
</BinaryCollaboration>

<MultipartyCollaboration name="MC:Create/Ship Purchase Order">
   <BusinessPartnerRole name="BPR:Buyer">
      <Performs initiatingRole="AR:Buyer"/>
      <Performs respondingRole="AR: Buyer" />
      <Transition fromBusinessState="BTA:Create Purchase Order"
                  toBusinessState="BTA:Ship Order"
                  conditionGuard="Success"/>
   </BusinessPartnerRole>
   <BusinessPartnerRole name="BPR:Seller">
      <Performs initiatingRole="AR:Seller"/>
      <Performs respondingRole="AR:Seller"/>

   </BusinessPartnerRole>
   <BusinessPartnerRole name="BPR:Shipper">
      <Performs initiatingRole="AR:Shipper"/>
      <Performs respondingRole="AR:Shipper" />
      <Transition fromBusinessState="BTA:Receive Order"
                  toBusinessState="BTA:Process Invoice"
                  conditionGuard="Success"/>
   </BusinessPartnerRole>
</MultipartyCollaboration>
```

Another possibility is to use the `onInitiation` capability of a transition. As we saw earlier, the transition fires when the request has been received successfully, and before the transaction completes. In this case, the receive order transaction is nested with the ship order transaction:

```
<MultipartyCollaboration name="MC:Create/Ship Purchase Order">
   <BusinessPartnerRole name="BPR:Buyer">
      <Performs initiatingRole="AR:Buyer"/>
      <Performs respondingRole="AR: Buyer"/>
   </BusinessPartnerRole>
   <BusinessPartnerRole name="BPR:Seller">
      <Performs initiatingRole="AR:Seller"/>
      <Performs respondingRole="AR:Seller"/>
   </BusinessPartnerRole>
   <BusinessPartnerRole name="BPR:Shipper">
      <Performs initiatingRole="AR:Shipper"/>
      <Performs respondingRole="AR:Shipper"/>
      <Transition onInitiation="true"
                  fromBusinessState="BTA:Ship Order"
                  toBusinessState="BTA:Recive Order"/>
   </BusinessPartnerRole>
</MultipartyCollaboration>
```

# Substitution Sets and Process Specification Reuse

The ebBPSS Specification was carefully designed to provide reuseable elements across various definitions. We have seen, for instance, that a collaboration definition may be used by another collaboration definition or a multiparty collaboration definition. It is expected that many organizations (such as the OAG, RosettaNet, and ACORD – http://www.OpenApplications.org, http://www.RosettaNet.org and http://www.Acord.org respectively) will publish horizontal and vertical process specifications. A horizontal process specification provides processes that can be used in any industries (such as 'Process Purchase Order'), while vertical process definitions are relevant to a single industry (such as the 'Price Protection' process in the IT supply chain). It will also inevitably happen that some of the parameters, such as timeouts or condition expressions, may not be suitable for particular business needs. The specification allows for substitution sets to be defined and overwrite existing parameters of a process definition. This capability allows for writing process specifications that have no document format definition, just abstract business document definitions. In this case, it is expected that different industry consortia or individual business partners will each specify the document formats they will be using.

A **substitution set** is a container for one or more `AttributeSubstitution` and/or `DocumentSubstitution` elements:

```
<SubstitutionSet name="OAGI" applyToScope="BTA:Insure shipment request">
   <DocumentSubstitution
       originalBusinessDocument=
      "http://www.openapplications.org/OAGI/v7/210_insure_shipment_007.dtd"
      substituteBusinessDocument=
      "http://www.openapplications.org/OAGI/v7/210_insure_shipment_008.dtd"
   />
   <AttributeSubstitution attributeName="timeToAcknowledgeReceipt"
                          value="P4H"/>
</SubstitutionSet>
```

# Identifying Elements Within and Outside a Process Specification Document

The specification was designed to be flexible in the way elements are referenced by each other. If elements are only referenced within the same file, we can use the traditional mechanism of ID/IDREF provided by XML DTD and Schema. ID/IDREF functionality requires all IDs to be unique within a document and that all IDREFs point to a defined ID value. It is expected that editing tools will implement the ID/IDREF mechanism, rather than their implementation by hand.

If elements need to be referenced across specification documents using includes, this mechanism cannot be used. We have chosen in this chapter not to use the ID/IDREF mechanism, but rather to use a logical name for each element. We have chosen to prefix this element with the type of element it is denominating, such that we can use `BC:Create Purchase Order`, `BT:Create Purchase Order` and `BTA:Create Purchase Order`.

Another alternative, which is more verbose, but removes any ambiguity such that you do not need to use namespace prefixes, is to use an XPath expression by that name. This is the approach recommended by the ebBPSS Specification:

```
fromAuthorizedRole='//InitiatingRole[@name=" Buyer"]'
```

is equivalent to:

```
FromAuthorizedRole="AR:Buyer"
```

Implementers should support both ways. The BPSS-recommended syntax is a little bit harder to read for humans, however, I am certain that you have already figured out quite a few pages ago that this specification was designed to be read by machines anyway.

# Packages and Includes

A ProcessSpecification can include another ProcessSpecification by reference (as an include).

For instance, this feature may be used to 'bind' business document definitions to a generic process specification:

```
<ProcessSpecification>
   <Include name="Open Applications Group Business Object Documents"
           uuid="123-456"
           uri="http://www.openapplications.org/OAGIS/v7.2/bods.xml"
           version="7.2"
   ...
</ProcessSpecification>
```

In addition, the contents of an ebXML Process Specification can be arranged in a recursive package structure. A <ProcessSpecification> is a package container, so it can contain packages within it. A <Package> in itself is also a package container, so it can contain further packages.

As stated in the BPSS version 1.01 (found at http://www.ebxml.org/specs/), page 101, lines 2946/2950 – "Finally, a Package at any level can have PackageContent. Types of PackageContent are BusinessTransaction, BinaryCollaboration, and MultiPartyCollaboration. PackageContent is always uniquely named within a package. Lower-level elements are uniquely named within their parent PackageContent."

Packages are often organized by BusinessArea and ProcessArea. This is a recommendation coming from UMM:

```
<Package name="BusinessArea:Insurance"/>
   <Package name="ProcessArea:Insure shipment"/>
      ...
```

Packages function as namespaces. We can choose to extend the naming convention that we used so far:

```
<BusinessTransaction
        name="BT:Insurance:Insure shipment:Insure shipment RFQ "/>
           ...
```

We can also use an XPath naming convention with reference packages:

```
<Performs
authorizedRole='//Package[@name="BusinessArea:Insurance"]/
Package[@name="ProcessArea:Insure shipment"] /BinaryCollaboration
[@name="BC:Insure shipment RFQ"]/InitiatingRole[@name="AR:Seller"]'/>
```

Ultimately, these BPSS documents are designed to be front-ended by an application and not authored by hand. The XPath naming convention is the most precise and should be the first choice for an implementation.

# The Business Service Interface

The ebBPSS was designed to be a protocol completely independent of the ebXML Messaging Service. The specification often references a "business service interface" (BSI)" which is in charge of enforcing the process specification. A typical architecture is represented below:

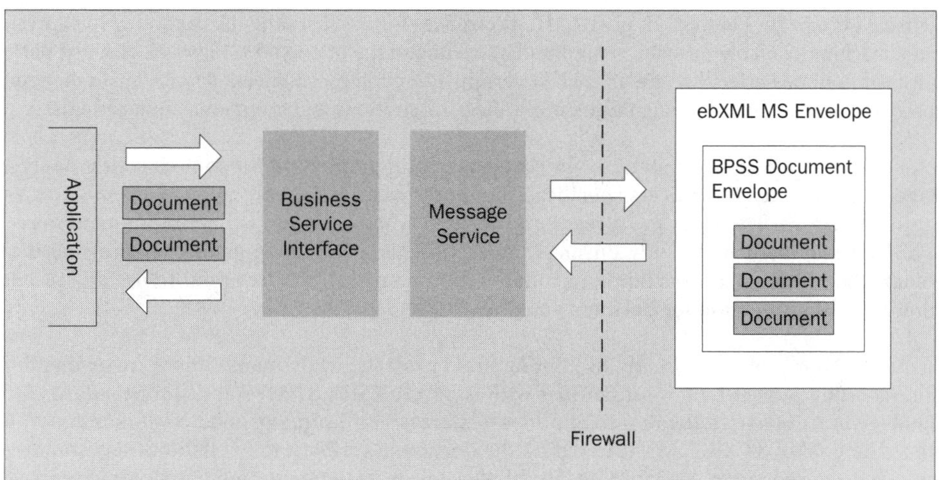


A business application is using the BSI to send and receive documents following a BPSS instance. The BSI is relying on the Messaging Service services such as guaranteed delivery, authentication, encryption, and so on, to manage the business document interchange with the corresponding business partner.

In addition, the BSI enforces the semantics and sequencing of business transactions and collaborations. In particular, as a minimum, the BSI:

- Detects the opening of new collaboration and transactions
- Detects the successful completion of a transaction

- Detects the failed completion of a transaction:
  - Timeouts
  - Control and Process Exceptions
  - `isPositiveResponse`
- Manages the notification of failure

Of course, ebXML does not specify the relationship between the BSI layer and the business application. In simple cases, a BSI can be directly added to or used by an application. If the collaborations involve more than one or a few applications, one might want to choose a different architecture by introducing a layer that will route documents and exceptions from applications to the BSI. A Business Process Management System is used typically in that capacity. We will explore this type of architecture in the next chapter.

# Conclusion

The ebBPSS is a major component of ebXML. It provides for the first time the capability to express formally and in a machine-readable format a shared understanding of the interactions between business partners. As such it might not be perfect (we are after all at version 1.0) but it represents and will remain the foundation for discovery and automatic configuration of business applications and communication systems.

The specification has some limitations. In particular, it might be hard for some business analysts to manage all the details of a process specification, in particular being able to build effective state-transition diagrams. The work has already started at ebXML to define collaboration patterns on top of ebBPSS, just like there are already business transaction patterns. These patterns, merely a set of choreographed business transaction and collaboration activities, will be easier to use and provide yet another level of abstraction for business analysts.

Today, ebXML is probably already used in multiple projects, while many others are evaluating the technology. The project I am most familiar with is **STAR/XML**. STAR stands for **Standards for Technology in Automotive Retail** (see http://www.starstandard.org/sigs/sigs_xml/default.htm for more details). The goal of STAR/XML is to define the document formats, the collaborations and the infrastructure necessary to carry out business between car dealerships and car manufacturers. The project involves all the major car manufacturers in North America, and all the DSPs (Dealership System Providers). All aspects of the relationship are covered: vehicles, parts, customer and prospect information, finance, or insurance, etc. STAR/XML is using the Open Applications Group (OAGi) architecture to model business document formats and the ebXML infrastructure for collaboration and communication infrastructure.

Collaborations as defined by ebXML are message based and pseudo-real time. This new paradigm is significantly impacting current IT infrastructures, which have been mostly operating on a batch-oriented mode. It is likely that to respond to these requirements, IT infrastructure will adopt a new generation of systems: for example, **Online Collaboration Processing** (**OLCP**) systems to complement their **Online Transaction Processing** (**OLTP**) and **Online Analytical Process** (**OLAP**) systems.

# Summary

In this chapter we have learned how to design business transactions as the building block of collaborations. We spent a fair amount of time looking at business transaction failures and talked about exception handling. We also explored the definition of binary and multi-party collaborations and how to specify the choreography of business transaction and collaboration activities. One of the key aspects is to decouple the choreography from the document format definitions. Finally, we learned how to make our process definitions more generic and reusable by others.

# 6

# Implementing BPSS

In Chapter 5 we learned what a "business collaboration" was, and all the necessary semantics used to exchange business documents. In this chapter, we are going to look at the benefits entailed by this concept and define its impact on current IT architectures.

Before we start, let us set the context of this chapter. ebXML was designed to deal with issues a company will face when it needs to integrate with hundreds of business partners, and when it needs to carry out several types of long running business activities. Let's take a concrete example. If a company has five core B2B processes they need to automate, each process on average has five documents and this company needs to do this with 100 partners, this company will have to deploy and manage 2500 different network end points!!! Don't forget that at any point in time, a single endpoint may change (document format, security model, URL, etc.) Let's imagine now that you are a big aerospace company and have nearly 30,000 suppliers, or a big car manufacturer with 2500 enterprise information systems, which need to interact with these network endpoints. You will get a headache just thinking about the resources it will take to build the integration between all this. When you are done, you also take a minute to think about suppliers that might need to develop specific implementations for each of its preferred customers. I often refer to this problem using the term "highly-connected systems". In this chapter, we are going to learn about the architecture of such systems.

We are going to cover many topics in this chapter to help you establish a vision (not necessarily *the* vision) of how all the pieces fit together:

- We start with a brief introduction to the π-calculus theory. This theory was designed to model communicating and mobile systems, and as such provides a very elegant foundation to understand the relationship of BPSS and the systems that support the communication with business partners.

- Next, we will spend a fair amount of time introducing an old concept, which has recently received a lot of interest: **Business Process Management Systems** (**BPMS**). Today, there are three major XML-based standards competing for the specification of business process definitions (again BPSS is a collaboration definition standard):
  - Business Process Markup Language (BPML – see http://www.bpmi.org)
  - XLANG (check out http://www.gotdotnet.com/team/xml_wsspecs/xlang-c/default.htm)
  - Web Service Flow Language from IBM (WSFL, see http://www-4.ibm.com/software/solutions/webservices/pdf/WSFL.pdf)

  These three standards are all based on Web Services. I'd be surprised if you have never heard of Web Services, but to continue our journey I will give you a three-page crash course on this new distributed computing model.
- In the last sections of the chapter, we will bring all the pieces together and show how ebXML collaborations can be implemented with a BPML, XLANG or WSFL BPMS.

# π-Calculus

The ubiquity of TCP/IP and the Internet has enabled many systems to communicate with their environment with great ease. Such interactive systems are actually becoming the norm. Surprisingly, efforts to model these categories of systems started only fairly recently, relative to the theory of sequential algorithmic processes (λ-calculus) – which is the foundation of all programming languages. The first steps of this theory can be traced back to the 1600s with the work of mathematician and philosopher, Blaise Pascal, who designed and built the first (mechanical) calculator.

The **π-calculus theory**, developed by Robin Milner in the late 1980s, is about modelling concurrent communicating systems. π-calculus theory also takes into account the notion of **mobility**, which can either be physical or, as in our case, virtual (movement of links between systems). In this chapter we will use the term mobility with respect to the notion of **'change'**: change of business partner, business document format, capabilities, etc. – any modification of an existing relationship between two companies may be associated with mobility.

The ebXML BPSS provides a formal description of the interactions between two entities whose states are completely disjointed. The very role of the messages exchanged as part of a collaboration is to synchronize these two states. ebBPSS was not based on a π-calculus foundation, but in this section we will show that these two formalisms are fairly well aligned. In addition, π-calculus is the foundation of two of the main Business Process Definition Languages: BPML from the BPMI consortium and XLANG from Microsoft (see references above), which we will study at the end of this chapter.

# Automata, State, Actions, and Interactions

At a high level, a company can be considered to be a very large automaton whose logical **state** consists of gigabytes or terabytes of data, and whose physical state is made of the raw materials, goods and money under its control. Its state is strictly bounded in the sense that it is owned and accessible in its entirety by the corporation, whilst being hidden from any other corporation. A company can change its state by initiating an **action** (such as shipping an order, or paying a supplier). When another corporation wants to change or query this state it is done via an **interaction.** Interactions usually trigger some internal actions based on business rules, which enable the corporation ultimately to synchronize its own state with one of its business partners.

The company's **actions**, when executed, characterize a transition from one state to another. Interactions and actions, when assembled together, form the enterprise business processes. Both the number of **actions** and **states** can be large for any given corporation. However, they are both finite.

Let's look in more details at an **automaton.** The classical theory, as the starting point of Milner's theory, specifies that an automaton over a set of actions ***Act*** has four ingredients:

- A set of states $\boldsymbol{Q} = \{q_0, q_1, \dots\}$
- A start state $q_0$
- A set of transitions which are triplets $(q, a, q')$ members of $\boldsymbol{Q} \times \boldsymbol{Act} \times \boldsymbol{Q}$
- A subset $\boldsymbol{F}$ of $\boldsymbol{Q}$ called the accepting states

In theory a business is deterministic, thus will obey the rule that for each pair of state and action $(q, a)$ there is at most one transition $(q, a, q')$.

An automaton can be represented with a directed graph, as shown below. States are represented in circles ($q_0$, $q_1$, ...), transitions are represented as arrows ($a$, $b$, $c$), and accepting states are represented with a double circle:

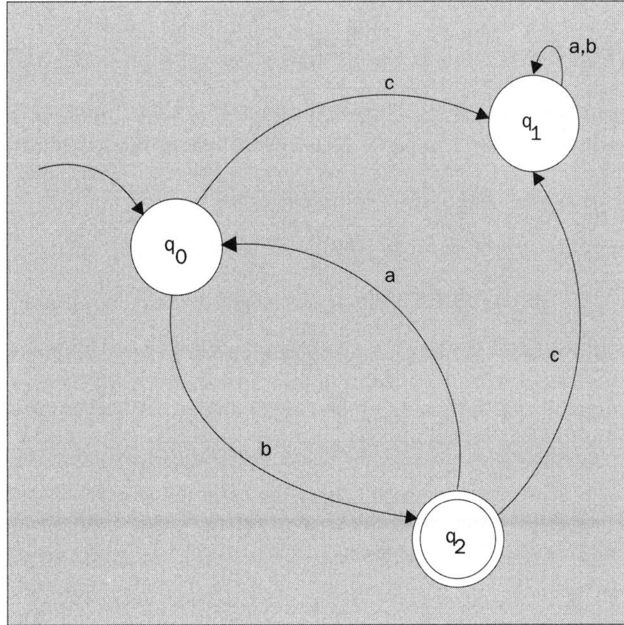


This model can be extended to introduce the notion of **events** and **conditions**, which may act as a **guard** to an action. Actions may be automatic; when one reaches a state $q_i$ an action $a$ occurs without any other preconditions. In other cases, a "condition" may decide whether action $a$ or $b$ will happen, again automatically. Lastly, an event, sometimes combined with a condition, may trigger an action (ECA model), which in turn will transition the automaton from a state to another.

When the number of potential states is large, this diagram becomes impractical and is often replaced by an activity diagram as we used in Chapter 5. This diagram is drawn from a different perspective. It does not show the specific states the automaton may take, but rather the controlled succession of activities (that is, actions) that may occur within a corporation. State-transition or activity diagrams are often referred to as **processes** or **sequential processes**.

When two corporations are engaging in B2B activities, they are each running their (internal) sequential process concurrently. These two processes must interact to reflect commitments, transfer of economic resources, and many other aspects of the business activity shared between the two business partners.

This causes the actions of a given corporation to be divided into two different sets: those that are **externally observable** and those that are **internal**. This is precisely the theoretical link between ebXML BPSS and the π-calculus theory. ebXML BPSS provides the framework to expose the externally observable actions (requesting and responding business activities) in a view shared by the two business partners involved. In addition (not addressed by π-calculus), it provides a framework for assembling these observable actions in non-repudiation and legally binding business transactions.

At this point, the automaton ***A*** (that is, the corporation) is considered as a black box and the externally observable actions can be represented with the following notation (in this case only two of them):

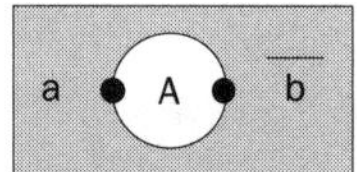


$a$ and $\overline{b}$ are called **labelled ports**. Each complementary pair $(\overline{b}, b)$ of ports represents a means of interaction between two automata. These are the points of synchronization between the automata.

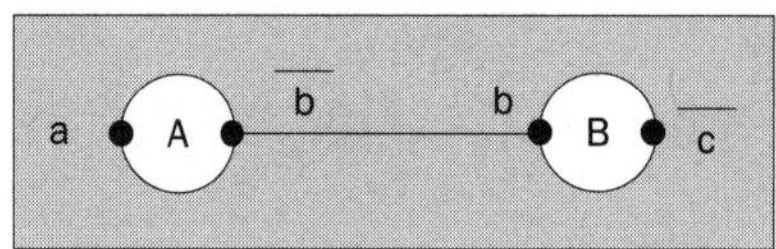


This graph is called a **flowgraph**. While the transition graph depicts the dynamic properties of a system, a flowgraph depicts the structure of the system, in other words the relationships between its components. An automaton can have any number of labelled ports, and a port may bear any number of arcs directed to any number of automata.

In BPSS, the points of synchronization are precisely the responding and requesting business activities: once these activities have been completed, the state of each company will be consistent with the one of its business partner.

If we look at a global picture we see that the two automata $A$ and $B$ are running with no particular dependence except that any action $b$ from $B$ must be synchronized with an action from $\overline{b}$ from $A$:

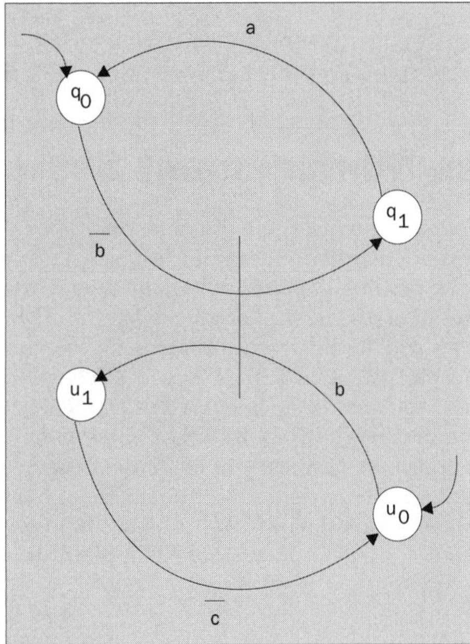


The synchronization is represented by a shared transition between their state-transition graphs. This notion of shared transitions was first introduced by Carl-Adam Petri in his **theory of automata**. The corresponding graphs have been known as **Petri nets**.

Let's draw some conclusions from this very short exposure to the π-calculus theory. First and foremost, there is no need to expose the details of the processes to model their interactions – it is enough to focus on the externally observable actions. Nothing prevents a corporation from exposing as much of its internal actions as it wishes (sometimes to obey regulatory requirements such as the ones in the aerospace or pharmaceutical industry, or yet to comply with standards such as ISO 9000), but it is completely separate from the specification of interactions. These internal actions do not become external once they are exposed; rather they remain internal since they are not part of the interaction. This is the ultimate goal of ebXML BPSS, providing a shared view of the interactions regardless of the actions that lead to any particular interaction. Most companies consider their internal actions as their core assets and therefore are very reluctant to expose them.

Second, interactions are solely supported by the actions of the two concurrent automata involved. In particular, interactions do not require a third automaton to manage them, unless chosen by design (such as a broker, or a market place between buyers and suppliers in typical B2B topologies).

Last, a set of enterprise information systems can be viewed as a communicating and mobile automata. Inside a corporation, they can be aggregated to form a single logical automaton. Once we reach the boundary of a corporation, automata may no longer be composed since corporations do not share any state, but rather synchronize their respective states when they communicate.

The π-calculus theory is far more elaborate than what was presented in this section. Our goal here was to introduce a few concepts that will be helpful in the following sections to understand how ebBPSS fits in with other technologies, and their importance in modeling business partner interactions.

In the next section, we are going to focus on the automaton itself, and introduce the concept of the Business Process Management System (BPMS) as a possible application model for the "automata". Of course, we will also establish the link with BPSS as their communication model.

# Business Process Management Systems

ebXML BPSS does not recommend any particular implementation model. The specification was designed to support a large variety of architectures. For instance, an existing application (such as an order entry application) may be modified by the addition of an ebXML module to allow it to communicate directly with business partners. Alternatively, an "ebXML adaptor" may enable a series of applications integrated together with an Enterprise Application Integration (EAI) framework to communicate with its business partners. Lastly, the lifecycle of collaborations may also be supported with a **BPMS**. BPMSs are one step towards the holy grail of IT architecture enabling the enterprise to be manageable at the business process level: with a BPMS business analysts are able to directly control the operations and constantly optimize the processes, or adapt the behaviour of their enterprise to changing economic or regulatory conditions. To be clear, this vision will not happen for at least another 3 to 5 years (if ever) but already, a new generation of BPMS products has appeared on the market, and they represent a very natural infrastructure to implement ebXML BPSS, as we shall see in this chapter.

We have seen in the previous section that BPSS models the interactions between two business automata. A BPMS can be viewed as a generic infrastructure to specify and implement these automata. In general, these products work on the basis of activity diagrams rather than state diagrams since they manage the transitions and do not necessarily control the state, which is itself captured as part of a variety of enterprise systems, or is made up of the goods and currency which belong to the company.

In this section we will review the notion of a *business process*, and the technologies that are part of this new generation of BPMS, and will finally look at how BPSS/BPMS is a key enabler of highly-connected systems.

## Business Processes

A **business process** can be defined as a precisely choreographed sequence of activities (that is, actions), which operate from a start state until an end state is reached. After the execution of a new activity, the process is in a new state. Business rules (such as *On Event* and *Condition* predicates) control the sequence of activities.

The term *business process* tends to be applied to anything that looks like a series of steps – it is probably one of the most overloaded terms in the industry. It has now reached the status of a buzzword, and unfortunately, everybody is using it in any kind of context to gain some marketing edge. We provide here a simple taxonomy of *business processes*. For the purpose of this discussion we will distinguish five concepts, all of which are referenced in the literature as *business processes*:

- Enterprise business processes
- Executable business processes
- ebXML business processes (that is, collaborations)
- Business process activities
- Workflows

An **enterprise business process** (**eBP**) is the description of steps needed to carry out a business activity regardless of the systems involved. They provide a high-level view of the steps involved and can be used to model, benchmark and document existing or future designs. Enterprise business processes are actually free to span multiple corporations because of their nature, which is not bound to systems. An example would be describing all the steps that are required to happen for a pair of shoes to be manufactured in Asia and appear at your favourite store at the mall.

An **executable business process** (**xBP**) is a kind of eBP whose life cycle is controlled by one, or a combination of BPMS. It is limited to run within a single corporation. One of the important characteristics of an eBP or xBP is that it is long running. Its execution is not limited to minutes or hours like the session of a web-based application – it rather spans days, months, or years. An xBP relies on specific interactions between users, systems, and business partners, which it ties together. This system provides all the facilities and services necessary for design and execution, and mediates the integration with its environment. As we will see in the later sections of this chapter, a BPML, XLANG or WSFL business process is an xBP.

An **ebXML business process** is, as we have seen in Chapter 5 and in the previous section, a business collaboration specification that can be used to specify how two concurrent executable business processes interact at the business level.

A **business process activity** (**BPa**) represents a short-lived interaction between users or, in certain cases, systems. BPas are often managed by a Session bean in a J2EE based application. A BPa can be viewed as one step in an executable business process – a typical example is a user browsing a catalogue and filling a shopping cart. Once the user is finished, he or she pushes the checkout button, which in turn completes the activity. The proper information is passed to a BPMS as part of a completion message. Overall, the concept of long running executable business processes is not part of the J2EE architecture – this architecture was solely designed to provide the services to build standalone web-based OLTP applications. Typically, in the current J2EE model, a developer has to hard code the long running state management.

Lastly, some people are talking about **workflow,** or (strangely enough) **business process workflow**. We can often associate workflow with "automated document management" such as the review of a proposal or a contract by a large number of people. The engine in charge of this task does not know much about the documents themselves and is merely routing them through different people while keeping an audit trail. There is little or no integration with enterprise systems, let alone with other partners.

In the remainder of this chapter we will focus on executable processes as one of the possible models to develop an ebXML BPSS implementation.

## Executable Business Processes Key Semantics

This field is evolving very rapidly and the semantics of a BPMS is still a work in progress. A consortium of over 100 companies (http://www.BPMI.org) is developing a specification of a business process definition (BPML). Some vendors, such as Microsoft, have also created their own specification (XLANG). More recently, IBM has released the WSFL specification, which deals with the choreography of Web Services. Previous work of the Workflow Management Coalition (http://www.WFMC.org) is less relevant, since it dealt mostly with document-based workflow and interoperability between these workflow engines, with very limited interaction models (chained and nested) in comparison to ebXML BPSS binary collaborations.

A modern BPMS needs to provide at its foundation a precise articulation between the **message flow**, **data flow**, and **control flow**. A business process is initiated by an event, which can be a business partner message or a timer event, for instance. In response, it initiates activities via the exchange of messages with other systems. When the activity completes, it sends a completion message to the BPMS. These messages usually contain data that makes up the data flow. Data is passed to activities, which in turn create new data or modify the existing data. The control flow specifies the production and consumption of the messages, which may be dependent either on the data flow as condition predicates on the content of documents or directly on the message flow itself.

Another key concept of a modern BPMS is the separation between **activities** and **services**. As we have seen, an activity is one of the steps that make up the business process definition. It is always carried out by an **activity performer** (user, system, or business partner). A performer is a physical entity, not a logical one, like an UML actor could be. Each performer offers a service, which is associated with an activity of the business process. There is a many-to-many relationship between activities and services. Sometimes, an activity may be implemented by multiple services since each performer may choose to implement the activity in a slightly different way. For instance, a (logical) activity could be dealing with "Process Purchase Order" while the corresponding (physical) services would be specialized, such as "Process an OAGI Process PO BOD over ebXML" or "Process a RosettaNet Purchase Order over RNIF2.0". This distinction is essential to bring the right level of decoupling in the architecture, and to select the physical implementation of an activity based on the context of the business process instance rather than hard code it in the business process definition. The indirection will typically be resolved at run-time via a performer profile. This capability enables us to change business partner profiles, or more generally, performer profiles, without affecting the business process definition.

The last set of semantics is relative to **transactions**. Unlike database transactions, business process transactions cannot lock resources for the duration of the business process. Hence, business process transactions cannot happen in isolation of their environment – they are said to be open. There is no general model in existence today to deal with transactions and business process state management. BPML is the most advanced in this direction. It is using some of the work that IBM pioneered. XLANG also provides some support for transactions.

*The use of a business process approach requires a change in the way we think about Object-Oriented Design when applied to business applications. A couple of years ago, I had seen an example on a leading ERP vendor's web site that illustrated the concept of a "business object". The example showed the "person" business object with "typical" business methods such as* `sendFax()`*, which is used when this person wants to send a fax to another person. This type of modeling is not very elegant because it couples three entities, which have little in common:*

1. *A business process participant ("person") which can either be a performer or a parameter you pass to a service*
2. *A business process activity ("sendFax") which is a service, maybe from the fax server itself*
3. *A document ("Fax"), which is part of the business process context*

*There is rarely any reason to associate a "fax" with the state of a "person", it rather belongs to the context of the business process. As a general rule, we should avoid adding business process state to business objects such as "person". This kind of business object should rather hold a profile and some form of "history", such as a purchase history or a HR history, which is part of its profile.*

*A better design is to use explicit business process objects, which enable the reuse of activities such as "sendFax" across any number of business process definitions. The parameters of this activity (documents to be transmitted, fax number of the recipient, etc.) should be looked up in the data flow of the business process instance. When you need to manage a lot of business process objects, a BPMS is a good idea.*

*A BPMS allows us to decouple "what do we do next" from "what do we do".*

# BPMS Key Technologies

XML, Web Services, and B2B middleware (such as ebXML) have been catalysts in the architecture of modern BPMS. The design of current products is already relying heavily on this trio.

At the first level, XML facilitates data exchange between systems and a BPMS. However, XML also provides a new perspective on information modelling, which fits in extremely well with the problem of modelling the context of a business process instance (the data required to keep track of the current state of the business process instance).

Web Services provide a common mechanism to interact with enterprise systems (local or remote) and match perfectly as an implementation of a logical activity. This promising technology is still in its infancy: some specifications and products exist today, but a lot of work remains to be done for a mainstream adoption of this technology.

Like Web Services on the enterprise system side, B2B middleware adds value to a BPMS because it isolates the details of the communication protocol used for any given partners. Some may have noticed that I do not consider Web Services as B2B middleware. I do not believe that in the current state of the Web Service specifications, this technology is viable to carry out business transactions. It does not have the semantics of ebXML, such as non-repudiation, guaranteed message delivery, or legally binding.

## XML

XML provides a generic way to exchange information regardless of platform, operating system, application, etc. The application of this technology has transformed traditional distributed computing models, which have evolved to a model now composed of network endpoints which consume or produce XML documents, in other words Web Services. However, XML is not just a data format like ASCII, it provides a clear advantage over other marshaling techniques because XML documents are both *extensible* and *semantically accessible*. Extensibility is pretty obvious since, by holding meta data and data, an XML document can be extended (adding new meta data and data) without necessarily breaking the initial document structure (that is, the ability to find existing information in the original data structure). Note that in order to be extensible, an XML document cannot be limited to any one schema. This is a new paradigm where unlike object instances bound to a class definition, XML documents may evolve freely from the schema that was used to create them. You might want to ask "*if you can freely add information, how do you find it?*" Well, this is when the second property comes into play: an XML document is also semantically accessible as opposed to structurally accessible like a C-structure or an object via its accessor methods. This was a very important concept in the now forgotten Objective-C. This is also partly why a Java reflection API was subsequently added into the language. In an XML document information may be queried or updated in a way that is relatively independent of the overall document structure (using relative XPath expressions for instance).

These two properties, though seemingly trivial, have significant implications on the behavior of XML network endpoints and Web Services in particular. They enable a level of decoupling between the requestor and the service provider, with no equivalent to date. For instance, additional information models may be supported by these network end points without impacting existing interactions, in the case where the owners of a network end point may not want to upgrade immediately to support a new information model. Furthermore, extraneous information could potentially be passed to, and pass through, a network end point without impacting its ability to operate. For instance, a style sheet may be applied by the service or the initiator of the service request itself, prior to processing the information. This ability is actually not supported formally in the current web service. Chained services may also add to an XML stream enabling dynamic chaining capabilities.

XML also provides a good information modeling capability and a set of technologies to handle the data flow of a business process instance. Earlier attempts in the workflow engine area had to deal constantly with data sources connectivity. Because it was difficult to integrate data sources, early designs were often reduced to manage the data flow as simple key-value pairs. On the other hand, today most data sources provide an XML gateway. Consequently, modeling a data flow as an XML document is going to make the integration with data sources or systems easier. An XML data flow provides a rich context to write business rules that govern the control flow of a business process definition. It supports natively the "document metaphor" which is common to all business process models. Lastly, XML can be easily transformed or queried with standard technologies (XSLT and XPath). Transformations are essential to a BPMS as it brings together software components, systems, partner systems that have been written independently of each other, without a common information model. As an XML document is semantically accessible, business rules and transformations may be expressed in a way that is independent of the overall document structure.

The fact that XML is extensible makes it the perfect technology to manage the context of a business process instance. Documents that participate in a business process may need to be extended to keep track of their life cycle (such as "a Purchase Order has been approved on a given date, by a specific person, with some comments"). This is actually key to the BPMS data flow: every document does not have a predictable lifec ycle. We can define what can happen to any document at any given time, but its life cycle depends on external events and conditions, which usually make the number of possible "states" for the document fairly large. XML, coupled with transformation technologies which trim these extensions whenever necessary, enables this paradigm almost natively.

The context of the business process instance needs to be persisted over long periods of time. There is a variety of ways to persist XML documents. There are native solutions, often referred to as XML databases. Relational database management systems provide some kind of XML adapter into their database but the storage of arbitrary XML document remains difficult. Some vendors do not even support attributes! Alternatively, some third-party vendors provide a complete XML layer on top of leading RDMS, performing the same kind of functionality as the native XML storage solutions.

Some BPMS vendors have chosen to manage the context of the business processes as XML but in memory. This is somewhat awkward since business processes typically run for days or weeks. This approach will clearly limit the scalability of their engine in terms of the number of processes they can manage. A better approach is to use caching when performance is needed, and transactional persistence when a process state changes rarely.

## B2B Middleware

Managing the business processes that interact with business partners is a high value add activity for a BPMS. The major issue is that by definition, a given organization has little control over the communication capabilities developed by its business partners. The least desirable approach is to have each partner develop an *ad hoc* communication system that your staff will have to deal with along with the several hundred other proprietary communication infrastructures of the remaining business partners.

The most desirable approach is to get all partners to use a well-defined communication protocol that supports all the semantics necessary to carry out any business activity without specific constraints to the users of this protocol (such as format of the documents, processes, etc.) ebXML is only one of them – the BizTalk Framework from Microsoft and the RosettaNet Implementation Framework (RNIF 2.0) are other possible choices.

It is unlikely that the market will be able to support more than one such communication protocol, simply because of the cost involved in maintaining interoperability and protocol gateways. Imagine if TCP/IP or HTTP did not have such a market share? It is likely that all the existing frameworks to date will ultimately merge into a single communication framework. For instance, the RosettaNet Consortium has expressed publicly that it plans to replace the RosettaNet implementation framework (RNIF 2.0) with ebXML. Other industry consortia, which deal solely with content and business processes have already publicly adopted ebXML as their infrastructure of choice (the Open Applications Group, ACORD, SWIFT to name a few).

The characteristic of a good implementation supporting such a communication framework is configurability. An implementation where business partner relationships would be encoded in a procedural manner would simply not scale to hundreds or thousands of partners, because the maintenance involved in the code would be horrendous. This points to one of the major contributions of ebXML, which had been originally identified by the ECO Framework back in 1999: Protocol Profiles and Protocol Agreements. As we will see in Chapter 8, a collaboration protocol profile (CPP) describes the capabilities of a given business partner with respect to a collaboration definition. This CPP can be published to an ebXML registry, and two CPPs may be composed to form a collaboration protocol agreement (CPA). A CPA contains all the information necessary to configure the B2B middleware. A CPA contains the technical details of the interactions such as transport, security mechanisms, whether guaranteed delivery or non-repudiation is required, and so on, as well as the document formats contained in the collaboration messages and the exact sequence of these messages.

Many commercial products are reaching maturity in this field. Most of them are actively working on an ebXML implementation. So, B2B middleware is both creating the need for a BPMS and impacting its architecture by isolating the BPMS from the details of the communication with business partners.

## Services

Services such as XML-based network end points are a necessary evolution towards highly-connected systems. One of the issues encountered with enterprise systems is the proliferation of APIs that are used to interact and transact with them. Even though component technologies such as CORBA, DCOM, or EJB have somehow simplified the integration work necessary for two systems to communicate, they have not specifically addressed the need to build communication systems which link hundreds or thousands of systems together. One of the shortfalls of this technology is a coupling between the end point (the component) and the API it provides. It also encourages the developer to implement very granular APIs with lots of method calls. Overall, these models have created systems that are brittle, and need a lot of maintenance on each side of the integration each time something changes on one of the sides.

In essence, the combination of XML documents as fully qualified arguments and services as network end points have provided a new way to design an API and evolve from a series of function calls or component invocations such as this:

```
foo(a,b,c)
component.bar(a,b,c)
```

into a Web Service invocation:

```
ServiceURI.invoke(operation,XML)
```

A service is actually a wrapper of an API as a combination of the **façade** and **command patterns**. Practically, a service call may be able to replace several if not dozens of function calls, in essence making the API simpler.

One of the key benefits of utilizing a global as opposed to local or proprietary naming service is that these network end points may be located anywhere without impacting the ability of a service consumer to find the service: a service is "mobile". It also enables us to dynamically discover services and interact with them without specific code, a broker, or supported knowledge. These concepts are not new: finding an object instance or a COM component has always been possible. What is new is leveraging the technologies of the Internet to do it. These technologies are so pervasive (compared to a given ORB); they enable service consumers to interact with services without much technological barrier.

A useful design guideline is to make the service stateless with respect to client invocations. Of course, a service may and should have an internal state (that could very well be its only value), but it should not maintain state between invocations. "Data rich" services are very important, since they can generate revenue for the corporation that owns the data. For instance, a corporate credit rating service would return the content of its database when a company name or identification number is provided.

Services are far less "brittle" than their function or component counterparts. A network end point may be easily physically relocated or made highly available with a clustering system. In addition, the invocation protocol may also support multiple input or output document formats, which enable the service to support new functionality without breaking existing relationships which is essential when hundreds of systems are "connected" to you and may not have the time or desire to upgrade their invocation mechanism when the service changes. This concept is, of course, not magic, and the price is often paid when parsing the XML document. Typically, the "document" would contain a variety of data, as well as processing instructions. To go back to our example, an *Insure shipment request* is a great example of such document. In one call, you pass hundreds of parameters and processing instructions.

Traditional APIs are designed to deal with tight integration between a few systems. Their usage simply does not scale when hundreds of application across company boundaries need to be integrated. Web Services are not just designed to solve this problem, but they prove extremely useful to address its requirements.

The major impact of a "Services-Based Architecture" is that it enables us to address the many-to-many problem of integrating disparate applications into a many-to-one, one-to-many approach. The figure below shows that if each application has a given API, then we need to integrate these applications two by two: each application is going to call the API of the other to achieve certain results. For instance, if we consider an order entry application which needs to integrate with 5 other enterprise systems locally and 100 systems in each of the company's customer. These 105 systems will have to know and invoke the Order Entry application API (if they can pass the firewall). Then, in order to be able to send back a confirmation, the order entry application will have to know and invoke the 105 different APIs. On the other hand, is we used a service-based approach, we can define a common information model (or always transform an application specific document format to a common information model). If we front end our 105 applications with a Web Service, we get the picture on the right, which creates $2N$ links as opposed to the picture on the left, which creates $N^2$ links.

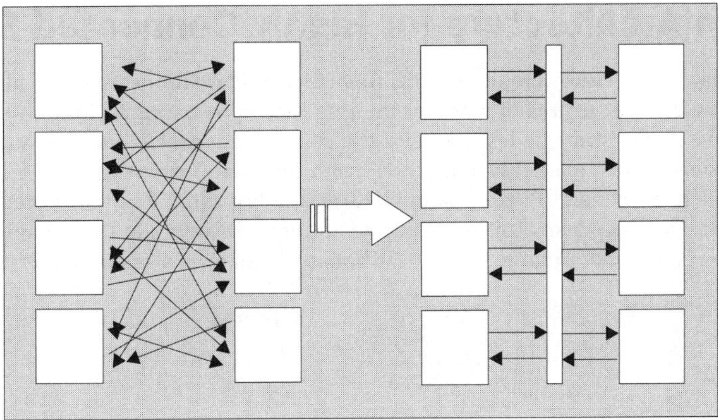

If we now plot the level of effort (in arbitrary time units) required for integrating *N* systems, the graphs are very eloquent:

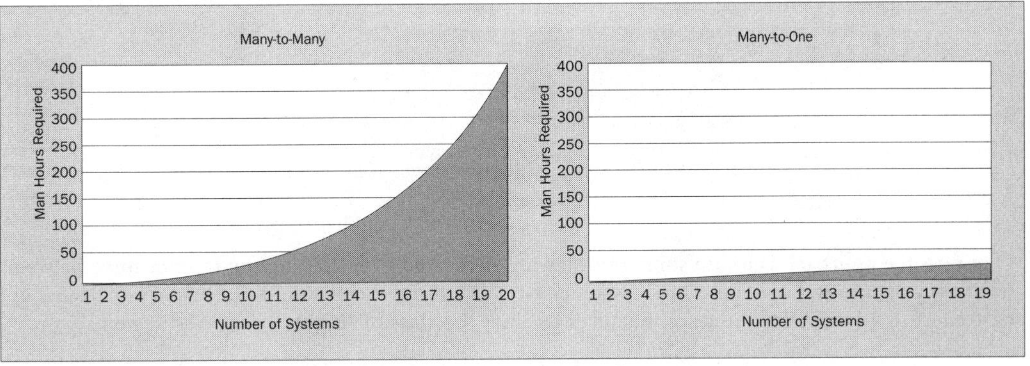


If we want a complete decoupling between the applications, the Web Services approach requires a broker that will find services, transform documents and deliver messages on behalf of an application. The broker can be based on a business process management system. On the other hand, services are extremely useful to the architecture of BPMS since they provide a fairly generic way to interact with any system that matches the key semantics of "activities" and "documents". The point we are making here is that it would be significantly harder to build a BPMS on the premises of traditional function-based or component-based APIs.

The software industry is already marching towards developing new products, which support this new evolution of distributed computing. It is supported by standards such as SOAP, UDDI, and WSDL, which are briefly reviewed in this book. If the development of the Web can teach us some lessons, the simplicity of the service concept will win the lion's share over the more sophisticated component model in the architecture of highly-connected systems.

# BPMS As an Architecture for Highly Connected Systems

Modern e-business architectures aim at establishing electronic relationships with all customers, channel partners, suppliers, etc., regardless of whether the relationship is based on human-to-server or server-to-server interactions. At the strategic level, one of the goals of this architecture should be to decouple the organization (business units, plants, systems, etc.) from the relationships (see the following figure). If your company is a large PC and Printer manufacturer, the last thing your customers (and suppliers) want to hear is they have to deal with two separate entities. However, at the organizational level, or with respect to the competition, it might make a lot of sense to create two separate entities.

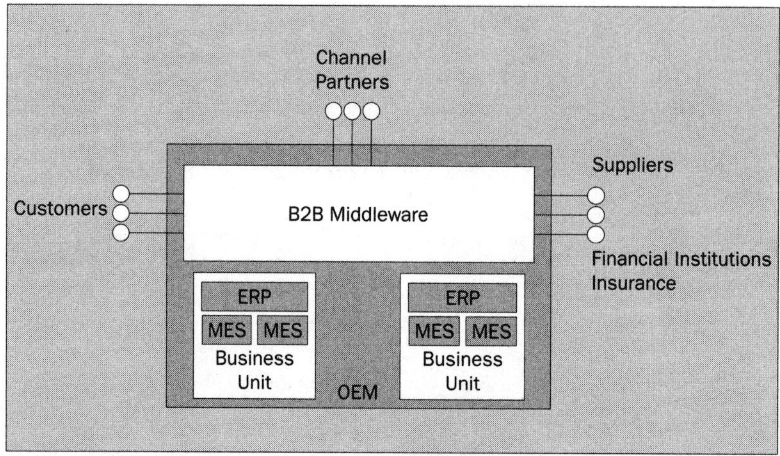


One possible approach is to use some middleware dedicated to managing the relationships between business partners and core enterprise systems. Because of the sheer number of business partners or customers involved, e-business architectures fall into the class of "highly connected systems".

## Architecture Requirements

The major barrier to implementing highly connected systems is not necessarily technology but rather cost. If you spend $100 (hardware, software licenses, labor, maintenance, support etc.) on each of the 2500 end points that we talked about in the introduction, you have already spent $2,500,000. And this is just for 100 business partners! The cost of such a project could easily run into several hundred million dollars for a given business community or industry. Even if this cost is not fully supported by a single corporation, the higher it is, the less likely it will be that the overall project will be successful, because partners will delay their decision to implement an expensive infrastructure. The complexity and technical risks will also be directly related to the cost of implementation, so the first and foremost principle of highly connected system architecture is to be **cost conscious**. The second, which is a corollary, is that it ought to be the **simplest possible**, but not simpler. The last principle of the architecture is that it has to be **fault-tolerant**. Within any given business community we cannot expect to have its partners up and running at all times with the correct configuration.

This problem is new, even in Internet times, and it may take a few years until a robust application model that deals with all its aspects and its complexity (mobility, scalability, security, business semantics, etc.) emerges.

It is also different from the traditional class of problems solved by EAI software. A lot of the EAI glue is dedicated to application synchronization within an enterprise. This glue is fairly static because the applications it ties together are also very static in nature with a well-defined API.

It is also significantly different from the problem of building large-scale web-applications supporting thousands of concurrent users, each doing personalized activities. In the B2B space, the problem is compounded by the fact that we are dealing with automated server-to-server interactions carrying out legally binding transaction and exchanging literally hundreds of types of events between each other. In the B2C space, a legally binding transaction merely results in a successful credit card transaction, which is equated to the will of the customer to purchase the selected goods at the given price, and most of the events can be related to a user pressing the checkout button.

## Highly Connected Systems

We now have everything at hand to introduce the architecture of highly connected systems (see the following figure). Not surprisingly, the core of the architecture is based on a Business Process Management System:

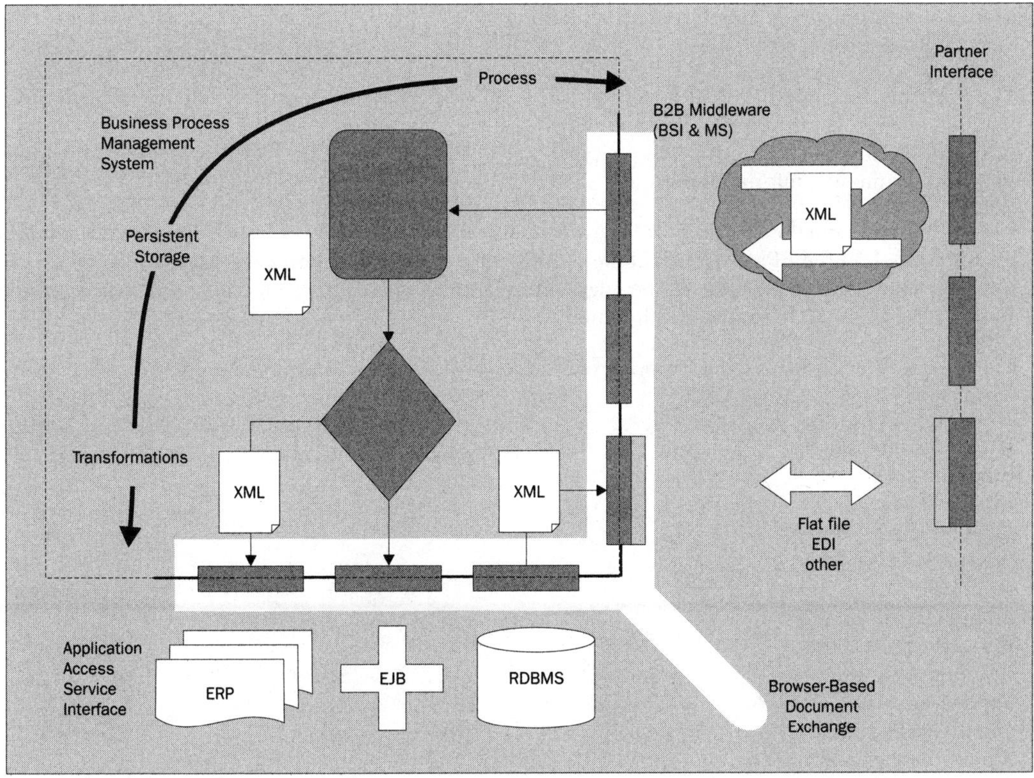


The BPMS acts as a bridge between an Application Service Interface (ASI) and the Business Service Interface (BSI). The ASI wraps all enterprise, legacy, and e-business applications into a set of Web Services. The BSI manages the interactions between executable business processes and the business partners. It provides a model of all the business partners, which can be used when resolving performers of activities.

Let's stop a moment and look at the role and importance of the BSI and an ebXML-based BSI. ebXML provides the most complete BSI specification to date compared to the one of XLANG (Port Maps) or WSFL (Global Models), which are the two other alternatives, as we will see in the following sections. Its openness enables us to model virtually any business interaction with any business partner. Without this modelling capability, the BPMS would have to support some of the semantics directly from the business process definition itself (for example, signals which would be implemented as a separate activity in the process definition). This would make it hard to scale the number of partners, simply because it would require a business process definition for each partner. A scalable BPMS should be able to handle all equivalent relationships with a single business process definition and a series of business partner profiles, which are used to establish the binding between activities and services at run-time.

Let's take an example where a business process definition involves interactions with two groups of partners out of five possible groups. If the BPMS architecture does not allow for this decoupling, and hard codes some of the communication protocol details into the business process definition, we could easily end up managing anywhere from 10 (5!/(3! x 2!) ) to 25 (5 x 5) slightly different business process definitions. If your BPMS manages one kind of business process, this might still be okay. If it manages 50 kinds of business processes, then it would be harder to deal with 1250 individual definitions. I have also seen the case where the URL of the participant is hard coded in the business process definition itself! I cannot imagine managing and maintaining 10,000 *Process purchase order* business process definitions, one for each supplier!

The third interface of a BPMS after ASI and BSI is browser-based document exchange. This is the paradox of automation: we can only automate if we are guaranteed that exceptions will be properly raised and resolved with the appropriate person or business partner employee approving a document, or filling out missing information.

The architecture should also support legacy formats such as EDI or flat files. However, data should only transit as XML in the BPMS as part of the business process instance contexts. All necessary transformations should be used on the edges of the architecture to go from and to other data formats, as well as from an XML format to another one.

Most products currently available on the market follow closely or loosely the model we just presented.

If we go back to the basic implementation model that we introduced in Chapter 5, we have now added a BPMS within the architecture to enable multiple applications (as opposed to one application) to be connected to a large number of partners using an ebXML infrastructure to communicate.

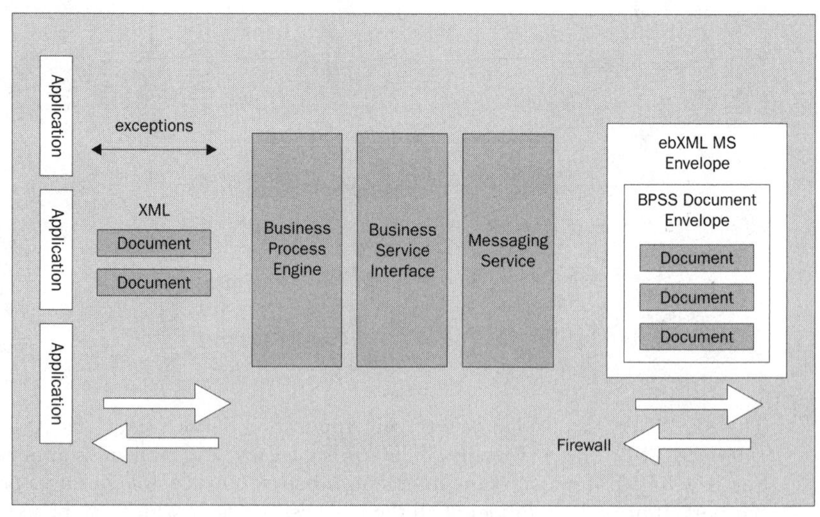

# An Introduction to WSDL

Before we go on and study the different Business Process Management System semantics, we will briefly look at the semantics of Web Services, because it is the basis of all three Business Process Definition Languages: BPML, XLANG and WSFL. If you are already familiar with this, just go to the last paragraph of this section (Web Service as a BPMS Unit of Work). We do not intend to explain in full details the semantics of Web Services – for a more complete view, look at Chapters 4 (*SOAP*) and 9 (*UDDI*), in this book, and take a look at *Professional Web Services* by Patrick Cauldwell *et al* (Wrox, ISBN 1-1861005-09-1).

Services already have well-developed specifications:

- SOAP: for the transport of information and communication infrastructure. Find the latest version of the W3C SOAP 1.1 note at http://www.w3.org/TR/SOAP/.
- WSDL: for the description of services being provided. See http://www.w3.org/TR/wsdl for the Specification.
- UDDI: for a directory of service providers and their respective capabilities that can be discovered by service consumers. Go to http://www.uddi.org to check out the Specification documents.
- XML Protocol (XMLP): this is a new effort from the W3C XML Protocol Group, which aims at building the next generation of RPC mechanisms to operate over the Internet. SOAP 1.2 is building on the work done by SOAP, WSDL, and UDDI. The latest version of the W3C Working Draft can be found at http://www.w3.org/TR/xmlp-reqs/ .

WSDL (Web Service Description Language) is the equivalent of **IDL** (Interface Definition Language) for distributed computing models (CORBA, DCOM). This XML grammar provides a formal framework to describe services in terms of protocols, servers, ports, and operations that can be invoked. It also includes input/output document formats, and the exceptions, which can be thrown by the service. WSDL is a joint proposal between Microsoft and IBM, now being worked on by the W3C as XML Protocol. The fundamental semantics of WSDL are as follows:

- `message`: A message is a potentially multi-part package of documents and context data that constitutes the unit of communication with a web service. Each part in a message is defined using some well-defined type system. The type system may be abstract and the wire format of the messages may not be defined by the type. Messages are in this sense abstract.
- `operation`: An operation is a basic interaction pattern supported by a Web Service. These are either one-way messages or request-response message pairs, with optional fault messages. Operations are defined in terms of incoming or outgoing messages with respect to the implementation of the service. Messages may be synchronous or asynchronous.
- `portType`: A port type is a named set of abstract operations, defined using abstract message types. For instance, in Java an `operation` would be a method, and a `portType` would be an interface.
- `binding`: A binding defines message format and protocol details for operations and messages defined by a particular port type. There may be multiple bindings for a given port type. The binding for a message defines the wire form of a message, typically in the context of a specific message format standard such as SOAP.
- `port`: A port is an externally visible target for a set of operations supported by a Web Service. A port minimally specifies a transport end point at which a binding is deployed.
- `service`: A (Web) Service is a group of related ports.

These relationships can be summarized in the class diagram below:

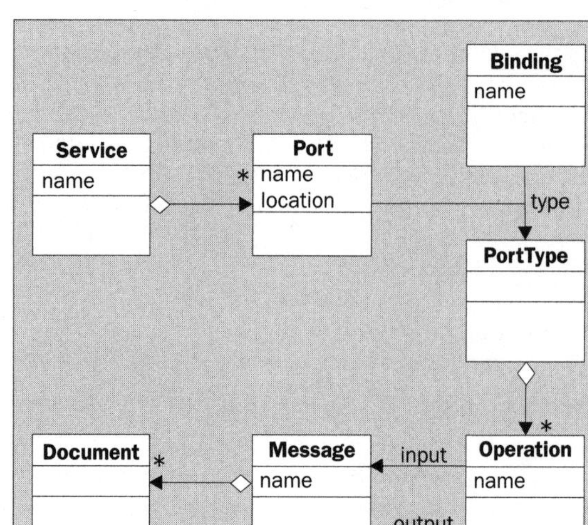


There are four basic types of operations relative to the request initiator or the service provider, which are summarized in the diagram below:

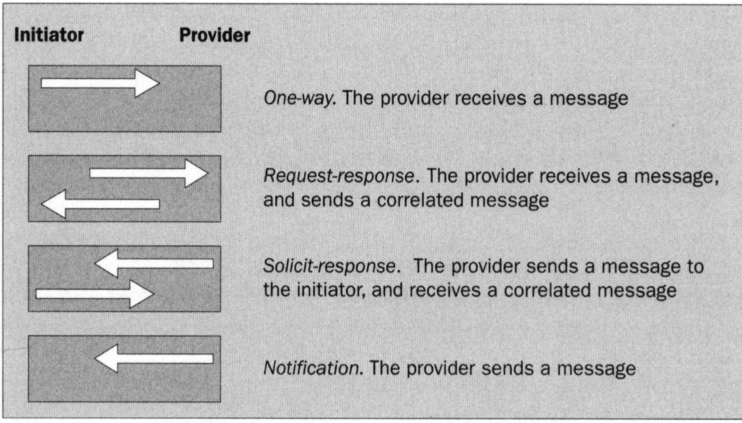


Let's take a simple example to show what a service definition looks like – we will look at the *Insure shipment* example. In this example, we will use SOAP binding – this example has no relation to ebXML; we are just expressing that documents can flow from company A to company B:

```
<definition
   xmlns:xsd="http://www.w3.org/1999/XMLSchema"
   xmlns:soap="http://schemas.xmlsoap.org/wsdl/soap/">

<!-- ******************************************************* -->
<!-- * Input, Output parameters                            * -->
```

```
<!-- ****************************************************** -->
   <message name="Msg:Insure shipment request">
      <part name="ISR" type="Ins_shp_req"/>
   </message>

   <message name="Msg:Contract">
      <part name="Contract" type="Contract"/>
   </message>

   <portType name="PT:Insure shipment request">
      <operation name="Op:Insure shipment request">
         <input message="Msg:Insure shipment request"/>
         <output message="Msg:Contract"/>
      </operation>
   </portType>

   <binding name="BD:SOAP:Insure shipment request"
         type="tns:Insure shipment request">
      <soap:binding style="document"
                transport="http://schemas.xmlsoap.org/soap/http"/>
      <operation name="O:Insure shipment request">
         <soap:operation soapAction="urn:InsuranceRequest"/>
         <input>
            <soap:body use="encoded"
             encodingStyle="http://schemas.xmlsoap.org/soap/encoding/"/>
         </input>
         <output>
            <soap:body use="encoded"
             encodingStyle="http://schemas.xmlsoap.org/soap/encoding/"/>
         </output>
      </operation>
   </binding>
   <service name="Srv:Insure shipment request">
      <port name="Pt:Insure shipment request"
            binding="tns:BD:SOAP:Insure shipment request">
         <soap:address
            location="http://www.YeOldInsurer.com/Request"/>
      </port>
   </service>
</definition>
```

## Exception Handling

WSDL specifies the exceptions thrown by a Web Service as faults. A fault is a message and is specified within the operation definition. The protocol used to raise the exception is specified in the <binding> element, just as it is for inputs and outputs.

For instance, we can add a fault to the previous example:

```
   <message name="Msg:Reject insurance request">
      <part name="Reject insurance request" type="reject_ins_req"/>
   </message>
```

```
...

<portType>
   <operation name="Op:Insure shipment request">
      <input message="Msg:Insure shipment request"/>
      <output message="Msg:Contract"/>
      <fault message="Msg:Reject insurance request"/>
   </operation>
</portType>

<binding name="BD:SOAP:Insure shipment request"
         type="tns:Insure shipment request">
   <soap:binding style="document"
            transport="http://schemas.xmlsoap.org/soap/http"/>
   <operation name="Op:Insure shipment request">
      <soap:operation soapAction="urn:InsuranceRequest"/>
      <input>
         <soap:body use="encoded"
          encodingStyle="http://schemas.xmlsoap.org/soap/encoding/"/>
      </input>
      <output>
         <soap:body use="encoded"
          encodingStyle="http://schemas.xmlsoap.org/soap/encoding/"/>
      </output>
      <fault>
         <soap:body use="encoded"
          encodingStyle="http://schemas.xmlsoap.org/soap/encoding/"/>
      </fault>
   </operation>
</binding>
</definition>
```

I don't want to go in to more details about WSDL and Web Services. I just want to illustrate that the semantics of WSDL and BPSS do not align very well. BPSS is both a communication protocol (signals, handshakes, etc.), and a "business interface" definition language. WSDL not match at all with the BPSS communication protocol, as WSDL and BPSS were designed to solve two very different problems (Remote Procedure Calls and Business Collaboration respectively). It just happens that they are both describing a choreography of message interchanges. Hence, all the messages used by a BPSS collaboration could be described by a WSDL definition.

We are now going to show how Web Services fits in with Business Process Management Systems before we pull together Web Services, collaborations, and BPMS.

## The Relationship Between Operations and BPMS Units of Work

An operation of a Web Service is a perfect match with the unit of work (that is, activity or action) of a BPMS: operations use "documents" as inputs or outputs – operations, like most activities of a business process, may be asynchronous, and are supported by an abstract definition, and various bindings. Consequently, a business process may be specified as a sequence of operation invocations:

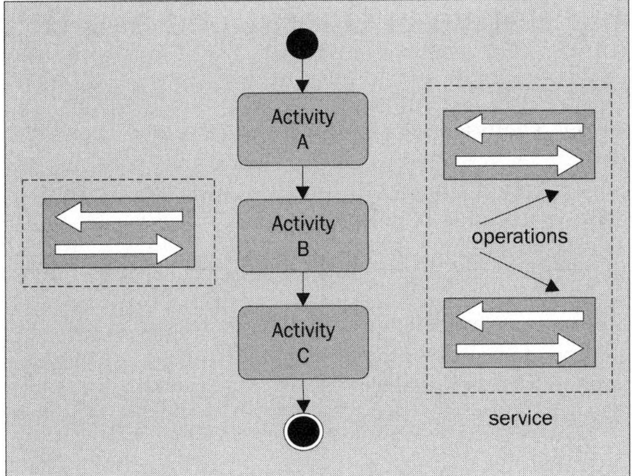


A business process may itself be wrapped as an operation, as part of a service. It is initiated with an incoming message (a one-way operation) and it may, as a result of the process execution, return an outgoing message (a notification):

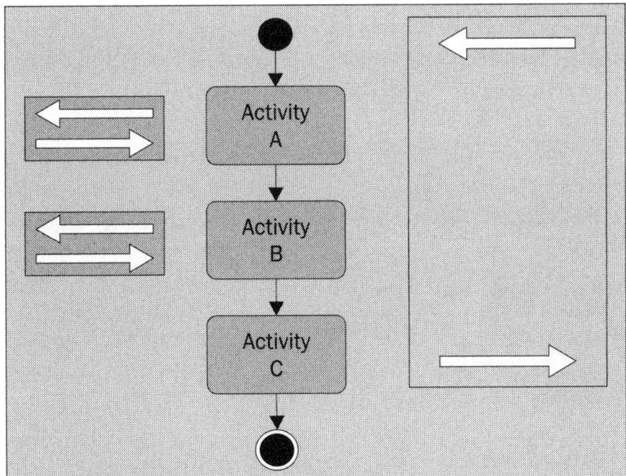


We have chosen a basic approach to illustrate the relationship between an activity and an operation in the diagrams shown above. There is more to the relationship of messages to a business process definition (as we will see in the next sections). A BPMS metamodel, which deals with the way to bring together message flow, data flow, and control flow, is still pretty much a work in progress. BPML, XLANG, and WSFL provide their own approach to that problem as we are going to see in the last part of this chapter.

## The Relationship Between Operations and BPSS Business Transactions

The mismatch between operations and BPSS business transactions originates from two sources:

- A business transaction is a complex exchange of messages (request, receipt, acceptance, response, receipt, notification of failure).
- A business transaction response is one out of many possible responses.

Several responses can actually be modeled with WSDL as "faults", as part of an abstract (that is without specific binding) `PortType`. This follows the design guidelines of a business transaction, where multiple possible responses are often used to signal exceptions (for example, Accept Order, Reject Order, Back Order, Order on hold).

We can consider two approaches to model the complex exchange of messages. The first one would be to create a specific binding with the ebXML communication protocol, just like the way in which WSDL supports a binding with SOAP. This protocol would have to be a combination of ebXML Messaging Service and BPSS.

Another approach is to wrap the **Business Service Interface** (**BSI**) into a set of services and operations. The BSI will implement the ebXML protocol and hide it from the BPMS perspective, operating as if business partners had a Web Service interface. In particular, the BSI will manage the correlation between business process instances and collaboration instances.

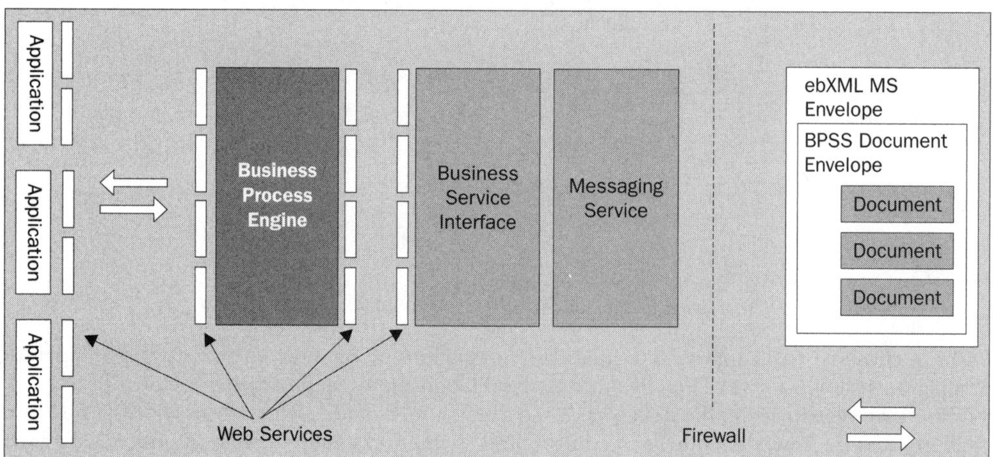


Yet another solution is to develop a BPMS metamodel, which supports both concepts independently: Web Services and business transactions. The BPMS metamodel would establish a direct relationship between all the business transaction model entities and the BPMS model entities. So far, it seems that no commercial product has decided to take that route. Most companies (such as Intalio, Inc. or Microsoft) are using an approach based on a Web Service only requiring a wrapper to the BSI layer as shown in the figure above. This approach serves as the basis for the following sections, which illustrate the binding between BPMS metamodel specifications and ebXML BPSS.

# Where Next?

Let's stop for a moment and look at where we are, and where we will go from here. We have learned that a company can be associated to a large automaton, ruled by a mighty business process management system that controls the lifecycle of *executable business processes* (xBP). The BPMS, if designed properly, helps connecting large number of business partners to the enterprise systems of the company. We have also learned that the communication between two automata (or companies) can and needs to be formalized as *externally observable actions.*

At the technical level, we have established that there is a good fit between the units of work of a BPMS and the operations of a Web Service. This extends to units of work running at or provided to a business partner, and to that effect ebXML business transactions can be wrapped into Web Service operations. I would like to stress that these operations are not external, since their URL is local, pointing to the BSI layer. The advantage of this approach is two-fold: Web Services do not have the necessary business semantics as of today, and furthermore, the logic of executable business processes is completely isolated from the semantics of ebXML such as signals, calculate business transaction failures, etc. The BMPS does not have to manage the details of the ebXML communication protocol; it only manages requests, responses, and exceptions, when they occur.

In the next three sections of this chapter we are going to "bind" ebXML BPSS to the three leading business process definition specifications (BPML, XLANG and WSFL). In other words, how can we define an executable business process definition, which will implement a given BPSS collaboration? Even if you are not planning to use any of these specifications, the following sections will still give you a solid introduction to the pieces necessary to implement BPSS in any kind of architecture.

# Binding Between BPML and BPSS

BPML business process definition is an ordered collection of activities: simple, complex, and process activities, as shown in this diagram:

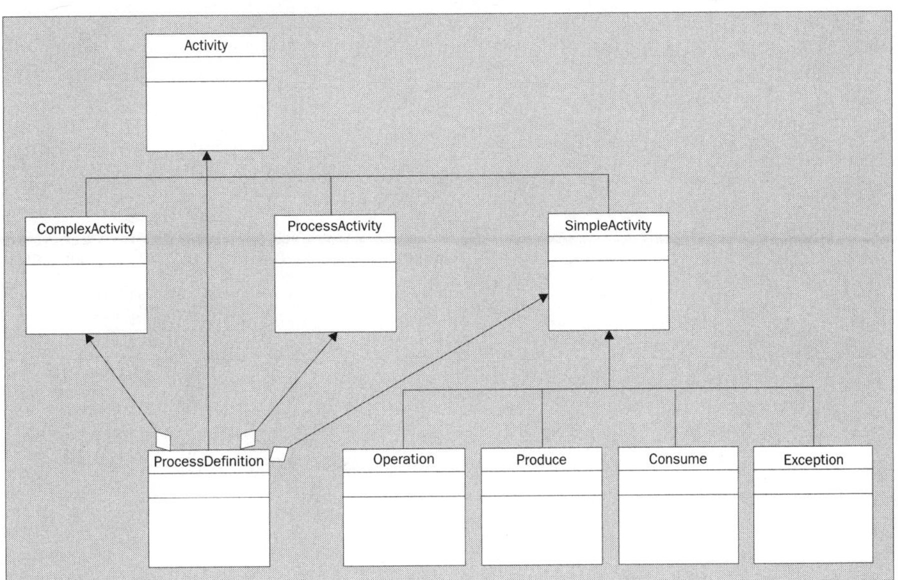

A complex activity is a collection of simple activities and complex activities. A process activity is an activity performed in the BPMS itself, such as a simple calculation.

There are four types of simple activities: **operation**, **produce**, **consume**, and **exceptions**. These types match precisely the classification of operations in WSDL since a **BPML:operation** can either be a WSDL request/response or solicit response operation, **BPML:produce** is equivalent to **WSDL:one way** and **BPML:consume** is equivalent to **WSDL:notification**. **BPML:exceptions** are associated with **WSDL:faults**.

Simple activities are made of messages (incoming and outgoing) that constitute the message and data flow of a business process:

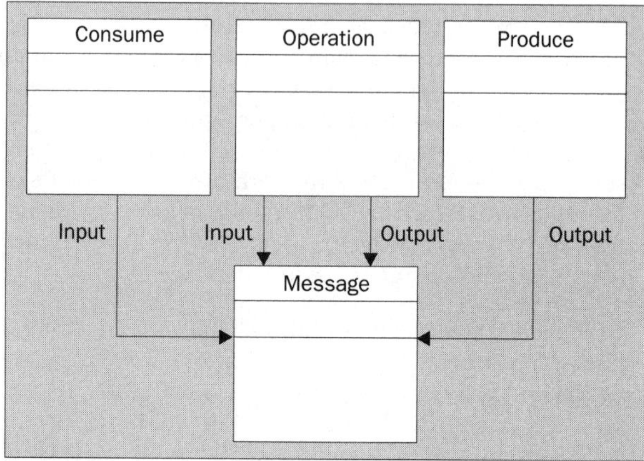


In BPML, messages are defined from the point of view of the BPMS and not necessarily from the point of view of the business partner, which sends or receives the message. Messages are abstract, just like in WSDL: nothing specifies their origin or destination.

Complex and process activities represent the control flow of the business process definition:

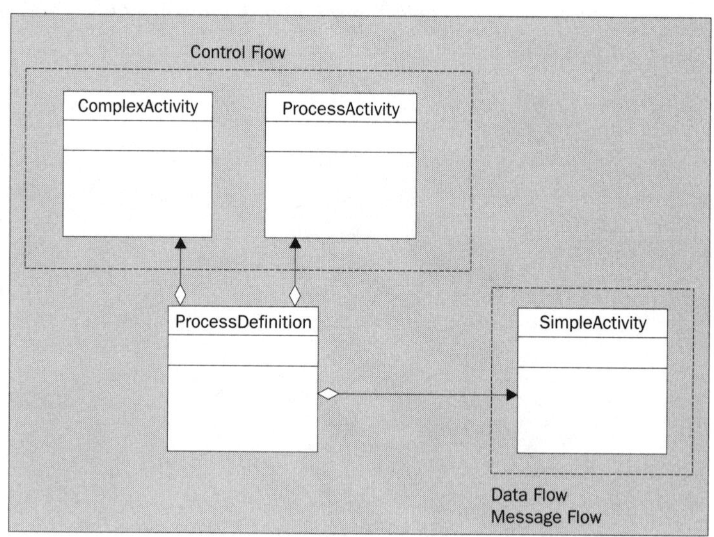

The binding between a process definition and a collaboration definition happens at two levels:

- The simple activity level, which deals with messages and their data content
- The complex activity level, which supports collaboration sequencing rules

So, now let's specifically look at these three levels of binding: Message, Data and Control flow binding.

# Message Flow Binding

We are looking at binding the collection of simple activities that involve the same participant with which the BPMS collaborates, to the business transaction activities of a BPSS binary collaboration definition (see figure below). BPML provides the concept of an **abstract** to group these activities in a single entity. Abstracts are used to model views of processes supported by participants, or to define reusable views of a process with regard to one or more participants.

An abstract need not be complete and may omit information that is not relevant outside the context of interaction with its participants.

A process can declare it supports one or more abstracts. This is actually the essence of a business process definition: a business process is a collection of collaborations between a role represented by the BPMS and any number of participants, which can be users, systems, or business partners. All simple activities can be associated with a given collaboration.

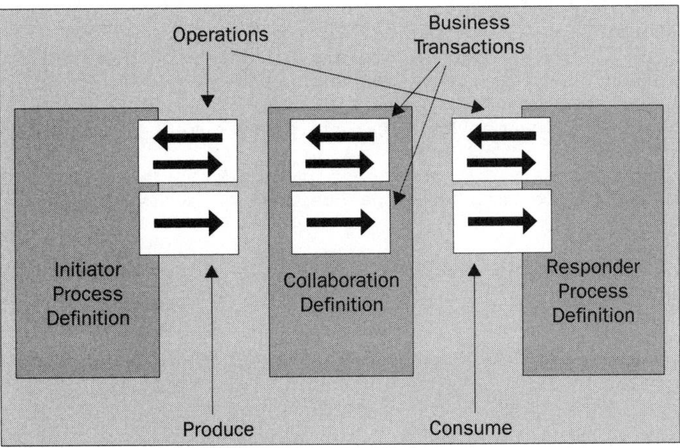


Consequently, an abstract is the representation of a particular collaboration from the perspective of the BPMS. A BPSS collaboration does not have any point of view; it merely represents the shared view of the message interchanges between two roles. A process definition may support as many abstracts as necessary, and one role may support more than one abstract.

There is no need for an abstract to model the sequencing rules of its collaboration. It is merely a series of simple activity definitions that will be sequenced within the process definition as complex activities. The process definition sequencing rules turn out to be substantially different from the collaboration sequencing rules. In the process definition, other activities, with specific and internal sequencing rules, will be interleaved with the simple activities that participate in the abstract. These internal activities and sequencing rules are completely independent from the collaboration definition.

An abstract definition is very simple – an example is provided below:

```
<abstract name="Ab:Insure shipment request" timeToPerform="2D">
   <message name="Msg:Insurance request" type="request"/>
   <message name="Msg:Contract" type="response"/>
   <message name="Msg:Reject insurance request" type="response"/>

   <operation name="Op:Insure shipment request">
      <input message="Msg:Contract"/>
      <output message="Msg:Insurance request"/>
   </operation>
   <exception name="Exc:Reject insurance request"
      <input message="Msg:Reject insurance request"/>
   </exception>
</abstract>
```

BPMI is currently working on a binding framework specification for ebXML, as well as other standards such as RosettaNet. There is no vocabulary or meta model that has been specified yet. The following example is just a tentative illustration of what a binding may look like:

```
<?xml version="1.0"?>
<! DOCTYPE "BPMLBinding.dtd" >

<!-- We are binding the abstract to the BPSS collaboration -->
<Bindings abstract="Ab:Insure shipment request" version="1.0">
   <Binding name="PlatinumCusotmers" type="ebXML:acord">
   <MessageBinding collaboration="CB:Insure shipment request"
               uri="http://Acord.org/…/InsuranceReq.xml">
      <operation name="Op:Insure shipment request">
         <input message="Msg:Contract">
            <ebBPSS:DocumentEnvelope BusinessDocument="BD:Contract"/>
         </input>
         <output message="Op:Insure shipment request">
            <ebBPSS:DocumentEnvelope BusinessDocument="BD:Insurance req"/>
         </output>
      </operation>
      <exception message="Exc:Reject insurance request">
         <ebBPSS:DocumentEnvelope BusinessDocument="Reject insurance req"/>
      </exception>
   </MessageBinding>
   <TimeToPerform duration="7D"/>
   <DataBinding>
      ...
   </DataBinding>
   <ProtocolBinding>
      <ebXMLProtocol>
         ...
      </ebXMLProtocol>
   </ProtocolBinding>
   <ParticipantRole name="Buyer"/>
   </Binding>

   <Binding name="RegularCustomers" type="ebXML:acord">
      <MessageBinding ref="CB:Insure shipment request"/>
      <TimeToPerform duration="30D"/>
      <ProtocolBinding>
         <ebXMLProtocol>
            ...
```

```
            </ebXMLProtocol>
        </ProtocolBinding>
        <ParticipantRole name="Buyer"/>
    </Binding>
</Bindings>
```

Note that, as in this example, several bindings may exist for the same (abstract or collaboration) association. This is a key design decision in the metamodel of a given BPMS, since this is what is going to relate participant profiles to the way the business process definition really behaves at run-time, once the performer of an activity is identified. BPML allows for both static and dynamic participants, therefore taking advantage of multiple possible bindings, one for each group of participants. A static participant is defined as part of the business process definition, whereas a dynamic participant is "passed" to a business process instance at run-time.

The fact that several bindings can be associated to a given abstract is essential in the architecture of highly connected systems. Within a large community of business partners, when a new version of a standard is available, it is unlikely that all partners will upgrade their systems at the same time. However, if they upgrade to a new format (such as OAGIS v8.0) or a new communication protocol (such as ebXML 2.0) it is also likely that a given business process definition will still be applicable, so only its binding will need to be updated. Ultimately, any given process definition which involves collaborations with business partners will have to support multiple bindings. 80% of these bindings are likely to be relative to different business document versions.

## Data Flow Binding

Data flow is a very important concept in BPMS systems. We have seen earlier that XML enables the modeling of the context of a business process instance as a set of structured documents. These are extensible, as the various activities of the business process operate on the documents, and semantically accessible, which enable the definition of business rules or transformations into participant format which are somewhat decoupled from the structure of the document itself. BPML is one of the first business process standards, which truly takes advantage of an XML data flow.

The binding is done via the concept of **assignment**. Assignments work both ways, with the information collected from or communicated to participants. The example below shows an 'Insure shipment request' document appended with the status value of the response document. It also shows that an 'Insure shipment request' could be created from the 'Purchase order' document, which was created as part of a previous activity and is now part of the business process context.

```
<abstract name="Ab:Insure shipment request" timeToPerform="2D">
   <message name="Msg:Insure shipment request" type="request">
      <xsd:element name="InsuranceRequest" type="acord:InsReq.dtd"/>
   </message>

   <message name="Msg:Contract" type="response">
      <xsd:element name="Contract" type="acord:Contract.dtd"/>
   </message>
   <operation name="Op:Insure shipment request">
      <input message="Msg:Contract"
         <!-- append request document with response from insurer -->
         <assign target="Contract/Accepted"
                 select="InsuranceRequest/Status"/>
      </input>
```

```
        <output message="Msg:Insure shipment request">
           <!-- Create request from purchase order -->
           <assign select="Msg:Purchase order"
                   target="Msg:Insure shipment request"/>
        </output>
     </operation>
  </abstract>
```

We have also added the message format definition. We have chosen an ACORD (http://www.acord.org/) format for the request and the response. These formats represent the internal format used by the BPMS to store its context. This format may itself be bound to various formats, maybe different versions of the ACORD specification or other standards such as OAGIS, xCBL, which all have a purchase order document. The data binding is specified at the document level, since documents may be reused over different messages within several collaborations. Let's take a look at what a document format binding (or data binding) looks like. Again, this is not part of BPML; it is just an illustration of what could be part of BPML.

```
<?xml version="1.0"?>
<! DOCTYPE "BPMLBinding.xsd" >
<Bindings abstract="Ab:Insure shipment request"
          version="1.0">
   <Binding name="PlatinumCusotmers" type="ebXML:ACORD">
      <MessageBinding name="CB:Insure shipment request">
         ...
      </MessageBinding>
      <TimeToPerform duration="7D"/>

      <DataBinding>
         <message ref="Msg:Insure shipment request">
            <ebBPSS:BusinessDocument ref="BD:Insure shipment request"/>
            <transformation uri="http://.../tsf/InsReq_ACORD_1_2.xslt"/>
         </message>

         <message ref="Msg:Contract">
            <ebBPSS:BusinessDocument ref="BD:Contract"/>
            <transformation uri="http://.../tsf/Contract_ACORD_1_2_.xslt"/>
         </message>
      </DataBinding>

      <ProtocolBinding>
         <ebXMLProtocol>
            ...
         </ebXMLProtocol>
      </ProtocolBinding>
      <ParticipantRole name="Buyer"/>
   </Binding>
   <Binding name="RegularCustomers" type="ebXML:OAG">
      ...
   </Binding>
</Bindings>
```

# Control Flow Binding

In this section, we are going to explore the rules that map collaboration sequencing rules into complex activities and BPML transactions. This section is based on the BPML specification, available at www.bpmi.org/. What we are going to do here is create a business process definition, the control flow of which supports the collaboration document envelope (that is, message) choreography.

Complex activities provide facilities to model (in parentheses, I have indicated the corresponding BPML tag names):

- Sequences of activities (`Sequence`).
- Activities happening in parallel (`All`).
- Conditional process branching (`Switch`).
- Conditional participant branching (`Choice`).
- Repeat of activities over a set of entities (`ForEach`).

An activity can either be a complex process, or simple activity. A conditional process branching is based on the information contained in the business process instance context – for instance, "if a shipment amount is greater than $10,000, it requires a manual approval process for the insurance contract". A conditional participant branching is a decision taken by a participant and communicated to the process instance as a message. For instance, an 'insure shipment request' order may be accepted or rejected by the insurer. This decision is communicated as part of a message to the buyer business process instance.

Time constrains may be associated to any activity as part of the control flow of the business process definition.

BPML, XLANG, and WSFL are among the few business process specifications to support transactional semantics – the Workflow Management Coalition (WfMC) does not support these semantics. In the business world, transactions are significantly different from database transactions. The traditional **ACID** (**Atomic, Consistent, Durable, Isolated**) properties of a database transaction are difficult to implement in real world business transactions. The major issue is the isolation of a database transaction. This property requires resource locking which is impractical in the business world. It would also preclude users from participating in a business process.

BPML supports two transaction models: **coordinated** and **extended**. They both provide an "all-or-nothing" guarantee for complex interactions between multiple participants. In a **coordinated transaction**, all participants agree to either complete the transaction or abort it. This model relies on a two-phase commit protocol and is also known as a closed, flat transaction due to its ability to support isolation. The **extended transaction** model relaxes the isolation requirement. There are two possible modes of recovery for such a transaction: backward recovery, where the transaction initiates some compensating activities that will cancel the effects of the failed transaction, and forward recovery, where the business process instance is allowed to continue its execution taking into account that the transaction failed. Compensating activities are used wherever the execution of an activity cannot be rolled back (such as when an order is shipped). These transactions are also known as open-nested transactions or *Sagas.* This model supports transaction interleaving with arbitrary nesting; in other words, a transaction may be composed of other transactions.

BPML transactions operate with users, partners, and systems without discrimination. They do not impose limits on duration and survive hardware or software failures.

Control flow binding is somewhat arbitrary, in the sense that somebody has to sit down and make decisions taking into account not only the collaboration, but also the internal context in which this collaboration will be executed. The best we can do is to establish production rules to transform a collaboration definition into the skeleton of a business process definition that only features those activities that involve the partner role of the collaboration. We may also develop an algorithm that takes an arbitrary business process definition and creates a collaboration definition for a given role.

If we take the example of Chapter 5, 'Insure shipment RFQ':

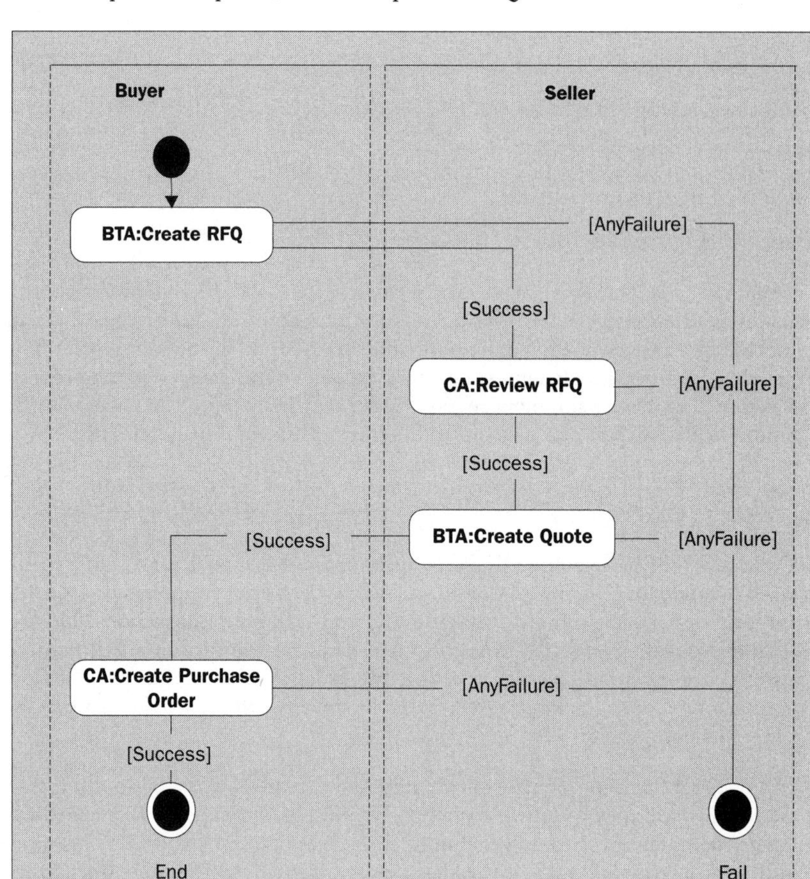


The corresponding BPML definition that supports this collaboration may look like this:

```
<abstract name="Insure shipment RFQ">
   ...
</abstract>
<process name="Ship Order">
   <supports abstract="Ab:Insure shipment RFQ"/>
   <sequence name="main">
      <completedBy duration="P10D"/>
      <operation name="Create RFQ">
         <participant select="insurer"/>
         <output message="Msg:RFQ">
         <input message="Msg:Accept RFQ">
            <assign target="RFQ_Status"
                    select="$(Msg:Accept RFQ)//Status/text()"/>
         </input>
      </operation>
      <exception code="TechnicalFailure">
```

```
         <complete/>
      </exception>
      <consume>
         <participant select="seller"/>
         <input message="Msg:Reject RFQ">
            <assign target="RFQ_Status"
                    select="Accept RFQ/Status/text()"/>
         </input>
      </consume>
      <switch>
         <case condition="[RFQ_Status='OK']">
            <!-- could have some internal
                 activities defined here -->
            <sequence name="reviewRFQ">
               ...
            </sequence>
            <otherwise>
               <complete/>
            </otherwise>
         </case>
      </switch>
   </sequence>
</process>
```

The review RFQ activity is a complex activity, which corresponds to this part of the collaboration (taken from Chapter 5):

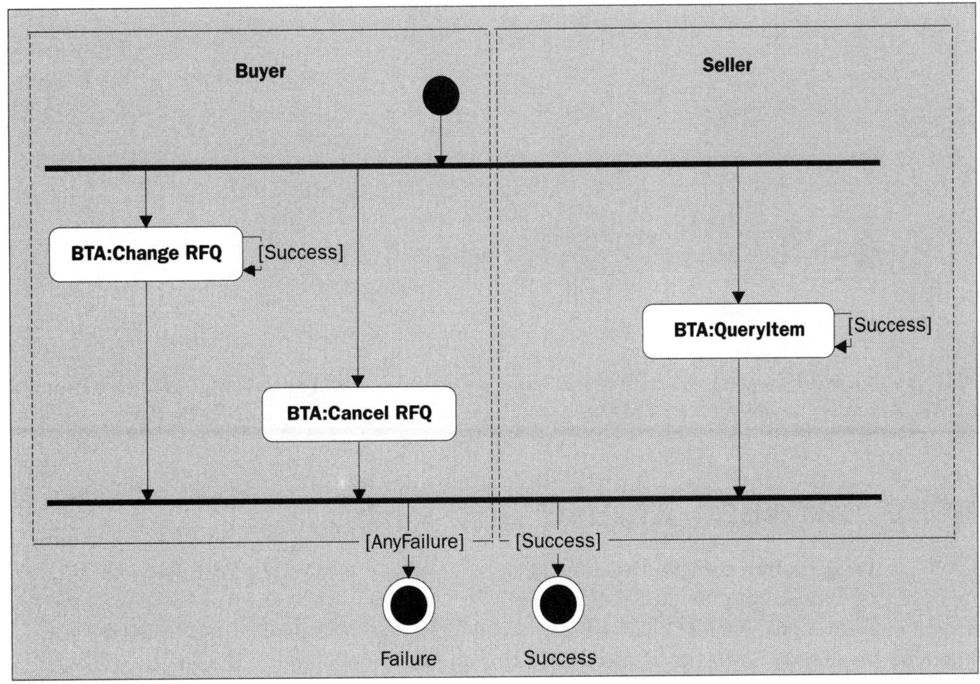

The corresponding code is as follows:

```
<process>
   <sequence name="reviewRFQ">
      <all>
         <sequence name="Change RFQ">
            <!-- Internal operation goes here -->
            <operation name="Change RFQ">
               <participant select="insurer"/>
               <output message="Msg:Change RFQ"/>
               <input message="Msg:Change Acknowledgement"/>
            </operation>
         </sequence>

         <sequence name="Cancel RFQ">
            <!-- Internal operation goes here -->
            <operation name="Cancel RFQ">
               <participant select="insurer"/>
               <output message="Msg:Cancel RFQ"/>
               <input message="Msg:Cancel Acknowledgement"/>
            </operation>
         </sequence>

         <sequence name="Query Item">
            <consume>
               <participant select="insurer"/>
               <input message="Msg:Query Item"/>
            </consume>
            <!-- Internal operation goes here -->
            <produce name="Response">
               <participant select="seller/">
               <output message="Msg:Response"/>
            </produce>
         </sequence>

         <exception code="TechnicalFailure>"
            <complete/>
         </exception>
      </all>
   </sequence>
   ...
</process>
```

BPML is still a work in progress. The consortium is currently working toward a precise binding to ebXML. Actually, the design of BPML metamodel is taking into account ebXML BPSS.

# Binding Between XLANG and BPSS

XLANG (www.gotdotnet.com/XLANG.htm) is an extension of WSDL, the Web Service Definition Language. It provides both the model of an orchestration of services as well as collaboration contracts between orchestrations. XLANG, like BPML, was designed with an explicit $\pi$-calculus theory foundation (see earlier, in the *$\pi$-calculus* section, for an introduction to this theory) .

## Message Flow

Actions are the basic constituents of an XLANG process definition. The four types of WSDL operations (**request/response**, **solicit response**, **one way**, and **notification**) can be used as XLANG actions. However, XLANG adds two other kinds of action: **timeouts** (deadline and duration) and **exceptions**. Timeouts cannot be properties of specific actions as they may apply to an arbitrary block of actions. Timeouts should be viewed as the action of sending a timeout event to the BPMS.

A process definition is specified within a service definition. The XLANG process definition specifies the behavior of the service. A service with a behavior represents an interaction spanning many operations; the incoming and outgoing operations of the XLANG service represent interactions with other services, therefore sequencing the operations of a given service is equivalent to orchestrating a series of services. The interaction has a well-defined beginning and end.

Since the interaction may be long running, a given service may initiate many different "process instances" based on the request of different clients. An instance can be started in two ways. A service may be explicitly instantiated by a background process or some application functionality or it may be implicitly instantiated with an operation. Each time the service receives a message corresponding to this operation, it will create a new business process instance. This operation is called an activation operation (in this case, the `activation` attribute has a value of `true`). Such an action must be an input with respect to its operation within the service definition. A service instance terminates when the process that defines its behavior ends.

For instance, a *purchase order service* may have two operations; one initiated by the buyer, which itself activates a process instance, and one initiated by the seller which, once completed, marks the end of the process. Here is the XLANG definition expressing that both operations happen one after another:

```
<XLANG:sequence>
   <XLANG:action operation="Op:Insure shipment RFQ" activation="true"/>
   <XLANG:action operation="Op:Insure shipment request"/>
</XLANG:sequence>
```

XLANG specifies the notion of **message correlation**. BPMI is currently working on that specific issue and it should be part of the final BPML specification. Let's look further into message correlation.

A service instance typically holds one or more conversations with other service instances representing other participants (users, enterprise systems, partners) involved in the interaction. It is possible that an enterprise system or a partner is not set up with a communication protocol that keeps track of the conversation. For instance, the only way to identify a given process instance might be to look up the purchase order or the invoice number. Sometimes, correlation patterns can become even more complex. The scope of correlation is not, in general, the entire interaction specified by a service, but may span a part of the service behaviour.

XLANG implements message correlation by providing a very general mechanism to specify correlated groups of operations within a service instance. A correlation set can be specified as a set of properties shared by all messages in the correlated group. The corresponding set of operations (in a single service) is called a correlation group. A correlation group would typically correspond to a BPSS collaboration. Whenever possible, it is better to keep track of the "collaboration ID" at the protocol level (ebXML protocol that is) rather than at the document level, even if XLANG allows you to work with data elements such as *Purchase Order Number*, which are inherently dependent on the document format. If the correlation is specified at the ebXML envelope level, the service which binds a collaboration to the business process just needs to keep track of all the open collaborations with their respective collaboration ID. An XLANG collaboration group has the same life cycle as an ebXML collaboration:

- Correlation groups are instantiated and terminated within the scope of their service instance. Correlation groups may go through several instantiations within the lifetime of a single service instance.
- The instantiation of a correlation group is triggered by a specially marked operation.
- The correlation group instance lifetime is determined by the lifetime of its context or service.

For instance, in our insure shipment request example, the correlation ID could be the purchase order number (for which the shipment is organized):

```
<correlation name="InsuranceRequestKeys">
   RequestProps:PONumber ContractProps:PONumber
</correlation>

<action operation="receiveQuote"
        correlation="PONumber QuoteNumber"
        correlationBegin="PONumber"/>
```

## Data Flow

Just like BPML, XLANG relies on an XML data flow, which is fed by the message flow and supports the control flow decisions. XLANG assumes that XML document types are specified with XML Schema (XLANG does not support DTDs). A property is bound to an element of an XML document with an XPath statement.

The following is an example of a property definition inside the 'Insure Shipment Request' schema:

```
<complexType name="InsureShipmentRequest"
xmlns:po="http://www.openapplications.org/OAGIS/v7.2/003_process_po_007.xsd">

   <annotation>
      <appInfo>
         <XLANG:propertyDef name="OrderNumber" path="//PONUMBER"/>
      </appInfo>
   </annotation>
   <element name="PONUMBER" type="string"/>
   <!-- Other elements of the Insure shipment request -->
</complexType>
```

Properties have globally unique qualified names (QNames). Properties may be either simple or structured. Simple properties are used mainly for correlation, while structured properties are used for passing port references and participant bindings for constructing dynamic participant topologies.

## Control Flow

The control flow of BPML is very similar to that of XLANG. Elements such as <sequence>, <switch>, and <all> have a similar meaning. In addition, XLANG provides support for looping with the <while> element, which specifies that a given fragment of the process definition is executed until a specified condition is no longer true. This is particularly useful to support ebXML collaboration patterns such as review or modify which may have recurrent business transactions.

Like in BPML, XLANG provides semantics to specify exceptions and exception handlers, with the <pick> construct:

```
<pick>
   <eventHandler>
      <action operation="Op:RejectInsuranceRequest"/>
      <sequence>
         <!-- add line item to order -->
         ...
      </sequence>
   </eventHandler>
</pick>
```

XLANG has introduced the notion of a context for local declaration of correlation sets and port references, exception handling, and transactional behaviour. A context provides and limits the scope over which declarations, exceptions, and transactions apply.

XLANG supports open transactions, but unlike BPML, it does not support coordinated transactions. XLANG transactions follow the model of long-running transactions, which are associated with compensating actions in case the transaction fails.

Since BPML and XLANG have nearly identical control flow, the XLANG business process definition, which supports our 'Insure shipment RFQ' collaboration, is similar to the BPML one we have built. As in the case of BPML, we recommend wrapping a BSI layer into a series of *services* rather than trying to map to business transactions and signals directly. The handshake is too difficult to implement at the business process definition level, because signals are not related to a unit of work – they are merely events, which represent the state of the unit of work.

One possible approach to write an XLANG process definition based on a collaboration definition is to write an XSLT that will translate an ebXML binary collaboration definition into a WSDL service definition. This definition becomes the basis of a collaboration XLANG process definition.

So let's go back to our 'Insure shipment RFQ' . Here is an example of the process definition of the Seller request for insurance:

```
<definitions name="Insure shipment RFQ"
             targetNamespace="http://example.com/rfq/initiator"
             xmlns:tns="http://example.com/rfq/initiator"
             xmlns:XLANG="http://schemas.microsoft.com/biztalk/XLANG/"
             xmlns="http://schemas.xmlsoap.org/wsdl/">

   <!-- An XLANG definition starts just like a service definition
        messages, portTypes, bindings, service. The service
        element contains the XLANG process definition -->

   <message name="Msg:Create RFQ">
      <part name="RFQ" type="acord:CreateRFQ"/>
   </message>

   <message name="Msg:Accept RFQ">
      <part name="AcceptRFQ" type="acord:AceptRFQ"/>
   </message>
```

```
<message name="Msg:Reject RFQ">
   <part name="RejectRFQ" type="acord:RejectRFQ"/>
</message>

<message name="Msg:Change RFQ">
   <part name="ChangeRFQ" type="acord:ChangeRFQ"/>
</message>

<!-- all other message definitions go here -->

<portType name="PT:Create RFQ">
   <documentation>
      This port sends the Insure shipment RFQ to the insurer
   </documentation>
   <operation name="Op:Create RFQ">
      <output message="Msg:Create RFQ"/>
      <input message="Msg:Accept RFQ"/>
   </operation>
   <operation name="Op:Reject RFQ">
      <input message="Msg:Reject RFQ"/>
   </operation>
</portType>

<portType name="PT:Review RFQ">
   <documentation>
      This port sends implements the RFQ review process
   </documentation>
   <operation name="Op:Change RFQ">
      <output message="Msg:Change RFQ"/>
      <input message="Msg:Change Acknowledgement"/>
   </operation>
   <operation name="Op:Cancel RFQ">
      <output message="Msg:Cancel RFQ"/>
      <input message="Msg:Cancel Acknowledgement"/>
   </operation>
   <operation name="Op:Query Item">
      <input message="Msg:Query Item"/>
      <output message="Msg:Respond Query"/>
   </operation>
</portType>

<!-- For the business transaction failures, we have two possibilities,
     1. add fault messages to all operations corresponding to
        business transaction failures
     2. Have an independent port type in charge of notifying the
        failure mode of the current operation, as shown below -->

<portType name="Failures">
   <documentation>
      This port receives failure notifications from the BSI component
   </documentation>
   <operation name="Technical Failure">
      <input message="Msg:Technical Failure"/>
```

```
      </operation>
      <operation name="Business Failure">
         <input message="Msg:Business Failure"/>
      </operation>
      <operation name="Time Out">
         <input message="Msg:Time Out"/>
      </operation>
   </portType>

   <!-- All the binding information goes here. We can assume that the BSI
        will be implemented to support SOAP on the BizTalk side, just like
        it does on the ebXML side -->
   <binding name="Create RFQ Binding"
            type="tns:Create RFQ">
      <!-- details omitted -->
   </binding>

   <binding name="Review RFQ Binding"
            type="tns:Review RFQ">
      <!-- details omitted -->
   </binding>

   <binding name="Failures Binding"
            type="tns:Failures">
   <!-- details omitted -->
   </binding>

   <!-- Here is the XLANG:behavior definition inside the service definition
     -->
   <service name="Process RFQ">
      <!-- please note that the URL of the BSI is local, the BizTalk server
           running the XLANG definition does not talk directly to the
           business partner, the BSI acts as an adapter, an ebXML
           adapter that is -->

      <port name="port:Create RFQ" binding="tns:Create RFQ">
         <soap:address location="http://BSI:2901/processrfq.jsp"/>
      </port>

      <port name="port:Review RFQ" binding="tns:Review RFQ">
         <soap:address location=" http://BSI:2901/processrfq.jsp"/>
      </port>

      <port name="port:Failures" binding="tns:Failures">
         <soap:address location=" http://BSI:2901/failures.jsp"/>
      </port>

      <XLANG:behavior>
         <XLANG:body>
            <XLANG:sequence>
            <!-- actions which lead to the preparation
                 of the RFQ go here -->
               <XLANG:action operation="Op:Create RFQ"
                             port="port:Create RFQ" activation="false"/>
```

```
            <!-- even though Create RFQ is the first observable action
                 between the buyer and the seller, it is not the action
                 that would have initiated the service -->

            <all>
               <XLANG:action operation="Op:change RFQ"
                             port="port:Review RFQ" activation="false"/>
               <XLANG:action operation="Op:cancel RFQ"
                             port="port:Review RFQ" activation="false"/>
               <XLANG:action operation="Op:Query Item"
                             port="port:Review RFQ" activation="false"/>
            </all>
            <pick>
               <eventHandler>
                  <XLANG:action operation="Op:Reject RFQ"
                             port="port:Create RFQ"/>
                  <!-- process completes -->
               </eventHandler>
               <eventHandler>
                  <XLANG:action operation="Op:Technical Failure"
                                port="port:Failures"/>
                  <!-- process completes -->
               </eventHandler>
               <eventHandler>
                  <XLANG:action operation="Time Out"
                                port="port:Failures"/>
                  <!-- process completes -->
               </eventHandler>
            </pick>
         </XLANG:sequence>
      </XLANG:body>
   </XLANG:behavior>

   </service>
</definitions>
```

There is often an issue when specifying the outgoing port addresses: it is rarely possible to know in advance the address of the outgoing message. XLANG allows us to specify that the address bound to these outgoing ports will be supplied dynamically. As with the correlation set, we are confronted with the problem of locating this information in the content of documents. In ebXML, the reply address is part of the Collaboration Protocol Agreement, which can be found at run-time in the participant profile. XLANG enables us to bind the address (and other parameters if necessary) to a property definition on a document. If this mechanism is more generic, it is also trickier, since it will strongly depend on the document formats, which may not have been designed to support the corresponding information. For instance, a purchase order will carry the contact information of the buyer, but it may not carry the URL to which the "acknowledge purchase order" should be sent. In general we recommend treating the ebXML header as a document and assigning all correlation sets and binding parameters to the ebXML header whenever possible. I would also recommend bringing the corresponding CPA within the business process instance context in order to leverage its information at run-time.

## Business Process Contracts

This part of XLANG overlaps with ebXML BPSS. However, unlike their name would suggest, contracts do not support any business-related semantics. It is merely a mapping between two port types that interact together. There is no notion of business transaction, non-repudiation, or legally binding transactions. The concept is actually fairly difficult to use in real life since the two port types need to support unidirectional messages in order to establish a contract. Consequently, if your business relationship requires a request followed by a response, they cannot belong to the same contract. A contract can only map ports that are "unidirectional": an input-only port will map to an output-only port and vice versa:

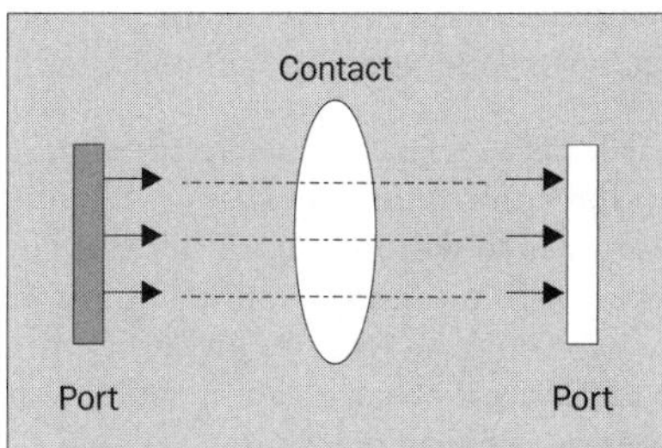


In the rare cases where this is applicable a contract definition would look like this:

```
<XLANG:contract>
   <XLANG:services refs="provider:Create RFQ
                        user:Create RFQ
                        provider:Accept RFQ
                       user:Accept RFQ"/>
   <XLANG:portMap>
      <XLANG:connect port="provider:Create RFQ/port:GetRFQ"
                     port="user:Create RFQ/port:SendRFQ"/>
      <XLANG:connect port="provider:Accept RFQ/port:SendAcceptRFQ"
                     port="user:Accept RFQ/port:GetAcceptRFQ"/>
   </XLANG:portMap>
</XLANG:contract>
```

## Binding Between WSFL and BPSS

The Web Services Flow Language (WSFL), is an XML language for the description of Web Services compositions as part of a business process definition. It was designed by IBM to be part of the Web Service technology framework and relies on and complements existing specifications like SOAP, WSDL, XMLP and UDDI. WSFL considers two types of Web Services compositions:

- The first type specifies an executable business process known as a `flowModel`.
- The second type specifies a business collaboration known as a `globalModel`.

The unit of work in WSFL is an **activity** – activities represent nodes in a linked graph. The `dataLink` and `controlLink` represent the data flow and the control flow between these activities. A `dataLink` specifies that its source activity passes data to the flow engine as part of the process instance context, which in turn has to pass (some of) this data to the target activity of the `dataLink`. Data always flows along `controlLinks`. However, the `controlLink` path does not have to be direct and can comprise multiple activities. The `dataLink` enables the specification of a mapping between a source and a target document if necessary.

If we go back to the π-calculus section, activity is associated with the concept of action. Once the corresponding activity is complete, the process instance reaches a given state. At this point another action may be triggered automatically based on the transition definition, and a new activity may start. A transition may be guarded by a condition, expressed as a function of the data flow. Events are associated with completion messages of an activity's operation, or can be an individual message (notification).

There is at most one `controlLink` between any two activities and the model must be a cyclic, therefore forbidding loops within the control flow. However, the model supports recurring activities using an exit condition mechanism, which will loop until the exit condition becomes true. The control flow model supports forks (activities with more than one outgoing transition) and joins (activities with more than one incoming transition). Activities with no incoming transitions are called start activities; similarly, activities with no outgoing transitions are called end activities. When a flow model is instantiated, all of its start activities are determined and scheduled.

One goal of WSFL is to enable Web Services as implementations for activities of business processes. Each activity is associated with a service provider responsible for the execution of the process step. This relationship defines the association between activities which participate in the control flow and operations offered by the service provider. Activities correspond to nodes in a graph. Thus, an activity can have an input message, an output message, and multiple fault messages. This is how the message flow is specified. Each message can have multiple parts, and each part is further defined in some type system. This is the binding between the message flow and the data flow.

If we take our *Insure shipment RFQ* example again, here is the corresponding WSFL executable business process (from the Seller perspective). This example is based on the same WSDL definition that was created for XLANG:

```
<flowModel name="Insure shipment RFQ" serviceProviderType="RFQPublic">

  <serviceProvider name="SP:Insurer" type="tns:insurer">
    <locator type="static" service="www.YeOldInsurer.com"/>
  </serviceProvider>

  <serviceProvider name="SP:local" type="seller"/>
  <!-- This activity is completely local, and its purpose is to
      create the RFQ that will be sent to the insurer -->
  <activity name="Create RFQ">
    <input message="tns:RFQ"/>
    <performedBy serviceProvider="SP:local"/>
    <implement>
      <internal serviceProviderType="SPT:RFQPrivate"
            portType="PT:RFQManagement"
            operation="Create RFQ">
        <plugLink>
          <source serviceProviderType="SPT:RFQPrivate"
                portType="PT:RFQManagement"
                operation="selectBook"/>
```

```
                <target serviceProviderType="SPT:someCicsTransactions"
                        portType="PT:cicsy" operation="T123"/>
            </plugLink>
         </internal>
      </implement>
   </activity>

   <!-- Activities relative to the collaboration -->
   <activity name="Send RFQ">
      <output message="Msg:Send RFQ"/>
      <input message="Msg:Accept RFQ"/>
      <fault message="Msg:Reject RFQ"/>
      <performedBy serviceProvider="SP:Insurer"/>
      <implement>
         <export>
            <target portType="PT:Send RFQ"
                    operation="Op:Send RFQ"/>
         </export>
      </implement>
   </activity>

   <activity name="Change RFQ">
      <output message="Msg:Change RFQ"/>
      <input message="Msg:Accept Change RFQ"/>
      <fault message="Msg:Reject Change RFQ"/>
      <performedBy serviceProvider="SP:Insurer"/>
      <implement>
         <export>
            <target portType="PT:Manage RFQ"
                    operation="Op:Change RFQ"/>
         </export>
      </implement>
   </activity>

   <activity name="Cancel RFQ">
      <output message="Msg:Cancel RFQ"/>
      <input message="Msg:Accept Cancel RFQ"/>
      <fault message="Msg:Reject Cancel RFQ"/>
      <performedBy serviceProvider="SP:Insurer"/>
      <implement>
         <export>
            <target portType="PT:Manage RFQ"
                    operation="Op:Cancel RFQ"/>
         </export>
      </implement>
   </activity>
   <activity name="Query Item">
      <input message="Msg:Query Item"/>
      <output message="Msg:Response Query"/>
      <performedBy serviceProvider="SP:Insurer"/>
      <implement>
         <export>
            <target portType="PT:Manage RFQ"
                    operation="Op:Query Item"/>
         </export>
      </implement>
   </activity>

   <activity name="Create Quote">
      <input message="Msg:Create Quote"/>
```

```
      <output message="Msg:Accept Quote"/>
      <fault message="Msg:Reject Quote"/>
      <performedBy serviceProvider="SP:Insurer"/>
      <implement>
         <export>
            <target portType="PT:Send RFQ"
                    operation="Op:Send Quote"/>
         </export>
      </implement>
   </activity>

   <!-- Now we need to write the control flow between all the activities -->

   <controlLink source="Create RFQ" target="Send RFQ"/>
      <!-- Fork -->
   <controlLink source="Send RFQ" target="Change RFQ"/>
   <controlLink source="Send RFQ" target="Cancel RFQ"/>
   <controlLink source="Send RFQ" target="Query Item"/>
      <!-- Join to Create Quote activity -->
   <controlLink source="Change RFQ" target="Create Quote"/>
   <controlLink source="Cancel RFQ" target="Create Quote"/>
   <controlLink source="Query Item" target="Create Quote"/>

   <!-- and the data flow between all the activities -->
   <dataLink source="RFQ" target="Quote"/>
   <dataLink source="Create RFQ" target="Send RFQ"/>
</flowModel>
```

## WSFL Global Models

As we have seen, WSFL provides a facility to model interactions between business partners: the **global model**. Notice that, as in the case of XLANG, a global model is merely a mapping between inputs and outputs. Business semantics (such as non-repudiation, quality of service, legally binding, etc.) cannot be specified by a global model. Fortunately, WSFL collaborations are a bit more useful than XLANG contracts, since it enables mapping with bi-directional services.

```
<globalModel name="Manage RFQ" serviceProviderType="RFQ">
   <serviceProvider name="SP:Insurer" type="insurer">
      <locator type="static" service="www.YeOldInsurer.com"/>
   </serviceProvider>

   <serviceProvider name="SP:local" type="seller">
      <export>
         <source portType="lifeCycle"
                 operation="spawn"/>
         <target portType="lifeCycle"
                 operation="buy"/>
      </export>
   </serviceProvider>
   <plugLink>
      <source serviceProvider="SP:local"
              portType="PT:Manage RFQ"
              operation="Op:Send RFQ"/>
      <target serviceProvider="SP:Insurer"
              portType="PT:processRFQ"
              operation="Op:getRFQ"/>
   </plugLink>
```

```
    <plugLink>
      <source serviceProvider="SP:local"
              portType="PT:Manage RFQ"
              operation="Op:Change RFQ"/>
      <target serviceProvider="SP:Insurer"
              portType="PT:processRFQ"
              operation="Op:receiveChangeRFQ"/>
    </plugLink>
    <plugLink>
      <source serviceProvider="SP:local"
              portType="PT:Manage RFQ"
              operation="Op:Cancel RFQ"/>
      <target serviceProvider="SP:Insurer"
              portType="PT:processRFQ"
              operation="Op:receiveCancelRFQ"/>
    </plugLink>
    <plugLink>
      <source serviceProvider="SP:Insurer"
              portType="PT:processRFQ"
              operation="PT:Query Item"/>
      <target serviceProvider="SP:local "
              portType="PT:Manage RFQ"
              operation="Op:receiveQueryItem"/>
    </plugLink>
    <plugLink>
      <source serviceProvider="SP:Insurer"
              portType="PT:processQuote"
              operation="Op:Create Quote"/>
      <target serviceProvider="SP:local "
              portType="PT:Manage Quote"
              operation="Op:receiveQuote"/>
    </plugLink>
  </globalModel>
```

# Summary

Together ebXML (and the ebXML BPSS), ebXML Core Components and Business Process Definition languages such as BPML, XLANG, and WSFL are creating the foundation for the next generation of IT infrastructure, enabling large scale flexible dynamic connectivity of the enterprise to its environment. The architecture of BPMS, supported by XML data flows, Web Services and B2B middleware constitutes a new application model based on a declarative programming environment where business logic is clearly separated in services (which perform the actions), and business rules (which make up the control flow). In this new model, actions can be quickly composed in new business processes. Furthermore, there is a layer of abstraction between activities, and services that enable the resolution at run-time of the unit of work that will be effectively initiated. The technology of BPMS is still a work in progress: most of the specifications are not yet finalized, and very few products exist today on the market; those that do are for the most part only at version 1.0. The BPMI.org member list provides an excellent source of vendors that currently offer or will offer a BPMS.

All three business process definition standards that have been discussed here are well on track to provide a complete set of semantics to describe executable business processes. ebXML BPSS complement each one of them by providing the most complete business partner interaction semantics. Business modelers and developers can take advantage of these formalisms to develop robust and scalable B2B solutions.

To implement BPSS, we have proposed a layered architecture based on an Application Service Interface (ASI), a Business Process Management Systems (BPMS), and a Business Service Interface (BSI), with a Web Service interface. The BSI relies on a Messaging Service layer for the transport, routing, and packaging of ebXML-compliant messages. The key is to develop a configurable business service interface, which manages and enforces collaborations, hiding the details of the interactions to the business process management system. If the number of collaborations that your company needs to support is small, the BPMS layer may be omitted or hard coded as components with your favourite application server, until more mature products appear on the market.

# 7

# ebXML Registry/Repository

The purpose of this chapter is to provide an introduction to a technology involved with the search for, storage of, and retrieval of business artifacts – the **ebXML Registry/Repository Specifications**. The chapter's intent is not to duplicate or simply summarize the available specifications and white papers, but rather to provide the reader with an overview of the technology and a discussion of how to implement it. It is assumed that the majority of readers will be interested in interfacing to a registry/repository, or procuring and installing one, rather than building one of their own.

> *For those who would like to program a registry or repository themselves we recommend that you study the specifications and participate in the related development efforts discussed later in the chapter.*

The ebXML specifications' goals are that of creating a platform-independent open registry/repository for housing the description and facilitating the exchange of business artifacts, and discovering businesses via collaboration profiles. The registry contains the descriptions of these business artifacts (like the index of a book), and the repository actually stores them (like the book's actual content).

Firm knowledge in this area is critical for programmers who are making the journey towards a full ebXML implementation, as a good solid registry/repository is essential for any worthwhile ebXML venture. However, ebXML's concepts of reusability and interoperability of business data can be fully realized only when the registry/repository elements are in place and in service. The ebXML Registry/Repository work is being enhanced at the time of this writing within OASIS, and these current shortcomings will be addressed in future versions of the specifications. There are two parts to the current specification:

- Registry Information Model v1.0 – provides information on the type of metadata that is stored in the *Registry* as well as the relationships among meta data. The relationships are industry ontologies providing a structured coded vocabulary, making a significant enhancement to current glossary-based mechanisms.

- Registry Services Specification v1.0 – defines the communication functionality of the Registry using the ebXML Messaging Service and an ebXML client (application), including query management and security aspects. The real power of the services is exposing new and interesting data – especially where that data is dynamic and where perhaps you may not know the answer beforehand.

Both can be found at http://www.ebxml.org/specs/index.htm#technical_specifications.

In this chapter we will look at:

- The registry and repository Use Case
- The benefits of a Registry-centric architecture
- Itemizing critical work leading to the specifications
- An overview of a Registry interface
- Tool suites, with examples of interface code and transformations
- The future of ebXML Registry/Repository work and possible enhancements

# Introduction To ebXML Registry/Repository

The **ebXML Registry/Repository** provides a set of services that enable sharing of information between interested parties for the purpose of enabling business process integration between such parties based on the ebXML specifications. The shared information is maintained as **Business Information Objects** (**BIOs**) in an **ebXML Repository** and is managed by the **ebXML Registry Services**. The repository item is used to refer to an object that has been submitted to a Registry (where meta data is 'registered' about the item) for storage and safekeeping (for example, an XML document or a DTD). Every repository item is described by a `RegistryEntry` instance.

A comparison of a registry/repository can be drawn to a library, where you first look at a book catalogue (be it on a computer or in paper format). After discovering the book you are interested in (via author name, title, ISBN, etc.), you are then directed to the physical book on the bookshelves. As shown in the following figure, the registry enables *discovery* and the repository enables *retrieval*:

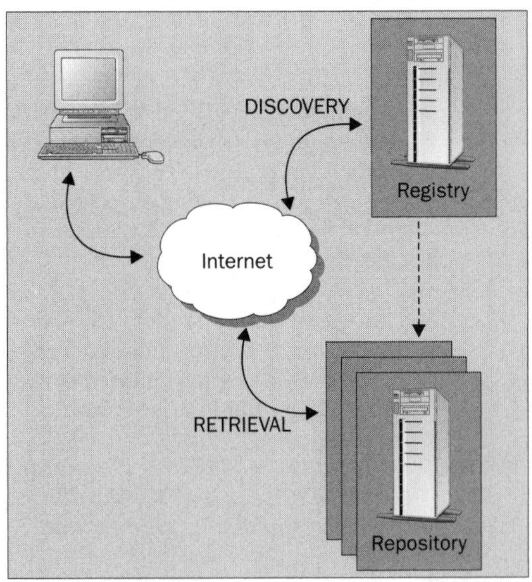

# Why Have a Separate Registry and Repository?

This is a question frequently asked by those learning about the architecture of the ebXML Registry/Repository, with another following closely on its heels: "We already have a repository – do we now need another?"

The answer to the second question is simple – no. In many cases, a repository exists prior to implementing ebXML. Metadata is already being captured and managed to some degree within the organization. It could be a database, a configuration management system, a version control mechanism, a modeling library, ERP, a content management system, or an in-house project. To implement ebXML it is only necessary to add a registry to the existing system, and not duplicate the existing repository with yet another housing facility for meta data.

The reason for separating registry from repository came about because at the time that the specifications were being developed, OASIS was building a repository for schemas – clearly ebXML wasn't defining the requirements for that, but something new. For e-business, the resolution of the store needed to be much higher, to meet the requirements of the most atomic business logical unit, and message/document-level registration would not have met such objectives. The initial technical objectives of the OASIS repository was never intended to meet the requirements of electronic commerce, but to capture the large array of schemas being developed. The initial OASIS repository, and the BizTalk repository were both at the resolution of the transaction or document, and not focused on core components. So, it came to be that the ebXML Registry would sit above the document repository, with the repository being able to handle *any* business artifact. The types of business artifacts required for e-business are detailed later in the chapter.

As implementers moved forward, incorporating ebXML technology into legacy systems, they discovered that what could have easily become a monolithic service design, where one component handles all tasks (registration of entities such as core components, and the storage mechanism for supporting information, for example, business process definitions) would have been inflexible for real use. A two-part solution with registry and repository is a perfect match for meeting real-world constraints, such as:

- Implementing ebXML within a organization with an install base of an existing repository, either product or in-house development
- Accessing multiple repositories

We'll see the latter point in action in the next two sections, where we'll look at further advantages of having the registry and repository as separate entities.

## Distributed Repositories

The two-part solution was applicable to other issues being faced by the workgroup. For example, it was always envisioned that content stakeholder (3rd party content sources) requirements (such as the DISA.org Repository) would be built into the ebXML specifications; these types of content source could be numerous. The registry became the answer to discovering these repositories – a mechanism through which the user would navigate. If a content owner wanted to charge for access to business artifacts, the registry would be the means to uncover the resource, with control being passed to the appropriate repository in which fees would be charged. The two-part solution was clean, and provided scalability to the architecture.

## Information Services

From an ebXML standpoint there are two ebXML workgroups, **Registry/Repository** and **Transport, Routing and Packaging (TRP)**, whose output specifications manifest themselves as software components. Other workgroups exist, that define content types to be stored in the registry/repository, and used, either by humans or the TRP during design and/runtime. The TRP Specification takes care of communication requirements, whereas the Registry/Repository Specifications take a general-purpose approach to handling the requirements of the other working groups – the registry/repository, due to its nature, needs to be a universal storage and management system.

In addition, during the requirements phase of ebXML, the registry/repository group recognized the need to provide **information services**. TRP constitutes one of these information services, and thus it was assumed that the Registry/Repository Working Group would address other services required for global e-business. Such services, as identified in the following figure, are workflow, transformation, logging, key (UID), search, indexing, and other middleware type services:

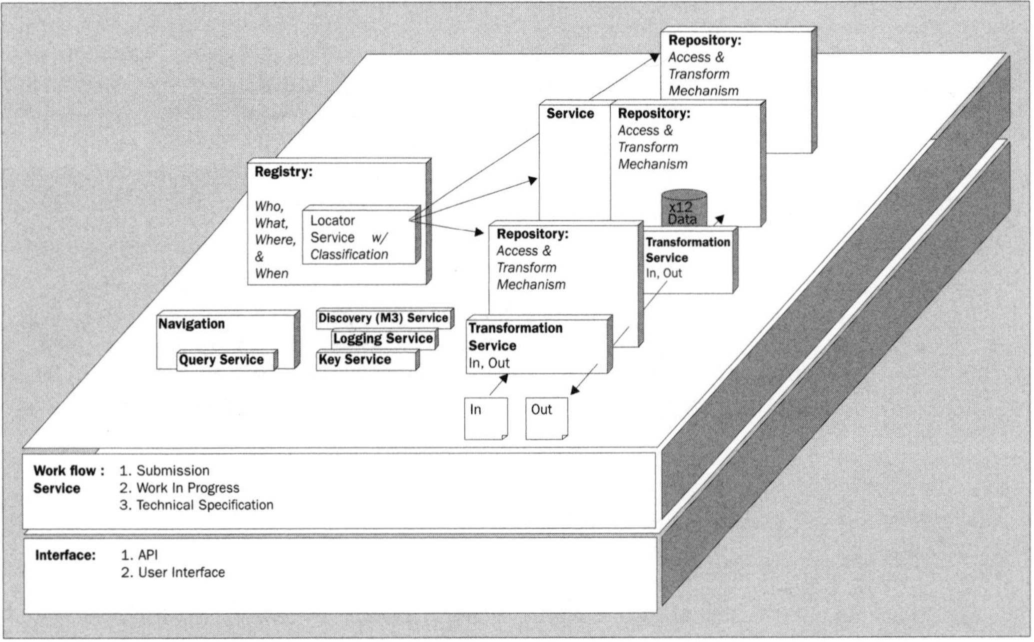


The thought at the time, which still remains today, was that these services would be modular and optional depending on business requirements. As shown, the registry/repository is simply a set of services with two interfaces: API and user interface. The services would add value, so each vendor could choose to incorporate them into their products in order to be competitive. Both of the tools discussed later in the chapter have done just this – they extend the base ebXML Registry functionality and thus prove that the workgroup assumption that a modular approach would be required was true. Perhaps you can think of other services that could be included (a collaborative notification service perhaps)?

# Why Use an ebXML Registry/Repository?

Now we have seen why ebXML defines a separate registry and repository, perhaps the most important question you will be considering is "what can an ebXML Registry/Repository do for me and my organization?" This self-centered question is the correct one to ask when dealing with the option of any technology – there needs to be a real business case in order to justify going ahead with any development work. Implementing a registry or interfacing to an external registry/repository can be an expensive undertaking, and the decision may well depend on the number of business artifacts deemed worthy of registering.

Other questions you might ask include "does the concept of managing my enterprise's meta data concern me, and if so, why? What are the likely returns on investment in time and other resources?" This section briefly addresses these issues, and will hopefully convince you that meta data management, as a business asset, is a worthwhile investment.

After reading this chapter, you might realize that a registry/repository solution may be exactly what your company needs; the issue then becomes a matter of to what degree your organization should be involved in the ongoing registry or core component standardization efforts. As you review the tradeoffs of various issues, don't be surprised if you find yourself championing a registry prototype implementation in your organization!

# What Does a Registry/Repository Offer?

In short, an ebXML Registry/Repository:

- Provides a mechanism for risk mitigation by allowing an organization to fully understand areas to be impacted with future changes by understanding its meta data, thus allowing changes to be made more efficiently. This will allow organizations to be more confident in moving forward with modifications, and understand that some changes may not appear to be critical, but in the long run they could mean the difference between being successful and being left behind.
- Promotes information reuse, again making companies more efficient.
- Enables collaborative development, for example by providing a collaboration mechanism between trading partners via a common access mechanism to trading partner owned registries.
- Allows access to industry components and nomenclature as a guide when modeling (UML), developing, and testing systems through the life cycle.
- Enables efficient version control.
- Extends the reach of electronic business to include the mapping and processing of data directly into the organizations' business systems.
- Promotes unified understanding and consistency of registered objects across domains.
- Covers a wider range of interactions among trading partners, such as real-time exchanges. The registry/repository infrastructure allows for the support of accurate communications by housing Collaboration Partner Profiles (CPP) and business processes templates and diagrams, which in the past have had to be relayed via telephone calls and e-mails.
- Takes advantage of next generation application software that can interact directly with the transmitted data from trading partners.

- Promotes selective access to registered objects.
- Ensures that business rules aren't buried in code or shackled to proprietary tools.

An ebXML Registry/Repository contains collections of standardized tags, business components (program code, both source and compiled), objects, style sheets, and industry terms and codes. The ebXML Registry/Repository was purposely architected without constraints as to the types of information that can or should be stored to facilitate e-business; these types of information tend to include:

- Common sets of data that can be exchanged among trading partners.
- Specific user community data.
- To encourage interoperability, provision of connections (links) to:
  - universal business or product databases such as GIS (Geographic Information System), D-U-N-S (D&B's Data Universal Numbering System for companies), and NAICS (North American Industry Classification System of business categories)
  - UPC (Universal Product Code)/EAN (European Article Numbering) product numbers, and
  - taxonomies such as the UDEF (Universal Data Element Framework)
- Holding temporary, non-versioned data to simplify exchange of information between trading partners.
- XML/EDI templates (see http://www.xmledi-group.org) and translation maps.
- Namespaces – both XML Namespaces and management of various naming areas within a community or organization.
- Provision of access to common mapping, scripting, workflow, and processing business components.
- Provision of access to common forms and screen displays that allow for human interaction with specific types of messages.

The ebXML Registry/Repository accounts for challenges such as generic-specific relationships, synonyms, multiple senses of terms depending on context, and methods to address exchange dependencies, through dynamic self-forming structuring to reduce loss or distortion of meaning. The idea of having a 'standard' word or tag for 'PartNumber' or a 'standard' document such as 'Purchase Order' is in the past. Our business vocabulary is changing at a great pace: meanings change, and words are borrowed and contain different meaning in each context. The registry mechanisms are not intended to duplicate failed mechanisms to force standardization, but rather to capture and use efficiently our business vocabulary now, and in the future. The registry mechanism is dynamic and context-sensitive, which through metrics should lead users to an understanding of the current state of business meaning by understanding better the relations between registered business artifacts. It does not simply attempt to 'dictionarize', but instead to provide a rich ontology of business communication.

## *Context Everywhere!*

The **ebXML Registry Information Model** (**RIM**) is founded on the use of **classifications** to manage and structure content within the registry. Classifications capture context and traversal, thus allowing for domain and subdomain context-centric interpretation. Context eases interpretation and reduces costs (improper interpretation can come with high costs). This is much like the file system of a computer operating system, but instead of allowing just one hierarchical path, classifications can provide any number of dimensions. For instance, the term "golf club" can be classified under "sporting instrument", and "restaurant/bar", giving more context to the meaning of the term.

Registries allow access to the objectives (and examples) of registered objects throughout the workflow within an enterprise or trading community. This leads to a situation with much more reuse situations – a core component now only needs to be defined once, and no matter where the component is being interpreted (transformed, routed, imported, etc.), whether internally, or externally during collaboration with a trading partner, the components context and definition can be easily accessed via the registry/repository mechanism, giving us **context everywhere**.

## Major Use Cases of Registry-Centric Operations?

Registries are infrastructure components that, once implemented, have a wide range of uses. The following figure depicts a model of a value-chain, showing how reuse and accurate communication between trading partners, internal heterogeneous applications, and professions can be achieved:

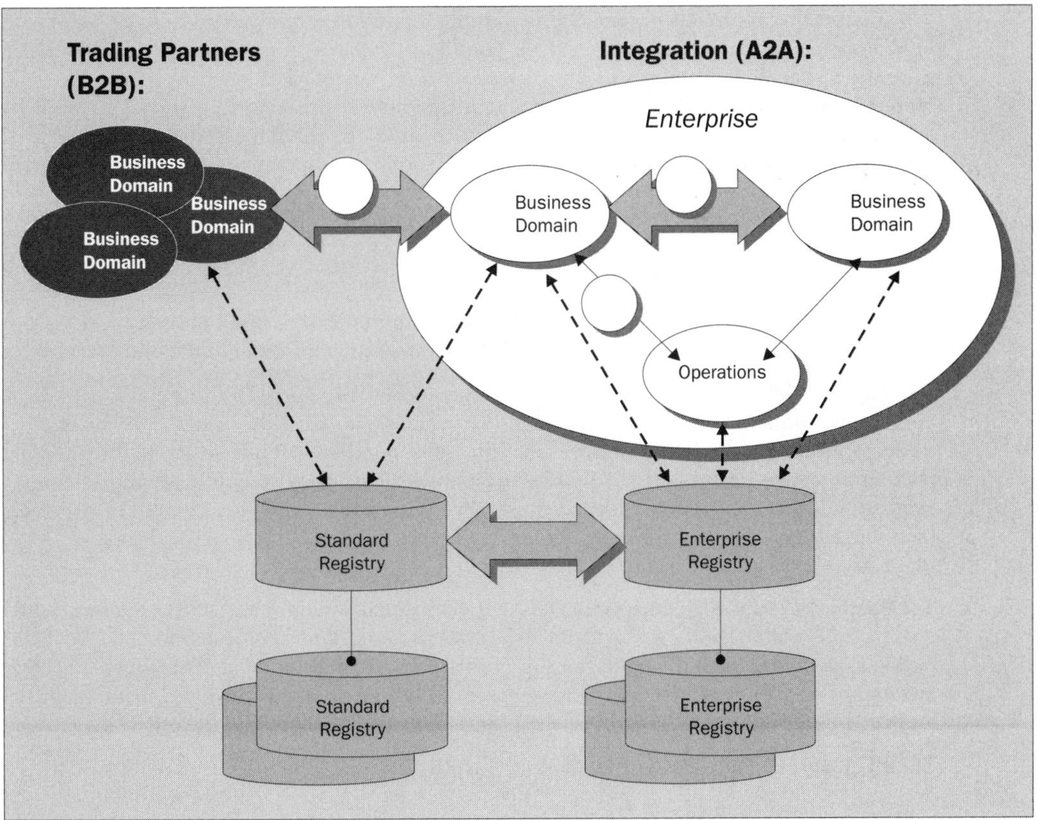


In the diagram there are two registry/repository pairs, one standards-based and one enterprise-based, each supporting different actions and requirements. As the white circles in the diagram show, registry-centric operations are used to facilitate the interactions across three very diverse challenge areas:

- The ebXML emphasis was certainly with the standards-based registry/repository to support *business-to-business (B2B) interactions.* The effort was concerned with optimizing business transactions among established business partners and preparing for business transactions with new partners. This discovery stage is important for companies expanding to new markets or geographies, new businesses or consortia in the setup phase, or for enabling companies to switch partners more flexibly (dynamic e-business). It also offers business opportunities for intermediaries (such as e-business brokers). For e-commerce to work for complex transactions, tools must be able to perform many of the traditional, robust document management and workflow functions, but also easily exchange information between trading partners, via the use of XML. Since these projects tend to be fairly dynamic, there is an emphasis on publishing and on the ability to update content rapidly and seamlessly.

- With enterprises finding the need to cache the information found in standard registries/repositories, and their own organization requirements, it is suspected that vendors will support the numerous organizations wanting the full capability to do both B2B and *application-to-application (A2A) integration.* Traditionally the A2A market space has flourished, as vendors shackled customers to proprietary mechanisms, formats, and protocols. Recently there has been a backlash by customers who have found themselves in this position, and who are now asking for open standards for A2A processes along the lines of the ones being developed for electronic commerce, or at the very least giving open access to the information. Adopting, and in some cases demanding from vendors, registry-centric solutions is one way to unshackle themselves and reduce costs. The A2A integration demand for registry-based products and implementations that build upon the work of ebXML will increase as organizations demonstrate success and returns are realized on their investments.

- Likewise, the registry can be used as an effective communication tool between those knowledgeable about the *business domain and the operations* or runtime of the organization.

  The business domain perspective (Business Operational View – BOV) addresses the operations, evolution, and management of the business (for example, people, problems, business processes, models, patterns, semantic interoperability, frameworks, industry dialects) within and across business areas (finance, accounting, corporate resource, administration, acquisition). Business domain experts must drive the business perspective from the business lines and support services that are responsible for the business enterprise and policy. They must lead efforts to define the 'What', 'Why', and 'Who' aspects of business operations.

  The operations technology perspective (ebXML Functional Service View – FSV) addresses the operations, evolution, and management of the systems and technical infrastructure that enable business operations (such as applications, products, software development, deployment, integration, trading partner setup). This perspective must be driven by the developers responsible for the 'How', 'When', and 'Where' aspects of business transactions within the organization.

  The BOV and FSV are further detailed in Chapter 2.

## What Are the Benefits of Registry-Centric Operations

The following diagram depicts the typical point-to-point interfaces (internal and external) of an enterprise:

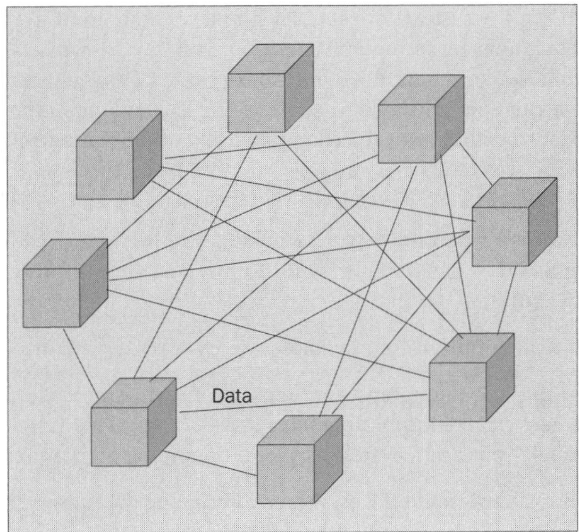


The business communication from sender and receiver is direct, but at the low levels very cumbersome. Each interface requires detailed knowledge of each other's application for mapping values; there is little in the way of sharing meta data between entities, as we have neither a standard format nor automation. Suffice to say that, because of this, the mapping task requires great technical skills. The task can't be based on lessons learned in the past because each interface is almost starting from scratch, with little or no reuse. For audit purposes there isn't a central control point, nor is there an end-to-end tracking mechanism. The perceived problem is that the number of mappings between endpoints (provided each endpoint maps to every other endpoint exactly once) is equal to `n(n-1)/2` (where `n` is the number of endpoints) – the number of mappings between the endpoints can become astronomical.

One architecture that can be applied to address the issues described above is a "hub n' spoke" pattern, creating an integration broker for the enterprise. Such a solution is depicted in the following diagram:

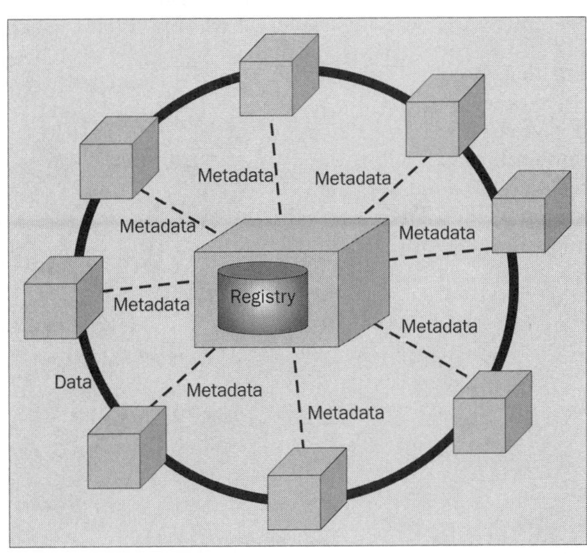

From a conceptual viewpoint the system looks much simpler than a point-to-point approach and it is therefore easy for business managers to buy into this approach, even from a 30,000' level. Looking closer at the benefits of this hub n' spoke scenario we find some very positive characteristics; primarily that, through centralization, we can add consistency, share expertise, and gain other controls required for robust message passing. However, it is important to recognize a few of the side effects of this solution:

- We have added another processing step, slowing the flow of information.
- We have added another possible area for mistakes to be made, leading to a potential loss of information; we now have two maps (point-to-hub and hub-to-point) whereas before we had just one (point-to-point).
- We have added a constraint to our architecture by forcing a centralized design.
- We have moved into a queuing environment, eliminating any solutions where synchronous communications are nearly impossible with heavy loads. This single-point integration could lead to bottlenecks if not architected with load-balancing techniques.
- Changes in the hub affect all interfaces, thereby impeding the fulfillment of business requirements.
- It is a possibly incomplete solution; if we don't constantly feed the hub with new domain reference tables, we will need to perform lookup processes at the endpoint (thus requiring a mapping or joining at the destination). For instance, if current manufacturing information is to be added to a purchase order, it can be added to the transaction at the hub if the hub is updated, or needs to be joined in at the receiving application. In some cases, at the application is not an option, with this information being added into note fields for users.
- There is a need for larger machines, as the computing power at the hub is taxing.
- The number of messages being passed around is doubled, thus requiring greater communication bandwidth.

The integration broker is likely to be a vendor solution that doesn't completely meet the business needs. The 30,000 foot view looks good until we implement and discover the new problems that have cropped up – the hub n' spoke approach tends to not decrease the organization's efforts, but rather the effort remains the same or even increases, but with a different set of problems.

The ideal solution is one that combines the best of both worlds, in other words, a hybrid solution, which gives us the optimum result and eliminates many of the problems associated with the point-to-point and hub n' spoke approaches. The following diagram depicts such a hybrid solution:

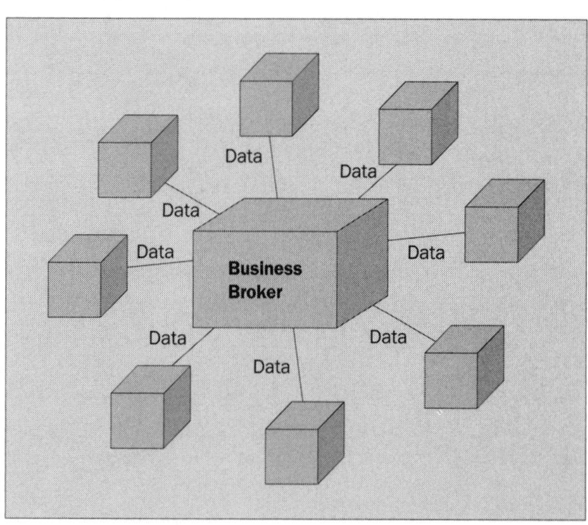

So what should be decentralized? The answer is the information – the transactions, the web queries, the Web Services, etc. (in other words, data). What do we keep centralized? The answer to the second question is meta data (context) and a few support functions such as end-to-end status mechanisms (logging, etc.). What about our `n(n-1)/2` problem? While mathematically correct, in business the actual set communication patterns is typically a very small subset of the theoretical possibilities – does every application in your business 'talk' to every other application? Of course not, but for sure the best, most accurate communication between each required exchange is direct understanding of each application's requirements. Note that the hybrid solution had only been economically feasible for medium to large enterprises in the last few years, before XML-based tools came to market and allowed smaller businesses to take advantage. Being that the hybrid solution is a distributed model, it allows the enterprise to coexist with centralized infrastructure components as well. It supports a mix – an enterprise balances its functions, and a distributed model adopts processes that work best in a synchronous environment. The bottom line is that the hybrid (registry-centric) approach isn't driven by technology but is instead properly guided by business requirements.

## Flexibility

The intent of the ebXML Registry Specifications was to be flexible, with ad-hoc extensions for tailoring to the specific application requirements of each user. Any XPath or XQuery can be formulated and executed as extensions. The registry, envisioned as a set of services, can be used in many industries for various purposes. Thus, the registry services provide a standard base upon which an organization may build to meet its customers' needs.

The concepts (for example, services, codes of practice, terminologies etc.) in an enterprise can be split up into four categories, each covered by one **domain** (domains are basically categories of scope):

- Internal concepts.
- Concepts shared with others in its industry.
- Concepts common to its resident country (or countries).
- Global concepts.

These domains contain differences (due to, for example, differing resolution of business needs between domains) and so our XML e-business systems must be written to accommodate these differences. For example, there may be different languages between domains, such as English to German, Chinese, Spanish, etc. Solutions must be reached through negotiation, replicated cross-references, and through mechanisms to repackage in a different manner appropriate to the domain.

## Return On Investment (ROI): Agility & Domain Knowledge

Enterprise agility, domain knowledge, and information services are important concepts central to becoming a world-class leader. Enterprise agility means moving fast, in the right direction, as opposed to sluggish movement or wasted motion. Superior domain knowledge is the fuel that propels an agile enterprise. Domain knowledge is achieved by leveraging the knowledge processes and information assets that traverse the many heterogeneous environments of the business domain. The XML information services provide a robust set of non-proprietary, interoperable, reusable information services that interconnect the enterprise while maintaining context everywhere. XML information services are the foundation for bringing together business and technology to enable domain knowledge and enterprise agility. Without a solid foundation and a registry/repository strategy, reaching the goal of becoming a world-class leader becomes difficult or impossible.

The following figure depicts building upon critical foundation components in order to achieve enterprise agility:

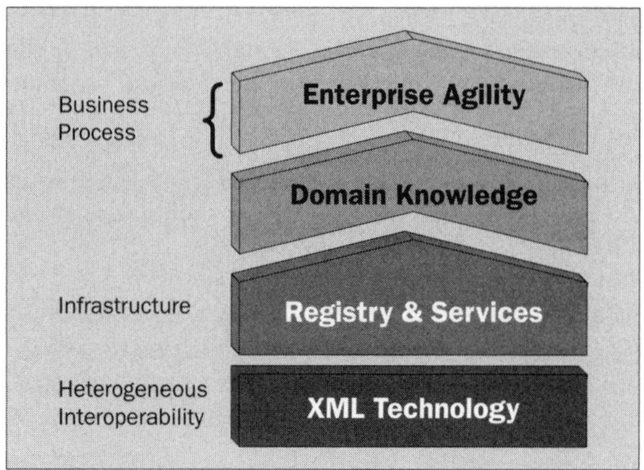


### *Enterprise Agility*

The agility of the business is driven by sound innovative decision-making that applies knowledge, experience, and ultimately wisdom to achieve the desired business outcome – the ability for an organization to quickly respond to its business environment in an effective manner. Decision cycles must operate at speeds that keep pace with compressing business and technology cycles, and meet the challenges inherent in today's climate (a series of external crises, such as terrorist attacks and financial turbulence). Ubiquitous access to information services that enable discovery, exchange, and application of business artifacts provides the foundation for responsive decision-making. Gains on return on investment are:

- Business-proficient personnel implement new capabilities using mechanisms that provide transparency from the technical underpinnings, giving greater independence, and thus the opportunity for business-driven solutions.
- The costs, quality, and delivery time cycles can be more effective because:
  - Proprietary mechanisms have been eliminated through the use of open system standards and best practices.
  - Information exchange has been elevated to a process based on loosely-coupled logical dependencies.

In the past, the ability of the enterprise to implement business capabilities was often limited by the boundaries of the supporting infrastructure. Since infrastructure is capital-intensive and permeates the enterprise, change is often a slow and expensive proposition. World-class leaders evolve their infrastructure through a forward-looking process that plans, budgets for, and implements change, adding capabilities and extending boundaries in anticipation of business needs – as opposed to a reactive process that lags behind and slowly adapts to business forces out of necessity.

### Domain Knowledge

Today, many organizations are selling the platitudes of moving up the information value chain (that is data, context, information, knowledge, experience, and wisdom) without addressing the granularity and foundational components that enable an enterprise to function at higher levels. It is best if decision makers have the ability to leverage the collective knowledge of the business domain as well as external knowledge sources. The corporate registry/repository maintains the linkage and semantic relationships required to extract, exchange, and translate information. Enabled by Registry Services, the management and use of BIOs (for example, meta data, business artifacts, information maps, and translation logic) is elevated from system-centric, technology-focused processes to enterprise-centric, business-driven services. BIOs are managed by Knowledge Brokers (KBs), either built in-house, or contained within off-the-shelf products,that understand their context and business value. Through enterprise-wide discovery and collaborative services, information can be refined, shared, and reused to achieve domain knowledge.

## Business Information Objects (BIOs)

The Lubash Pyramid below depicts the required artifacts that an organization considers should be registered and managed. The Lubash Pyramid developed at the US Defense Finance and Accounting Services (DoD-DFAS) highlights those critical items required for business integration, either within a trading community or an enterprise. Any information valued as a business asset should be controlled. The Pyramid provides a meta data management view of the Zachman framework (http://www.zifa.com). Those familiar with the Zachman framework should recognize the bottom layers (Inputs, Outputs). Also, Controls covers the six verticals of the framework. These layers abstract to WHAT, HOW, WHERE, and WHO, WHEN, WHY. The Lubash Pyramid builds on the framework and specifically identifies Specifications, Workflow, Contract, Presentation, Relationships, and Directory Services. The highlighting of these components/layers makes a distinction between requirements of interoperability of information and integration.

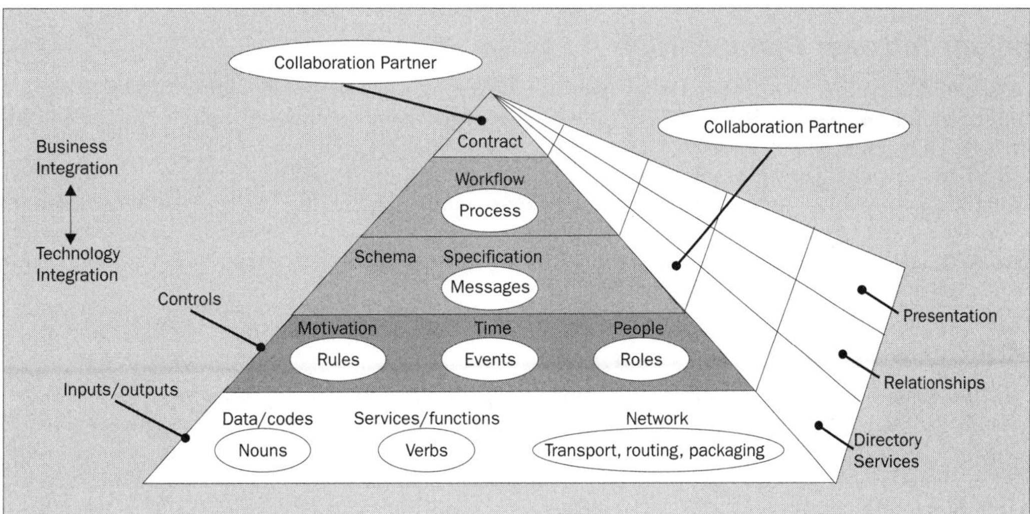


This model highlights the requirements placed on the registry/repository's classification mechanisms to handle the permutations and relationships required for taking full advantage of the power of the registry and what the registry can bring to the value chain. The model possibly demonstrates that a registry, or at the very least a database, is required for information management. ebXML Registry/Repository opens the door and specifies registry services for handling these registered business artifacts.

# Who Is to Host the Registry?

This is the number one question to be asked, if there is a master registry, who is to bring it online? The answer has been deferred, and the community is learning through deduction which players aren't willing to maintain such a registry. The issue is that the cost of such an undertaking is no small sum. The trend thus far is for building focused registries, with sound business models to address identifiable objectives. It is no surprise then that ebXML Registries are being developed around communities of interest (we'll discuss some of these later in the chapter).

# Should We Bring a Registry Online?

To answer this question, you need to perform an honest self-evaluation of your ranking in your industry, or consider how well you could support your industry's members in becoming agile in today's global economy. We have seen that registries enhance community, increase communication, and not only make the community stronger but each participating member as well. In simple terms, understand which category you fall into (Standards and Medium+ Communities, Small Communities, or Medium+ Organizations – discussed in more detail shortly) and develop a plan to gain capability. In either case gains are made by the participating organizations as a result of making their organization more competitive. For example, through discussion at a meeting, other members learned that one participant, a very large and successful multinational corporation known for its leading technology, was changing its engineering practices to align with the techniques learned from the community meeting. This by-product of working with or bringing online a registry-centric community of interest was considered just as valuable to the corporation than the reuse and sharing of business artifacts, a capability the corporation valued very much. When performing the evaluation, remember not to discount any underlying benefits of participating in a registry-centric community.

## *Medium To Large Communities*

Associations that define vocabularies or metrics for their industry should strongly consider implementing an ebXML Registry/Repository – the larger the community, the larger the benefit from bringing a registry online. However, in some respects this is balanced out – the larger the community is, the greater the challenge is to implement reuse, and the greater the problem of communication. If your community is medium to large sized, then bringing a registry online should certainly be considered. Various capabilities can be brought online in phases, to assure success and to insure that users' needs are met at each milestone. As the implementation progresses, links or feeds to and from other registries could be added for exchanging taxonomies.

## *Small Communities*

Small communities gain most, not by bringing a registry online, but instead by joining one or more established registries in their business domain(s). The first time you encounter the registry, it will typically be because you have been asked to review materials stored there in order for you to exchange information. The key here would be to architect the registry into the strategic design, and take into consideration the registry owner's strategy when procuring tools and services so that they don't preclude the use of a registry-centric information services-based architecture. Survival of small companies can be traced to effective networking, for which participation is key, to exchange ideas, etc.

# How Does Registry/Repository Fit?

The following figure is an ebXML diagram showing the registry and repository used as a design time business library for registration and discovery. Providing storage for business process (BP) diagrams and configurations, other business documents, core and domain component (CC) definitions along with collaboration protocol profiles and agreements (CPPs and CPAs – see Chapter 8 for more details), the registry is used to help the modeler or programmer when performing his or her tasks. Some tool suites extend the registry to include support during runtime for transformations to access lookup tables, in addition to querying CPPs and CPAs.

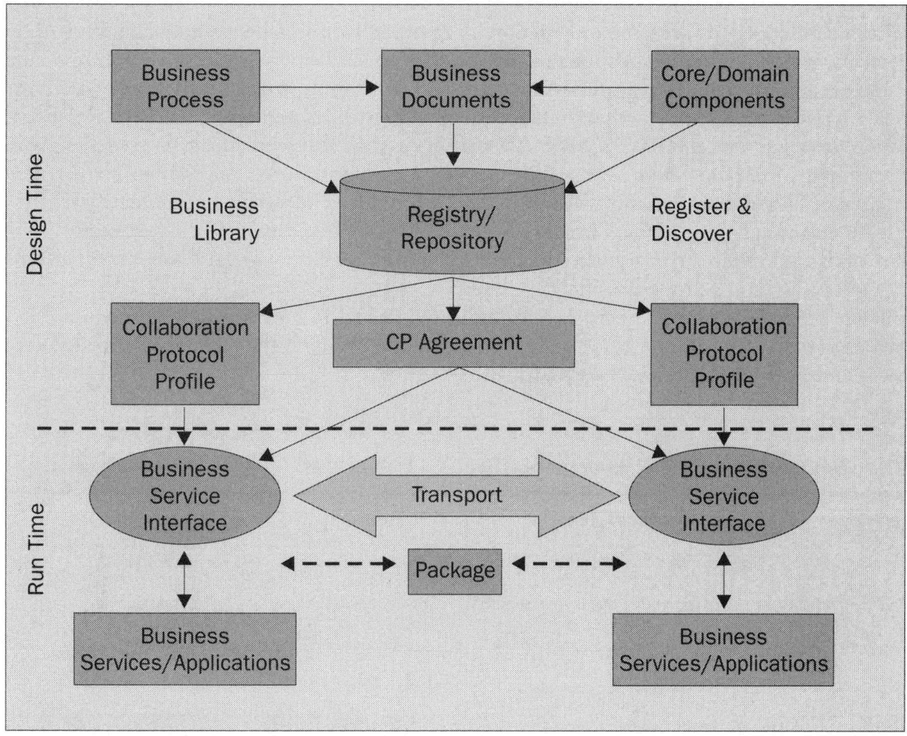


## Semantic Alignment

Is it possible to incorporate ebXML messages without investing in registry technology, without interfacing with a registry, or maintaining an organizational or standard registry? For sure, many ebXML implementations will use the Transport, Routing and Package (TRP) Specification(s) to exchange information between trading partners or collaborate with internal applications, and much can be gained by implementing just this limited use of the technology. This first step would be an improvement in many ways, but doesn't allow for a solution to the semantic alignment problem that occurs in real business.

Seamless integration or semantic interoperability for all organizations was one of the hurdles facing ebXML. Prior to ebXML, the train of thought was to devise a standard vocabulary – one dictionary of terms. With the current, single dictionary approach to data standardization, the 'tagname' that was standardized often did not mesh with data definitions for an organization's internal operations. As a result, the standard terms became overloaded and used for different meanings. Thus, the standard terms became placeholders with meanings described in documents particular to trading partners and not part of the automated process. The overloading was primarily due to a rigid approach to configuration management of the 'standardized' dictionary and the attempt to reuse elements in a relational manner. The dictionary also lacked critical information such as the rationale behind the selection or the relation of entries in the dictionary.

The deficiencies associated with the one dictionary approach led to a better understanding of the requirements, which in turn established the basis for the ebXML specifications. ebXML extends the dimension of the dictionary into a multi-dimensional classification structure (taxonomy), and provides the classification structure online in a distributed model, with user-defined and already established simple application programming interfaces (APIs). This allows a common mechanism for accessing various industry domains from anywhere on the Internet, and for the industries to add their taxonomies without knowing the details of other domains. Additionally, it provides **UIDs (Universal Identifiers)** for keying this information and role-based business processes models to provide context to the taxonomy. In short, the right answer is to provide a rich dynamic taxonomy to provide context-everywhere mechanisms.

The following figure lists four standards and their equivalents in each standard. The task for the registry/repository is to house this type of cross-reference between the standards – for lookup purposes, and to ease mapping between each format.

| Legacy PDM* | MIL-STD-2549 | X12 (EDI) | STEP AP203 |
|---|---|---|---|
| Part number | Part product identifier | Product/service ID | Part number |
| Supplier | Part product name | Product/service name | Supplier name |
| Contract number | Contract document identifier | Entity (supplier) name | Contract number |
| Doc Type | Contract product quantity | Buyer's contract number | Component quantity |
| | Document type code | Report type code | |

As shown in the next diagram, partners don't have to agree on the tag names in the XML instance to map from one domain or application to the other. The figure depicts the use of the ebXML UID (named BizCode in the XML/EDI framework) mapping through a schema declaration. An alternative mechanism would be to store the crosswalk with UID references in the registry/repository. The mapping crosswalk can be accessed and transformations defined, either with a process constraint on the component (UID), or as a collection of transformation maps and business rules such as an exchange definition.

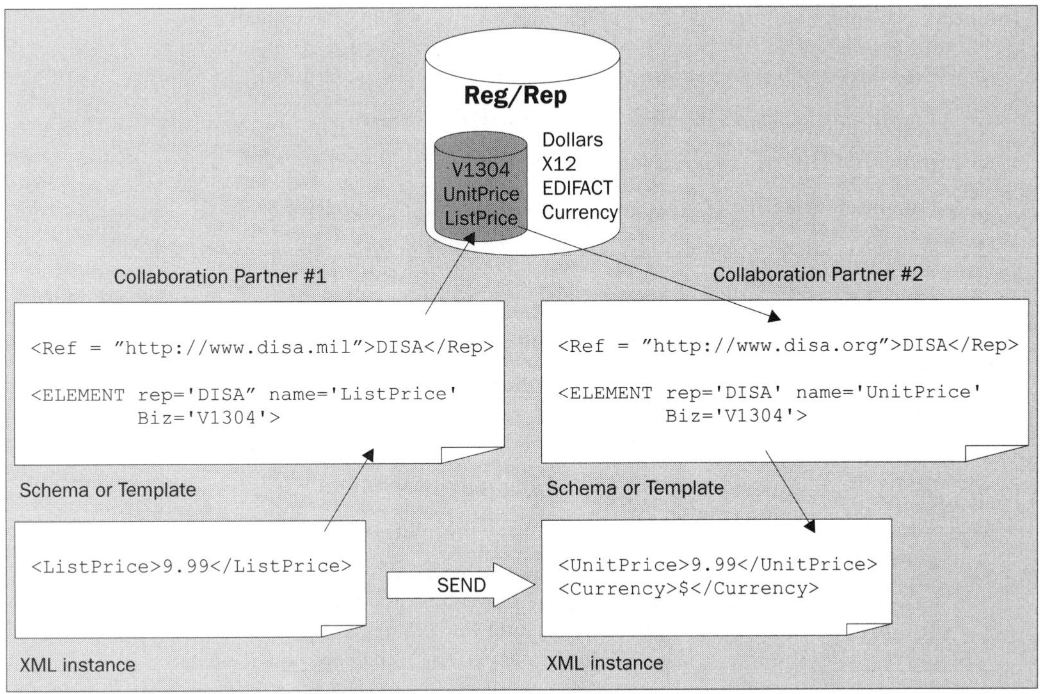


Registries use ebXML UIDs (discussed in greater depth in Chapter 10) to reference and allow for interrogation of information concerning items, picture masks, appropriate values, default values, help, definitions, links to validation classes, and constraints. As shown, UIDs are a simple mechanism for registries/repositories to handle. The option of handling the UID and other references can be restricted to design time or extended to runtime processing, depending on the application. Products exist today that provide for automated mapping between XML vocabularies, dialects, schemas, and various standards for reuse through the ebXML mechanism.

Traditional EDI has long addressed this consideration with code and element dictionaries, but has not provided the blueprint for the cross-referencing. Instead, individual EDI tool vendors have provided their own industry-specific vocabularies mapped to the standards. In the ebXML Registry/Repository for each industry, a glossary would equate a specific identifier to the equivalent UID. An industry could create a UID 'ListPrice' label for the logical unit with a UID 'VI304'. When collaboration partner #1 in the industry transmits outside the industry's domain and interacts with enterprises (collaboration #2) in other domains, the UID is used to relate precisely to VI304. Collaboration partner #2 can also convert tags to their nomenclature ('UnitPrice') if needed, or to EDIFACT, X12, etc. As a result, by using an ebXML Registry/Repository collaboration, partners in a vertical industry can use the business terms and rules with which they are familiar, yet still relate easily to other business domains.

The search for a mechanism for effectively cross-referencing domains has been elusive for decades – it is this reuse which allows large savings of resources. Imagine with an ebXML mechanism in place how various industry 'standards' could be crosswalked once, and users could then reuse references registered in a common registry/repository. The same mechanism could be used between various product formats, say, all major accounting packages. The registry/repository, coupled with UIDs, is one critical component of the integration solution.

The prime advantages of using UIDs coupled with a registry-centric approach are:

- Cross-reference information is housed in the ebXML repositories.
- Transformations are simplified through a linking process.
- Allows for effective reuse of logical units.
- Provides for international language transformation for global e-business.
- Simple one-link linking mechanism in the DTD or in XML Schema archetypes.
- The information "attached" is managed and extensible, allowing for knowledge additions.
- Attributes and relationships can be interrogated further.
- Same mechanism for industry, international standards, as well as for enterprise vocabulary; converting 'price' in German, Japanese, and Indian, a very much needed attribute for global e-business.
- Allows for transient definitions with lifetimes for transactions.
- Allows for the collection of metrics on business language.
- Allows the repository to learn business languages quickly, and subscribe to standards. For instance, if we were to query the registry and return two uses of 'Amount' and see that the two are very similar in function, but one has hundreds of users and the other only a few users, the query guides the user to the *de facto* standard of use – the core component.

# Technology Base

The set of ebXML Registry/Repository specifications is quite possibly one of the most advanced collections of thought on the housing and access of meta data for e-business. The specifications are built on a base of information technology and so it is advisable, before beginning development in this area, to review the work listed below or risk repeating work that has already been done. This section should help you to better understand the basis from which the ebXML Registry/Repository evolved.

Registry/repository technology takes from XML-based directory mechanisms, configuration management, topic maps, nomination submission standard workflow processing, database storage, and UML modeling tools. The ebXML Registry/Repository effort moves forward to better define how best to communicate through semantic alignment. The effort is at an early stage, with the version 1.0 specification addressing quite a broad and unique range of topics, including (multiple) classification, and searching/querying. A study of related efforts preceding the ebXML initiative assisted in providing solid input into the registry/repository vision and, as should be the case, the lessons learned from these related efforts continue to influence the direction of the ebXML Registry/Repository TC. This is typically achieved by the stakeholders, simply by participating in the initiative:

- XML/EDI Group Framework (1997) includes five components critical for e-business: XML, EDI, Registry, Templates, Agents (see http://www.XMLedi-group.org).
- BSR (Basic Semantic Register) is an International Standards Organization (ISO) effort, with roots in the BSI/Beacon project. For more, follow this URL: http://comelec.afnor.fr/servlet/ServletForum?form_name=cForumPage&file_name=TC154WG1%2FPUBLIC%2FWEB%2FENGLISH%2Fcontent.htm&login=invite&password=invite.

- UDEF, the Universal Data Element Framework, is an attempt to map various data standards (CALS, STEP, X12 EDI, etc.) into a single framework using sets of object classes and properties to define data elements. See http://www.udef.com for more information.
- The NIST Identifier Collaboration Service (NICS) project, funded through the Advanced Technology Program, has established an experimental collaborative registry for XML – see http://pitch.nist.gov/nics/.
- The Resource Description Framework (RDF) integrates a variety of applications, from library catalogs and worldwide directories to syndication and aggregation of news, software, and content, to personal collections of music, photos, and events, using XML as interchange syntax. The RDF specifications provide a lightweight ontology system to support the exchange of knowledge on the Web. This work is part of the W3C Semantic Web Activity. See http://www.w3.org/2001/sw for more on semantic web activity, and http://www.w3.org/RDF/ for more on the Resource Description Framework.
- Directory Services Markup Language (DSML) – for managing data about people, resources, and processes, which is very synergistic with LDAP. See http://www.dsml.org/ for more information.
- NCITS/L8 is backing an effort whose prime sponsor is the US EPA. The EPA has already invested a couple of million dollars in what they call the EDR (Environmental Data Registry) and seen its use expanding into HCFA and DOD – see http://www.epa.gov/edr/.
- UREP – the Universal REPository from UNISYS is an XML-based extensible information system that defines, integrates, and manages meta data and business data – check it out at http://www.unisys.com/marketplace/urep/.
- Ontology Markup Language (OML) – valuable features of RDF/Schemas, conceptual graphs (CGIF), SHOE, and previous versions CKML. See http://www.ontologos.org/IFF/..%5COML/OML%200.3.htm for more.
- XML Metadata Interchange Format (XMI) "specifies an open information interchange model that is intended to give developers working with object technology the ability to exchange programming data over the Internet in a standardized way" – http://www.omg.org provides more information.
- Metadata Information Clearinghouse – Metadata Subcommittee of the AAP launched MICI, an interactive repository where questions or comments can be posted, and threaded discussions can be conducted. For more on this, go to http://domino.wileynpt.com/NPT_Pilot/Metadata/mici.nsf.
- Component Registry is an open resource to provide critical component documentation for the industry's large and growing collection of JavaBeans, Enterprise JavaBeans (EJBs), and COM software components. See http://www.componentregistry.com/ for more information.
- IBM's alphaWorks has released XML Registry/Repository (XRR), a data management tool that supports registration, searching, and delivery for XML artifacts including schemas (DTD, XSD), style sheets (XSL) and instance documents (WSDL). The repository provides access to registered objects using standard identifiers (URLs). For more on this, follow the link: http://www.alphaworks.ibm.com/tech/xrr.
- The BizTalk Framework is an industry initiative, started by Microsoft, and supported by a community of XML standards users. The Biztalk Framework homepage can found at http://www.biztalk.org/.
- xmlTree – the leaves of xmlTree are XML content resources. Some of the leaves on xmlTree represent XML interfaces, which you can query using parameters. Find it here: http://www.xmlTree.com

- OASIS - the Organization for the Advancement of Structured Information Standards, is a non-profit, international consortium steered by XML.org (a vendor neutral consortium) dedicated to accelerating the adoption of product-independent formats (XML) based on public standards. Go to the http://www.oasis-open.org/cover/ and http://www.oasis-open.org/html/rrpublic.htm sites for more information.
- The EEMA EDI/EC Work Group has proposed to CEFACT the establishment of a global repository for the translation of XML tags in UN/EDIFACT and human language on the Internet. The EEMA EDI Working Group is prepared to assist in the setup and operation of such a repository, which could be crucial in the advancement of the use of EDI over the Internet. For more on this group, go to http://www.editie.nl/edifact/xml-edi.htm.
- ISO/IEC 11179-1 is the International Standards Organization's framework for the Specification and Standardization of Data Elements composition, including meta data. The 11179 standard is the basis for a document, 'Concept of Operations for a Data Registry,' which addresses registration of data elements as they are described in the 11179 standard. ISO/IEC 11179-3 is being revised to incorporate the notions of the American National Standards Institute (ANSI) X3.285 standard: Metamodel for the Management of Shareable Data. This new version, known as the 'registry metamodel (MDR3),' extends the original version to include registering objects – referred to as the '11179 registry metamodel'. The X3.285 standard specifies the structure of a data registry as a conceptual data model and provides the attributes for identifying the characteristics of data that are necessary to clearly describe, inventory, analyze, and classify data. All other parts of the ISO/IEC 11179 standard also are being harmonized to use the same terminology as the 11179 registry metamodel. For more on this, check out http://www.sdct.itl.nist.gov/~ftp/l8/other/coalition/Coalition.htm.

## Comparison with UDDI

As we shall discuss in Chapter 9, Universal Description, Discovery and Integration (UDDI) is based around the concept of standard registry services that provide Yellow Page (business type classification), White Page (general contact information), and Green Page (how to invoke services) business functionality. The fundamental difference between UDDI and ebXML is that UDDI aims to create a standard registry for companies that will accelerate the integration of systems around Net Marketplaces, while ebXML is working to standardize how XML is used in general business-to-business (B2B) integration. The following points characterize the similarities and differences of the two efforts:

- ebXML Repositories are intended to be for more general-purpose storage (only business searches). UDDI is more specialized in the type of information stored, geared only towards supporting the information contained in the Yellow, White and Green pages.
- One strength of ebXML is in the classification and relationships between business artifacts; much of UDDI is flat space listings.
- ebXML reusability stems from its granularity and sharing these atomics at the enterprise level – UDDI sharing is focused at the process level.
- UDDI is verb-centric (Web Services), whereas ebXML core components are noun-centric, with processes handled in UML or form-driven definitions.
- UDDI is a less comprehensive initiative in that no attempt is made to allow enterprise reuse of its business vocabulary or create a 'standard' nomenclature; that is, with UDDI all business services must be associated with a business entity.

The core of the UDDI model is therefore focused particularly on middleware connectivity, and using XML itself to describe the systems that companies use to interface with one another. UDDI plans to do this by storing information about companies' integration profiles and capabilities in a shared directory that other companies can access via a set of XML standards currently being worked on.

> *The trend for registry products on the market is to capture the capabilities of UDDI, 11179, and ebXML. (References "Requirements for an XML Registry." By Joseph M. Chiusano, Terence J. Schmitt, and Mark Crawford. Logistics Management Institute (McLean, VA, USA). Report EP005T4. May 2001.* (http://xml.gov/lmi/registryreport.pdf)*) The two commercial products listed later in this chapter offer the combined attributes of both UDDI and ebXML functionality. Convergence is certainly on the horizon with these two complementary approaches, either through learning from each other's efforts, from products incorporating both mechanisms, and/or formally at some future date, through a standardization process.*

For a good example of_UDDI working together with an ebXML Registry, check out the *Using UDDI to find ebXML Registry/Repository white paper,* found at http://www.ebxml.org/specs/index.htm.

### *Web Front-ended UDDI Support*

SalCentral (http://www.salcentral.com/) and XMethods (http://www.xmethods.com/) are examples of a centralized brokerage that can help customers find Web Services and help Web Service providers advertise their functionality, using specialist searching facilities and quality assurance checking. It is mentioned here because these web sites complement UDDI and Web Services, by allowing for searching the UDDI servers for Web Services as well as those registered at the web sites themselves. In addition, the web sites offer Web Service providers the ability to categorize their products and differentiate their Web Service from the crowd, using a unique value added service – classifications.

# ebXML Registry/Repository Details

In this part of the chapter we'll look at the various interfaces to the Registry Service and Registry Information Model.

## Services

The Registry Services Specification v1.0 defines six types of interfaces with Registries. The first three cover connections directly to the registry and the next three apply to connections to the end-user:

- `RegistryService` – the service that permits access to the registry's two main functions, `ObjectManager` and `ObjectQueryManager`.
- `ObjectManager` – a function that allows an organization to submit data objects (CPPs, schemas), edit or modify the object characteristics, or remove objects.
- `ObjectQueryManager` – provides a service for searching objects listed in the registry, performing browse, drill-down, or ad hoc queries.
- `RegistryClient` – a service that links the user's client to the registry services.
- `ObjectManagerClient` – a service, which calls back the client after submission of requests to the `ObjectManager` service, with notification of the results of the query.

- `ObjectQueryManagerClient` – a callback service for requests submitted earlier to the `ObjectQueryManager`.

## Registry Information Model

Registered items may have the following attributes as defined in registry information model (RIM) v1.0:

- **Association** – Defines the relationship between a registry entry and other objects, and can cover potentially complex many-to-many relationships. The RIM has 15 predefined associations to describe these relationships:

| | |
|---|---|
| `RelatedTo` | Defines that the source `RegistryObject` is related to target `RegistryObject`. |
| `HasMember` | Defines that the source `Package` object has the target `RegistryEntry` object as a member. Reserved for use in Packaging of `RegistryEntries`. |
| `ExternallyLinks` | Defines that the source `ExternalLink` object externally links the target `RegistryEntry` object. Reserved for use in associating `ExternalLinks` with `RegistryEntries`. |
| `ExternallyIdentifies` | Defines that the source `ExternalIdentifier` object identifies the target `RegistryEntry` object. Reserved for use in associating `ExternalIdentifiers` with `RegistryEntries`. |
| `ContainedBy` | Defines that the source `RegistryObject` is contained by the target `RegistryObject`. |
| `Contains` | Defines that the source `RegistryObject` contains the target `RegistryObject`. |
| `Extends` | Defines that the source `RegistryObject` inherits from or specializes the target `RegistryObject`. |
| `Implements` | Defines that the source `RegistryObject` implements the functionality defined by the target `RegistryObject`. |
| `InstanceOf` | Defines that the source `RegistryObject` is an *Instance* of target `RegistryObject`. |
| `SupersededBy` | Defines that the source `RegistryObject` is superseded by the target `RegistryObject`. |
| `Supersedes` | Defines that the source `RegistryObject` supersedes the target `RegistryObject`. |
| `UsedBy` | Defines that the source `RegistryObject` is used by the target `RegistryObject` in some manner. |
| `Uses` | Defines that the source `RegistryObject` uses the target `RegistryObject` in some manner. |

| | |
|---|---|
| `RelatedTo` | Defines that the source `RegistryObject` is related to the target `RegistryObject`. |
| `ReplacedBy` | Defines that the source `RegistryObject` is replaced by the target `RegistryObject` in some manner. |
| `Replaces` | Defines that the source `RegistryObject` replaces the target `RegistryObject` in some manner. |

- **AuditableEvent** – provides the ability to generate an audit trail for the entry. This ability includes associating registered users as part of the audit trail.
- **Classification** – Defines ways of categorizing registry entries, and since classifications can vary significantly from one industry to another, registries need the flexibility to use their own classification schemes. A classification associates the registry entry with a `ClassificationNode` – a branch in the tree structure making up that scheme.
- **ExternalIdentifier** – offers an additional means of identifying the registered item, such as a D-U-N-S or UCC/EAN company identifier.
- **ExternalLink** – Provides a way for an object to reference Internet-based resources outside the registry, for example, a schema that references another schema.
- **Organization** – Describes the entity submitting the entry to the registry, including references to parent organizations.
- **Package** – Provides a way of grouping entries together, and also allows for managing this group as a whole, for example for querying all items associated with a package.

These interfaces are summarized in the following diagram:

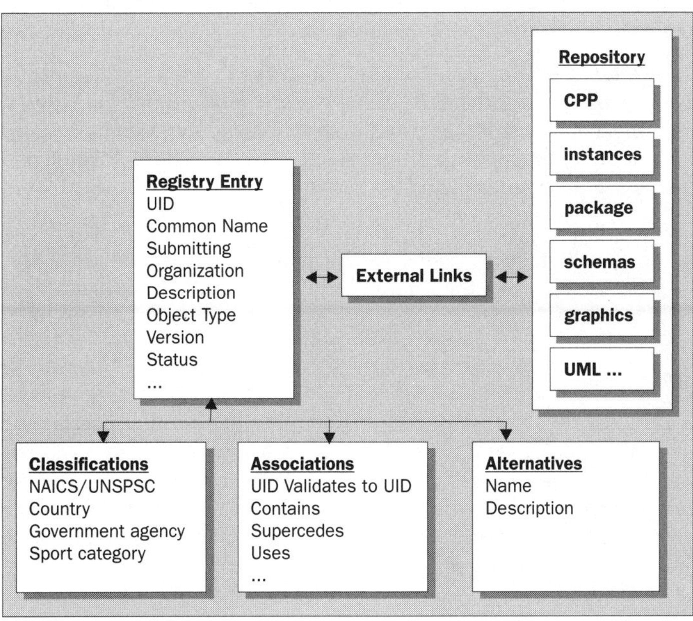

The ebXML Registry provides a key new functionality using the RIM information trees, which can be navigated based on business domains and required business functions. RIM mechanisms are functionally directed; therefore an end-user would expect to navigate a taxonomy in a directed domain path search to locate the particular business action. Such domain-based decision trees within topics on top of a semantic net provide an adjunct interface to the traditional keyword or dictionary style searches.

Put simply, the concept is "select what you want to do from this list provided from what is already known concerning context, and only the logical business units are displayed with prompting for more information". For instance, a user may navigate one of the tree hierarchies to a location within a financial investment repository, the commodities section, and a BUY action, and then find the items required for performing that task, and the standard transactions, times and schedules, special conditions (such as limits and edge requirements) and events provided for it. RIM mechanisms also then identify the individual data elements and detail their relationship with other elements, both inside and outside their industries.

There are many usages of the term "registry", so it is important to understand specifically how ebXML registries differ from others. The RIM mechanisms can provide domain taxonomies, thesauri, and (in future implementations) 'intelligent' user prompts driven with extensive use of collaborative technology in adapting pathways both during the language modeling and production/searching phases.

# Asking Questions of the Registry

The following Structured Query Language (SQL) search mechanisms are allowed as options on ebXML Registries:

- Get Root `ClassificationNodes` Request – `ClassificationNodes` are branches in the tree structure of the scheme used to classify the content of the registry. This request retrieves a list of root `ClassificationNodes`, defined as those without parents, or the top-most nodes in the tree. (See the example later in this section.)
- Get Classification Tree Request – Each `ClassificationNode` has a subtree attached that represents part of the classification scheme for the substance of the registry's content. This request returns the classifications listed under this node. The request allows searchers to specify the number of layers to drill down in the tree structure; a value of 1 for example returns the immediate children and no more.
- Get Classified Objects Request – With this request, the searcher specifies a precise list of classifications for the registry to query. This request returns the entries matching the `ClassificationNodes` in the list and those in descendant branches of the tree structure under those nodes.

## *Filtered Queries*

ebXML Registries also support filtered queries, which provide for more precise and complex searches. Filtered queries use the semantics and structure of the RIM, rather than the classification scheme of the subject matter used in browses and drill-down queries. Registries use the RIM structure mainly for submitting and managing objects. However, the meta data assigned to objects for these management functions can also be used for queries. Registries provide a list of queries, and in some cases the core/domain components schema, for a greater degree of query options.

The simple XML `FilterQuery` utilizes a formal XML structure based on *Predicate Clauses.* Predicate Clauses are utilized to formally define the constraint mechanism, and are referred to simply as **Clauses** in the Services specification. The following is one of the compound query examples listed in the specification:

```
("Smoker" = False) AND ("Age" =< 45)):
```

```
<?xml version="1.0" encoding="UTF-8"?>
<!DOCTYPE Clause SYSTEM "Clause.dtd" >
<Clause>
   <CompoundClause connectivePredicate="And">
      <Clause>
         <SimpleClause leftArgument="Smoker">
            <BooleanClause booleanPredicate="False"/>
         </SimpleClause>
      </Clause>
      <Clause>
         <SimpleClause leftArgument="Age">
            <RationalClause logicalPredicate="EL">
               <IntClause e-dtype="int">45</IntClause>
            </RationalClause>
         </SimpleClause>
      </Clause>
   </CompoundClause>
</Clause>
```

## Semantic Rules

The semantic rules used in these `RegistryEntryQuery` messages vary from one set of meta data to another, since they use different structures, or associations, either as source or target relationships of the object, as well as the specific registry entries associated with the object. Each `<RegistryEntryQuery>` XML element has a `<RegistryEntryFilter>` element with the desired filtering given in subsequent child elements representing the different types of RIM meta data.

## Retrieving Meta Data

Once these queries have identified specific registry entries or repository objects, searching users can then implement a similar approach to retrieve the meta data associated with the entries or the objects themselves. The `GetRegistryEntry` command allows for adding the same filtering arguments used to search for the specific entries. It returns the meta data for the registry entry identified. The `GetRepositoryItem` command has a comparable but not identical set of arguments, since repository items may have a different storage protocol compared to the registry entries. Users can retrieve specific content from a repository using the `GetContentRequest` command. This request lists the references to the objects, perhaps generated through the queries described above. A successful request message will return a corresponding `GetContentResponse` message with the specified object as payloads. Since the response may include multiple payloads, each item is individually identified in the manifest of the ebXML header for the response message. (See Chapter 13, where we discussed the areas of TRP.)

## Complex Queries

Registries for ebXML objects may also provide support for more complex queries based on SQL, although not required, as is the case for browse/drill-down and filtered queries. ebXML specifies the syntax of SQL found in a subset of ISO/IEC standard 9075:1992, Database Language SQL. The following is an example of such a query:

```
SELECT id FROM ExtrinsicObject WHERE name LIKE '%Amount%' AND
    majorVersion >= 1 AND (majorVersion >= 2 OR minorVersion > 3);
```

For more on these queries, check out Appendix C of the ebXML Registry Services Specification (http://www.ebxml.org/specs/ebRS.pdf).

# Configuration Control

Much of the focus of the specification was on specifying the rules for registering business information objects and their management over their life cycle. A registered object goes through four stages in its life cycle: submission, approval, deprecation, and removal.

There are two distinct classes of objects – `ExtrinsicObject` and `InstrinsicObject`, each with their own rules for management. `ExtrinsicObject` applies to those items submitted from external sources to registries, such as a UML diagram, where the properties of the object are not automatically known or understood. They are accepted but there doesn't exist explicit functionality for operating on them. `InstrinsicObject` covers those properties and characteristics already defined by the registry, and are those normally attached to objects already registered. Because of this, `InstrinsicObjects` are more flexible in use with applications.

The following figure shows the major areas of interest for configuration auditing a registry for configuration identification, change management, and configuration status accounting as a guest visits the registry. Note the processes required and the policy of configuring registered objects, compared to the alternative of just posting changes without control on the items. Organizations must make a determination on which artifacts need to be configured and controlled due to this additional expense to the organization:

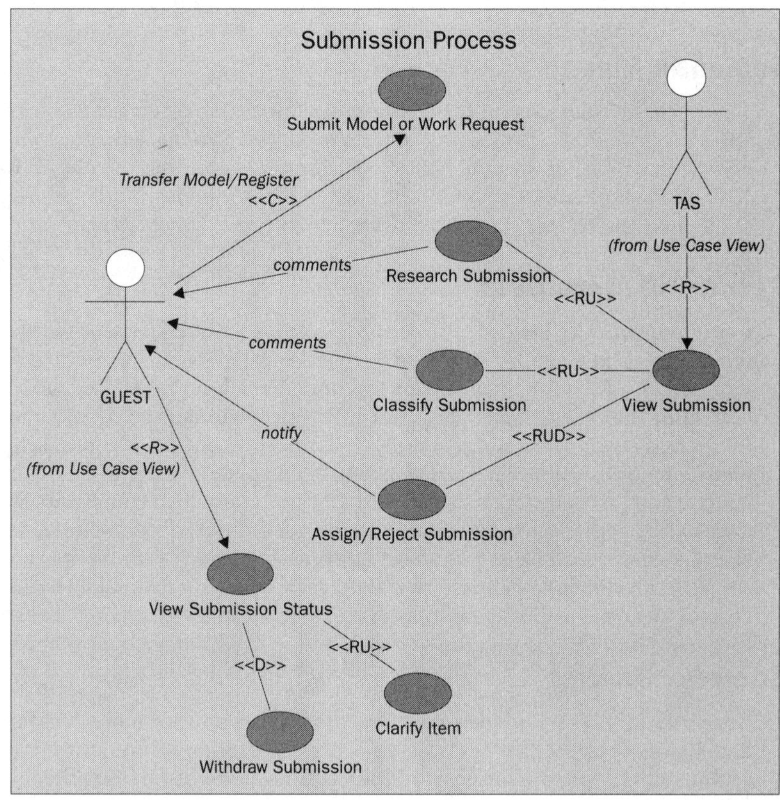

### Security

This section only discusses security as it applies to the ebXML registry/repository. For general ebXML security refer to Chapter 15. ebXML considers the registries to be public resources, and all content submitted to an ebXML Registry might be discovered and read by any user accessing the service.As a result, registries must make their content available in the clear. The ebXML Registry/Repository must secure its contents, authenticate the identity of authorized users, and provide role-based access control. To protect the submission integrity, content interchange may have a digital signature that ensures that no one has tampered with the content through transport or within the registry. Also, the signature verifies that content is associated with the submitting organization. In some registries, such as public registries, the signature requirement will probably not be optional for exchanges and stores. These registries must implement authentication mechanisms using credentials based on digital certificates and signatures. The ebXML Registry specifications require authentication of parties seeking access on a per-request basis, with future support for session-based authentications.

The registry specification defines three distinct roles with different levels of access. Public registries must implement default access-control policies that reflect these roles and privileges:

- **Registry guest** – Unauthenticated visitors to the registry that are entitled to read-only access to the registry objects.
- **Content owner** – Submitter of content to the registry from an organization, who has access to all procedures in the registry dealing with that content.
- **Registry administrator** – The party responsible for the management and operation of the registry, and with access to all procedures on all registry objects.

## Working with Repositories

In this section we will take a look at examples of tools on the market today – many more products are expected as version 1.0 of the specifications have been completed and released. We'll also see some examples to give programmers a flavor of the solution sets available to them as systems are architected and implementations are developed. Technology vendors are approaching ebXML, and specifically the usage of the registry/repository, from a variety of vantage points, including traditional EDI, workflows, traditional enterprise application integration (EAI) or middleware, and traditional ERP.

## Tool Suites

The following tools provide a base for submitting information into an ebXML Registry/Repository. Examples of information the suites support are XML Schema and documents, business process descriptions, business context descriptions, UML models, business collaboration information, and Core Components. Each offers a registry/repository implementation that provides support for middleware services such as database connectivity, transaction management, and security, along with TRP support for interfacing to ebXML Registry clients.

### XML Global Technologies

**GoXML™ Central Registry** (http://www.xmlglobal.com) offers an open platform that enables participation in global electronic marketplaces, supporting version 1.0 of the ebXML RIM and Registry Services Specification. Central Registry provides a GUI (and programming interfaces) to allow easier interaction with registry artifacts for programmers AND business users.

Central Registry uses commonly accepted standards, specifications, protocols and methodologies, specifically ebXML and UDDI, and provides a modular, scalable platform that facilitates integration with backend systems with a multitude of connectors to backend systems, and plug-ins for IBM's MQSI. It supports W3C Specifications on ad-hoc querying of XML content, such as XQuery and XPath (in the current version). Components such as TRP can be embedded into best-in-class business applications.

Coupling GoXML™ Transform allows for registry-based mapping using ebXML UIDs during design and runtime, allowing for enterprise management of the organization's business objects throughout the value-chain. GoXML Transform provides drag-and-drop mapping capabilities, automatic document recognition, an extensive library of mapping templates, support for EDI transactions, and a native XML repository. Central Registry is a complete lightweight package for users as well as developers.

### Sun Microsystems

Suns offering is **JAXR** (**Java API for XML Registries** – see http://www.sun.com), which provides an API for a set of distributed registry services that enables business-to-business integration between business enterprises, using the protocols being defined by ebXML.org, OASIS, and ISO 11179. This registry/repository implementation can be used to submit, store, retrieve, and manage resources to facilitate ebXML-based business-to-business partnerships and transactions. EJB provides the foundation for implementation of the RIM. In addition, the JAXR specification assumes that all communication between registry and registry clients will be based on the **Java API for XML Messaging** (**JAXM**) specification. Sun suggests using the following software components:

- A JDK (1.2.2 or later – go to http://java.sun.com/ to download)
- An application server environment; this implementation includes complete instructions for deploying the registry/repository using the following iPlanet Application Server environment components (for more information, and evaluation copy downloads, go to http://www.iplanet.com/):
  - iPlanet Application Server 6.0 or other J2EE implementation
  - iPlanet Web Server 4.1 SP7 (not 5.0, as the *Hook* feature wasn't carried forward)
  - iPlanet Directory Server 4.1x (comes with iAS 6.0)
- A database server – Sybase or Oracle are recommended as the registry database (for more information, go to http://www.oracle.com/ or http://www.sybase.com/, respectively).

## Examples

Included here are two examples of interfacing with an ebXML-compliant registry. In the first we dive into a code example of a client interface, depicting a query asking the registry for the root classification node. The second is a walk-through of a scenario in which a transformation tool interrogates the registry for information concerning elements in a transaction to be mapped using its UIDs both at design time and runtime.

### Registry Service Example

The two key factors to understanding ebXML registry interfacing are the registry access functions themselves and the ebXML TRP SOAP calls needed to transport the requests and responses.
In this section we present sample Java source code that implements the registry accessing. When compiled, `SimpleRegistryClient.java` builds a simple ebXML TRP message and sends it to an ebXML Registry. The body includes a query, compliant with RSS 1.0, that asks for the root classification node of the registry.

The ebXML TRP library itself is available with this book and can be downloaded from the Wrox web site. There is also a special URL that provides a live registry implementation that you can use to test out the sample program. This provides an actual ebXML Registry services interface, located at http://registry.xmlglobal.com, and this address is used by the sample Java program.

`SimpleRegistryClient.java`, included in the code download for this book, is just 100 lines of code, but illustrates each piece of the required interfacing. The following represents a tree schematic of the source code:

```
ebXML library object declarations
Swing UI object declarations
XML DOM handlers declarations

Start
      SimpleRegistryClient
      SetConfigProperties
         InitComponents
         SetButtonAction(getrootnodes)
         DisplaySwingUIpanel
      getrootnodes
         createnewXMLDOMinstance
         buildXMLrequestheader
         sendSynchronousMessage(request)
         response.getdefaultpayload
            catch invalidmessage
            catch transportexception
            catch IOexception
            catch messagingexception
            displayresultstopanel
```

While experienced Java programmers should find this relatively straightforward and obvious, we will review the main pieces here to make the details clear. This will particularly help other programmers looking to use different languages such as C# with .NET to create the same interface. Note that any language can be used to implement the registry server interfacing, since the query/response mechanism is done with XML SOAP messages via a simple HTTP-based dialogue, and clearly any software language with the correct HTTP protocol connections can exchange these messages with the server.

The first piece of the Java code is simply to do with the user interface (UI), and provides the Swing library with the necessary action functions so that when the "Retrieve Root Classifications" button is pressed, then the correct action of `getrootnodes` proceeds.

Once the user has entered in the URL of the registry service they wish to access, and pressed the "Retrieve" button, the program then connects to that address and exchanges the XML SOAP messages. The interaction control is set using the `initSystemProperties()` class (in this example these values are hard coded in the Java source code for simplicity). The values of `systemProperties` are stored for use by the ebXML TRP library objects. Notice that the library functions automatically construct the XML for the ebXML SOAP message format and details. You should refer to the section in this book on the ebXML TRP for full details of the envelope and SOAP interchange mechanics. In this registry chapter we are only concerned with the "payload" itself, and the request and response formats that are sent and received from the client Java application.

We have chosen to implement one of the base ebXML Registry services for this example. Since most registry content discovery must start from the classification nodes and proceed from there, this is clearly one of the fundamental registry service methods that can be invoked. The following screenshot shows the response details:


```
<?xml version="1.0" encoding="UTF-8" ?>
<!DOCTYPE ReturnRegistryEntryResult (View Source for full doctype...)>
<ReturnRegistryEntryResult>
  <RegistryEntryMetadata>
    <RegistryEntry majorVersion="1" minorVersion="0" status="Approved" userVersion=""
        stability="Dynamic" expirationDate="02022002" id="non-unique?" name="my
        name" description="my description">
      <SlotList/>
      + <Slot name="NAICS" slotType="Classification">
        + <ValueList>
            <Value>51113</Value>
            <Value>51114</Value>
          </ValueList>
        </Slot>
      + <Slot name="NAICS" slotType="Classification">
        - <ValueList>
            <Value>51113</Value>
          </ValueList>
        </Slot>
      </SlotList>
    </RegistryEntry>
    <Classification majorVersion="1" minorVersion="0" status="Approved" userVersion=""
        stability="Dynamic" expirationDate="02022002" id="non-unique?" name="my
        name" description="my description" classifiedObject="IDREF_REQUIRED"
        classificationNode="IDREF_REQUIRED" />
```


*There is a whole set of these primitive access methods and they all operate in the same fashion. Therefore, it is relatively straightforward to modify the example to use a different query request. There are also the* `filterquery` *alternatives that allow constrained content-based queries against the registry.*

The figure above shows the detail of the XML response that is returned. The data shown is just a representative sample. The structure of the associated DTD is shown in the following figure, since this helps in the understanding of the overall detail that can be returned by this particular query. The ebXML registry specifications show one giant DTD of these, but each subpiece is in fact intended to be a standalone DTD, as can be seen in this example.

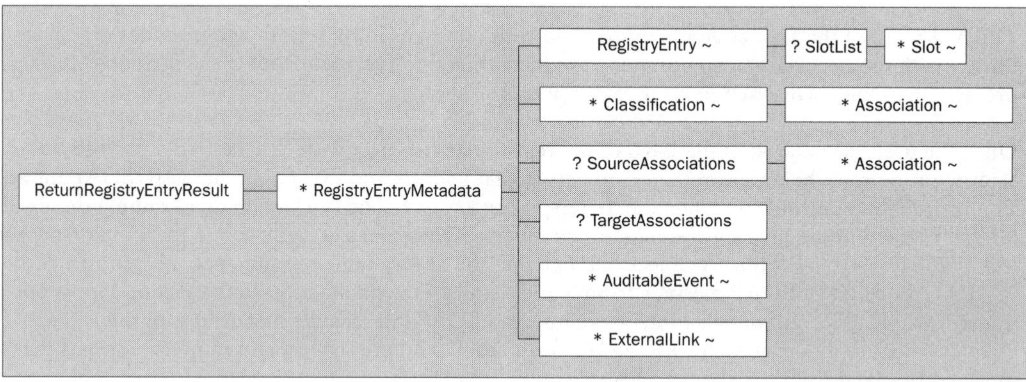

The figure shows the main element level components of the DTD. The data is shown as empty elements to simplify the diagram. Live queries to the registry will obviously return actual data.

This completes the roundup of the XML and source code associated with the example of accessing the ebXML Registry server from a Java enabled client using an existing ebXML TRP library implementation.

## Transformation Example

A registry can aid transformations during both design and runtime. The following walk-through is simple and straightforward but conveys the power of managing the enterprises meta data in a shared registry. As you begin to use the same components over the value chain, the reuse can be huge, especially when we consider the timesaving in auto-transformations.

### Design Time

As shown in the following screen shot, a dialog box is presented to the user with options for how to handle elements identified via a UID on the inbound schema. In addition, a matching algorithm can match on element and attribute names to core and domain components found in the registry. The user can also bring up the component for review to inspect other facets of the unit. The registry's user interface can be invoked for browsing and querying, full navigation of the registry is allowed, perhaps using a message schema as the guide to learn more about its use and to digest any annotations to assist in the mapping process.

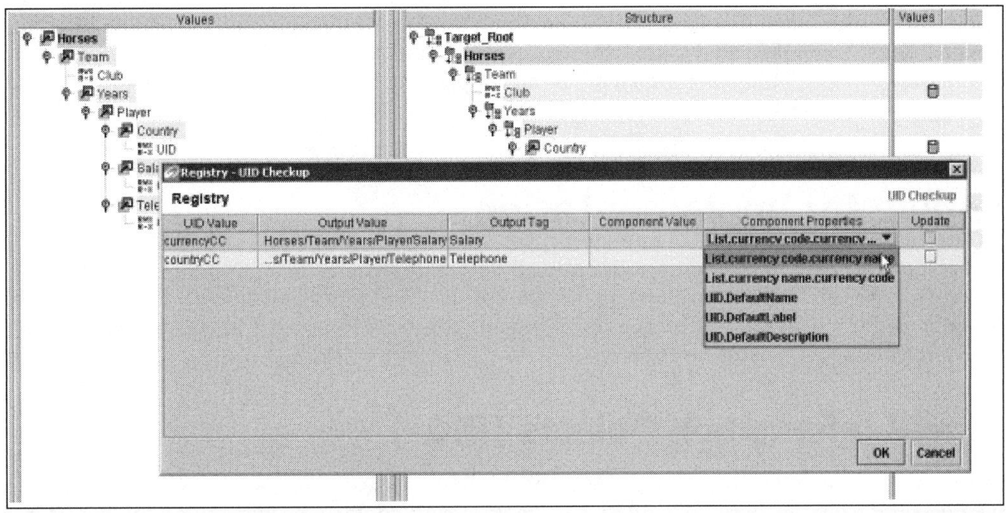


In either case, the user is presented with a list of the type information specific to the inbound element that may be included in the output structure. An example XML snippet returned by the ebXML Registry used to populate the transformation user dialog box can be found in the following code listing:

```
<extensions>
   <component CodeList="true" Propertylist="true" UID="countryCC">
      <properties>
         <ElementName>coreComponentXYZ</ElementName>
         <Label>countryCC</Label>
         <Description>
            countryCC for currency and country codelists
         </Description>
```

```
        </properties>
        <ExtensionDefinitions>
            <Extension type="codeLists">
                <Item type="UID">callCL</Item>
                <Item type="UID">currencyCL</Item>
                <Item type="UID">countryCL</Item>
            </Extension>
         </ExtensionDefinitions>
    </component>
</extensions>
```

The appropriate meta data is shown in the dropdown edit box under Component Properties. This can be an alias (alternative name) or some other attribute related to the core or domain component, such as long name or description. In the previous example, with `UnitPrice` lookup, the user will have the option of selecting `ListPrice` and may decide to include the `Currency` element as well.

#### *Runtime*

If late linking is required in the transform, such as a conversion between a country code and its full name, it can be achieved by identifying and selecting the appropriate cross-reference data values and the elements to map. This dynamic lookup can also be defined to work the other way, which is to go from full name to country code. It can be accessed on core components residing in the registry, a repository, or file system. In addition, different lookup values can be accessed depending on where the lookup takes place in the value chain, varying the constraints allowed and specific to the elements used. Likewise, the lookup can be performed differently depending on regional characteristics to assist in the globalization of the element.

# Planning for Implementation

This section lists the tasks typically accomplished during implementation. This isn't intended to be complete, rather an aid to understanding the process and 'food for thought' on how to best plan for development. It is split into two stages: identifying data to be incorporated in the registry/repository and identifying requirements for registry services.

## Business Information Objects (BIOs)

This stage is concerned with data migration, which involves discovering, analyzing, and propagating meta data (for example, business models, data capture methodology, business rules) for import into the registry/repository. Data migration will involve the following broad steps:

- Evaluate tools to assist in data migration task.
- Review existing data and activity models.
- Prepare models and other data for registration.
- Define extraction transformations.
- Register and filter models.
- Register other data.

- Run classification sequences on registered business artifacts.
- Design and set up information model.
- Define role-based security measures for various business artifacts and assign personnel to roles.
- Develop user interface for navigation.
- Structure registered business artifacts into BIOs.
- Work with XML-based consortiums to influence standards.
- Manage the BIOs configurations.
- Adjust process based on feedback.
- Continue to add capabilities as the process and data migration matures.

## Registry

This stage involves defining registry services, in addition to those specified by ebXML, that address internal structure, business artifacts, patterns, use case and scenarios, crosswalks (mappings), message specification, collaboration partner profiles (CPPs), and collaboration partner agreements (CPAs). Some examples of such services offering additional functionality are described in this section.

The registry could provide new functionality to the organization using the ebXML RIM set of classification structures (or taxonomies) as a baseline that can be navigated based on business domains and required business functions. The RIM is functionally directed; therefore an end-user can navigate in a directed domain path search to locate the particular business action or component. This domain-based decision tree, with topics that reside on top of a semantic net, provides an adjunct interface to the traditional keyword or dictionary style searches. The user navigating the registry will see only the components that are applicable in the context of their search. For instance, a user may navigate one of the hierarchies to find the general ledger located within an accounting repository, and then find the chart of account items required to perform the task, then find the standard transactions, and then find the times, schedules, special conditions (such as limits and edge requirements), and events.

The RIM identifies the individual data elements and details their relationship with other elements (both inside and outside the business domain). The RIM can provide data dictionaries, thesauri, and "intelligent" user prompts driven by extensive use of collaborative technology used in adapting pathways, both during language modeling and production/searching functions.

As discussed previously, a critical aspect of the registry is the crosswalk entries. A crosswalk is a set of transformations applied to business components and their link mechanisms to analogous business components. Crosswalk development is the intellectual task of business experts, as they must determine the semantic mapping of elements between the source and target meta data. The task involves specifying a mapping of each element in the source meta data with a semantically equivalent element in the target meta data.

The organization will achieve harmonization throughout the business domain by creating and maintaining only one set of prime components and mapping other components to the prime components as required. The first step toward harmonization is to extract the common terminology, properties, organization, and processes used by many of the business functions and then create a generic framework for developing new, or updating existing, components. Because similar procedures can be applied to related components, the implementation and the development of new crosswalks are simplified.

The harmonization tasks include:

- Identifying common terminology and establishing a formal definition for each term. A shared vocabulary prevents misinterpretation of the standards and lays the foundation for subsequent harmonization efforts.
- Identifying the classes and superclasses, or if not in a class, identifying the processes (verbs) for noun-type functions or the objects (nouns) for verb-type functions.
- Identifying position or positions in the RIM.
- Extracting concepts that can be generalized and used in a common way. For example, determine if the meta data element is mandatory, optional, or mandatory based on certain conditions; determine if the meta data element can occur only once or multiple times; determine the organization of meta data elements relative to each other, such as hierarchical parent-child relationships and constraints imposed on the value of the element (for example free text, numeric range, date, or a controlled vocabulary).

The shared properties can then be expressed and used in a similar fashion. The crosswalk mechanism simplifies operational runtime data transformations through a linking and business rules process. Historically, these transformations were maps at the document level only. By managing the meta data at the enterprise level there is a better probability that the maps can be configured once for all instances in the organization.

Crosswalk attributes and relationships can be defined as templates that establish a common, implicit negotiation protocol at the business enterprise view. Because business interactions can be complex and potentially require specialized knowledge, data manipulation agents may ensure that users can express their requirements in high-level, natural language supplementing templates. The registry service automatically creates appropriate rule templates and XML syntax (if required) to match user requirements and broker the entire interchange. Additionally, the registry service specifies registry meta data requirements and structures in detail and evaluates the local repository toolset, if one exists, relative to registry requirements, including performing gap analysis and formulating solutions.

Extension of registry functionality includes providing active linking to other registries for the ability to handle peak loads, and system reliability, and linking to external communities.

# Ongoing Registry/Repository Efforts

Several organizations have already begun to implement version 1.0 of the ebXML Registry/Repository specifications. In this section we'll take a look at a sample of the efforts that are underway.

## OASIS

In June 2001 members of the existing OASIS Registry/Repository TC expanded their charter to embrace the ebXML Registry/Repository Specification. The OASIS ebXML Registry TC (http://www.oasis-open.org/committees/regrep/) develops specifications to achieve interoperable registries and repositories, with an interface that enables submission, query, and retrieval of the contents of the registry and repository. Further, the Registry TC seeks to develop specifications that serve a wide range of uses, from general-purpose document registries to real-time business-to-business registries. Additionally, as part of its specification development work, this TC explores and promotes various emerging models for distributed and cooperating registries.

## KIEC Korea ebXML Central Registry & Repository

The **Korea Institute for Electronic Commerce** (**KIEC** – the KIEC homepage, hosted in Korean, can be found at http://www.ebxml.or.kr/registry/index.html) has an online ebXML Registry/Repository prototype to promote electronic business within Korean industries by utilizing advanced ebXML technology. In accordance with the development of the ebXML specifications at OASIS, the functionalities and services of the Korea ebXML Central Registry & Repository will be synchronously upgraded. The current Korea ebXML Central Registry & Repository supports registration and search of CPPs, XML DTDs, and Schemas.

KIEC believes in the concept of distributed registries and repositories: As they say, "There will surely be many ebXML registries and repositories in Korea to serve the need of specific industries and sectors." One sector-specific ebXML Registry/Repository is already being developed. The GxmlHub, really the offspring of KIEC's Korea ebXML Central Registry & Repository, is being developed by Korea Trade Network to serve the trade sector. The Korea ebXML Central Registry & Repository will maintain standard business content for Korean industry; also, as one step to overcome the digital divide, it will serve the role of a sector-specific ebXML Registry/Repository for those sectors that cannot afford to have their own ebXML Registry/Repository.

## DISA DRIve

The Data Interchange Standards Association (DISA) is moving forward with its DISA Registry Initiative (DRIve) project (http://www.disa.org/drive/) with contributions of software, systems, and technical expertise to create the architecture for, and operation of, a registry of data objects. The DRIve registry will meet the requirements of the ebXML Registry/Repository specifications. DRIve will support organizations under the DISA umbrella, including:

- Accredited Standards Committee (ASC) X12.
- Open Travel Alliance (OTA).
- Interactive Financial eXchange (IFX) Forum.
- Mortgage Industry Standards Maintenance Organization (MISMO).
- Open Philanthropy eXchange (OPX) Forum.
- Hotel Electronic Distribution Network Association (HEDNA).

Registering ebXML-based core components for the semantics of these standards and specifications into a framework that is consistent with that of the ebXML distributed registry and repository vision will have a far-reaching impact.

## DoD SHADE XML Registry

The US Department of Defense (DoD) has an initiative (for more information, see http://diides.ncr.disa.mil/xmlreg/index.cfm) to improve data interoperability within DoD communities, items to browse and use that satisfy DoD system or database requirements. Shared Data Engineering (SHADE) is responsible for data services and other data-related infrastructure for the Common Operating Environment (COE) that promote interoperability and software reuse in a secure, reliable, and global-networked environment.

The COE's data service infrastructure is implemented as sets of shared schema, data management and data access services, build-time and runtime tools, server development and operating procedures, and technical guidance for supporting COE-based mission applications. The primary objective of the registry is to migrate many redundant, dissimilar but overlapping data stores to standardized COE-compliant data services built from "plug-and-play" components that blend multiple data technologies. The following namespaces have been identified: Acquisition Logistics, Configuration Management, Combat Support, Controlled Exports, DoD Enterprise, Finance and Accounting, Geospatial and Imagery, General Military Intelligence, Ground Operations, Logistics, Meteorological and Oceanographic, Product Data, Personnel, System Engineering, Supply, Tracks and Reports, and Transportation. Plans are for DoD SHADE to adopt ebXML interfaces.

## XML.gov

Recently, General Services Administration (GSA) published a request for a proposal for an ebXML Registry/Repository in support of collaboration with US Federal Agencies and US State governments, with an implementation timeline in early 2002. The XML.gov web site (http://www.xml.gov/ – linked from http://.www.firstgov.gov/) will contain the front-end interface that allows access to the registry, with future plans to add features from the latest W3C specifications on querying XML content, such as XQuery and XSQL.

*Note: these query capabilities are included in the scope of the ebXML specifications under the ad hoc query provisions that vendors can provide. Combined with the standard query mechanisms these provide a complete suite of capabilities to access and manage content within the registry.*

Preferably, maintenance of the registry implementation will not require any specialized tools, associated database storage will utilize standard file-system access, and web-based maintenance can be achieved using the maintenance web forms – allowing administrators full access to the registry system to control user access, security, review content, and even extend these through a web services interface. Additionally, having the database layer itself include an administrative user interface that allows repair and recovery of the content within the database, along with a Query-by-Example (QBE) wizard that helps novice staff quickly learn how to directly access content using advanced XML querying syntax, is an underlying objective of the ebXML Registry implementation.

## Next Steps

You should now have a thorough understanding of the purpose of the ebXML Registry/Repository and may have decided that your organization could benefit from such an implementation. What are the next steps? What areas need your experience and skills to push the envelope with XML technology? In short, the next steps in the journey will be defined by those who have the desire to advance the technology, and will be fueled by your imagination. The following areas could provide interesting products to supplement the state of the specifications today:

- XML-based Information Services – the initial vision of the registry is that it would serve the community of interest and include infrastructure functionality in addition to passive storage and retrieval.
- User Interface – using the registry-centric approach, dynamically generating user interfaces.
- CASE Tool support – the automation of UML to XMI to XML Schemas to core components.

- Consistent procedures and policies – using the registry to provide a meta-architecture for development, where the registry/repository provides consistency to the organization through reuse of procedures, etc.
- Resource accounting – logging usage to provide a self-sustaining system of selling information, and calculating royalties and micro-payments for transactions, as an alternative to wholesale blocks or rental periods.
- UDDI & WSDL family of standards' influence – bringing together the verb and noun-based approaches to provide a more flexible and complete offering, with a services front-end user interface program that uses registry references for semantic interpretation.
- Notifications – using the registry to discover people in the community of interest, or to receive e-mails notifying changes to components of interest, and to provide a basis for collaborative development.
- Classifications – provide auto-classification tools to assist organizations in identifying concepts in a dynamic environment of operations, to provide constant feedback.

# Summary

In this chapter we learned the value of an ebXML Registry, and how the architecture provides a link to existing repositories. Without a solid foundation and a registry/repository strategy, reaching the goal of enterprise agility or implementation of knowledge management will continue to be elusive or unattainable. To meet this challenge, we see vendors bringing products to market to support the organizations who are adopting ebXML as part of their eBusiness strategy. We discovered that even though the work of ebXML ended in May of 2001, the work is based on years of development and continues to evolve through extensions to the core specifications. Discussed are the issues an organization would need to consider implementing an ebXML Registry/Repository with tasks outlined, which should be carried out to take the first step.

Hopefully this chapter has prepared you to begin thinking about how a registry/repository can help your organization, and has either enabled you to make the decision to delay implementation for the time being, or inspired you to begin your development at once. In either case you should now have enough knowledge and material available to back any decision you make concerning the use of a registry-centric architecture. By all means revisit the chapter, read the specifications, research the base technology efforts, attend registry initiatives, and participate in helping to define this change agent for achieving enterprise agility.

# 8

# Collaboration Protocol Profiles and Agreements

One of the limitations of many currently operational e-business application infrastructures is that they have mainly managed to automate what are essentially **static** business relations among business partners. By 'static', we mean that the business partners that had the system constructed already knew each other, already had business arrangements and plan to continue their relationship over a longer time. The e-business system simply automates the execution of those arrangements. To justify an e-business system in such an environment, the return on investment for the project is often estimated not on a potential for new business opportunities or expanding sales. It is often judged instead on reductions in administrative/other costs, reductions in the time taken to execute processes, or supply chain management related benefits obtained through improved information sharing, such as optimizing inventory levels using just-in-time (JIT) manufacturing.

The next, more challenging, step in e-business is to use technology to support a move towards more **dynamic** business relations. By 'dynamic', we mean not just that the e-business infrastructure supports businesses in finding (or allowing themselves to be found by) new partners that they can do business with. A dynamic e-business infrastructure should also help to automate the process of setting up e-business collaboration agreements, perhaps on a more ad hoc, time-limited basis. Such agreements are often called electronic **trading partner agreements** (**TPAs**).

The **Collaboration Protocol Profiles/Collaboration Protocol Agreements** (**CPP/CPA**) specification is the implementation of trading partner agreements in the ebXML framework, and the topic of this chapter. While we'll only discuss ebXML CPPs and CPAs, it is worth noting that ebXML's facilities in this area have benefited from prior work, such as that done in CommerceNet and in particular IBM's work on a markup language for trading partners, called tpaML. The tpaML was donated to OASIS prior to the ebXML project and further developed as part of it; the schema for ebXML CPP/CPA shares many elements with the tpaML DTD.

Apart from supporting dynamic e-business relations, there is an important architectural principle in the separation of two different classes of information:

- Information needed for the interaction with specific parties.
- Information relating to a general business process or collaboration, which is relevant to any instantiation of the collaboration with a specific business partner, and can be managed independently of the particular parties you collaborate with.

This separation gives you a handle to scale your e-business system to support new business processes and new business parties independently.

We'll start the chapter by giving a high-level introduction to the general topic of partner agreements and to the position of CPP and CPA in the overall ebXML framework. Next, we'll dive into detailed discussion of the specifications, with some examples from the International Trade Transaction (ITT) case we met in Chapter 2. Some of the issues briefly discussed in the first section are worked out in more detail in the other sections of this chapter.

So here's the order of proceedings for this chapter:

- First, we'll give a high-level overview of CPAs and CPPs, and their context.
- The main chapter body is a discussion of the XML structure of CPP and CPA documents, following the organization of the XML Schema for CPP/CPA. Discussion of CPA formation is interleaved with this discussion.
- Next, we'll present another way of thinking about how the aspects of business interactions in an ebXML based e-business solution are controlled – by CPP and CPA documents, in relation to other ebXML specifications.
- After this, we discuss some adoption strategies for CPP/CPAs when implementing an ebXML solution.
- Finally, we'll summarize the main issues of the chapter and point to further work.

# Introducing CPP and CPA Documents

The term **trading partner agreement** (**TPA**) is a general term that can cover both technical and business-related agreements, or a combination of both. The technical agreements are discussed in detail in this chapter and include transport protocols and security policies. At the business level, a TPA needs to provide a reference to the business process that both partners agree to implement, each performing their role in a particular collaboration, and perhaps also to other (often non-electronic) contractual arrangements, terms and conditions etc. that companies have agreed to.

The ebXML **collaboration protocol agreements**, or **CPAs**, are machine interpretable versions of such TPAs. A particular CPA is an XML document that conforms to the schema for CPA documents. This schema is provided and documented in the ebXML specification for protocol profiles and agreements. The specification is available at http://www.ebxml.org/specs/ebCPP.pdf. As it is mentioned so often in this chapter, we'll refer to it as ebCPP from now on, following the conventions used in the ebXML specifications themselves. As the word "protocol" suggests, they are more focused on the technical aspects of interaction between business partners than on the business-related aspects. You can think of CPAs as the bridge between the transport layer and the business layer:

- At the **transport** layer, you look at an ebXML system as an XML-based, secure e-business messaging system.
- At the **business** layer, you are thinking in terms of the function of those messages within business processes, business collaborations and business transactions among business partners.

The CPA layer connects the two layers. If you were to trace the message traffic in an operational ebXML system in an attempt to link a specific message to the business transaction activity that it implements, or vice versa, the CPA provides the information you would need to get started. We'll dive into the specifics of how this works later in this chapter.

In terms of the **UN/CEFACT Modeling Method** (**UMM**) process for ebXML projects (see Chapter 2), you can think of the CPA as configuration information for the "Business Service View". You would work on CPAs in the "Design" workflow of your ebXML project. We will occasionally reference the business modeling, requirements and analysis workflows when we reference some of the "artifacts" you would produce in these workflows if you use UMM. In the "Implementation" workflow, your complementary actions would be to use a CPA in one of two ways:

- As **documentation** for a custom interface layer between a higher-level business process handler or enterprise systems and the lower-level transport layer. You can implement this layer using the XML tools and/or programming languages of choice.
- As **configuration** information for a CPA-compliant ebXML middleware product. In this case, you can think of the software product as having solved the "generic" problem of protocol arrangements, and the CPA document as specific configuration parameters for such a system.

The same two options for implementation are available to **business process specification schema** (**BPSS**) business process specifications (see Chapter 5). Both the CPA and BPSS specifications are instances of the general trend from lower-level procedural programming to middleware products that allow configuration by declarative, executable specifications. We'll go into the advantages and disadvantages of the two approaches later in this chapter.

A CPA also provides a mechanism for two business partners to negotiate variable properties, override default values specified in the business process specification, or specify the time interval during which the agreement is valid. A single organization can use, say, HTTP as transport protocol to collaborate with one partner and SMTP with another partner, and yet perform the same role in the same business collaboration in both cases. This offers a lot of flexibility and opportunities for optimization to users and implementers of the ebXML infrastructure.

Now that we've introduced CPAs and shown how they fit in with the overall ebXML framework, an obvious question is: what steps do two organizations need to take to create a CPA, and what are the inputs to that process? Here, there are several options, including the following:

- One option is that the CPA is formed from scratch or from a template where only a few parameters need to be set, or from an expired previous version of the CPA. There need not be any other input documents and the CPA is directly used to further configure or implement the ebXML system.
- The CPA might be built into a custom software package, implicit in its terms of use or agreed explicitly as part of the software installation procedure. You can think of this as a special case of the previous option.
- Another option is to create the CPA on the basis of similarly structured documents called **collaboration protocol profiles** (**CPPs**).

The following diagram visualizes these options, where we have viewed the second option as a special case of the first option, and "A" as issuer of the software product or of the CPA template.

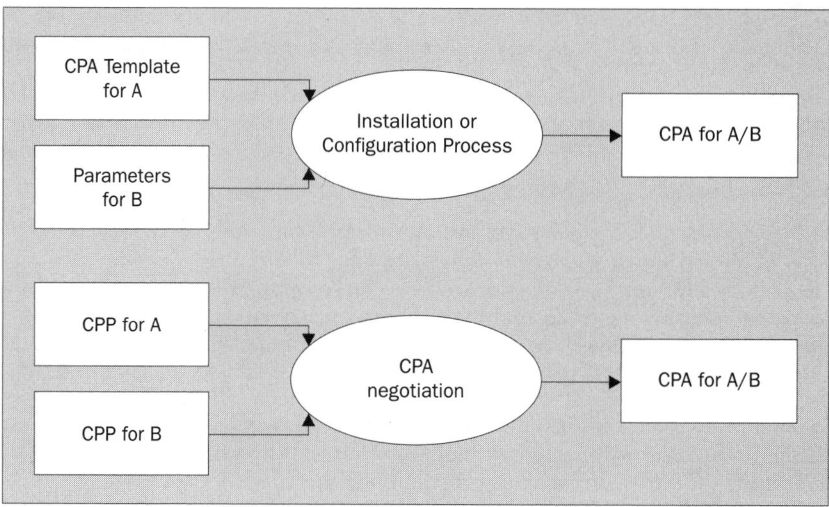


A CPP, like a CPA, is an XML document; a CPP conforms to the schema for CPP documents. This schema is provided (in DTD and XML Schemas forms) in Appendices C and D of the ebCPP specification (http://www.ebxml.org). A CPP describes the e-business capabilities of a single business partner. In general, it will provide a multitude of options for negotiation with potential business partners.

Let's look at the ITT case introduced in Chapter 2 for some examples. An insurance company may provide, at the business level, many insurance services apart from providing international transport insurance (through the 'Insurer' role, in the 'Prepare For Export' use case). At the technical level, the company may support various protocols, perhaps including proprietary protocols or the use of private value added networks (VANs). A potential customer, such as the espresso-machine vendor, will only be interested in collaboration with this company because it wants to act as 'Exporter' in a specific business process that requires an 'Insurer' as business partner. Similarly, the company probably won't be interested in all the transport protocols supported by the 'Insurer', as long as there is one compatible set of transport parameters on which they agree.

While the CPA is, in principle, a *private* agreement between two organizations, any company (for example the insurance company) that wants to expand its business will be interested in publishing its CPP on its web site, and in making the CPP available via a public registry. This will enable potential customers (such as the exporting company) to browse through the registry, probably using the business process as an access path, and find that CPP. If the CPP **matches** that company's protocol profile (which, preferably, would also be specified as a CPP document), they can propose a draft CPA to the 'Insurer'. Possibly after some negotiation, a final CPA is agreed upon, and their systems can be configured to implement the agreement.

Again, there is an obvious next question: what do we mean by **matching** and how does the matching process work? The ebCPP specification document for CPP/CPA explains why, at the moment, you cannot create a CPA from two CPPs in a completely automatic fashion; we'll go into the reasons why in more detail later in this chapter. This is not as problematic as it might seem at first glance, because in parallel to negotiating the CPA, the organizations will probably need to make other business-level arrangements that (at least in the foreseeable future) will require human intervention. However, further automation in this area clearly remains a challenge for future developments and perhaps poses an interesting potential application area (and business opportunity) for agent technology.

Now that we've given a high-level overview of CPA and CPP and their context, let's take a look at the XML structure of CPP and CPA documents (following the organization of the XML Schema for CPP/CPA), and consider the formation of a CPA document.

# Structure of CPP and CPA Documents

The ebCPP Specification document provides a specification for CPP and CPA XML documents in XML DTD and XML Schema formats. Because of the use of XML Schema data typing, the XML Schema version is strictly more constraining and informative, but otherwise the two schemas are equivalent. The structure of documents defined by these schemas provides a good handle to come to an understanding of the specifications. In our discussion, we will provide examples from CPP documents related to the International Trade Transactions case introduced in Chapter 2. Specifically, we've adopted the following structure for this section – we will discuss:

- The `<CollaborationProtocolProfile>` and `<CollaborationProtocolAgreement>` elements, root elements of CPP and CPA documents, respectively. In this section we'll also discuss additional CPA-specific information.
- The party identification and party reference information elements, `<PartyId>` and `<PartyRef>`.
- Digital certificates, which are put in place in CPP/CPA documents using `<Certificate>` structures.
- The `<CollaborationRole>` and `<ServiceBinding>` elements.
- Elements for defining delivery channels and packaging – `<DeliveryChannel>`, and the `<Packaging>` structure.
- The `<Transport>` and `<DocExchange>` elements.

To facilitate discussion and comparison, each section contains corresponding information from CPPs and the CPA. In this chapter, we'll focus on providing a succinct tutorial introduction with examples, and cross-references to further specifications. We cover most (but not all) of the material covered in the ebCPP Specification, which remains the definitive reference.

## The Document Element

The CPP and CPA documents have root elements that act as containers for the collaboration information provided by one business partner (in the case of a CPP) or of the agreements reached between the two partners (in the case of a CPA). These elements mainly serve to define a number of namespaces and the prefixes used to refer to them throughout the document, as well as an optional `version` attribute, which provides elementary versioning information.

XML Namespace prefixes are used to label elements that are derived from the specific namespace, and allow reference to the namespace without having to put the verbose URI on all elements. The URI is not (at least, not necessarily) an address for a downloadable XML Schema document, but merely serves for identification. Namespaces are defined in the W3C Specification, *Namespaces in XML* (http://www.w3.org/TR/1999/REC-xml-names-19990114/) and discussed in many introductory XML textbooks, such as *Beginning XML Second Edition* (Wrox, ISBN 1-861005-59-8).

The namespace URIs and suggested prefixes are:

- `http://www.ebxml.org/namespaces/tradePartner` (prefix `tp`, or without prefix if used as default namespace) is the namespace for the elements in the CPP and CPA specifications.
- `http://www.w3.org/2001/XMLSchema-instance` (prefix `xsi`) is the URI for XML Schema instances. It is needed at the document element itself to prefix the `xsi:schemaLocation` attribute. This attribute references a namespace for the CPP/CPA schema itself, allowing you to validate CPP/CPA documents using generic validating XML parsers.
- `http://www.w3.org/1999/xlink` (prefix `xlink`) is the namespace for the W3C XLINK Specification (http://www.w3.org/TR/xlink/). CPP/CPA uses these links for several external references.
- `http://www.w3.org/2000/09/xmldsig#` (prefix `ds`) is the URI for the W3C Digital Signature Specification. These allow parties to digitally sign the CPP or CPA documents.

## A CPP Template

The following is a template for a CPP, with substructures omitted. Note that this template includes both a reference to the DTD (using the `DOCTYPE` declaration) and to the XML Schema version of the CPP schema. The presence of two "schema" references is rather redundant but useful in situations where some validation or editing software uses DTDs, and some uses XML Schemas. In a project you will probably use just one of these, with the XML Schema version likely becoming preferred, as support for XML Schema becomes increasingly more widespread. Also note that in production systems, you would reference schemas stored at public locations or repositories rather than having such references resolved locally. For performance reasons, production ebXML systems will probably ignore the referenced schema anyway and validate the CPP/CPA XML documents using pre-parsed, cached or compiled representations of the CPP/CPA schemas.

```
<?xml version="1.0" encoding="UTF-8"?>
<!DOCTYPE CollaborationProtocolProfile SYSTEM "cpp-cpa-v1_0.dtd">
<CollaborationProtocolProfile
   xmlns="http://www.ebxml.org/namespaces/tradePartner"
   xmlns:xsi="http://www.w3.org/2000/10/XMLSchema-instance"
   xmlns:xlink="http://www.w3.org/1999/xlink"
   xmlns:ds="http://www.w3.org/2000/09/xmldsig#"
      xsi:schemaLocation="cpp-cpa-v1_0.xsd.xml"
       tp:version="1.1">
   <PartyInfo>
      <!-- Information about the Party -->
   </PartyInfo>
   <Packaging id="pk.emv.01">
      <!-- Information about packaging of message payload -->
   </Packaging>
   <ds:Signature>
```

```
      <!-- Optional digital signature -->
   </ds:Signature>
   <Comment xml:lang="en">
      <!-- ... -->
   </Comment>
</CollaborationProtocolProfile>
```

A given CPP document can have multiple `<PartyInfo>` and `<Packaging>` elements. We'll discuss packaging later in this chapter. Multiple `<PartyInfo>` elements can be useful if a party wants to present itself as multiple parties, for instance to reflect an organization in multiple business units or geographic divisions, or because the organization can do business as different legal entities. (As you'll see when we discuss `<PartyInfo>`, this differs from having multiple business identifiers for a single party, which can be accommodated by a multiple `<PartyId>` elements within a single `<PartyInfo>`).

Only one of these multiple `<PartyInfo>` elements is actually involved in a particular CPA. This is a demonstration of the formation of a CPA from CPPs by process of narrowing down from multiple alternatives to a single selection, a general pattern that you will see again and again in this chapter.

## A CPA Template

The following is a template for a CPA. As you see, it is structured similarly to a CPP:

```
<CollaborationProtocolAgreement
   xmlns="http://www.ebxml.org/namespaces/tradePartner"
   xmlns:xsi="http://www.w3.org/2000/10/XMLSchema-instance"
   xmlns:xlink="http://www.w3.org/1999/xlink"
   xmlns:ds="http://www.w3.org/2000/09/xmldsig#"
   xsi:schemaLocation="http://www.ebxml.org/namespaces/tradePartner/cpp-cpa-
v1_0.xsd"
   cpaid="EspressoMachineVendorAndItsInsurer"
   version="1.0">
   <Status value="signed"/>
   <Start>2001-11-26T07:21:00Z</Start>
   <End>2001-12-26T07:21:00Z</End>
   <ConversationConstraints invocationLimit="100"
                            concurrentConversations="4"/>
   <PartyInfo>
      <!--Identification information for the first business partner,
          see next section -->
   </PartyInfo>
   <PartyInfo>
      <!-- The other business partner -->
   </PartyInfo>
   <Packaging id="pk.emv.01">
      <!-- Information about packaging of message payload -->
   </Packaging>
   <ds:Signature>
      <!-- Optional digital signature -->
   </ds:Signature>
</CollaborationProtocolAgreement>
```

While the CPA schema actually allows one or many `<PartyInfo>` elements, the current standard only supports bilateral agreements involving exactly two partners. In a collaboration involving multiple partners, these partners should create pair-wise CPAs, but only if they are involved in business collaborations. In the ITT case discussed in Chapter 2, the number of business partners involved is quite high, but the main flow of events only involves one or two core partners, 'Exporter' and 'Freight Forwarder', who are involved with more than one other business partner. These two partners need to create CPAs with all those partners, but there is no need for, say, the 'Carrier' to make arrangements with the 'Chamber of Commerce', as they never exchange information, at least not in this context.

The `cpaid` attribute provides a unique identifier for this agreement. It is used by the ebXML messaging service as header information. As a result, each incoming message can be traced to the CPA document. The ebXML layer in the e-business system should maintain a lookup table from this identifier to the CPA documents (or information derived or compiled from these CPA documents) so that it can retrieve the protocol agreement information needed to further process the information.

The CPA also records additional information not derived from information in the source CPPs:

- The `<Status>` element records whether the CPA is `proposed`, `agreed` or `signed`. A `proposed` CPA is one that a partner like 'Importer' (or rather its ebXML-based e-business system) might send to 'Exporter', indicating that it wants to engage in e-business collaboration. If 'Exporter' agrees to this, they can return the CPA with `agreed` status. Finally, the status can be set to `signed` if both parties digitally sign the CPA.
- The `<Start>` and `<End>` elements indicate the interval during which new business process instances governed by this CPA can be started.
- The `<ConversationConstraints>` element allows you to specify a limit on how often a new business process governed by the CPA can be started and how many such conversations can be ongoing at the same time.

The values for `Status` make sense when you can think of CPA negotiation as a kind of a business process in itself, where the CPA is the business document that is exchanged and modified until (hopefully) an agreement is reached. If you want to automate this negotiation process itself using an e-business system, the partners probably need a CPA to get started. Such a CPA will probably be built into ebXML-compliant software, to bootstrap the overall CPA formation process. Negotiation protocols are part of the work list of the OASIS CPPA technical committee that continues the work in this field after the ebXML project.

Note that the interval between `<Start>` and `<End>` is different from the duration of an individual business conversation, which may vary from sub-second transactions to processes that take weeks or months to complete. When the time indicated by the `<End>` element has arrived, the CPA expires, and no new conversations can be initiated, but existing transactions are allowed to complete. Here, ebXML reflects common practice in workflow management systems. If you're wondering about ways to constrain duration of processes and of associated business conversations, these can be controlled using the `timeToPerform` properties of the UMM process analysis model (Chapter 2) and the ebXML Business Process Specification Schema (Chapter 5).

Let's step back for the moment and look at what the parameters specified in the `<Start>`, `<End>` and `<ConversationConstraints>` elements allow you to do. They control business conversation with a *specific* partner, either for business reasons or for technical reasons:

- You may want to reduce the number of concurrent connections due to the **technical** limitations (such as performance) of the back-end system – perhaps the underlying system locks partner-specific resources (in a database system), or it was not designed for concurrent processes at all. Note that this is not sufficient to prevent cases where your system is overloaded by multiple concurrent requests from different partners, as the CPA only limits the number of conversations with individual partners, not the number of current conversations with all partners collectively.
- Pricing strategies, product availability or seasonal limitations are examples of **business** reasons to limit the number of invocations or the validity interval of the CPA.
- To a limited extent, you can also use these limitations to safeguard against fraud or hacking. (However, they are no substitutes for professional software and policies for prevention and detection of fraud or intrusion!)

Time- and invocation-limited agreements also make sense in the general context of **dynamic** e-business. CPAs enable companies to engage in business relations for a limited time or for a limited amount of transactions. Automated formation of CPAs from CPPs reduces the administrative cost of making such arrangements and therefore increases the overall flexibility and efficiency of e-business relations.

The `<Comment>` element in CPP and CPA documents can be used as a generic placeholder for document meta information. One use might be to reference legal documents. In a CPP, you could use the `<Comment>` element to reference your general terms and conditions on your web site or deposited with the 'Chamber of Commerce' in your country. In a CPA, you could use it to reference a contract your company has signed with another party.

# Party Identification and Reference

The `<PartyInfo>` element has two sub-elements that provide information about the organization that issues the CPP. They are:

- The `<PartyId>` element, which provides a logical identifier for the party.
- The `<PartyRef>` element, which can store references to other (descriptive) information about the party.

While we use URLs as a way to uniquely identify and access resources on the Internet, there is no equivalent universal identification schema for businesses, and ebXML does not provide one. This is not unfortunate (and perhaps even desirable), as there are many established schemas or systems that allow for unique identification of parties that can be re-used. The `<PartyId>` element has string content and a `type` attribute that also has a string value. You can use the attribute value to identify a classification schema and the content of the element to provide an identifier within that classification schema. Here are some examples of classification schemas for businesses:

- Dun and Bradstreet (a company that collects data on businesses for risk assessment, marketing etc.) have developed the D-U-N-S (Data Universal Numbering Service) system to uniquely identify businesses worldwide. More information is available at http://www.dnb.com. According to Dun and Bradstreet's web site, the D-U-N-S numbering scheme covered 62 million individual businesses in September 2001 (http://www.dnb.com/english/D-U-N-S/default.asp).

- Many businesses are classified in industry-specific registries, for instance the Uniform Code Council for the grocery and retail industry (http://www.uc-council.org), and SWIFT for worldwide financial institutions (http://www.swift.com).
- National Chambers of Commerce and government tax agencies also have unique identification schemes (such as company VAT numbers) that are referenced in (non-electronic) business documents such as invoices.

Assuming a hypothetical classification scheme "abc" and an identifier "1234567890" within that scheme, the party identification could look like this:

```
<PartyId type="abc">1234567890</PartyId>
```

To summarize, so far we've seen two pieces of party identification information: a classification scheme and an identifier within that scheme. As a third dimension (but this is not encoded in the CPP/CPA schema), the classification schema itself can be registered using a "meta"-classification scheme. If you do not know the "abc" classification scheme (or, say, you want to find out who "abc" is so you can go to their web site to look up the company identified by them as 1234567890), you could look it up in a "registry of registries". There are three common standards in this area:

- In EDIFACT, the "Interchange Sender" and "Interchange Recipient" segments in the interchange header can have a 0007 "Partner identification code qualifier" (see http://www.unece.org/trade/edifact/untdid/d422_s.htm). Similarly, in many EDIFACT message bodies, you can use the NAD segment that encodes party addresses. This segment has a 3055 data element, "Code list responsible agency code" (see http://www.unece.org/trade/untdid/d01b/tred/tred3055.htm), which provides mapping codes for numerous classification systems. This element complements the 3039 "Party identifier" code and the 1131 "Code list identification code" elements that correspond to the CPP counterparts discussed above. (The URLs for these are like the 3055 data element, with appropriate number changes).
- ANSI ASC X12's I05 serves a similar purpose (see http://grants.nih.gov/grants/era/X12Headers_Trailers.pdf).
- ISO 6523, EDIRA. According to EDIRA Web site, "the EBIC (EDIRA Business Identifier Code) is designed for use as a prefix to a business identifier. The prefix joined with the business identifier is a worldwide unique identification. This allows the recipient of a business identifier to easily identify the issuing organization as well as any appropriate data validation and verification information." More information available at http://www.edira.com.

There can be multiple <PartyId>s if a single organization is classified according to multiple classification schemes. One or more D-U-N-S numbers may be in use because of acquisitions and mergers. In addition to D-U-N-S, a company may have EAN GLNs (Global Location Numbers – see http://www.ean-int.org/locations.html). In the US, a common carrier will have a SCAC (Standard Carrier Alpha Code, see http://www.nmfta.org/) used as its primary identifier, in addition to the D-U-N-S. US Banks are identified using ABA Routing numbers (American Bankers Association – for more information, see http://www.aba.com/Products/PS98_Routing.htm). These would be multiple identifiers for a single organization.

The <PartyRef> element is an XLink simple link. It does not constrain the type or structure of the information referenced. Typically, you would use it to reference pages at the organization's web site that provide background information about the organization, its products and services:

```
<PartyRef xlink:type="simple"
          xlink:href="http://www.espressomachine.it/index.xhtml">
   Espresso Machine Vendor web site
</PartyRef>
```

A common requirement for business registries is to present more types of information in a structured way, such as address information and contact information (e-mail, telephone). You could store that information in a structured XML document and use <PartyRef> to point at that document. Alternatively, you could extend the CPP to incorporate that information inline. This is the approach taken in the case study presented in Chapter 16.

As mentioned before, a single CPP can have multiple <PartyInfo> elements. These have their own <PartyId> substructures that identify the organization that provides the business interfaces described in the <CollaborationRole> elements, enclosed within the same <PartyInfo> element.

#### *Party Identification and Reference in the Formation of a CPA*

In forming a CPA from two CPPs, one <PartyInfo> element is selected for each of the parties bound by the CPA that determines the legal identity of the party for the purpose of the business agreement.

## Certificates

You can add <Certificate>s within the <PartyInfo> structure. A certificate consists of a single <ds:KeyInfo> subelement, and is referenced from various other positions for diverse reasons like authorization, message and transport encryption:

```
<Certificate certId="cert.01">
      <ds:KeyInfo>...</ds:KeyInfo>
</Certificate>
```

Digital certificates are technical components of a public key-based security infrastructure. They are used to identify business parties and to expose their public keys and encryption preferences. The <KeyInfo> element is drawn from the Digital Signature Namespace and defined in the XML Signature Syntax and Processing Specification, developed by the W3C (http://www.w3.org/TR/xmldsig-core/).

The general topic of e-business security is discussed in Chapter 15.

## Collaborations and Services

Understanding the <CollaborationRole> element is key to understanding how the various ebXML specifications complement and relate to each other. It associates the ability of a party to fulfill a particular role in a business collaboration at a business process level, with the "channels" and message headers used to actually transmit business information and business signals. The following fragment is drawn from the CPP of the exporting coffee equipment company:

```
<CollaborationRole>
   <ProcessSpecification
      name="PrepareForExport"
      tp:version="4.3"
```

```
        xlink:href="PrepareForExport.bpss.xml" />
     <Role
        name="Insurance requestor"
        xlink:href="PrepareForExport.xml#bc.ir.1"/>
     <CertificateRef certId="cert.emv.01"/>
     <ServiceBinding channelId="ch.emv.01" packageId="pk.emv.01">
        <Service>IssueRequestForInsurance</Service>
        <!-- Preferably, use HTTP across the board -->
     </ServiceBinding>
     <ServiceBinding channelId="ch.emv.02" packageId="pk.emv.01">
        <Service>IssueRequestForInsurance</Service>
        <!-- SMTP is acceptable as alternative protocol -->
     </ServiceBinding>
  </CollaborationRole>
```

The <CollaborationRole> element has the following structure:

- The <ProcessSpecification> element identifies a business process specification document. The CPP asserts the capability of a party to perform a particular role within a business collaboration defined in that document.
- The <Role> element identifies this role precisely, in the context of the process specified in the <ProcessSpecification> sibling element.
- The <ServiceBinding> element provides a binding of the message traffic associated with the fulfillment of this role to a particular channel and to a particular content packaging specification.

We'll discuss each of these in turn.

### The <ProcessSpecification> Element

Operational ebXML systems automate business interactions between parties that collaborate to execute a collaborative business process. The <ProcessSpecification> element in the CPP references a process specification document that describes these collaborative interactions formally. It asserts certain capabilities of a party with respect to the processes described in that document. In this case, the process has been described using the ebBPSS notation (see Chapter 5), although the URI only provides the reference and no information about the specific process specification language used. The BPSS model is stored in a document called PrepareForExport.bpss.xml:

```
  <ProcessSpecification
     name="PrepareForExport"
     version="4.3"
     xlink:href="PrepareForExport.bpss.xml" />
```

Note that the href attribute is actually a URI, rather than a file name; this means that the document could be stored elsewhere, for example in a public business process registry. In a real-life situation, this file would be stored at a public location, from which both the exporting company and its (potential) business partners can reference it. An operational system can regularly compare the value of the version attribute with the value of the version attribute within the referenced process document to make sure the CPP and CPA remain up to date.

## The <Role> Element

The `<Role>` element provides a pointer into the process specification document. To really understand the relationship between CPP/CPA and BPSS, you need to understand both of them. Fortunately, at this point you don't need to possess a full, formal understanding of the information in BPSS process specification documents and their structure. This is because you only need to understand some basic BPSS concepts to understand how CPP/CPA relates to it, and because BPSS is in essence just an additional view on the UMM models we introduced in Chapter 2. We'll informally provide that basic information in the next few paragraphs and recapitulate UMM concepts and terminology as needed.

So before we move on, we'll briefly outline some BPSS process modeling concepts that are relevant to CPP/CPA, without actually going into a discussion of BPSS itself. A business process may involve many parties and potentially complex interactions between them; however, at the lowest level all ebXML messages are sent from exactly one partner to exactly one other partner. Even if a party needs to contact a third party before it is able to respond to a request, you can still view this composite conversation as two separate (but interrelated) bilateral conversations, with one intermediate partner talking to the other two.

An example of such a decomposition of a multiparty relation into multiple binary relations is given in the following diagram. It displays eight organizations that have business relations. In this case, there are two "pivotal" business partners, one of which is related to four other organizations and one to two other organizations. The six other business partners only have to deal with one other organization.

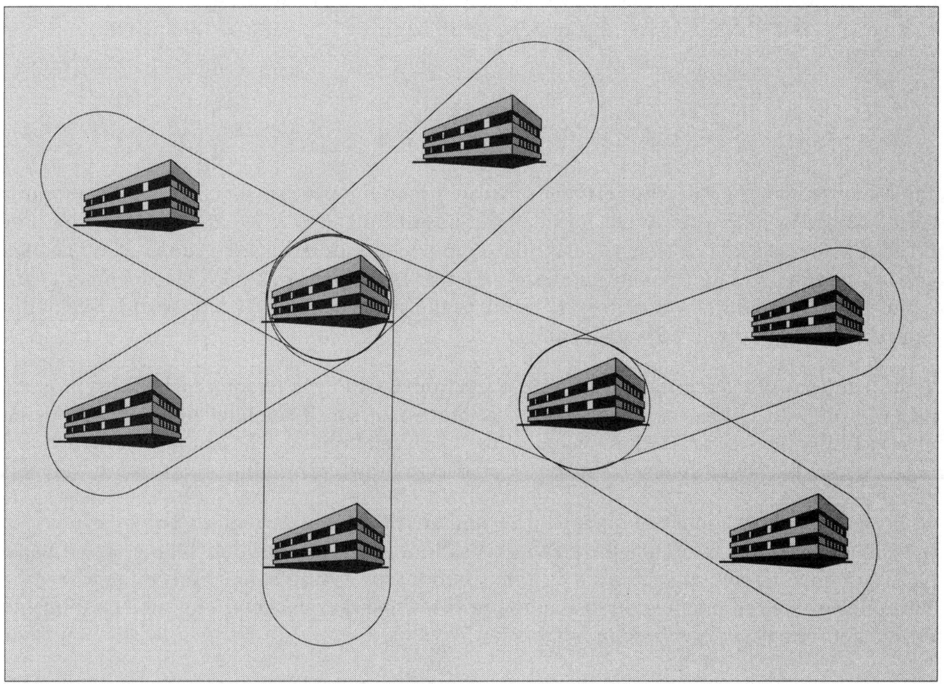

The "worst case scenario" for a decomposition of a multiparty involving *n* partners requires in the order of *n(n-1)* binary collaborations, but many practical situations will be more like this picture, with one or a few pivotal partners. This is because many organizations like to limit the number of organizations they have contractual agreements with. If particular services can only be fulfilled using third parties, those are then engaged in a subcontractor relationship. The prime contractor takes the full business responsibility for these services and "owns" the ultimate customer relationship.

In the ITT case, we have a clear illustration of this. Most activities involve the 'Exporter', who needs to perform various administrative tasks to prepare ordered products for export. The various organizations 'Exporter' deals with are not exchanging information among themselves. The 'Freight Forwarder' uses a third party 'Carrier' to perform the actual transport, but retains contractual responsibility to his customer.

This bilateral collaboration level is the main level of interest to CPP/CPA, and in BPSS it is referred to as `<BinaryCollaboration>`s (we'll get to the two other levels a few paragraphs down from here). These in turn roughly correspond to UMM `Collaboration` objects, which you would identify and model in the Business Requirements workflow in the UMM process modeling methodology.

The `<Role>` element in a CPP or CPA `<CollaborationRole>` structure serves to reference such a collaboration element. In a `<BinaryCollaboration>` there is a named initiating role and a named responding role, both encoded as string-valued attributes, as well as an ID-valued attribute used for identification. You can use one of these string values as value for an attribute of the `<Role>` element that is conveniently called `name`. In the following example, drawn from the CPP for the exporting company, this attribute has the value `Insurance requestor`. The insurer itself will have a similar entry in its CPP, but with the value `Insurance provider`:

```
<Role
    name="Insurance requestor"
    xlink:href="PrepareForExport.xml#bc.ir.1"/>
```

In addition to naming the role, the relevant substructure in the process specification document is referenced using the `href` attribute. The value of this attribute is a URI that points into the process specification document to the binary collaboration in which `Insurance requestor` is specified. Here we are assuming the XLINK convention that references like `#bc.ir.1` on XML documents are unique (at document level) identifier references, and link to the substructure that carries an ID-valued attribute with specified value in the BPSS document.

This is the main way of referencing a business process from a CPP: you reference a business process and associate yourself with a binary collaboration in that process, in which you fulfill either the "requesting" role or the "responding" role, as selected by shared values of `name` attributes. The actual XML structure can be referenced via the link, but this may be mostly of interest to browsers or other tools to work with ebXML.

If your business collaborations are fairly simple, and are mostly single request/response pairs, this will be the main way you will reference process specifications. This will certainly be the case if you are comparing an ebXML solution against a custom solution; for example, one built using a Web Services Toolkit. In this case, you might want to skip the next few paragraphs now. The subject of business process collaborations is expanded on in Chapter 5.

The complete story is a bit more complex than we've presented it to be so far. To be precise, there is one layer "above" the binary collaboration level and one below. For reference, we'll provide a table before going into this discussion, to show all the levels in relation to one another, the elements they contain, the link elements that connect the levels to adjacent ones, and the relevant ebXML components and corresponding UMM workflow for each level:

| Level (element names) | Link(s) to adjacent level | Relevant ebXML component | UMM workflow |
|---|---|---|---|
| MultiPartyCollaboration | BusinessPartnerRole<br>Transition | BPSS | Business modeling |
| BinaryCollaboration | BusinessTransactionActivity<br>CollaborationActivity<br>Fork<br>Join | | Requirements |
| BusinessTransaction | | | Analysis |
| CollaborationRole | Role | CPP/CPA | Design |

First of all, at the higher level, there is a <MultiPartyCollaboration> element in BPSS that provides a listing of <BusinessPartnerRole> elements. This corresponds to the Process objects identified in the UMM business modeling and business requirements workflows. Each of these provides a reference to roles in, and <Transition>s between, one or more <BinaryCollaboration> elements, and has a name attribute itself. You can reference this name attribute as a shortcut for an enumeration of all the various individual roles in binary collaborations. As we'll see in the discussion of service bindings, this assumes the default channel and packaging for all collaborations are the same, which is unlikely if there are many different types of business transactions in the overall process.

The lower level is relevant because, unfortunately, not all business collaborations are single request/response transactions, and relating to them from a CPP or CPA inherits that complexity. The problem is that the conversation within a binary collaboration can be quite complex in itself. It may involve many different requests and responses. Even between two parties, and within a single business process conversation, there may be multiple outstanding requests (parallelism), or the course of a conversation may depend on the business information exchanged (conditionalism).

The building blocks for <BinaryCollaboration>s are <BusinessTransaction>s. A business transaction involves a single request and an optional response (for instance, a notification does not require a formal response). A transaction can sometimes be used multiple times, across different collaborations and even within a single collaboration. In UMM, you would identify business transactions in the business analysis workflow. In BPSS, the use of a transaction in a collaboration is called a <BusinessTransactionActivity>. You can specify the sender and recipient roles at this level similarly to the way you do this at the collaboration level. (See Chapter 5 for discussion of <Fork>, <Join> and <CollaborationActivity>.) When we discuss the <Override> element below, you'll see that you can provide separate service bindings for different business transactions in a single binary collaboration if you want to.

So, in summary, the level of binary collaborations is the first and probably most important level you can address from a CPP or CPA document. It is certainly the only level you will need to worry about if your involvement in a collaboration is rather simple and requires only a single, simple request/response message exchange. In BPSS, you can generalize over all binary collaborations using the <BusinessPartnerRole> substructure of <MultiPartyCollaboration>s, and the level of <BusinessTransaction>s is the third level. The actual referencing mechanism is the same and uses shared values for name attributes.

Before we move on to discussing service bindings, we'll just make two more general remarks. First, note that we have only been talking about "referencing" process descriptions. This reference is just an assertion that the party can fulfill the referenced role; it is not a fact that somehow follows from this reference. It also does not mean that the party uses the BPSS at all to configure its ebXML system, even though a CPA and BPSS jointly do provide enough information to automatically configure a complete business interface.

Second, parties can also reference processes described in other notations besides BPSS as long as they agree (at the CPA stage) how to interpret that notation and how to appropriately configure their e-business systems. Some alternative approaches to process notation are discussed in Chapter 6. Note that a CPP or CPA does not "know about" the language used to specify the process, and just references a specification document.

### Process Specification and Role and the Formation of a CPA

If we limit ourselves to binary collaborations, two CPPs can be said to **match** for process specification and role if one party's CPP asserts the ability to fulfill one role and the other party's CPP the other. This is true both for simple binary collaborations that consist of a single request/response, and for complex binary collaborations that consist of a potentially complex, graph-structured flow of transaction activities.

The story is more complex for multiparty collaborations, and the ebCPP Specification avoids any discussion of these. One problem is that, although a multiparty collaboration builds on constituent binary collaborations, no single party necessarily gets to see the "bigger picture" of knowing whether or not there are parties and agreements to execute all binary collaborations in the overall multiparty collaboration. Also, in forming the actual agreements, one party may want to define conditions on its CPA with another party that references that partner's CPA with a third party, which the current specification cannot express. Overall, this is clearly an underdeveloped area in the specification.

## The <ServiceBinding> Element

Where the `<Role>` and `<ProcessSpecification>` elements establish a relation between one party (in the case of a CPP) or two parties (in the case of a CPA) and the roles they perform in particular business processes, the `<ServiceBinding>` element associates the performance of these messages to specific communication channels and to specific ways of packaging content:

```
<ServiceBinding channelId="ch.emv.01" packageId="pk.emv.01">
   <Service>IssueRequestForInsurance</Service>
   <!-- Preferably, use HTTP across the board -->
</ServiceBinding>
<ServiceBinding channelId="ch.emv.02" packageId="pk.emv.01">
   <Service>IssueRequestForInsurance</Service>
   <!-- SMTP is acceptable as alternative protocol  -->
</ServiceBinding>
```

The channels and packaging definitions themselves are defined elsewhere in the CPP/CPA document, as we'll discuss later in this chapter. The `ch.emv.01` and `pk.emv.01` attribute values are ID references to the defining elements. All interesting information is encoded by those referenced elements. The use of references (rather than including the referenced structures as substructures) in the `<ServiceBinding>` element enables re-use – there may be many `<CollaborationRole>` elements that share the same channel definition. This is an instance of the more general pattern of representing many-to-many relations in XML. We'll see the same pattern at work in the `<DeliveryChannel>` element, discussed later in this chapter.

In a single <CollaborationRole> element in a CPP, there can be multiple <ServiceBinding> elements. The **order** of such elements is significant, and represents a **preference**. For instance, the example indicates that the party prefers to use channel ch.emv.01, which (if we look at the definition) uses HTTP as communication protocol, to channel ch.emv.02, which uses SMTP. (The reason might be that a synchronous protocol is more appropriate given the nature of the transactions associated with this role.) In other cases, the reverse might be true, and the various orders can reflect this.

## *The <Override> Element*

A <ServiceBinding> element is contained within a <CollaborationRole> element. Its scope is determined by the <Role> element and can cover a business transaction within a specific business transaction activity, or all business transactions involved in a binary collaboration or entire business process. You can define exceptional bindings for specific business transactions in such a scope using the <Override> element. It has an action attribute, which references a specific business transaction activity by name.

As an example, let's assume that 'Freight Forwarder' specifies a <CollaborationRole> that governs its collaboration with a 'Carrier' to perform transport-related activities. This collaboration involves multiple business transaction activities. One of these activities is 'Prepare for Delivery', that invokes the business transaction ConfirmDelivery, with identifier bs.4 in the BPSS document. The following example is a CPP fragment for Freight Forwarder's CPP that specifies that another channel is to be used for this business transaction:

```
<ServiceBinding channelId="ch.ff.02" packageId="pk.ff.01">
   <Service>ProvideTransport</Service>
   <Override action="Confirm Delivery"
             channelID="ch.ff.03"
             packageId="pk.ff.01"
             xlink:href="PrepareForExport.xml#bs.4"/>
</ServiceBinding>
```

There are some issues that you should be aware of when you start to use <Override> in practice:

- The <Override> element is only useful if the <Role> element indirectly references multiple transactions, through multiple business transaction activities. This means that you can use it with binary collaborations that have a complex internal structure or at multiparty collaboration level, but not for collaboration roles associated with business transaction activities, where you're only binding a single transaction to a service.
- You can only reference a single action once, as you must unambiguously bind a transaction to a service.
- To be meaningful, at least one of the values of the channelID or packageID should differ from the values specified at <CollaborationRole> level.
- If the <Role> element references a name of a <BusinessPartnerRole>, its scope covers transactions in multiple binary collaborations in the overall process. However, if you're creating a CPA between two parties, some of the overrides are irrelevant as they reference transactions with other roles than the two represented in the CPA, so you don't need to copy those from the CPP.

So, while the mechanism of CPPs and CPA formation is not really hard to understand, there are many minor issues hidden in the details of interactions of the various specifications.

The <Service> element provides a textual name for the service. This is a string that is used as content for an element in the ebXML message service header that is also called <Service> (see http://www.ebxml.org/specs/ebMS.pdf). The specification allows you to specify different values for this element for the various <ServiceBinding>s in a single <CollaborationRole>, if you can think of a reason why that might be useful.

Earlier, we saw that you can use the cpaid attribute in a message sent to you to find the associated CPA. As a single CPA can cover many business service interfaces between two organizations, the <Service> element identifies which of your business services is being accessed. This is one reason to have <CollaborationRole>s associated with the business process at the level of <BinaryCollaboration>s or even lower, at <BusinessTransactionActivity> level, rather than at the top-level business process element <MultiPartyCollaboration>. The value of the <Service> element is more informative if limited to one or just a select number of business collaborations. Another reason is that the referenced packageId in <ServiceBinding> will be a physical reflection of the structure of business documents and attachments exchanged. In BPSS, these are expressed at the level of <BusinessTransaction>s.

In a <CollaborationRole> element, you can reference certificates using the standard ID/IDREF mechanism. These certificates are used here for business process authorization, in contrast to their use in channels where they are used for message security.

### Service Binding and the Formation of a CPA

In forming a CPA, one of the <ServiceBinding>s is selected based on a compatibility check between the sending party and the receiving party and on the preferences expressed by the order of the substructures in the source CPPs. We saw a pattern of "narrowing down" from multiple options to a single option with the <PartyInfo>, and this is another instance of this pattern.

> *The meaning of "compatibility" in this context will become clear when we look into the channel and packaging definitions.*

The occurrence of <Override> elements further complicates this. It means that you don't have to look at just the role in a binary collaboration, but at all constituent business transaction activities (as the <Override> element essentially partitions these into different groups) and ensure that they match.

<ServiceBinding>s from two CPPs can be said to **match** if the referenced channels and document exchange match. The specification does not tell what happens if two CPPs have incompatible string content for their <Service> elements; but presumably one of the two parties could easily agree to perform a string translation somewhere in their ebXML handler. Similarly, it is probably wise to rename ID attributes and references to them in each of the constituent CPPs to make them unique and prevent ID clashes.

The specification requires companies to take their preferential order expressed in CPPs into account, but if, for instance, Party A's first service binding is compatible with Party B's second and Party A's second service binding with Party B's first, an unspecified negotiation process is referred to. This is one of many areas in which initial product implementations and experience in applying ebXML will need to build up some best practices. The CPA formation process may also be used more dynamically than described here, as hinted at in the ebCPP Specification. For instance, if your receiving party's HTTP service does not respond and you know they also accept SMTP-based messages, you may switch to using that protocol, just like you eventually pick up the phone or send a fax if someone doesn't answer their e-mail for a while.

# Channels and Packaging

A <ServiceBinding> element has two IDREF attributes that associate a collaboration role with a particular channel and particular package. The first of these describes a party's message receiving capabilities and the second one is concerned with the way multiple message components are assembled in a MIME package and security is applied.

## *The <DeliveryChannel> Element*

The <DeliveryChannel> element identifies at a technical level how a party can receive particular messages. Essentially, it is a pairing of a particular transport and a particular named set of document exchange parameters, plus some additional specification of channel properties in the <Characteristics> element:

```
<DeliveryChannel
   channelId="ch.ic.01"
   transportId="tr.ic.01"
   docExchangeId="dx.ic.01">
   <Characteristics
      ...   />
</DeliveryChannel>
```

Because multiple <DeliveryChannel>s can refer to different combinations of channel and transport definitions, they are not included in the XML document as a substructure, but instead referenced using an IDREF mechanism. This is another instance of the pattern of using ID/IDREF to express many-to-many relations, like we saw earlier in the discussion of service bindings.

The <Characteristics> element is empty and serves to carry a number of attributes, all of which are optional. The following example shows all attributes that can validly appear on the element:

```
<Characteristics
   syncReplyMode="none"
   nonrepudiationOfOrigin="true"
   nonrepudiationOfReceipt="false"
   secureTransport="false"
   confidentiality="false"
   authenticated="true"
   authorized="false" />
```

The syncReplyMode attribute allows you to specify whether a synchronous reply is requested if the transport protocol (like HTTP for instance, but unlike SMTP) supports synchronous communication. The value none indicates asynchronous communication, and is the default if no value is specified. You can use other values to indicate that return information, either technical information (signals) or substantive business information (response), or both, needs to be included synchronously. The distinction between business signals and business response is discussed in the chapters on UMM and BPSS (Chapters 2 and 5).

The other attributes are primarily concerned with document-level (as opposed to transport-level) security. They can also be specified on the definition of business transactions in BPSS, or be inferred by classifying a business transaction as one of six business "patterns" identified in UMM. You can read about these attributes and their meaning in Chapters 2, 5, and 15, respectively. Their specification in CPP/CPA documents is a way for parties to bilaterally override the values specified in the process specification documents. The ability for parties to benefit from, but not be tied down by, BPSS specifications is an important and very useful feature of the ebXML model.

A `<DeliveryChannel>` element, and therefore all properties set (modified) by the `<Characteristics>` element, is associated with a `<CollaborationRole>` and sets these properties for all business transactions in the scope of that element. This is another reason why we recommend that you associate `<CollaborationRole>`s with `<BinaryCollaboration>`s (or even with `<BusinessTransactionActivity>`s, if you read the part of our discussion on the `<Role>` element), as this allows you fine-grained control over these properties. If you were to associate them with `<BusinessPartnerRole>` elements, you would enforce these settings for all transactions defined in all binary collaborations defined in the BPSS document.

### DeliveryChannel and the Formation of a CPA

As with `<CollaborationRole>`, matching two instances of `<DeliveryChannel>`s largely reduces to matching the associated (referenced) transport and document exchange elements. Matching of security attributes is a complex issue discussed in some detail in Appendix F of the ebCPP Specification. We won't go further into this here.

## Packaging

So far, we've seen how CPPs and CPAs indirectly reference business collaborations, and we've been talking about messages being exchanged all along, but so far we haven't discussed what kind of **content** is being exchanged at all. In the context of ebXML, there are two levels at which you can talk about content:

- At the **logical** level, there is the issue of wanting to express that the requesting business activity of some business transaction involves transmission of an XML document conforming to a particular XML Schema.
- At the **physical** level, there is the issue of being able to pack, and unpack, the structured and unstructured information into a format that can be transported by the messaging layer.

The logical level is not addressed at the level of CPP/CPA at all. As the terms "activity" and "business transaction" indicate, it is properly addressed at the business process specification level, as described in Chapter 5.

> *In case you are curious how to get at that information from a CPP/CPA, here's the quick answer: follow the references from the `<CollaborationRole>` element to definitions of `<BusinessTransaction>`s in the BPSS file, these reference `<BusinessDocument>`s and `<Attachment>`s. The referenced business documents can have links to XML Schemas external to the BPSS file.*

The physical level of packaging content is expressed in the CPP using the `<Packaging>` element. Essentially, this element provides a notation for secure, composite MIME structures. There can be multiple `<Packaging>` elements in a CPP, referenced by different `<ServiceBinding>`s.

This is another instance where CPP/CPA acts as the link between business layers in ebXML and the messaging layer. In this case, it also pinpoints the responsibility of the CPP designer to keep the two levels synchronized, as the package structure should mirror the business document and attachment distinguished at the logical level.

In our model of the ITT case, there is a business transaction named 'Perform Pre-shipment Inspection' that results in a "clear report of findings" if no abnormalities have been detected. We've assumed that this document consists of an XML message and a paper form that contains handwritten notes. The paper form is scanned and attached as a binary file to the XML message. The CPP is responsible for defining a packaging that can support this. Such a package would consist of two components, or building blocks, that contain the business document and the attachment, respectively. Next, you use these building blocks to build a composite structure. So the overall structure will be as follows:

```
<Packaging id="pk.psi.01">
   <ProcessingCapabilities parse="true" generate="true" />

   <SimplePart id="sp.crof" mimetype="text/xml"/>
   <!-- clear report of findings -->

   <SimplePart id="sp.sdi" mimetype="image/tiff"/>
   <!-- for the scanned document image -->

   <!-- other SimpleParts could go here -->

   <CompositeList>
      <Composite id="cp.psi.01"
                 mimetype="multipart/related">
         <Constituent idref="sp.crof"/>
         <Constituent idref="sp.sdi"/>
      </Composite>
      <!-- other Composites could go here -->
   </CompositeList>
</Packaging>
```

The `<Packaging>` element has an `id` attribute to allow it to be referenced from `<ServiceBinding>`s. Each `<SimplePart>` element has an obligatory `id` attribute to allow straightforward reference from `<Composite>` elements. `<SimplePart>` and `<Composite>` elements also require a `mimetype`, and can have a `mimeparameters` attribute. The first provides a value for the MIME content type of the component's content and the second provides any additional MIME parameters needed to process the message. MIME is specified in the IETF RFC 1521 (search for this at http://www.ietf.org/rfc.html).

In the displayed document fragment, the `<SimplePart>` elements only have attributes and no content. If you want, you can use a `<NamespaceSupported>` sub element with `<SimplePart>`s that have XML content, to express additional extensions supported, for instance security extensions. An example of these would be the OASIS Security Assertion Markup Language (SAML). The main URL for the OASIS security services technical committee is http://www.oasis-open.org/committees/security/.

```
<SimplePart id="sp.crof" mimetype="text/xml">
<NamespaceSupported
    location="http://www.oasis-open.org/committees/security/docs/draft-sstc-
schema-assertion-15.xsd"> http://www.oasis-
open.org/committees/security/docs/draft-sstc-schema-assertion-15.xsd
</NamespaceSupported>
</SimplePart>
```

The <ProcessingCapabilities> element, with Boolean-valued attributes `parse` or `generate`, can encode whether the messaging subsystem has processing limitations with respect to the document components included in the `Packaging`; the default value is `true`. You could set `parse` to `true` and `generate` to `false` if you can process certain information in receive mode only. Clearly, at least one of them should have value `true`.

#### Packaging and the Formation of a CPA

Appendix F of the ebCPP Specification http://www.ebxml.org/specs/ebCPP.pdf considers document-packaging capabilities to be one of the most complex matching problems. It involves matching simple and composite MIME types, and there are complications due to asymmetric parse/generation `ProcessingCapabilities` and the presence of `NamespaceSupported` specifications for security.

## Transport and Document Exchange

The <Transport> and <DocumentExchange> elements are at the lowest levels in the CPP/CPA documents, and they provide the direct interface to the ebXML messaging service. We'll discuss them in turn.

### The <Transport> Element

Now that we've arrived at the discussion of the <Transport> element, we've reached an important milestone in this chapter. Namely, we've now covered enough of CPP/CPA to be able to trace from a fairly abstract concept like "collaborations", down to something as specific and low-level in nature as a specific port or an e-mail address used by the ebXML adaptor at the receiving party's end, and back up again. In a sense, this means we have covered the full ebXML "protocol stack". The following diagram visualizes this:

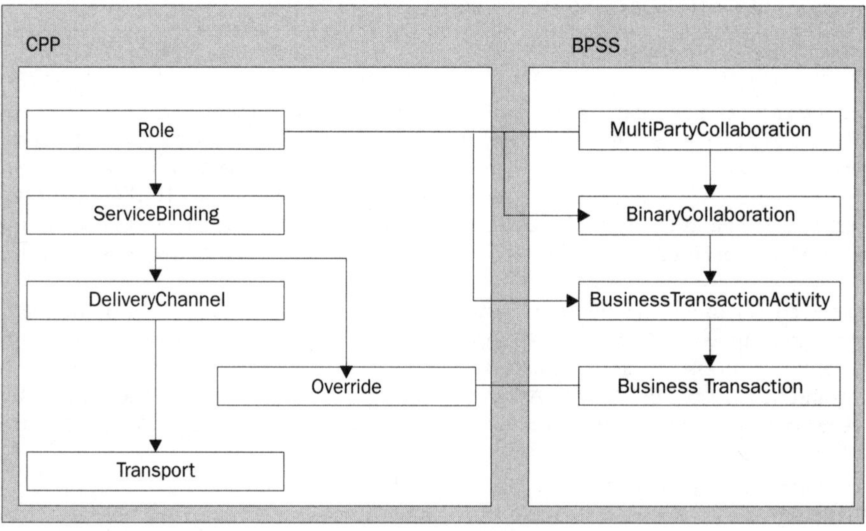

The <Transport> element is referenced by <DeliveryChannel>s, which are referenced by <ServiceBinding>s, which are referenced by <CollaborationRole>s, which define <ServiceBinding>s for <BusinessTransaction>s, which implement <BusinessTransactionActivity>s that make up specific <BinaryCollaboration>s.

In this diagram, the arrow that links <Role> to <MultiPartyCollaboration>, <BinaryCollaboration> and <BusinessTransactionActivity> represents alternatives, as explained in the discussion of the <Role> element.

The association of <Override>and <BusinessTransaction> represents an exceptional binding for a specific <BusinessTransaction> as explained in the section that discusses the <Override> element.

The following fragment shows a <Transport> element from the exporting company's CPP:

```
<Transport transportId="tr.emv.01">
   <SendingProtocol version="1.1">HTTP</SendingProtocol>
   <ReceivingProtocol version="1.1">HTTP</ReceivingProtocol>
   <Endpoint
      uri="http://services.espressomachine.it/ebxmlhandler"
      type="request"/>
   <TransportSecurity>
     <Protocol version="3.0">SSL</Protocol>
     <CertificateRef certID="cert.emv.01"/>"
   </TransportSecurity>
</Transport>
```

The <Transport> element consists of a combination of one or more <SendingProtocol>, <ReceivingProtocol> and <Endpoint> elements. In a CPP, multiple occurrences of these indicate that the party supports multiple protocols or endpoints. For a CPA, you will select one of these as agreed with the other party.

To carry ebXML message traffic, a protocol needs to be able to carry MIME-encoded content, and this includes HTTP, FTP and SMTP, support of which (the specification indicates in section 7.5.13) is mandatory for ebXML-compliant middleware. One of the really nice features of ebXML and the model of CPP/CPA is that if two parties both support some other exotic transport that happens to be able to transport MIME content, they can go ahead and use that without requiring any changes to any of the ebXML specifications. Another thing to note is that a small (or mobile) business with only a dial-up connection to the Internet can have its ebXML mail traffic delivered at a post office, which it periodically accesses using a protocol like POP3 or IMAP.

For further discussion of the specific details of each of the three standard transport protocols, I'll refer you to the ebCPP Specification (Section 7.5.15).

### *Transport and the Formation of a CPA*

The <Transport> element has a substructure for protocols and security, so CPA formation needs to look into both of these. At the protocol level, you need to compare the <SendingProtocol> of one to the other party's <ReceivingProtocol>, and vice versa, to establish that each of the two parties speaks a language the other party understands.

The two parties also need to agree on transport security protocol and versions of these. As mentioned in the ebCPP Specification, a CPA negotiation process might require one partner to upgrade or downgrade to other (versions of) protocols. Mismatches between versions may be acceptable if higher versions of a protocol are backward compatible with earlier versions.

## The <DocExchange> Element

The <DocExchange> element is an element that contains additional configuration information related to the exchange of messages over a <DeliveryChannel> using a particular messaging service. CPP/CPA documents may contain multiple <DocExchange> substructures if the information specified at this level differs for the various channels.

At the moment, the schema only allows a single <ebXMLBinding> subelement inside <DocExchange>, which provides information for the ebXML messaging service, but it might be extended in the future to support other message protocols. In that case, parties will presumably decide to use a single messaging service, and record that choice in the final CPA:

```
<DocExchange docExchangeId="dx.emv.01">
   <ebXMLBinding version="1.0">
      <ReliableMessaging ...>
         <!-- ... -->
      </ReliableMessaging>
      <NonRepudiation>
         <!-- ... -->
      </NonRepudiation>
      <DigitalEnvelope>
         <!-- ... -->
      </DigitalEnvelope>
      <NamespaceSupported ...>
         <!-- ... -->
      </NamespaceSupported>
   </ebXMLBinding>
</DocExchange>
```

The subelements of <ebXMLBinding> can be grouped in two categories, one concerned with reliable messaging and one with security.

### Reliable Messaging

The <ReliableMessaging> element has three attributes and three subelements. The three attributes are:

- A required `idempotency` attribute, which allows you to specify whether or not (value `true` or `false`, respectively) the ebXML message should check for duplicate messages.
- The required `deliverySemantics` attribute, which has two possible values and allows you to specify that you want the messaging service to guarantee that a message is to be delivered exactly once (value `OnceAndOnlyOnce`). If you don't, use the attribute value `BestEffort`, which indicates that the messaging service is not expected to provide reliable messaging functionality.
- `messageOrderSemantics`. If `deliverySemantics` is set to `OnceAndOnlyOnce`, the value of the attribute `messageOrderSemantics` allows you to request the receiving ebXML message handler to pass on messages to the receiving application in the order they were sent by the sending application (value `Guaranteed`). The default is to not perform this check (value `NotGuaranteed`).

The three subelements are:

- The <Retries> element – allows you to specify how often an application should attempt to resend a request message after a timeout of receipt or acceptance acknowledgement.
- The <RetryInterval> element – allows you to set a retry interval, in seconds between each retry.
- The <PersistDuration> element – allows you specify that the receiving application should store received messages for a duration expressed in the element content:

```
<ReliableMessaging
   deliverySemantics="OnceAndOnlyOnce"
   idempotency="true"
   messageOrderSemantics="Guaranteed">
   <Retries>5</Retries>
   <RetryInterval>120</RetryInterval>
   <PersistDuration>P40D</PersistDuration>
</ReliableMessaging>
```

The P40D value in the above example indicates this period has a duration of 40 days. If <PersistDuration> is unspecified, the ebXML message handler is free to delete messages once they are transferred to the enterprise system that handles the business process internally.

Chapters 13 and 14 provide more information on ebXML and messaging frameworks.

### *Security Information*

The other subelements of <ebXMLBinding> are security-related. Here, we'll just summarize the main elements in the ebCPP Specification. Security in e-business is sufficiently complex and is of critical importance, so has been given its own chapter in this book, which will address all these issues in detail – see Chapter 15.

The <NonRepudiation> element allows you to specify that messages sent be signed using a digital signature. If absent, messages sent are not digitally signed. If present, it needs sub-elements to express the signing protocol, the function used to generate the signature, and the certificate reference:

```
<NonRepudiation>
   <Protocol version="2000/10/31">
      http://www.w3.org/2000/09/xmldsig#
   </Protocol>
   <HashFunction>sha1</HashFunction>
   <SignatureAlgorithm>rsa</SignatureAlgorithm>
   <CertificateRef certID="cert.emv.01"/>
</NonRepudiation>
```

The <Protocol> element names the (version of the) technology used to sign the message; the example references the W3C XML Digital Signature Specification (XML Signature Syntax and Processing – http://www.w3.org/TR/xmldsig-core/). The <HashFunction> element identifies the algorithm used to compute the digest of the message that is to be signed. The <SignatureAlgorithm> identifies the algorithm used to compute the value of the digital signature.

The <CertificateRef> element references a <Certificate> element elsewhere in the XML document.

The <DigitalEnvelope> element configures message encryption. It allows you to specify the security protocol to be used, the encryption algorithm and the certificate used:

```
<DigitalEnvelope>
   <Protocol version="2.0">S/MIME</Protocol>
   <EncryptionAlgorithm>DES-CBC</EncryptionAlgorithm>
   <CertificateRef certId="N03"/>
</DigitalEnvelope>
```

The <NamespaceSupported> element was discussed previously, in the section on *Packaging*. In this context, it allows you to specify that your ebXML message handler supports other security-related standards, identified using their namespaces.

```
<NamespaceSupported
 location="http://ebxml.org/project_teams/transport/xmldsig-core-schema.xsd"
 version="1.0">http://www.w3.org/2000/09/xmldsig</NamespaceSupported>
```

### *Document Exchange and Formation of a CPA*

As usual, the CPA will reflect agreements on the various substructures encoded in this element. For instance, the reliable messaging attributes provide information on the order in which messages are sent and on the potential for duplicates. If you have designed the receiving application based on the assumption that messages are sent in order and exactly once, you will need to make sure the messaging system and sending application guarantee this.

The security subelement provides references to several security-related specifications, such as specifications for signing and encrypting messages. This means that the CPA formation needs to know which (versions) of these specifications are compatible with each other.

# CPP/CPA and other ebXML Specifications

Now that we've gone through the XML structure of CPP and CPA documents, it is perhaps useful to return to a statement we made in the introduction to this chapter to see if we can make it a bit more precise. We indicated that CPPs and CPAs describe the e-business capabilities of a particular party, and can logically be viewed as the specification for the business service layer between business process specifications and the transport specification. This means that the CPP and CPA are less abstract than business process specifications, but more abstract than messages processed by transport, routing and messaging. The following list attempts to position CPP/CPA more precisely within the overall ebXML framework:

- Business process modeling provides an overview of business processes, business collaborations and business transactions between parties identified using role labels (see Chapter 2). The BPSS specification (see Chapter 5) is a representation of this information in an executable XML format. These descriptions provide a blueprint for all possible conversations between all possible instantiations of these roles to specific parties. They provide no information about the transport protocol used for business transactions.
- For a given business process, the CPP layer narrows this down to all conversations involving one particular party in a particular role. For any collaboration involving that party in the collaboration, the CPP specifies a number of optional transport protocols.

- The CPA models a subset of conversations governed by a particular BPSS involving two specific partners and the use of specific protocols for the individual business transactions. The CPA still generalizes over all such conversations. If derived from two CPPs, the set of conversations governed by the CPA will be the intersection of the conversations modeled by the two source CPPs, performed using a particular protocol.
- Messages transferred at the messaging services level always involves two specific partners, are exchanged over a specific protocol and relate to a specific business conversation.

*In this description, we use the term **conversation** to talk about the message traffic associated with all business transactions in a specific activation of a business collaboration relation (or "unit of business") between two parties. The concept of conversations is also relevant to and discussed in the context of ebXML messaging (see the ebXML Message Service Specification at http://www.ebxml.org/specs/ebMS.pdf) and Chapter 13 of this book). Another term sometimes used is **dialog**.*

It is as important to note where CPP/CPA has links to other areas of ebXML as it is to note where CPP/CPA is independent of other parts of the framework. Three particular areas are noteworthy:

- While CPPs and a CPA reference business process specifications and roles, they do not specify that these specifications need to be in ebXML BPSS format. CPP/CPA can work with any XML business process specification format that allows roles to be referenced using XLINK links.
- Like BPSS, CPP/CPA is independent of the specific payload message format. Perhaps surprisingly, this means that you can use CPA to configure a system where all message content is expressed in a non-XML format, such as EDIFACT or another EDI standard.
- CPP/CPA requires that the message service use the textual content of the `Service` element as routing information (see ebCPP, section 7.5.7), but it does not prescribe the use of the ebXML messaging service.

These points are important because, even though BPSS is a very capable format, innovation does not end with it, as witnessed by activities reported on in Chapter 6. Similarly, while the ebXML Message Service Specification provides a messaging service designed to support ebXML, other messaging services are in use or under development. An example might be the work currently being done within the W3C on the basis of the SOAP submission. The relative independence of the various ebXML specifications ensures their interoperability with alternative or future implementations, flexibility in choosing software components to implement ebXML systems and protection of investment in ebXML solutions.

# CPP/CPA in an ebXML System

A separate issue from the generic benefits of CPP/CPA in e-business systems is the issue of what supporting CPP/CPA means for a practical ebXML system, both for developing new systems and for maintaining existing systems, and what implementation and adoption strategies you can adopt. At the time of writing, practical implementation of these specifications in software products is just starting, so there clearly is a need for experimentation to build up "best practices" that we can build on. Given that background, the content of this section is very preliminary.

As mentioned in the introduction to this chapter, there are, broadly speaking, two main alternative approaches in the use of CPP/CPA. These alternatives represent extremes, practical systems will be somewhere between these two.

- You can limit the use of CPPs and CPAs to **document** your e-business abilities and bilateral protocol agreements, respectively.
- You can use CPPs and CPAs to automatically **configure** ebXML compliant e-business middleware software.

The first scenario assumes there are no direct, program-controlled relations between the e-business system, the CPP/CPA documents and business process descriptions. The CPP and CPA documents are created and updated manually in parallel to the development and maintenance of the e-business system. The developer team takes the responsibility to keep the CPP/CPA specifications and the software implementation synchronized. All functionality that a CPP specifies and a CPA agrees to perform in an e-business collaboration then needs to be implemented in a custom software layer and/or the CPP, and derived CPAs need to reflect the capabilities of the software layer.

This scenario may be attractive if the e-business system supports essentially a fixed set of roles in high volume and/or high value business processes, and assumes fixed policies on, for example, protocols supported and security policies, that can be viewed as a template. The costs of developing the custom system can be justified in relation to these known business processes and may be competitive in relation to a middleware product. The fixed assumptions on protocol policies can be hard coded into the e-business system. The limited variable data (URLs, party identification) is relatively easy to manage using some lookup mechanism, preferably integrated with the backend system and a directory service.

The other scenario assumes an ebXML middleware system that generically supports ebXML messaging services, CPP/CPA and BPSS. As stressed throughout this chapter, a CPA and BPSS together provide all the information to completely configure an ebXML message handler that can map between arbitrary ebXML messages and the appropriate business transaction activities. The main value added to the BPSS management component by the CPP/CPA component is to offer maximum per-partner configurability and separation of partner-specific information from business process specific information.

This scenario is attractive if the e-business system needs to support many business processes and many business partners, and needs to be dynamically configurable: new partners being enrolled or replaced, and new business processes supported. The fixed costs of purchasing, configuring, implementing and managing a generic middleware product will be competitive if they can be spread over many processes, few of which would perhaps individually justify the costs of developing a point software solution.

# Summary and Further Work

As stated in the introduction, you can argue that collaboration protocol profiles (CPPs) and collaboration protocol agreements (CPAs) provide two benefits to the ebXML infrastructure:

- They support dynamic e-business, allow partial automation of the configuration of your systems to work with new partners, and can be limited to specific intervals or number of transactions. They support business discovery in not just publishing information about a company, but also about its capabilities to fulfill roles in business processes.
- They allow an architecturally clean separation between implementing a new business process and signing up a new (or discontinuing an existing) business partner, thus offering scalability and manageability.

Hopefully, these features will lower the cost of e-business implementations, increase their flexibility and improve their scalability. Together, this should allow more and smaller companies to automate more business processes with more partners, and to make e-business solutions economically feasible for lower volume transactions. The CPP/CPA specification is still very new, and there are some deficiencies and open issues with the current version, as noted on several occasions in this chapter. Further experience in implementing and using the specification will pinpoint more errors and omissions in it.

One account of such a practical implementation is the case study presented in Chapter 16 of this book. It is quite likely that many projects that will use CPP/CPA in the near future, will work with extended subsets of CPPs and will adopt approaches to CPA formation that are project-specific, rather than implementing generic, highly automated CPA negotiation functionality.

After the 18 month ebXML project completed in June 2001, work in the field of CPP/CPA has been continued in the context of an OASIS technical committee, the **OASIS Collaboration Protocol Profile and Agreement Technical Committee (CPPA TC)**. A first priority for this committee prior to addressing new activities, has been to fix any outstanding errors in the specification or inconsistencies with other specifications. At its web site, http://www.oasis-open.org/committees/ebxml-cppa/, the activities of this committee are documented. The committee has a public mailing list, archived at http://lists.OASIS-open.org/archives/ebxml-cppa/.

# 9

# UDDI

**Universal Description, Discovery, and Integration** (**UDDI**) is a specification for XML-based business registries (see http://www.uddi.org/specification.html for the specification documents). In this chapter we will start by explaining UDDI concepts and then cover this specification in detail – the data structures and APIs. We will also introduce some implementations, and then go through a case study, which uses the UDDI registry for publishing business and service information and searching the registry to find such information.

The work being done in the UDDI consortium seems to parallel some of the efforts in ebXML. In this chapter we will cover the areas of overlap, the differences between UDDI and ebXML registry and repository, and will also explore how these two specifications can coexist.

## UDDI Overview

UDDI enables a company to list definitions of itself, its services, and preferred means of conducting business transactions. These can be listed either publicly in a global registry or in a private registry exposed to trusted partner companies. Potential customers can then search for, and interact with, the registered businesses.

UDDI was initiated by three companies: IBM, Microsoft, and Ariba in early 2000 – the first version (UDDI V1) was released in September 2000. Since then more than 300 companies have signed up as supporters (called the 'advisory group'). These companies are listed at the UDDI.org web site (http://www.uddi.org). The direction of the UDDI specification is, however, guided by a smaller set of companies called the UDDI Working Group. These currently include IBM, Microsoft, Ariba, HP, SAP, Oracle, Intel, Accenture, Fujitsu, Verisign, Sun Microsystems, Compaq, Commerce One, and i2 Technologies.

The UDDI specification defines data structures for modeling businesses, their services, and service type information in the registry, and APIs for publishing, querying, and deleting this information. There are additional specifications for operators of UDDI registries, and these cover issues such as replication of information between the registries. This chapter does not cover in detail the specifications for UDDI registry operators.

The latest version of the UDDI specification is version 2. However, most commercially available UDDI implementations, such as Microsoft's and IBM's (see below), support version 1 only. UDDI version 2 implementations should be available by the end of 2001. Some of these implementations are introduced later in this chapter, in the *UDDI Implementations* section. UDDI V2 contains additional functionality for publisher assertions. These allow for businesses to describe relationships they have with other businesses. Another major enhancement is support for third parties to validate taxonomies. This feature allows for data in the registry to be more trustable. Both of these are described in more detail later in the chapter.

Currently the UDDI project is an industry initiative, but will eventually be handed to a standards body. This will most likely occur after the next iteration of the UDDI specifications (version 3). This version of the specification is still under design. Some of the functionality likely to be addressed includes greater support for geographic locations of businesses (latitude, longitude), which would be useful to mobile users; also, there will hopefully be better query capabilities and subscription functionality for supporting externally cached data.

In addition, UDDI proposes a global registry infrastructure called the **Universal Business Registry** (**UBR**). This is also sometimes referred to as the "UDDI cloud" or the "Service cloud". This is essentially a set of operator nodes that maintain the business and service data and replicate all the information to the other operator nodes. A service provider would need to sign up at one of the operator nodes in order to be able to publish its information. This information is then replicated to other operator nodes within 24 hours and users can then find this information at any of the other nodes in the cloud. The service provider can, however, modify or delete information only at the operator node where he is signed up. This simplifies the UDDI protocol from handling conditions of simultaneous and conflicting changes.

At the time of writing this chapter there were two operator nodes in existence. These are run by IBM (see http://www-3.ibm.com/services/uddi/) and Microsoft (see http://uddi.microsoft.com) respectively and, as we have already said, support the UDDI version 1 protocol.

More operator nodes will appear soon – HP (see http://uddi.hp.com/) and SAP (see http://www.sap.com/) will be joining these operator nodes by the end of 2001. Around this time, all the operator nodes would start supporting UDDI version 2. However, they would maintain backward compatibility to version 1 for clients that haven't upgraded.

UDDI is a part of a software stack for **Web Services**. A Web Service is a self-contained application or component that has the following characteristics – it can be described in a service description language, and this description can be published. Client programs can find these descriptions, bind to the service so described and finally invoke the services. UDDI provides the registry piece of this stack. The other components include SOAP and WSDL:

- **SOAP** (Simple Object Access Protocol) is a XML protocol for exchanging information. It is often used for a platform-independent mechanism for remote procedure calls (RPC) and is commonly used over an HTTP transport. UDDI messages are transported over SOAP. See Chapter 4 for more on SOAP.

- **WSDL** (Web Service Definition Language) is an XML format for describing Web Services. A WSDL document for a Web Service defines it in terms of its interface, its protocol bindings, and its deployment details. WSDL allows for separation of the definition of endpoints of a service from their actual network deployment and data structures. The latest version of the WSDL specification is available at http://www.w3.org/TR/wsdl.

The following figure illustrates the interactions between a service provider, operator nodes, and a user:

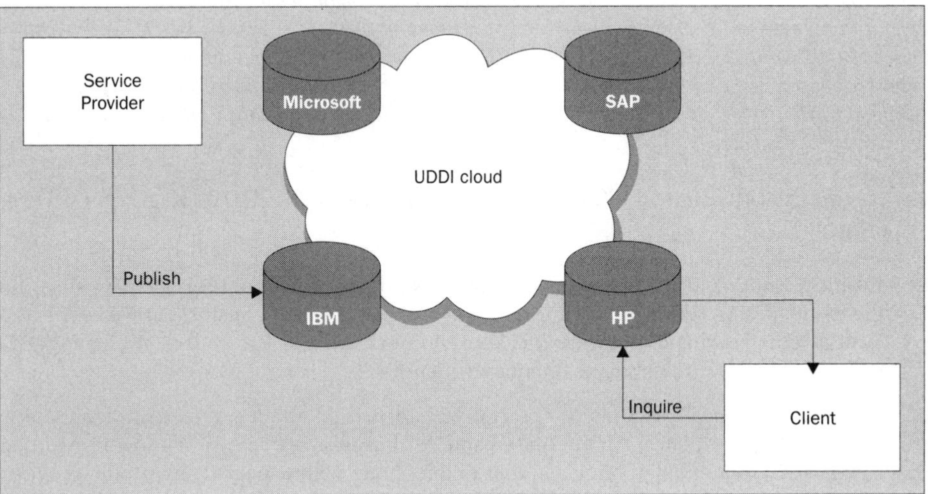


The UDDI UBR is not the only way that a UDDI registry can be deployed. Companies can also host private UDDI registries. Some use cases of such private registry deployments are:

- **B2B marketplace deployment**. A closed B2B marketplace could run a local version of a UDDI. This kind of marketplace can then provide value added services such as service monitoring, ensuring that participants in the UDDI registry have been vetted by a rigorous selection procedure, and also ensuring that all entries pertain to the market segment of interest. In such a deployment, publish and find operations could be restricted to the legitimate businesses registered with the marketplace. Such a deployment might not be free (unlike the global registry) and may charge a fee, either from the service providers or from the users, for providing such value added services.

  A variant of the above is a business partner UDDI registry catalog, in which the registry is hosted behind one partner's firewall and only trusted, or 'vetted', partners can access the registry.

- **Portal deployment**. Yet another deployment of the registry could be in a web portal that has the registry behind a firewall. External users of the portal would be allowed to carry out find operations on the registry. However, publish operations would be restricted to services internal to the portal.

- **Intranet deployment**. An intranet is another way to deploy the UDDI registry. This allows applications in different departments of an organization to publish and find services, and would be useful for large corporations. These kinds of deployments are called **Internal Enterprise Application Integration UDDI**, as they allow corporations to deploy and advertise intranet Web Services. Check out http://www.alphaworks.ibm.com/tech/UDDIreg for an example of a UDDI registry designed for a private intranet.

These private registries allow for value added services that are not provided by the UBR.

> *The UBR does not restrict how the service is described, hence a company could describe its services by a variety of means – it could be a URL pointing to a text description of the service, or a description in* ***Web Services Definition Language (WSDL)****, or whatever means the company desires to use. While this allows for flexibility, it severely restricts the ability of an application to do anything meaningful with the results of a find operation. Instead, if the description were modeled in a way that was well defined, for example using WSDL (this is a recommended best practice), an application could use dynamic find and bind operations on the service. Private UDDI deployments can thus restrict publishing to allow only WSDL-based service descriptions, or only screened and approved businesses; and hence can provide a target-rich environment to users. Private registries could also selectively propagate some information to the UBR or even publish information about themselves in the UBR.*

Finally, we come to the nature of information that is published in the UDDI Registry. UDDI defines five data structures:

- **Business Entities**. The business entity contains information about service providers. It contains the name, description, contact information, and zero or more business services. Borrowing a term from telephone directories, this kind of information is also called "White Pages", as it is structured based on the business name or identity.
- **Business Services**. This contains descriptive information about services, and contains zero or more binding templates. An alternate name for business services is "Yellow Pages" because it is organized in a manner similar to that in telephone yellow pages – by products or services offered, or geographic location. Some mechanisms of classification (called classification taxonomies) supported by UDDI are discussed later in the chapter.
- **Binding Templates**. Binding templates have technical information about how a service can be accessed. They also contain references to service type definitions.
- **Service Type Definitions**. The service type definitions are used for descriptions of service or taxonomy specifications. They form the basis of technical fingerprints. For example, two services tagged by the same service type key are understood as having the same access interface. Service type definitions are more commonly called **tModels**.
- **Publisher Assertions**. Publisher assertions capture information about the relationship between two business entities. These can be asserted by one or both parties concerned; however, to be visible to the world matching assertions are needed from both.

These data structures are described in greater detail in the *UDDI Data Structures* section later in this chapter.

# UDDI Usage Model

The usage model of the UDDI UBR envisages different roles. Some of these roles are:

- Registry operators
- Standards bodies or industry consortiums
- Service providers

- Taxonomy providers
- Information validators
- Information aggregators, business portals, and online marketplaces
- Registry users

The registry operators refer to the four operators of the UDDI Business Registry – namely IBM, Microsoft, HP, and SAP. This Business Registry has a role analogous to the role that DNS (Domain Name Service) has in the Internet infrastructure. It enables users to locate businesses, services, and service specifications.

The UDDI usage model would involve standards bodies and industry consortiums (or even the service providers themselves) publishing the descriptions of the services in the form of service type definitions (tModels). Later in the chapter we see an example of this – a tModel for a RosettaNet PIP (Partner Interface Process). The tModels do not contain the actual service definitions, and instead have a URL which points to the location where these are stored. These definitions can be in any form, however UDDI recommends using WSDL.

Next, the service providers implement and deploy Web Services conforming to these service type definitions. They then publish information about their business and the services they offer in the UDDI registry. The published data also contains the end point of the Web Service. The business and service information can also be tagged using business identifiers such as **Dun and Bradstreet's Data Universal Numbering System (D-U-N-S)**, or by product and service classifications tags based on standard taxonomies like **UNSPSC** (**Universal Standard Products and Services Classification**) and **NAICS** (**North American Industrial Classification System**). These identifiers and taxonomies are further explained later in the chapter in the *Classification and Identification Taxonomy* section.

> *For more on these three tagging conventions, see below, or visit* http://www.dnb.com, http://www.unspsc.org, *and* http://www.naics.com/, *respectively. More on NAICS can also be found at* http://www.census.gov/epcd/www/naics.html.

Prospective users could then query the UDDI registry based on various criteria such as the name of the business, the NAICS/UNSPSC product classification categories, or even services that implement a given service type definition. From the business details found, the users can obtain the end points of the Web Service.

These users can then get the details of the service type definition from the location specified. As mentioned earlier, the UDDI registry only contains the URL pointing to the service interface definition (for example, a URL to a WSDL file) and not the definition itself.

Finally, now that the user has the service end point, and also details on how to exchange messages with it, they can invoke the Web Service.

The following diagram summarizes this basic usage model:

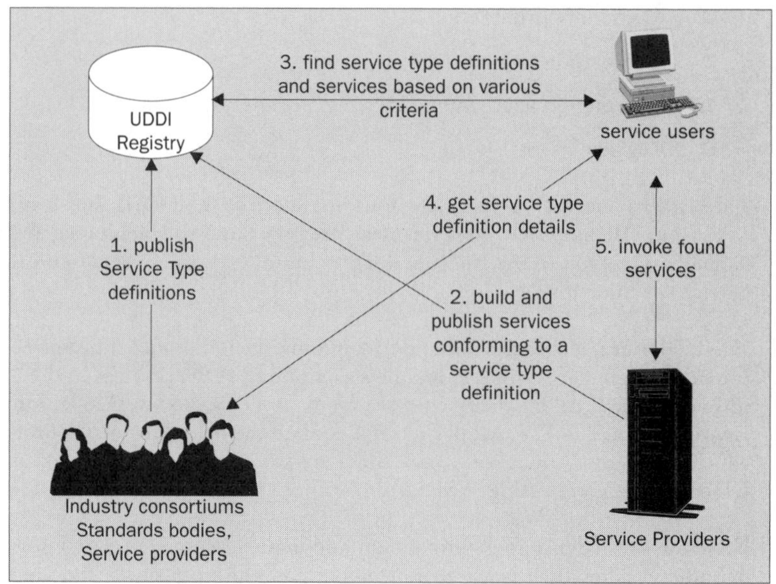


The other roles described earlier, such as taxonomy providers, information validators, and aggregators, provide additional added value over this basic model.

# Classification and Identification Taxonomies

As mentioned earlier, UDDI supports the use of standard industry and service classification taxonomies. This is supported by defining canonical service type definitions (tModels) for each of these taxonomy schemes. Businesses then tag their business and service definitions using these canonical definitions, thus enabling users to find businesses in a specific industry, product category, or geographical location. Examples include:

- The **Standard Industrial Classification** (**SIC**) classifies establishments by their primary type of activity. This is a US classification mechanism, and dates back to the 1930s. More information on SIC can be found at http://www.census.gov/epcd/www/sic.html. It is now being replaced by NAICS. Mappings between the SIC and NAICS have been published, and can be viewed at http://www.census.gov/epcd/www/naicstab.htm.
- The **North American Industrial Classification System** (**NAICS**) is a classification mechanism specific to the US, Canada, and Mexico. As the name suggests, it defines classification codes for industries. For example, mining companies have been assigned a NAICS classification code "21", non oil and gas mining companies the value "212", and under that hierarchy, coal mining companies have the NAICS code "2121.

  The following example shows how a business would use this. The `<categoryBag>` element in the example contains classification information. It contains one or more `<keyedReference>` elements for each of the classification tags. The `tModelKey` is the unique service type key. This attribute uniquely identifies the entry to be a NAICS-based classification entry. The specific value is given by the `keyValue` attribute (2121 for coal mining companies). The `keyName` attribute is provided for human readability of the `keyValue`. More details on these XML elements are given later in the *UDDI Data Structures* section.

```
<categoryBag>
   <keyedReference tModelKey="uuid:c0b9fe13-179f-413d-8a5b-5004db8e5bb2"
                   keyName="NAICS:Coal mining Companies"
                   keyValue="2121" />
   ...
   </categoryBag>
```

- The **Universal Standard Products and Services Classification** (**UNSPSC**) is an open, global coding system for classifying products and services. It is used extensively in electronic catalogs, procurement applications, and accounting systems. It is a new system, and is supposed to supersede the **Dun & Bradstreet Standard Product and Services Classification** (**SPSC**) and the United Nations Development Program's **United Nations Common Coding System** (**UNCCS**). It uses a hierarchical code for classification, consisting of the product segment, product family, class, commodity, and business type. For example, mining machinery and accessory companies have the UNSPSC code "20". Under this, quarrying machinery and equipment manufacturers have the code "2010", and still further down the hierarchy, cutting equipment manufacturers have the UNSPSC code "201015". The following code fragment shows how this would be implemented:

```
<keyedReference keyName="UNSPSC: Cutting Equipment Manufacturers"
                keyValue="201015"
                tModelKey="UUID:DB77450D-9FA8-45D4-A7BC-04411D14E384"/>
```

  As in the previous example, the `tModelKey` indicates that this entry belongs to the UNSPSC classification taxonomy, and the `keyValue` of `201015` indicates that the service provider is a cutting equipment manufacturer.

- Geographic taxonomies are a location-based classification for business organizations. UDDI supports the **ISO 3166** standard (see http://www.niso.org/3166.html for more information, and a list of the codes). This defines standard numeric and 2-or 3-letter alphabetic codes for countries and regions. For example, businesses in California would have "US-CA" as their ISO 3166 geographic taxonomy code, as can be seen in the following example:

```
<keyedReference keyName="California" keyValue="US-CA"
                tModelKey="uuid:61668105-B6B6-425C-914B-409FB252C36D"/>
```

  **GeoWeb** is another standard for geographic taxonomies, proposed by Microsoft (http://uddi.microsoft.com). It allows for a more fine-grained geographic classification than ISO 3166. The following example shows the classification tag for California in GeoWeb taxonomy:

```
<keyedReference keyName="California" keyValue="301364"
   tModelKey="uuid:297aaa47-2de3-4454-a04a-cf38e889d0c4"/>
```

In addition to *classification* taxonomies, there is support in UDDI for *identification* taxonomies. These allow businesses to tag their business information published in the UDDI registry using standard identification schemes such as the D-U-N-S identifier, Thomas register, or even country-specific mechanisms such as tax ID codes in the USA. More information can be found at http://www.dnb.com for D-U-N-S and at http://www.thomasregister.com for the Thomas register.

A new feature in UDDI version 2 is support for third-party validated taxonomies. This aims to solve a problem with fictitious content in the V1 registry, and make registry data more trustable. This feature involves participation from third parties, like those specializing in identity verification services. It would provide two kinds of checks- first to ensure that the data published in the taxonomy is correct data, and second that the business entity publishing this data actually belongs to the category it claims to be. For more details, see the *Providing a Taxonomy for Use in UDDI Version 2* paper on the UDDI best practices site (http://www.uddi.org/bestpractices.html).

# UDDI Implementations

There are a number of UDDI implementations available, although at the time of writing most supported UDDI version 1 only. These implementations include the following:

- **UDDI4J.** UDDI4J is a client implementation of the UDDI and is available in open source from http://www.uddi4j.org/. UDDI4J is UDDI 2.0 complaint and was co-developed by IBM and HP, based on code released earlier by IBM for the UDDI 1.0 version. At the time of writing, there are plans to package it along with IBM Web Services Toolkit (WSTK) and HP Web Services Platform (WSP). More about these products is given below.
- **IBM Web Services Toolkit** (**WSTK**). IBM's Web Services Toolkit includes a UDDI client API in Java (UDDI4J), a UDDI private registry implementation, and tools including a Web Services browser. UDDI4J can be downloaded from http://www.alphaworks.ibm.com/tech/webservicestoolkit.
- **Microsoft UDDI SDK**. The Microsoft UDDI SDK provides an API for Visual Studio developers to interact with UDDI registries. This API can be used in all languages supported by Visual Studio – Visual Basic/VBScript, C#, etc. Microsoft UDDI SDK can be downloaded from http://uddi.microsoft.com/developer/.
- **HP Web Services Platform** (**WSP**). The HP UDDI implementation is part of its Web Services Platform and includes a private UDDI registry, a Java client API (UDDI4J), and a UDDI browser tool. This is available at http://www.hp.com/go/webservices.
- **Idoox WASP UDDI**. The WASP UDDI implementation from Idoox provides a distributed, DNS-like UDDI implementation that allows for hierarchical organization of registries and also for selective replication. This is available from http://www.idoox.com/products/index.html and includes a private UDDI registry and a Java SDK.
- **MindElectric UDDI**. MindElectric's UDDI implementation can be downloaded from http://www.themindelectric.com/products/uddi/uddi.html. It is a Java implementation too, and includes both a UDDI private registry and a client SDK.
- **jUDDI**. jUDDI is a freeware UDDI implementation in Java, developed by Bowstreet. It includes both a UDDI private registry and a client SDK. It can be downloaded from http://www.juddi.org.
- **pUDDIng**. pUDDIng is yet another freeware UDDI implementation in Java. It can be downloaded from http://www.opensorcerer.org. It includes a private registry as well as a client SDK, and is the first UDDI 2.0 compliant implementation.
- **UDDI::Lite**. UDDI::Lite is a freeware client library in Perl for interacting with UDDI registries. It is packaged along with SOAP::Lite, a SOAP client library in Perl. Both are available from http://www.soaplite.com/.

These implementations provide users with APIs for programmatically interacting with the UDDI registry. Some of them also provide tools for users to publish and browse the UDDI registry. Shown below is one such tool from HP – the **Registry Composer**. It is being used to find all businesses named 'Hewlett-Packard' and then to drill down to get detailed information about them:

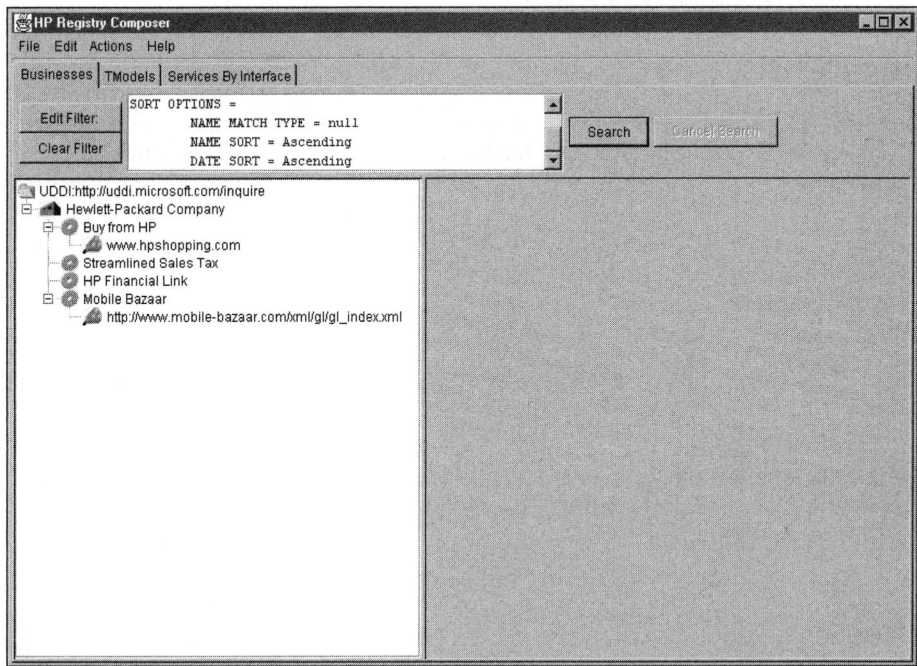


# UDDI Data Structures

The UDDI specification defines five XML data structures – the following diagram shows the interrelation between them:

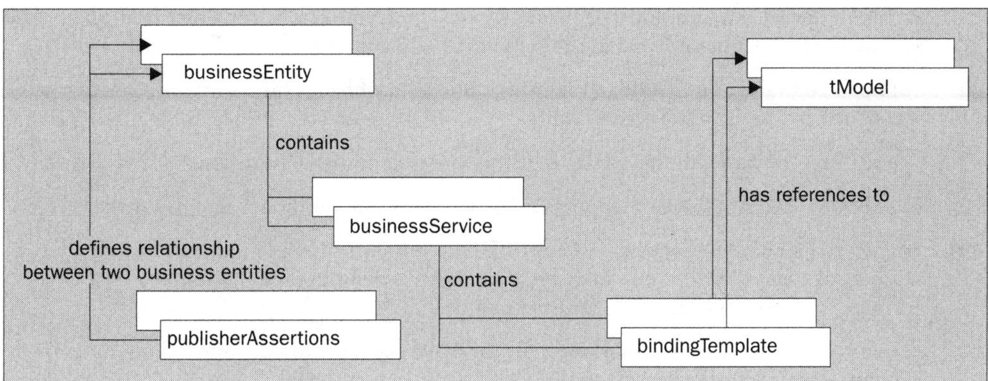

The <businessEntity> is an enclosing structure containing zero or more <businessService>s. Each <businessService> in turn contains zero or more <bindingTemplate>s. The <bindingTemplate>s may have references to a <tModel> (using the unique tModel keys). Relationships between each <businessEntity> are captured using <publisherAssertions>. These data structures are explained in greater detail below.

## Business Entity

The Business Entity (<businessEntity> data structure) contains information about the service provider company. The specification (which takes the form of an XML Schema fragment) for a business entity is as follows:

```
<element name = "businessEntity">
   <complexType>
      <sequence>
         <element ref = "discoveryURLs" minOccurs = "0"/>
         <element ref = "name" maxOccurs = "unbounded"/>
         <element ref = "description" minOccurs = "0"
                  maxOccurs = "unbounded"/>
         <element ref = "contacts" minOccurs = "0"/>
         <element ref = "businessServices" minOccurs = "0"/>
         <element ref = "identifierBag" minOccurs = "0"/>
         <element ref = "categoryBag" minOccurs = "0"/>
      </sequence>
      <attribute ref = "businessKey" use = "required"/>
      <attribute ref = "operator"/>
      <attribute ref = "authorizedName"/>
   </complexType>
</element>
```

The <businessEntity> contains:

- businessKey: A unique business key, which is an identifier for the <businessEntity>. This service key is assigned to the <businessEntity> by the UDDI operator node when it registers, using a well-defined algorithm – the DCE UUID (**U**niversal **U**nique **Id**entifier) algorithm is required by the UDDI specifications. These keys are guaranteed to be unique across all operator nodes. Further details of this algorithm can be obtained from the UUID Internet Draft document listed in the reference section at the end of the chapter.
- authorizedName: The name of the individual that publishes the <businessEntity>. This is assigned by the UDDI operator node.
- operator: The name of the UDDI registry operator site where this entry is published.
- <discoveryURLs>: URLs that point to alternative discovery mechanisms for the service.
- <name>: The name of the organization. UDDI allows for multiple names, and provides support for names in different languages. The names need to be qualified by an xml:lang attribute to denote the language that the name is in.
- <description>: A short description for the business. This too can have multiple entries, but only one for a particular language.

- <contacts>: Contact information for the organization. There can be more than one contact information entry in this element.
- <businessServices>: A list of business services that this business entity provides (see below).
- <identifierBag>: A list of name-value pairs that act as alternative identifiers for the company. For example, the US Tax code ID, D-U-N-S identifier, Thomas register ID, etc. These allow clients to search a company using alternative identification names. The example below shows IBM's business entity structure, and its D-U-N-S ID "00-136-8083" published in it. A company could have multiple entries in this field.
- <categoryBag>: A list of name-value pairs that tag the business entity with specific classification information. This could be in the form of industry taxonomy classifiers (for example UNSPSC) or geographic classifiers.

## Business Service

The business service models descriptive information about a family of services offered by a company. The top-level <businessEntity> described earlier can contain one or more <businessService> entries for each of these service families. The <businessService>, as the name suggests, contains the business service information. This information includes:

- serviceKey: A unique service key that identifies this service. This service key is assigned by the operator node when the service is registered.
- businessKey: The business entity key – this is the <businessEntity> that contains this service. In case the <businesssService> is fully contained within a <businessEntity>, the businessKey is optional. However, UDDI supports **service projection**, that is, sharing of <businessService>s between two or more <businessEntity>s. In this case, the businessKey would be different from the publishing <businessEntity>'s businessKey. Also, when a <businessService> is taken in isolation, say as a result of a find_service() API call (discussed later) that returns <businessService>s, then having a businessKey allows users to browse through the parent <businessEntity>.
- <name>: The name of this service family. Like in <businessEntity>s, there can be multiple name elements in <businessService>.
- <description>: A text description of the service family. These too can have multiple entries, with one for each language.
- <bindingTemplates>: The binding templates, giving the technical service description. More on binding templates is given below.
- <categoryBag>: A list of name-value pairs that tag the business entity with specific taxonomy information. These, as discussed earlier, can be product, service, or geographic codes. The example below for a "Buy from IBM" service shows it classified under multiple classification codes – for example, for database software (UNSPSC code 43161501) etc.

The <businessService> structure specification is given below:

```
<element name = "businessService">
   <complexType>
      <sequence>
```

```
            <element ref = "name" maxOccurs = "unbounded"/>
            <element ref = "description" minOccurs = "0"
                     maxOccurs = "unbounded"/>
            <element ref = "bindingTemplates"/>
            <element ref = "categoryBag" minOccurs = "0"/>
         </sequence>
            <attribute ref = "serviceKey" use = "required"/>
            <attribute ref = "businessKey"/>
      </complexType>
   </element>
```

## Binding Template

Binding information contains technical information about a Web Service. This information helps clients to connect and then invoke the service. The complete list of attributes contained in the <bindingTemplate> structure (the structure that models binding information) is:

- bindingKey: A unique binding key identifying this binding template. This again is a unique ID assigned by the operator node.
- serviceKey: The business service key – this is the key of the <businessService> element that contains this binding template. The serviceKey is optional when the <bindingTemplate> is contained within a <businessService>. However, when it is taken in isolation, say as a result of a find_binding() API call (discussed later) that returns <bindingTemplate>s, then having a serviceKey allows users to browse through the parent <businessService>.
- <description>: A text description of the binding template.
- <accessPoint>: The access point for the information. This contains the entry point for the service. Valid access point values can include the URL, e-mail address, or even a phone number. The access point has a urlType attribute, and valid values that it can contain include http, https, ftp, fax, phone, and mailto.
- <hostingRedirector>: This points to another binding template, and is used when the access point is not specified.
- <tModelInstanceDetails>: A list of tModels info structures. A tModel acts as a fingerprint for the service – more information on tModels is given below.

The following fragment shows the structure definition for a binding template:

```
   <element name = "bindingTemplate">
      <complexType>
         <sequence>
            <element ref = "description" minOccurs = "0"
                     maxOccurs = "unbounded"/>
               <choice>
                  <element ref = "accessPoint" minOccurs = "0"/>
                  <element ref = "hostingRedirector" minOccurs = "0"/>
               </choice>
            <element ref = "tModelInstanceDetails"/>
          </sequence>
```

```
            <attribute ref = "bindingKey" use = "required"/>
            <attribute ref = "serviceKey"/>
      </complexType>
   </element>
```

An example <businessEntity> is shown below, with enclosed <businessServices> and <bindingTemplate>s. This <businessEntity> contains information about a company (Hewlett-Packard), and the services it provides. The UDDI registry data may get updated by the company, and so should be taken as an example, and not actual UDDI registry data. It is however based on information that was published in the UDDI registry at the time the chapter was written. Some of the information in this <businessEntity> has been edited to make it shorter and more suitable for an example. A complete version of this <businessEntity> can be found in the code download for this book, at http://www.wrox.com/.

The <businessEntity> contains the name of the company (<name> element), textual descriptions (<description> element), contact information (<contact> element), categorization information (<categoryBag>), alternative identifiers for the company (<identifierBag>), and the enclosed business services (<businessService> element).

The operator attribute that can be seen below refers to the UDDI operator where this <businessEntity> is registered. The UDDI operator assigns both the authorizedName as well as the (unique) businessKey.

```
<businessEntity authorizedName="HewlettPackard Company"
                operator="Microsoft Corporation"
                businessKey="2E97C41AFD624AB8BF9F1F3231AB3373">
   <discoveryURLs>
      <discoveryURL useType="businessEntity">
http://uddi.microsoft.com/discovery?businessKey=2E97C41AFD624AB8BF9F1F3231AB3373
      </discoveryURL>
   </discoveryURLs>
   <name>HewlettPackard Company</name>
   <description xml:lang="en">
      A leading global provider of computing and imaging solutions and services
      is focused on making technology and its benefits accessible to all.
   </description>
```

Next comes the contact information for HP, including its corporate headquarters and offices in Latin America:

```
   <contacts>
      <contact useType="">
         <description xml:lang="en">Headquarters</description>
         <personName>HewlettPackard Company</personName>
         <phone useType="">18006377740</phone>
         <email useType="">
            http://www.hp.com/solutions1/eservices/contact/eml_contact_form.html
         </email>
         <address useType="" sortCode="">
            <addressLine>3000 Hanover St.</addressLine>
            <addressLine>Palo Alto, CA 94304</addressLine>
```

```
        </address>
      </contact>
      <contact useType="">
        <description xml:lang="en">Latin America</description>
        <personName>HewlettPackard Company</personName>
        <phone useType="">(305) 2674220</phone>
        <address useType="" sortCode="">
          <addressLine>Waterford Building, 9th Floor</addressLine>
          <addressLine>5200 Blue Lagoon Drive</addressLine>
          <addressLine>Miami, Florida 33126 USA</addressLine>
        </address>
      </contact>
    </contacts>
```

Now comes the enclosed <businessServices>. These contain the service name, description, and classification information (<categoryBag> element). Each <businessService> also contains zero or more <bindingTemplate>s:

```
    <businessServices>
      <businessService serviceKey="979C498DC9DD4F9096434E8338ACE2A6"
                       businessKey="2E97C41AFD624AB8BF9F1F3231AB3373">
        <name>Buy from HP</name>
        <description xml:lang="en">
          This service enables direct purchasing from HP through the HPShopping
          web site.
        </description>
        <bindingTemplates>
          <bindingTemplate bindingKey="C55FD09DE7EB43319C2A7FE2C94FEE3F"
                           serviceKey="979C498DC9DD4F9096434E8338ACE2A6">
            <description xml:lang="en">
              A URL to hpshopping's web site.
            </description>
            <accessPoint URLType="http">www.hpshopping.com</accessPoint>
            <tModelInstanceDetails />
          </bindingTemplate>
        </bindingTemplates>
        <categoryBag>
          <keyedReference tModelKey="UUID:DB77450D9FA845D4A7BC04411D14E384"
                          keyName="Electronic Components and Supplies"
                          keyValue="32" />
          <keyedReference tModelKey="UUID:DB77450D9FA845D4A7BC04411D14E384"
                          keyName="Communications and computer supplies"
                          keyValue="4318" />
          <keyedReference tModelKey="UUID:DB77450D9FA845D4A7BC04411D14E384"
                          keyName="Print utility software"
                          keyValue="43162505" />
        </categoryBag>
      </businessService>
    </businessServices>
    <identifierBag>
      <keyedReference tModelKey="UUID:8609C81EEE1F4D5AB2023EB13AD01823"
                      keyName="HP Headquarters"
                      keyValue="009122532" />
    </identifierBag>
    <categoryBag>
      <keyedReference tModelKey="UUID:DB77450D9FA845D4A7BC04411D14E384"
                      keyName="Hardware and accessories"
```

```
                    keyValue="4317" />
      <keyedReference tModelKey="UUID:DB77450D9FA845D4A7BC04411D14E384"
                      keyName="Software"
                      keyValue="4316" />
    </categoryBag>
  </businessEntity>
```

## tModel

The binding information discussed above defines how to contact a Web Service. Access information alone is often not sufficient, as a programmer would need to know a lot more information about the Web Service. This could be information about what are the kinds of methods that the service exposes, what is the data format expected, and so on – a lot of this information is application specific. This information is kept in a `<tModel>` (see details below), and has been kept deliberately vague. It has a key, a name, an optional description, and a URL that points to a location that has more description related to the service or taxonomy:

- `tModelKey`: A unique tModel key identifying the tModel. These keys are assigned by the operator node in a manner similar to the business, service, and binding keys.
- `authorizedName`: The name of the individual that published this tModel information.
- `operator`: The name of the UDDI registry operator site where this information is published.
- `<name>`: The name of the tModel.
- `<description>`: A description of the tModel.
- `<overviewDoc>`: A reference to remote instructions or descriptions related to the tModel. For example, this could contain a URL pointing to the WSDL description of the Web Service.
- `<identifierBag>`: A list of name-value pairs used to record identification numbers for this tModel.
- `<categoryBag>`: A list of name-value pairs used to record classification information for this tModel.

The structure definition for a tModel is given below:

```
  <element name = "tModel">
    <complexType>
      <sequence>
        <element ref = "name"/>
        <element ref = "description" minOccurs = "0"
                 maxOccurs = "unbounded"/>
        <element ref = "overviewDoc" minOccurs = "0"/>
        <element ref = "identifierBag" minOccurs = "0"/>
        <element ref = "categoryBag" minOccurs = "0"/>
      </sequence>
      <attribute ref = "tModelKey" use = "required"/>
      <attribute ref = "operator"/>
      <attribute ref = "authorizedName"/>
    </complexType>
  </element>
```

A tModel has two main uses: it defines a "technical fingerprint" for the service (when used in binding templates), and it defines an abstract namespace reference (when used in category and identifier bags). Let's look at some examples of where a `tModelKey` is used:

- Used in a binding template, the tModel key refers to a technical service type. It defines the "technical fingerprint" for the service and thus helps a client program to determine if a web service implements a particular programming interface (and hence is compatible with the client program).

```
<bindingTemplate bindingKey="6D8F8DF0-3AAF-11D5-80DC-002035229C64"
                 serviceKey="894B5100-3AAF-11D5-80DC-002035229C64">
   <description xml:lang="en">Register to ShopIBM</description>
   <accessPoint URLType="https">https://someurl</accessPoint>
   <tModelInstanceDetails>
      <tModelInstanceInfo tModelKey="UUID:68DE9E80-AD09-469D-8A37-088422BFBC36"/>
   </tModelInstanceDetails>
</bindingTemplate>
```

- The tModel key in a category element defines the type of taxonomy. For example, different tModel keys would identify NAICS, UNSPSC, and other taxonomy types. The tModel key shown in the example below is the one for UNSPSC codes:

```
<categoryBag>
     <keyedReference keyName="UNSPSC: Database software"
                     keyValue="43161501"
                     tModelKey="UUID:DB77450D-9FA8-45D4-A7BC-04411D14E384"/>
```

- In an <identifierBag> element, the tModel key is the type of the identifier – for instance the D-U-N-S number or taxpayer ID number.

```
<identifierBag>
     <keyedReference keyName="D-U-N-S"
                     keyValue="00-136-8083"
                     tModelKey="UUID:8609C81E-EE1F-4D5A-B202-3EB13AD01823"/>
```

- In a business relationship (publisher assertion structure), the tModel key is the type of the relationship. In the example below, it is used to define the relationship to be that of a "holding company". Publisher assertions are new in UDDI 2.0, and are discussed later.

```
<publisherAssertions generic="2.0" operator="www.ibm.com/services/uddi/"
                     authorizedName="John J. Doe" xmlns="urn:uddi-org:api_v2">
   <publisherAssertion>
      <fromKey>F5E65...</fromKey>
      <toKey>A237B...</toKey>
      <keyedReference tModelKey="uuid:807A2C6A-EE22-470D-ADC7-E0424A337C03"
                      keyName="Holding Company"
                      keyValue="parent-child">
      </keyedReference>
   </publisherAssertion>
</publisherAssertions>
```

- In an address structure, the tModel key specifies the organization structure of the address – for example addresses in the USA would be formatted differently from those in other countries. Again, this use is new in version 2.0.

For example, an organization could define a structure for addresses with keyValues for different components – "10" for street name, "20" for street number etc. Then, it would publish a tModel for this standard. Users could then use this known tModelKey (uuid:A345... in the example below) to specify addresses in their contact information.

```
<address useType="office" tModelKey="uuid:A345...">
   <addressLine keyName="Street" keyValue="10">Elm Court</addressLine>
   <addressLine keyName="Street number" keyValue="20">180</addressLine>
   <addressLine keyName="City" keyValue="40">Sunnyvale</addressLine>
   <addressLine keyName="Country" keyValue="70">USA</addressLine>
</address>
```

Appendix I of the *UDDI Programmer's Specification* (http://www.uddi.org/specification.html) also defines a set of **canonical** tModels. Some of these are defined for the industry standard taxonomies (NAICS, UNSPSC etc.).

A sample <tModel> entry in the UDDI registry is shown below. It is, as the description specifies, a <tModel> for the RosettaNet PIP for enabling trading partners to request and provide quotes. RosettaNet defines a set of standards for information technology, an electronic component, and a semiconductor manufacturing supply chain. It is also a consortium of more than 400 of the world's leading companies in this area, and was formed in early 1998 in response to business needs for open business-to-business process standards. RosettaNet PIPs (Partner Interface Process), define business processes between trading partners. Further information on RosettaNet can be found at http://www.rosettanet.org/

As can be seen, the specification is not stored in the UDDI registry; instead the <tModel> has a URL (<overviewURL> element) pointing to where this can be found. Besides the URL, the <tModel> contains a name and textual description of the <tModel>.

```
<tModel tModelKey="uuid:2c4c2263-daec-4dd0-80ba-337fb729f74e"
        operator="Microsoft Corporation"
        authorizedName="Suhayl Masud">
   <name>Rosettanet-org:PIP3A1:RequestQuote:vB01.00.00A</name>
   <description xml:lang="en">
      Supports a process for trading partners to request and provide quotes
   </description>
   <overviewDoc>
      <description xml:lang="en">
         This is the compressed file that contains the specification in a word
         document, the html message guideline document, and the xml dtds
      </description>
      <overviewURL>
  http://www.rosettanet.org/rosettanet/Doc/0/K96RPDQA97A1311M0304UQ4J39/3A1_RequestQuote.zip
      </overviewURL>
   </overviewDoc>
</tModel>
```

This example highlights another area where UDDI can be useful. UDDI is agnostic to the process of interaction between users after they find each other. This enables, for instance, RosettaNet users to find each other.

## Publisher Assertion

Publisher assertions are used for modeling business relationships. These can be published by one or both business entities, however, for an assertion to be visible to users of the UDDI registry, both business entities must publish the same information in the assertions. This prevents businesses from claiming a relationship unilaterally. However, if a publisher is responsible for both the business entities, then publishing just one assertion is enough.

The `<publisherAssertion>` structure contains the following:

- The `<fromKey>`, the first business entity the assertion is made for.
- The `<toKey>`, the second business entity the assertion is made for.
- The `<keyedReference>`. This designates the relationship type.

The structure definition for the publisher assertion is shown:

```
<element name = "publisherAssertion">
   <complexType>
      <sequence>
         <element ref = "fromKey"/>
         <element ref = "toKey"/>
         <element ref = "keyedReference"/>
      </sequence>
   </complexType>
</element>
```

A sample publisher assertion is given below. It models a relationship between a holding company and its subsidiary:

```
<publisherAssertion>
```

The `<fromKey>` contains the `businessKey` of the first business that the assertion is made for:

```
   <fromKey>82...</fromKey>
```

The `<toKey>` contains the `businessKey` of the second business:

```
   <toKey>A237B...</toKey>
```

The tModel below is the canonical tModel for a business relationship description. The valid `keyValues` in this tModel are *parent-child* (for organizational hierarchies such as holding company/subsidiary relationships), *peer-peer* (for entities on equal footing, for example partner companies, or departments in a company), and *identity* (for indicating that the two business entities represent the same company): Identity relationships can be used by identification authorities to confirm the identity of a business.

```
   <keyedReference tModelKey="uuid:807A2C6A-EE22-470D-ADC7-E0424A337C03"
                   keyName="Holding Company"
                   keyValue="parent-child">
   </keyedReference>
</publisherAssertion>
```

To summarize, the information that is stored in the UDDI registry allows the user to determine **who** the business entity represents, **what** they do, **where** the services they provide can be found, and **how** they can be accessed.

The data in the `<businessEntity>` data structure, with the name of the business and identifiers like the D-U-N-S number, or the Tax ID number provides information on **who** the business entity is. The classification information, like UNSPSC, SIC and NAICS codes for product and geographic classification, as well as the text description stored in the `<businessService>` data structure give an answer to **what** the business does. The `<bindingTemplate>` contains details on **where** the service is, and this can be specified as a URL, an e-mail address, a fax number or a phone number. Finally, the `<tModel>` describes on **how** the service can be accessed. This is usually in the form of a reference to information about the service interface.

# UDDI API

UDDI defines XML-based APIs for interacting with the registry. Using these APIs, it is possible to add, delete, and modify the data published in the registry, and also to search for this data. The UDDI publishing API is targeted for the former, and the latter can be done using the inquiry API.

## Inquiry API

The UDDI inquiry API has two usage patterns – browse and drill down. A programmer would use a browse pattern (`find_xx()` API calls) to get a list of all entries of a certain type and then use the drill down pattern (`get_xx()` API calls) to get additional information on a specific entry. For example, a `find_business()` call would first be issued to locate all businesses in a specific category area, and then a `get_BusinessDetail()` call would be used to get additional information about a specific business. The specific inquiry API calls are described below.

### *find_binding()*

This is used to locate specific bindings within a registered business service. It takes as arguments the service key, which is a unique identifier for a business service, the technical fingerprints for the desired services (sent as a list in `<tModelBag>`) and some optional search criteria. This call returns the binding template(s) that matches the search criteria. The binding templates have information on invoking services. The syntax of this call, as given in the UDDI v 2.0 Programmer API document, is:

```
<find_binding serviceKey="uuid_key" [ maxRows="nn" ] generic="2.0"
              xmlns="urn:uddi-org:api_v2" >
  [<findQualifiers/>]
   <tModelBag/>
</find_binding>
```

A sample `find_binding` message is given below. In the example, we show the HTTP headers as well as the SOAP envelope tags. In all other UDDI messages in this case study, we will skip them, and show only the UDDI message payload.

```
POST / HTTP/1.1
Content-Length: 439
Connection: close
User-Agent: HP-SOAP/2001-06-15-11:11:28
SOAPAction: ""
Content-Type: text/xml; charset="UTF-8"

<?xml version="1.0" encoding="UTF-8" ?>
<SOAP:Envelope SOAP:encodingStyle="http://schemas.xmlsoap.org/soap/encoding/"
               xmlns:SOAP="http://schemas.xmlsoap.org/soap/envelope/">
   <SOAP:Body>
      <find_binding serviceKey="uuid_key" generic="2.0"
                    xmlns="urn:uddi-org:api_v2" >
         <findQualifiers>
            <findQualifier>sortByNameAsc</findQualifier>
         </findQualifiers>
         <tModelBag>
            <tModelKey>uuid:6a7826c8-bbb4-c5ec-768b-7d5c4fb690b7</tModelKey>
         </tModelBag>
      </find_binding>
   </SOAP:Body>
</SOAP:Envelope>
```

Error messages, if any, are passed back through a "Disposition Report" (more explanation on this is given later). There can be two cases in which this call can fail, and the error codes for these are:

- `E_invalidKeyPassed`. Invalid key for service or tModel.
- `E_unsupported`. Invalid values were passed in the find qualifiers.

These errors are returned in a `dispositionReport` message. A sample `dispositionReport` is shown below with SOAP headers. This particular error message indicates that the `findQualifier` specified was invalid.

```
<?xml version="1.0" encoding="UTF-8" ?>
<Envelope xmlns="http://schemas.xmlsoaporg.org/soap/envelope/">
   <Body>
      <Fault>
         <faultcode>Client</faultcode>
         <faultstring>Client Error</faultstring>
         <detail>
            <dispositionReport generic="2.0" operator="OperatorURI"
                               xmlns="urn:uddi-org:api_v2" >
               <result errno="10050" >
                  <errInfo errCode="E_fatalError">
                     The findQualifier value passed is unrecognized: exitNameMatch
                  </errInfo>
               </result>
            </dispositionReport>
         </detail>
      </Fault>
   </Body>
</Envelope>
```

A successful find_binding() call returns a <bindingDetail> message. In case the search resulted in no matches, an empty <bindingDetail> (that is, no <bindingTemplate>s) will be returned.

```
<bindingDetail generic="2.0" operator="uddi.someoperator" truncated="true"
               xmlns="urn:uddi-org:api_v2">
   <bindingTemplate bindingKey="somekey" serviceKey="somekey" >
   </bindingTemplate>
   [<bindingTemplate/>]
</bindingDetail>
```

The **find qualifiers** mentioned earlier have the following syntax:

```
<findQualifiers>
   <findQualifier>fixedQualifierValue</findQualifier>
   [<findQualifier>fixedQualifierValue</findQualifier> ...]
</findQualifiers>
```

The values that can go in the find qualifier are given below. These are self descriptive in their meaning, and they modify the default search behavior of the inquiry methods. The UDDI API document also defines precedence rules for them.

- exactNameMatch overrides the default behavior of lexical order matches.
- caseSensitiveMatch overrides the default behavior of case-insensitive matches.

*exactNameMatch and caseSensitiveMatch can be combined but are equal in precedence.*

- sortByNameAsc specifies that the results should be sorted on the name field in the ascending alphabetic order.
- sortByNameDesc specifies that the results should be sorted on the name field in the descending alphabetic order.

*sortByNameAsc and sortByNameDesc are mutually exclusive, but equal in precedence.*

- sortByDateAsc specifies that the results should be sorted on the date last updated in an ascending order.
- sortByDateDesc specifies that the results should be sorted on the date last updated in descending order.

*sortByDateAsc and sortByDateDesc are mutually exclusive, but equal in precedence.*

- orLikeKeys: When a <categoryBag> or <identifierBag> contains multiple entries, those in the same namespace, that is with the same tModelKey, are logically ORed for the search and not ANDed.
- orAllKeys: Logically OR all keys in the <categoryBag> and <tModelBag>, instead of ANDing them (the default behavior).
- andAllKeys: Logically AND all keys in the <identifierBag> instead of ORing them.

*orLikeKeys, orAllKeys and andAllKeys are mutually exclusive. <categoryBag>s and <identifierBag>s are not present in the find_binding() call, but other find API calls (find_business(), find_service() and find_tModel()) have them. Therefore, orLikeKeys, orAllKeys and andAllKeys are applicable only for those calls.*

- soundex: Does a "sound-alike" search on the names.
- combineCategoryBags: This find qualifier is used only in find_business() calls (see below). This qualifier indicates that the category bag entries in the business service should be combined with that of the business entity while performing a search.
- serviceSubset: This find qualifier too is used only in find_business() calls. It indicates that only the category bag entries of the business service should be used for the search.

## find_business()

This method helps locate one or more business entities that match search criteria. The search can be performed on the partial name of the business, the business identifiers, the category/classification identifiers or the technical fingerprints of the services. The operator node might truncate the search result if the number of businesses is too large – UDDI does not define what being too large means, and individual operator nodes would be defining this for themselves. The syntax of the call is given below:

```
<find_business [maxRows="nn"] generic="2.0" xmlns="urn:uddi-org:api_v2" >
   [<findQualifiers/>]
   [<name/> [<name/>]...]
   [<discoveryURLs/>]
   [<identifierBag/>]
   [<categoryBag/>]
   [<tModelBag/>]
</find_business>
```

In case multiple names are supplied in a find_business() call, they are ORed together while performing a search.

The possible errors for this call include:

- E_nameTooLong. The partial name value passed exceeds the maximum name length designated by the operator site.
- E_tooManyOptions. More than five names arguments passed.
- E_unsupported. One of the findQualifier values passed was invalid.

A successful find_business() returns a businessList. This contains <businessInfo>s, which is a summarized form of <businessEntity>.

```
<businessList generic="2.0" operator="uddi.sourceOperator" truncated="true"
              xmlns="urn:uddi-org:api_v2">
   <businessInfos>
      <businessInfo businessKey="F5E65..." >
         <name>Some Business Name</name>
            <serviceInfos>
               <serviceInfo serviceKey="3D45...">
               <name>Some Service Name</name>
            </serviceInfo>
         </serviceInfos>
      </businessInfo>
      [<businessInfo/>...]
   </businessInfos>
</businessList>
```

## *find_relatedBusinesses()*

This is used to locate information about business entity registrations that are related to the business entity. The business entity's unique key is passed as the input parameter. This functionality is used to manage registrations of business units and relate them based on organization hierarchies or business partner relationships. This call returns a list of related business entities. The syntax for this call is:

```
<find_relatedBusinesses generic="2.0" xmlns="urn:uddi-org:api_v2">
    [<findQualifiers/>]
    <businessKey/>
    [<keyedReference/>]
</find_relatedBusinesses>
```

Possible errors from this call include:

- `E_invalidKeyPassed`. A `uuid_key` or `tModelkey` value passed did not match with any known `businessKey` or `tModelkey` values.
- `E_unsupported`. The `findQualifier` values passed was invalid.

A successful `find_relatedBusinesses()` call will return a `<relatedBusinessesList>` message. A sample message is shown below. In cases where no businesses matched, zero `<relatedBusinessInfo>`s are returned. Each `<relatedBusinessInfo>` contains information about a business relationship that a given `<businessEntity>` has.

```
<relatedBusinessesList generic="2.0"
                       operator="uddi.someoperator"
                       [truncated="false"]
                       xmlns="urn:uddi-org:api_v2">
    <businessKey/>F5E65...</businessKey>
    <relatedBusinessInfos>
        <relatedBusinessInfo>
            <businessKey>A237B...</businessKey>
            <name>Business Name</name>
            <description>Business Description</description>
            <sharedRelationships direction="toKey">
                <keyedReference tModelKey="uuid:807A2..."
                                keyName="Subsidiary"
                                keyValue="parent-child">
                [<keyedReference/>...]
            </sharedRelationships>
        </relatedBusinessInfo>
        [<relatedBusinessInfo/>...]
    </relatedBusinessInfos>
</relatedBusinessesList>
```

As mentioned earlier, one-sided assertions are not visible. Hence these will not be returned by the `find_relatedBusiness()` call.

## *find_service()*

The `find_service()` method returns a list of business services that match the search conditions. The input parameters to this method are the unique business entity key, the partial name of the service, a list of category references for the service, and other search qualifiers.

```
<find_service businessKey="uuid_key" " [maxRows="nn"] generic="2.0
              xmlns="urn:uddi-org:api_v2" >
   [<findQualifiers/>]
   [<name/> [<name/>]... ]
   [<categoryBag/>]
   [<tModelBag/>]
</find_service>
```

The find qualifiers are the same as described in find_binding(). The errors that can occur in this call are given below. These are returned in a dispositionReport as described earlier.

- E_invalidKeyPassed. The uuid_key value passed did not match with any known businessKey key or tModelkey values.
- E_nameTooLong. The partial name value passed exceeds the maximum name length as specified in the UDDI data structure specification. Currently, a name field can be up to 255 characters in length.
- E_unsupported. Can be one of multiple causes – the error text would have more details. Some possible causes are invalid findQualifier values, or a blank name value.

A successful find_service() returns a <serviceList>, as shown below. A <serviceList> contains a <serviceInfos> element with zero or more <serviceInfo>s. A <serviceInfo> is a summarized version of a <businessService>.

```
<serviceList generic="2.0" operator="uddi.sourceOperator" [truncated="false"]
             xmlns="urn:uddi-org:api_v2">
   <serviceInfos>
      <serviceInfo serviceKey="somekey" businessKey="somekey">
         <name/>
      </serviceInfo>
   </serviceInfos>
</serviceList>
```

## find_tModel()

This method, as the name suggests, finds tModels. The input is a partial name of the tModel, a list of business identifiers, or a list of category/classification identifiers, in addition to other find qualifiers. The business identifiers are logically ORed with each other while the category identifiers are ANDed in the search query.

```
<find_tModel [maxRows="nn"] generic="2.0" xmlns="urn:uddi-org:api_v2" >
   [<findQualifiers/>]
   [<name/>]
   [<identifierBag/>]
   [<categoryBag/>]
</find_tModel>
```

The find qualifiers are the same as described for find_binding(). In case of an error, the disposition report will contain the following errors:

- E_nameTooLong. The partial name value passed exceeds the maximum name length designated by the operator site.
- E_unsupported. One of the findQualifier values passed was invalid.

A successful find_tModel() call returns a tModelList message. This contains a <tModelInfos> with zero or more <tModelInfo>s – zero in a case where the search resulted in no matches. A <tModelInfo> is a summarized form of a <tModelDetail>.

```
<tModelList generic="2.0" operator="uddi.sourceOperator" [truncated="false"]
            xmlns="urn:uddi-org:api_v2">
   <tModelInfos>
      <tModelInfo tModelKey="uuid:34D5...">
         <name>Proprietary XML purchase order</name>
      </tModelInfo>
   [<tModelInfo/>...]
   </tModelInfos>
</tModelList>
```

## get_bindingDetail()

This method returns the run-time binding template information (<bindingTemplate> structure) used for invoking methods against a business service. The <bindingTemplate>s specified by the <bindingKey>s are the input parameters to the call.

```
<get_bindingDetail generic="2.0" xmlns="urn:uddi-org:api_v2">
   <bindingKey/>
   [ <bindingKey/> ...]
</get_bindingDetail>
```

The error that can be returned by this call is:

- E_invalidKeyPassed. One of the uuid_key values passed did not match with any known bindingKey key values.

A successful get_bindingDetail() call returns a <bindingDetail> message containing one or more <bindingTemplate>s.

```
<bindingDetail generic="2.0" operator="uddi.someoperator" truncated="true"
    xmlns="urn:uddi-org:api_v2">
   <bindingTemplate>
   [<bindingTemplate/>...]
</bindingDetail>
```

## get_businessDetail()

The get_businessDetail() method returns the complete businessEntity object for one or more business entities. The input parameter is a list of <businessKey>s that uniquely specify the business entity.

```
<get_businessDetail generic="2.0" xmlns="urn:uddi-org:api_v2">
   <businessKey/>
   [<businessKey/>...]
</get_businessDetail>
```

The error that can be returned by this call is:

- E_invalidKeyPassed. One of the uuid_key values passed did not match with any known businessKey key values.

A successful get_businessDetail() call returns a <businessDetail> message containing one or more <businessEntity>s.

```
<businessDetail generic="2.0" operator="uddi.sourceOperator" truncated="true"
                xmlns="urn:uddi-org:api_v2">
   <businessEntity/>
   [<businessEntity/>...]
</businessDetail>
```

## get_businessDetailExt()

This method is identical to the get_businessDetail() method, but returns extra attributes in case the source registry is not an operator node:

```
<get_businessDetailExt generic="2.0" xmlns="urn:uddi-org:api_v2">
   <businessKey/>
   [<businessKey/> ...]
</get_businessDetailExt>
```

The errors that can be returned by this call are:

- E_invalidKeyPassed. One of the uuid_key values passed did not match with any known businessKey key values.
- E_unsupported. The operator node does not implement the extended detail function.

A successful get_businessDetailExt() call returns a <businessDetailExt> message containing one or more <businessEntityExt>s.

```
<businessDetailExt generic="2.0" operator="uddi.sourceOperator" truncated="true"
                   xmlns="urn:uddi-org:api_v2">
   <businessEntityExt/>
   [<businessEntityExt/>...]
</businessDetail>
```

## get_serviceDetail()

The get_serviceDetail() method returns the complete businessService object for one or more business services specified by their service keys:

```
<get_serviceDetail generic="2.0" xmlns="urn:uddi-org:api_v2">
   <serviceKey/>
   [ <serviceKey/> ...]
</get_serviceDetail>
```

The error that can be returned by this call is:

- E_invalidKeyPassed. One of the uuid_key values passed did not match with any known serviceKey key values.

A successful get_serviceDetail() call returns a <serviceDetail> message containing one or more <businessService>s.

```
<serviceDetail generic="2.0" operator="uddi.sourceOperator" [truncated="false"]
               xmlns="urn:uddi-org:api_v2">
   <businessService/>
   [<businessService/>...]
</serviceDetail>
```

### *get_tModelDetail()*

This method returns the tModel details. One or more tModelKeys can be passed as an argument:

```
<get_tModelDetail generic="2.0" xmlns="urn:uddi-org:api_v2">
   <tModelKey/>
   [<tModelKey/> ...]
</get_tModelDetail>
```

The error that can be returned by this call is:

- E_invalidKeyPassed. One of the uuid_key values passed did not match with any known tModelKey key values.

A successful get_tModelDetail() call returns a <tModelDetail> message containing one or more <tModel>s.

```
<tModelDetail generic="2.0" operator="uddi.sourceOperator" [truncated="false"]
              xmlns="urn:uddi-org:api_v2">
   <tModel/>
   [<tModel/>...]
</tModelDetail>
```

All the inquiry methods can have their results truncated by the operator site. If this is the case, the truncated attribute in the response is set to true. The methods can control the number of rows desired using the maxRows input parameter. However, typically, operator nodes truncate result sets of more than 1000 rows. Currently there is not provision in the API to get the remaining rows in the result set – this functionality is being actively investigated for the next iteration of the UDDI specification (V3). For now, users should refine their search criteria in case the result set is so large that it gets truncated.

## Publishing API

The publishing API essentially allows programs to save and delete the five data types supported by UDDI and described earlier in the UDDI information model.

These calls are used by service providers and companies to publish and unpublish information about themselves in the UDDI registry. These API calls require authenticated access to the registry, unlike the inquiry API. All these calls, except for `get_authToken()`, require an authentication token to be passed as a parameter. The authentication token is an opaque data value – it is up to the operator node to implement a mechanism for generation of the authentication token, and these tokens are not portable across operator nodes. The publishing API provides two calls – `get_AuthToken()` and `discard_authToken()` – for getting an authentication token and invalidating it respectively. The `get_AuthToken()` call takes the user ID and credentials and returns the token. The user ID and password for this call is set when the user sets up a publisher account at an operator node. The UDDI operators provide a web-based interface for setting up a publisher account, and these often involve entering some contact information about the business. This token is then used in all subsequent publishing calls – these and other calls are discussed in greater length later.

The following figure shows the web interface for IBM's UDDI node (https://www-3.ibm.com/services/uddi/protect/registry.html). This web interface allows first-time users to register and create an account – this is required in case a user wishes to start publishing data in the registry. The web interface also allows users to browse the data in the UDDI registry. The case study later in the chapter walks you through an example registration at a UDDI operator node.

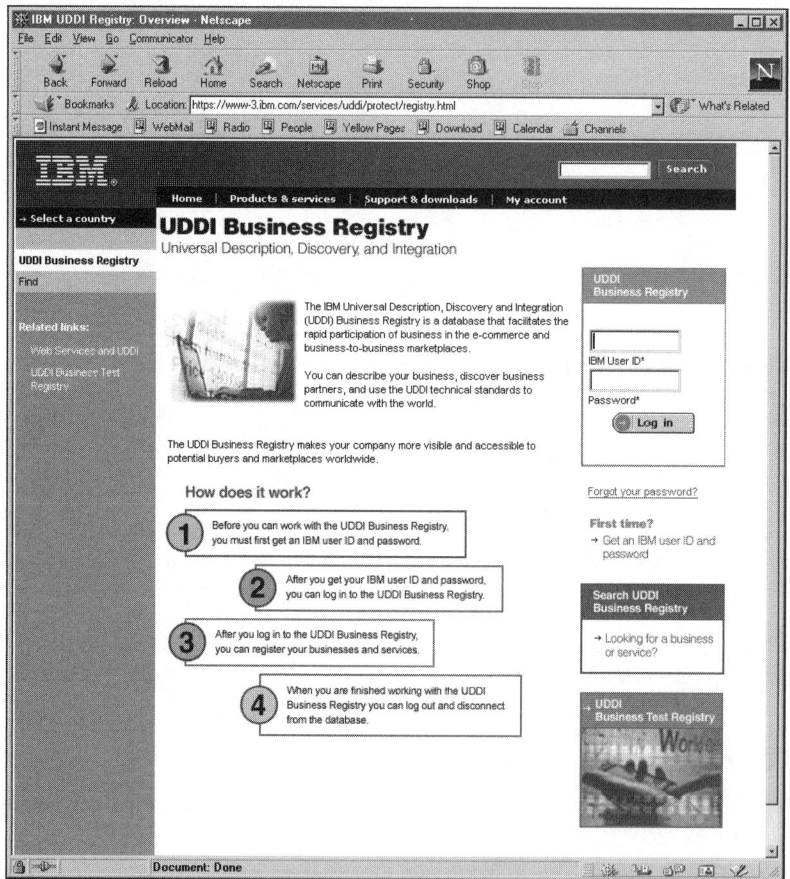

The corresponding web site for Microsoft is at http://uddi.microsoft.com (shown below).

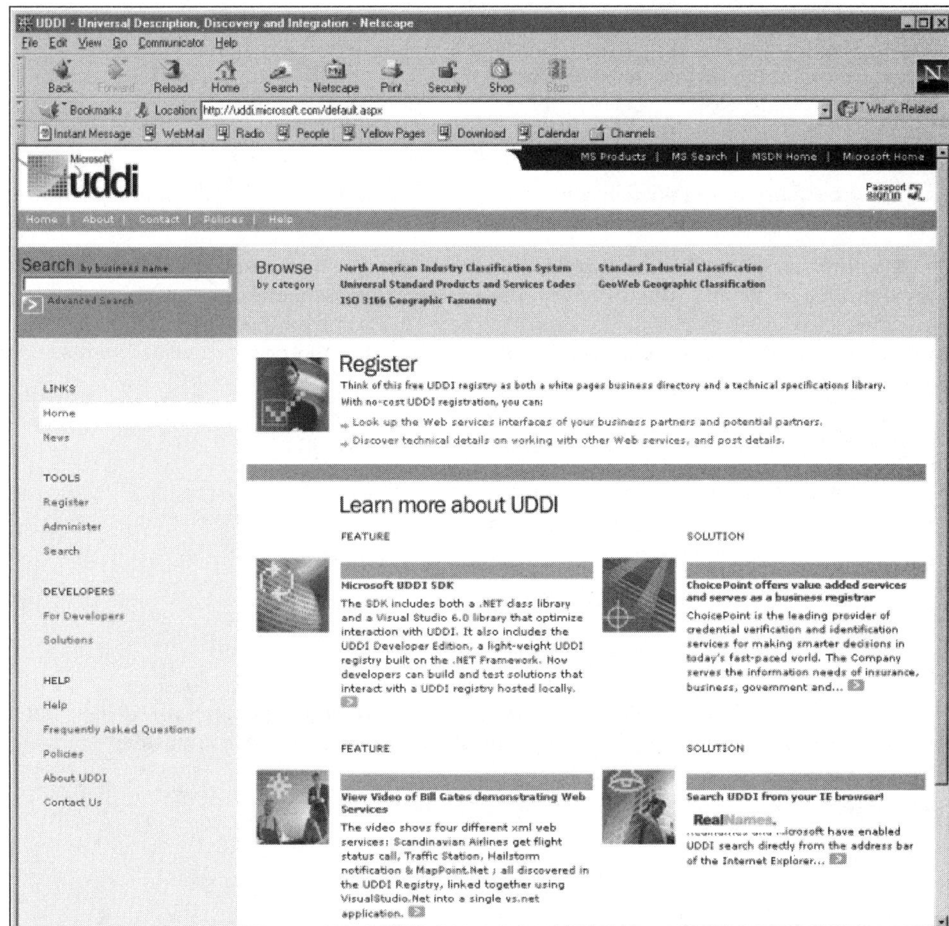


## *delete_binding()*

This method call removes one or more binding templates from the registry. The binding templates to be deleted are specified by their unique binding keys. The calls syntax is given below and, as can be seen, it takes one or more binding keys as input:

```
<delete_binding generic="2.0" xmlns="urn:uddi-org:api_v2">
   <authInfo/>
   <bindingKey/>
   [<bindingKey/> ...]
</delete_binding>
```

The errors that can occur in this call are:

- E_invalidKeyPassed. One of the uuid_key values passed did not match with any known bindingKey values. No partial results will be returned – if any bindingKey values passed are not valid, this error will be returned.
- E_authTokenExpired. The authentication token value passed in the authInfo argument is no longer valid because the token has expired.
- E_authTokenRequired. The authentication token value passed in the authInfo argument is either missing or is not valid.
- E_userMismatch. One or more of the bindingKey values passed refers to data that is not controlled by the individual who is represented by the authentication token.

A successful delete_binding() call results in a <dispositionReport> message with a success indicator as shown below.

```
<dispositionReport generic="2.0" operator="OperatorURI"
                   xmlns="urn:uddi-org:api_v2" >
   <result errno="0" >
      <errInfo errCode="E_success" />
   </result>
</dispositionReport>
```

## delete_business()

Removes one or more <businessEntity> structures from the registry. The business entities to be deleted are specified by their unique business keys. The syntax of this call is shown below, and it takes one or more business keys along with the authentication information as its parameters:

```
<delete_business generic="2.0" xmlns="urn:uddi-org:api_v2">
   <authInfo/>
   <businessKey/>
   [<businessKey/> ...]
</delete_business>
```

The errors that can occur in this call are:

- E_invalidKeyPassed. One of the uuid_key values passed did not match with any known bindingKey values. No partial results will be returned – if any bindingKey values passed are not valid, this error will be returned.
- E_authTokenExpired. The authentication token value passed in the authInfo argument is no longer valid because the token has expired.
- E_authTokenRequired. The authentication token value passed in the authInfo argument is either missing or is not valid.
- E_userMismatch. One or more of the bindingKey values passed refers to data that is not controlled by the individual who is represented by the authentication token.

A successful call results in a <dispositionReport> message with a success indicator.

A delete_business() call should be issued with care, as all contained <businessService>s and <bindingTemplate>s also get deleted. Any <publisherAssertion>s involving this <businessEntity> is also deleted. However <tModel>s are not affected by this call.

## *delete_service()*

Removes one or more <businessService> structures from the registry. The business services to be deleted are specified by their unique service keys:

```
<delete_service generic="2.0" xmlns="urn:uddi-org:api_v2">
   <authInfo/>
   <serviceKey/>
   [<serviceKey/> ...]
</delete_service>
```

The errors that can occur in this call are:

- E_invalidKeyPassed. One of the uuid_key values passed did not match with any known bindingKey values. No partial results will be returned – if any bindingKey values passed are not valid, this error will be returned.
- E_authTokenExpired. The authentication token value passed in the authInfo argument is no longer valid because the token has expired.
- E_authTokenRequired. The authentication token value passed in the authInfo argument is either missing or is not valid.
- E_userMismatch. One or more of the bindingKey values passed refers to data that is not controlled by the individual who is represented by the authentication token.

A successful call results in a <dispositionReport> message with a success indicator. Deleting a <businesService> also removes all contained <bindingTemplates>.

## *delete_tModel()*

Removes one or more <tModel> structures from the registry. The <tModel>s to be deleted are specified by their unique tModelKeys.

```
<delete_tModel generic="2.0" xmlns="urn:uddi-org:api_v2">
   <authInfo/>
   <tModelKey/> [<tModelKey/> ...]
</delete_tModel>
```

The errors that can occur in this call are:

- E_invalidKeyPassed. One of the uuid_key values passed did not match with any known bindingKey values. No partial results will be returned – if any bindingKey values passed are not valid, this error will be returned.
- E_authTokenExpired. The authentication token value passed in the authInfo argument is no longer valid because the token has expired.

- E_authTokenRequired. The authentication token value passed in the authInfo argument is either missing or is not valid.
- E_userMismatch. One or more of the bindingKey values passed refers to data that is not controlled by the individual who is represented by the authentication token.

A successful call results in a <dispositionReport> message with a success indicator. Deleting a tModel causes it to go into a deprecated or hidden state. The effect of this is that the tModel is invisible to a find_tModel() call, and save API calls (save_business(), save_service() etc.) that contain this tModelKey fail. However, a get_tModelDetail succeeds. This provides support to existing users of the tModel, while discouraging new users. A subsequent save_tModel() call passing the same information and tModelKey will restore the tModel.

## discard_authToken

This call informs the UDDI site that the authentication token may be discarded, and all subsequent calls using this token are to be rejected.

```
<discard_authToken generic="2.0" xmlns="urn:uddi-org:api_v2">
   <authInfo/>
</discard_authToken>
```

Once a client has finished publishing to the UDDI registry, it should expire the token using this call. The error that can occur in this call is:

- E_authTokenRequired. The authentication token value passed in the authInfo argument is either missing or is not valid.

A successful call results in a <dispositionReport> message with a success indicator.

## get_authToken()

This call is used to obtain an authentication token. The input parameters are username and credentials/password. The token obtained is used for all subsequent calls that require authentication. This token is valid until it either expires or is invalidated by a discard_authToken() call. The expiry time for an authentication token is UDDI operator dependent.

```
<get_authToken generic="2.0" xmlns="urn:uddi-org:api_v2"
               userID="someLoginName" cred="someCredential">
</get_authToken>
```

The error that can occur in this call is:

- E_unknownUser. The operator site that received the request does not recognize the userID and/or credential argument values passed to be valid.

A successful call results in a <authToken> message containing the authentication token.

```
<authToken generic="2.0" operator="uddi.someoperator"
          xmlns="urn:uddi-org:api_v2" >
   <authInfo>some opaque token value</authInfo>
</authToken>
```

A UDDI registry implementation need not use this kind of login-based mechanism for authentication. It could use alternative means of getting a token, or could use a certificate-based authentication scheme that directly passes an authentication token (in this case the certificate value) with each published API message. In such an implementation, the use of `get_authToken()` and `discard_authToken()` messages would not be required.

## get_registeredInfo()

The `get_registeredInfo()` call returns an abbreviated list of all business entity keys and `tModelKeys` that are controlled by the individual whose credentials are passed as input to the call:

```
<get_registeredInfo generic="2.0" xmlns="urn:uddi-org:api_v2">
   <authInfo/>
</get_registeredInfo>
```

The errors that can occur in this call are:

- `E_authTokenExpired`. The authentication token value passed in the `authInfo` argument is no longer valid because the token has expired.
- `E_authTokenRequired`. The authentication token value passed in the `authInfo` argument is either missing or is not valid.

A successful `get_registeredInfo` method call results in a `<registeredInfo>` message as shown below. It contains all `<businessInfo>`s and `<tModelInfo>`s that are published by the requestor.

```
<registeredInfo generic="2.0" operator="uddi.sourceOperator" [truncated="false"]
                xmlns="urn:uddi-org:api_v2">
   <businessInfos>
      <businessInfo/>
      [<businessInfo/>...]
   </businessInfos>
   <tModelInfos>
      <tModelInfo/>
      [<tModelInfo/>...]
   </tModelInfos>
</registeredInfo>
```

## save_binding()

The `save_binding()` call is used to save or update a complete `<bindingTemplate>` structure. One or more binding templates may be passed to the call, as shown in the syntax of the call below:

```
<save_binding generic="2.0" xmlns="urn:uddi-org:api_v2">
<authInfo/>
<bindingTemplate/> [<bindingTemplate/>...]
</save_binding>
```

The errors that can occur in this call are:

- `E_invalidKeyPassed`. One of the `uuid_key` values passed did not match with any known `bindingKey` values. No partial results will be returned – if any `bindingKey` values passed are not valid, this error will be returned.

- E_authTokenExpired. The authentication token value passed in the authInfo argument is no longer valid because the token has expired.
- E_authTokenRequired. The authentication token value passed in the authInfo argument is either missing or is not valid.
- E_userMismatch. One or more of the bindingKey values passed refers to data that is not controlled by the individual who is represented by the authentication token.
- E_accountLimitExceeded. User account limits have been exceeded.

A successful save returns a <bindingDetail> message containing one or more <bindingTemplate>s. Any bindingKeys left empty are assigned unique values by the UDDI registry.

```
<bindingDetail generic="2.0" operator="uddi.someoperator" truncated="true"
               xmlns="urn:uddi-org:api_v2">
   <bindingTemplate>
   [<bindingTemplate/>...]
</bindingDetail>
```

## save_business()

This method is used to save or update a business entity structure. One or more business entity structures may be passed to this call, and it updates these in the registry. Since the business entity contains the business services, which in turn contain the binding templates, this call is very broad in its effect!

```
<save_business generic="2.0" xmlns="urn:uddi-org:api_v2">
   <authInfo/>
   <businessEntity/> [<businessEntity/>...]
</save_business>
```

The errors that can occur in this call are as follows:

- E_invalidKeyPassed. One of the uuid_key values passed did not match with any known bindingKey values. No partial results will be returned – if any bindingKey values passed are not valid, this error will be returned.
- E_authTokenExpired. The authentication token value passed in the authInfo argument is no longer valid because the token has expired.
- E_authTokenRequired. The authentication token value passed in the authInfo argument is either missing or is not valid.
- E_userMismatch. One or more of the bindingKey values passed refers to data that is not controlled by the individual who is represented by the authentication token.
- E_accountLimitExceeded. User account limits have been exceeded.
- E_invalidValue. The given keyValue did not correspond to a category within the taxonomy identified by a tModelKey value within one of the <categoryBag>elements provided.
- E_valueNotAllowed. Restrictions have been placed by the taxonomy provider on the types of information that should be included at that location within a specific taxonomy. The validation routine chosen by the operator site has rejected this businessEntity for at least one specified category.

A successful save_business() call returns a <businessDetail> message containing one or more <businessEntity>s. Any businessKeys, serviceKeys or bindingKeys left empty are assigned unique values by the UDDI registry.

```
<businessDetail generic="2.0" operator="uddi.sourceOperator" truncated="true"
                xmlns="urn:uddi-org:api_v2">
   <businessEntity/>
   [<businessEntity/>...]
</businessDetail>
```

## save_service()

This method is used to save or update a business service structure. It takes as input one or more business service structures, and updates the registry with it. This can be seen in the syntax for the call below:

```
<save_service generic="2.0" xmlns="urn:uddi-org:api_v2">
   <authInfo/>
   <businessService/> [<businessService/>...]
</save_service>
```

The errors that can occur in this call are as follows:

- E_invalidKeyPassed. One of the uuid_key values passed did not match with any known bindingKey values. No partial results will be returned – if any bindingKey values passed are not valid, this error will be returned.
- E_authTokenExpired. The authentication token value passed in the authInfo argument is no longer valid because the token has expired.
- E_authTokenRequired. The authentication token value passed in the authInfo argument is either missing or is not valid.
- E_userMismatch. One or more of the bindingKey values passed refers to data that is not controlled by the individual who is represented by the authentication token.
- E_accountLimitExceeded. User account limits have been exceeded.
- E_invalidValue. The given keyValue did not correspond to a category within the taxonomy identified by a tModelKey value within one of the <categoryBag> elements provided.
- E_valueNotAllowed. Restrictions have been placed by the taxonomy provider on the types of information that should be included at that location within a specific taxonomy. The validation routine chosen by the operator site has rejected this businessEntity for at least one specified category.

A successful save_service() call returns a <serviceDetail> message containing one or more <businessService>s. All serviceKeys and bindingKeys left unassigned are assigned unique values by the UDDI registry.

```
<serviceDetail generic="2.0" operator="uddi.sourceOperator" [truncated="false"]
               xmlns="urn:uddi-org:api_v2">
   <businessService/>
   [<businessService/>...]
</serviceDetail>
```

## save_tModel()

The save_tModel() method is used to add or update <tModel> structures. As can be seen from the syntax below, it takes one or more <tModel> structures as input:

```
<save_tModel generic="2.0" xmlns="urn:uddi-org:api_v2">
   <authInfo/>
   <tModel/> [<tModel/>...]
</save_tModel>
```

The errors that can occur in this call are as follows:

- E_invalidKeyPassed. One of the uuid_key values passed did not match with any known bindingKey values. No partial results will be returned – if any bindingKey values passed are not valid, this error will be returned.
- E_authTokenExpired. The authentication token value passed in the authInfo argument is no longer valid because the token has expired.
- E_authTokenRequired. The authentication token value passed in the authInfo argument is either missing or is not valid.
- E_userMismatch. One or more of the bindingKey values passed refers to data that is not controlled by the individual who is represented by the authentication token.
- E_accountLimitExceeded. User account limits have been exceeded.
- E_invalidValue. The given keyValue did not correspond to a category within the taxonomy identified by a tModelKey value within one of the <categoryBag > elements provided.
- E_valueNotAllowed. Restrictions have been placed by the taxonomy provider on the types of information that should be included at that location within a specific taxonomy. The validation routine chosen by the operator site has rejected this <businessEntity> for at least one specified category.

A successful save_tModel() call returns a <tModelDetail> message containing one or more <tModel>s.

```
<tModelDetail generic="2.0" operator="uddi.sourceOperator" [truncated="false"]
              xmlns="urn:uddi-org:api_v2">
   <tModel/>
   [<tModel/>...]
</tModelDetail>
```

## add_publisherAssertions()

Adds a relationship to the existing set of assertions about relationship. The syntax of this call is:

```
<add_publisherAssertions generic="2.0" xmlns="urn:uddi-org:api_v2" >
   <authInfo/>
   <publisherAssertion>
      <fromKey/>
      <toKey/>
      <keyedReference/>
   </publisherAssertion>
   [<publisherAssertion/> ...]
</add_publisherAssertions>
```

As can be seen, the publisher assertions consist of a "from" key, a "to" key, and a keyed reference. This is explained in more detail earlier in the section on *UDDI Data Structures.*

The following errors are relevant for this call:

- E_invalidKeyPassed. One of the uuid_key values passed did not match any known businessKey or tModelKey values.
- E_authTokenExpired. The authentication token value passed in the authInfo argument is no longer valid because the token has expired.
- E_authTokenRequired. The authentication token value passed in the authInfo argument is either missing or is not valid.
- E_userMismatch. Neither of the businessKey values passed in the embedded <fromKey> and <toKey> elements is controlled by the publisher account associated with the authentication token.

A successful call results in a <dispositionReport> message with a success indicator.

## delete_publisherAssertions()

This method deletes a specific assertion about a business relationship from the assertion collection of a particular publisher account. Deleting an assertion effectively invalidates the business relationship based on that assertion. The syntax for this call is shown below.

```
<delete_publisherAssertions generic="2.0" xmlns="urn:uddi-org:api_v2" >
   <authInfo/>
   <publisherAssertion>
      <fromKey/>
      <toKey/>
      <keyedReference/>
   </publisherAssertion>
   [<publisherAssertion/> ...]
</delete_publisherAssertions>
```

The following errors can occur in this call:

- E_assertionNotFound. No such matching assertion was found in the publisher's matching collection.
- E_authTokenExpired. The authentication token value passed in the authInfo argument is no longer valid because the token has expired.
- E_authTokenRequired. The authentication token value passed in the authInfo argument is either missing or is not valid.

A successful call results in a <dispositionReport> message with a success indicator.

## get_assertionStatusReport()

This method is used to get a status report on publisher assertions involving a <businessEntity>s controlled by a publisher account. This report helps in managing the publisher assertions.

```
<get_assertionStatusReport generic="2.0" xmlns="urn:uddi-org:api_v2">
   <authInfo/>
   [<completionStatus/>]
</get_assertionStatusReport>
```

The optional completion status is used to restrict the result set. It can have one of following three possible values:

- status:complete returns only the publisher assertions that are complete to be returned, that is, there are matching assertions from both parties involved.
- status:toKey_incomplete returns only those publisher assertions where the party who controls the <businessEntity> referenced by the <toKey> value in an assertion, has not made a matching assertion to be listed.
- status:fromKey_incomplete returns only those publisher assertions where the party who controls the <businessEntity> referenced by the <fromKey> value in an assertion, has not made a matching assertion to be listed.

The errors that can occur in this call are:

- E_invalidCompletionStatus. The completionStatus value passed is unrecognized.
- E_authTokenExpired. The authentication token value passed in the authInfo argument is no longer valid because the token has expired.
- E_authTokenRequired. The authentication token value passed in the authInfo argument is either missing or is not valid.

On successful completion, an <assertingStatusReport> is returned. A sample <assertionStatusReport> is shown below.

```
<assertionStatusReport generic="2.0" operator="uddi.someoperator"
                       xmlns="urn:uddi-org:api_v2">
   <assertionStatusItem completionStatus="status:toKey_incomplete">
      <fromKey>F5E65...</fromKey>
      <toKey>A237B...</toKey>
      <keyedReference tModelKey="uuid:F5E65…" keyName="Subsidiary" keyValue="1"
      </keyedReference>
      <keysOwned>
         <fromKey>F5E65</fromKey>
      </keysOwned>
   </assertionStatusItem>
   [<assertionStatusItem/>...]
</assertionStatusReport>
```

## get_publisherAssertions()

The get_publisherAssertions() method returns the active set of publisher assertions for a publisher. The syntax for the call is:

```
<get_publisherAssertions generic="2.0" xmlns="urn:uddi-org:api_v2" >
   <authInfo/>
</get_publisherAssertions>
```

The errors that can occur in this call are:

- E_authTokenExpired. The authentication token value passed in the authInfo argument is no longer valid because the token has expired.
- E_authTokenRequired. The authentication token value passed in the authInfo argument is either missing or is not valid.

A successful method call results in a <publisherAssertions> message (as shown below), containing all the assertions registered of the given publisher.

```
<publisherAssertions generic="2.0" operator="uddi.someoperator"
                     authorizedName="J. Doe"
                     xmlns="urn:uddi-org:api_v2">
   <publisherAssertion/>
   [<publisherAssertion/>...]
</publisherAssertions>
```

## set_publisherAssertions()

The set_publisherAssertions() call is used to save the entire set of publisher assertions. It replaces any exiting assertions in the registry.

```
<set_publisherAssertions generic="2.0" xmlns="urn:uddi-org:api_v2" >
   <authInfo/>
   <publisherAssertion>
      <fromKey/>
      <toKey/>
      <keyedReference/>
   </publisherAssertion>
   [<publisherAssertion/>...]
</set_publisherAssertions>
```

The errors that can occur in this call are:

- E_invalidKeyPassed. One of the uuid_key values passed did not match any known businessKey or tModelKey values.
- E_authTokenExpired. The authentication token value passed in the authInfo argument is no longer valid because the token has expired.
- E_authTokenRequired. The authentication token value passed in the authInfo argument is either missing or not valid.
- E_userMismatch. Neither of the businessKey values passed in the embedded <fromKey> and <toKey> elements is controlled by the publisher account associated with the authentication token.

A successful method call results in a <publisherAssertions> message (as shown below), containing all the assertion, sent in the set_publisherAssertions() call.

```
<publisherAssertions generic="2.0" operator="uddi.someoperator"
                     authorizedName="J. Doe"
                     xmlns="urn:uddi-org:api_v2">
   <publisherAssertion/>
   [<publisherAssertion/>...]
</publisherAssertions>
```

# Case Study: A Tulip Bulb Business

Let's look at an example of a business and see how it can use the UDDI registry for publishing information about itself and its services. We will first look at the business need, and then go over the steps taken by the company to publish information in the UDDI UBR, and the steps taken by the client to discover and interact with the company. The steps taken by the company to publish this information are as follows:

- The company decides on how customers would access its services. These could be accessed either by conventional mechanisms such as phone, e-mail, fax, etc., or programmatically using Web Services.
- In case it desires programmatic access, it develops and deploys Web Services. These Web Services are components that expose some of their public methods to SOAP calls. These calls are typically transported over HTTP. The company then generates interface descriptions for these Web Services as WSDL documents.
- It then registers with a UDDI registry operator node and gets credentials (typically in the form of a username/password combination) for publishing its information.
- The company publishes new service type definitions (tModels) in the UDDI registry for the services that are accessible as Web Services, and this contains the URL to the WSDL document describing the service. There are canonical tModels already published in the UDDI registry for services accessible via non-programmatic mechanisms such as phone, etc.
- It then publishes a `<businessEntity>` structure for the entire company, containing all the services it provides. The services are described in a `<businessService>` structure that is contained in a `<businessEntity>`. Each `<businessService>` contains zero or more `<bindingTemplates>`. The `<bindingTemplate>` contains access information for the service, and as services could have more than one access mechanism, hence there can be more than one `<bindingTemplate>`. For instance, one `<bindingTemplate>` would be for access via the phone and would contain a phone number as its `<accessPoint>`. The `<bindingTemplate>` corresponding to the Web Service would have a URL as its `<accessPoint>`, and so on. The `<bindingTemplates>` also contain `tModelKeys`, and the `<bindingTemplate>` for the Web Service would have the key for the `<tModel>` published earlier containing the WSDL description for accessing the service.

Customers can now locate the company in various ways. Some of these are as follows:

- Search by company name.
- Search for all companies in that particular product or service category. This would be based on specific industry classification codes for such companies and this would be one of the things published in the Business Entity.

- Know the service type definition and search for all companies that provide services conforming to this definition. This kind of search is useful when the service type definition (tModel) is a well-known definition, such as one that is published by a standards body or an industry consortium. Individual companies then implement services as described by these tModels and customers can search for all companies that do so.

In this case study we will see an example of a customer performing a search based on the product classification. Once the customer locates the service that he wishes to use, he can get the `<accessPoint>` for the services from the `<bindingTemplate>`, and the interface description for it from the corresponding tModel; and thus interact with the business.

In this case study we will show XML messages for publishing and querying the UDDI registry so that we can better understand the underlying UDDI data structures and API. Users would typically write code in some programming language such as Java, Visual Basic, Perl, etc., to perform these steps. See the *UDDI Implementations* section earlier in the chapter for some of the software toolkits available from different vendors. In addition, some of these vendors also provide GUI tools that allow users to publish and search for information in the UDDI registry without writing code.

In our case study we have a fictitious company called Tulip Mania Inc., based in San Jose, California, that sells tulip bulbs over the Internet. While it has a dedicated clientele in both northern and southern California, the company feels that it would be able to reach a worldwide market by publishing information about its business and services in the UDDI UBR. This will also enable clients to know how to buy tulip bulbs from the company (specified using UDDI service type definitions) and also where to buy them (specified by the `<accessPoint>` for the service in the `<bindingTemplate>`s).

Tulip Mania used to sell its bulbs either over the phone, or by using its web site. The Tulip Mania web site has a catalog of the tulips types that are available for sale, and their prices. It also has a form on its web site that users can fill in. This form collects information about the user's shipping address, number, type of tulips desired, and credit card information.

Now, in addition to these ordering methods, Tulip Mania has developed a Web Service that customers can programmatically invoke to get information on tulip availability and prices. They also can use this Web Service to place an order for tulip bulbs. The Web Service method for placing a tulip order takes as input the number and type of bulbs, shipping address, and credit card information. It processes this information and generates a receipt with the shipping details and order tracking number. The methods of this Web Service can be invoked using SOAP RPC conventions. Customers wishing to use Tulip Mania's Web Service can determine how to interact with it using a WSDL specification of the service interface. This Web Service is deployed in a SOAP server and can be accessed via the fictitious URL http://www.tulip-mania.com/soap/servlet/rpcrouter.

Tulip Mania hosts this WSDL description on its web site and publishes a service type definition (tModel) containing a URL pointing to it in the UDDI Business Registry. In our example, the WSDL is accessible at the fictitious URL http://www.tulip-mania.com/wsdl/BuyBulb_Service.wsdl.

## Registering Tulip Mania

Before publishing anything, Tulip Mania needs to sign up with a UDDI operator node. At the time of writing, there are two operator nodes for the UDDI business registry in operation– IBM's (http://www-3.ibm.com/uddi) and Microsoft's (http://uddi.microsoft.com). Tulip Mania decided to register with IBM's UDDI operator node, and signed up at their web site for a free account. To do this, they pointed their browser to IBM's registry signup page at http://www-3.ibm.com/services/uddi/ (see screenshot overleaf). These screenshots should only be taken as an example of a UDDI registration process. They were taken at the time of writing, so the user interface as well as the process may have changed.

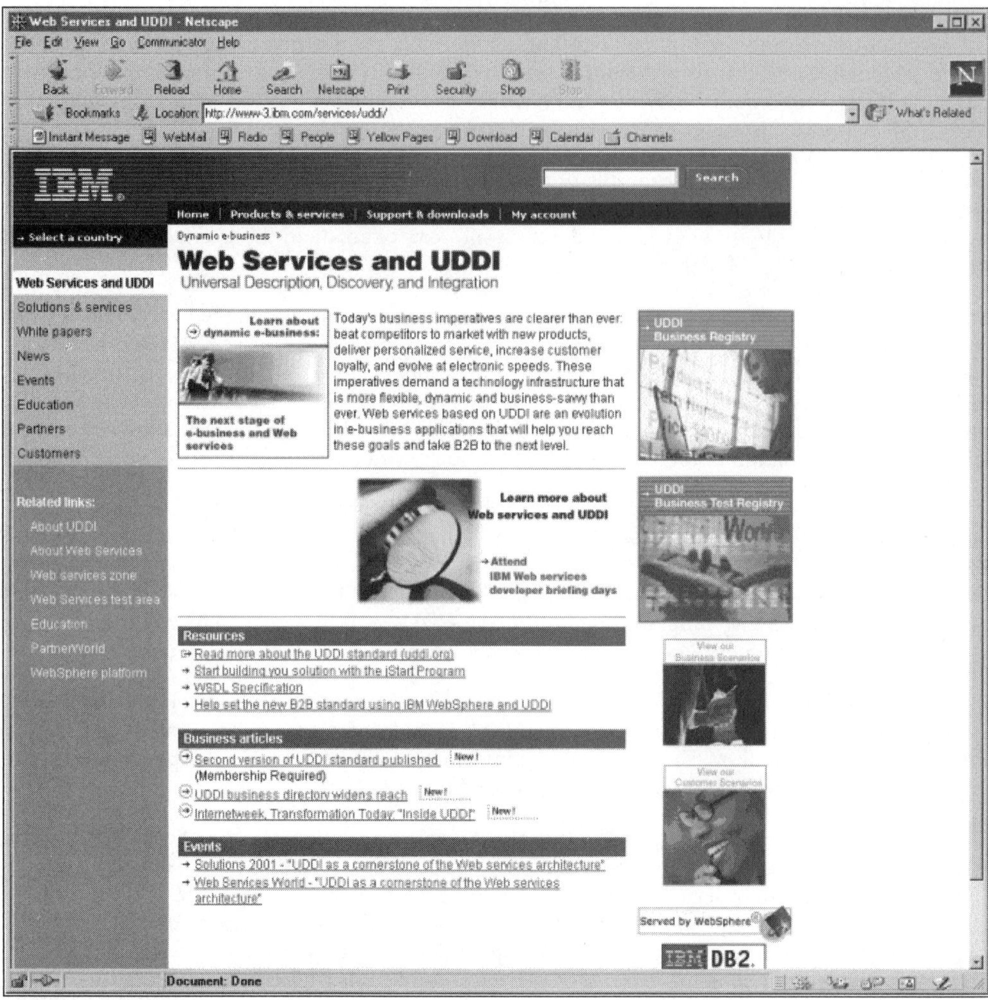


Next they selected the "UDDI Business Registry" link. There is also a UDDI Business Test Registry link on this page. It is advised that you use this test registry for testing and experimentation before uploading data into the (production) Business Registry.

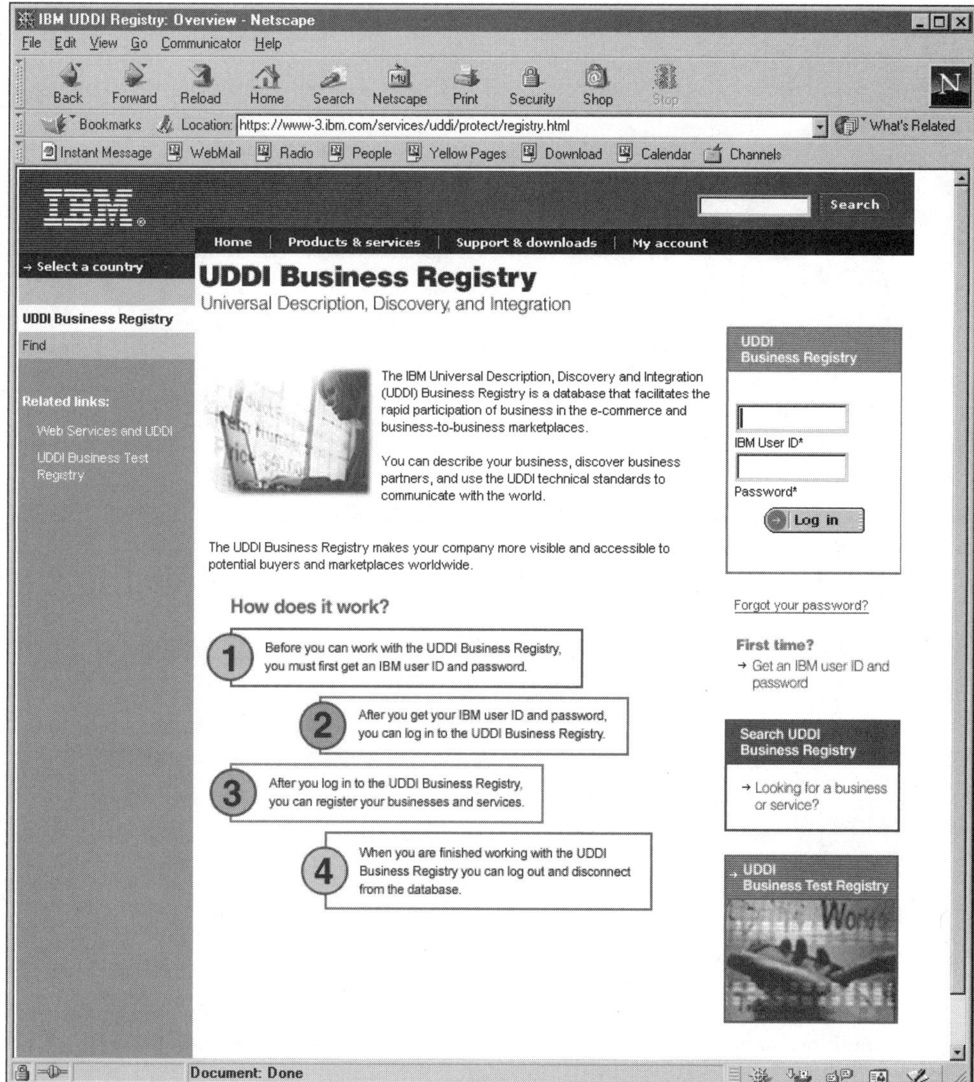


Since they needed to create an account, they clicked on the "Get an IBM user ID and password" link. This took them to a Registration page and then a signup form, where they selected a username, set a password, and filled in the required information about themselves – including an e-mail address.

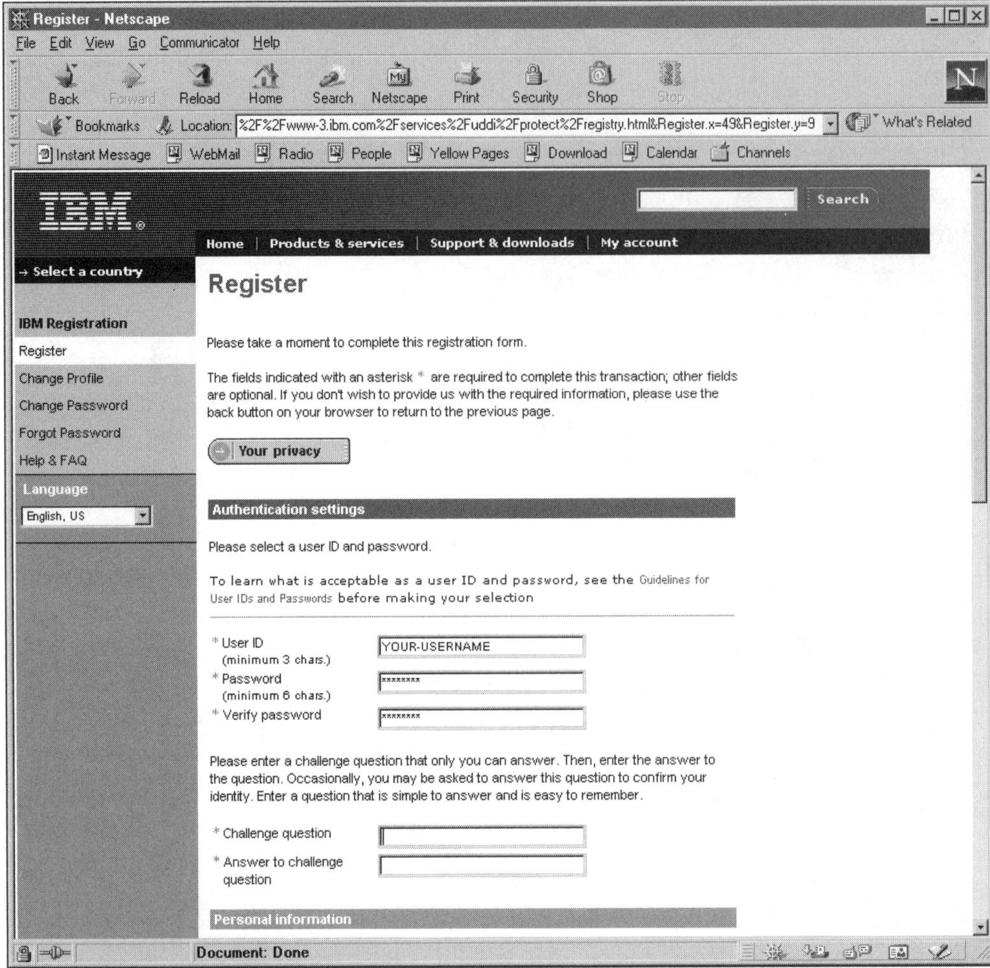


After filling and submitting this form, they were required to confirm the data entered and accept the terms and conditions of usage. Following that, a confirmation e-mail was sent to the account created.

The e-mail contained an activation code that was required when logging in to the UDDI registry via the web interface for the first time. Once this was done, the account was activated and ready to use.

Tulip Mania could now publish data into the registry either via the web interface at https://www-3.ibm.com/services/uddi/protect/registry.html, programmatically, or by using a tool.

The first step before being able to publish programmatically was to get an authentication token. This was done by sending a `get_authToken` request over HTTPS to the publishing URL at IBM. The `get_authToken` request sent is shown below.

The `userID` and `cred` parameters contain the username and password that was set up earlier when Tulip Mania registered at IBM's registry node. The `generic` attribute specifies the version of the UDDI protocol used for the message, which is 2.0 for UDDI version 2.0. The other attributes of this message include the namespace qualifier (`xmlns`) which should be `urn:uddi-org:api_v2` for UDDI 2.0.

```
<get_authToken generic="2.0" xmlns="urn:uddi-org:api_v2"
   userID="YOUR-USERNAME"
   cred="YOUR-PASSWORD" >
</get_authToken>
```

On sending this request to the IBM operator node, Tulip's client program got back the following response. The message contained the <authInfo> element with the authentication token string.

```
<authToken generic="2.0" operator="www.ibm.com/services/uddi"
                          xmlns="urn:uddi-org:api_v2" >
   <authInfo>TOKEN_VALUE</authInfo>
</authToken>
```

Now that Tulip Mania has an authentication token, it can publish the tModel. This is done using the save_tModel() UDDI method as shown below.

It passes the authentication token that it received earlier in the <authInfo> element. This is required so that the publishing operations can be validated. Later, if the company desires to modify or delete this tModel, it will need to get a new authentication token based on its username and password. If any other user tries to do this, it would get an authentication error back from the registry. The tModel being saved contains the name of the tModel (buy_bulbs) and the URL for the WSDL description of the service (the fictitious URL http://www.tulip-mania.com/wsdl/BuyBulb_Service.wsdl). Since the tModel is being published for the first time, the tModelKey being passed is empty. This tells the UDDI registry to assign a new key for it. In case the user wishes to update an existing tModel, the tModelKey should be sent in the save_tModel message.

```
<save_tModel generic="2.0" xmlns="urn:uddi-org:api_v2">
   <authInfo>TOKEN_VALUE</authInfo>
   <tModel tModelKey="">
      <name>buy_bulbs</name>
      <overviewDoc>
         <overviewURL>http://www.tulip-mania.com/wsdl/BuyBulb_Service.wsdl
         </overviewURL>
      </overviewDoc>
   </tModel>
</save_tModel>
```

On successful completion of this operation, the UDDI registry sends back the tModel in a tModelDetail structure. This has the tModelKey filled in. We need to save this tModelKey for later use. We will be publishing it along with the Business Entity.

```
<tModelDetail generic="2.0" operator="www.ibm.com/services/uddi" truncated="false"
         xmlns="urn:uddi-org:api_v2">
   <tModel tModelKey="uuid:CCB..."
         authorizedName="AJ00000"
         operator="www.ibm.com/services/uddi">
      <name>directory_tmodel</name>
      <overviewDoc>
         <overviewURL>
            http://www.tulip-mania.com/wsdl/BuyBulb_Service.wsdl
```

```
            </overviewURL>
        </overviewDoc>
    </tModel>
</tModelDetail>
```

Tulip Mania can either write a client program to save the tModel information for it, or use a tool for this purpose. The screenshot below shows one such tool, the HP Registry Composer. This tool, as mentioned earlier, is packaged along with the HP Web Services Platform and is available at http://www.hp.com/go/webservices/.

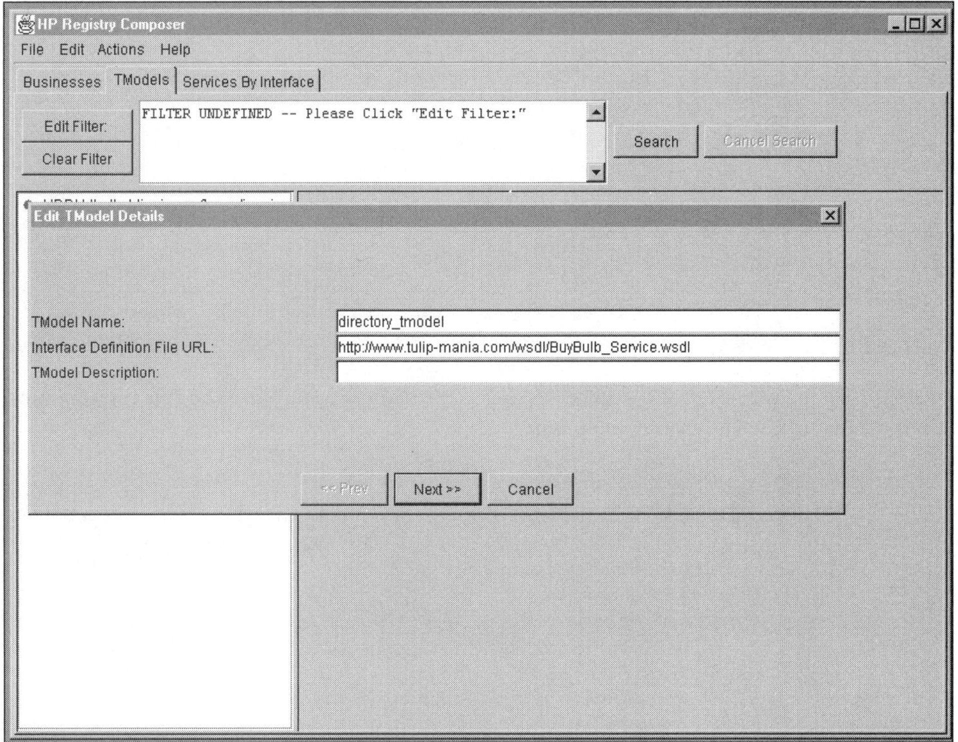


After the service type definition had been successfully published, Tulip Mania could publish information about its business and services. This is done using the save_business() UDDI method as shown below. The business entity published contains the name of the business (<name> element), a textual description (<description> element), contact information with name, e-mail address, phone, and postal address of the contact person(s) (<contact> element). It also contains <businessServices>, which in turn contains <bindingTemplates>. The businessKey, serviceKey and bindingKey are passed as empty strings, and this tells the UDDI registry to assign new key values for them. The response message to a save_business() call would contain a successfully published <businessEntity> with all the key values assigned. In case the company wishes to modify a <businessEntity> that it had published earlier, it would issue a save_business() method call with these key attributes set to the assigned values.

```
<save_business generic="2.0" xmlns="urn:uddi-org:api_v2">
   <authInfo>AUTH_TOKEN</authInfo>
   <businessEntity businessKey="">
      <name>Tulip Mania Inc</name>
      <description xml:lang="EN">We sell tulip bulbs</description>
      <contacts>
         <contact useType="business">
            <personName>N. O. Body</personName>
            <phone useType="work">1-800-000-000</phone>
            <email useType="work">nobody@nospam.tulip-mania.com</email>
            <address useType="work">
               <addressLine>123 Tulip Road</addressLine>
               <addressLine>San Jose</addressLine>
               <addressLine>CA 95122</addressLine>
            </address>
         </contact>
      </contacts>
      <businessServices>
         <businessService serviceKey="" businessKey="">
         <name>Buy Tulips</name>
         <bindingTemplates>
            <bindingTemplate bindingKey="" serviceKey="">
               <description xml:lang="en">Buy tulips over the phone</description>
               <accessPoint URLType="phone">1 888 000 0000</accessPoint>
```

The `tModelKey` below (`UUID:38E12427-5536-4260-A6F9-B5B530E63A07`) is the canonical tModel for a service that is invoked via the telephone.

```
               <tModelInstanceDetails>
                  <tModelInstanceInfo
                     tModelKey="UUID:38E12427-5536-4260-A6F9-B5B530E63A07"/>
                  </tModelInstanceDetails>
               </bindingTemplate>
               <bindingTemplate bindingKey="" serviceKey="">
                  <description xml:lang="en">Buy tulips over the web</description>
                  <accessPoint URLType="http">
                     http://www.tulip-mania/cgi-bin/buy.pl
                  </accessPoint>
```

The `tModelKey` in this case (`UUID:68DE9E80-AD09-469D-8A37-088422BFBC36`) is the canonical tModel for a service that is invoked via a web browser.

```
                  <tModelInstanceDetails>
                     <tModelInstanceInfo
                        tModelKey="UUID:68DE9E80-AD09-469D-8A37-088422BFBC36"/>
                  </tModelInstanceDetails>
               </bindingTemplate>
```

Finally, for the Web Service, the `accessPoint` contains the URL of the SOAP server hosting the Web Service, and the `tModelKey` is that of the tModel we published earlier.

```
            <bindingTemplate bindingKey="" serviceKey="">
               <description xml:lang="en">
                  Buy tulips using a Web Service
               </description>
               <accessPoint URLType="http">
                  http://www.tulip-mania.com/soap/servlet/rpcrouter
               </accessPoint>
               <tModelInstanceDetails>
                  <tModelInstanceInfo  tModelKey="uuid:CCB.."/>
               </tModelInstanceDetails>
            </bindingTemplate>
         </bindingTemplates>
      </businessService>
   </businessServices>
```

The business can be tagged using alternative identifiers. In this case study, we use a D-U-N-S number for the company. Other schemes for business identifiers could be specific national/regional codes, for example US tax identifiers. The `tModelKey` shown (`UUID:8609C81E-EE1F-4D5A-B202-3EB13AD01823`) is the UDDI canonical tModel for the D-U-N-S identification taxonomy. Canonical tModels are defined for such standard taxonomies in the UDDI specifications and have well-known, published `tModelKeys`.

```
   <identifierBag>
      <keyedReference keyName="D-U-N-S" keyValue="00-111-1111"
                      tModelKey="UUID:8609C81E-EE1F-4D5A-B202-3EB13AD01823"/>
   </identifierBag>
```

We also put the product classification category in the Business Entity. We are using UNSPSC's category code for tulip bulbs in this example. The `tModelKey` shown (`UUID:DB77450D-9FA8-45D4-A7BC-04411D14E384`) is the canonical tModel for UNSPSC classification taxonomy.

```
   <categoryBag>
      <keyedReference
         keyName="UNSPSC:Tulip seeds, bulbs, seedlings or cuttings"
         keyValue="10151901"
         tModelKey="UUID:DB77450D-9FA8-45D4-A7BC-04411D14E384"/>
```

In addition, since Tulip Mania currently operates only in California, it also adds this geographic location information to the `categoryBag`. It uses the ISO 3166 geographic taxonomy for this, and the tModel shown below is the canonical tModel for this taxonomy.

```
      <keyedReference keyName="California" keyValue="US-CA"
                      tModelKey="uuid:61668105-B6B6-425C-914B-409FB252C36D"/>
   </categoryBag>
  </businessEntity>
</save_business>
```

On successful publication of this data, the business entity is sent back in a `<BusinessDetail>` structure with all the business, service, and binding keys assigned. This also contains the `businessKey` for the saved `<BusinessEntity>`. This is used later for publisher assertions.

### *Adding Publisher Assertions*

Tulip Mania aims to achieve world domination in the tulip bulb marketplace. To further this goal, it went on an acquisition spree funded in part by its high stock value. It bought a Dutch company called Tulpenwoede BV for getting into the European tulip bulb market. Tulpenwoede would function as a subsidiary company, and Tulip Mania wanted to publish information about this relationship in the UDDI registry. Tulpenwoede, being a progressive tulip company, already had an entry in the UDDI registry. So Tulip Mania published a `publisherAssertion` specifying this relationship.

```
<add_publisherAssertions generic="2.0" xmlns="urn:uddi-org:api_v2" >
   <authInfo>AUTH_TOKEN</authInfo>
<publisherAssertion>
```

The `<fromKey>` contains the `businessKey` of the first business that the assertion is made for. In this case it is the `businessKey` for Tulip Mania, which was obtained as a result of the `save_business()` call.

```
         <fromKey>82...</fromKey>
```

The `<toKey>` contains the `businessKey` of the second business. In this example it is the `businessKey` for Tulpenwoede.

```
         <toKey>A237B...</toKey>
```

The tModel below is the canonical tModel for a business relationship description. The valid `keyValues` in this tModel are *parent-child* (for holding company/subsidiary relationships), *peer-peer* (for partner companies) and *identity* (for indicating that the two `businessEntities` represent the same company).

```
         <keyedReference tModelKey="uuid:807A2C6A-EE22-470D-ADC7-E0424A337C03"
                         keyName="Holding Company"
                         keyValue="parent-child">
         </keyedReference>
      </publisherAssertion>
</add_publisherAssertions>
```

Tulpenwoede BV has to publish a corresponding publisher assertion in the UDDI registry to make this relationship visible. This mechanism of requiring two assertions ensured that nobody else could assert a relationship without consent from both the parties involved. To do this, Tulpenwoede would first need to issue a `get_assertionStatusReport()` call to its UDDI operator site. Note that Tulpenwoede and Tulip Mania need not have registered with the same UDDI operator node. The `completionStatus` value of `status:toKey_incomplete` indicates that we are interested in those assertions in which the party referred in the `toKey` of the `<publisherAssertion>` has not made a matching assertion. The `AUTH_TOKEN2` contained in the `<authInfo>` element is the authorization token that Tulpenwoede obtained using a `get_authToken()` call (not shown here) passing its username and credentials.

```
<get_assertionStatusReport generic="2.0" xmlns="urn:uddi-org:api_v2" >
   <authInfo>AUTH_TOKEN2</authInfo>
   <completionStatus>status:toKey_incomplete</completionStatus>
</get_assertionStatusReport>
```

The result of a get_assertionStatusReport() call would contain all unmatched assertions listed against its businessEntity in a <assertionStatusReport> message as shown below. The <keysOwned> element contains the keys that the publisher (in this case Tulpenwoede) manages.

```
<assertionStatusReport generic="2.0" operator=" www.ibm.com/services/uddi"
                       xmlns="urn:uddi-org:api_v2">
   <assertionStatusItem completionStatus="status:toKey_incomplete">
      <fromKey>82...</fromKey>
      <toKey>A237B...</toKey>
      <keyedReference tModelKey=" uuid:807A2C6A-EE22-470D-ADC7-E0424A337C03"
                      keyName="Holding Company" keyValue="parent-child"
      </keyedReference>
      <keysOwned>
         <toKey>A237B…</toKey>
      </keysOwned>
   </assertionStatusItem>
   [<assertionStatusItem/>…]
</assertionStatusReport>
```

Tulpenwoede can then send the exact same <publisherAssertions> to its UDDI operator node in a add_publisherAssertions() call, similar to the one shown earlier for Tulip Mania. The publisher assertion is now visible, and will be returned by all subsequent find_authToken() calls, as shown below.

## Finding Tulip Mania

Let's see how potential tulip customers can locate Tulip Mania, and determine how to do business with them. The customer in question does not know the name of the company; otherwise it could have searched in the UDDI registry based on the business name.

Instead, it searches based on the categorization of tulip companies using the find_business() method call. The Java program given below shows how a user could do this programmatically. This program uses UDDI4J, which is an open-source UDDI 2.0 API implementation co-developed by IBM and HP.

A complete version of the program below can be found in the code download for this book at http://www.wrox.com/

```
/**
   * The FindBusinessByLocators class finds a business based on UNSPSC,
   * NAICS or ISO-3166 locators.
   * @author Vivek Chopra
*/
public class FindBusinessByLocators {

   public static void main (String args[]) {
```

The command line argument process is shown below. This program has been designed to be generic in nature, and takes three command line arguments – the Inquiry URL of the UDDI registry against which the program should be run, a tag for the classification taxonomy to search in (NAICS, UNSPSC or ISO 3166), and the classification keyValue.

```
/* Process command line arguments */
if (args.length != 4) {
   System.out.println ("usage: java wrox.ebXML.examples UDDI_INQUIRY_URL "
                       + "[NAICS|UNSPSC|ISO3166] keyValue keyName\n");
   System.out.println ("An empty keyName can be passed as \"\"");
   System.exit (1);
}
```

Next, we construct an `UDDIProxy` object. The `UDDIProxy` class models the UDDI registry – it has all the UDDI methods (`inquiry()` and `publish()`) that interact with the registry.

```
/* Construct a UDDIProxy object- this represents a UDDI server
   * and the actions that can be invoked against it.
*/
UDDIProxy uddiProxy = new UDDIProxy ();
```

We then set the Inquiry URL in the `uddiProxy` to that passed through the command line. In case this URL is not a well-formed URL, a `MalformedURLException` is thrown.

```
/* Set the inquiry URL */
try {
   uddiProxy.setInquiryURL (args[0]);
   System.out.println ("Set Inquiry URL [" + args[0] + "]");
}
catch (MalformedURLException e) {
   System.err.println ("Malformed inquiry URL [" + args[0] + "]");
   e.printStackTrace ();
   System.exit (1); /* fatal error */
}
```

We then construct a `<categoryBag>` for the search, setting in it the appropriate classification taxonomy `tModelKey` (NAICS, UNSPSC or ISO-3166) and the actual `keyValue`. The `keyValue` indicates the particular category that we are interested in. In the case of companies in the "Tulip seeds, bulbs, seedlings or cuttings" business the `keyValue` will be 10151901. These and other UNSPSC codes are listed at http://www.unspsc.org

```
/*  Find businesses (businessEntity) that match the UNSPC/
 *  NAICS/ISO3166 locator
*/
KeyedReference keyedReference = new KeyedReference();

if (args[1].equals ("NAICS")) {
   keyedReference.setTModelKey (TModel.NAICS_TMODEL_KEY);
}
else if (args[1].equals ("UNSPSC")) {
   keyedReference.setTModelKey (TModel.UNSPSC_TMODEL_KEY);
}
else if (args[1].equals ("ISO3166")) {
   keyedReference.setTModelKey (TModel.ISO_CH_TMODEL_KEY);
}
else {
```

```
        System.err.println ("Invalid locator tag [" + args[1]
                            + "]. Must be one of NAICS, UNSPSC, ISO3166");
        System.out.println ("usage: java wrox.ebXML.examples UDDI_INQUIRY_URL "
                            + "[NAICS|UNSPSC|ISO3166] keyValue\n");
        System.exit (1);
    }

    /* Set the keyName and keyValue from the passed parameters */
    keyedReference.setKeyValue (args[2]);
    if (args.length > 3)
        keyedReference.setKeyName (args[3]);

    Vector keyedReferenceVector = new Vector ();
    keyedReferenceVector.addElement (keyedReference);

    CategoryBag categoryBag = new CategoryBag ();
    categoryBag.setKeyedReferenceVector (keyedReferenceVector);
```

Next, we construct a `findQualifier`, and set it to `sortByNameAsc`. This will give us the businesses sorted in the ascending alphabetic order of the name field.

```
    FindQualifier findQualifier = new FindQualifier ();
    findQualifier.setText ("sortByNameAsc");
    Vector findQualifierVector = new Vector ();
    findQualifierVector.addElement (findQualifier);

    FindQualifiers findQualifiers = new FindQualifiers ();
    findQualifiers.setFindQualifierVector (findQualifierVector);
```

Finally, we call the `find_business()` method, passing it the `categoryBag` and the `findQualifiers`. The result is returned in a `businessList` structure, and we print out the names of the found businesses. In case no matching business is found, we print out an appropriate error message and quit. This call could also result in a UDDI-related exception (`UDDIException`), or a SOAP transport layer-related exception (`TransportException`) – appropriate error information is displayed in these cases.

```
    BusinessList businessList = null;
    try {
         businessList =
         uddiProxy.find_business
                (null, /* names        */
                 null, /* discoveryURL  */
                 null, /* identifiedBag */
                 categoryBag,
                 null, /* tModelBag     */
                 findQualifiers,
                 0);   /* max_rows      */
    }
    catch (UDDIException e) {
          DispositionReport dispositionReport = e.getDispositionReport ();
          System.err.println ("Error finding businesses: "
                              + dispositionReport.getErrCode() + ": "
```

```
                                   + dispositionReport.getErrInfoText());
           System.exit (1); /* fatal error */
     }
     catch (TransportException e) {
        System.err.println ("SOAP related error finding businesses");
        e.printStackTrace ();
        System.exit (1); /* fatal error */
     }

     BusinessInfos businessInfos = businessList.getBusinessInfos ();
     Vector businessVector = null;
     if (businessInfos != null)
         businessVector = businessInfos.getBusinessInfoVector();

     /* Select one business out of the list- we select the first one */
     if (businessInfos == null || businessVector.isEmpty()) {
         System.err.println ("No Business found matching the specified locator "
                             + args[1] + ":" + args[2] +". Sorry!");
         System.exit (1);
     }

     System.out.println ("Found " + businessVector.size()
                           + " <businessEntity>s:");

     for (int i = 0; i < businessVector.size() ; i ++) {
        System.out.println ((i + 1) + ". " +
             ((BusinessInfo)businessVector.elementAt(i)).getNameString ());
     }
   }
 }
```

To run this program, you will first need to carry out the following setup procedure:

- Add `uddi4j.jar` (the main UDDI4J jar file) to the CLASSPATH. This can be downloaded from http://www.uddi4j.org/.
- Add Xerces to your CLASSPATH. This example used Xerces 1.3.1, which can be downloaded from http://xml.apache.org/xerces-j/index.html.
- Add a soap library to the CLASSPATH. UDDI4J supports three SOAP transports – Apache SOAP 2.2 (get it from http://xml.apache.org/soap/index.html), Axis (obtain from http://xml.apache.org/axis/index.html), and HP SOAP (available at http://www.hp.com/go/webservices, and also bundled along with the HP Web Services platform – this includes UDDI4J and a private UDDI registry implementation). Alternatively, you could download IBM Web Services toolkit from http://www.alphaworks.ibm.com/tech/webservicestoolkit, which comes with, among other things, Apache SOAP, Axis and UDDI4J.
- Select a specific SOAP transport using the `TransportClassName` System property. The supported SOAP transports are Apache SOAP, Axis, and HP SOAP. The default transport setting is for Apache SOAP. See the UDDI4J documentation for further details.
- Put any additional jar files required in the CLASSPATH. Apache SOAP (which is being used in this example) requires Javamail (available from http://java.sun.com/products/javamail) and Java Activation framework (available from http://java.sun.com/products/beans)

- In case you are behind a proxy server, you may need to set the following System properties appropriately:
    - `http.proxyHost`: Host name of the HTTP proxy
    - `https.proxyHost`: Host name of the HTTPS proxy
    - `http.proxyPort`: Port number of the HTTP proxy
    - `https.proxyPort`: Port number of the HTTPS proxy

In addition, UDDI4J also allows you to turn tracing of the UDDI messages on or off using the `logEnabled System` property. Please see the release notes of UDDI4J for further details.

Now we are ready to compile and run this program. First we set the CLASSPATH. Some of the directories specified may be different on your system.

```
C:\install> set CLASSPATH=C:\libs\xerces-1.3.1.jar;
        C:\lib\uddi4j.jar;C:\lib\soap.jar;C:\lib\mail.jar;C:\lib\activation.jar;.
```

Next, we compile the program:

```
C:\install> javac –d . FindBusinessByLocators.java
```

Finally we run the program by passing the Inquiry URL of a UDDI registry node (IBM in this case), the classification taxonomy name (UNSPSC) and the classification `keyValue` (10151901 for companies in the "Tulip seeds, bulbs, seedlings or cuttings" business).

```
C:\install> java wrox.ebXML.examples.FindBusinessByLocators
        http://www-3.ibm.com/services/uddi/inquiryapi UNSPSC 10151901
        "UNSPSC:Tulip seeds, bulbs, seedlings or cuttings" 10151901
```

This program will send a `find_business` request to the UDDI registry, and display all the matching businesses. If none are found, it will display a "No Business found" message. You can try this program out as a generic client program and use it to browse companies in various other classification categories.

This `find_business()` method call shown above sends the following XML message to the UDDI registry:

```
<find_business generic="2.0" xmlns="urn:uddi-org:api_v2">
   <findQualifiers>
      <findQualifier>sortByNameAsc</findQualifier>
   </findQualifiers>
   <categoryBag>
      <keyedReference keyValue="10151901"
                      keyName="UNSPSC:Tulip seeds, bulbs, seedlings or cuttings"
                      tModelKey="UUID:DB77450D-9FA8-45D4-A7BC-04411D14E384"/>
   </categoryBag>
</find_business>
```

The third parameter in `keyedReference`, namely the `keyName`, is optional in UDDI V2, and the program above could very well be executed as shown below:

```
C:\install> java wrox.ebXML.examples.FindBusinessByLocators
        http://www-3.ibm.com/services/uddi/inquiryapi UNSPSC 10151901
```

Users could use the `logEnabled` System property to turn logging on. The exact logging mechanism is implemented at the SOAP transport level, and may have different behavior. For example, Apache SOAP (the default SOAP transport) sends these trace messages to the command window. HP SOAP has two additional System properties – `hpsoap.logFileName` and `hpsoap.logDirectory` allow redirecting the log messages to a file. Log messages get sent to the command window in case the `hpsoap.logFileName` property is not set.

Users behind a firewall can use the `http.proxyHost` and `http.proxyPort` System properties to set the proxy host and port number respectively, as shown below:

```
C:\install> java –Dhttp.proxyHost=YOUR_PROXYHOST
            –Dhttp.proxyPort=YOUR_PROXYPORT
             wrox.ebXML.examples.FindBusinessByLocators
             http://www-3.ibm.com/services/uddi/inquiryapi UNSPSC 10151901
```

Note that the search need not be done at the UDDI registry node where Tulip Mania was registered. The Business Registry nodes replicates the information published at other nodes in the UDDI Business Registry cloud.

A successful `find_business()` call will return a `businessList` structure containing `<businessInfo>`s (a `<businessInfo>` is a summarized version of a `<businessEntity>`):

```
<businessList generic="2.0"
              xmlns="urn:uddi-org:api_v2"
              operator="www.ibm.com/services/uddi" truncated="false">
   <businessInfos>
      <businessInfo businessKey="82...">
         <name>Tulip Mania</name>
         <description xml:lang="en">We sell tulips</description>
         <serviceInfos>
            <serviceInfo serviceKey="C7..."
                         businessKey="82...">
               <name>Buy Tulips</name>
            </serviceInfo>
         </serviceInfos>
      </businessInfo>
      <businessInfo>
         ...
      </businessInfo>
   </businessInfos>
</businessList>
```

The client then selects one business out of the `<businessInfo>`s, and this happens to be Tulip Mania. He then drills down to get the entire `<businessEntity>` for the company. From the `<bindingTemplate>`, the client can determine how to interact with Tulip Mania in case it desires to place an order for tulips. It could be either via the phone, the company web site, or programmatically using the `accessPoint` for the Web Service.

```
<get_businessDetail generic="2.0" xmlns="urn:uddi-org:api_v2">
   <businessKey>82...</businessKey>
</get_businessDetail>
```

This results in a businessDetail structure containing the entire Business Entity that we had published earlier. This contains information on the services that the company provides and access information for the services.

## Using the Web Service

In case the client wishes to use the Web Service, he can grab the tModelKey for it and use it to get the tModel. From this tModel, the client can get the WSDL description for the Web Service. Thus, it has details on how to interact with the service (from the interface description in the WSDL file) and also where to access the service (from the service end point in the <accessPoint> element of the <bindingTemplate>). It then can make a method call serialized using SOAP RPC conventions and sent over HTTP. Details of method invocation over SOAP are not covered in this chapter, but can be found in Chapter 4, *SOAP*.

In case the customer wants to buy tulips in Europe, it could get all related companies of Tulip Mania, and discover that it has a subsidiary company in Europe that it can do business with.

This can be done using the find_relatedBusinesses() UDDI method as shown below. This takes the business key of the company (Tulip Mania's business key in this case) as input.

```
<find_relatedBusinesses generic="2.0" xmlns="urn:uddi-org:api_v2" >
   <businessKey>82…</businessKey>
</find_relatedBusinesses>
```

This results in <relatedBusinessesList> message as show below. It contains information about all related businesses (<relatedBusinessInfo>) and the nature of the relationship ("parent-child", as indicated by the keyValue attribute). The *direction* attribute indicates the position of Tulip Mania in this relationship – it owns the fromKey, and hence it is the parent company.

```
<relatedBusinessesList generic="2.0" operator=" www.ibm.com/services/uddi"
                       truncated="false" xmlns="urn:uddi-org:api_v2">
   <businessKey>82...</businessKey>
   <relatedBusinessInfos>
      <relatedBusinessInfo>
         <businessKey>A237B…</businessKey>
         <name>Tulpenwoede B.V</name>
         <description>We see tulips too</description>
         <sharedRelationships direction="fromKey">
            <keyedReference tModelKey="uuid:807A2..."
                            keyName="Holding Company"
                            keyValue="parent-child">
         </sharedRelationships>
      </relatedBusinessInfo>
   </relatedBusinessInfos>
</relatedBusinessesList>
```

## UDDI and ebXML

UDDI and ebXML appear to have overlapping areas, especially between UDDI and the ebXML Registry and Repository specification. However, as we shall see, there are distinct differences between their scope and implementation. We'll also see that there can be coexistence between them.

The major points of distinction between UDDI and ebXML are:

- UDDI is a registry specification as compared to ebXML, which defines a registry and a repository. A registry contains information about resources – it is an 'index of things'. A repository is a 'holder of things'. The resources themselves are stored external to the registry.

  In UDDI a tModel can describe the specification of how to access a service – this specification could be in the form of a WSDL document, however, this document is not stored in the registry – only the URL pointing to it is stored.

  ebXML on the other hand defines both – a registry and a repository. The ebXML registry would have information on the business and service specification. For example, it would contain information on where to locate specific Collaboration Protocol Profiles (CPPs – see Chapter 8 for more on these), schemas, process models, etc. These specifications would be stored in the ebXML repository.

- UDDI's Universal Business Registry has a replicated registry model. There are multiple operator nodes in the registry cloud, and each node replicates the entire content of the other registry nodes. The UDDI specifications also define protocols for replication between the operator nodes.

  ebXML, on the other hand, defines a distributed registry model. Each registry owner manages its own information, and hence there is no need to replicate the information. These ebXML registry nodes would be maintained by specific industry groups, marketplaces, exchanges, or individual companies.

- Besides these design differences, the information contained in the UDDI and ebXML registries is different too. UDDI registries contain information about businesses (in the form of `<businessEntity>` structures or white pages), their services (`<businessService>` structures or yellow pages), information on how to interact with these services (`<bindingTemplate>` structures), and finally service type definitions (tModels).

  ebXML registries contain information about businesses and services, and have indexes to the specifications stored in the ebXML repository. These, as mentioned earlier, could be CPPs, schemas, process models, core components, and classification and categorization schemes.

UDDI is an evolving specification, and it remains to be seen if its direction brings it closer to where ebXML is. Already there are proposals on how UDDI and ebXML can work together towards the common goal of enabling a single global electronic marketplace. One use case promoted by the ebXML Registry Project Team is using UDDI to discover ebXML Registry/Repositories. This is useful as, unlike UDDI, there is no central ebXML registry, and thus clients could use UDDI as an entry point to discover ebXML registries and repositories.

# Using UDDI To Find an ebXML Registry/Repository

The ebXML Registry Project team, in an attempt to define ways in which ebXML and UDDI could work together, have proposed a white paper (available at http://www.ebxml.org/specs/rrUDDI.pdf) on how the UDDI registry can be used to find an ebXML Registry/Repository (Reg/Rep). ebXML, unlike UDDI, does not have a Universal Business Registry model, and hence UDDI can fulfill this need.

The steps in this process are:

## 1. Defining the ebXML Reg/Rep Canonical tModel

The ebXML standards body would need to define a canonical tModel. The <tModel> still needs to be defined, but may possibly look something like this:

```
<tModel tModelKey="uuid:563726c8-bbb4-c5ec-768b-7d5c4fb690b7">
   <name>ebXML RegRep</name>
   <description lang="en">ebXML conformant registry/repository</description>
   <overviewDoc>
      <description lang="en">EbXML Reg/Rep Specification</description>
      <overviewURL>
         http://www.ebxml.org/project_teams/registry/private/Registry.dtd
      </overviewURL>
   </overviewDoc>
   <categoryBag>
      <keyedReference tModelKey="uuid:C1ACF26D-9672-4404-9D70-39B756E62AB4"
                      keyName="uddi: A specification "
                      keyValue="specification"/>
      <keyedReference tModelKey="uuid:C1ACF26D-9672-4404-9D70-39B756E62AB4"
                      keyName="uddi: An XML specification "
                      keyValue="xmlSpec"/>
      <keyedReference tModelKey="uuid:C1ACF26D-9672-4404-9D70-39B756E62AB4"
                      keyName="uddi: Using SOAP messages "
                      keyValue="soapSpec"/>
   </categoryBag>
</tModel>
```

The <tModel> would act as a technical fingerprint for ebXML Reg/Rep registrations. As can be seen, the <tModel> would not contain any details about the Reg/Reps, but instead have a URL pointing to the location where further information could be found. In this proposed <tModel>, this would be in the form of the DTD (document type definition) for the ebXML registry (Registry.dtd).

## 2. Creating a UDDI business registration for the ebXML Reg/Rep

Each business that runs a Reg/Rep would need to publish a Business Entity for it, containing a service that refers to the Reg/Rep tModel defined earlier. The <businessEntity> below shows a Reg/Rep for a flower marketplace.

```
<businessEntity businessKey="AZ...">
   <name>Flower Marketplace</name>
   <description lang="en"> This is a Flower marketplace Reg/Rep</description>
   <contacts>
      <contact useType="work">
```

```
            <personName>Some Body</personName>
            <email useType="primary">some.body@nospam.com</email>
         </contact>
      </contacts>
      <businessServices>
         <businessService serviceKey="">
            <name>Search Registry</name>
            <description lang="en">Search the Flower Registry</description>
            <bindingTemplates>
               <bindingTemplate bindingKey="">
                  <accessPoint URLType="http">
                     http://www.someurl.com
                  </accessPoint>
```

The business service is then tagged with the `tModelKey` for the ebXML Reg/Rep:

```
                  <tModelInstanceDetails>
                     <tModelInstanceInfo
                        tModelKey="uuid:563726c8-bbb4-c5ec-768b-4fb690b7">
                        <description lang="en">ebXML RegRep</description>
                     </tModelInstanceInfo>
                  </tModelInstanceDetails>
               </bindingTemplate>
            </bindingTemplates>
         </businessService>
      </businessServices>
```

We also publish categorization information indicating that this is a business that deals in flowers and related products. This enables clients to easily locate it.

```
      <categoryBag>
         <keyedReference keyName="UNSPSC:Flower seeds, bulbs, seedlings and cuttings"
                         keyValue="101519"
                         tModelKey="UUID:DB77450D-9FA8-45D4-A7BC-04411D14E384"/>
           <keyedReference keyName="UNSPSC:Floral plants"
                           keyValue="101616"
                           tModelKey="UUID:DB77450D-9FA8-45D4-A7BC-04411D14E384"/>
          <keyedReference keyName="UNSPSC:Cut flowers"
                          keyValue="101617"
                          tModelKey="UUID:DB77450D-9FA8-45D4-A7BC-04411D14E384"/>
      </categoryBag>
   </businessEntity>
```

## 3. Finding an ebXML Reg/Rep

A client could then search for all Reg/Reps published in the UDDI registry. The call below searches for all business entities that have services implementing the Reg/Rep `<tModel>` (specified by using the canonical Reg/Rep `tModelkey`).

```
   <find_business xmlns="urn:uddi-org:api_v2" generic="2.0" maxRows="100">
      <tModelBag>
         <tModelKey>uuid:563726c8-bbb4-c5ec-768b-7d5c4fb690b7</tModelKey>
      </tModelBag>
   </find_business>
```

It could even refine the search a bit more by looking for all Reg/Reps that are classified using specific categorization values. In this example below, it is searching for a Reg/Rep dealing with floral plants (101616 is the UNSPSC code for floral plants).

```
<find_business xmlns="urn:uddi-org:api_v2" generic="2.0" maxRows="100">
   <tModelBag>
      <tModelKey>"uuid:563726c8-bbb4-c5ec-768b-7d5c4fb690b7"</tModelKey>
   </tModelBag>
   <categoryBag>
      <keyedReference tModelKey="uuid:DB77450D-9FA8-45D4-A7BC-04411D14E384"
                      keyName=""
                      keyValue="101616" />
   </categoryBag>
</find_business>
```

These `find_business()` calls return a `BusinessList` with one or more `<BusinessInfo>` structures – one for every business entity that matches the search criteria.

```
<businessList xmlns="urn:uddi-org:api" generic="2.0"
   operator=" www.ibm.com/services/uddi " truncated="false">
   <businessInfos>
      <businessInfo businessKey="....">
         <name>Flower marketplace </name>
         <description lang="en">
            This is a Flower marketplace Reg/Rep
         </description>
         <serviceInfos>
            <serviceInfo serviceKey="....">
               <name>Search the Flower Registry</name>
            </serviceInfo>
         </serviceInfos>
      </businessInfo>
      </businessInfo>
         ...
      </businessInfo>
   </businessInfos>
</businessList>
```

The client could then take the `<businessKey>` from one of the found `<businessInfo>`s, and drill down to get the entire `<businessEntity>`.

```
<get_businessDetail xmlns="urn:uddi-org:api_v2" generic="2.0" maxRows="100">
   <businessKey>...</businessKey>
</get_businessDetail>
```

This would return a `<businessDetail>` structure containing the Business Entity that was published earlier. The client could then extract information out of it, specifically the URL for searching the Reg/Rep, which was published as the `<accessType>` element.

In addition to the Registry/Repository tModels, the ebXML Core Components, CPPs, and Business Process Definitions could also be defined in the UDDI registry as canonical tModels. UDDI can thus be used as an entry point to discover not only Reg/Reps, but also ebXML-enabled businesses.

# Summary

In this chapter we learned about UDDI concepts and protocol specifications, and were introduced to some implementations available – both commercially and in freeware. UDDI does not specify standards for how users should interact with each other after discovery in the registry. This allows existing standardization efforts to interoperate with UDDI. In this chapter we saw an example of UDDI being used to discover ebXML Registry/Repositories, and also compared UDDI with ebXML Registry/Repository specification.

To summarize, the topics we covered in this chapter include:

- An overview of UDDI
- UDDI Usage Models
- Classification and Identification taxonomies
- UDDI Implementations
- UDDI Data structures
- UDDI API
- A Case Study for UDDI
- Comparison between ebXML and UDDI

Further information on UDDI can be obtained from the UDDI web site at http://www.uddi.org.

# 10

# ebXML Core Components

Many of the individual technological aspects of ebXML are not especially novel. Certainly there is nothing new about the concept of a registry and repository system, and the world has already used several messaging formats, each of which promises to be the latest and greatest. Most of the information within the collaboration protocol profiles/agreements (CPPs and CPAs – see Chapter 8 for more on these) work was already defined in IBM's Trading Partner Agreement Markup Language (TPAML – see http://xml.coverpages.org/tpa.html).

What makes ebXML *really* stand apart from previous efforts is the work of two of the ebXML specification groups. In particular, the **Business Process Modeling** and **Core Components** teams have defined new methods for business choreography and defining and using business information. In this chapter we are going to look specifically at the pieces of business information called **core components**, and the work of the core components project team. Unless otherwise noted, all Core Component Project Team work, including specifications, technical reports and white papers, is available from the ebXML web site at http://www.ebxml.org/.

## Background To ebXML Core Components

ebXML defines a core component as "a building block that contains pieces of business information, which go together because they are about a single concept". Core components are reusable pieces of business information, horizontal to many business processes. Examples of core components could be things like "Business Party Details" or "Date of Purchase Order". At the outset, it appears extremely simple to define semantics for these items; however, for true interoperability there is an additional piece we must add.

Businesses enter into business processes with each other. Before engaging in such a process, a business must design the process. This refers to a state in ebXML called the design time (or design phase). During design time, business information is bound to the process, which in turn is bound to two or more business parties via the CPA mechanism. (It may help to think of the information as nouns, or things, and the business processes as verbs, or actions.)

The design of a specific business process captures the information and exchange requirements, identifying the sequence, timing, and purpose of each exchange. The business information bound to each process is essentially the same information; however, slight modifications are made to fulfill requirements that are unique to a business process within a certain **context**. The context drivers of a business process may modify the way the business information is used. Some examples of context drivers are "business process = procurement" and "geopolitical = European Union". The contexts essentially guide how the base set of business information must be adapted for use in a narrower context.

The ebXML core components project team delivered a document called *Context and the re-Usability of core components v. 1.04*, along with two other context-relevant documents – the *Catalog of Context Drivers v. 1.04*, and *Document Assembly and Context Rules v. 1.04* (Latest copies of these documents are always available at http://www.ebxml.org/*)*. The latter describes the procedures and schemas for assembling documents using contextually driven core components. The business information is what must be represented by the core components. Context drivers are derived from information contained in both the business process and the CPP and CPA documents.

*At the time of writing this book, the complete set of information required to drive the contextual modifications of core components is not present in the CPP and CPA documents in a format to which programmers can write code to access on a consistent basis. The CPP/CPA project team did not define an XML schema for capturing geographical and geopolitical information for the owners of the CPPs. A project team will be working on this deliverable and it should be forthcoming in the next round of revisions to the specifications. Therefore, the description of the context mechanism forms an important part of the core components work.*

At this point, rather than reprinting all the information contained in the ebXML core components project team documents, I encourage readers to go to www.ebxml.org/specs/ to download and read the core components related documents. There is a lot of information to digest and I do not wish to restate the entire work of the core components team in this chapter.

## Developing Reusable Core Components

Core components can be either **atomic** or **aggregate** in their composition. The former means that a component cannot be further divided into subsections, while the latter indicates it is composed of several smaller (atomic or aggregate) components. Aggregate and atomic components can be constructed into documents. When this is done at design time, the actual components can be modified to meet the needs of the business based on the context in which they will be used. The following figure, taken from the ebXML core components team documentation, demonstrates this:

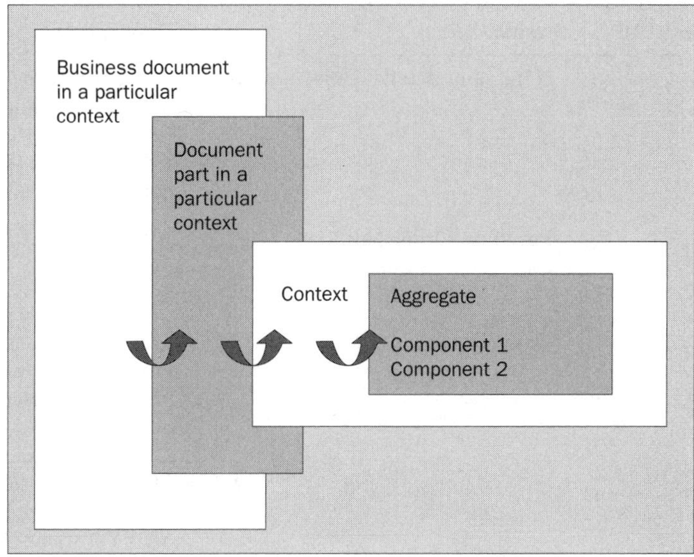


Let's look at a very simple ebXML-enabled scenario to examine how this works. Imagine that company "A", a French shoe manufacturer, installs an ebXML server, builds a CPP document, and places it in a registry. In the CPP they advertise the capability to engage in an electronic ordering business process that allows other business to purchase their shoes in bulk. Company "B", a European Union (EU) shoe distributor with offices in Luxembourg, comes along and discovers the CPP document of company "A". They wish to engage in the CPP-referenced business process for bulk ordering of shoes. The business process details that the following information must be sent to company "A" (this is somewhat simplified for the purposes of explanation):

```
Name and details (Company B)
Purchase Order Number
Date of order
Order details (Shoe model, Shoe size, Color)
Subtotal amount before taxes
Total amount.
```

This information could easily be modeled into core components if it was specific only to the two companies above; however, now we want this business process and the business information to be reusable on a global basis – this adds a layer of complexity to how we describe the core components.

The first thing we might do is to build a set of core components for the business transaction, by abstracting at a high level the information about each of the previous pieces of information. This would allow us to build the following table. Note that UID is short for Unique Identifier, which refers to a unique ID for each component.

| Core Component UID | Name | Description |
|---|---|---|
| 01 | Name and details (Company B) | The party name and details, including a unique identifier issued by an agency of record. Address formats vary from country to country. |
| 02 | Purchase Order Number | A String used to indicate the purchase order number (format – String). |
| 03 | Date of order | The date of the order. A good idea is to express it in ISO-8601 (the International Time and Date Standard Notation, YYYY-MM-DD, for example, the 7th of March 2001 is 2001-03-07). However, it might be in DD-MM-YYYY if we are in Europe, or MM-DD-YYYY in the USA. |
| 04 | Order details::Shoe model | The shoe model (format – String). Can be in English, French, or other languages. |
| 05 | Order details::Shoe size | The shoe size. Can be expressed in European or North American standard sizes. |
| 06 | Total amount | The total amount of the invoice that will be generated if this order is fulfilled in whole. Can be expressed in US dollars or Euros (note that in a more formal modeling process, we would include a qualifier for currency code). |

The above table is over-simplified from what would be acceptable in an actual production environment, however, it should serve as an abstract guide. Right away we can see how the physical representation of many of these core components would vary slightly, based on the context in which a business process was engaged. For instance, if the companies are both European, the shoe size can be expressed in European sizes (for example, 43-45). Alternatively, if both companies are North American, the shoe sizes could be in North American format (for example, 10½). Accounting for the possibility that one company was in Europe and the other was in North America, it could be required to state the sizes in both European and North American values.

We will specifically examine two of these core components and how they are going to be influenced based on the geographical and geopolitical context-driven information. The information will be expressed differently than if company "A" and company "B" were in North America, for example the "Total amount" (UID 06) could be modified to be expressed in Euros instead of US dollars.

So why do we need the core components to be contextually modified at design time? One of the great promises of ebXML is the reusability on a global scale of the business processes and methodologies, including business information. If we let everyone define their own information in whatever format they choose, interoperability will be a complete nightmare. Let's examine the two core components again to see how they might differ depending on whether they are used in North America or Europe:

| UID | Name | Description | Geographical Context = North America | Geographical Context = Europe |
|---|---|---|---|---|
| 03 | Date of order | The date of the order. | Expressed in ISO-8601 format of YYYY-MM-DD. | Expressed in EU format of DD-MM-YYYY. |
| | | | Element name is | Element name is |
| | | | `<Date format="ISO-8601">` | `<DateDeFacture format="EU">` Note that even though core component elements and attributes can be expressed in any language, it is probable that most will use English names. Using English names is not a requirement. |
| | **Example:** | | 2001-08-07 | 07-08-2001 |
| 06 | Total amount | The total amount of the invoice that will be generated if the entire order is fulfilled. | Expressed in US dollars, uses a period as a decimal indicator. | Expressed in Euros, uses a comma to separate major and minor currency values. |
| | | | Element name is | Element name is |
| | | | `<InvoiceAmount>` | `<QuantiteDeFacture>` |
| | **Example:** | | `<InvoiceAmount currencysymbol="$" currency="USD">57.99` | `<QuantiteDeFacture currencysymbol="E" currency="EUR">61,34` |

So, we can see that in order to have reusable business processes and reusable business information, we can use the context driver and contextual modification mechanisms to keep the information sets common to all industries.

## ebXML Core Component Project Team

Before we go into more technical details, we need to look at the work done by the ebXML core components team. The team declared their mandate as:

> *"The objective of the ebXML Core Components Project Team is to define a process, by which information components can be discovered, catalogued in sufficient detail, and analysed to identify which components are core components. The creation of such a catalogue will enable interoperability across industries that utilize electronic commerce."*

A common misconception of ebXML's deliverables is that ebXML was going to deliver all the core components, and business messages built using those core components, to the world. This is simply not true, for two major considerations. First, the team had a huge task in trying to establish a methodology for capturing information about core components and the higher-level abstractions of what they represented. Second, even if the team delivered a set of core components, there would immediately be huge waiting lists to add to the base set based on business needs. We have learned from the experiences of EDI that we need the means for businesses to *extend* standards to be able to meet their own requirements. When using EDI, a single business cannot simply *extend* the EDI standard by adding additional data elements.

### Overview of ebXML Core Component Work

The core components team started working on several documents simultaneously. These documents included the following, which are all available at the ebXML.org web site:

- Naming Conventions for core components
- Core Component Analysis and Discovery
- Core Component Catalog and Guide
- Document Assembly and Context Rules
- Core Component Structure
- Catalog of Context Drivers
- Context and Reusability of core components
- Relationships of ebXML Technical Reports
- The Core Component Catalog

This diagram (courtesy of ebXML.org) illustrates the relationships among the papers listed above:

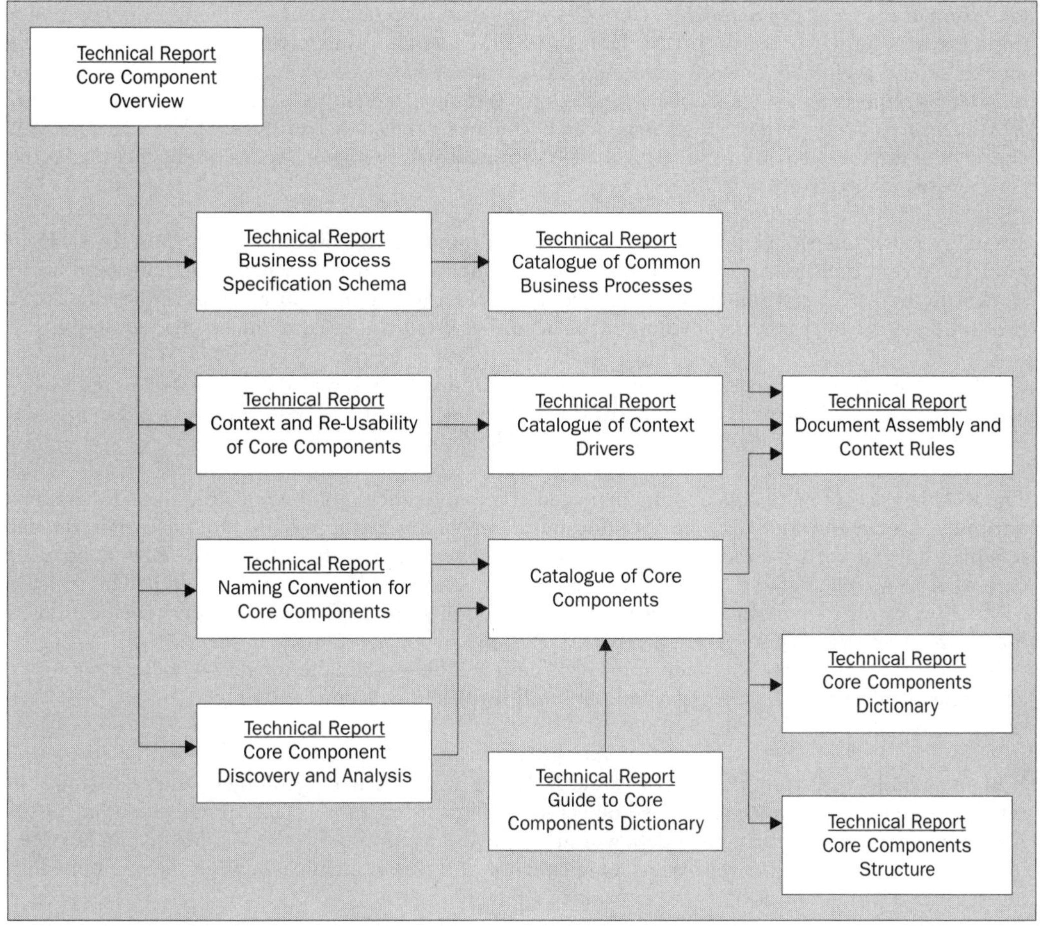


The team did deliver a substantial amount after their initial 18 month work plan; however, there are a few things that the team did not deliver which are critical to those who wish to implement ebXML.

The most conspicuous absence is the lack of a formal schema definition for defining how a core component should be defined and represented in XML. This is probably the first thing any programmer will look for in this chapter if they are in a hurry to begin implementation. But don't worry, I will explore "best practices" solutions for these two items, with caveats about how adopting them will affect interoperability.

# Implementing Core Components

If you have read the ebXML technical report entitled *Core Component Analysis and Discovery* and you are familiar with a modeling language such as UML, you will probably be able to capture the business information needed for a simple exchange of data under the umbrella of a single process. I recommend you try at least one of these before beginning any production work.

A portion of the work of the ebXML Core Components Group talks about modeling core components using a syntax largely based on UMM. UMM uses UML models as its primary methodology and these models should preferably be converted into XML syntax for use within ebXML, although this is not a mandatory requirement – the lack of a formal and terse requirement to build core components into XML instances of components is an issue which I believe needs to be resolved. ebXML is about XML, and a lot of the functionality needed for the entire infrastructure to work relies on the fact that core components are available in XML syntax.

There are many theories about how to derive XML instances of those components from the UML models. Since this chapter is aimed primarily at developers who will be seeking to understand how to work with the XML representations of core components, I will redirect discussions of the UML to XML conversion to the http://www.ebtwg.org web site and its related core components discussion lists.

The logical storage mechanism for a core component is an ebXML registry. Because the registry has an associated **Registry Information Model** (**RIM**), we need to examine exactly what we need to express in our core component and what its relationship is to the RIM.

The RIM consists of meta data about a managed object referenced by the registry. The RIM has many attributes associated with each piece of information, including, but not limited to, the owner, the date it was placed in the registry, and the classifications and associations of the object. The RIM doesn't really care what XML schema language is used to describe the managed object, nor should it. The registry has a job of performing content management operations defined in the ebXML Registry specifications, via the `ObjectManager()` interface, and ebXML Registry query operations via the `ObjectQueryManager()` interface. Our focus here will be on the functionality of using core components referenced via a registry, and this will lead us to concentrate on the `ObjectQueryManager()` interface.

When you build a program that queries an ebXML registry for a managed object, the registry will first return the metadata about the managed object to the registry client interface, along with a link to the managed object. The registry meta data will likely be packaged into the ebXML Messaging Service format. The following figure represents a logical view of the relationships between the components and messages in a `getManagedObjectResponse()` type of request:

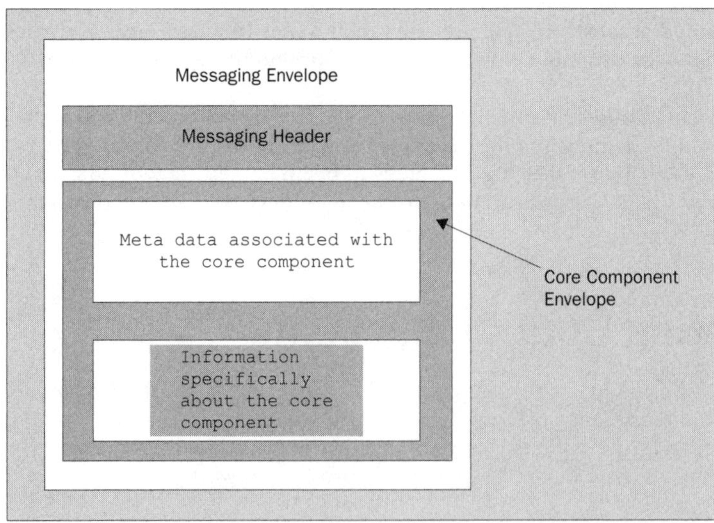

*Note that the ebXML RegistryInformation Model (RIM) specification provides an exact schema for building the* `getRegsitryItemResult` *type message.*

The meta data returned as part of the `getManagedObjectReponse()` message can be captured in the following DTD fragment. Note that this is actually derived from the ebXML RIM. Documentation can be found in Chapter 7, *ebXML Registry/Repository*, and Chapter 16, *Implementing ebXML* (a case study).

```
<!ENTITY % ObjectAttributes "
   id                ID      #IMPLIED
   name              CDATA   #IMPLIED
   description       CDATA   #IMPLIED">

<!ENTITY % RegistryEntryAttributes " %ObjectAttributes;
   majorVersion        CDATA   '1'
   minorVersion        CDATA   '0'
   status              CDATA   #IMPLIED
   userVersion         CDATA   #IMPLIED
   stability           CDATA   'Dynamic'
   expirationDate      CDATA   #IMPLIED">

<!ENTITY % IntrinsicObjectAttributes " %RegistryEntryAttributes;">

<!ELEMENT ReturnRegistryEntryResult
        (RegistryEntryMetadata*)>

<!ELEMENT RegistryEntryMetadata
        (RegistryEntry,
         Classification*,
         SourceAssociations?,
         TargetAssociations?,
         AuditableEvent*,
         ExternalLink*)>

<!--*********RegistryEntry TREE*********-->
<!ELEMENT RegistryEntry (SlotList?)>
<!ATTLIST RegistryEntry
       %RegistryEntryAttributes;>
<!ELEMENT SlotList (Slot*)>
<!ELEMENT Slot (ValueList?)>
<!ATTLIST Slot
   name                CDATA   #REQUIRED
   slotType            CDATA   #IMPLIED>
<!ELEMENT ValueList (Value*)>
<!ELEMENT Value (#PCDATA)>

<!--*********Classification Tree*********-->
<!ELEMENT Classification EMPTY>
<!ATTLIST Classification
   %IntrinsicObjectAttributes;
   classifiedObject    IDREF   #REQUIRED
   classificationNode IDREF   #REQUIRED>

<!--*******SourceAssociations AND TargetAssociations Tree*******-->
```

```
<!ELEMENT SourceAssociations ( Association* )>
<!ELEMENT TargetAssociations ( Association* )>
<!ELEMENT Association EMPTY>
<!ATTLIST Association
   %IntrinsicObjectAttributes;
   sourceRole          CDATA  #IMPLIED
   targetRole          CDATA  #IMPLIED
   associationType     CDATA  #REQUIRED
   bidirection         (true | false) "false"
   sourceObject        IDREF  #REQUIRED
   targetObject        IDREF  #REQUIRED>

<!--********AuditableEvent Tree**********-->
<!ELEMENT AuditableEvent EMPTY>
<!ATTLIST AuditableEvent
   %ObjectAttributes;
   eventType           CDATA  #REQUIRED
   registryEntry       IDREF  #REQUIRED
   timestamp           CDATA  #REQUIRED
   user                IDREF  #REQUIRED>

<!--********ExternalEvent Tree***********-->
<!ELEMENT ExternalLink EMPTY>
<!ATTLIST ExternalLink
   %IntrinsicObjectAttributes;
   externalURI         CDATA  #IMPLIED>
```

The very last line of this DTD gives us the URI to the core component if it is an extrinsic object (of type unknown to the registry).

# Designing the Core Component

Let's now look at the abstract information model for a core component implementation. The core component can be broken down into a logical model too. The outer wrapper will likely be a `<CoreComponent>` element that will allow programs to quickly identify the returned managed object as such. The composition can be marked up in three sections:

- A header-type section dealing with the top-level logical information and meta data information not included in the RIM. This information can include, but is not limited to, the UID, the physical location of the master copy of the core component, and copyright/statement of intended use type information.
- A default **assembly block** of XML that describes how to use this core component and the basic structure of it in its default state. The basic structure can include the XML element `name`, names of any attributes, the default allowable content for both the element and the associated attributes (sometimes expressed as an enumerated list), and a section open for extensions.
- The third block is extendable – it includes one or more assembly blocks, each of which is specific to one or more specific context drivers that may be applicable.

Let's look at the logical representation of the core component XML fragment, followed by a sample core component XML file. The logical model of the core component fragment contains a wrapper element (in our case we use `<CoreComponent>`), and some meta data (not the same as the RIM meta data) housed in the `<MetaInformation>` element. This is followed by a `<DefaultAssembly>` element (we wrapped the default assembly in the `<DefaultAssembly>` element for easy programmatic access to this branch). After that there are zero or more `<Assembly>` elements, each of which house the assembly details and context rules governing their use.

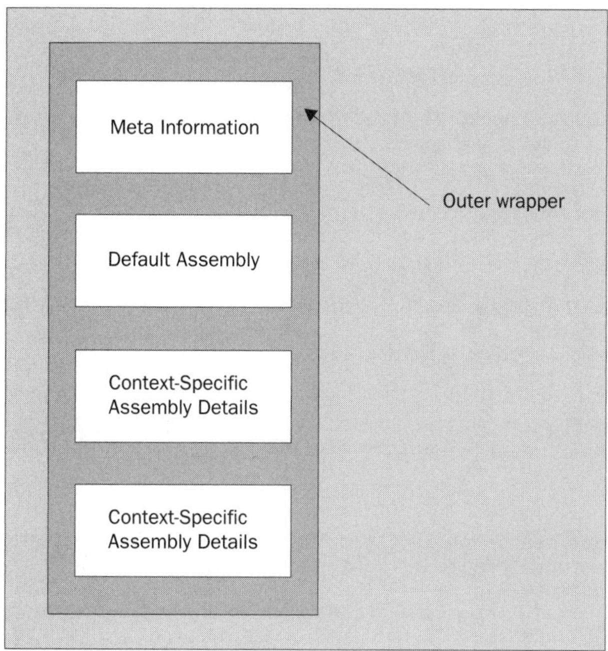


The XML Schema for expressing this was not fully defined by the ebXML project team; however, there are sufficient details that allow the easy creation of such schemas. The problem is that if everyone creates their own schemas for core components, obviously interoperability is affected due to the fact that programmers cannot write code to consistently access information inside instances of core components. The following example is based on "best practices" defined by a small set of developers, and has been successfully implemented. It contains assembly fragments based on James Clark's RELAX NG Schema format. Implementer's could just as easily use the W3C Schema format in place of the RELAX NG Schema fragment. RELAX NG is a relatively new schema format spearheaded by James Clark – RELAX NG Schemas are relatively simple, yet contain enough meta data to meet most schema needs. You can find out more information about this schema type at http://www.thaiopensource.com/relaxng/.

> *The following fragment can be validated against a RELAX NG Schema by using Jing, a RELAX NG validating parser. Because ebXML is not tied to any one schema language, I have included the schema for this core component in W3C Schema format in the code download for this chapter, available from* http://www.wrox.com/. *The following model may be implemented using other schema formats, including "plain old" DTDs.*

We'll break this down, section by section. The code starts by declaring default namespaces for RELAX NG grammar, as well as attributes to specify the default. This is followed by some basic and self-explanatory documentation and extensibility declarations. The <Documentation> element has several attributes that correspond to the RELAX NG Schema (written in RELAX NG). These can include name, description, usage, copyright, license, commentary, note, and code that should give you enough flexibility to tell all about the core component.

```
<?xml version="1.0" encoding="UTF-8"?>

<CoreComponent type="" xmlns:rng="http://relaxng.org/ns/structure/0.9"
               defaultLocale="en_CA"> <!--(noun | verb | other)-->
   <MetaInformation>
      <Behaviour isExtensable="true" isRestrictable="false" />
      <Documentation type="description">
         This is a core component for defining a monetary value.
      </Documentation>
      <Documentation type="copyright">
         (c)2001 XML Global Technologies, Inc. All rights reserved.
      </Documentation>
      <Documentation type="license">
         Redistribution and use in source and binary forms, with or without
         modification, are permitted provided that such redistributions
         retain this copyright notice.
      </Documentation>

      <Identifiers>
         <Indentifier type="primary" value="URN:UID:com-xmlglobal:80032"/>
      </Identifiers>

      <ExplanationOfUse>
         <!--type can be "AssemblyDoc", "Fragment", "Atomic" or "Any"-->
         <Usage type="Fragment" instance="Element"/>
         <!--instance can be
                     ( element | attribute | attributeGroup | Any )-->
      </ExplanationOfUse>
   </MetaInformation>
```

The next section starts with the <DefaultAssembly> element, which can have only one child element of <Assembly>. This outer wrapper allows programmers to quickly locate the default assembly of a core component, rather than having a program iterate through each of the other <Assembly> elements trying to match a default='true' type of string.

```
   <DefaultAssembly>
      <Assembly>
```

Each <Context> element contains two distinct branches – <BaseDetails> and <ExtendedDetails>. The <BaseDetails> branch contains the basic information for the core component. The next declarations are the XML element name and label, along with a localized description:

```
      <BaseDetails>
         <ElementName>InvoiceAmount</ElementName>
         <Label>Invoice Amount</Label>
         <Description>
            Represents a monetary amount for the total of an Invoice
         </Description>
```

Attributes and elements can both be constrained, by including the <PhysicalDetail> element as a direct child – see example below. The physical detail element can constrain based on datatype, a regular expression mask, and minimum and maximum length attributes. This core component schema allows POSIX, GNU, ORO, JAKARTA, and PERL as regular expression formats. The <SchemaFacet> element can also reference W3C schema datatypes, such as xsd:date, xsd:string, and xsd:int.

```
    <Attributes>
       <Attribute name="UID" value="com-xmlglobal-registry:80010"/>
       <Attribute name="symbol" complexTypeRef="" value="$" type="FIXED">
          <PhysicalDetail><!--if we want to constrain values-->
             <Constraints minLength="1" maxLength="1">
                <Regexp mask="OK | NOT_OK" type="ORO" comment="" />
             </Constraints>
          </PhysicalDetail>
       </Attribute>
       <Attribute name="currency" value="USD"/>
    </Attributes>

    <ExtensionDefinitions>
       <!--further descriptions and masks, transforms, SQL, EDI basically
           a type of extension in a particular dialect or business rules
           (human readable business stuff)-->
       <Extension type="">
          <Item type="elementarygrammar">Noun</Item>
       </Extension>
    </ExtensionDefinitions>

    <PhysicalDetail><!--David owns this branch-->
       <Constraints minLength="" maxLength="">
          <Regexp mask="" type="ORO" comment="" />
       </Constraints>
          <SchemaFacet syntax="xsd" value="xsd:int"/>
          <PermittedValues/>
    </PhysicalDetail>
 </BaseDetails>
```

Next comes the <ExtendedDetails> portion of the assembly branch. The RELAX NG assembly component expresses how to represent both an atomic core component as well as aggregates. The structure and abilities of RELAX NG make it ideal for declaring assemblies of several atomic or aggregate core components into larger aggregate core components.

You will also notice the <Association> element. This seems to be made redundant by the "associations" contained inside the ebXML Registry Information Model, but it is quite different. Each XML vocabulary in the world has elements that may be semantically identical to elements in other languages, including ebXML-type core components. Because these types of semantic associations are very sensitive and can change with context, we include the <Association> branch inside each <Assembly> element. The attributes establish the **Universally Unique Identifier** (**UID**) of the element in the other XML vocabulary, the taxonomy, a relationship of "identical", similar", or "related", and the registry that can be queried to find more details about that element. This association is unique to the specific <Assembly> branch it is contained within.

```
      <ExtendedDetails>
         <Context locale="en_CA"/>
         <Associations>
            <Association reference="UID:foocom:112"
                         taxonomy="FooCom-Library"
                         relationship="similar"
                         name=""
                         registry="http://foocom.com:2345" />
            <Dependency/>
         </Associations>
            <!-- RELAX NG grammar is used for assembling aggregate core
               components. Thanks James C.!-->
         <rng:grammar ns="http://relaxng.org/ns/structure/0.9">
            <rng:start>
               <rng:ref name="invoiceAmount" />
            </rng:start>
            <rng:definition name="invoiceAmount">
               <rng:element ns="UID:com-xmlglobal-registry:80010"
                            name="InvoiceAmount">
                  <rng:attribute name="UID">
                     <rng:choice>
                        <rng:value>
                           UID:com-xmlglobal-registry:80010
                        </rng:value>
                     </rng:choice>
                  </rng:attribute>

                  <rng:attribute name="symbol">
                     <rng:choice>
                        <rng:value>$</rng:value>
                     </rng:choice>
                  </rng:attribute>

                  <rng:attribute name="currency">
                     <rng:choice>
                        <!--any ISO 4217 currency code can go here-->
                        <rng:value>USD</rng:value>
                        <rng:value>FRF</rng:value>
                     </rng:choice>
                  </rng:attribute>

               </rng:element>
            </rng:definition>
         </rng:grammar>
            <Processes/><!--any-->
      </ExtendedDetails>
   </Assembly>
</DefaultAssembly>
```

You will notice that the next <Assembly> element has a <ContextGroups> element inside the <ExtendedDetails> element. The <ContextGroups> element contains one or more <Context> elements, each of which describes the context in a series of one or more <Rule> elements. The enumerations for the values of the rule types were taken directly from the ebXML core components project team's *Context Drivers for core components v. 1.04* document (see http://www.ebxml.org/), and two more were added to the XML global definition – `Language` and `Custom`. `Language` was added due to the requirements of the system being implemented, and on later examination it made sense since the language is not always tied to the geopolitical context driver. A good example of this is Canada, where both English and French are required. The `Custom` value was added for future extensibility. The context drivers specified by ebXML that were incorporated are `Business Process`, `Industry`, `Geopolitical`, `Product`, and `Official Constraints`. The `Business Process` context values are based on classifications under major categories such as "procurement" or "advisement", but also reference specific UIDs for each process to allow for precision.

The `Geopolitical` drivers are a bit more complex. While any ISO 3166 country code can help, the schema also allows for other values, such as "EU" (European Union economic zone) and "NAFTA" (North American Free Trade Agreement). There is not any declared enumerated code list for possible value types. Languages, likewise, were based on ISO 639 language codes. For additional information on ISO 3166, 638, 8601 or others, simply type in "ISO XXXX" in a search engine like Google and it should point you to a suitable page.

`Industry` and `Product`, while similar, have subtle differences. The possible values for industrial classifications are initially recommended to be:

- North American Industry Classification System (NAICS – http://www.naics.com/)
- International Standard Industrial Classification (ISIC – http://www.un.org/)
- UNiversal Standard Products and Services Classification (UNSPSC – http://eccma.org/unspsc/)
- OTHER (for extensibility)

The `Product` context is set to a choice of:

- UNSPSC, Standard Industry Trade Classification (SITC – http://www.un.org/)
- United Nations Statistical Division (UNSD – http://esa.un.org/)
- Harmonized Standards (HS)
- Classification for the Purposes of non Profit Institutions (COPI)
- OTHER

Lastly, `Official Constraints` (which describes data use contexts resulting from official sources, such as legal constraints, specifications, business requirements, etc.) can take any value that fits in this category, such as ISO/W3C Specifications, regulatory and legislative contexts like national and state laws and customs, and contractual and trading partner agreements.

Here is that next <Assembly> structure:

```
<!--Start of another Context-->
<Assembly>
   ...
   <ExtendedDetails>
      <!--This allows users to specify which context drives the
          selection of this Assembly branch-->
      <ContextGroups>
         <Context ID="com-xmlglobal-registry:80011:00001">
            <!--<!ATTLIST Rule type (BusinessProcess CDATA #IMPLIED
                                     Industry CDATA #IMPLIED
                                     Geopolitical CDATA #IMPLIED
                                     Product CDATA #IMPLIED
                                     OfficialContraints CDATA #IMPLIED
                                     Role CDATA #IMPLIED
                                     Language CDATA #IMPLIED
                                     Custom CDATA #IMPLIED)> -->
            <!--Procurement Process-->
            <Rule type="BusinessProcess"
                   name="procurement"
                  value="com-xmlglobal-registry:90002"/>
            <Rule type="GeoPolitical" value="EU"/>
               <!--ISO-3166 language codes-->
            <Rule type="Language" value="FR"/>
               <!--( NAICS | ISIC | UNSPSC | OTHER )-->
            <Rule type="INDUSTRY"
                  classificationScheme="SIC"
                  value="5139"
                  label="Shoes - wholesale"/>
            <Rule type="Product"
                  classificationScheme="UNSPSC"
                  value="53.11.16.01.00"
                  label="chaussures - hommes"/>
               <!--classificationScheme(UNSPSC | SITC | UNSD |
                                        HS | COPI | OTHER)-->
         </Context>
         <Context>
            <!--another context can go here if it uses the same CC
                format described in this assembly-->
         </Context>
      </ContextGroups>
      ...
   </ExtendedDetails>
   ...
</Assembly>
```

All of the <Rule> elements within a <Context> element are considered a group joined by a logical "AND", while each branch of <Context> is considered to be in a logical "OR" relationship. That is to say, the preceding core component assembly would have been the correct block to choose if the Business Process matched a value of "com-xmlglobal-registry:90002" AND the Geopolitical value matched "EU" AND the Industry matched an SIC classification of "5139" AND the Language value matched "FR" AND the Product value matched "53.11.16.01.00". If either of these tests failed, this particular assembly would not be the correct choice.

The assembly has been optimized via an ID for the <Context> element, with a unique value. This allows for more efficient context matching; however, systems must have prior knowledge of the ID values.

If you examine the first <Assembly> element, in the example directly opposite, after the <DefaultAssembly> branch, you will notice these items are in French:

```
        <ElementName>QuantiteDeFacture</ElementName>
        <Label>Quantite de Facture</Label>
        <Description>
           Repr&#233;sente une quantité&#233;mon&#233;taire pour
           le total d'une facture.
        </Description>
```

Because elements can have attributes associated with them, we have to make sure we can represent this inside the core component. Each ebXML core component has at least one attribute that must be present in all instance documents. This is the Universally Unique Identifier attribute. It does not have to be specifically written in each instance – by using the DTD mechanism for a fixed value attribute for an element, when the instance document is parsed by a validating parser, the attribute will be inherently available as part of the document. I will explain how this works later. The following XML fragment is the complete <Assembly> branch for an alternative contextual representation of the core component.

```
  <!--Start of another Context-->
  <Assembly>
     <BaseDetails>
        <ElementName>QuantiteDeFacture</ElementName>
        <Label>Quantite de Facture</Label>
        <Description>
           Repr&#233;sente une quantit&#233; mon&#233;taire pour le
           total d'une facture.
        </Description>

        <Attributes>
           <!--UID never changes-->
           <Attribute name="UID" value="com-xmlglobal-registry:80010"/>
              <!-- &#8364; is the Euro symbol entity reference
                   for ISO-8859-1 -->
           <Attribute name="symbol" value="&#8364;" type="FIXED"/>
           <Attribute name="currency" value="EUR"/>
        </Attributes>

        <PhysicalDetail>
           <!--element physical detail does not change
               from default but can be overridden here. -->
           <SchemaFacet syntax="xsd" value="xsd:int" />
        </PhysicalDetail>
     </BaseDetails>

     <ExtendedDetails>
        <!--This allows users to specify which context drives
            the selection of this Assembly branch-->
        <ContextGroups>
           <Context ID="com-xmlglobal-registry:80011:00001">
              <!--<!ATTLIST Rule type (BusinessProcess CDATA #IMPLIED
```

```
                                          Industry CDATA #IMPLIED
                                          Geopolitical CDATA #IMPLIED
                                          Product CDATA #IMPLIED
                                          OfficialContraints CDATA #IMPLIED
                                          Role CDATA #IMPLIED
                                          Language CDATA #IMPLIED
                                          Custom CDATA #IMPLIED)> -->
            <!--Procurement Process-->
            <Rule type="BusinessProcess"
                  name="procurement"
                  value="com-xmlglobal-registry:90002"/>
            <Rule type="GeoPolitical" value="EU"/>
               <!--ISO-3166 language codes-->
            <Rule type="Language" value="FR"/>
               <!--( NAICS | ISIC | UNSPSC | OTHER )-->
            <Rule type="INDUSTRY"
                  classificationScheme="SIC"
                  value="5139"
                  label="Shoes - wholesale"/>
            <Rule type="Product"
                  classificationScheme="UNSPSC"
                  value="53.11.16.01.00"
                  label="chaussures - hommes"/>
               <!--classificationScheme(UNSPSC | SITC | UNSD |
                                          HS | COPI | OTHER)-->
         </Context>
         <Context>
            <!-- another context  here if it uses the same core
                 component format described in this assembly -->
         </Context>
      </ContextGroups>
      <rng:grammar xmlns="http://relaxng.org/ns/structure/0.9">
         <rng:start>
            <rng:ref name="quantiteDeFacture" />
         </rng:start>
         <rng:definition name="quantiteDeFacture">
            <rng:element ns="UID:com-xmlglobal-registry:80010"
                         name="QuantiteDeFacture">

               <rng:attribute name="UID">
                  <rng:choice>
                     <rng:value>
                        UID:com-xmlglobal-registry:80010
                     </rng:value>
                  </rng:choice>
               </rng:attribute>

               <rng:attribute name="symbol">
                  <rng:choice>
                     <rng:value>&#8364;</rng:value>
                  </rng:choice>
               </rng:attribute>

               <rng:attribute name="currency">
```

```
                    <rng:choice>
                        <!--this is now a specific value for
                            the context-->
                        <rng:value>EUR</rng:value>
                    </rng:choice>
                </rng:attribute>

            </rng:element>
        </rng:definition>
    </rng:grammar>
  </ExtendedDetails>
</Assembly>
```

## Overall Architecture

Let's examine the overall architecture for how a business document is built based on context-driven core components.

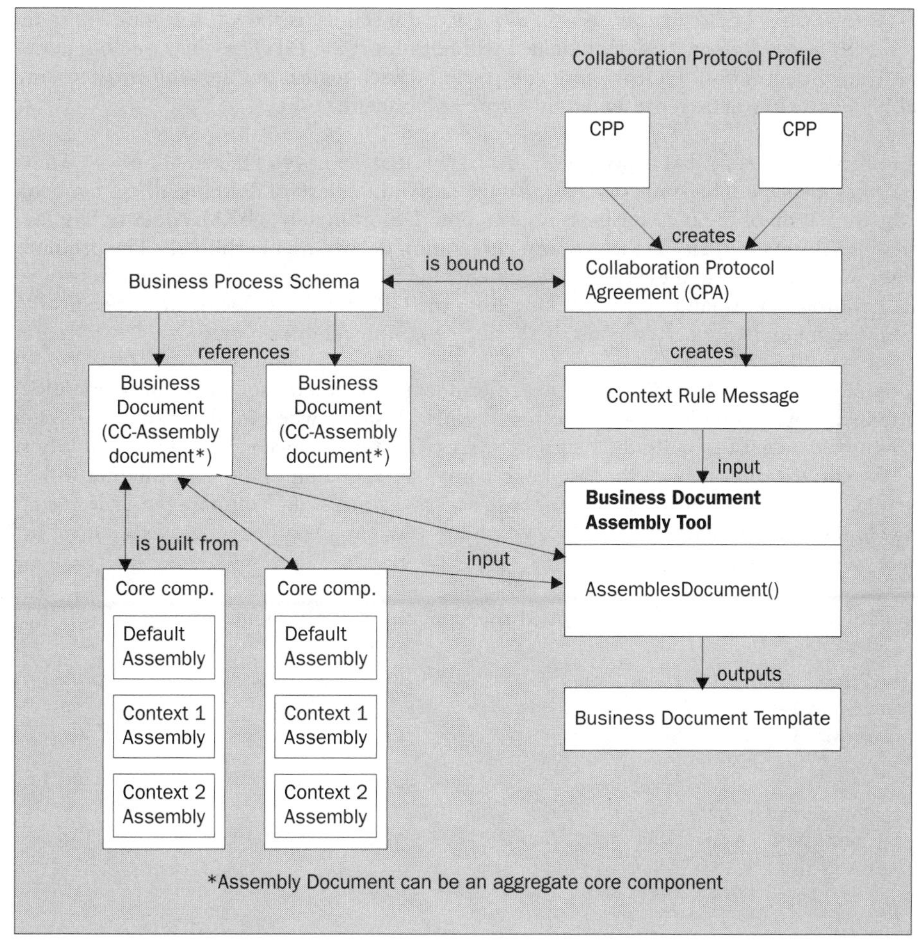

In the depiction above, we can see the entire design time process of creating our business information for the exchange. This entire sequence of events could eventually be automatically facilitated. The first step is the creation of a CPA document from binding a specific business process to two or more (more being unlikely) CPP documents. The Business Process Schema references the business information that is included in a specific business transaction. That business information is expressed as an **assembly document** as defined by the core components project team. It is important to note that the assembly document can also be a core component itself – do you remember the `<Usage>` element from the core component example?

```
<ExplanationOfUse>
   <!--type can be "AssemblyDoc", "Fragment", "Atomic" or "Any"-->
   <Usage type="Fragment" instance="Element"/>
   <!--instance can be ( element | attribute | attributeGroup | Any )-->
</ExplanationOfUse>
```

If the `type` attribute for `<Usage>` is set to `AssemblyDoc`, that core component, by itself, represents an entire business document.

The DTD for assembly documents, as well as an actual instance, is shown in section 7.2 of the *Document Assembly and Context Rules v. 1.04* document. I will not repeat the DTD for the assembly document. The assembly document is built up from core components. Each logical business information entity in the assembly document can be represented by a core component.

There is another message that is present in the system that we haven't talked about yet. That is the **context rules message**. The context rules message is given the task of defining all the contexts that will drive the formation of the final business information. Unfortunately, ebXML does not define how to capture this information, although such implementation details are not difficult. The problem once again lies with the fact that if everyone implements their own context rule mechanisms, interoperability suffers. Important information is also lacking from the CPP and CPA documents, specifically the lack of a formal schema to define party details, including geographical information.

In my opinion, the ebXML-defined context rules document violates several of the principles of XML by trying to incorporate pseudo code, expressed as XML. Instead, when implementing the system, programmers may wish to build their own messages. Of course, once again interoperability suffers. The goal of the context rules message should be to convey information to the program that will assemble the business information, not define logic for constructing the message. Compare the example context rules message to the ebXML-defined one. My own philosophy has always been "leave the logic in the program, not in the data".

The modified (and much simplified) context rules document looks like this:

```
<?xml version="1.0"?>
<ContextRules ID=" com-xmlglobal-registry:80010:00001">
   <Condition type="BusinessProcess"
              name="procurement"
              value="com-xmlglobal-registry:90002"/>
   <Condition type="GeoPolitical" value="EU"/>
   <Condition type="Language" value="FR"/>
   <Condition type="INDUSTRY"
              classificationScheme="SIC"
              value="5139"
```

```
                label="Shoes - wholesale"/>
    <Condition type="Product"
                classificationScheme="UNSPSC"
                value="53.11.16.01.00"
                label="chaussures - hommes"/>
</ContextRules>
```

The first thing that you might notice is the `ID` attribute of the `<ContextRules>` element. This is present to provide an efficient match if the `ID` value is the same as the value in the core component. We have used a URN type identifier, which should allow vertical trading communities to quickly and easily identify and use their own contextual core components.

# Building a Simple Program

Let's look at the code we can write to work with core components and context rules message. Because there is lots to do with core components during the design time, we will assume that the type of query we are giving to the registry is a `returnManagedObject()` type query, as defined within the Registry Services specification. This could return the entire details of the managed object back to your application, sent back as the payload of an ebXML message.

*Note: it is not always required to return the entire object in an ebXML message. When developing programs to work with core components, it is highly recommended to abstract the transport layer from your program, in alignment with most generally accepted principles of object-oriented design. It is also possible that the registry metadata may not be returned or may be returned in a format other than the XML metadata syntax shown above. Therefore, the example below will concentrate mainly on working with the core components specific XML fragment.*

We will build a simple command line tool that will read two XML files as input (the context rules message and a core component fragment), then return one fragment of XML as output. The output will be the actual XML fragment that will be used in the business document template.

*Note: in a full-blown implementation, our tool would read in an assembly document and construct the entire business message template. This would involve making several calls to the simple tool we will build.*

For demonstration purposes we will work in Java. To try this code, use JDOM Build 7 (earlier version will not work) and the `crimson.jar` and `jaxp.jar` files in your classpath. The example is built using JDK 1.3; the JDOM is available from http://www.jdom.org/. When compiling, please use the `[-deprecation]` flag, which will report errors associated with outdated libraries.

```
// $Id:$
// package com.xmlglobal.ebxml.cc;
import java.io.*;
import java.util.*;
import org.jdom.*; // build 7.  < 6 may not work.
import org.jdom.input.SAXBuilder;
import org.jdom.output.*;

/******************************************
   *
```

```
    *  You will need to place crimson.jar, jdom.jar
    *  and jaxp.jar into your classpath
    *  (c) 2001 Duane Nickull, Matt Mackenzie - XML Global Technologies, Inc.
    *  All rights reserved.  You may use, distribute or modify this code
    *  freely as long as this message remains intact.
    *
    *  Changed 25.09.01 by D. Nickull to work with updated CC model in CVS
 */

public class AssemblyUtils {
   static Namespace rngNs =
          Namespace.getNamespace("http://relaxng.org/ns/structure/0.9");
   public AssemblyUtils() { }

   public static Element extractAssembly(Element cc, Element cr)
         throws Exception {
      // Grabs the ID from the Context Rules message.
      String contextId = cr.getAttributeValue("ID");

      // Create a list of Context Assemblies in memory.
      List asms = cc.getChildren("Assembly");

      Element result = null; // initialize

      // Iterate through the List
      for (int i = 0; i < asms.size(); i++) {
         Element asm = (Element)asms.get(i);
         //System.out.println(asm);
         //Grab each Element
         List ctxts =
 asm.getChild("ExtendedDetails").getChild("ContextGroups").getChildren("Context");

         // Since there can be more than one Context,
         // we have to test them all
         for (int ii = 0; ii < ctxts.size(); ii++) {
            Element ctxt = (Element)ctxts.get(ii);

            // Grab the ID attributes value
            String ctxtId = ctxt.getAttributeValue("ID");

            // Test it against the Context Rules value.
            // Beware of funny results with evaluating null values!
            if (ctxtId !=null && ctxtId.equals(contextId)) {

               // If it matches, grab the branch of rng grammar or element
               Element rng =
                 asm.getChild("ExtendedDetails").getChild("grammar",rngNs);
               if (rng == null) rng =
                 asm.getChild("ExtendedDetails").getChild("element", rngNs);

               // Test to see if we found anything.
               if (rng == null)
                  throw new Exception("No RNG schema found in assembly");

               // Return branch as fragment
               return rng.detach();
            }
         }
      }
      throw new Exception("Evidently, something is wrong with your XML.");
```

```
    }

    public static void main(String[] args) {
       if (args.length < 2) {
          System.out.println(
             "Usage: java " + AssemblyUtils.class.getName() +
             "<CoreComponent.xml> <ContextRules.xml>");
             System.exit(-1);
          }
          try {
               Element coreComp =
                  new SAXBuilder().build(args[0]).getRootElement();
               Element contRule =
                  new SAXBuilder().build(args[1]).getRootElement();

               // test the Context Rules document. Not needed if
               // validated at parse time.
               if (!contRule.getName().equals("ContextRules")) {
                   System.err.println ("The input does not appear to be " +
                                       "a valid context rules document.");
               System.exit(-1);
          }

          Element target = null;

          // If we call this code from another program we feed it two args
          // and get the fragment returned.
          try {
             target = AssemblyUtils.extractAssembly(coreComp, contRule);
             XMLOutputter xo = new XMLOutputter("    ", true);
             xo.output(target, System.out);
          }
          catch (Exception e) {
             System.err.println("Error extracting assembly: " +
                                e.getMessage());
             System.exit(-1);
          }
       }
       catch (Exception e) {
          System.err.println("XML Parser error: " + e.getMessage());
       }
    }
 }
```

When we run the program we must give it two arguments – a core components document and a context rules document. The program is written to work with the two samples of those files included in this chapter (they can also be found in the code download, as `Component.xml` and `ContextRules.xml`, respectively). The program will execute and return a fragment of XML based on the context (for more on running the example, see the `README.txt` file in the code download). The result looks like this (assuming your `<ContextRules>` context `ID` attribute is set for the value that corresponds to the German context):

```
<?xml version="1.0" encoding="UTF-8"?>
<rng:grammar xmlns=http://relaxng.org/ns/structure/0.9>
   <rng:start>
      <rng:ref name="rechnungsbetrag" />
   </rng:start>
   <rng:definition name="rechnungsbetrag">
```

```
        <rng:element ns="UID:com-xmlglobal-registry:80010"
                     name="Rechnungsbetrag">

          <rng:attribute name="UID">
            <rng:choice>
              <rng:value>
                UID:com-xmlglobal-registry:80010
              </rng:value>
            </rng:choice>
          </rng:attribute>

          <rng:attribute name="symbol">
            <rng:choice>
              <rng:value>$</rng:value>
            </rng:choice>
          </rng:attribute>

          <rng:attribute name="currency">
            <rng:choice>
              <rng:value>DEM</rng:value>
            </rng:choice>
          </rng:attribute>
        </rng:element>
      </rng:definition>
    </rng:grammar>
```

The idea is that for each core component in an ebXML assembly document you would repeat this process and eventually assemble a complete schema for a business message instance that is part of an ebXML business exchange. The output schema would allow users to build their output document by a number of means, ranging from manual input (maybe using HTML-type forms) all the way up to a fully-automated process involving a product that can resolve semantic equivalencies and build a mapping template from traditional data sources.

So what should a programmer do if there are no matching assemblies available based on the context drivers? ebXML did not specify any default messages or procedures, so you are basically on your own. Properly defined error messages are needed within ebXML and will hopefully develop over time.

## Referencing Core Components from Document Instances

The XML instance that follows the rules of the schema above could look like this:

```
<Rechnungsbetrag UID=" UID:com-xmlglobal-registry:80010"
                 symbol="$"
                 currency="DEM">
</Rechnungsbetrag>
```

Each element that is built from a core component has a universally unique identifier as an attribute, which can be used to reference the core component. Because ebXML did not define a mechanism for parsers of these messages to know the URI of a registry that can help you retrieve a copy of the core component, a "best practice" is to use the format shown above, with the URI of the registry used as a URN type identifier. The way to locate the core component from the above example would be to go to the registry interface at http://registry.xmlglobal.com and query for a managed object with a UID of `com-xmlglobal-registry:80010`. This is by no means a permanent or preferred long-term method for accessing core components, however it is used today.

## Representing Aggregate Core Components

The example shown above represents a basic atomic value. What do we do if we want to represent a more complex structure for a core component? Thanks to James Clark and the RELAX NG group, we have a very robust mechanism for presenting such aggregate components. Look once again at the `<rng:grammar>` structure within the core component:

```
<rng:grammar ns="http://relaxng.org/ns/structure/0.9">
   <rng:start>
      <rng:ref name="fullName" />
   </rng:start>
   <rng:definition name="fullName">
      <rng:element ns="UID:com-xmlglobal-registry:80010" name="FullName">
         <rng:attribute name="UID">
            <rng:choice>
               <rng:value>UID:com-xmlglobal-registry:80345</rng:value>
            </rng:choice>
         </rng:attribute>
            ...
      </rng:element>
   </rng:definition>
</rng:grammar>
```

Imagine we want to build a structure that represents a person's full name, built from two or more other names, which themselves are represented as atomic core components. We can easily modify this branch as follows:

```
<rng:grammar ns="http://relaxng.org/ns/structure/0.9">
   <rng:start>
      <rng:ref name="fullName" />
   </rng:start>
   <rng:definition name="fullName">
      <rng:element ns="UID:com-xmlglobal-registry:80345" name="FullName">

         <rng:attribute name="UID">
            <rng:choice>
               <rng:value>UID:com-xmlglobal-registry:80345</rng:value>
            </rng:choice>
         </rng:attribute>
         <ref name="nameGroup"/>
      </rng:element>

      <rng:define name="nameGroup">
         <rng:element ns="UID:com-xmlglobal-registry:80356 name="firstName">
            <rng:text/>
            <!—these should also have UID attributes-->
         </rng:element>
         <rng:element ns="UID:com-xmlglobal-registry:80357
                     name="lastName">
            <rng:text/>
         </rng:element>
      </rng:define>
   </rng:definition>
</rng:grammar>
```

The RELAX NG schema language is actually perfectly suited for core components. It has an inherent mechanism for defining named patterns (think of aggregate core components). Note once again that the RELAX NG schema embedded in core component can act as the assembly document. A core component can be a complete document, such as a "Purchase Order" or an "Invoice". This means far less complexity for implementing a system.

# Future Core Components Development

I have mentioned on several occasions that the ebXML core components work has some technology gaps that need to be addressed. Luckily, the core components work will continue along its development path. While the ultimate contribution will come from actual business users, there are several groups working hard to advance the methodology and technology surrounding core components.

Pursuant to a Memorandum Of Understanding (MOU) between OASIS and UN/CEFACT, all infrastructure-related work will continue to be developed under the auspices of OASIS, and all content-related work (including business process schemas and business information – in other words core components) will be developed under UN/CEFACT. UN/CEFACT has a proposed restructure which *may* eventually include a new electronic business working group (eBWG). This has not been formally convened at the time of writing this book. In the meantime, a transitional group called the Electronic Business Transitional Work Group (eBTWG), has been set up to continue the work of ebXML. To add to the confusion there are at least two other groups conducting work in the arena of core components.

The Universal Business Language (UBL) group, a now OASIS Technical Committee lead by Jon Bosak of Sun, has emerged as a contender for developing a set of ebXML-specific business messages, based on a set of core components, to be used openly across many businesses. The group home page is at http://www.oasis-open.org/committees/ubl/. UBL has decided to use Commerce One's xCBL 3.0 (an early XML vocabulary which stands for XML Common Business Library) as the starting point for developing their business messages, and will continue work throughout 2001-2. Once complete (or near complete), the IP of this group may likely be turned over to an internationally accredited standards' body.

The EDIFACT Working Group of UN/CEFACT and the ANSI ASC X12 groups have initiated a Joint core components (JCC) team that started in the fall of 2000. The CE/FACT Steering Committee (CSG) has unequivocally stated its support for this ongoing work. UN/CEFACT (http://www.unece.org/cefact/) looks after the future needs of EDIFACT (http://www.unece.org/trade/untdid/welcome.htm) while ASC X12 (a North American Flavour of EDI) is under the auspices of ANSI (http://www.ansi.org).

Individuals who are interested in the future of this work are encouraged to become part of the teams. The guidelines on how to join and what skills are required are available at http://www.ebtwg.org/.

# Summary

In this chapter, we reviewed the work of the ebXML Core Components team, looked at ways to implement core components and some of the shortcomings in the specifications. The core components schema in this chapter is not by any means the definitive schema for core components, however, it can be used for now. Future work in core components will be interesting, and will likely yield changes to the current work in this area. There are more details on implementing core components in Chapter 16, along with other implementation details on related ebXML Specifications.

ebXMLFoundationsProfessional

# 11

# Other Standards for Payload

In the previous chapter we saw how the ebXML Core Component libraries can be used to generate schemas for message content in the ebXML framework. However, there are many reasons why alternative payloads might be used, particularly when migrating from an existing system. Indeed, ebXML has been designed to support such incremental adoption.

This chapter should encourage you to integrate your ebXML solutions with existing and emerging initiatives. However, to do so successfully requires an appreciation of the issues involved with using non-ebXML payloads. Primarily, the areas of concern are **integrity** of messaging information and the **interoperability** of the payload data across applications.

In this chapter we shall examine two types of payload: first some commonly used XML-based message contents, and then other structured data formats (as used in existing EDI exchanges). Where possible, these are described using documents or messages that could apply to our ITT P&SI case study, such as the 'Advanced Shipping Notice' document and the 'Request for Inspection' business processes. We shall also discuss the combination of various payload types in a mixed message business scenario. Finally, we'll consider how the goal of interoperability can be achieved and the way forward for using non-ebXML payloads.

## Why Use Other Payloads?

The first question to ask when considering non-ebXML payloads is "*What is an ebXML payload?*" By definition, ebXML core components are syntax-neutral, so it is legitimate to claim that *any* payload is compliant if it bases itself upon the ebXML Core Component library definitions and extension methodology. Unfortunately, there are a few factors that make such a strategy difficult to implement:

- **Availability** – at the time of writing, only skeletal parts of the ebXML Core Component library are in place. Moreover, the documents that are in place are not yet ratified (see Chapter 10 for more on core components).
- **Legacy systems** – the e-commerce marketplace is already littered with various services, standards, and initiatives that have their own defined payloads for messages.
- **Inducement** – despite the vision of an "open" marketplace, the reality is that some enterprises, initiatives, and technology providers have already provided technical and commercial attractions to adopt and retain alternative payloads.

These all help to explain why ebXML has been designed to accommodate *any* type of payload. ebXML achieves this by separating the content of the payload from the ebXML infrastructure.

So, on one level, we can say that ebXML does not care what type of payload it carries. However, in order to make this assertion, we have to assume that the non-ebXML payload *itself* is also aware of this separation. In practice, most documents used in e-business exchanges carry some pieces of data for dealing with their disposition. The way these payloads are processed within the ebXML infrastructure will affect the available level of data integrity.

In addition, ebXML strives to encourage interoperability between applications. A payload business document that has not been described using ebXML core components would not provide the advantage of allowing enterprises to align their business processes automatically.

So, when using alternative payloads, we need to consider both of these factors.

# Message Integrity

Within any messaging service, there is normally a clear differentiation within each message between the transaction data and the controlling information necessary for identification and processing of this data. Note that neither should be confused with the information that may be used by the data transport mechanism involved. The information we are concerned with here relates to actual business transactions, such as order placements and requests for inspection.

*Transport layer protocols identify the protocol connection points for origin and delivery of the message container. The relationship between this and a business transaction may be complex, for example involving many different types of business transactions carried within one transport exchange.*

Because designers of business transactions seek to keep their payload independent of the messaging services involved, it is common for designers to define message control information as part of the payload content. In this way, the designers can insure that the necessary identification, security, and audit facilities are available to the users of their payloads, regardless of how they are exchanged. Unfortunately, this also means that any transport routing or packaging services also requiring this data will duplicate it. This is similar to the way snail mail correspondents often use the sender's and recipient's addressing details both on the letterhead (the transaction layer) and on the envelope (the message service layer).

As with any case of data duplication, this raises the problem of synchronizing these values – or risking potential contradiction and the subsequent loss of data integrity. Under such circumstances, a message payload may contain addressing details that disagree with the message services protocol. If this happens, which address should the application consider correct? Similarly, if this message control information is used for redirecting the payload, then a routing application may choose the wrong destination for the data. Adding to the complexity is the fact that, given the modular nature of many business-to-business system interfaces, separate applications may be involved in these decisions.

Obviously, it would be advisable to align this information, but to do so requires an appreciation of various data elements and where they differ or relate to others. So we shall be looking at the relationship between various payloads and the ebXML Message Service (ebMS). Although the ebXML framework does not mandate the use of ebXML Message Services for its payloads, some key points need to be considered where they *have* been adopted. Of course, where the ebXML Message Services are *not* used for handling payloads, many of these concepts will still apply – but the implementation details are outside the scope of this chapter.

By revisiting Section 4 of the ebMS specification (http://www.ebxml.org/specs/ebMS.pdf) we can establish where these duplicated elements may be found:

> *"This [the ebMS] specification focuses on defining a communications-protocol neutral method for exchanging the electronic business messages. It defines specific enveloping constructs that support reliable, secure delivery of business information. Furthermore, the specification defines a flexible enveloping technique that permits ebXML-compliant messages to contain payloads of any format type. This versatility ensures that legacy electronic business systems employing traditional syntaxes (that is, UN/EDIFACT, ASC X12, or HL7) can leverage the advantages of the ebXML infrastructure along with users of emerging technologies."*

As we discussed in Chapter 13, the ebXML Message Service should be viewed as a set of extensions to the SOAP protocol. These extensions aim to provide the security and reliability features necessary to support international electronic business.

The following diagram illustrates the basic structure of an ebXML message:

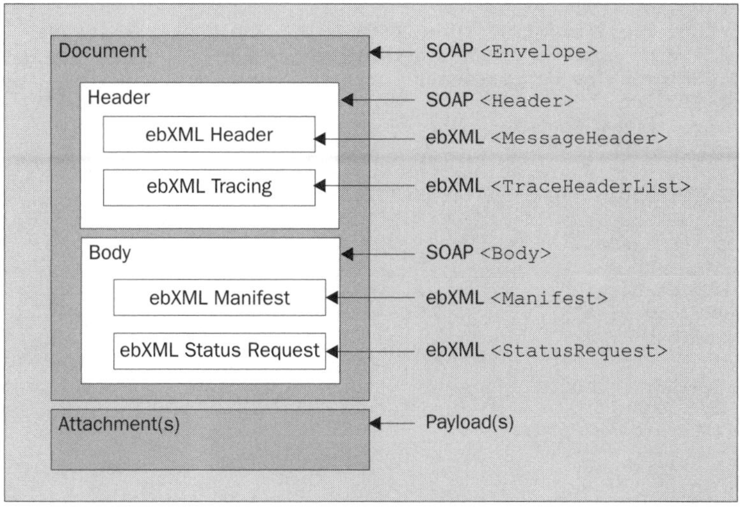

In revisiting this structure, we should remind ourselves of a few key points:

- Payloads are contained within MIME attachments to the overall message.
- The message structure is independent of the transport mechanism used.
- ebXML extensions are located in both the SOAP envelope header and body.

When using any type of payload, it is advisable to review certain elements within the SOAP `<Header>` to ensure integrity with the data in the payload. For example, payloads that use intermediary services may need to examine the ebXML `<TraceHeaderList>` element. For the purposes of this discussion, we shall focus on the `<MessageHeader>` element extension within the SOAP envelope header. This mandatory element has, potentially, more associations with data elements that may be duplicated within the payload content than any other.

The following fragment demonstrates the structure and potential content of an ebXML `<MessageHeader>` element:

```
<SOAP-ENV:Envelope
      xmlns:SOAP-ENV="http://schemas.xmlsoap.org/soap/envelope/"
      xmlns:xsi="http://www.w3.org/2000/10/XMLSchema-instance"
      xsi:schemaLocation="http://schemas.xmlsoap.org/soap/envelope/
      http://ebxml.org/project_teams/transport/envelope.xsd" ...>
  <SOAP-ENV:Header
      xmlns:eb="http://www.ebxml.org/namespaces/messageHeader"
      xsi:schemaLocation="http://www.ebxml.org/namespaces/messageHeader
      http://ebxml.org/project_teams/transport/messageHeaderv0_99.xsd" ...>
    <eb:MessageHeader id="..." eb:version="1.0"
                      SOAP-ENV:mustUnderstand="1">
      <eb:From>
        <eb:PartyId eb:type="urn:duns">123456789</eb:PartyId>
      </eb:From>
      <eb:To>
        <eb:PartyId>mailto:requests@inspectionservices.com</eb:PartyId>
      </eb:To>
      <eb:CPAId>
        http://inspectionservices.com/cpas/noexistingCPA.xml
      </eb:CPAId>
      <eb:ConversationId>20020101-120000-00001</eb:ConversationId>
      <eb:Service eb:type="myservicetypes">
        PreShipmentInspectionRequest
      </eb:Service>
      <eb:Action>New Request</eb:Action>
      <eb:MessageData>
        <eb:MessageId>mid:UUID-2</eb:MessageId>
        <eb:Timestamp>2002-01-01T12:00:00Z</eb:Timestamp>
        <eb:RefToMessageId>mid:UUID-1</eb:RefToMessageId>
      </eb:MessageData>
    </eb:MessageHeader>
  </SOAP-ENV:Header>
  <SOAP-ENV:Body ...>
    <eb:Manifest ...>
      ...
    </eb:Manifest>
  </SOAP-ENV:Body>
</SOAP-ENV:Envelope>
```

Within the <MessageHeader> element above, there are several controlling data elements we should be aware of (and we'll remind ourselves of their purpose in the process):

- The <From> and <To> parties. These elements identify both the party that originated the message and the intended recipient of the message, respectively. Whilst ebXML recommends that these contain URIs (as seen in the <To> element), they may contain other identifiers such as a DUNS number (as shown in the <From> element).
- The <CPAId> collaboration protocol. This element is a string that identifies the parameters governing the exchange of messages between the parties. Whilst this may be an ebXML collaboration protocol agreement (CPA), it may be a reference to any document agreed by the parties involved.
- The <ConversationId> transaction set identification. This element is a string uniquely identifying the set of related messages that make up a set of business transactions between the <From> and <To> parties. Typically, these are used for reporting and audit purposes.
- The <Service>. This element identifies the business services or 'sets of related actions' that use the message.
- The <Action>. Within a <Service>, the <Action> element identifies a specific business process. In this case, this is the original request made for an inspection of these goods.
- The <MessageData> message identification. This element provides a means of uniquely identifying an ebXML message instance. This should not be confused with the <ConversationId> element, which defines a *series* of messages. For example, if this message was re-sent then the <MessageData> value would change but the <ConversationId> value would not. The <RefToMessageId> child element allows for a thread of messages to be maintained.

As we examine various types of alternative payloads we shall return to these data elements – we shall establish where and how they are related. We will see that many payloads really do have the potential to duplicate the data used in the ebXML Message Service protocol. And of course, when developing applications to manipulate alternative payloads it is advisable to attempt to synchronize these data values.

# Interoperability

ebXML promotes application interoperability by encouraging the use of a common specification schema for defining a business process metamodel. It is this metamodel schema that can be used to define individual business processes themselves.

This is similar to the way in which database *manufacturers* use metamodels for their database management systems, while database *designers* use these metamodels to define application databases. For example, a business process is specified within the ebXML framework using the ebXML Business Procces Specification Schema, or ebBPSS (as discussed in Chapter 5). The business process models resulting from the application of this schema, along with any business documents described using core components in the given context, allow enterprises to align their application interfaces. This level of interoperability means not only providing syntactic recognition but semantic understanding as well.

These business process models may also be referenced in ebXML collaboration protocol profiles and/or agreements (CPPs and CPAs), more about which can be found out in Chapter 8.

Any business process models specified will normally reference a set of required business documents. These business documents may either be assembled from ebXML core component libraries, or defined by some external document specification using non-ebXML formats and vocabularies. This relationship is shown in the following diagram:

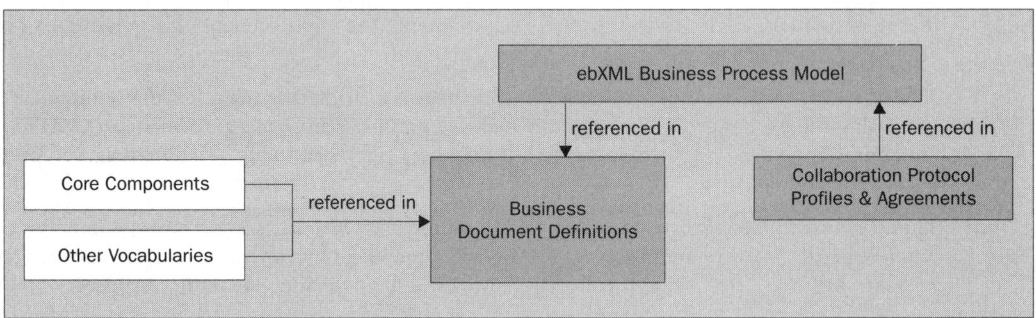


To encourage interoperability, any payloads used should be defined as part of an ebXML business process model. This specification is available at http://www.ebxml.org/specs/ebBPSS.pdf. As an example, here is a sample fragment from an ebXML business process specification that might be used in the P&SI case study application, which we introduced in Chapter 2:

```
<BusinessTransaction name="Perform Pre-Shipment Inspection">
   <RequestingBusinessActivity name="Prepare for Shipping">
      <DocumentEnvelope BusinessDocument="PreShipmentInspectionRequest"/>
   </RequestingBusinessActivity>
   <RespondingBusinessActivity name="Report of Findings">
      <DocumentEnvelope BusinessDocument="ReportOfFindings"/>
   </RespondingBusinessActivity>
</BusinessTransaction>
```

From this we can see that the `Prepare for Shipping` activity requests the `Perform Pre-Shipment Inspection` transaction. This transaction uses the document known as `PreShipmentInspectionRequest`. In response the transaction expects the document known as `ReportOfFindings`. None of these are necessarily ebXML messages.

As we shall see when we examine some alternative payloads, many of these also have their own equivalent methods for specifying business processes, transactions, and documents. The developers' challenge is to ensure that both the syntax *and* the semantics are understood by their applications.

# Using XML-Based Payloads

There are several reasons why various flavors of XML documents are likely to be used as payloads in ebXML exchanges. First, XML syntax has some benefits as a data exchange format, such as:

- Explicit structure definitions are available.
- XML documents have some degree of human-readability, and considerable machine-readability (both in terms of structure and data).

- XML supports Unicode for internationalization.
- XML documents are text based.
- XML is not tied to any particular technology or computing platform.
- XML is an Internet-friendly technology.

Secondly, there is a widely-held, altruistic view of XML as the open, lightweight, and independent language for the next generation of Internet services (including Web Services). Finally, a standard using XML in its title is likely to attract XML-based technologies!

However, as we know, the XML standard only defines a meta-language. Formalized XML vocabularies are needed to conduct business-to-business exchanges of XML documents. These vocabularies describe what data should look like (syntax) as well as how they are to be interpreted (semantics). An increasing number of XML vocabularies are being promoted by various organizations and industry initiatives. Examples include the e-BIS-XML project from the UK-based Business and Accounting Software Developers Association (BASDA –see http://www.basda.org) and the Global XML Invoice Specification project being developed by Visa (http://www.visa.com/). In fact, at the time of writing, there are 57 e-commerce projects registered with the xml.org web site (http://www.xml.org/xml/industrySectorList.jsp?CATEGORY=19). By necessity, many of these projects are developing their own specific XML vocabularies.

In this section we examine some of the more common XML vocabularies in use today. Understandably, many of these involve large, sophisticated architectures that we cannot hope to cover entirely in one chapter. Therefore, we have selected pertinent components to demonstrate the overall role and structure of these initiatives.

Whilst all these vocabularies may define their payloads as XML documents, they remain frustratingly different in their syntax and semantics. This frustration was one of the catalysts for the ebXML initiative.

## The Open Applications Group (OAGI)

The **Open Applications Group, Inc** (**OAGI**, see http://www.openapplications.org/) is an industry-driven initiative to promote "plug-and-play" software components across platforms and applications. Their focus is both Enterprise Application Integration (EAI) and, increasingly, B2B application integration (e-business). OAGI publish and maintain the **OAGI Integration Specification** (**OAGIS**) (http://www.openapplications.org/downloads/oagidownloads.htm). We shall examine the recently-released OAGIS version 7.1 for one example of a common standard for XML payloads.

OAGIS does not specify business processes or transport protocols. Their architecture defines a set of specification structures known as **Business Object Documents** (**BODs**). BODs describe business objects, including the exchange control details and the actual data to carry out the requested business event. The following quotation is taken from an OAGI news article, http://www.openapplications.org/news/010730.htm:

> *"[OAGIS] defines over 182 XML-based business objects (BODs) for business-to-business and application-to-application integration in e-Commerce, purchasing, manufacturing, logistics, human resource management and finance. It is expected that OAGI support for ebXML will significantly accelerate broad-based adoption of this specification."*

Obviously, this is a significant base upon which the OAGI intends to offer ebXML support. However, the current XML architecture of OAGIS is based on a message service similar to, but not the same as, ebXML. If we look more closely, we can see two areas where developers need to take care when integrating OAGIS payloads within their ebXML framework – **message integrity** and **interoperability**. We shall look at these in turn, in the following sections.

## Message Integrity and OAGIS

Whilst OAGIS does not mandate the messaging services to be used, we can see from the OAGIS BOD model that there are some obvious overlaps with the ebMS specification:

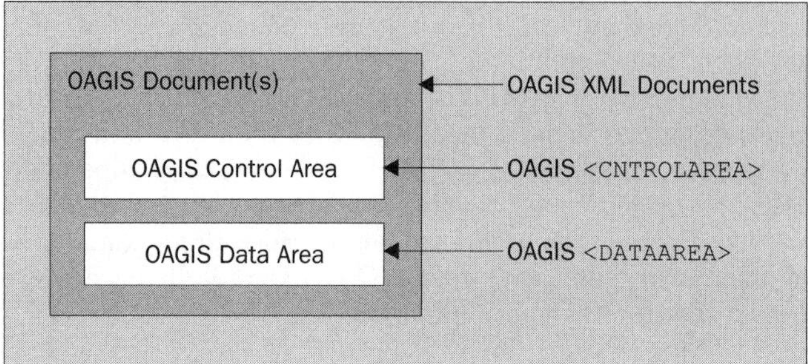


As can be seen, OAGIS documents use a <CNTROLAREA> element for messaging information. Including this within each BOD gives the potential for duplication of data within every message sent as an ebXML payload. If we look inside this element we can see where some of these duplications may be found.

Within the <CNTROLAREA> element, there is a <BSR> (business service request) element containing <VERB>, <NOUN>, and <VERSION> values for the given transaction type. The BSR defines the action that the sender application wants the receiver application to perform. In addition, <SENDER> and <DATETIME> elements are also contained in the <CNTROLAREA> element.

By using the following fragment, we can see that the <CNTROLAREA> element has several data items that may overlap with those used by the ebMS <MessageHeader> element:

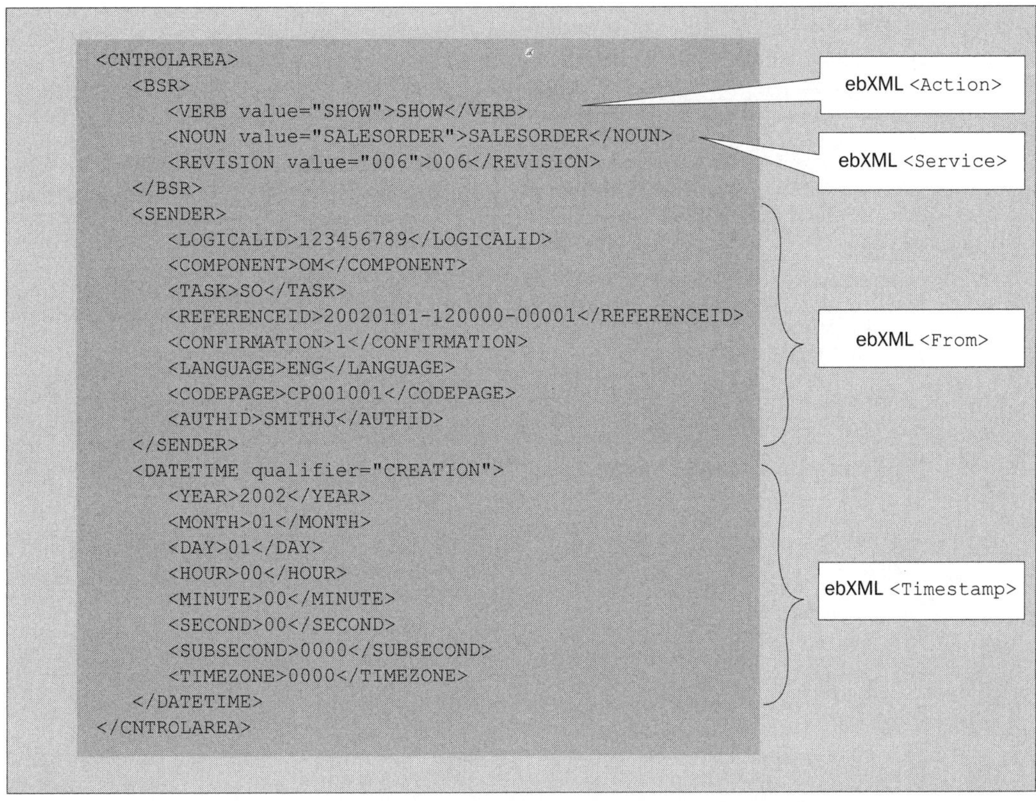
<CNTROLAREA>
<BSR>
<VERB value="SHOW">SHOW</VERB>
<NOUN value="SALESORDER">SALESORDER</NOUN>
<REVISION value="006">006</REVISION>
</BSR>
<SENDER>
<LOGICALID>123456789</LOGICALID>
<COMPONENT>OM</COMPONENT>
<TASK>SO</TASK>
<REFERENCEID>20020101-120000-00001</REFERENCEID>
<CONFIRMATION>1</CONFIRMATION>
<LANGUAGE>ENG</LANGUAGE>
<CODEPAGE>CP001001</CODEPAGE>
<AUTHID>SMITHJ</AUTHID>
</SENDER>
<DATETIME qualifier="CREATION">
<YEAR>2002</YEAR>
<MONTH>01</MONTH>
<DAY>01</DAY>
<HOUR>00</HOUR>
<MINUTE>00</MINUTE>
<SECOND>00</SECOND>
<SUBSECOND>0000</SUBSECOND>
<TIMEZONE>0000</TIMEZONE>
</DATETIME>
</CNTROLAREA>
ebXML <Action>
ebXML <Service>
ebXML <From>
ebXML <Timestamp>

Some of these elements may have a direct correlation with each other. For example, the <LOGICALID>, has the same value here that we would expect to find in the <PartyId> element of the ebXML <MessageHeader>.

Even where some of these values have a less direct correlation, it should be feasible to deduce one set of values from the other. For example, we can map the value atttributes of both the <VERB> element and the <NOUN> element to the equivalent ebMS <MessageHeader> elements, <Service> and <Action>.

Once these relationships have been recognized, the diligent developer should insure these values stay synchronized.

## Interoperability and OAGIS

Currently OAGIS does not define many of the documents used in our case study scenario. Therefore, we shall use the nearest structural equivalent, the 'Show Sales Order' BOD (revision 006), for explanatory purposes. The following is an example of this BOD:

```
<SHOW_SALESORDER_006>
   <CNTROLAREA>
      <BSR>
         <VERB value="SHOW">SHOW</VERB>
         <NOUN value="SALESORDER">SALESORDER</NOUN>
```

```
            <REVISION value="006">006</REVISION>
        </BSR>
        <SENDER>
            <LOGICALID>123456789</LOGICALID>
            <COMPONENT>OM</COMPONENT>
            <TASK>SO</TASK>
            <REFERENCEID>20020101-120000-00001</REFERENCEID>
            <CONFIRMATION>1</CONFIRMATION>
            <LANGUAGE>ENG</LANGUAGE>
            <CODEPAGE>CP001001</CODEPAGE>
            <AUTHID>SMITHJ</AUTHID>
        </SENDER>
        <DATETIME qualifier="CREATION">
            <YEAR>2002</YEAR>
            <MONTH>01</MONTH>
            <DAY>01</DAY>
            <HOUR>00</HOUR>
            <MINUTE>00</MINUTE>
            <SECOND>00</SECOND>
            <SUBSECOND>0000</SUBSECOND>
            <TIMEZONE>0000</TIMEZONE>
        </DATETIME>
    </CNTROLAREA>
    <DATAAREA>
        <SHOW_SALESORDER>
            <SOHEADER>
                <SALESORDID>S0001</SALESORDID>
                <SALESORG index="1">ORG12345</SALESORG>
                <PARTNER>
                    <NAME index="1">CIMBALI</NAME>
                    <ONETIME>0</ONETIME>
                    <PARTNRID>CIM001</PARTNRID>
                    <PARTNRTYPE>INTERNATIONAL</PARTNRTYPE>
                </PARTNER>
                <SALESINFO>
                    <SALESORG index="1">SO_EASTCOAST</SALESORG>
                    <SALESPERSN>BOB</SALESPERSN>
                </SALESINFO>
            </SOHEADER>
            <SOLINE>
                <QUANTITY qualifier="ORDERED">
                    <VALUE>1</VALUE>
                    <NUMOFDEC>0</NUMOFDEC>
                    <SIGN>+</SIGN>
                    <UOM>EACH</UOM>
                </QUANTITY>
                <SOLINENUM>1</SOLINENUM>
                <DESCRIPTN>ESPRESSO MACHINE</DESCRIPTN>
                <ROUTINGID>100</ROUTINGID>
                <SUBSFLAG>0</SUBSFLAG>
                <UPC>000012121212</UPC>
            </SOLINE>
        </SHOW_SALESORDER>
    </DATAAREA>
</SHOW_SALESORDER_006>
```

Firstly, we should note that the `<CNTROLAREA>` may contain values related to the ebXML BPSS. For example, the `<VERB>` and `<NOUN>` elements may also relate to the value for the `<BusinessTransaction>` element within the BPSS.

Secondly, the application layer data elements such as `<PARTNER>` and `<QUANTITY>` use fixed tag names. Applications processing these messages will need to understand the semantics and context of these tag names.

Finally, the elements `<SALESORD>` and `<PRTNRID>` have values that presumably relate to code sets within the individual business processes. All applications processing this data will need access to these code sets.

To use their own phrase, the OAGI has been "good citizens" in their involvement with ebXML. Recently, they announced their intention to work towards convergence with the core components effort by initially adopting the ebXML naming conventions for XML tags and by cross-referencing OAGIS XML tags to the UID in the core components specification.

One the basis of such statements, it is feasible that these two initiatives will be closely aligned in the future.

# RosettaNet

RosettaNet (http://www.rosettanet.org/), like OAGI, is an industry consortium. However, RosettaNet's approach is to provide a broader range of standardization within a narrower field of application, namely the high-technology and computer components industries. The RosettaNet model spans three areas:

- Message exchange protocols – known as the **RosettaNet Implementation Framework** (**RNIF**).
- Process definitions – known as **Partner Interface Processes** (**PIPs**).
- Industry-specific data sets – such as partner and product codes used in payload content.

## *Message Integrity and the RosettaNet Implementation Framework (RNIF)*

The RosettaNet Implementation Framework, or RNIF, defines XML documents for specifying the transport, routing, and packaging of business data. The current version of RNIF (validated 02.00.00), has been expanded to include features for security, signaling, and trading partner agreements.

RosettaNet separates its messages into distinct XML documents consisting of a `<Preamble>`, `<DeliveryHeader>`, `<ServiceHeader>`, and `<ServiceContent>`, which are packaged as related MIME-encoded messages. The following diagram shows this structure:

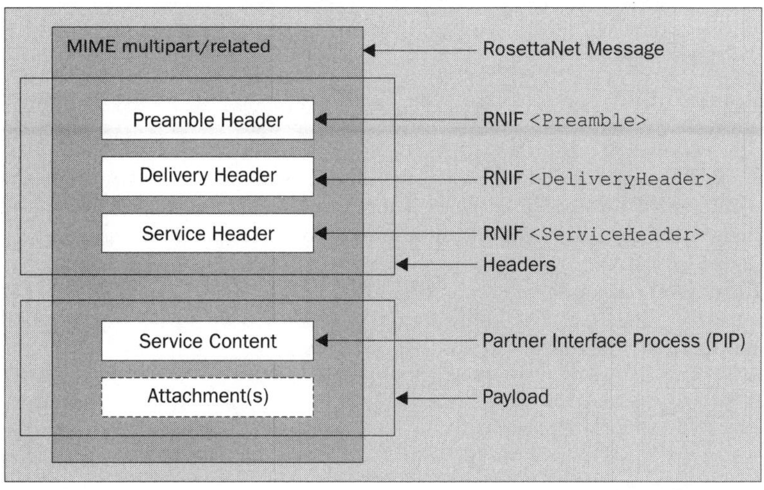

Despite outward appearances, RosettaNet and ebXML have followed similar philosophies with the architecture of their messaging services. Most importantly for our examination, this means RosettaNet payloads have been designed without any message control data. This avoids the likelihood of conflict and duplication of the sort we discovered within OAGIS messages. One can simply transport RosettaNet payloads within ebXML Message Services transparently.

However, there is a possibility that an entire "RosettaNet message" may be used as the payload in an ebXML environment. In this case, we are faced with similar issues to those with the OAGIS BODs. The RNIF `<DeliveryHeader>` and `<ServiceHeader>` elements both contain data that duplicates that of the ebMS layer. The following fragment contains a number of overlaps between a sample RosettaNet `<DeliveryHeader>` element and various equivalent ebMS elements:

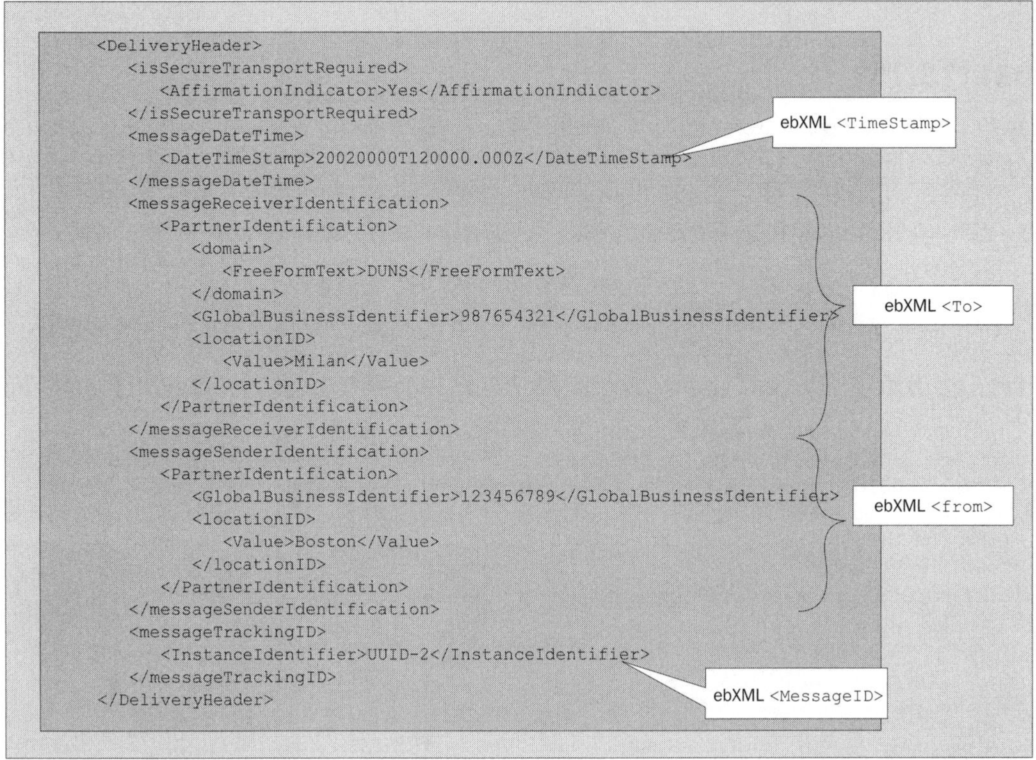

```
<DeliveryHeader>
   <isSecureTransportRequired>
      <AffirmationIndicator>Yes</AffirmationIndicator>
   </isSecureTransportRequired>
   <messageDateTime>
      <DateTimeStamp>20020000T120000.000Z</DateTimeStamp>
   </messageDateTime>
   <messageReceiverIdentification>
      <PartnerIdentification>
         <domain>
            <FreeFormText>DUNS</FreeFormText>
         </domain>
         <GlobalBusinessIdentifier>987654321</GlobalBusinessIdentifier>
         <locationID>
            <Value>Milan</Value>
         </locationID>
      </PartnerIdentification>
   </messageReceiverIdentification>
   <messageSenderIdentification>
      <PartnerIdentification>
         <GlobalBusinessIdentifier>123456789</GlobalBusinessIdentifier>
         <locationID>
            <Value>Boston</Value>
         </locationID>
      </PartnerIdentification>
   </messageSenderIdentification>
   <messageTrackingID>
      <InstanceIdentifier>UUID-2</InstanceIdentifier>
   </messageTrackingID>
</DeliveryHeader>
```



In addition, the RNIF `<ServiceHeader>` has a `<GlobalBusinessActionCode>` that equates to the `<Service>` within ebXML Message Services. Therefore, in situations where an entire RosettaNet message is being exchanged, these values will also need synchronizing.

Fortunately, RosettaNet has announced intention to publish RNIF version 3.0 as an ebXML Message Services-compliant specification. The following quote is taken from a press release published by RosettaNet on http://www.rosettanet.org/, on April 25, 2001:

*"RosettaNet today announced its intent to support the ebXML Messaging Service Specification for the secure transfer, routing and packaging (TRP) of electronic information. Future releases of RosettaNet's Implementation Framework (RNIF), which serves as a guide for e-business process development and implementation, will include support for the ebXML Messaging Service Specification, in an effort to achieve interoperability goals across industries. "*

This leaves the issue of application interoperability with RosettaNet payloads. To appreciate this, we'll need to examine the philosophy behind the RosettaNet's PIPs.

## Interoperability and Partner Interface Processes (PIPs)

RosettaNet's PIPs are XML-based documents that define business processes between trading partners. This is somewhat analogous to the business process models produced by applying the ebXML Business Process Specification Schema. Each PIP specification includes a description of the business document(s) to be exchanged (including the data elements involved), together with a business process definition (including an information flow diagram which describes the choreography of these documents).

The individual business documents involved in a PIP are exchanged in a container that packs together other related entities such as headers, attachments, and digital signatures. Refering back to the RosettaNet message structure diagram, we can see that this container is known as a **RosettaNet message**.

The true "payload" is the business content described by the service header; it comprises the service content and any optional attachments. In terms of interoperability issues, we will focus our attention on this content.

RosettaNet categorizes two types of content used in its PIPs: **signal messages**, which are effectively one-way and require no response, and **action messages**, which initiate a dialog of document exchanges. For example, a signal message may provide notification of a catalog item change, whereas an action message may place an order on that item.

*It should be noted that these are actions required by the applications processing the data, rather than responses (such as delivery acknowledgments) that may be required from a message handling system.*

The specifications for data elements used in any payload are constructed from components taken from either the RosettaNet technical component dictionary (for Information Technology components) or the RosettaNet business property dictionary. These are available from RosettaNet at http://www.rosettanet.org/.

RosettaNet publishes the syntax of these messages as XML DTDs. However, to encourage greater interoperability, RosettaNet also describes the semantics involved using PIP specification documents. These PIPs define the business process definitions, purposes, process flows, start and end dates, partner role descriptions, and business process activity controls, as well as the actual business data to be exchanged.

For example, here is the UML sequence diagram taken from the PIP for 'Notify of Advance Shipment' (PIP3B2). The 'Advance Shipment Notification' contains information on when a product was shipped, its expected date of arrival, how the product shipped, and details of its contents:

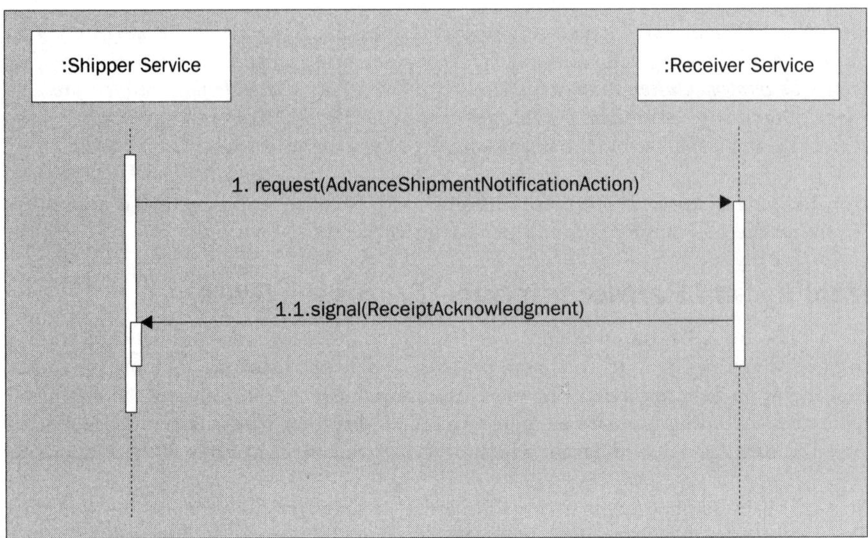


This PIP document, in turn, references the DTD for `<Pip3B2AdvanceShipmentNotification>`, a fragment of which is shown here:

```
<!ELEMENT Pip3B2AdvanceShipmentNotification (AdvancedShipmentNotification,
                                             fromRole,
                                             GlobalDocumentFunctionCode,
                                             thisDocumentGenerationDateTime,
                                             thisDocumentIdentifier,
                                             toRole)>
<!ELEMENT AdvancedShipmentNotification (BuyingPartner,
                                        OriginatingPartner,
                                        SellingPartner,
                                        Shipment)>
<!ELEMENT BuyingPartner (purchasedBy)>
<!ELEMENT purchasedBy (PartnerDescription)>
<!ELEMENT PartnerDescription (BusinessDescription,
                              ContactInformation?,
                              GlobalPartnerClassificationCode? )>
<!ELEMENT BusinessDescription (GlobalBusinessIdentifier,
                               NationalBusinessTaxIdentifier?,
                               RegionalBusinessTaxIdentifier?,
                               GlobalSupplyChainCode?)>
<!ELEMENT GlobalBusinessIdentifier (#PCDATA)>
<!ELEMENT NationalBusinessTaxIdentifier (BusinessTaxIdentifier,
                                         GlobalCountryCode)>
<!ELEMENT BusinessTaxIdentifier (#PCDATA)>
<!ELEMENT GlobalCountryCode (#PCDATA)>
<!ELEMENT RegionalBusinessTaxIdentifier (BusinessTaxIdentifier,
                                         regionName)>
<!ELEMENT regionName (FreeFormText)>
```

To better understand these elements, we can examine their corresponding definitions in the RosettaNet business property dictionary. For example, the <GlobalDocumentFunctionCode> and <GlobalPartnerClassificationCode> elements are defined as:

```
<FundamentalBusinessDataEntities>
   <NAME>GlobalDocumentFunctionCode</NAME>
   <DEFINITION>
      Code identifying the function of a document as either a request
      or a response.
   </DEFINITION>
   <Type>String</Type>
   <Min>1</Min>
   <Max/>
   <Repr/>
</FundamentalBusinessDataEntities>
```

```
<FundamentalBusinessDataEntities>
   <NAME>GlobalPartnerClassificationCode</NAME>
   <DEFINITION>
      Code identifying a partner's function in the supply chain.
   </DEFINITION>
   <Type>String</Type>
   <Min>1</Min>
   <Max/>
   <Repr/>
</FundamentalBusinessDataEntities>
```

Using the above architecture, RosettaNet follows the philosophy of ebXML. At the risk of appearing impudent, we could view RosettaNet as an early prototype implementation of an ebXML framework!

The similarity of the RosettaNet PIPs to the ebXML BPSS, and of the RosettaNet property dictionaries to ebXML core components, would indicate that convergence of these two initiatives is technically feasible, advantageous and likely, at some stage in the future.

# The XML Common Business Library (xCBL)

The **XML Common Business Library** (**xCBL** – see http://www.xcbl.org/) is a set of XML business documents and its associated components library, developed by Commerce One. The xCBL philosophy is to encourage users to utilize the xCBL component library when building their own specific business documents.

The designers of xCBL attempted to exploit the semantic knowledge of existing EDI standards such as ASC X12 and UN/EDIFACT and the investment many organizations already made in this technology. The current version, xCBL 3.0, has been jointly developed with SAP and has the support of Microsoft, Sun, and Compaq.

*We'll cover both EDI standards, ASC X12 and UN/EDIFACT, later in this chapter.*

In XML terms, xCBL tends to be element-focused, rather than attribute-focused. This leads to some lengthy and deep document structures, as can be seen in this example fragment from the xCBL 3.0 'Advanced Shipment Notice':

```
<AdvanceShipmentNotice>
   <ASNHeader>
      <ASNNumber>
         <Reference>
            <RefNum>ASN:00-1</RefNum>
         </Reference>
      </ASNNumber>
      <ASNIssueDate>20020101T00:00:00</ASNIssueDate>
      <ASNOrderNumber>
         <BuyerOrderNumber>000000001</BuyerOrderNumber>
      </ASNOrderNumber>
      <ASNPurpose>
         <ASNPurposeCoded>Original</ASNPurposeCoded>
      </ASNPurpose>
      <ASNType>
         <ASNTypeCoded>Actual</ASNTypeCoded>
      </ASNType>
      <ASNStatus>
         <ASNStatusCoded>CompleteOrder</ASNStatusCoded>
      </ASNStatus>
      <ASNCurrency>
         <Currency>
            <CurrencyCoded>LRE</CurrencyCoded>
         </Currency>
      </ASNCurrency>
      <ASNLanguage>
      <Language>
         <LanguageCoded>en</LanguageCoded>
      </Language>
      </ASNLanguage>
      <ASNDates>
         <DeliveryDate>20020102T09:00:00</DeliveryDate>
      </ASNDates>
      <ASNParty>
         <OrderParty>
            <BuyerParty>
               <Party>
                  <NameAddress>
                     <Name1>Central Perk</Name1>
                     <POBox POBoxPostalCode="249"></POBox>
                     <PostalCode>20012</PostalCode>
                     <City>Boston</City>
                     <Region>
                        <RegionCoded>USNY</RegionCoded>
                     </Region>
                  </NameAddress>
               </Party>
            </BuyerParty>
         </OrderParty>
      </ASNParty>
   </ASNHeader>
</AdvanceShipmentNotice>
```

From this we can see how we have to traverse the `OrderParty/BuyerParty/Party/NameAddress` path to get to the actual `<Name1>` element which holds the name of the party ordering the goods. This is probably indicative of xCBL's EDI origins.

Another feature of xCBL is that it does not concern itself with any messaging control data. The minor exception to this is the xCBL component, `<MessageID>`, which may be used for message audit and control information. Here is a sample fragment of this element:

```
<ListofMessageID>
   <MessageID>
      <IDNumber>UUID-1</IDNumber>
      <IDAssignedBy>
         <IDAssignedByCoded>PurchaseManager</IDAssignedByCoded>
      </IDAssignedBy>
   </MessageID>
</ListofMessageID>
```

From this, it would appear that the xCBL `<IDNumber>` element is the same as the ebXML `<MessageId>` element. Fortunately, this element appears only as an optional component within the one xCBL element (`<OrderNumber>`).

Therefore, in terms of message integrity, it is a straightforward task to encapsulate any xCBL document as part of the ebXML message payload.

xCBL's support for ebXML business process models and core component libraries lies in the convergence of the two initiatives. Currently, xCBL 3.0 provides some basic business patterns which could be implemented as ebXML business process models. Also, as with RosettaNet, the xCBL component libraries have the potential to be aligned with any emerging ebXML Core Components definitions. Indeed, given Commerce One's involvement with the Core Components work of ebXML, it is safe to assume that future versions of will evolve in an ebXML-compliant way.

From the brief examinations of OAGIS, RosettaNet, and xCBL, we can see that several XML-based initiatives are converging on ebXML core components and business process modeling as a means of achieving interoperability.

The missing piece in this strategy is the specification in an XML vocabulary of what ebXML core components will look like. As has been discussed, if the ebXML core components are syntax-neutral, developers will need a set of XML grammatical components that will allow them to unambiguously identify the business documents to be exchanged in a particular business context. To provide this, a **Universal Business Language** (**UBL**) Technical Committee has recently been established by OASIS.

## UBL

The **Universal Business Language**, from OASIS (http://oasis-open.org/committees/ubl/), will be a synthesis of existing XML business document libraries.

The aims of the UBL are to develop an internationally-recognized set of XML grammatical components that will allow trading partners to identify the business documents to be exchanged in a particular business context.

The project is starting from a set of mutually agreed-upon changes to xCBL 3.0 based on industry experience with other XML and EDI business libraries. These will be harmonized as far as practical with the ebXML specifications.

The first task is to align the vocabulary and structures of UBL with the work of the ebXML Core Components initiative and with the vocabulary and structures of other existing business libraries, such as RosettaNet and OAGIS.

The second phase will be to implement a mechanism for the generation of context-specific schemas for basic business documents and their components through the application of transformation rules to a common XML source library.

## EDI-derived Vocabularies

Chapter 12 describes in some detail how groups such as XEDI.org are recasting EDI directories into XML syntax. In the case given this is based on the ANSI ASC X12 standard, but similar attempts are underway for UN/EDIFACT directories as well.

However, whilst such a strategy may be intellectually satisfying, it is difficult to see what attraction this will have to those wishing to implement e-commerce. The risk with adopting these vocabularies is the potential loss of interoperability strengths of XML and inheritance of the restrictions of EDI syntaxes. For example, EDI standards tend to be very comprehensive, generic definitions of structured data messages. In practice, these standard messages are not used *per se*. Instead, customized subsets, known as **message implementation guidelines**, are used to specify the precise structure of the data to be exchanged. It is these customized messages that determine the interoperability of EDI systems, not the official standards themselves. This has led to an enormous number of incompatible implementations, even based on the same EDI standard. Changing syntax to XML will not avoid this problem.

Many EDI practitioners have recognized the need to think beyond using yet another syntax when developing e-commerce applications. Hopefully, the work of ebXML Core Components and its various implementation projects will circumvent unnecessary investment in these strategies.

# Integrating ebXML with EDI Payloads

Despite its poor press of late, **Electronic Data Interchange** (**EDI**) systems have at least helped define the problems of e-business, even if they haven't given us very appealing solutions. Given that EDI has a global knowledgebase of 30 years experience, it is not surprising that companies such as Commerce One choose to base their xCBL vocabulary on this semantic knowledge. Furthermore, EDI systems are well established in many larger enterprises and so are likely to remain as legacy systems for some time.

Therefore, it is likely that at some point someone will want to use EDI messages as part of their ebXML payloads. As with XML-based documents, the issues of message integrity and data interoperability still apply.

We shall focus our EDI discussion on the two dominant standards: the United Nation's UN/EDIFACT (http://www.unece.org/trade/untdid/) and the American National Standards Institute Accredited Standards Committee's (ANSI ASC) X12 (http://www.x12.org). Both share similar architectures, although varying syntaxes.

## UN/EDIFACT

First, **UN/EDIFACT** (ISO 9735) has been around since 1988 and was developed mainly from the European GTDI standard. Managed by the United Nations, it is the global standard for EDI. As an EDI standard it is entirely data-centric and does not formally describe the processes their messages participate in. The overall structure used by UN/EDIFACT is given in the following diagram:

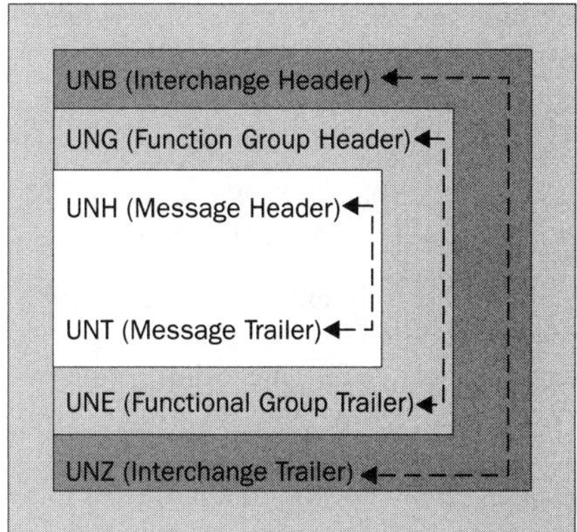


From this we can see the three levels of hierarchy (**interchange**, **functional group**, and **message**) and the EDIFACT "tags" (UNB–UNZ, UNG–UNE, and UNH–UNT) used to mark the start (header) and end (trailer) of each section. These sections are nested, in that each may repeat inside the outer section. That is, an interchange may contain many functional groups and each functional group may contain many messages.

The message service layer information is carried primarily in the interchange and functional group "headers". One communication exchange should always contain only one interchange. This may contain several functional groups. Different functional groups are used to encapsulate different message types. For example, using our P&SI case study scenario, one interchange between our coffee shop and the overseas inspection service may contain several 'Request for Inspection' messages and a single 'Purchase Order' message. The response may include several 'Inspection Status' messages and an 'Invoice' message. In both cases, each message type would be contained in its own functional group.

Once again, because UN/EDIFACT is designed to be message service-independent, the UNB–UNZ, UNG–UNE, and UNH–UNT envelopes are likely to contain details very similar to those used by the ebXML Message Service. Here is an example of a UN/EDIFACT interchange:

```
UNB+UNOA:1+123456789:DN+987654321:DN+020101:010100+UUID2++INSREQ+X+1+NOCPA+1'
UNH+1000003+INSREQ:D:01A:UN:EX01'
BGM+610+1001+1'
DTM+137:200201011200:203'
NAD+CN++IMPEX DUESSELDORF GMBH:57 KOENIGSTRASSE:ALTSTADT DUESSELDORF 4000 GERMANY'
DOC+700+:21+EI'
UNT+6+1000003'
UNZ+1+UUID2'
```

*Note that the +, : and ' characters are used here as data field delimiters*

For our discussion we shall focus on the interchange header segment, the `UNB`. This example translates as follows:

| UN/EDIFACT | Description | ebXML Equivalent |
|---|---|---|
| `UNB` | Is the segment tag code. | |
| `UNOA:1` | Identifies version 1, level A of the syntax rules and Controlling Agency UNO. | |
| `123456789:DN` | Identifies the sender of the transmission in code with a qualifier of `DN` (Data Universal Numbering Systems, or D-U-N-S) to identify the code set being used. | `From/PartyId` |
| `987654321:DN` | Identifies the recipient of the transmission in code (qualified by `DN`), plus a subaddress code. The subaddress code for onward routing may be used if the functional grouping facility, (which also provides for sub-ddressing), is not used. | `To/PartyId` |
| `020101:010100` | `020101` is the date and `010100` is the time of the preparation of the transmission. This is the date/time that the interchange is assembled for transmission. | `MessageData/Timestamp` |
| `UUID2` | Is the unique interchange control reference for this transmission, allocated by the sender of the interchange. | `MessageData/MessageId` |
| `INSREQ` | Is an example of an application reference. | `Service` |
| `X` | Is a processing priority code, using a code defined in the Interchange Agreement. | |
| `1` | Indicates that the sender is requesting an acknowledgment for the interchange. | |
| `NOCPA` | Is an example of a code specified in the Interchange Agreement, which identifies the type of communications agreement under which the interchange is controlled, (or left blank if not used). | `CPAId` |
| `1` | Indicates that this is a test transmission. The field is set to zero for transmission of live data. | |

As with our XML-based payloads, these field values should be synchronized with the ebXML Message Service elements. The use of interchanges and group structures is not strictly enforced by many EDI networks and software interfaces. Therefore, it is possible that only the `UNH` messages themselves are exchanged. In any case, both the `UNG` (if used) and `UNH` data fields may also contain messaging control and reference data that should be checked.

## ANSI ASC X12

Here is our familiar structure diagram, this time for **ASC X12** interchanges:

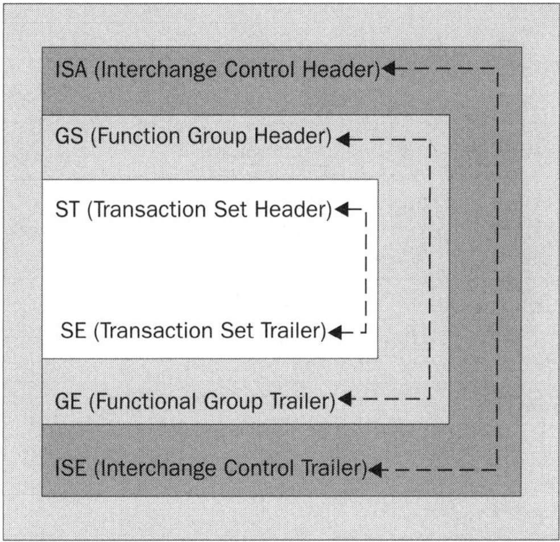


Apart from its use of different tag names, this resembles the structure of UN/EDIFACT. As you would expect, ASC X12 also contains similar message control information in its `ISA-ISE`, `GS-GE` and `ST-SE` envelopes. As can be seen from the following fragment, the same concepts apply as we saw with UN/EDIFACT:

```
ISA*00*KNOCKKNOCK*00**DN*123456789*DN*987654321*020101*1200*U*00200*000000002*0*P*
>
GS*SN*8888888*123456789*020101*1538*000000043*X*003010
ST*856*0001
BSN*00*12345*921225*111559*0001
HL*1**S
NTE*DEL*020
TD1*CTN25*256****G*160*KG
N1*ST**92*020
HL*2*1*0
PRF*90056459-R10***921207
TD1*CTN25*20
TD5******CC
REF*IA*987456
PKG*S*36*VI*P02
MAN*GM*98765432101111222333
HL*4*3*I
LIN**EN*9398500041331
SN1**12*EA
HL*7*2*P
PKG*S*36*VI*P02
MAN*GM*98765432102222111333
HL*8*7*I
CTT*11
SE*46*0001
GE*1*000000043
IEA*1*000000043
```

*Note: here, the * character is used as a data field delimiter. The field numbers count across, so `ISA06` follows the sixth * character in the ISA segment.*

The following codes are used:

| Code | Description | ebXML Equivalent |
|---|---|---|
| ISA01 | Authorization Information Qualifier | |
| ISA02 | Authorization Information | |
| ISA03 | Security Information Qualifier | |
| ISA04 | Security Information | |
| ISA05 | Interchange ID Qualifier | |
| ISA06 | Interchange Sender | From/PartyId |
| ISA07 | Interchange ID Qualifier | |
| ISA08 | Interchange Receiver ID | To/PartyId |
| ISA09 | Interchange Date | ISA09 and ISA10 are equivalent to MessageData/Timestamp |
| ISA10 | Interchange Time | |
| ISA11 | Interchange Standards ID | |
| ISA12 | Interchange Version ID | |
| ISA13 | Interchange Control Number | |
| ISA14 | Acknowledge Requested | deliveryReceiptRequested |
| ISA15 | Test Indicator | |
| ISA16 | Subelement Separator | |

As with UN/EDIFACT, the use of interchanges and groups structures is not strictly enforced by many EDI networks and software interfaces. Therefore, it is possible that only the transaction sets themselves are exchanged. In any case, both the `GS` and `ST` data fields may also contain messaging control and reference data that will need examination.

# Mixed Payloads

Up to now, we have concentrated on examining isolated cases of non-ebXML payloads. However, experience tells us that in practice we are likely to encounter a hybrid of varying documents formats and standards. A valuable example of this is best described by referring to the ebXML Proof of Concept demonstration scenario.

# The ebXML Proof of Concept Scenario

As part of the ebXML standards development process, a parallel stream known as the **Proof of Concept team** was established to implement ebXML specifications as they were emerging, and to assist in the development of these standards by testing their strength when coding real world applications.

The end product of this was a sophisticated implementation involving a range of varying payloads. These involved 32 different organizations (including industry and software vendors) in three different business cases. The 'Procurement' scenario involved seven different roles exchanging seven different types of payloads. Some of these have been discussed in this chapter. The processes involved were modeled using the ebXML BPSS and these, together with the relevant CPPs were registered in (and subsequently discovered from) an ebXML registry.

These are described in the following diagram:

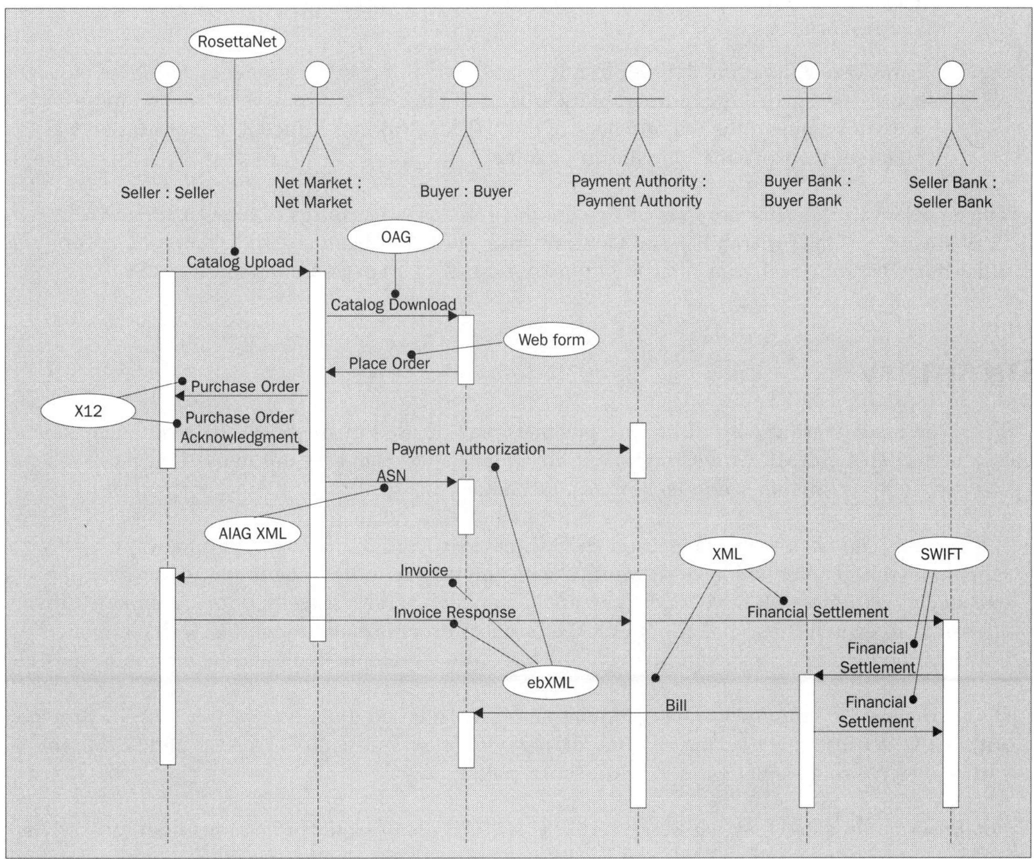

This business process model illustrates the process of purchasing using a third-party intermediary, in this case a Net Market provider. The Seller party has uploaded their product catalog details to the Net Market, from whence the Buyer downloads their required item details and produces a purchase order. Once the Seller acknowledges the order, the Net Market requests payment authorization from the party responsible for paying for the goods (perhaps the Buyer's head office or a credit agency). After the Net Market generates a shipping notice advising the goods are dispatched, the Seller sends their Invoice. This triggers a sequence of exchanges between the Buyer's bank and the Seller's bank resulting in a bill being presented to the Buyer.

From a messaging perspective, there are a few points to make with this scenario:

- The demonstration proved the technical infrastructure of ebXML – that is, that the message services, registry interfaces, collaboration protocols, and specification schema could support a reasonably complex and realistic business scenario.
- The demonstration proved that this infrastructure could carry a range of different payloads in various formats.
- However, without the definitions and specification of core components that these payloads could reference, the interoperability aspects of the ebXML framework remain unproven. Therefore, one of the major values of the ebXML Proof of Concept demonstration was to highlight the work that remains to be done.

The excellent work of this group is being continued under the auspices of the OASIS ebXML Implementation, Interoperability and Conformance Technical Committee. For more details on this and other demonstration scenarios refer to http://www.oasis-open.org/committees/ebxml-iic/.

# Summary

There are many reasons why alternative payloads may be used in an ebXML environment, such as the lack of available ebXML Core Component libraries, the fact that they are in use in legacy systems already, and possibly other non-technical inducements.

It is not only *legitimate* to exchange non-ebXML payloads within the ebXML framework, it is *encouraged.* Hopefully, this chapter will have shown that with careful attention to the message integrity, the exchanging of non-ebXML payloads is an area where ebXML Message Services is 'do-able'. If you choose to go even further, and adopt ebXML business process models together with component libraries, then future interoperability with ebXML Core Components should be a smooth transition.

In this chapter we examined some commonly-used XML-based initiatives such as OAGI, RosettaNet, and xCBL. We also saw how the EDI standard payloads, such as UN/EDIFACT and ANSI ASC X12, can be integrated in similar ways to XML-based messages.

Finally we commented that, whilst the recent ebXML Proof of Concept demonstration proved the technical infrastructure of ebXML and its ability to carry diverse types of payloads, it also emphasized that the work of standardizing on core components still needs to be done.

The missing piece in this strategy is the specification in an XML vocabulary of what ebXML Core Components will look like. Hopefully, the work of groups such as the OASIS UBL project will avoid this fragmentation of XML vocabularies and provide the practical basis for such ebXML-compliant documents.

# 12

# Using XML/EDI Message Payload Content

To summarize what we have seen of the ITT (International Trade Transaction) case so far in this book, the business collaborations that make up the ITT case are executed as a series of message exchanges over the ebXML messaging service. The CPA document associates these exchanges with collaborations and business transaction activities in a BPSS document. The BPSS document in turn associates business transactions to externally specified business document schemas. These schemas are to be used as notation for the message payload. As we saw in Chapter 10, the actual message formats are not in the scope of any of the ebXML technical specifications, but are discussed in the technical reports produced by the Core Components working group.

Depending on the type of applications or projects you are working on, you can adopt various strategies for the design of these messages. You can:

- Reuse an existing XML vocabulary, such as the ones described in Chapter 5. Some of these are mature and cover common business processes.
- Track the progress of the work of the ebXML Core Components team, and adopt their results as they become available. Chapter 10 provides a discussion and a practical approach to this strategy.
- Develop and implement an (entirely or partly) *ad hoc* XML vocabulary, specific to the project in question.
- Derive XML Schemas from UML models of the information to be encoded in some (partly) automatic fashion.

Another source for definitions of message payload content is existing EDI message sets. Chapter 11 has provided an overview of the X12 and UN/EDIFACT message formats and shown how they relate to the ebXML framework. The bodies that maintain these standards also provide extensive libraries of existing business messages. These EDI message libraries are potentially relevant for many e-business projects, because they are very comprehensive and have been proven to work successfully in high-volume production systems. UN/EDIFACT, in particular:

- covers many message types not covered by any XML-based framework (for instance, it provides ten times more message types than xCBL).
- has been fine-tuned over many years to cover the requirements of real-life production systems, and takes details into account that are easy to oversee if you start from scratch.
- is aimed at international commerce and has many refinements for differences in legal and financial systems globally that are unaccounted for in many national standards.

Therefore, if you familiarize yourself with EDI syntax and become aware of the vast libraries of EDI message specifications, you open up a major source of information for ebXML (or other e-business) applications. At present, no XML-based e-business framework beats EDI in terms of coverage of business processes and market validation by successful high-volume production systems.

If you find a message in one of these directories, you could use it in one of two ways:

- You can use the EDI notation as payload in an ebXML infrastructure. This might be a first step in opening up an existing EDI infrastructure, where you use the ebXML transport layers to transport EDI content.
- You can also adopt the "semantics" of the EDI message, but use an XML-based format to express this content instead of the EDI notation.

You can transport information in native EDI format because ebXML messages can carry arbitrary MIME-encoded content. The ebXML documents don't explore this option, however approaches to transporting EDI content using the public Internet are described at the IETF *Electronic Data Interchange-Internet Integration* page. IETF RFC 1767, *MIME Encapsulation of EDI Objects*, provides a description of the applicable Content-Types for EDI. Base64 encoding would be needed, so that non-printable EDI delimiters don't violate MIME's encoding conventions.

> *The two documents mentioned above can be found at http://www.ietf.org/html.charters/ediint-charter.html and http://www.ietf.org/rfc/rfc1767.txt.*

The second approach is more interesting for projects where you don't want to use non-XML formats, but want to benefit from the EDI libraries as much as possible. In this chapter we will look at two strategies to do this, and will show how this would work in practice by applying it to a specific message type. As this book assumes familiarity with XML but not with EDI, we will first provide a brief introduction to the EDI syntax, focusing on the UN/EDIFACT standard. The sample we will use is the "Inspection Request Message" defined by the UN/EDIFACT `INSREQ` message type (see http://www.unece.org/trade/untdid/d01a/trmd/insreq_c.htm). In the ITT case, such an inspection can be requested as one of the final activities in the 'Prepare for Export' stage.

The `INSREQ` message type is just one of a very large number of messages specified in the UN/EDIFACT D01A (First Draft of 2001) Directory, accessible on-line at http://www.unece.org/trade/untdid/directory.htm.

*Note that at this point we are not providing a technical or business justification for moving (or not moving) from EDI notation to XML, in case your project is with an organization that already uses EDI, but are focusing on the practical issue of designing an XML notation that is capable of re-encoding the knowledge of e-business processes and business information embedded in the EDIFACT message specification.*

# UN/EDIFACT Syntax

To understand an EDIFACT message specification, first of all you need an understanding of its syntax, which in turn requires you to know some terminology for syntactic constructs. EDIFACT syntax is quite cryptic, as you'll see in a while, but actually not very complex. We'll describe this in a bottom-up fashion:

- A **simple data element** consists of a single data element value.
- A **composite data element** consists of two or more component data elements.
- A **segment** consists of stand-alone data elements and/or composite data elements. It is identified by the first data element, called the **segment tag**.
- A **segment group** consists of exactly one **trigger segment** of a particular type, optionally followed by other segments or segment groups.
- A **message** consists of segments or groups of segments.

Note that the EDI term *element* is not to be confused with the XML term *element.* EDIFACT messages, segment groups, segments, and composite data elements specify the position of each of their children, indicate whether they are optional or mandatory, and set a limit on the number of occurrences.

*When referring to EDI `elements`, we will write them in code style, but without the pointy brackets, as opposed to XML `<element>`s.*

All EDIFACT messages share a common header/trailer structure that provides an envelope for the message payload body. This envelope is discussed in Chapter 11, so we can focus on the message body in this chapter. The "Interchange" and "Function Group" wrapper for the actual message include a formal encoding of the message type. This allows an EDIFACT message handler to unambiguously identify the type and purpose of a message and process its content accordingly.

The following fragment from the `INSREQ` Inspection Request Message definition identifies a segment group with two segments. The first, and trigger, segment is the `CTA` (contact information) segment:

```
Pos    Tag Name                                          S   R
0170       ----- Segment group 6  ------------------ C   99--------+||
0180   CTA Contact information                           M   1         |||
0190   COM Communication contact                         C   99--------++|
```

This example, copied verbatim from the message definition, expresses positional information in the first column, which we can safely ignore as they are implicitly carried over to the XML counterpart we will create later in this chapter. The `Tag` column provides the three-character segment identifier tag of the segments in the group, `CTA` and `COM` in this particular case. The `Name` column provides a textual description of these segments, such as `Contact information` for CTA. The next column provides information whether the segment is mandatory (`M`) or not (`C`).

In this case, the CTA segment is obligatory, but the COM segment is optional. The next column provides information on how many occurrences of a segment or segment group there can be in the message. This shows that there must be exactly one CTA segment and up to 99 COM segments. The segment group can also occur up to 99 times within the message. The other + and | characters at the right are textual indications of the nesting of structures in the EDI message. You'll see better examples of that later.

The CTA segment itself is defined as a simple data element CONTACT FUNCTION CODE and a composite data element, DEPARTMENT OR EMPLOYEE DETAILS:

```
010    3139 CONTACT FUNCTION CODE                        C    1 an..3

020    C056 DEPARTMENT OR EMPLOYEE DETAILS               C    1
       3413  Department or employee name code            C      an..17
       3412  Department or employee name                 C      an..35
```

The CONTACT FUNCTION CODE is a data element identified using its numeric code (3139); it has basic field type information and a limited, enumerated value range. The an..3 text means the field has 1 to 3 characters (an signifies "alphanumeric") The following fragment, for data element 3139, shows two out of several dozen allowed values, the first one, and another one that is relevant to the example:

```
Desc: Code specifying the function of a contact (for example
      department or person).

   Repr: an..3

   Code Values:

   AA    Insurance contact
            Department/person to contact for matters regarding
            insurance.   ...

   MC    Material control contact
            Department/person responsible for the
            controlling/inspection of goods.
   ...
```

The other element, DEPARTMENT OR EMPLOYEE DETAILS, is a composite data element. It is composed of two other simple data elements, 3413 and 3412.

The following (default) service characters allow you to tokenize an EDIFACT message stream:

- Segments are terminated using the single quote (') character.
- Components of composite data elements are separated using the colon (:) character.
- The plus sign (+) character precedes composite and simple data elements.

The higher-level structure of an EDIFACT message stream can be reconstructed deterministically and unambiguously because the "tag" identifies the segment and the "trigger" segment indicates segment group structure. With this information, an example fragment can be constructed as follows:

```
CTA+MC+DTE:L. Ventura'COM+lino@espressomachine.it:EM'
```

The following figure shows a parse tree for this structure:

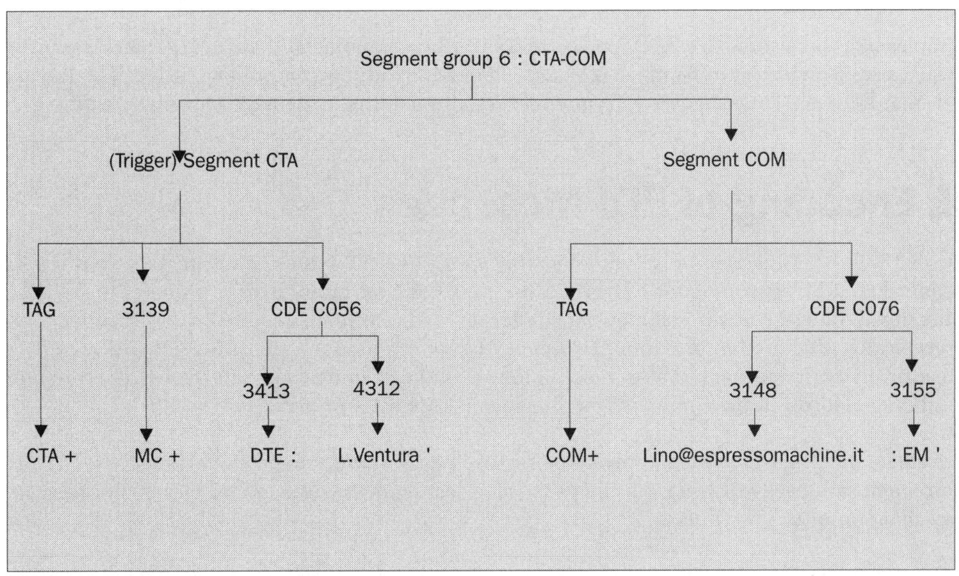


In this figure, various data elements are used that we describe briefly in the following table. Note that with simple data elements, the "Datatype" column provides field length constraints. The various components jointly express the meaning of the fields. For example, the value "`EM`" for element `3155` indicates that the preceding field value needs to be interpreted as an e-mail address. This is why it is called a **qualifier** data element.

| Identifier | Compound/ Simple | Name | Datatype (for simple elements) | Value |
|---|---|---|---|---|
| `3139` | Simple | Contact function code | an..3 | MC |
| `C056` | Compound | Department or employee details | | |
| `3413` | Simple | Department or employee name code | an..17 | DTE |
| `4312` | Simple | Department or employee name | an..35 | L. Ventura |
| `C076` | Compound | Communication contact | | |
| `3148` | Simple | Communication address identifier | an..512 | `lino@espressomachine.it` |
| `3155` | Simple | Communication address qualifier | an..3 | EM |

Another example of such **co-constraints** is in the `DTM` composite element used elsewhere in this message. Here, the element `2379` (date or time or period format code), expresses the required format of type `2380` (date or time or period value). For example, a value `204` for `2379` requires the content of `2380` to be in the `CCYYMMDDHHMMSS` format ("calendar date including time with seconds").

Examples like these show that EDIFACT syntax is more economical than XML in terms of overall message size, which used to be more relevant when bandwidth was more expensive. The downside of this is that EDIFACT messages are cryptic and require external code tables for interpretation.

## XML Encoding of EDI Messages

Now that we've familiarized ourselves a bit with the EDIFACT syntax, it's time to look at ways to define an equivalent XML encoding for EDIFACT message content. From the discussion of the EDIFACT syntax, it will be clear that it is somewhat similar to XML; both are generic representations for hierarchically structured information. However, the representations are sufficiently different to support a great diversity in approaches. We'll look into two of these, one developed by the XEDI initiative and the other developed in the context of the European XML-EDI project.

To evaluate the proposals, we'll apply some requirements to the proposed XML encoding. These requirements are partly drawn from the proposal documents themselves and clearly not relevant in every situation or to everyone.

- **General**: the approach should not be applicable to just a subset of EDI messages, but should extend to the full EDIFACT (or other EDI) message type directory.
- **Natural**: naming, structure, and organization of the XML schema should mirror the data it transports and the information it models. Admittedly a fairly subjective criterion.
- **Non-arbitrary**, or **objective**: different people applying the same methodology should come up with (roughly) similar results. This affects decisions on both naming and representing information as XML attributes, subelements, or content.
- **Automated**: this is a stronger version of the previous requirement, and states that given an arbitrary EDI message, it should be possible to generate the corresponding XML document without requiring manually created mapping definitions (such as style sheets or schemas).
- **Bi-directional**: the approach should not just support conversion from EDI messages to XML messages, but also back from the XML representation to the EDI notation.
- **Multilingual**: the approach should support situations where the sender and receiver of a message speak different languages. This is relevant because XML encourages the use of human-readable element names, and hence introduces a language dependency.
- Support **structural validation**: validate completeness and correctness of requirements on order, presence, and cardinality of types of children.
- Support **data-type validation**: the XML should support validation against enumerated value lists, field length constraints, and (preferably) also co-constraints as discussed previously.
- Support **built-in cross-references** to EDI data; to enable existing EDI programmers, who are mostly familiar with the EDI representation, to work with the XML counterparts of this data.

Before discussing the two approaches, we can make two further preliminary remarks:

- The EDIFACT message specifications are very generic and hence contain a level of completeness and detail that is unnecessary in most projects. Practical applications typically specify their subset in a Message Implementation Guidelines (MIG) document. If available, they are a better starting point than the full-blown EDIFACT specifications.
- As mentioned earlier, message headers and trailers are omitted; in an ebXML context, the ebXML message header (discussed in Chapter 13, *ebXML Messaging*) fulfills their role.

# XEDI

The company XML Solutions developed the **XEDI** approach for encoding X12, the North American EDI standard. The web site http://www.xedi.org/ is used to market the approach and includes references to and contributions from some of its users. The web site publishes a number of white papers (see http://www.xedi.org/whitepapers.html) that illustrate its use. Although the approach covers X12, the basic approach carries over to EDIFACT, with some assumptions on our part noted in the following discussion.

The key feature of the XEDI approach is that a *single* XML Schema is used to encode *any* EDI message. It uses a few elements and attributes to generically encode any EDI message. These are:

- `<transactionSet>` corresponds to an entire message.
- `<loop>` corresponds to a repeatable segment group.
- `<segment>` encodes an EDI segment.
- `<element>` corresponds to an EDI element.
- The `<transactionSet>`, `<segment>`, and `<element>` elements have a `code` attribute that references the EDI identifier, and a `name` element that encodes the human-readable name.
- The `<value>` child element of these three main elements encodes the human-readable value as its content and the abbreviated value as the value of the `code` attribute, if the value is from an enumerated value set.

The two EDIFACT elements used in our introduction to EDIFACT syntax could be encoded using the following XEDI syntax:

```
<loop code="CTA">
   <name>Contact information</name>
   &lt;segment code="CTA">
      <name>Contact information</name>
      <element code="3139">
         <name>Contact function code</name>
         <value code="MC">Material control contact</value>
      </element>
      <!-- begin of composite element:
         C056 DEPARTMENT OR EMPLOYEE DETAILS -->
      <element code="3413">
         <name>Department or employee name code</name>
         <value>DTE</value>
      </element>
      <element code="3412">
```

```
        <name>Department or employee name</name>
        <value>L. Ventura</value>
      </element>
      <!-- end of composite element -->
    &lt;/segment&gt;
    &lt;segment code="COM"&gt;
      <name>Communication contact</name>
      <element code="3148">
        <name>Communication address identifier</name>
        <value>DTE</value>
      </element>
      <element code="3155">
        <name>Communication address qualifier</name>
        <value code="EM">Electronic mail</value>
      </element>
    &lt;/segment&gt;
  </loop>
```

Note that we have assumed that the <loop> element encodes EDI segment groups and that the content of its <name> element is copied from the trigger segment; the white papers have no examples of loops allowing us to verify that assumption. Also note that the XEDI DTD does not have an XML element for EDI composite elements such as C056, as indicated by the XML comments in the fragment, so we have encoded that information as comments. The DTD could be extended with some <compositeElement> element if required, and would then facilitate bi-directional conversion.

```
  <compositeElement code="C056">
    <name>DEPARTMENT OR EMPLOYEE DETAILS</name>
    <element code="3413">
      <name>Department or employee name code</name>
      <value>DTE</value>
    </element>
    <element code="3412">
      <name>Department or employee name</name>
      <value>L. Ventura</value>
    </element>
  </compositeElement>
```

As discussed in the XEDI white papers, XEDI-encoded messages can easily be extended for multilingual situations by allowing multiple occurrences of elements with language attributes indicating which text is relevant in a given language, such as:

```
    <name xml:lang="en">Department or employee name code</name>
    <name xml:lang="nl">Naamcode van afdeling of medewerker</name>
```

As there are only a few elements in XEDI, the DTD can be translated easily as well.

The XEDI approach scores quite well against the list of requirements specified. It is clearly general, non-arbitrary, bi-directional, multilingual, and provides built-in cross-references to the EDI structure. It is also highly automated, though not completely as the information on mapping codes like EM to ElectronicMail has to be represented in a data dictionary (the XEDI documentation includes a DTD and sample data from such a data dictionary). In a project, use of XEDI means that if you have built a conversion program from one EDI message set to XML, you've essentially built all such programs, which is a major advantage. However, XEDI fails some of the criteria.

The ability to use names of elements and attributes to reflect the information that a document encodes and its structure is key to the XML philosophy (inherited from the SGML philosophy). In this sense, XEDI certainly fails the requirement of being a "natural" encoding of EDI data (however problematic that concept is). In a sense, it is reminiscent of Rainbow, an early SGML encoding of word processor documents. To illustrate the idea of Rainbow, let's look at the title of this chapter. While it is true that it could be encoded in XML in either of the following two ways, we would assume that once people decide to migrate to XML, it should be possible to express it as something like this:

```
<Chapter>
   <Title>
      Using XML/EDI Message Payload Content
   </Title>
      ...
</Chapter>
```

...rather than something like this, which is what Rainbow would give you:

```
<para paraType="chapter title - PRODUCTION" font-family="FrGothHeavy"
                                            font-size="26">
   Using XML/EDI Message Payload Content
</para>
```

However, the main purpose of Rainbow was to facilitate document conversion. Software that converts from a document format like Microsoft Word documents to a Rainbow XML representation is very generic and reusable. It conveniently encodes all possibly relevant information in the word processor document and makes no assumptions about the conversion target. Rainbow-style encoded documents are much easier to process than word processor documents, as you can use generic XML tools to manipulate Rainbow XML documents. Therefore, converting to Rainbow is very useful as a first step in a (multi-stage) conversion chain. Although not positioned as such by its developers, XEDI would be very useful as an intermediate data representation for the same reasons.

Another way to look at XEDI would be to compare it to a generic DTD that attempts to capture the structure of any well-formed XML document. Like XEDI, such a DTD would only have a few elements (`<Element>`, `<Attribute>`, `<Text>`, `<ProcessingInstruction>`, `<CDATASection>`, `<DoctypeDeclaration>`, `<EntityReference>` etc.), and a well-formed XML document like this:

```
<a att="val">aa <b> bb </b> more aa </a>
```

...could be represented like:

```
<Element name="a">
<Attribute name="att">val</Attribute>
<Text>aa </Text>
<Element name="b"><Text>bb </Text></Element>
<Text>more aa </Text>
</Element>
```

Any well-formed XML document would trivially satisfy this DTD, but that fact wouldn't make the schema more useful for any particular application space. The main problem is that XML is not just about being able to describe data, but also about being able to *validate* documents.

The original EDIFACT message definition specifies that the "Communication Contact" (COM) segment requires two elements, a 3148 "Communication Address Identifier", and a 3155 "Communication Address Qualifier", and this is information that EDI message handlers validate. These systems can reject messages where one of these two children is omitted or has the wrong type. However, this ability to validate messages is lost with XEDI, as XEDI messages by design trivially satisfy the XEDI schema. The XEDI DTD can check that a <segment> has <element> children, but it cannot validate any additional constraints that are expressed in the EDI message definition (or are expressible in an XML DTD that distinguishes separate XML elements for the various EDI elements). This is an example of structural validation. Similar remarks apply to simple content datatype validation. XML Schema Part II – Datatypes (found at http://www.w3.org/TR/xmlschema-2/) can express EDI field constraints, but again a generic schema like XEDI does not encode such constraints, irrespective of the schema language used.

In an e-business message context, not supporting validation is perhaps the most important deficiency of XEDI. A strict schema declaratively specifies a set of constraints that generic schema validation software can apply. Together, the schema and the XML validation software replace ad hoc validation software that would be expensive (not to mention tedious...) to write and maintain. XEDI requires (and perhaps assumes) other components (such as an EDI infrastructure) for this, and provides limited value over the native EDI format.

Before concluding our discussion of XEDI, we should mention that what we have been discussing is what people involved in XEDI call the "indirect" approach in public mailing list discussions. In a posting to the ebxml-dev list on 19/07/2001, John Evdemon of XML Solutions refers to a "direct" approach (not described in the publicly available white papers), which is more similar to the approach discussed in the next section. This approach would support validation but would also lose some of the advantages of the indirect approach, such as multilingualism.

## European XML/EDI Project

The European XML-EDI project was carried out in the context of the European Commission's ISIS framework. In September 2001, the results of the currently completed project were made available from http://palvelut.tieke.fi/edi/isis-xmledi/. The following discussion informally paraphrases some of the mapping conventions discussed in *Rules for Mapping Existing EDIFACT MIGs to XML DTDs* by M. Bryan, found at http://palvelut.tieke.fi/edi/isis-xmledi/d2/rules2.htm. Before we get into the details of the approach proposed by the project, you should note the following:

- The approach assumes that an XML developer applies these conventions when creating a schema for the EDIFACT message. The conversion is therefore objective but not automatic, and is open to arbitrary naming decisions.
- DTDs allow you to attach additional information that is not present in the document. This information can either be fixed attribute values (encoded using the #FIXED notation) or default information (encoded as default for an enumeration). XML/EDI takes advantage of this to omit predictable information from messages that is useful for processing and/or self-documentation purposes (thus keeping them small).

The XML **root element** name of the message is selected by the developer, and indicates the purpose of the message, using upper camel case capitalization conventions. For the INSREQ message, a reasonable name in the English language would be <InspectionRequestMessage>. In the schema, the developer can reference the EDIFACT message type identifier as a #FIXED value. In the EDIFACT representation, that information would be in the UNH header segment. In this and following ATTLIST declarations, we only reference attributes relevant to the discussion.

```
<!ATTLIST InspectionRequestMessage
   UN-EDIFACT:Id CDATA #FIXED "INSREQ:D:01A:UN">
```

This represents a common use of `#FIXED` values in XML. It means that any XML parser that uses DTD information will interpret an XML document that starts with:

```
<InspectionRequestMessage ...>
   ...
</InspectionRequestMessage>
```

as if the document had contained:

```
<InspectionRequestMessage UN-EDIFACT:Id="INSREQ:D:01A:UN" ...>
   ...
</InspectionRequestMessage>
```

This saves space in the document, and uses the DTD and the XML parser to provide an alternative view on the XML tree structure. Other fixed EDI header information (data elements and values) can be encoded similarly. The full XML DTD also defines the `UN-EDIFACT` and other namespaces.

**Segment groups** are represented as XML elements named after the "trigger" segment, with "`Group`" appended to the name. The `CTA` segment triggers segment group 6, so we might call it `ContactInformationGroup`. Each segment is represented by its own XML element. The schema definition of the XML element can encode a reference to the original EDIFACT segment identifier, as demonstrated here:

```
<!ATTLIST ContactInformation
   UN-EDIFACT:Segment CDATA #FIXED "CTA">
```

Sometimes an EDIFACT message contains multiple segment groups with the same trigger segment. These are differentiated at message level using qualifier data elements and in the message documentation. For instance, there are multiple "name and address" segment groups in the `INSREQ` message. In the XML rendering, we will create separate elements for these based on the qualifier value, with a fixed value for the qualifying attribute.

According to the `INSREQ` message definition, multiple `COM` segments are allowed in group 6. Such multiple occurrences are contained in a container element, named after the plural form of the contained element's name:

```
<!ELEMENT ContactInformationGroup (ContactInformation,
                                   CommunicationContacts?)>
<!ELEMENT CommunicationContacts    (CommunicationContact+)>
```

A data element with a fixed value set is encoded as an attribute on the XML element that represents the containing EDI segment. Another fixed attribute, named `UN-EDIFACT:Attributes`, can be used to document the mapping from data element identifiers to attribute names. Its value is a string-encoded list of identifier-name pairs. The list in the following example has just one such pair:

```
<!ATTLIST ContactInformation
   UN-EDIFACT:Attributes CDATA  #FIXED "3139 ContactFunctionCode"
   ContactFunctionCode  (InsuranceContact | MaterialControlContact)
   #REQUIRED>
```

We'll discuss an alternative XML representation of this information later.

This representation omits the mapping from the expanded values `InsuranceContact` and `MaterialControlContact` to code values like `AA` and `MC`. The document suggests a reference to an external mapping document. Such a document would be similar to the XEDI data dictionary. The document reference can also be encoded using a fixed attribute.

A data element that is not selected from a pre-defined element is represented by an XML element:

```
<!ELEMENT DepartmentOrEmployeeName (#PCDATA)>
<!ATTLIST DepartmentOrEmployeeName
   UN-EDIFACT:Element CDATA #FIXED "3413">
```

However, if there is only one such data element in a segment (for instance because all other elements are represented as attributes), the segment structure is flattened and the content of the data element directly becomes the content of the segment. This is the case with the `<CommunicationAddressQualifier>` data element in the `<CommunicationContact>` segment:

```
<!ELEMENT CommunicationContact (#PCDATA) >
<!ATTLIST CommunicationContact
   UN-EDIFACT:Element CDATA #FIXED "C076"
   CommunicationAddressQualifier (ElectronicMail | Telephone |
                                 X400Address | Telefax) #REQUIRED>
```

(We've assumed that the value for the `UN-EDIFACT:Element` attribute should reflect the fact that `<CommunicationContact>` is based on a composite data element in the EDIFACT definition. You could also argue that the value should be `3148`, the code for the EDIFACT "communication address identifier". Also note that we've copied just four members of the full EDIFACT value set for the `<CommunicationAddressQualifier>` into this DTD fragment.)

As the project was concluded before XML Schema became a W3C Recommendation, it only discusses XML DTD representations, which cannot express datatype limitations. The overall approach of XML/EDI is as applicable with more expressive schema languages as it is with DTDs, and can therefore benefit from the extended datatype checking facilities offered by these languages.

The following is an XML/EDI encoding of the fragment of segment group 6 that we previously presented as EDIFACT and XEDI:

```
<ContactInformationGroup>
   <ContactInformation ContactFunctionCode="MaterialControlContact">
      <DepartmentOrEmployeeDetails>
         <DepartmentOrEmployeeNameCode>DTE</DepartmentOrEmployeeNameCode>
         <DepartmentOrEmployeeName>L. Ventura</DepartmentOrEmployeeName>
      </DepartmentOrEmployeeDetails>
   </ContactInformation>
   <CommunicationContacts>
      <CommunicationContact CommunicationAddressQualifier="ElectronicMail">
         lino@espressomachine.it
      </CommunicationContact>
   </CommunicationContacts>
</ContactInformationGroup>
```

The information expressed by fixed or default attributes is omitted in this, as the XML parser will provide it.

Like XEDI, XML/EDI addresses most of the requirements we identified. It is general, natural, and also has built-in cross-references to EDI data. Importantly, it provides significant support for validation. With a DTD encoding of the schema, you can already rely on standard XML validation tools to check presence, cardinality, and order of subelements, and check that attribute values are selected from specified value sets. With XML Schema datatypes, you can also check field length.

The project has also looked into ways to deal with some co-constraints among data elements within a segment. Again, see http://palvelut.tieke.fi/edi/isis-xmledi/d2/rules2.htm for discussion. Due to the way the XML/EDI mapping is set up, not all kinds of co-constraints validation are possible. As an example of this, in the fragment displayed above you can see that the value `ElectronicMail` for the attribute `CommunicationAddressQualifier` restricts the type of the content of the `<CommunicationContact>` element. This would be solved by a more complex translation that combines the qualifier and the identifier in a single XML element name, for example something like:

```
<CommunicationContact>
   <ElectronicMail>lino@espressomachine.it</ElectronicMail>
</CommunicationContact>
```

We'll adopt this structure for the full `INSREQ` message schema.

Apart from co-constraint validation, XML/EDI also does not address some of the other requirements we started out with. In particular, it assumes the process is manual, and relies on subjective human judgment in the selection of names. Some of the structural flattening rules greatly complicate bi-directionality, as the EDI generator would have to know how and where to introduce the additional structure. The deliverables of the project do not discuss the issue of multilingual support. However, this can be accommodated using mechanisms similar to those used by XEDI, for example:

```
<!ATTLIST InspectionRequestMessage
   xml:lang               NMTOKEN #FIXED "en"
   AlternativeNameIn_nl   CDATA    #FIXED "InspectieVerzoekBericht"
   AlternativeNameIn_de   CDATA    #FIXED "..."
   UN-EDIFACT:Id  CDATA  #FIXED "INSREQ:D:01A:UN">
```

The XEDI white paper mentions some drawbacks of using (potentially long) natural language names as elements, names, as used in XML/EDI and similar approaches:

- It is claimed that style sheets or conversion tools cannot generically reference XML elements that correspond to an arbitrary EDI element, segment, or data element. But this information is encoded in fixed attributes.
- Long names are harder to remember and more easily misspelled. This is only an issue in the (probably not very likely) case that the payload content is created manually or without editing tools.
- A natural language name can just encode one language and hence this approach is less acceptable in a multiple-language environment.

We've shown that XML/EDI can encode alternative language descriptions and names in a way similar to XEDI. With XSLT, it is also possible to use XPath patterns that look at the language independent EDIFACT back-references (provided by fixed attributes in the schema) rather than at language dependent element names. The following fragment shows an XSLT template that processes any XML element that claims to express information in an EDIFACT "CTA" segment:

```
<xsl:template match="*[UN-EDIFACT:Segment='CTA']">
   <!-- process ContactInformation structure -->
</xsl:template>
```

This would combine the best of both worlds: the long name would be useful for developers and other human consumers of the message, and the attribute name would make any processing code robust against changes in (or translations of) names.

Similarly, it is easy to write style sheets that rename elements using the "AlternativeNameIn_XX" attribute values, should this be required for any particular reason.

## Summary of XEDI and XML/EDI

As we've seen, both XEDI and the approach proposed by the XML/EDI project allow you to use XML as an alternative notation for information in EDIFACT messages. The two approaches are very different:

- The ("indirect") XEDI approach provides a very lightweight, generic encoding of EDI messages. Its main advantage is that the mapping from and back to EDI format is completely predictable and therefore requires no separate development of mapping code (other than providing the data dictionary). The main limitation is that its XML representation does not support validation.
- The XML/EDI guidelines provide a methodology for mapping EDIFACT messages to an XML representation. The resulting representations have insightful names and structure and support structural and data type validation. The drawback is that schemas and style sheets need to be developed and maintained for each project, which could be a burden on the developer team.

The main use for XEDI seems to be in e-business projects that build on (or need to interface with) existing EDI implementations. The XML/EDI approach and similar proposals seem to be more appropriate in projects that want to benefit from the EDI knowledge base but have no need (or limited needs) to interface with existing EDI systems. We'll adopt this approach in the remainder of this chapter.

# XML/EDI Encoding of the INSREQ Message

In this section, we'll provide a walkthrough of the INSREQ message, fragments of which we've used throughout the discussion to compare the two approaches to mapping EDI to XML. Our discussion will be organized as follows:

- As a reference, we'll first provide the complete EDI structure, taken from the EDIFACT message directory specification.
- Next we'll describe a DTD that encodes the EDIFACT message, largely along the lines of the XML/EDI project.

- Then we'll provide an XML instance of an inspection request document based on this schema.
- Finally, we'll provide some comments on the results of this translation.

As you'll notice, even a relatively simple message like `INSREQ` already requires a non-trivial DTD. However, this is not just true for both EDI-derived message standards, but also for XML business-to-business vocabularies.

## INSREQ Message Specification

The following is taken directly from the UN/EDIFACT D01A directory. This specification uses the same notations as the sample we discussed earlier. This more complete example also shows how the -, + and | characters are used to express nesting. There's no need to try to understand this syntax diagram completely now, as we'll walk through the various pieces of it in the remainders of this chapter to explain how it describes the structure of the message. (The `X` after position `0290` is an irrelevant revision mark that indicates this segment was in previous versions of the EDIFACT syntax and is removed with this release.)

```
4.3.1   Segment table

Pos     Tag Name                                    S   R

0010    UNH Message header                          M   1
0020    BGM Beginning of message                    M   1
0030    DTM Date/time/period                        M   99

0040        ----- Segment group 1  ---------------- C   99----------+
0050    RFF Reference                               M   1           |
0060    DTM Date/time/period                        C   9-----------+

0070        ----- Segment group 2  ---------------- M   99----------+
0080    NAD Name and address                        M   1           |
0090    LOC Place/location identification           C   99----------+

0100        ----- Segment group 3  ---------------- M   99----------+
0110    DOC Document/message details                M   1           |
                                                                    |
0120        ----- Segment group 4  ---------------- C   99---------+|
0130    RFF Reference                               M   1          ||
0140    DTM Date/time/period                        C   99---------+|
                                                                    |
0150        ----- Segment group 5  ---------------- C   99---------+|
0160    NAD Name and address                        M   1          ||
                                                                   ||
0170        ----- Segment group 6  ---------------- C   99--------+||
0180    CTA Contact information                     M   1         |||
0190    COM Communication contact                   C   99--------++|
                                                                    |
0200        ----- Segment group 7  ---------------- C   999--------+|
0210    LIN Line item                               M   1          ||
0220    PIA Additional product id                   C   99         ||
0230    IMD Item description                        C   99         ||
```

```
0240    DTM Date/time/period                    C    99          ||
0250    RFF Reference                           C    99          ||
0260    FTX Free text                           C    9           ||
                                                                 ||
0270        ----- Segment group 8 ------------- C    999--------+||
0280    NAD Name and address                    M    1          |||
0290  X GIS General indicator                   C    99         |||
0300    LOC Place/location identification       C    99         |||
0310    QTY Quantity                            C    99         |||
0320    QVR Quantity variances                  C    99         |||
0330    RFF Reference                           C    99         |||
0340    FTX Free text                           C    9          |||
                                                                |||
0350        ----- Segment group 9 ------------- C    999-------+|||
0360    GIN Goods identity number               M    1         ||||
0370    RFF Reference                           C    99--------++++
0380    UNT Message trailer                     M    1
```

# XML/EDI DTD for INSREQ

This document provides a representation of the UN/EDIFACT D01A INSREQ Inspection Message Request message type. It is reasonably complete in terms of structure but not in code value lists. The methodology applied to derive this XML representation from the EDIFACT representation is essentially based on the XML/EDI methodology, with some exceptions noted.

The DTD is structured in a top-down format; we'll start with the top-level element, then discuss segment groups, segments, composite data elements, and end with simple data elements. First of all, however, we provide some useful parameter entities. The first of these defines an EDIFACT URL for namespace definition purposes:

```
<!-- INSREQ DTD schema:

-->

<!ENTITY % edifact-url "'http://www.unece.org/trade/untdid/d01'">
<!ENTITY % edifact-ns  "xmlns:UN-EDIFACT CDATA #FIXED  %edifact-url;">
```

Next, we use the `CommunicationContact` parameter entity as an approximation for a UML abstract class that covers various communication contacts (the four we've listed here are a tiny subset of the complete set). You can use this parameter entity in content models. They all share a fixed value for the EDIFACT segment reference. The second parameter entity is for use in `ATTLIST` declarations:

```
<!ENTITY % CommunicationContact
   "(ElectronicMail | Telephone | X400Address | Telefax )">
<!ENTITY % CommunicationContact.Atts
   " %edifact-ns; UN-EDIFACT:Segment CDATA #FIXED 'COM' ">
```

Similarly, the following parameter entities are intended for use by elements that specialize the EDIFACT `NAD` (name and address) segment. In the EDIFACT directory, this segment has a qualifier element to indicate which party's address is being described. The message definition for `INSREQ` outlines which qualifier value is to be used in one of three contexts. By distinguishing separate elements, the appropriate party can be selected where needed.

The first parameter entity is for use in content models, the second one is for use in attribute lists. It relates three attributes to their EDIFACT data element counterparts:

```
<!ENTITY % NameAndAddress.Content
   "(PartyIdentificationDetails, NameAndAddressDescription+,
     PartyName+, Street+, City )">
<!ENTITY % NameAndAddress.Atts
   "%edifact-ns;
   UN-EDIFACT:Segment    CDATA #FIXED 'NAD'
   UN-EDIFACT:Attributes CDATA #FIXED '3035 PartyFunctionCodeQualifier
                                       3251 PostalIdentificationCode
                                       3207 CountryNameCode'
   PostalIdentificationCode  NMTOKEN   #IMPLIED
   CountryNameCode           NMTOKEN   #IMPLIED
   ">
```

The documentation of `INSREQ` indicates that segment group 2 serves to identify the supplier party and the inspection party. The XML schema encodes this strictly.

Note that all segment groups after group 3 (Document/message details) are actually embedded within these `DocumentOrMessageDetailsGroup` elements.

```
<!-- MESSAGE ELEMENT -->

<!ELEMENT InspectionRequestMessage (SupplierParty,InspectionParty,
                                    DocumentOrMessageDetailsGroup+)>
<!ATTLIST InspectionRequestMessage %edifact-ns; >
```

We've reorganized the first part of the message a bit. First of all, segment group 1 is omitted as we simply assume there have been no previous inspections to refer to. Segment group 2 is replaced by specialized party elements:

- `<SupplierParty>`
- `<InspectionParty>`

If you need to reference all parties, you could create a parameter entity.

For simplicity, we've omitted place/location information. So, the first element that we need to look at corresponds to segment group 3:

```
<!ELEMENT DocumentOrMessageDetailsGroup (DocumentOrMessageDetails+,
                                         ReferenceGroup*,
                                         IssuerPartyGroup?,
                                         LineItemGroup*)>
```

Segment group 4 contains references to contracts or purchase orders that are at the basis of the shipment:

```
<!ELEMENT ReferenceGroup (Reference, DateTimePeriod*)>
```

Segment group 5 consists of a single NAD segment, representing the document issuer, so we don't create a separate segment group to hold it, as specified in the XML/EDI guidelines. Group 5 embeds segment group 6.

```
<!ELEMENT IssuerPartyGroup (IssuerParty, ContactInformationGroup*)>
```

Segment group 6 conveys contact information. You can reference multiple contacts by repeating the entire group. You can specify multiple means of communicating with a single contact using the <CommunicationContacts> elements:

```
<!ELEMENT ContactInformationGroup (ContactInformation,
                                   CommunicationContacts*)>
```

Segment group 7 encodes the actual items that are to be inspected. The group is repeated for each individual item. Per item, you can specify additional product information, descriptions, and the party to whom the goods are to be delivered:

```
<!ELEMENT LineItemGroup (LineItem, AdditionalProductId*,
                         ItemDescription*, DeliveryPartyGroup*) >
```

Segment group 8 encodes the delivery party. It is essentially a NAD segment with quantity information that back-references the particular line item that is delivered to this party:

```
<!ELEMENT DeliveryPartyGroup (DeliveryParty, Quantity?,
                              GoodsIdentityGroup*)>
```

The specific items that are delivered to the party (a subset of the ensemble of what is referenced by the line item) can be referenced (for example using serial numbers) in segment group 9:

```
<!ELEMENT GoodsIdentityGroup (GoodsIdentityNumber, Reference*)>
```

This concludes the segment group level.

Next, we'll provide an alphabetical listing of all Segments. These are all very similar. Essentially, each references the segment it is derived from by its code. The Segments also reference any fixed value set data elements that are represented as attributes.

<AdditionalProductId> functions specify additional or substitutional item identification codes:

```
<!ELEMENT AdditionalProductId (ItemNumberIdentification)>
<!ATTLIST AdditionalProductId
   %edifact-ns;
   UN-EDIFACT:Segment    CDATA   #FIXED   "PIA"
   UN-EDIFACT:Attributes CDATA   #FIXED
                         '4347 ProductIdentifierCodeQualifier'
   ProductIdentifierCodeQualifier  (AdditionalInformation |
                                    SubstitutedBy |
                                    SubstitutedFor |
                                    ProductIdentification |
```

```
                                    SuccessorProductId |
                                    PredecessorProductId |
                                    AlternateProductIdentification) #REQUIRED >
```

Refer back to the definition of the `CommunicationContact` entity at the beginning of this file. It encodes a disjunction of elements that can all occur as content for the `<CommunicationContracts>` element:

```
<!ELEMENT CommunicationContacts (%CommunicationContact;)+>

<!ELEMENT ContactInformation (DepartmentOrEmployeeDetails)>
<!ATTLIST ContactInformation
   %edifact-ns;
   UN-EDIFACT:Segment   CDATA          #FIXED   "CTA"
   ContactFunctionCode (InsuranceContact | MaterialControlContact)
   #REQUIRED >

<!ELEMENT DeliveryParty (%NameAndAddress.Content;)>
<!ATTLIST DeliveryParty
   %NameAndAddress.Atts;
   PartyFunctionCodeQualifier CDATA   #FIXED "DeliveryParty">
```

The function of this next segment is to identify documents and details directly related to it:

```
<!ELEMENT DocumentOrMessageDetails (DocumentMessageName,
                                    DocumentMessageDetails?)>
<!ATTLIST DocumentOrMessageDetails
   %edifact-ns;
   UN-EDIFACT:Segment    CDATA    #FIXED "DOC">

<!ELEMENT ElectronicMail        (#PCDATA)>
<!ATTLIST ElectronicMail
   %CommunicationContact.Atts;
   UN-EDIFACT:Segment           CDATA #FIXED "COM"
   CommunicationAddressQualifier CDATA #FIXED "EM">
```

The next segment serves to give specific identification numbers, either as single numbers or ranges:

```
<!ELEMENT GoodsIdentityNumber  (IdentityNumberRange,
                                (IdentityNumberRange,
                                 (IdentityNumberRange,
                                  IdentityNumberRange?)?)?) >

<!ATTLIST GoodsIdentityNumber
   %edifact-ns;
   UN-EDIFACT:Segment    CDATA #FIXED "GIN"
   UN-EDIFACT:Attributes CDATA #FIXED
      "7405 ObjectIdentificationCodeQualifier"
      ObjectIdentificationCodeQualifier (ReleaseNumber |
                                         SerialNumber |
                                         BatchNumber |
                                         MarkingOrLabelNumber) #REQUIRED>
```

```
<!ELEMENT InspectionParty (%NameAndAddress.Content;)>
<!ATTLIST InspectionParty
   %NameAndAddress.Atts;
   PartyFunctionCodeQualifier CDATA #FIXED "PartyPerformingInspection">

<!ELEMENT IssuerParty (%NameAndAddress.Content;)>
<!ATTLIST IssuerParty
   %NameAndAddress.Atts;
   PartyFunctionCodeQualifier
      CDATA #FIXED "DocumentOrMessageIssuerOrSender">
```

`ItemDescription` is greatly simplified, omitting two of the composite data elements (`C272` and `C273`) in the EDIFACT definition; we've defined a fixed value for data element `7077` and use the `#PCDATA` content of the element for data element 7008, "Item description". The permissible values for `ItemCharacteristicCode` is a very incomplete subset of EDIFACT values:

```
<!ELEMENT ItemDescription (#PCDATA)>
<!ATTLIST ItemDescription
   %edifact-ns;
   UN-EDIFACT:Segment       CDATA    #FIXED    "IMD"
   UN-EDIFACT:Attributes    CDATA    #FIXED
                                     '7077 DescriptionFormatCode
                                     7081 ItemCharacteristic
                                     3453 LanguageNameCode'
   DescriptionFormatCode    CDATA    #FIXED    "FreeForm"
   ItemCharacteristicCode     (GeneralProductForm |
                               EndUseApplication |
                               Product |
                               Quality |
                               MaterialDescription |
                               EuropeanCommunityRiskClass |
                               Colour |
                               WineGrowingRegion |
                               CorrosionResistance ) #IMPLIED
   LanguageNameCode               NMTOKEN #IMPLIED>

<!ELEMENT LineItem          (LineItemIdentifier, ItemNumberIdentification?) >
<!ATTLIST LineItem
   %edifact-ns;
   UN-EDIFACT:Segment     CDATA #FIXED "LIN"
   UN-EDIFACT:Attributes CDATA #FIXED
                         '1229 ActionRequestOrNotificationDescription'
   ActionRequestOrNotificationDescription (Added | Deleted | Changed |
                                           PendingAwaitingReview)
   #IMPLIED>

<!ELEMENT NameAndAddress (PartyIdentificationDetails,
                         NameAndAddressDescription+,
                         PartyName+, Street+, City )>

<!ATTLIST NameAndAddress %edifact-ns; >
```

We've simplified the `Quantity` segment a bit. Its PCDATA content is data element `6060`:

```
<!ELEMENT Quantity (#PCDATA) >
<!ATTLIST Quantity
   %edifact-ns;
   UN-EDIFACT:Segment      CDATA  #FIXED "QTY"
   UN-EDIFACT:Attributes   CDATA  #FIXED
                                  '6063 QuantityTypeCodeQualifier
                                 1229 ActionRequestOrNotificationDescription'
      QuantityTypeCodeQualifier (DiscreteQuantity |
                                  SplitQuantity |
                                  OrderedQuantity) #REQUIRED >

<!ELEMENT SupplierParty (%NameAndAddress.Content;)>
<!ATTLIST SupplierParty %NameAndAddress.Atts;
   PartyFunctionCodeQualifier CDATA #FIXED "Supplier">

<!ELEMENT Telefax        (#PCDATA)>
<!ATTLIST Telefax
   %CommunicationContact.Atts;
   UN-EDIFACT:Segment             CDATA #FIXED "COM"
   CommunicationAddressQualifier CDATA #FIXED "FX">

<!ELEMENT Telephone        (#PCDATA)>
<!ATTLIST Telephone
   %CommunicationContact.Atts;
   UN-EDIFACT:Segment             CDATA #FIXED "COM"
   CommunicationAddressQualifier CDATA #FIXED "TE">

<!ELEMENT X400Address        (#PCDATA)>
<!ATTLIST X400Address
   %CommunicationContact.Atts;
   UN-EDIFACT:Segment             CDATA #FIXED "COM"
   CommunicationAddressQualifier CDATA #FIXED "XF">
```

This concludes the alphabetical segment summary. If you're interested in how this translates to an XML document, you could look at the end of this chapter where we've included a sample document instance. What follows here is a similar alphabetical list of all composite data elements:

```
<!ELEMENT DepartmentOrEmployeeDetails
         (DepartmentOrEmployeeNameCode, DepartmentOrEmployeeName)>
<!ATTLIST DepartmentOrEmployeeDetails
   %edifact-ns;
   UN-EDIFACT:Element CDATA #FIXED "C056">

<!ELEMENT DepartmentOrEmployeeName (#PCDATA)>
<!ATTLIST DepartmentOrEmployeeName
   %edifact-ns;
   UN-EDIFACT:Element CDATA #FIXED "C082">
```

The content of this element is the value of data element `1000`, "Document Name":

```
<!ELEMENT DocumentMessageName (#PCDATA)>
<!ATTLIST DocumentMessageName
   %edifact-ns;
   UN-EDIFACT:Element    CDATA #FIXED "C002"
   UN-EDIFACT:Attributes CDATA #FIXED "1001 DocumentNameCode"
   DocumentNameCode      (PurchaseOrder |
                          ShippingInstructions |
                          PackingList)
#IMPLIED>
```

PCDATA content of `DocumentMessageDetails` is data element `1366` (document source free form description):

```
<!ELEMENT DocumentMessageDetails (#PCDATA) >
<!ATTLIST DocumentMessageDetails
   %edifact-ns;
   UN-EDIFACT:Element    CDATA #FIXED "C503"
   UN-EDIFACT:Attributes CDATA #FIXED "1004 DocumentIdentifier
                                      1373 DocumentStatusCode
                                      3453 LanguageNameCode"
   DocumentNameCode      (PurchaseOrder |
                          ShippingInstructions |
                          PackingList) #IMPLIED
   DocumentStatusCode    (Accepted |
                          Archived |
                          EnclosedInFirstTransmission |
                          AlreadyOnFileWithReceiver |
                          PreviouslySubmitted ) #IMPLIED
   LanguageNameCode      NMTOKEN          #IMPLIED>

<!ELEMENT IdentityNumberRange (ObjectIdentifier, ObjectIdentifier?)>
<!ATTLIST IdentityNumberRange
   %edifact-ns;
   UN-EDIFACT:Element    CDATA #FIXED "C208">
```

The PCDATA content of `PartyIdentificationDetails` encodes the `7140` item identifier element:

```
<!ELEMENT ItemNumberIdentification (#PCDATA)>
<!ATTLIST ItemNumberIdentification
   %edifact-ns;
   UN-EDIFACT:Element          CDATA  #FIXED    "C212"
   UN-EDIFACT:Attributes       CDATA  #FIXED    "7143 ItemTypeIdentificationCode"
   ItemTypeIdentificationCode (UniversalProductCode |
                               InternationalArticleNumberingAssociation |
                               VendorsPartNumber ) #IMPLIED >
```

The PCDATA content of `PartyIdentificationDetails` encodes the 3039 `PartyIdentifier` element:

```
<!ELEMENT PartyIdentificationDetails (#PCDATA)>
<!ATTLIST PartyIdentificationDetails
   %edifact-ns;
```

```
   UN-EDIFACT:Element          CDATA  #FIXED     "C082"
   UN-EDIFACT:Attributes       CDATA  #FIXED     "3055
                                                 CodeListResponsibleAgency
                                                 1131
                                                 CodeListIdentificationCode"
   CodeListResponsibleAgency  CDATA  #IMPLIED
   CodeListIdentificationCode CDATA  #IMPLIED>

<!ELEMENT Reference           (ReferenceIdentifier?,
                               DocumentLineIdentifier?)>
<!ATTLIST Reference
   %edifact-ns;
   UN-EDIFACT:Element          CDATA  #FIXED     "C506"
   UN-EDIFACT:Attributes       CDATA  #FIXED     "1153 ReferenceCodeQualifier"
   ReferenceCodeQualifier (ContractNumber |
                          StandardNumberOfInspectionDocument |
                          InitialSampleInspectionReportNumber |
                          TransportContractReferenceNumber) #REQUIRED >
```

This completes the list of composite data elements. Finally, here follows a list of data elements:

```
<!ELEMENT City (#PCDATA) >
<!ATTLIST City
   %edifact-ns;
   UN-EDIFACT:Element          CDATA #FIXED "3164" >

<!ELEMENT DepartmentOrEmployeeNameCode (#PCDATA)>
<!ATTLIST DepartmentOrEmployeeNameCode
   %edifact-ns;
   UN-EDIFACT:Element          CDATA #FIXED "3412" >

<!ELEMENT DocumentLineIdentifier (#PCDATA)>
<!ATTLIST DocumentLineIdentifier
   %edifact-ns;
   UN-EDIFACT:Element          CDATA #FIXED "1156" >

<!ELEMENT LineItemIdentifier (#PCDATA)>
<!ATTLIST LineItemIdentifier
   %edifact-ns;
   UN-EDIFACT:Element          CDATA #FIXED "1082" >

<!ELEMENT NameAndAddressDescription (#PCDATA) >
<!ATTLIST NameAndAddressDescription
   %edifact-ns;
   UN-EDIFACT:Element          CDATA #FIXED "3124" >

<!ELEMENT ObjectIdentifier (#PCDATA)>
<!ATTLIST ObjectIdentifier
   %edifact-ns;
   UN-EDIFACT:Element         CDATA #FIXED "7402" >

<!ELEMENT PartyName (#PCDATA) >
<!ATTLIST PartyName
```

```
   %edifact-ns;
   UN-EDIFACT:Element          CDATA #FIXED "3036" >

<!ELEMENT ReferenceIdentifier (#PCDATA)>
<!ATTLIST ReferenceIdentifier
   %edifact-ns;
   UN-EDIFACT:Element          CDATA #FIXED "1154" >

<!ELEMENT Street (#PCDATA) >
<!ATTLIST Street
   %edifact-ns;
   UN-EDIFACT:Element          CDATA #FIXED "3042" >
```

## XML Instance for INSREQ

The following XML instance document conforms to the INSREQ DTD discussed above:

```
<!DOCTYPE InspectionRequestMessage SYSTEM "insreq.dtd">
<InspectionRequestMessage>
   <SupplierParty PostalIdentificationCode="03j8e2"
                  CountryNameCode="IT">
      <PartyIdentificationDetails
         CodeListResponsibleAgency="Italian Customs">
         Customs reference number for seller
      </PartyIdentificationDetails>
      <NameAndAddressDescription>
         Sales department
      </NameAndAddressDescription>
      <PartyName>
         Exporting company name
      </PartyName>
      <Street>
         Street
      </Street>
      <City>
         Italian city where company is based
      </City>
   </SupplierParty>
   <InspectionParty PostalIdentificationCode="03j8e2"
                    CountryNameCode="IT">
      <PartyIdentificationDetails
         CodeListResponsibleAgency="Italian Customs">
         Customs reference number for pre-shipment inspection Company
      </PartyIdentificationDetails>
      <NameAndAddressDescription>
         Sales department
      </NameAndAddressDescription>
      <PartyName>
         Name of inspection company
      </PartyName>
      <Street>
         Street
```

```
      </Street>
      <City>
         City where they're based
      </City>
   </InspectionParty>
   <DocumentOrMessageDetailsGroup>
      <DocumentOrMessageDetails>
         <DocumentMessageName DocumentNameCode="PurchaseOrder">
            Reference of buyer's purchase order
         </DocumentMessageName>
      </DocumentOrMessageDetails>
      <IssuerPartyGroup>
         <IssuerParty PostalIdentificationCode="03j8e2"
                      CountryNameCode="IT">
            <PartyIdentificationDetails
               CodeListResponsibleAgency="Italian Customs">
               Customs reference number for seller
            </PartyIdentificationDetails>
            <NameAndAddressDescription>
               Some Street
            </NameAndAddressDescription>
            <PartyName>
               Exporting company name
            </PartyName>
            <Street>
               Street
            </Street>
            <City>
               City where company is based
            </City>
         </IssuerParty>
         <ContactInformationGroup>
            <ContactInformation
               ContactFunctionCode="MaterialControlContact">
               <DepartmentOrEmployeeDetails>
                  <DepartmentOrEmployeeNameCode>
                     DTE
                  </DepartmentOrEmployeeNameCode>
                  <DepartmentOrEmployeeName>
                     L. Ventura
                  </DepartmentOrEmployeeName>
               </DepartmentOrEmployeeDetails>
            </ContactInformation>
            <CommunicationContacts>
               <ElectronicMail>
                  lino@espressomachine.it
               </ElectronicMail>
            </CommunicationContacts>
         </ContactInformationGroup>
      </IssuerPartyGroup>
      <LineItemGroup>
         <LineItem
            ActionRequestOrNotificationDescription="PendingAwaitingReview">
            <LineItemIdentifier>
```

```
            000001
          </LineItemIdentifier>
        </LineItem>
        <ItemDescription ItemCharacteristicCode="Product"
                         LanguageNameCode="en">
          Elite Espresso Maker
        </ItemDescription>
        <ItemDescription ItemCharacteristicCode="Quality"
                         LanguageNameCode="en">
          Excellent
        </ItemDescription>
        <DeliveryPartyGroup>
          <DeliveryParty PostalIdentificationCode=""
                         CountryNameCode="USA">
            <PartyIdentificationDetails
              CodeListResponsibleAgency="DunAndBradStreet">
              D-U-N-S Number for coffee machine importing company
            </PartyIdentificationDetails>
            <NameAndAddressDescription>
              Corporate purchasing
            </NameAndAddressDescription>
            <PartyName>
              Name of buyer
            </PartyName>
            <Street>
              Some street
            </Street>
            <City>
              City in USA where buyer is based
            </City>
          </DeliveryParty>
          <Quantity QuantityTypeCodeQualifier="OrderedQuantity" >
            1
          </Quantity>
        </DeliveryPartyGroup>
      </LineItemGroup>
    </DocumentOrMessageDetailsGroup>
</InspectionRequestMessage>
```

# Summary

Existing EDI libraries provide very valuable standard message definitions for numerous application areas and business processes. In an ebXML project, you can benefit from that knowledge in several ways. You can actually use EDI message content, as the messaging service allows you to transport EDI payload content as easily as XML content. This is particularly useful if you have to work with an existing EDI system that will remain operational. An alternative in that situation is to use XEDI, which provides an easy way to use an XML encoding of EDI content. This has some drawbacks – in particular you cannot use standard XML validating parsers, so you would need to write such validation code yourself or rely on an EDI translator.

If you don't have to integrate with an existing EDI infrastructure, you can still benefit from the knowledge expressed in the EDI message libraries, using an approach like the one proposed by the XML/EDI project. While the EDI syntax is cryptic and unfamiliar to most XML programmers, it is not very complex and if you're like most developers, you will be able to repeat the exercise we've gone through for the "Inspection Request Message" for other messages of interest to your particular project in less than a day.

The sample message we've looked at shows that the general approach for encoding EDIFACT messages in XML advocated by the XML/EDI project can be applied successfully and methodically to create XML e-business message payload content. In an actual project, the schema we've generated would just be a starting point, and there are many ways in which it can be modified or extended, two of which we'll mention here.

In ebXML, the above payload would be wrapped in a message that references a CPA. This CPA provides information about parties that is encoded, redundantly, in the EDIFACT message. You might decide to omit this information from the message or only provide it if it differs from what the parties involved agreed on.

The way XML/EDI produces DTDs is influenced by the limited capabilities of DTDs. DTDs can perform limited validation of attribute values but not of element text content. In XML Schema, you can also specify datatype constraints on text content of element, so you are free to use elements to represent this information.

- The relationship between the ebMS and other ebXML components (like the CPP), as they are relevant for messaging functionality
- An introduction to ebXML **message service handlers**, and the services required of a message service handler

There's a lot to cover in this chapter! The basic mechanisms are quite straightforward, and we build on the concepts covered in Chapter 4, *SOAP*. We believe that there are no inherently difficult areas in this chapter on ebMS – understanding is very much helped by the fact that ebMS messages are **self-describing** XML documents. The only problem we anticipate is in acquiring a concrete feeling for the terminology used, and we hope to guide you through that process.

# An Overview of the ebXML Messaging Service

As we've mentioned in earlier chapters, the **ebXML Messaging Service** (**ebMS**) is one of the infrastructural components of ebXML. The goal of the ebMS team was to come up with a specification which allows for a robust, yet low-cost messaging implementation. ebMS does that by tapping into the existing infrastructure of SOAP: ebMS extends the SOAP message structure with additional constructs to support secure and reliable messaging, necessary for communication in a B2B e-business framework.

There are two key areas in which ebMS extends SOAP:

- Reliable messaging: SOAP and ebMS, like most other messaging systems built on TCP/IP, rely on the notion that underlying protocol layers are considered to be 'unreliable' in nature. This is related to the issue of operation in a distributed environment like the Internet, where the basic form of communication is inherently asynchronous. In this environment, when a sender issues a message he is not able to rely on receipt or reply by their recipients; thus, it's possible for any of the following situations to arise without the sender's knowledge:
    - Delivery of a message can take a relatively long time (relative, that is, to messaging in a non-distributed environment).
    - A message may fail to reach its recipient – for example, because a machine goes offline or crashes, or because gateway buffers overflow, or because phone wires get cut.
    - Messages leaving the sender in a particular order may reach their recipient in a different order.

  ebMS specifies a messaging service framework that extends the messaging functionality offered by SOAP by defining additional mechanisms for routing, guaranteed delivery, and ordered delivery. ebMS also specifies behaviors for the message service handler (MSH) – the piece of software which takes care of execution of the ebMS-defined tasks at each node.
- Security: Secure messaging in ebXML relies heavily on the use of 'digital signatures' through which messages can be 'signed'. Digital signatures offer a means by which authentication, authorization, message integrity and non-repudiation are made possible. We will discuss this in more depth in Chapter 15, along with specific examples.

# 13

# ebXML Messaging

If the ebXML framework is to allow parties to exchange purchase orders, invoices, and other business documents, then it needs to provide some kind of **messaging service** that facilitates that exchange.

Within the ebXML infrastructure, the **ebXML Messaging Service** (**ebXML MS** or **ebMS**) is the component that provides the services needed for business document exchange. A messaging service should take care only of the mechanics of message exchange; not the message payload. The ebXML Messaging Service follows this model.

In the early days of the ebMS development, the ebMS designers had wanted to develop their own messaging system. At that time, they found that other XML-based initiatives (like SOAP) were not sufficiently flexible to meet the needs of ebXML. It wasn't until the release of the SOAP With Attachments (SWA) proposal that their approach changed, and the ebMS designers refocused their efforts on SOAP. In the meantime, SOAP had gathered some serious momentum. These factors, coupled with the fact that SOAP is an 'open' XML-based protocol, made SOAP an obvious choice on which to build ebMS.

The decision to build ebMS on SOAP left just two areas to be addressed in an ebXML Messaging Service, that were not covered in SOAP itself: namely, security and reliable messaging. These are exactly the areas covered by the ebXML Messaging Service.

In this chapter, we're going to cover:

- The way in which the ebXML Messaging Service extends the SOAP message structure
- The basic concepts and constructs of reliable messaging, and how ebMS says we should deal with them

## ebMS Interfaces

ebMS offers three interfaces:

- The **message service interface**, which defines the operations that local objects need to perform, if they are to use the communication services offered by ebMS.
- The **service handler interface**, which specifies the structure and meaning of the ebXML messages which pass between the message service interface and the transport service interface. This interface is used to implement the communication protocol (including the MSH).
- The **transport service interface**, which is used to specify the mapping to the underlying transport protocol or transport mechanism (such as HTTP).

An essential part of these interfaces is the Message Service Handler, which provides the actual functionality. Let's now take a closer look at the MSH.

## The Message Service Handler

The functions that need to be provided by a message service handler (MSH) are:

- **Message packaging** – wrapping the message structure of an ebXML message (envelope, header, body) into its SOAP with Attachments (SWA) container. We'll study this in more detail shortly.
- **Header processing** – creating the SOAP header elements around the primary data as passed on by the application. Processing is based partly on parameters specified by the **collaboration protocol agreement** (**CPA**; see Chapter 8). Generated data may include digital signatures, timestamps, and a unique identifier. As part of the header processing, the header is **parsed** by the receiving MSH as it extracts the ebMS header information.
- **Reliable messaging** – handling the delivery and acknowledgment of ebXML messages. The reliable messaging service includes a behavior for acknowledgment of messages, a retransmission and timeout mechanism, a description of persistency for message storage, and an error notification mechanism.
- **Security services** – describing digital signature creation and verification, authentication, and authorization. These services can be used by other components of the MSH including the header processing and header parsing components.
- **Error handling** – handling the reporting of errors encountered during the processing of a message.

Let's expand on this overview. This next diagram shows the ebMS functionality in more detail:

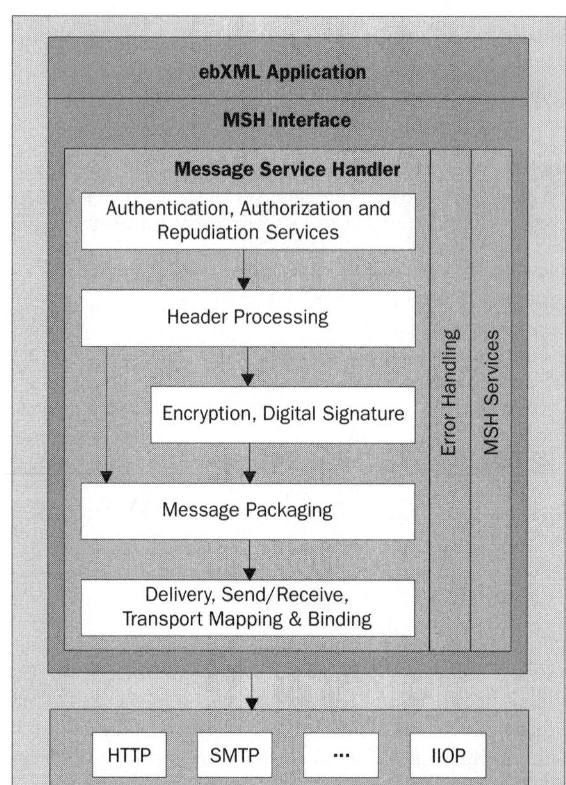


Let's briefly look at a basic ebMS message flow from one application to another. On its way, the message flows through the sending and receiving MSH, possibly passing through intermediary MSHs, all offering the relevant functionality to process the message:

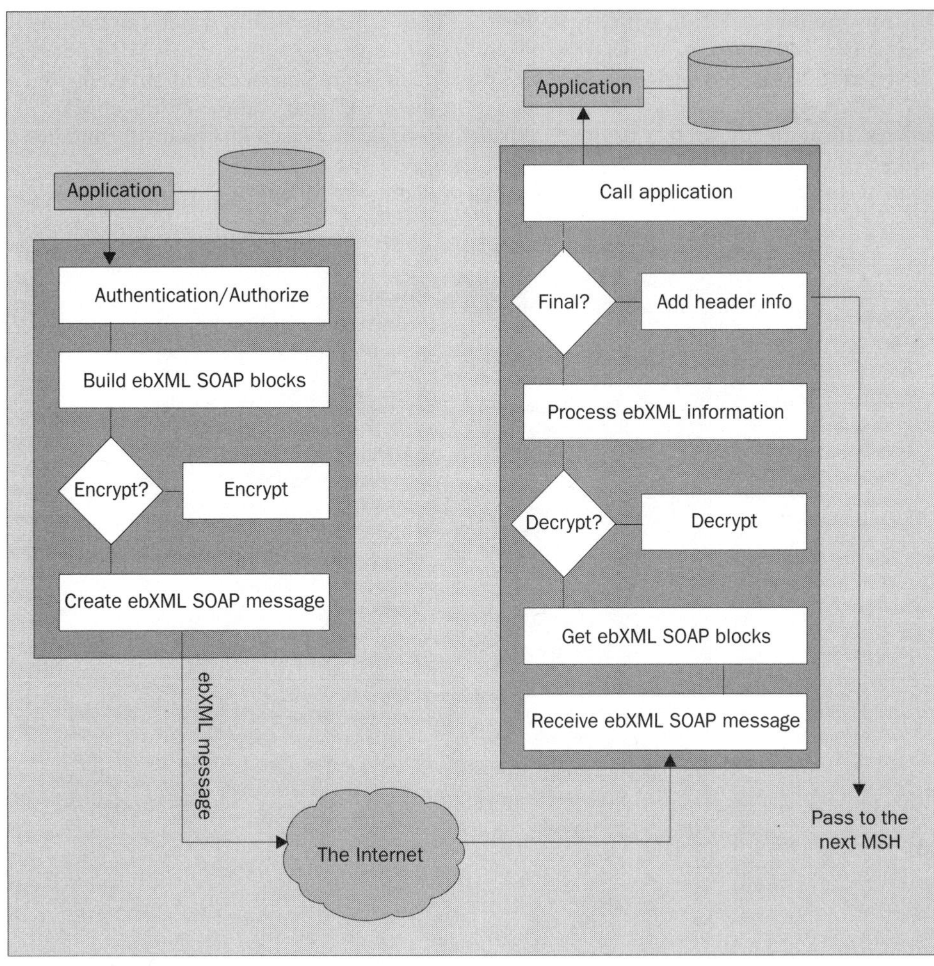


This diagram shows the flow of an ebMS message (which, remember, is just an XML document), using a familiar encapsulation mechanism. ebMS extends the basic SOAP message structure with its own header and body extensions (as we shall see in more detail later).

*In particular, the exact processing of the message shown here is subject to the exact reliability and quality of service requirements of the system. We'll meet these concepts later in the chapter.*

# ebMS Message Structure

ebXML messages are structured according to the **SOAP with Attachments** (**SWA**) specification that we met in Chapter 4. An ebMS **message package** may consist of the following MIME parts:

- The header container, containing a SOAP 1.1-compliant message. This SOAP XML document is referred to as a **SOAP message**.

- Any number of MIME parts, containing the application payloads, which can themselves contain XML documents, EDI messages, or any arbitrary file type. Each MIME part is referred to as a **payload container**. (It's possible to build a message with no payload containers, and store payload information in the SOAP body; however, the ebMS specification advises that payload information *should* be placed in a payload container.)

The general structure of an ebXML message is illustrated in the following diagram:

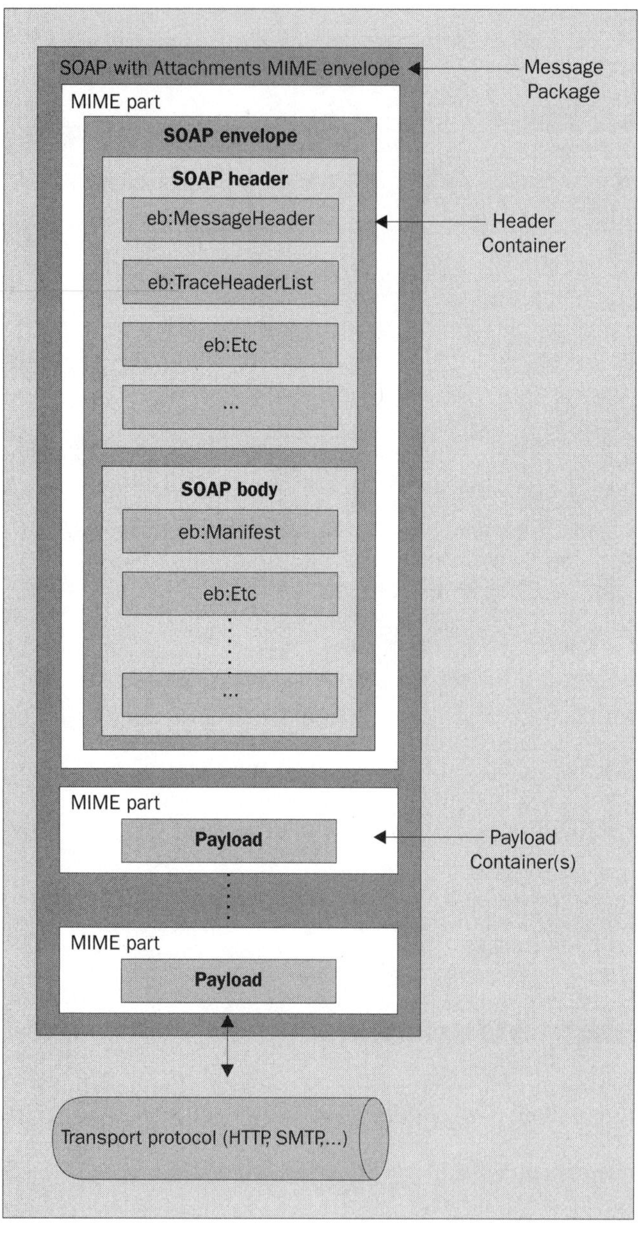

The following code is an example ebXML message package. It consists of a MIME header and two MIME packages. The first MIME package is the header container that contains the SOAP message. The second MIME package, the payload container, contains an encoded `.gif` file:

```
MIME-Version: 1.0
Content-Type: Multipart/Related;
boundary=MIME_boundary; type=text/xml;
start="<contract8987665.xml@wrox.com>"
Content-Description: Writer information, including
contract and draft manual.

--MIME_boundary
Content-Type: text/xml; charset=UTF-8
Content-Transfer-Encoding: 8bit
Content-ID: contract8987665.xml@wrox.com

<SOAP-ENV:Envelope        xmlns:SOAP-
ENV="http://schemas.xmlsoap.org/soap/envelope/">
   <SOAP-ENV:Header>...</SOAP-ENV:Header>
   <SOAP-ENV:Body>...</SOAP-ENV:Body>
</SOAP-ENV:Envelope>

--MIME_boundary
Content-Type: image/gif
Content-Transfer-Encoding: binary
Content-ID: contract8987665.gif@wrox.com
Content-Location: http://www.wrox.com/contract8987665.gif

...binary GIF image...
-MIME_boundary-
```

Header Container
SOAP Message
Payload Container
Payload

As for all ebXML messages, the `Content-Type` of the MIME header is `Multipart/Related`, and the `type` of the SOAP message is `text/xml`. The (optional) `start` parameter points to the first element in the MIME encapsulation – that is, the SOAP 1.1 message. The `Content-Description` is also optional, and may contain a human-readable description of the message.

As we mentioned above, the SOAP body element *should not be used for payload data*; rather, it should be used to contain the SWA equivalent of a number (zero-or-more) of payload containers, within a message package. We'll return to this later. The message package will contain an ebXML `<Manifest>` element, which is used to identify and reference any payload containers. (It's not shown in this code fragment; it's an ebXML extension of the SOAP body, and we'll meet it properly later in the chapter.) A payload may contain arbitrary blocks of data, such as simple text, XML documents, EDI (for example ANSI ASC X12 or UN/EDIFACT) messages, images, other binary data, or complex nested objects.

> *The following point should be obvious, but we'll just mention it for the sake of clarity. When two parties take part in an exchange of data, in order for the data to be useful to both parties, there must be prior agreement between those parties on the structure and interpretation of the payload. Messaging services typically don't deal with message semantics or interpretation of message content – their purpose is only to deliver the message payload to the receiving application.*

*The specification of the process governing message exchange within ebXML is described in the ebXML Business Process Specification Schema (ebBPSS), and is discussed in Chapter 5. Also, Chapters 10 and 11 will give further information on how ebXML handles payloads.*

Here's another fragment. This one shows part of an ebXML message that contains two payload containers with different *types* of payload:

```
--MIME_boundary
Content-Type: image/gif
Content-Transfer-Encoding: base64
Content-ID: contract8987665.gif@wrox.com
Content-Location: http://www.wrox.com/contract8987665.gif
...binary GIF image...
--MIME_boundary
Content-Type: application/xml
Content-Transfer-Encoding: utf-8
Content-ID: invoice232.xml@wrox.com

<invoice>
   <invoicedata>
      <!-- Invoice detail information -->
   </invoicedata>
</invoice>
--MIME_boundary--
```

The first payload container contains a GIF file, transferred in binary format. The second container contains an XML document with invoice information.

# ebXML and SOAP

As we've just seen, an ebXML message package consists of two MIME parts. The first part, the header container, contains a SOAP 1.1-compliant message. The second part, the payload container, contains the application payload.

The ebMS specification defines a set of extensions for the SOAP header and body elements. The SOAP message is similar in structure to those we saw in Chapter 4, except that the header is **obligatory**. It's interesting and instructive to compare the SOAP and ebXML message layouts, and the following diagrams allow us to do that. The first diagram shows the SOAP message structure:

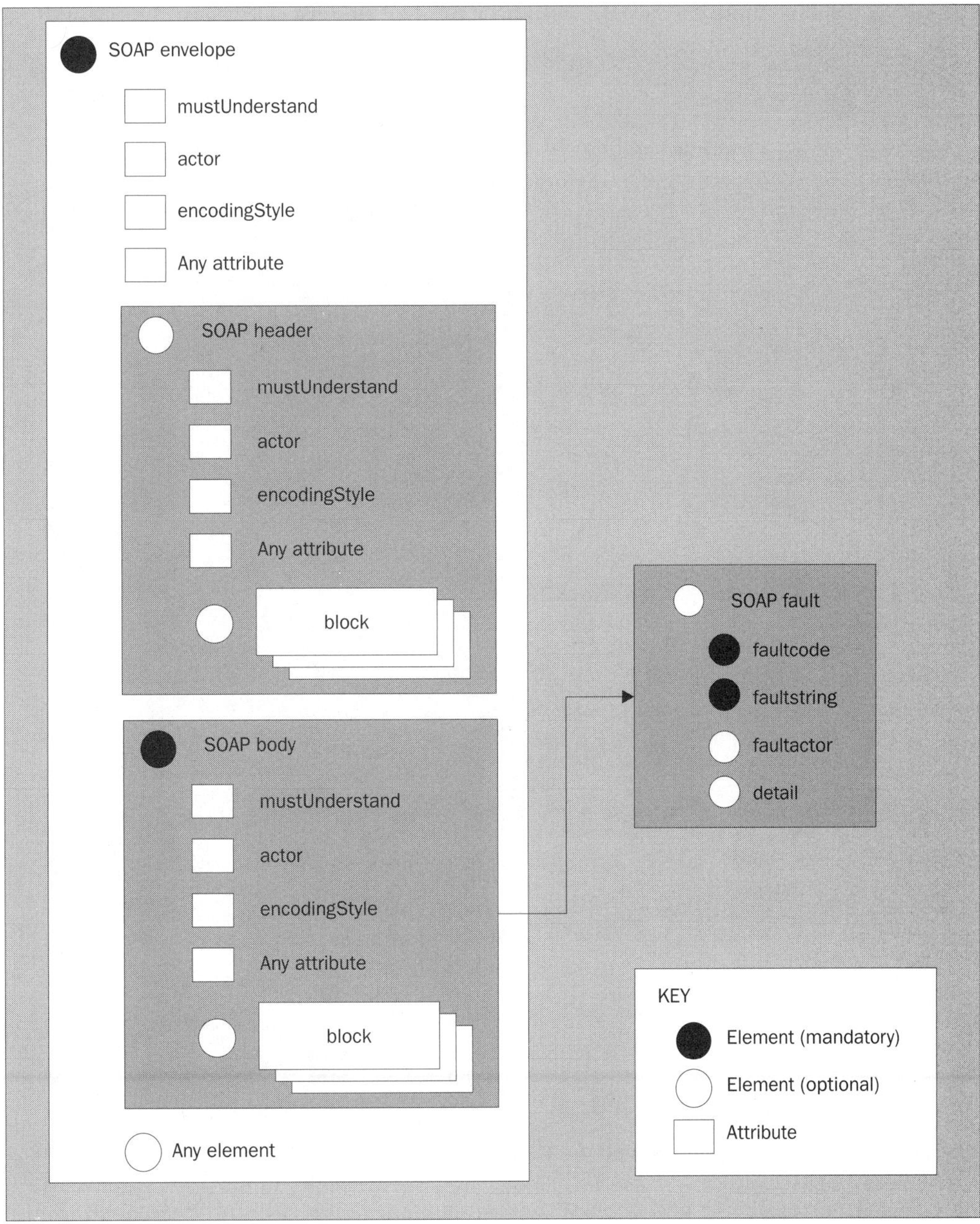
SOAP envelope
mustUnderstand
actor
encodingStyle
Any attribute
SOAP header
mustUnderstand
actor
encodingStyle
Any attribute
block
SOAP body
mustUnderstand
actor
encodingStyle
Any attribute
block
Any element
SOAP fault
faultcode
faultstring
faultactor
detail
KEY
Element (mandatory)
Element (optional)
Attribute

The second diagram shows the message with ebXML SOAP message extensions:

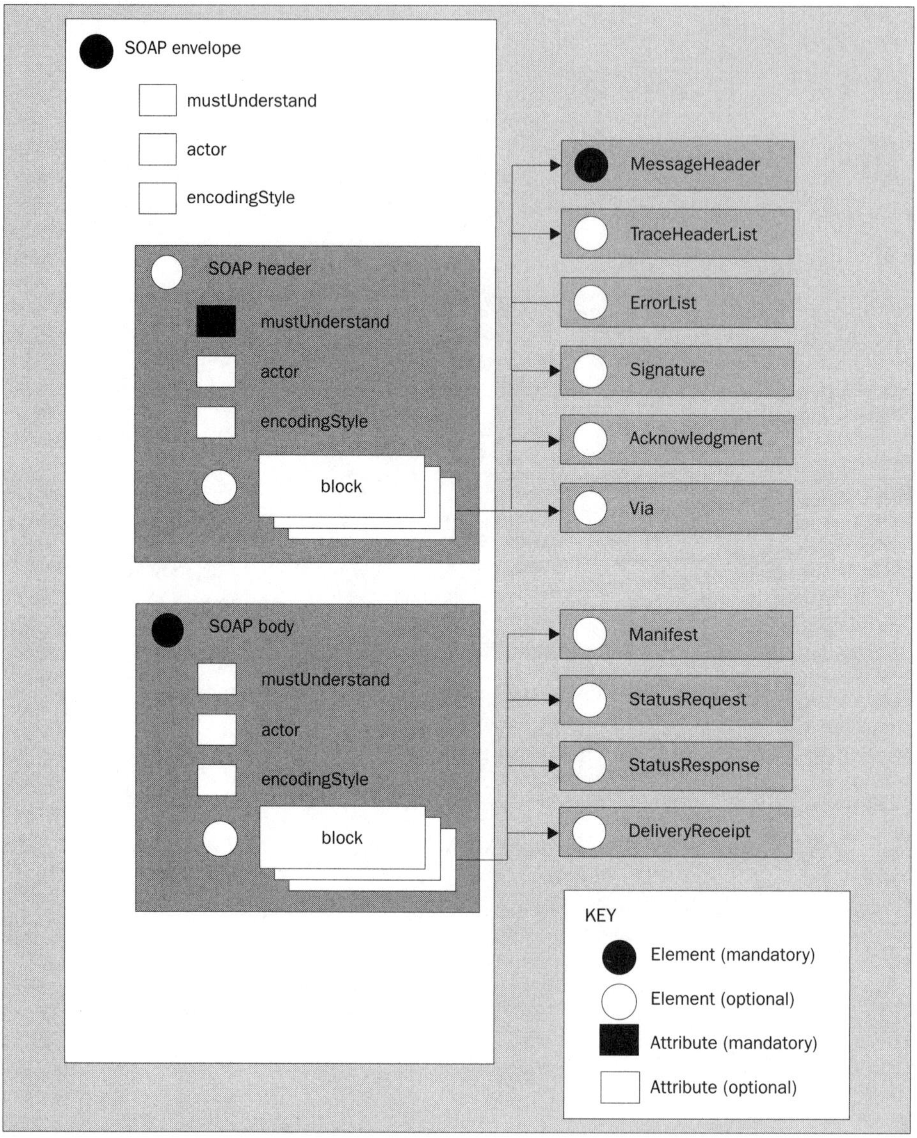

*When we say that an element or attribute is mandatory, we mean that (according to the schema) the element or attribute must be present in the document. For elements, this means that an empty element may be sufficient (for example `<SOAP-ENV:Body/>`). For attributes, it means that the attribute must be present with any value, for instance, `<SOAP-ENV:Header SOAP-ENV:mustUnderstand="1">`.*

## The ebXML Message Envelope

The envelope is the outermost part of the message. Just as in SOAP, this is the designated area for 'general' information, and thus **namespace** information. The namespace for the ebXML messages used in ebMS is `http://www.ebxml.org/namespaces/messageHeader`.

The envelope thus defines the outline of the ebXML SOAP message, like this:

```
<SOAP-ENV:Envelope
     xmlns:SOAP-ENV="http://schemas.xmlsoap.org/soap/envelope/"
     xmlns:eb="http://www.ebxml.org/namespaces/messageHeader">
  <SOAP-ENV:Header SOAP-ENV:mustUnderstand="1">
     <!--eb:ebXML header extension -->
  </SOAP-ENV:Header>
  <SOAP-ENV:Body>
     <!--eb:ebXML body extension -->
  </SOAP-ENV:Body>
</SOAP-ENV:Envelope>
```

We'll fill in the gaps in the following sections.

## Global Attributes in the ebXML Message

As we've seen with SOAP, there are a few important global attributes; let's discuss them here briefly:

- The `SOAP-ENV:mustUnderstand` attribute

  If you've read the Chapter on SOAP, then the purpose of this attribute should come as no surprise to you. Each header extension contains a required SOAP `mustUnderstand` attribute, namespace-qualified to the SOAP namespace (`http://schemas.xmlsoap.org/soap/envelope/`). It indicates that all the receiving MSHs in the chain must successfully be able to process the contents of the current element (extension) or else the message must be rejected in accordance with SOAP. This attribute must have a value of `1` (signifying "true").

- The `eb:version` attribute

  You may recall that in Chapter 4 we learned that SOAP's versioning mechanism was based on its namespace. In ebXML, the `version` attribute works rather differently: any ebXML extension contains a required `version` attribute, whose value must match that of the ebMS specification. Currently, the value of the `version` attribute must be `1.0` – because we're still at version 1.0 of this spec. Potentially, this allows a single ebXML SOAP document to use extension elements from different versions of ebXML at the same time.

- The `eb:id` attribute

  The optional `id` attribute is also new to us. It is an XML ID type and is used on extension blocks to allow the unique identification of the current element within the SOAP message. The creation of the ID is up to the developer of the MSH and therefore implementation-dependent. (Later in this chapter, we'll see this unique identification of messages being used when an MSH, having sent a message, inquires on the status of that message.)

### ebXML Message Header Extension Blocks

Recall (from our description of SOAP in Chapter 4) that we use the term **block** to describe a block of data seen as a *single computational unit* by a processing node. In the SOAP message, the `<Header>` element is the first child element of the SOAP envelope element, and is meant to be used as an area for auxiliary data (authentication, transactions, routing, etc.). So let's see how the ebXML-defined extensions make use of this area. ebXML defines the following header blocks:

- `<MessageHeader>` – a required element meant to contain **routing information** for the message (`To/From`, etc.) as well as other context information about the message.
- `<TraceHeaderList>` – an optional element used for the **identification of the MSHs** that sent and should receive the message. It is used in a multi-hop scenario where an audit trail of intermediaries is traced.
- `<ErrorList>` – an optional element containing (a list of) **errors** that are being reported against a message.
- `<Signature>` – an optional element containing a **digital signature** based on the XML DSIG specification.
- `<Acknowledgment>` – an optional element to be used by a receiving MSH to let the sending `MSH` know that a previous message has been received.
- `<Via>` – an optional element used to exchange 'transport'-related information to the next ebXML MSH, typically in a multi-hop scenario. We'll discuss this in more detail later.

The following diagram summarizes these ebXML header extensions:

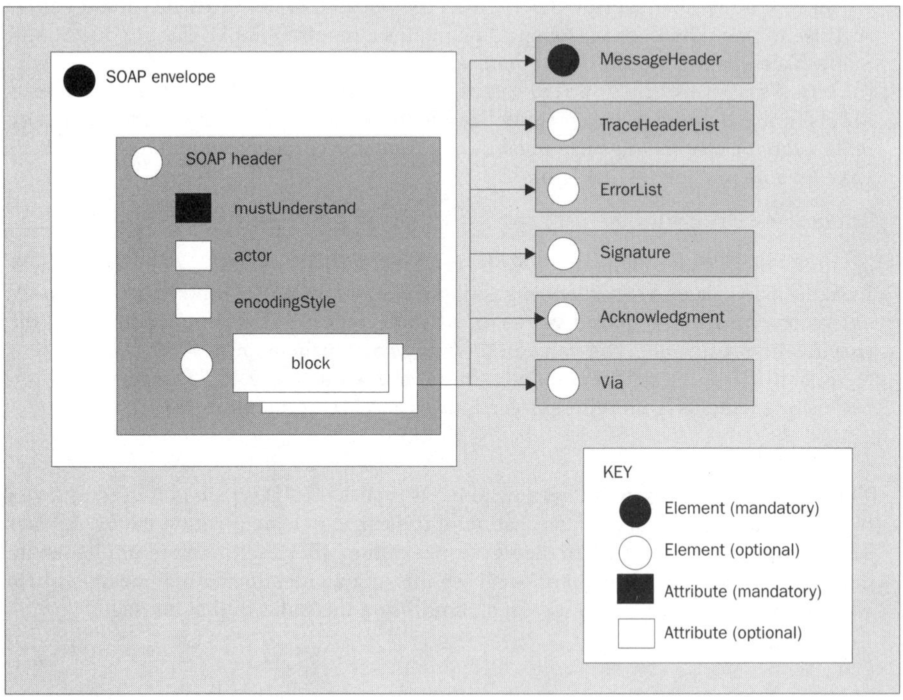

The six header blocks mentioned are composed of quite a few elements and attributes themselves, used in the different processing scenarios offered by the MSH. But before we go into further detail let's first get an overview of the ebXML message body extension blocks.

### ebXML Message Body Extension Blocks

Again, as in SOAP, the `<Body>` element is the second child element of the envelope element. An ebXML message extends the SOAP `<Body>` element with the following extension blocks:

- `<Manifest>` – an optional element, you can think of this as being the table of contents for the data in the payload container or elsewhere (for example on the Internet). The `<Manifest>` element contains references and descriptive information on the payload. In SOAP, the `<Body>` element is used to contain payload information; therefore the `<Body>` is a logical place for the `<Manifest>` element.
- `<StatusRequest>` – an optional element used to identify the message whose status is being requested.
- `<StatusResponse>` – an optional element used by an MSH when responding to a request on the status of a message that was received earlier.
- `<DeliveryReceipt>` – an optional element used by the `To` party that received a message, to let the `From` party know the message was received.

We can represent the ebXML body extensions diagrammatically as follows:

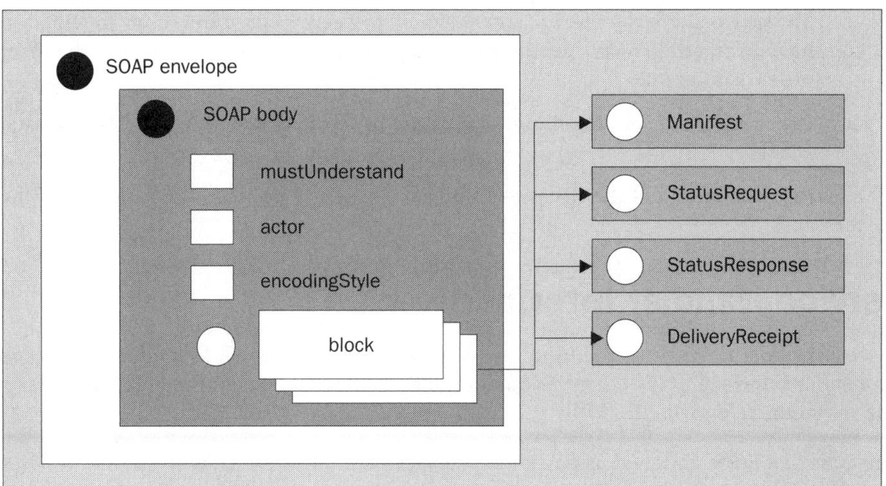


As with the header extension blocks, the body blocks consist of several elements and attributes. Later in the chapter we'll take a closer look at some sample messages, further explaining these elements as we meet them.

# ebXML MSH Processes

The <Header> and <Body> extension blocks we have just discussed are used for describing and requesting messaging functionality provided by the MSH. For instance, the <StatusRequest> body block is used to request information about the status of sent messages. We'll be looking at some examples of how the different blocks are used in different messaging scenarios, and explaining the content of the blocks.

In the remainder of this chapter, we'll cover the following base functionalities and their extension block settings:

- **ebMS message transfer** – sending of messages using a **single-hop** (direct sender-to-receiver) or **multi-hop** (via intermediary nodes) scenario.
- **ebMS message transport** – the transport of ebXML messages via the HTTP protocol.
- **Message service handler services** – a set of defined basic services offered by the MSH to obtain information on messages for the MSH, and not directly related to message transfers between applications using the MSH.
- **Quality of Service** – a number of base technologies that allow for robust and reliable messaging, containing:
  - **Reliable messaging** – an interoperable protocol such that two MSHs can "reliably" exchange messages.
  - **Message order** – the mechanism designed to keep track of the order in which messages have been sent. Allows for the reordering of received messages in case the receiving order is different.
  - **Error reporting and handling** – reporting of errors detected in ebXML messages between MSHs.
- **Security** – definition of the necessary steps to secure the messages and transfer of the messages.

# The Service Handler Interface

Before we talk about the processes and related extension blocks, we will first take a closer look at the **service handler interface**. It is defined as one of the three components in the ebXML Messaging Service, used for communication with the MSH.

The functions that are mentioned as part of the service handler interface are:

- `Send()` – sends an ebXML message. Values for the parameters are derived from the ebXML message headers.
- `Receive()` – indicates the ability to receive an ebXML message.
- `Notify()` – provides notification of expected and unexpected events (error handling).
- `Inquire()` – provides a method of querying the status of the specified ebXML message interchange via the MSH services. This message status can be one of `unAuthorized`, `notRecognized` and `Received` – we'll meet these message statuses properly later in the chapter.

Besides these functions, the MSH should also provide functionality to interface with internal systems, including the routing of received messages to internal systems, and error notification.

*Note that there is no fixed specification or definition provided to describe the functions and parameters that must be offered by this interface. A number of abstract functions, providing access to the base functionality, are mentioned, but no further detail is specified. This can easily lead to an incompatibility between service handler interface (API) implementations from different MSH vendors.*

*In spite of the current lack of direction, it may be possible to develop an implementation that minimizes potential incompatibility issues (although it can't guarantee to eliminate them). We could interpret the specification by implementing each of the functions with only a single parameter and a single result (both being an ebXML message), like this:*

```
Public ebXMLMessage Send(ebXMLMessage value)
```

# ebMS Message Transfer

Message transfer in ebXML is very similar to the mechanisms we've already encountered in SOAP. Messages can be sent directly from the sender to the receiver (a so-called **single-hop message transfer**), or they can be sent via one or more intermediary MSHs (a **multi-hop message transfer**).

## Single-hop Message Transfer

The following code is an example of an ebXML message that will be sent via a single-hop mechanism, meaning it will be sent from the sending MSH directly to the receiving MSH:

```
<SOAP-ENV:Envelope
      xmlns:SOAP-ENV="http://schemas.xmlsoap.org/soap/envelope/"
      xmlns:eb="http://www.ebxml.org/namespaces/messageHeader">
   <SOAP-ENV:Header SOAP-ENV:mustUnderstand="1">
      <eb:MessageHeader eb:id="19650205" eb:version="1.0"
                        SOAP-ENV:mustUnderstand="1">
         <eb:From>
            <eb:PartyId>urn:tamino.com:id:PartyA</eb:PartyId>
         </eb:From>
         <eb:To>
            <eb:PartyId>urn:wrox.com:id:PartyB</eb:PartyId>
         </eb:To>
         <eb:ConversationId>20010730-114115</eb:ConversationId>
         <eb:MessageData>
            <eb:MessageId>20010812.111203@wrox.com</eb:MessageId>
            <eb:Timestamp>2001-08-12T11:12:03Z</eb:Timestamp>
         </eb:MessageData>
      </eb:MessageHeader>
   </SOAP-ENV:Header>
</SOAP-ENV:Envelope>
```

The first few lines in this sample should be familiar, with namespace information, and `version` and `mustUnderstand` attributes. Now let's have a look at the other elements in this fragment, and their purpose.

### The <MessageHeader>, <From>, <To> and <PartyId> Elements

The first new element we encounter is the `<MessageHeader>` element, which must be present. It contains routing information for the message (`<From>` and `<To>`, etc.) as well as other context information about the message.

Stepping through this message, things should look familiar up until we reach the `<From>` and `<To>` elements – these are `<MessageHeader>` elements that we've mentioned in passing in this chapter, but this is the first time we've met them formally. As you've probably guessed, `<From>` is a required element that identifies the party that sent the original message. Similarly, `<To>` is a required element that identifies the party that is the intended recipient of the message.

Both `<From>` and `<To>` consist of one or more `<PartyId>` child elements. A `<PartyId>` element contains a business entity identifier which we'll describe in more detail in a moment. If multiple `<PartyId>` elements are present, they must all identify the same organisation. Having multiple `<PartyId>` elements is particularly useful when transport of a message between the parties involves multiple intermediaries that use different resolving mechanisms (for example if one MSH is capable of resolving the D-U-N-S number, while another can only resolve URLs).

### The <ConversationId> Element

Moving on we find another required element, `<ConversationId>`, used to identify messages that belong to a communication exchange between two parties. The entire exchange can be seen as a conversation. This conversation could consist of a single message and reply, or it might consist of a number of messages going back-and-forth between the two parties over time. The party initiating the conversation determines the value of the `<ConversationId>` – the value should be unique to the `From` and `To` parties. All messages in this conversation will use the same `ConversationId`. The generation of a `ConversationId` is implementation-specific; in the sample the `ConversationId` is `20010730-114115`, which is generated using a timestamp mechanism (which is a commonly-used technique). Note that MSH implementations must provide ways to handle IDs generated by others.

### The <MessageData>, <MessageId>, <Timestamp>, <RefToMessageId>, and <TimeToLive> Elements

The next element new to us 'in practice' (we mentioned it earlier in our enumeration of the ebXML header blocks) is `<MessageData>`:

```
<eb:MessageData>
   <eb:MessageId>20010812.111203@wrox.com</eb:MessageId>
   <eb:Timestamp>2001-08-12T11:12:03Z</eb:Timestamp>
   <eb:RefToMessageId>20010812.11159@tamino.com</eb:RefToMessageId>
</eb:MessageData>
```

This required element uniquely identifies an ebXML message. It can contain four elements:

- The required `<MessageId>` is used to uniquely identify the message. It conforms to the `Content-ID` and `Message-ID` URLs as defined in the IETF RFC2392 (see http://www.ietf.org/rfc/rfc2392.txt). The local part (`20010812.111203` in the sample) is implementation-dependent. In this case we have used a common technique of combining a time/datestamp with the host's domain name.
- The required `<Timestamp>` is an XML Schema `timeInstant` datatype, and represents the time the `<MessageHeader>` was created.

- The optional `<RefToMessageId>` contains the `MessageId` value of an earlier ebXML message, to which this message is related. This can either be present with a value, or not present at all. The `RefToMessageId` is used in `error messages` and `acknowledgment messages`, containing the `MessageId` of the originating message. It is also used in a `StatusRequest` or `StatusResponse` message and contains the message whose status is being queried. We will meet the `RefToMessageId` again during the coverage of these types of messages later in this chapter.
- It's also possible to include an (optional) `<TimeToLive>` element, which would be used to indicate the time by which the message should be delivered and processed by the `To` party's MSH.

### *The <TraceHeaderList> Element*

After the MSH receives the message, a `<TraceHeaderList>` element (containing a single `<TraceHeader>` element) can be added. This optional ebXML header extension block contains information about the transmission of messages between MSHs, and is only added in case of a multi-hop scenario to pass information on to the next node. The following sample shows a message containing both the `<MessageHeader>` and the `<TraceHeaderList>`:

```
<SOAP-ENV:Envelope
      xmlns:SOAP-ENV="http://schemas.xmlsoap.org/soap/envelope/"
      xmlns:eb="http://www.ebxml.org/namespaces/messageHeader">
   <SOAP-ENV:Header SOAP-ENV:mustUnderstand="1">
      <eb:MessageHeader eb:id="19650205" eb:version="1.0"
            SOAP-ENV:mustUnderstand="1">
         <eb:From>
            <eb:PartyId>urn:tamino.com:id:PartyA</eb:PartyId>
         </eb:From>
         <eb:To>
            <eb:PartyId>urn:wrox.com:id:PartyB</eb:PartyId>
         </eb:To>
         <eb:ConversationId>20010730-114115</eb:ConversationId>
         <eb:MessageData>
            <eb:MessageId>20010812.111203@wrox.com</eb:MessageId>
            <eb:Timestamp>2001-08-12T11:12:03Z</eb:Timestamp>
         </eb:MessageData>
      </eb:MessageHeader>
      <eb:TraceHeaderList eb:version="1.0" SOAP-ENV:mustUnderstand="1"
            SOAP-ENV:actor="http://schemas.xmlsoap.org/soap/actor/next">
         <eb:TraceHeader>
            <eb:Sender>
               <eb:PartyId eb:type="urn:duns">06-358-7745</eb:PartyId>
               <eb:Location>http://tamino.com/FromPartyMsh</eb:Location>
            </eb:Sender>
            <eb:Receiver>
               <eb:PartyId eb:type="urn:duns">99-358-7945</eb:PartyId>
              <eb:Location>http://wrox.com/ToPartyMsh</eb:Location>
           </eb:Receiver>
           <eb:Timestamp>2001-08-12T11:12:03Z</eb:Timestamp>
         </eb:TraceHeader>
      </eb:TraceHeaderList>
   </SOAP-ENV:Header>
</SOAP-ENV:Envelope>
```

The first few lines in this sample should be familiar from the earlier examples in this chapter, with namespace information, and version and mustUnderstand attributes.

The <TraceHeaderList> element must contain an actor attribute. This attribute contains the value http://schemas.xmlsoap.org/soap/actor/next. As we saw in our discussion of SOAP in Chapter 4, this value indicates that the <TraceHeaderList> element must be processed by the 'next' MSH (that is, the one receiving the message).

### The <TraceHeader> and <Sender> Elements

Moving further through the sample we meet the required <TraceHeader> element, which can be used repeatedly in a <TraceHeaderList> block. It contains information on – in this case – a single transmission of a message between two instances of an MSH. A <TraceHeader> element is appended to the <TraceHeaderList> before transmission of a message. Let's look in some more detail at the structure of the <TraceHeader> element itself (this one has an additional <TraceMessage> element, which we'll explan in a moment):

```
<eb:TraceHeader>
   <eb:Sender>
      <eb:PartyId eb:type="urn:duns">06-358-7745</eb:PartyId>
      <eb:Location>http://tamino.com/FromPartyMsh</eb:Location>
   </eb:Sender>
   <eb:Receiver>
      <eb:PartyId eb:type="urn:duns">99-358-7945</eb:PartyId>
      <eb:Location>http://wrox.com/ToPartyMsh</eb:Location>
   </eb:Receiver>
   <eb:Timestamp>2001-08-12T11:12:03Z</eb:Timestamp>
   <TraceMessage>Message processed successfully</TraceMessage>
</eb:TraceHeader>
```

The first two elements we meet within the <TraceHeader> are the required <Sender> and <Receiver> elements. As you have probably guessed, the <Sender> element identifies the party that sent the message, and the <Receiver> element identifies the message's intended receiver. Both elements are similarly structured, in that they each contain a required <PartyId> element and a required <Location> element.

### The <PartyId> Element

A <PartyId> element contains business entity identifiers; in the above example, a D-U-N-S (Dun and Bradstreet's Data Universal Numbering System) number has been used. Potentially this could contain other types of identifier, such as Chamber of Commerce numbers, VAT numbers, or even e-mail addresses. The type attribute of the <PartyId> element is used to indicate the domain to which the used <PartyId> belongs. This domain must be mutually understood and agreed upon by the sender and receiver.

If no type is specified, then the PartyId must be a URI (otherwise the receiving MSH has to report an error, with the errorCode set to Inconsistent and severity set to Error).

### The <Location> Element

The <Location> element is used to specify the URL of the sender's MSH. In our sample, for illustration, we used the fictional URL http://wrox.com/ToPartyMsh.

### The <Timestamp> and <TraceMessage> Elements

The `<Timestamp>` element must also be present; it contains information on the time the `<TraceHeader>` element was created. Additional elements can be added containing application-specific information. The above sample illustrates an additional `<TraceMessage>` element, which contains information on the process status of the message. An optional `id` attribute can be added to the `<TraceHeader>` element, to uniquely identify it within the `TraceHeaderList`.

To summarize, here's the diagrammatic representation of the `TraceHeaderList` block structure:

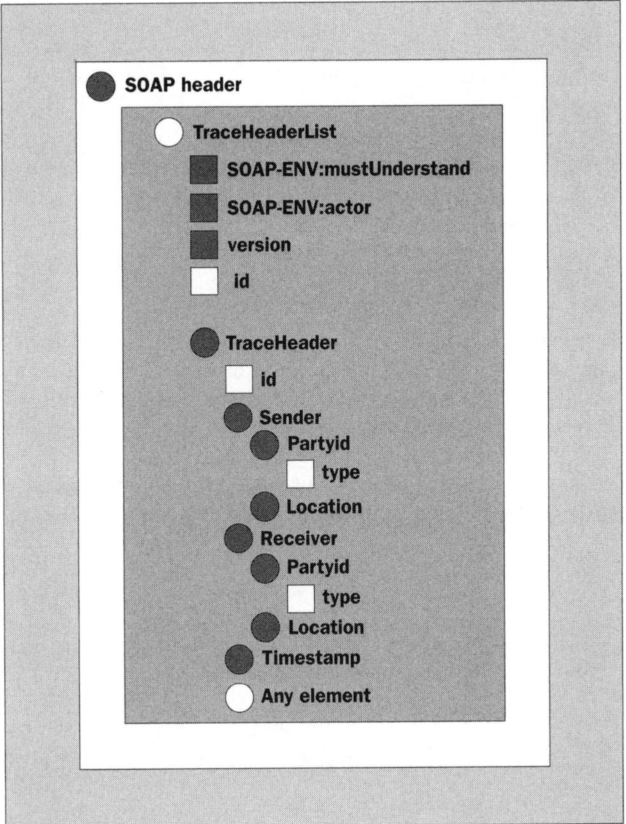


Now that we've covered a single-hop message transfer, let's make things slightly more difficult and move on to its multi-hop counterpart.

## Multi-hop Message Transfer

As we've seen in SOAP, multi-hop messages are sent via one or more intermediary parties. This is illustrated in the following figure:

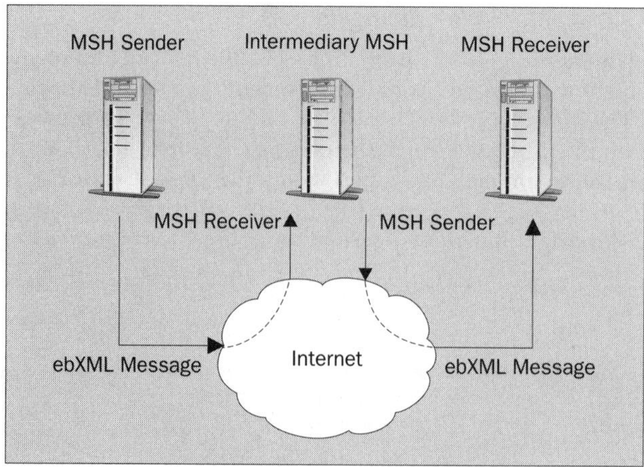


*In contrast with, for instance, e-mail forwarding and global e-mail handling, there is currently no global infrastructure support for either SOAP or ebMS. As the technology moves forward we expect better support in this area.*

By definition, multi-hop messages pass through various intermediaries, and therefore reliability of multi-hop messages is an issue that needs specific attention. Shortly we'll look at reliable messaging features of ebMS (building on acknowledgments and timeouts) in the context of multi-hop transfers, but before we do that, let's first look at some sample messages.

The following samples involve a message being sent from a sender (Party A) to a receiver (Party C) via an intermediary MSH (Party B), in a multi-hop scenario. Below is a typical sample message from Party A to Party B:

```
<SOAP-ENV:Envelope
      xmlns:SOAP-ENV="http://schemas.xmlsoap.org/soap/envelope/"
      xmlns:eb="http://www.ebxml.org/namespaces/messageHeader">
   <SOAP-ENV:Header SOAP-ENV:mustUnderstand="1">
      <eb:MessageHeader eb:id="19650205" eb:version="1.0"
                        SOAP-ENV:mustUnderstand="1">
         <eb:From>
            <eb:PartyId>urn:tamino.com:id:PartyA</eb:PartyId>
         </eb:From>
         <eb:To>
            <eb:PartyId>urn:wrox.com:id:PartyC</eb:PartyId>
         </eb:To>
         <eb:ConversationId>20010730-114115</eb:ConversationId>
         <eb:MessageData>
            <eb:MessageId>20010812.111203@wrox.com</eb:MessageId>
            <eb:Timestamp>2001-08-12T11:12:03Z</eb:Timestamp>
         </eb:MessageData>
      </eb:MessageHeader>
      <eb:Via SOAP-ENV:mustUnderstand="1" eb:version="1.0"
              SOAP-ENV:actor="http://schemas.xmlsoap.org/soap/actor/next">
         <eb:Service>urn:services:FlowController</eb:Service>
         <eb:Action>LogMessage</eb:Action>
      </eb:Via>
   </SOAP-ENV:Header>
</SOAP-ENV:Envelope>
```

The message looks very similar to that which we saw in the single-hop example, earlier in the chapter – until we reach the group of elements and attributes that begin with the <Via> element (which we've highlighted above). In what follows, we'll just focus on where the multi-hop example differs from the single-hop example.

### The <Via> Element

The <Via> element is an optional ebXML header extension block, used to transfer information between any two MSHs in the chain (From-to-intermediary, or intermediary-to-intermediary, or intermediary-to-To).

The <Via> element is used to hold data that can vary from one hop to another. It consists of the required mustUnderstand and version attributes, and (optionally) the id attribute to uniquely identify the <Via> element. We also see the familiar, and required, actor attribute in our sample.

The <Via> element can also contain up to three additional attributes which we didn't meet in the single-hop example. They are, of course, all optional:

- syncReply – an XML Schema Boolean, which indicates whether the underlying data communication protocol is synchronous (for example, HTTP). The sample above takes the default value, false, indicating an asynchronous transfer (for example, via SMTP). If syncReply is true, the MSH will return the response in the payload of the reply message.
- reliableMessagingMethod – contains the value ebXML (default) or Transport. More on this later when we describe reliable messaging.
- ackRequested – indicates to the receiving MSH whether an acknowledgment message is requested and, if so, what type – Signed, Unsigned, or None (default). Again, more on this later.

The <Via> element can also have a number of (optional) child elements. They're outlined here:

- <Service> – identifies the service that processes the message. There is a similar element in the <MessageHeader>, and we'll cover this in more detail later.
- <Action> – identifies the service that processes the message. As with the <Service> element, there is a similar element in the <MessageHeader> and we'll cover this in more detail later.

*Note that if the <Action> element is present, then the <Service> element must also be present (and vice versa). In the above sample, the requested process (or Action) is LogMessage, and the Service providing the process is urn:services:FlowController.*

- <CPAId> (not covered in this example) – specifies the parameters that govern the exchange of messages between two MSHs. It is identical to the <CPAId> element in the <MessageHeader> (see later), except that the parameters identified by *this* <CPAId> element apply just to the exchange of messages between the two MSHs (rather than between the parties identified in the <To> and <From> elements of the <MessageHeader>). This allows different parameters, transport protocols, etc., to be used on different hops when a message is passed through intermediaries.

*If the <CPAId> element is present, these values should be used instead of the values identified by the <CPAId> in the <MessageHeader> element.*

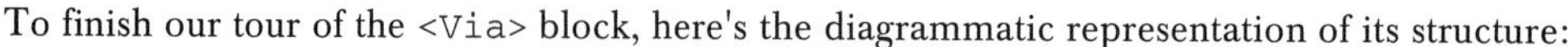

To finish our tour of the <Via> block, here's the diagrammatic representation of its structure:

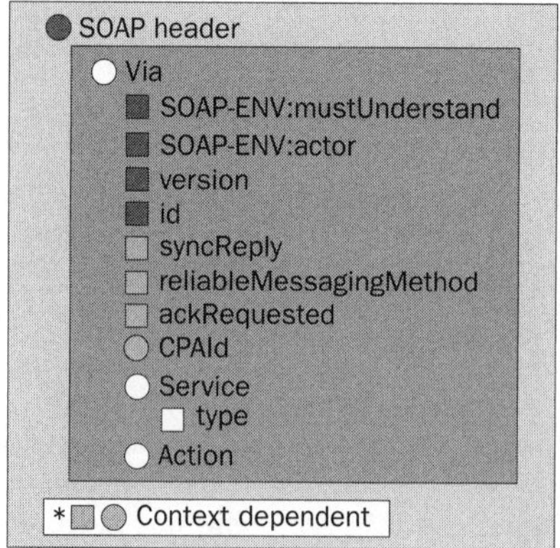


The receiving MSH (in this case the intermediary Party B) adds the <TraceHeaderList> element before transmitting it to the next MSH (Party C). The <TraceHeaderList> element will only be added in the case of a multi-hop scenario, and then only once, by the first intermediary MSH. Ultimately, the <TraceHeaderList> element will contain enough children to surmise the complete transfer information for the message.

The MSH also adds a <TraceHeader> element, which contains the information describing the single transmission of the message between these two adjacent MSHs. An MSH will only add a <TraceHeader> element to the <TraceHeaderList> if (and when) the MSH has to pass the message to a next MSH in the chain (and thus it's only used in a multi-hop scenario).

In the code sample above, the message has just been received from Party A by Party B. Party B has not yet processed the message, so there is no trace information present. In processing the message, Party B recognizes that it must pass the message on to Party C. So it adds a <TraceHeaderList> element, and a <TraceHeader> expressing the single transfer trace information from Party A to Party B, producing the following message, which is then sent to Party C:

```
<SOAP-ENV:Envelope
......xmlns:SOAP-ENV="http://schemas.xmlsoap.org/soap/envelope/"
......xmlns:eb="http://www.ebxml.org/namespaces/messageHeader">
   <SOAP-ENV:Header SOAP-ENV:mustUnderstand="1">
      <!-- eb:MessageHeader element as before ... -->
      <!-- eb:Via element as before ... -->
      <eb:TraceHeaderList eb:version="1.0" SOAP-ENV:mustUnderstand="1"
            SOAP-ENV:actor="http://schemas.xmlsoap.org/soap/actor/next">
         <eb:TraceHeader>
            <eb:Sender>
               <eb:PartyId>urn:wrox.com:id:PartyA</eb:PartyId>
               <eb:Location>http://tamino.com/PartyAMsh</eb:Location>
            </eb:Sender>
            <eb:Receiver>
               <eb:PartyId>urn:wrox.com:id:PartyB</eb:PartyId>
               <eb:Location> http://wrox.com/PartyBMsh</eb:Location>
            </eb:Receiver>
            <eb:Timestamp>2001-08-12T11:12:04Z</eb:Timestamp>
```

```
            </eb:TraceHeader>
        </eb:TraceHeaderList>
    </SOAP-ENV:Header>
</SOAP-ENV:Envelope>
```

When Party C receives this message, it can process it. Party C recognizes that it is the final receiver of this message (and not an intermediary). It too can add a `<TraceHeader>` element to the `<TraceHeaderList>` element. This expresses the message transfer from Party B to Party C. Note that, unlike intermediary MSHs, the final receiver is *not obliged* to add `TraceHeader` information:

```
<SOAP-ENV:Envelope
......xmlns:SOAP-ENV="http://schemas.xmlsoap.org/soap/envelope/"
......xmlns:eb="http://www.ebxml.org/namespaces/messageHeader">
    <SOAP-ENV:Header SOAP-ENV:mustUnderstand="1">
        <!-- eb:MessageHeader element as before ... -->
        <!-- eb:Via element as before ... -->
        <eb:TraceHeaderList eb:version="1.0" SOAP-ENV:mustUnderstand="1"
                SOAP-ENV:actor="http://schemas.xmlsoap.org/soap/actor/next">
            <!-- eb:TraceHeader element summarizing transmission
                                        from A to B, as before ... -->
            <eb:TraceHeader>
                <eb:Sender>
                    <eb:PartyId>urn:wrox.com:id:PartyB</eb:PartyId>
                    <eb:Location>http://wrox.com/PartyBMsh</eb:Location>
                </eb:Sender>
                <eb:Receiver>
                    <eb:PartyId>urn:wrox.com:id:PartyC</eb:PartyId>
                    <eb:Location> http://wrox.com/PartyCMsh</eb:Location>
                </eb:Receiver>
                <eb:Timestamp>2001-08-12T11:12:05Z</eb:Timestamp>
            </eb:TraceHeader>
        </eb:TraceHeaderList>
    </SOAP-ENV:Header>
</SOAP-ENV:Envelope>
```

The message is the same as before, except for the additional information in the `<TraceHeaderList>` element and its children.

### *The <MessageHeader> Element*

We met parts of the `<MessageHeader>` element earlier, when we discussed the single-hop message transfer. As we know, the `<MessageHeader>` must be present in all ebXML messages – it's a child element of the SOAP `<Header>` element, containing routing information (`To`/`From`, etc.) for the payload and other processing-related information about the message.

In the multi-hop situation, we meet some more elements of the `<MessageHeader>`. We'll use the following fragment (showing the structure of the `<MessageHeader>` element within the SOAP message) to aid our study:

```
<SOAP-ENV:Envelope
        xmlns:SOAP-ENV="http://schemas.xmlsoap.org/soap/envelope/"
        xmlns:eb="http://www.ebxml.org/namespaces/messageHeader">
    <SOAP-ENV:Header SOAP-ENV:mustUnderstand="1">
        <eb:MessageHeader eb:id="19650205" eb:version="1.0"
```

```
            SOAP-ENV:mustUnderstand="1">
         <eb:From>
            <eb:PartyId eb:type="urn:duns">06-358-7745</eb:PartyId>
            <eb:PartyId eb:type="SAG">ONIMAT</eb:PartyId>
         </eb:From>
         <eb:To>
            <eb:PartyId>mailto:john.doe@wrox.com</eb:PartyId>
         </eb:To>
         <eb:CPAId>http://www.wrox.com/ebXML/defaultAgreement.xml</eb:CPAId>
         <eb:ConversationId>20010730-114115</eb:ConversationId>
         <eb:Service type="wrox">
            urn:www.wrox.com/orderProcessing
         </eb:Service>
         <eb:Action>ATPCheck</eb:Action>
         <eb:MessageData>
            <eb:MessageId>20010812.111203@wrox.com</eb:MessageId>
            <eb:Timestamp>2001-08-12T11:12:03Z</eb:Timestamp>
            <eb:RefToMessageId>20010812.11159@tamino.com</eb:RefToMessageId>
         </eb:MessageData>
         <eb:QualityOfServiceInfo eb:deliverySemantics="OnceAndOnlyOnce"
            eb:messageOrderSemantics="Guaranteed"
            eb:deliveryReceiptRequested="Unsigned"/>
         <eb:Description xml:lang="en">
            ATP check for order 19650205
         </eb:Description>
         <eb:Description xml:lang="nl">
            ATP controle voor bestelling 19650205
         </eb:Description>
      </eb:MessageHeader>
   </SOAP-ENV:Header>
</SOAP-ENV:Envelope>
```

### The <CPAId> Element

The <CPAId> is a required element used to identify the parameters governing the exchange of messages between the parties. We came across its cousin when we discussed the <Via> element a moment ago. The MSH resolves the mutually agreed CPAId, which must be unique within a namespace. In the sample above, the CPAId is a URI pointing to the governing information at http://www.wrox.com/ebXML/defaultAgreement.xml.

The <CPAId> element can also reference a CPA via the cpaid attribute of the <CollaborationProtocolAgreement> element. If the message exchange is under a CPA, then the information offered by the reliable messaging parameters of the CPA is used to determine the required reliability for the exchange. Since no appropriate handling of conflicts in CPAs is defined in the ebXML MS specification, the MSHs should first check for the ability to deal with these conflicts before it uses them.

> *If a receiver chooses to generate an error as a result of a detected inconsistency, then it must report it with an errorCode of Inconsistent and a severity of Error. If it chooses to generate an error because the CPAId is not recognized, then it must report it with an errorCode of NotRecognized and a severity of Error.*

### The <Service> Element

The next new element is `<Service>` – a required, application-specific element that identifies the service that acts on the message.

ebXML defines a set of **standard services** for the MSH that are identified using the reserved URI `www.ebxml.org/messageService`. These reserved services include **ping**, **acknowledgment** and **message status request** services (we'll meet all three of these services in various MSH scenarios, later in this chapter).

In the previous sample, the requested `Service` is an `orderProcessing` service that is identified by specifying a URI. The optional `type` attribute can be used to tell the parties sending and receiving the message how to interpret the content of the `<Service>` element. In the previous sample, the type is set to `wrox` – indicating that the specified service value conforms to the `wrox` definition, and allows for specifying, for instance, a non-URI service value, such as the value of this element:

```
<eb:Service type="wrox">orderProcessing</eb:Service>
```

If the `type` attribute is not present, the content of the `<Service>` element must be a URI (otherwise the MSH should report an error with an `errorCode` of `Inconsistent` and a `severity` of `Error`).

### The <Action> Element

The required `<Action>` element identifies the process within the service that will process the message. The `Action` is a defined activity, conforming to the ebBPSS specification, which is unique within the service in which it is defined. So, combining the above `Service` and `Action` tells us that the MSH will perform an `ATPCheck` offered by the `orderProcessing` service.

### The <QualityOfServiceInfo> Element

The next new element we meet is `<QualityOfServiceInfo>` – an optional element which is used to identify the quality of service with which the message is delivered:

```
<eb:QualityOfServiceInfo eb:deliverySemantics="OnceAndOnlyOnce"
   eb:messageOrderSemantics="Guaranteed"
   eb:deliveryReceiptRequested="Unsigned"/>
```

In the above sample the message will be sent exactly once, and the messages will be processed in the order in which they were sent by the `From` party. After the message has been received, an unsigned `<Acknowledgment>` message will be sent to the `To` party. This behavior is specified via the three attributes of the `<QualityOfServiceInfo>` element, as will be explained in the *Reliable Messaging...* section later in this chapter.

### The <SequenceNumber> Element

The optional `<SequenceNumber>` element (not demonstrated in this sample) is used to indicate the sequence in which a receiving MSH must process messages. It will be covered later in this chapter, when we talk about the subject of message order.

### *The <Description> Element*

Finally, the `<MessageHeader>` can have any number of `<Description>` child elements (it's optional, so there may be no `<Description>` children at all). The purpose of `<Description>` is to provide a human-readable description of the intent of the message. The language of the description is defined by a required `xml:lang` attribute. Each occurrence should have a different value for `xml:lang`. In the previous sample, two descriptions for the message are defined – one in English (`xml:lang="en"`) and one in Dutch (`xml:lang="nl"`).

To summarize this section, here's the revised diagrammatic representation of the `<MessageHeader>` block:

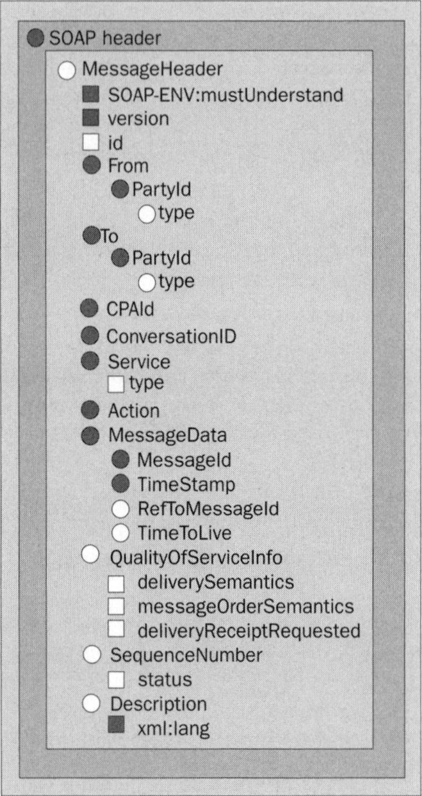


# ebMS Message Transport

All messages, including the single- and multi-hop messages that we've described above, must be sent using a standard communication protocol. The ebMS specification allows for transporting the message using a variety of communication protocols. However, only two are described in more detail, and they are the same protocols described in SWA – namely HTTP and SMTP.

In order to understand the necessary settings and possibilities of referencing payloads from within the ebXML message, we will use the following example that shows an ebXML message `POST`ed over HTTP:

```
POST /processOrder HTTP/1.1
Host: www.wrox.com
Content-Type: Multipart/Related; boundary=MIME_boundary; type=text/xml;
   start="order8987665.xml@wrox.com"
Content-Length: 2490
SOAPAction: "ebXML"
Content-Description: Ability To Promise (ATP) validation.

--MIME_boundary
Content-Type: text/xml; charset=UTF-8
Content-Transfer-Encoding: 8bit
Content-ID: order8987665.xml@wrox.com

<?xml version='1.0' encoding="UTF-8"?>
<SOAP-ENV:Envelope
      xmlns:SOAP-ENV="http://schemas.xmlsoap.org/soap/envelope/"
      xmlns:eb="http://www.ebxml.org/namespaces/messageHeader">
   <SOAP-ENV:Header SOAP-ENV:mustUnderstand="1">
      <eb:MessageHeader eb:id="19650205" eb:version="1.0"
                        SOAP-ENV:mustUnderstand="1">
         <eb:From>
            <eb:PartyId eb:type="urn:duns">06-358-7745</eb:PartyId>
         </eb:From>
         <eb:To>
            <eb:PartyId eb:type="urn:duns">99-358-7945</eb:PartyId>
         </eb:To>
         <eb:CPAId>http://www.wrox.com/ebXML/defaultAgreement.xml</eb:CPAId>
         <eb:ConversationId>20010730-114115</eb:ConversationId>
         <eb:Service type="wrox">
            urn:www.wrox.com/orderProcessing</eb:Service>
         <eb:Action>ATPCheck</eb:Action>
         <eb:MessageData>
            <eb:MessageId>20010812.111203@wrox.com</eb:MessageId>
            <eb:Timestamp>2001-08-12T11:12:03Z</eb:Timestamp>
            <eb:RefToMessageId>20010812.11159@tamino.com</eb:RefToMessageId>
         </eb:MessageData>
         <eb:QualityOfServiceInfo eb:deliverySemantics="OnceAndOnlyOnce"
            eb:messageOrderSemantics="Guaranteed"
            eb:deliveryReceiptRequested="Unsigned"/>
      </eb:MessageHeader>
   </SOAP-ENV:Header>
   <SOAP-ENV:Body>
      <eb:Manifest eb:id="Man01" eb:version="1.0">
         <eb:Reference eb:id="ATPOrder"
                       xlink:href="cid:order2389877.xml@wrox.com"
                       xlink:role="http://www.wrox.com/ebXML/order">
            <eb:Schema eb:location="http://www.wrox.com/ebXML/order.xsd"
                       eb:version="1.0"/>
            <eb:Description xml:lang="en-us">
               ATP Check for order 2389877</eb:Description>
         </eb:Reference>
      </eb:Manifest>
   </SOAP-ENV:Body>
</SOAP-ENV:Envelope>
```

```
--MIME_boundary
Content-ID: order2389877.xml@wrox.com
Content-Type: text/xml

<?xml version="1.0" encoding="UTF-8"?>
<order>
   <ordernumber>2389877</ordernumber>
   <item partnumber="989.546.880">
      <quantity>3</quantity>
      <price currency="USD">11.00</price>
   </item>
</order>
--MIME_boundary--
```

The first part, until the actual start of the message, is created in the same way as defined for SWA messages, thus:

- The `Content-Type: Multipart/Related` MIME header and associated parameters, from the ebXML message envelope, must appear as an HTTP header.
- The mandatory `SOAPAction` HTTP header field must be included in the HTTP header and could, for instance, have a value of `ebXML`, as in the above sample.
- All other MIME headers that constitute the ebXML message envelope must also become part of the HTTP header.
- All ebXML message parts that follow the ebXML message envelope, including the MIME boundary string, constitute the HTTP entity body. This includes the SOAP envelope containing the ebXML parts and all attachments, including the trailing MIME boundary strings.

Other headers with semantics defined by MIME specifications, such as `Content-Transfer-Encoding` and the `MIME-Version: 1.0` header, must *not* appear as an HTTP header. However, HTTP-specific MIME-like headers defined by HTTP 1.1 may be used with the semantic defined in the HTTP specification.

The message itself contains two parts: an **ebXML message** and an **XML payload**. The first part of the ebXML message, as usual, contains the various attributes and the required `<MessageHeader>` that are contained in the SOAP header. What's new is the SOAP body, containing the optional SOAP body extension block, `<Manifest>`.

### The <Manifest> Element

`<Manifest>` is used to identify data items associated with the message. These items can be included as part of the message (as payload document(s) contained in a payload container), or as remote resources accessible via a URL. By referencing payload data instead of adding it to the SOAP body, it is easier to directly extract a particular payload associated with an ebXML message. It also allows an application to determine whether it can process the payload without having to completely parse the payload.

The Manifest element can be represented graphically as follows:

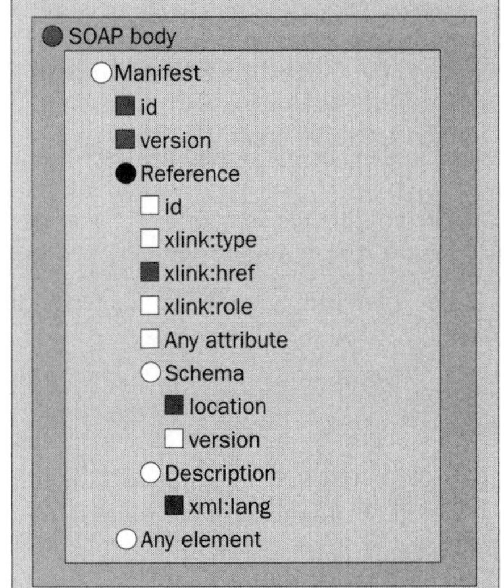


Aside from the required version attribute and the optional id attribute, the <Manifest> element consists of:

- <Reference> element(s) – one or more elements containing the information for referencing the payload. This is described in more detail below.
- Any other element(s) – optional elements, containing application-specific information, can be added.

The <Manifest> element in our sample above is the element is used for referencing the MIME payload, referenced via cid:order2389877.xml@wrox.com.

### The <Reference> Element

Each <Reference> element is an XLink simple link, and contains a number of attributes and elements for referencing the payload information. It contains the following attributes:

- id – an optional attribute containing the XML ID for the <Reference> element. In the sample the id has the value of ATPOrder.
- xlink:type – an optional attribute set to the value simple, which defines the element as being an XLink simple link, expressing a one-way hyperlink.
- xlink:href – a required attribute conforming to the W3C XLink specification, and containing the URI of the payload object referenced. In the sample, the URI of the payload object, a MIME payload, refers to a Content-ID as defined in RFC 2392 – cid:order2389877.xml@wrox.com.
- xlink:role – an optional attribute containing a URI that, according to the XLink specification, identifies a resource that describes the payload object or its purpose.
- Other namespace-qualified attributes can be added. However, receiving MSHs may ignore any foreign namespace attributes other than those defined above.

Child elements of the `<Reference>` element include:

- `<Schema>` – an optional element containing attributes to reference the schema(s) used to define the instance document identified in the parent `<Reference>` element. The required `location` attribute contains the URI of the schema, and the `version` contains a version identifier of the schema.
- `<Description>` – an optional element containing any number (or possibly none) of human-readable descriptions of the payload object referenced by the parent `<Reference>` element. It is similar to the `<Description>` element in the `<MessageHeader>`, thus allowing for multi-language support via the `xml:lang` attribute.
- Optional additional elements for adding application-specific information. (The ebMS specification refers to these as '#wildcard elements'.)

# ebMS MSH Services

In addition to the standard message transfer functionality we've mentioned, the MSH may support two other services allowing basic availability and message information functionality:

- The **Message Status Request Service** allows an MSH to request information about the status of a previously sent message.
- The **MSH Ping Service** allows a sending MSH to check whether the receiving MSH is alive.

Later in this chapter, we'll give an implementation of the MSH Ping service and hence illustrate the necessary steps, software, and tools required to develop one of the base functions of an MSH. For now, let's focus on the Message Status Request Service.

## The Message Status Request Service

The Message Status Request Service works by using the following two steps:

- First, a **message status request** message is sent to an MSH. This message contains details regarding a previously sent message.
- Then, the MSH receiving the request responds with a **message status response** message.

An MSH will always respond to message status requests for messages that have been sent reliably. An MSH *may* also respond to message status requests for messages that have *not* been sent reliably. For this reason, an MSH should not use the Message Status Request Service to implement reliable messaging.

### The Message Status Request Message

The message status request message is, as the name already tells us, a message that is used to obtain information about the status of another message that has already been sent. A message status request message is in fact a normal ebXML message that contains no ebXML payload. It consists of a SOAP header and a SOAP body, as shown here.

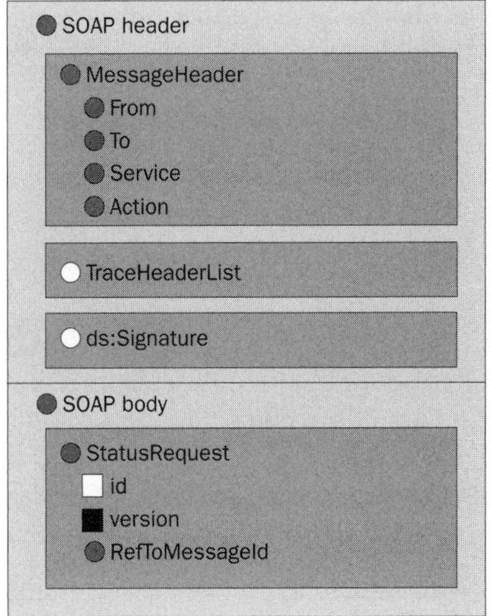


The interesting points to note here are:

- The <From> element identifies the party that created the message status request message.
- The <To> element identifies a party that should receive the message. If a <TraceHeader> was present on the message whose status is being checked, this must be set using the Receiver of the message. All <PartyId> elements present in the <Receiver> element should be included in this <To> element.
- The <Service> element contains the value uri:www.ebxml.org/messageService/ (this is the reserved URI we met earlier in the chapter, indicating that the service is an ebXML message service) .
- The <Action> element contains a <StatusRequest> element.
- The <RefToMessageId> element contains the MessageId of the message whose status is being queried.

This will result in a message that might look as follows:

```
<SOAP-ENV:Envelope
      xmlns:SOAP-ENV="http://schemas.xmlsoap.org/soap/envelope/"
      xmlns:eb="http://www.ebxml.org/namespaces/messageHeader">
   <SOAP-ENV:Header SOAP-ENV:mustUnderstand="1">
      <eb:MessageHeader eb:id="19650205" eb:version="1.0"
                        SOAP-ENV:mustUnderstand="1">
         <eb:From>
            <eb:PartyId>urn:tamino.com:id:PartyA</eb:PartyId>
         </eb:From>
         <eb:To>
            <eb:PartyId>urn:wrox.com:id:PartyB</eb:PartyId>
         </eb:To>
```

```
            <eb:Service>uri:www.ebxml.org/messageService/</eb:Service>
            <eb:Action>StatusRequest</eb:Action>
         </eb:MessageHeader>
      </SOAP-ENV:Header>
      <SOAP-ENV:Body>
         <eb:StatusRequest eb:version="1.0">
            <eb:RefToMessageId>20010812.11159@tamino.com</eb:RefToMessageId>
         </eb:StatusRequest>
      </SOAP-ENV:Body>
   </SOAP-ENV:Envelope>
```

As you can see, there is nothing new concerning the header extension blocks – except for the possibility of adding security and encryption by using the `ds:Signature`. We'll cover that later.

### The <StatusRequest> Element

The most important item (besides the `<MessageHeader>`, of course) is the `<StatusRequest>` element, an optional ebXML SOAP body extension block used to identify an earlier message whose status is being requested.

The `<StatusRequest>` element consists of a required `version` attribute and an optional `id` attribute. It also contains a required `<RefToMessageId>` child element, which itself contains the `MessageId` of the message whose status is being requested. In the sample above, the Party A MSH is contacting Party B MSH, with a request for information on the status of message `20010812.11159@tamino.com`.

### The Message Status Response Message

When the `To` party receives the message status request message, it should generate a message status response message. This consists of a SOAP header and body but no ebXML payload, as shown:

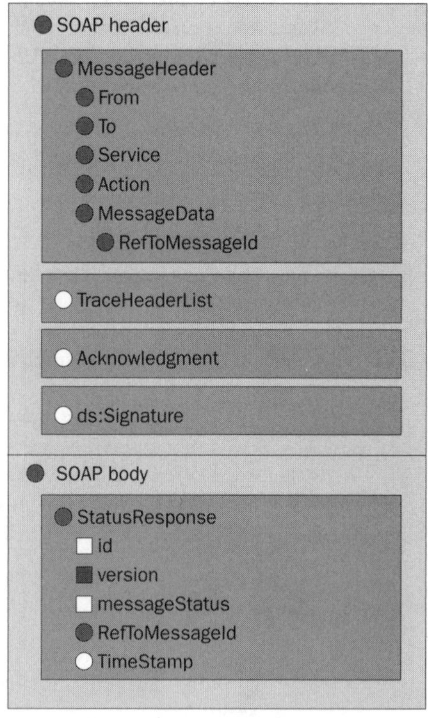

Here:

- The <From> element identifies the sender of the message status response message.
- The <To> element is set to the value of the <From> element in the message status request message.
- The <Service> element contains the value uri:www.ebxml.org/messageService/, just like the corresponding element in the message status request message.
- The <Action> element contains a <StatusResponse> element.
- The <RefToMessageId> element in the header identifies the message status request message. Note that here, the RefToMessageId identifies the request that this response is responding to, *not* the message whose status is being queried.
- The <RefToMessageId> element in the body contains the MessageId of the message whose status is being reported.

A typical message is as follows:

```
<SOAP-ENV:Envelope
      xmlns:SOAP-ENV="http://schemas.xmlsoap.org/soap/envelope/"
      xmlns:eb="http://www.ebxml.org/namespaces/messageHeader">
   <SOAP-ENV:Header SOAP-ENV:mustUnderstand="1">
      <eb:MessageHeader eb:id="19650206" eb:version="1.0"
            SOAP-ENV:mustUnderstand="1">
         <eb:From>
            <eb:PartyId>urn:tamino.com:id:PartyB</eb:PartyId>
         </eb:From>
         <eb:To>
            <eb:PartyId>urn:wrox.com:id:PartyA</eb:PartyId>
         </eb:To>
         <eb:Service>uri:www.ebxml.org/messageService/</eb:Service>
         <eb:Action>StatusResponse</eb:Action>
         <eb:MessageData>
            <eb:RefToMessageId>19650205</eb:RefToMessageId>
         </eb:MessageData>
      </eb:MessageHeader>
   </SOAP-ENV:Header>
   <SOAP-ENV:Body>
   <eb:StatusResponse eb:version="1.0" eb:messageStatus="Received">
      <eb:RefToMessageId>20010812.11159@tamino.com</eb:RefToMessageId>
      <eb:Timestamp>2001-08-12T12:36:30Z</eb:Timestamp>
   </eb:StatusResponse>
   </SOAP-ENV:Body>
</SOAP-ENV:Envelope>
```

Again, the only new features here are the option to add security and encryption (by <ds:Signature>) and reliable messaging (by asking for acknowledgment of message reception as defined in reliable messaging). Both will be covered later.

The message refers to the <StatusRequest> message via the <RefToMessageId>, containing the ID 19650205 of this message, in the <MessageData> element.

#### The <StatusResponse> Element

Let's look briefly at the important part – the `<StatusResponse>` element. It's an optional ebXML SOAP body extension block used by an MSH to respond to an inquiry on the processing status of a message sent previously. It consists of a required `version` attribute, an optional `id` attribute, and:

- `messageStatus` – an optional attribute, indicating the status of the message identified by the `<RefToMessageId>` element. There are three valid values:
    - `UnAuthorized` – indicates that the *status request* is either *not authorized* or *not accepted* by the MSH.
    - `NotRecognized` – indicates that the *message* is *not recognized.*
    - `Received` – indicates that the *message* has been *received* by the MSH.
- `<RefToMessageId>` – a required element that contains the `MessageId` of the message whose status is being reported.
- `<Timestamp>` – an optional element containing the time (as an XML Schema `timeInstant`) that the message, whose status is being reported, was received. If the message is `NotRecognized`, or the request was `UnAuthorized`, then the `Timestamp` can be omitted.

In the sample above, the message with ID `20010812.11159@tamino.com` is being reported as having been `Received` at `2001-08-12T12:36:30Z`.

## The MSH Ping Service

The MSH Ping service enables one MSH to determine if another MSH is operating. Unsurprisingly, it involves the first MSH sending an MSH Ping message to a second MSH, which (if all is well) responds to the first MSH with an MSH Pong message.

### The MSH Ping Message

An **MSH Ping** message consists of an ebXML message. It contains a SOAP header and body, but no ebXML payload:

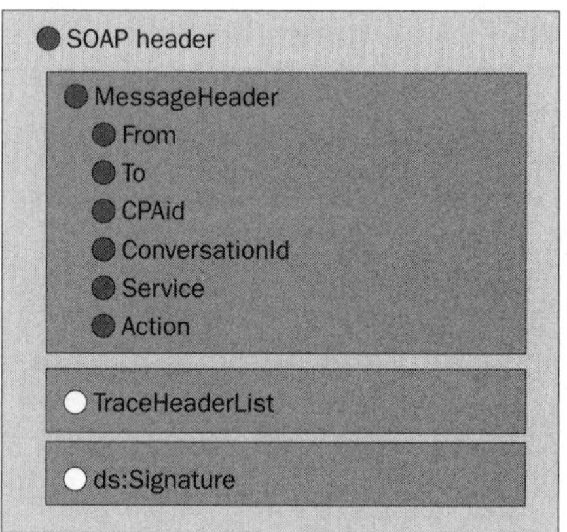


Recall that in the diagram, the black discs represent required elements, and white discs represent optional ones. Here, in the Ping message:

- The `<From>` element identifies the party creating the MSH Ping message.
- The `<To>` element identifies the party that is to receive the MSH Ping message.

- The <CPAId> element identifies the mutual agreement.
- The <ConversationId> element contains a unique identifier that is generated by the pinging MSH and used throughout the Ping-Pong exchange.
- The <Service> element contains the value of the reserved URI `uri:www.ebxml.org/messageService/`, indicating that this is an ebXML service.
- The <Action> element contains the value `Ping` – indicating that this is the Ping message.

This will result in a message like this:

```
<SOAP-ENV:Envelope
      xmlns:SOAP-ENV="http://schemas.xmlsoap.org/soap/envelope/"
      xmlns:eb="http://www.ebxml.org/namespaces/messageHeader">
   <SOAP-ENV:Header SOAP-ENV:mustUnderstand="1">
      <eb:MessageHeader eb:id="19650205" eb:version="1.0"
            SOAP-ENV:mustUnderstand="1">
         <eb:From>
            <eb:PartyId>urn:tamino.com:id:PartyA</eb:PartyId>
         </eb:From>
         <eb:To>
            <eb:PartyId>urn:wrox.com:id:PartyB</eb:PartyId>
         </eb:To>
         <eb:CPAId>
            http://www.wrox.com/ebXML/defaultAgreement.xml
         </eb:CPAId>
         <eb:ConversationId>20010810-034639GMT+02:00</eb:ConversationId>
         <eb:Service>uri:www.ebxml.org/messageService/</eb:Service>
         <eb:Action>Ping</eb:Action>
      </eb:MessageHeader>
   </SOAP-ENV:Header>
</SOAP-ENV:Envelope>
```

In summary, it's just a standard message with a specific `Service` and `Action`, which tell the receiving MSH (Party B) that the sending MSH (Party A) is pinging it.

### The MSH Pong Message

When the `To` party receives the MSH Ping message, it generates an **MSH Pong** message. This also consists of a SOAP header and body but no ebXML payload:

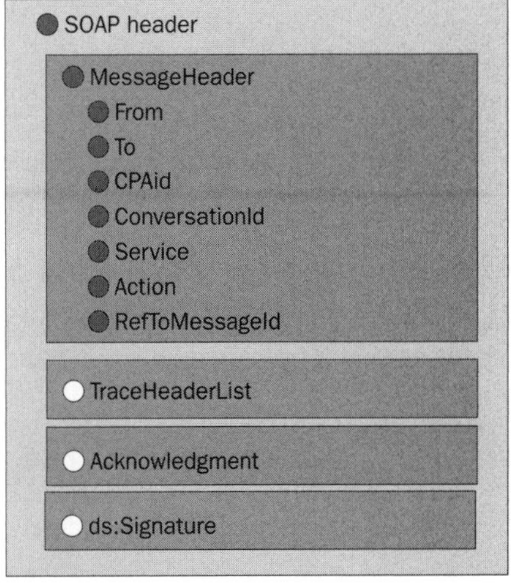

The Pong message is similar in structure to the Ping message, with a few differences:

- The <From> element identifies the creator of the MSH Pong message.
- The <To> element identifies the party that generated the MSH Ping message.
- The <ConversationId> element contains the same ConversationId as the Ping message, since they belong to the same conversation.
- The <Action> element contains the value Pong, to show that this is an MSH Pong message.
- The <RefToMessageId> element identifies the MSH Ping message to which this message is responding.

So, MSH Pong looks like this:

```
<SOAP-ENV:Envelope
      xmlns:SOAP-ENV="http://schemas.xmlsoap.org/soap/envelope/"
      xmlns:eb="http://www.ebxml.org/namespaces/messageHeader">
   <SOAP-ENV:Header SOAP-ENV:mustUnderstand="1">
      <eb:MessageHeader eb:id="19650206" eb:version="1.0"
                          SOAP-ENV:mustUnderstand="1">
         <eb:From>
            <eb:PartyId>urn:tamino.com:id:PartyB</eb:PartyId>
         </eb:From>
         <eb:To>
            <eb:PartyId>urn:wrox.com:id:PartyA</eb:PartyId>
         </eb:To>
         <eb:CPAId>
            http://www.wrox.com/ebXML/defaultAgreement.xml
         </eb:CPAId>
         <eb:ConversationId>20010810-034639GMT+02:00</eb:ConversationId>
         <eb:Service>uri:www.ebxml.org/messageService/</eb:Service>
         <eb:Action>Pong</eb:Action>
         <eb:MessageData>
            <eb:RefToMessageId>19650205</eb:RefToMessageId>
         </eb:MessageData>
      </eb:MessageHeader>
   </SOAP-ENV:Header>
</SOAP-ENV:Envelope>
```

Again, it's just a standard message – this time, with a specific Service and Action that tell the pinging MSH that this is a reply to its Ping request.

## Implementing the MSH Ping Service

In the following section, we'll take a look at an implementation of the MSH Ping service. The full code listing, and information on required software and setup, is available at http://www.wrox.com. We'll briefly list the software needed for the application; then we'll step through the more interesting parts of the code.

We'll look at a number of helper classes; then we'll build an MSH client to issue the Ping request, and an MSH server to handle the Ping request and reply with a Pong message.

### Software Used

The sample application is based on the Apache SOAP toolkit in combination with Tomcat (see http://xml.apache.org/soap/index.html and http://www.apache.org/dist/jakarta/tomcat respectively for downloads and installation instructions). Then the JDOM beta 7 (http://www.jdom.org/downloads/index.html) is used for building the required XML blocks.

### Building the ebXML Ping and Pong Messages

The creation of both the `Ping` and `Pong` messages basically involves building an ebXML message without payload, containing the necessary ebXML header elements (SOAP blocks) inside the SOAP header.

The first step is to create the SWA message to be transferred as the ebXML message. When I used the SOAP toolkit classes I got some headaches – like issuing exceptions within the pre-compiled SOAP packages when adding the ebXML extension elements to the header, body and envelope. A workaround is used to build both the necessary SOAP parts (`<Envelope>`, `<Header>`, and `<Body>`) and allow for adding the SOAP blocks, or better still the ebXML extensions.

But before hopping to the listing let's first take a look at the overall structure of the example to get an idea of what files are used:

- The `Ping.java` file contains the code for the client application, which sends the Ping message. It constructs the ebXML Ping message by using our SOAP helper classes (see below) to construct the envelope, header and body and adding the necessary ebXML message extensions. The result returned from the MSH server is printed to the output device.
- The `MSH.java` file contains the source code for the implementation of the `inquire()` interface of the MSH. Depending on the service request, it will react with an appropriate reply; thus in case of the Ping it will build the Pong message and reply it to the sender. Note that it also prints the received request to the output device.
- The `MessageHeader.java` file contains the source for a helper class, which builds the ebXML `<MessageHeader>` element. It allows for setting the appropriate subordinate elements like `<To>`, `<From>` and `<CPAId>`.
- The `ebXMLSOAPEnvelope.java` file contains the source for a helper class which builds the SOAP envelope, adds the appropriate ebXML namespaces and offers a method for adding SOAP blocks (`<Header>` and `<Body>`) to the envelope.
- There are two similar helper classes, contained in `ebXMLSOAPHeader.java` files and `ebXMLSOAPBody.java`.
- Finally, `DeploymentDescriptor.xml` contains the service description used for deployment with the Apache SOAP toolkit.

### The ebXMLSOAPEnvelope, ebXMLSOAPHeader, and ebXMLSOAPBody Helper Classes

Since `ebXMLSOAPEnvelope`, `ebXMLSOAPHeader`, and `ebXMLSOAPBody` classes are used to generate the SOAP parts. They're all very similar, so we'll only examine the `ebXMLSOAPHeader` here. First, here's the code used to define the base ebXML SOAP header:

```
public class ebXMLSOAPHeader
{
  private Element ebXMLHeader;
  private Namespace ebNS;
```

```
    private Namespace soapNS;
    public ebXMLSOAPHeader()
    {
        ebNS = Namespace.getNamespace("eb",
           "http://www.ebxml.org/namespaces/messageHeader");
        soapNS = Namespace.getNamespace("SOAP-ENV",
           "http://schemas.xmlsoap.org/soap/envelope/");
        ebXMLHeader = new Element("Header", soapNS);
        ebXMLHeader.addNamespaceDeclaration(soapNS);
        ebXMLHeader.setAttribute("mustUnderstand", "1", soapNS);
        ebXMLHeader.addContent("\n");
    }
```

The ebXMLSOAPHeader class is used to build up the SOAP header. It will create a new XML element, named <Header>, and will add attributes for both the ebXML and SOAP namespaces to the <Header> element. Finally it will add the mustUnderstand attribute (which, recall, is mandatory in an ebXML environment). It adds the linefeed, \n, just to enhance readability of the output – since reading a large string on one line is rather difficult. So the result from this piece of code is:

```
<Header xmlns:eb="http://www.ebxml.org/namespaces/messageHeader"
   xmlns:SOAP-ENV="http://schemas.xmlsoap.org/soap/envelope/"
   SOAP-ENV:mustUnderstand="1">\n</Header>
```

The ebXMLSOAPHeader class's addExtension() method, shown below, is used to add an XML element to the <Header>. The added <elm> element could be a simple element, or it could be a complete tree (such as the ebXML <MessageHeader>):

```
    public void addExtension(Element elm)
    {
        ebXMLHeader.addContent(elm);
        ebXMLHeader.addContent("\n");
    }
```

The toString() method generates a String datatype output from the XML element:

```
    public String toString()
    {
      return new XMLOutputter().outputString(ebXMLHeader);
    }
```

Finally, of course, we need to get hold of the <Header> element in its native form. Thus, the ebXMLSOAPHeader class provides a getebXMLSOAPHeader() method:

```
    public Element getebXMLSOAPHeader()
    {
      return ebXMLHeader;
    }
  }
```

As mentioned, the ebXMLSOAPEnvelope and ebXMLSOAPBody classes are very similar to the ebXMLSOAPHeader class, and use similar constructs as those described above.

### The MessageHeader Helper Class

Now that the SOAP basics are constructed, we can move on to the next step: the creation of the ebXML extensions. Since we're executing a Ping and returning a Pong, the only required extension is the <MessageHeader>. The MessageHeader class allows for the creation of the <MessageHeader> extension, and the setting and getting of the various required and optional elements:

```
public class MessageHeader
{
  private Element msgHeader;
  private Namespace ebNS;
  private Namespace soapNS;
  public MessageHeader()
  {
      ebNS = Namespace.getNamespace("eb",
         "http://www.ebxml.org/namespaces/messageHeader");
      soapNS = Namespace.getNamespace("SOAP-ENV",
         "http://schemas.xmlsoap.org/soap/envelope/");
      msgHeader = new Element("MessageHeader", ebNS);
      msgHeader.addNamespaceDeclaration(ebNS);
      msgHeader.addNamespaceDeclaration(soapNS);
      msgHeader.setAttribute("mustUnderstand", "1", soapNS);
      msgHeader.setAttribute("version", "1.0", ebNS);
      msgHeader.addContent("\n");
  }
```

msgHeader contains the newly created XML <MessageHeader> element. Both the namespace attributes to the <MessageHeader> element, and the mandatory mustUnderstand and version attributes are added. Again, the linefeed \n is added for readability. So the result is:

```
<MessageHeader xmlns:eb="http://www.ebxml.org/namespaces/messageHeader"
   xmlns:SOAP-ENV="http://schemas.xmlsoap.org/soap/envelope/"
   SOAP-ENV:mustUnderstand="1" eb:version="1.0">\n</MessageHeader>
```

If we're looking from the MSH perspective, we will not start with a new <MessageHeader>, but with one that we have received. The MessageHeader class has a MessageHeader() method, which is used to initialize a received <MessageHeader> element – and thus allow the information contained within the received <MessageHeader> (like <To> and <From>) to be retrievable, as we'll see a little later:

```
  public MessageHeader(org.w3c.dom.Element elm)
  {
      ebNS = Namespace.getNamespace("eb",
         "http://www.ebxml.org/namespaces/messageHeader");
      soapNS = Namespace.getNamespace("SOAP-ENV",
         "http://schemas.xmlsoap.org/soap/envelope/");
      msgHeader = new org.jdom.input.DOMBuilder().build(elm);
  }
```

The MessageHeader class contains various methods for setting and getting its elements. Since the methods are very similar, only the significant lines are shown. The MessageHeader class's setId() method is, unsurprisingly, used for setting the Id attribute of the <MessageHeader> element:

```
    public void setId(String value)
    {
        msgHeader.setAttribute("id", value, ebNS);
    }
```

The MessageHeader class has a number of methods which allow values to be assigned to the various elements within the MessageHeader. These methods are all quite similar; we'll only examine the setFrom() and setMessageData() methods here. The setFrom() method creates a <From> element, adds a child <PartyId> to it, and adds the specified value to the <PartyId>. As you can see, the creation of the <From> and <PartyId> elements use the ebNS namespace, that contains the namespace definition:

```
    public void setFrom(String value)
    {
        Element elm = new Element("From", ebNS);
        Element childElm = new Element("PartyId", ebNS);
        childElm.addContent(value);
        elm.addContent(childElm);
        elm.addContent("\n");
        msgHeader.addContent(elm);
        msgHeader.addContent("\n");
    }
```

The outcome of the setFrom() method would be:

```
  <eb:From>
     <eb:PartyId>...specified value...</eb:PartyId>
  </eb:From>
```

Similar methods are present for setting the <To>, <CPAId>, <ConversationId>, <Service> and <Action> elements.

The setMessageData() method is similar, but is shown here because it is also required to deal with the *optional* elements of the <MessageData> element:

```
    public void setMessageData(String messageId, String timeStamp,
                                String refToMessageId, String timeToLive)
    {
        Element elm = new Element("MessageData", ebNS);
        Element childElm = new Element("MessageId", ebNS);
        childElm.addContent(messageId);
        elm.addContent(childElm);
        elm.addContent("\n");
        childElm = new Element("Timestamp", ebNS);
        childElm.addContent(timeStamp);
        elm.addContent(childElm);
        elm.addContent("\n");
        if (refToMessageId!=null)
        {
          childElm = new Element("RefToMessageId", ebNS);
          childElm.addContent(refToMessageId);
```

```
        elm.addContent(childElm);
        elm.addContent("\n");
      }
      if (timeToLive!=null)
      {
        childElm = new Element("TimeToLive", ebNS);
        childElm.addContent(timeToLive);
        elm.addContent("\n");
      }
      msgHeader.addContent(elm);
      msgHeader.addContent("\n");
  }
```

The outcome of the `setMessageData()` method could be something like:

```
<eb:MessageData>
   <eb:MessageId>20010810.034641@wrox.com</eb:MessageId>
   <eb:Timestamp>2001-046-10T03:46:41Z</eb:Timestamp>
   <eb:TimeToLive>20s</eb:TimeToLive>
</eb:MessageData>
```

And as we've seen with the SOAP header, we offer the opportunity to retrieve the `<MessageHeader>` both in its native format (using `getMessageHeader()`) and as a string (using `toString()`):

```
  public String toString()
  {
    return new XMLOutputter().outputString(msgHeader);
  }
  public Element getMessageHeader()
  {
    return msgHeader;
  }
```

If we're starting with a received `<MessageHeader>` element, we'll need to be able to get the information from it. The following `get...()` methods are used for retrieving the information, and are thus (almost) opposites of the corresponsing `set...()` methods.

The `getId()` method is used to get the value of the `id` attribute. As shown below, where we can see that the `id` attribute belongs to the `ebNS` namespace definition:

```
  public String getId()
  {
    return msgHeader.getAttributeValue("id", ebNS);
  }
```

Shown below is the `getTo()` method, used to get the value of the child `<PartyId>` element of the `<To>` element:

```
  public String getTo()
  {
    return msgHeader.getChild("To", ebNS).getChildText("PartyId", ebNS);
  }
```

So, nothing exciting here; similar methods are available to retrieve the `<From>`, `<CPAId>`, `<ConversationId>`, `<Service>`, `<Action>` and `<MessageData>` elements and `MessageId`, `TimeToLive`, `RefToMessageId` and `Timestamp` attributes too.

#### The MSH Client

The client application will issue the Ping message. This means that it first has to construct the SWA message containing the SOAP envelope, SOAP header (including the <MessageHeader> extension), and SOAP body. After the construction of the message, it can be sent to the MSH. The result returned from the MSH server is printed to the screen, as we will see in the *Run the Application* subsection, a few pages from here.

The `Ping` class contains one method, `main()`, where the argument is the URL of the MSH the `Ping` has to be sent to. We'll step through the `main()` method a bit at a time:

```
public class Ping {
  public static void main (String[] args) throws Exception {
    if (args.length != 1) {
      System.err.println ("Usage: java " + Ping.class.getName () +
                                                   " URL-ebXML-MSH");
      System.exit (1);
    }
```

> *In the example, the server is the default SOAP* `messagerouter`*, so we can start the* `Ping` *application by typing:*
>
> *java Ping http://localhost:8080/soap/servlet/messagerouter*
>
> *There are more details on setup and execution with the source code that supports this book, at http://www.wrox.com/.*

The next step is to build the Ping request, using the helper classes to set up the ebXML <MessageHeader> and SOAP parts. As shown below, we start by creating the <MessageHeader> and setting the various required elements like <From>, <To>, <CPAId> and the <ConversationId> (which itself contains a <timeStamp> value):

```
    MessageHeader msgHeader = new MessageHeader();
    msgHeader.setFrom("urn:duns:800008");
    msgHeader.setTo("urn:duns:700007");
    msgHeader.setCPAId("http://www.wrox.com/ebXML/defaultAgreement.xml");
    SimpleDateFormat formatter =
                            new SimpleDateFormat ("yyyyMMdd-hhmmsszzz");
    String cid = formatter.format(new Date());
    msgHeader.setConversationId(cid);
```

The next step is to define the <Service> and <Action> as specified by the Ping message description:

```
    msgHeader.setService("uri:www.ebxml.org/messageService/");
    msgHeader.setAction("Ping");
```

To finalize the <MessageHeader> information we need to set the <MessageData> elements. The <MessageId> and <Timestamp> are set, the optional <TimeToLive> and <RefToMessageId> are not:

```
formatter = new SimpleDateFormat ("yyyyMMdd.hhmmss");
String mid = formatter.format(new Date())+"@wrox.com";
formatter = new SimpleDateFormat ("yyyy-mmm-dd'T'hh:mm:ss'Z'");
String tid = formatter.format(new Date());
msgHeader.setMessageData(mid,tid,null,null);
```

Now we can start creating the SOAP parts, thus create the SOAP header and add the ebXML `<MessageHeader>` extension to it.

```
ebXMLSOAPHeader ebXMLHeader = new ebXMLSOAPHeader();
ebXMLHeader.addExtension(msgHeader.getMessageHeader());
```

The SOAP body should contain an element that is used by the SOAP messagerouter in order to figure out what to do. In this case, we would like to use the `inquire()` service that offers access to the Ping functionality, thus we add an element with the name `inquire`:

```
ebXMLSOAPBody ebXMLBody = new ebXMLSOAPBody();
ebXMLBody.addElement("inquire");
```

So now we need to create the ebXML message, thus create a SOAP envelope and add the header and body to it:

```
ebXMLSOAPEnvelope ebXMLEnvelope = new ebXMLSOAPEnvelope();
ebXMLEnvelope.addSOAPBlock(ebXMLHeader.getebXMLSOAPHeader());
ebXMLEnvelope.addSOAPBlock(ebXMLBody.getebXMLSOAPBody());
```

The next bit looks a bit funny, but I've spent some time getting it to work and this does the trick. First we create a `StringReader` that takes our envelope as a string. We parse the envelope to see if it's a valid SOAP message, and finally `unmarshal` the message:

```
StringReader strMsg = new StringReader(ebXMLEnvelope.toString()+"\n");
DocumentBuilder xdb = XMLParserUtils.getXMLDocBuilder();
Document doc = xdb.parse (new InputSource (strMsg));
if (doc == null) {
  throw new SOAPException (Constants.FAULT_CODE_CLIENT,
                                                 "parsing error");
}
Envelope ebXMLMessage = Envelope.unmarshall (doc.getDocumentElement ());
```

In fact, this was all preparation before getting to the real stuff – sending the message itself. Sending the message just uses standard SOAP mechanisms, thus creating a `Message` and using the `send()` method in order to send the ebXML Ping message:

```
Message msg = new Message ();
msg.send (new URL (args[0]), "urn:msh", ebXMLMessage);
```

The result returned from the MSH, thus the Pong message, is printed to the screen:

```
SOAPTransport st = msg.getSOAPTransport ();
BufferedReader br = st.receive ();
String line;
```

```
      while ((line = br.readLine ()) != null) {
        System.out.println (line);
      }
    }
  }
```

### *The MSH Server*

The final step is to build an MSH server that receives the `Ping` message and answers by sending the Pong message.

The `MSH` class offers a public method, `inquire()`, which is one of the abstract defined interfaces of the MSH. The `inquire()` method is used as entry point for both the Ping and Message Service Request message.

The first step in the `inquire()` method is to get all parts of the ebXML message, thus the SOAP header and body that are in the received envelope, `env`:

```
public class MSH {
  public void inquire (Envelope env, SOAPContext reqCtx,
    SOAPContext resCtx) throws MessagingException, IOException
  {
    String msgResult = "";
    Header header = env.getHeader();
    Body body = env.getBody();
```

Since we're implementing the `Ping` function, the next few steps are focussed on getting the ebXML `MessageHeader` extension from the SOAP header and establishing what `<Service>` and `<Action>` are requested. If the `<Service>` is the reserved `www.ebxml.org/messageService/`, we should act according to the `<Action>` – which can be either a `Ping` or a `StatusRequest`. In case of a `Ping`, the result will be created using the `setPong()` method (which we'll meet it a moment), and returned to the issuer of the `Ping` request:

```
    Vector parms = header.getHeaderEntries();
    for(int i=0; i < parms.size(); i++)
    {
      Element elm = (Element)parms.get(i);
      if (elm.getLocalName().equals("MessageHeader"))
      {
        MessageHeader resMessageHeader = new MessageHeader(elm);
        if (resMessageHeader.getService().equals("uri:www.ebxml.org/messageService/"))
        {
          if (resMessageHeader.getAction().equals("Ping"))
          {
            msgResult = setPong(resMessageHeader);
          }
        }
      }
    }
    // send back the result
    resCtx.setRootPart(msgResult, "text/xml");
  }
```

The creation of the `Pong` request is in fact similar to the creation of the initial `Ping` message, except that most of the information is retrieved from the received `<MessageHeader>`, as we will see below. The `To` and `From` values are swapped, and the `CPAId`, `ConversationId` and `Service` values are copied. The `Action` is (of course) a `Pong` instead of a `Ping`. The `<MessageData>` is built from scratch, but now contains a `<RefToMessageId>` that contains the `id` of the original Ping message:

```
    private String setPong (MessageHeader elm)
    {
      MessageHeader msgHeader = new MessageHeader();
      msgHeader.setFrom(elm.getTo());
      msgHeader.setTo(elm.getFrom());
      msgHeader.setCPAId(elm.getCPAId());
      msgHeader.setConversationId(elm.getConversationId());
      msgHeader.setService(elm.getService());
      msgHeader.setAction("Pong");
      SimpleDateFormat formatter = new SimpleDateFormat ("yyyyMMdd.hhmmss");
      String mid = formatter.format(new Date())+"@wrox.com";
      formatter = new SimpleDateFormat ("yyyy-mmm-dd'T'hh:mm:ss'Z'");
      String tid = formatter.format(new Date());
      msgHeader.setMessageData(mid,tid,elm.getMessageId(),null);
      ...
    }
  }
```

The `setPong()` method also performs the creation of the ebXML message, using the helper classes to create the envelope that contains the header, body and ebXML extension. That code is omitted from the fragment above.

### Running the Application

Once the classes have been compiled, the test application can be executed. The first step is to register (or deploy) the service using the Apache SOAP toolkit administration tool, or by using the command line interface. As mentioned earlier, a more detailed description on compilation and running the example is provided in the download section at http://www.wrox.com.

The definition of the service providing the MSH inquire interface (the interface to the Ping service) can be found in the file `DeploymentDescriptor.xml`, as shown below:

```
<isd:service xmlns:isd="http://xml.apache.org/xml-soap/deployment"
             id="urn:msh" type="message">
  <isd:provider type="java"
                scope="Application"
                methods="inquire receive send notify">
    <isd:java class="wrox.msh.MSH" static="false"/>
  </isd:provider>
  <isd:faultListener>
    org.apache.soap.server.DOMFaultListener
  </isd:faultListener>
</isd:service>
```

The command to deploy the SOAP service using the `DeploymentDescriptor.xml` is as follows:

```
Java org.apache.soap.server.ServiceManagerClient
   http://localhost:8080/soap/servlet/rpcrouter
   deploy DeploymentDescriptor.xml
```

Now the service is deployed, and the `Ping` command can be executed. The following figure shows the command to execute the application, and the resulting `Pong` message which is sent from the MSH server:

```
E:\WINNT\System32\cmd.exe
C:\foo\msh>java wrox.msh.Ping http://localhost:8080/soap/servlet/messagerouter

<SOAP-ENV:Envelope xmlns:SOAP-ENV="http://schemas.xmlsoap.org/soap/envelope/">
<SOAP-ENV:Header SOAP-ENV:mustUnderstand="1">
<eb:MessageHeader xmlns:eb="http://www.ebxml.org/namespaces/messageHeader" SOAP-
ENV:mustUnderstand="1" eb:version="1.0">
<eb:From><eb:PartyId>urn:duns:700007</eb:PartyId>
</eb:From>
<eb:To><eb:PartyId>urn:duns:800008</eb:PartyId>
</eb:To>
<eb:CPAId>http://www.wrox.com/ebXML/defaultAgreement.xml</eb:CPAId>
<eb:ConversationId>20011005-055619GMT+01:00</eb:ConversationId>
<eb:Service>uri:www.ebxml.org/messageService/</eb:Service>
<eb:Action>Pong</eb:Action>
<eb:MessageData><eb:MessageId>20011005.055625@wrox.com</eb:MessageId>
<eb:Timestamp>2001-056-05T05:56:25Z</eb:Timestamp>
<eb:RefToMessageId>20011005.055619@wrox.com</eb:RefToMessageId>
</eb:MessageData>
</eb:MessageHeader>
</SOAP-ENV:Header>
<SOAP-ENV:Body SOAP-ENV:mustUnderstand="1">
</SOAP-ENV:Body>
</SOAP-ENV:Envelope>

C:\foo\msh>
```

The figure below shows the server application – you can see the `Ping` message that is received by the MSH `inquire` interface:

```
E:\WINNT\System32\cmd.exe - tomcat run

2001-10-05 04:46:49 - ContextManager: Adding context Ctx( /examples )
2001-10-05 04:46:49 - ContextManager: Adding context Ctx( /soap )
2001-10-05 04:46:49 - ContextManager: Adding context Ctx( /admin )
Starting tomcat. Check logs/tomcat.log for error messages
2001-10-05 04:46:49 - ContextManager: Adding context Ctx(  )
2001-10-05 04:46:49 - ContextManager: Adding context Ctx( /test )
2001-10-05 04:46:52 - PoolTcpConnector: Starting HttpConnectionHandler on 8080
2001-10-05 04:46:52 - PoolTcpConnector: Starting Ajp12ConnectionHandler on 8007

Processing MessageHeader...

<eb:MessageHeader xmlns:eb="http://www.ebxml.org/namespaces/messageHeader" xmlns
:SOAP-ENV="http://schemas.xmlsoap.org/soap/envelope/" SOAP-ENV:mustUnderstand="1
" eb:version="1.0">
<eb:From><eb:PartyId>urn:duns:800008</eb:PartyId>
</eb:From>
<eb:To><eb:PartyId>urn:duns:700007</eb:PartyId>
</eb:To>
<eb:CPAId>http://www.wrox.com/ebXML/defaultAgreement.xml</eb:CPAId>
<eb:ConversationId>20011005-044732GMT+01:00</eb:ConversationId>
<eb:Service>uri:www.ebxml.org/messageService/</eb:Service>
<eb:Action>Ping</eb:Action>
<eb:MessageData><eb:MessageId>20011005.044732@wrox.com</eb:MessageId>
<eb:Timestamp>2001-047-05T04:47:32Z</eb:Timestamp>
</eb:MessageData>
</eb:MessageHeader>
```

# Reliable Messaging in ebMS

Data transmitted across a network is normally transmitted in a **best effort** way, which simply means that the network will do its best to transfer the data unit to its desired destination. Best effort means that if something goes wrong and the data unit gets lost, corrupted, misdelivered, or in any way fails to reach its intended destination, the network does nothing – it made its best attempt, and that is all it has to do. It does not make any attempt to recover from the failure. Best effort delivery is sometimes called an **unreliable service**.

Best effort delivery does not just mean that data units can get lost. Sometimes they can get delivered out of order, and sometimes the same packet can get delivered more than once.

Messages sometimes get lost or become corrupted (and are thus discarded) while in transit. A protocol that wants to deliver messages in a **reliable** way must be able to cope with this problem. When talking about reliable messaging it's useful to start with the general concept of **Quality of Service,** usually abbreviated as QoS, which refers to the notion that a network protocol may treat some of its data units (packets, frames, messages) differently than others. This is accomplished by making use of two fundamental mechanisms: **acknowledgments** and **timeouts**:

- An **acknowledgment** is a small control message that a node sends back to its peer saying that it has received an earlier message. Typically, this control message consists of header data only, without a payload. The receipt of an acknowledgment indicates to the sender of the original message that its message was successfully delivered.
- If the sender does not receive an acknowledgment after a reasonable amount of time, then it resends the original message. This mechanism is called a **timeout**. While this mechanism is simple enough, it isn't trivial to find an appropriate and practical value for the timeout. This is especially true on the Internet, where latency or jitter (the variation in latency) is still very much a problem.

Note that 'resending the original message' means retransmission of that identical message. An identical message is defined by the ebMS specification as "a message that contains, apart from an additional `<TraceHeader>` element, the same ebXML SOAP `<Header>`, `<Body>`, and ebXML payload as the earlier message that was sent." By resending messages, we may introduce a further problem: that of **duplicate messages**. (A duplicate message is defined by the ebMS specification as "a message that contains the same `MessageId` as an earlier message that was received" which is a pragmatic enough definition to be useful.) In a messaging service like ebMS we need to cope with that, as we shall see later.

Related to the reception of duplicate messages is **idempotent delivery**, which indicates that a message is delivered to the receiving application exactly once. This means that even if the MSH receives the message multiple times, it has to filter out the duplicates. And let's mention **ordered delivery**, which addresses the problem that messages may not arrive in the sequence in which they were sent.

We'll mention one last problem related to timeouts – that of distinguishing between a message that is indeed lost, and one that is merely late in arriving. There are no magic solutions here, other than trying to find an optimum timeout value.

## *ebMS Reliable Messaging Elements*

Now that we've introduced the problem area, let's take a look at the reliable messaging and ordered delivery features of ebMS. The parameters necessary to implement reliable messaging can be found in three different places:

- The <QualityOfServiceInfo> block, in the message header.
- The <ReliableMessaging> block in the ebXML CPA (Chapter 8). The <CPAId> element (in the message header) specifies a CPA, which in turn contains the <ReliableMessaging> block.
- The <Via> element, in the SOAP header, which repeats some elements from the <QualityOfServiceInfo> block.

The following diagram shows where these elements can be found within the message. It's also worth mentioning the <ConversationId> element again here, for its role in ordered delivery.

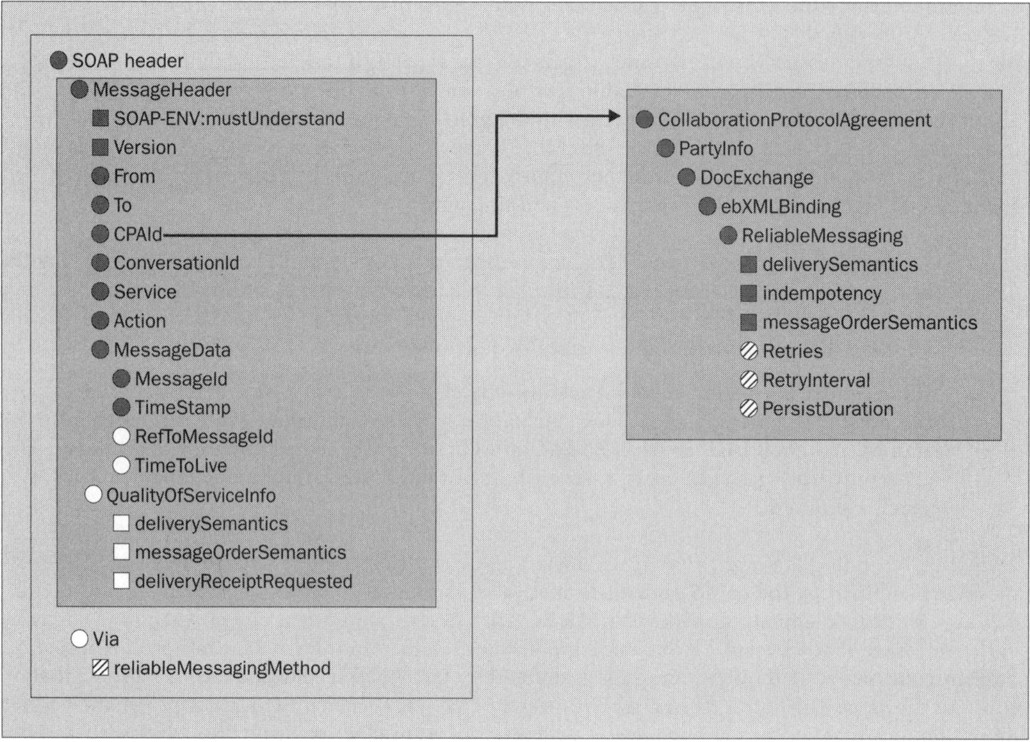


After we've looked at some of these parameters in more detail we'll move on to the corresponding MSH message processing.

### *The <QualityOfServiceInfo> Element*

The optional <QualityOfServiceInfo> block (in the message header) specifies the message services requested for the messages being delivered. It only needs to be present if any of the attributes within the element need to be set to a non-default value. The <QualityOfServiceInfo> element has the following three optional attributes:

- The deliverySemantics attribute is used by the From party MSH to indicate whether the message must be sent reliably. (We'll go into more detail on what this means in a minute.) This attribute can be specified here in the <MessageHeader>, or in the CPA. The deliverySemantics attribute can take one of the following values:

- BestEffort – the default, indicating that the message is sent unreliably. In this case, the value of the reliableMessagingMethod attribute in the <Via> element is ignored.
    - OnceAndOnlyOnce – the message must be sent using a (<Via>) reliableMessagingMethod that will result in the application at the To party receiving the message once and only once.
- The messageOrderSemantics attribute indicates whether the message is passed to the receiving application in the order the sending application specified (by means of the <SequenceNumber> within the <MessageHeader>). It can also be specified here in the <MessageHeader>, or in the CPA, and can take any of the following values:
    - NotGuaranteed – the default, indicating that messages *may* be passed to the receiving application in a different order from that specified by the sending application.
    - Guaranteed – the messages *must* be passed to the receiving application in the order specified by the sending application.
- The deliveryReceiptRequested attribute is used by a From party to indicate whether a message received by the To party should result in the To party returning an acknowledgment message containing a <DeliveryReceipt> element (more on that shortly). The acknowledgment indicates that an MSH (possibly an intermediate MSH) has received the message. Valid values for deliveryReceiptRequested are:
    - None – the default, indicates that no delivery receipt is requested.
    - Unsigned – requests that an unsigned delivery receipt is requested.
    - Signed – requests that a signed delivery receipt is requested. So this option supports the non-repudiation feature we mentioned earlier.

A sample fragment of a <QualityOfServiceInfo> element might be:

```
<eb:QualityOfServiceInfo eb:deliverySemantics="OnceAndOnlyOnce"
   eb:messageOrderSemantics="Guaranteed"
   eb:deliveryReceiptRequested="Unsigned"/>
```

### The <Via> Element

As we saw earlier, the <Via> element is an optional ebXML header extension block used to transfer information to the next MSH. The <Via> element is used to hold data that can vary from one hop to the next. Here, we will only repeat the attributes of <Via> that are relevant to reliable messaging, namely:

- reliableMessagingMethod – an optional attribute that can take the values ebXML (default) or Transport.
- ackRequested – an optional attribute to indicate to the receiving MSH whether an acknowledgment message is requested, and if so, which type. The valid types are None (default), Signed, or Unsigned.

## The CPA <ReliableMessaging> Element

As we mentioned above, the following description is not part of the ebXML MS specification – it's from the ebXML CPA specification. The parameters we'll discuss here are referenced via the <CPAId> element in the ebXML message header. We will just briefly discuss some of those attributes and elements which have particular relevance to messaging; see Chapter 8 for more in-depth information.

The <ReliableMessaging> element contains three attributes and three child elements. The elements must either be all present or all absent:

- The deliverySemantics attribute is identical to the <QualityOfServiceInfo> element's attribute of the same name, which we covered above.
- The idempotency attribute is a required attribute, specifying whether the party requires that all messages exchanged be subject to an idempotency test (detection and appropriate processing of duplicate messages) in the document-exchange layer.
- The messageOrderSemantics attribute is identical to the <QualityOfServiceInfo> element's attribute of the same name, which we covered above.
- The <Retries> element contains an integer value that specifies the maximum number of times a sending MSH should attempt to resend an unacknowledged message. We'll see the importance of this parameter when we look at MSH message processing shortly.
- The <RetryInterval> element contains a time value (as an XML Schema timeDuration), specifying the timeout a sending MSH must wait between retries, if an acknowledgment message is not received.

*For MSH implementations this is of key importance, and it is somewhat surprising that this is specified in the ebXML CPA and not in the ebXML MS.*

- The <PersistDuration> element contains the minimum length of time that data from a reliably-sent message is kept in persistent storage by a receiving MSH. For example, we can specify that the data has to be kept in persistent store for at least 30 seconds by using the element <PersistDuration>30S</PersistDuration>. The minimum length of time is 0, and the maximum is restricted only by the amount of persistent storage available. Note that this element is an XML Schema timeDuration datatype, so we use that mechanism to specify the desired unit of time.

  If the PersistDuration has expired since the message was first sent, a sending MSH should not resend a message with the same MessageId. If a message cannot be sent successfully before PersistDuration has passed, then the sending MSH should report a delivery failure. We will discuss persistency in more detail later, but this is our first indication that ebXML specifies persistent storage as a failure recovery mechanism.

This diagram shows the relevant reliable messaging related elements and attributes of the ReliableMessaging element in the CPA definition:

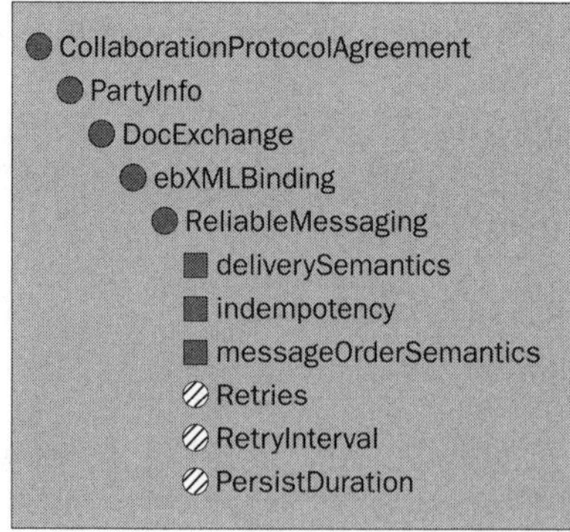

## *ebMS Acknowledgment Mechanisms*

The 'self-describing' nature of XML had its disadvantages, as we will see here when we consider **message acknowledgments**. There are several ways to request a confirmation and/or specific 'reports'. This may sound a bit vague – indeed, we think this could be more clearly covered in the ebMS specification. Four such mechanisms are listed below:

- Recall that we have already covered a way to request a message confirmation – the Message Status Request Service. However, as we've already noted, this is not intended to be used as such; this is because while an MSH will *always* respond to message status requests for messages that *have* been sent reliably, it may *also* respond to message status requests for messages that have *not* been sent reliably.

- A second (and more appropriate) way to ask for a confirmation is to send a `<MessageHeader>` with both of the following settings:

```
<eb:Service>
   http://www.ebxml.org/namespaces/messageService/MessageAcknowledgment
</eb:Service>
<eb:Action>
   Acknowledgment
</eb:Action>
```

  Apart from the obligatory elements, this acknowledgment message must contain a `<MessageData>` element with a `RefToMessageId` that has the same value as the `<MessageId>` element in the message being acknowledged.

- In addition, extra status information may be reported if specified with the parameters `ackRequested` (which results in a returned `<Acknowledgment>` element) or `deliveryReceiptRequested` (which results in a returned `<DeliveryReceipt>` element).

Let's discuss these last two elements (`<Acknowledgment>` and `<DeliveryReceipt>`) in a bit more detail.

### *The <Acknowledgment> Element*

This type of acknowledgment uses the optional header extension block – aptly named `<Acknowledgment>`. It is used by the receiving MSH to confirm to the sending MSH that it has received a message. It is triggered if the `ackRequested` attribute of the `<Via>` element has a value of `Signed` or `Unsigned`. The `<Acknowledgment>` element looks like this.

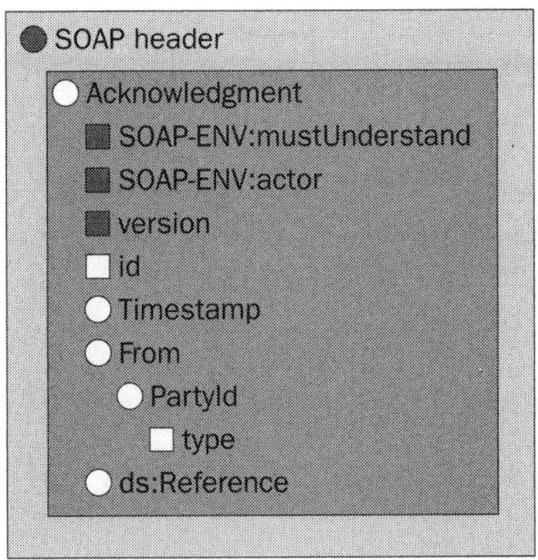

Apart from the required mustUnderstand and version attributes, and optional id attribute, the <Acknowledgment> element consists of:

- An actor attribute – a required attribute that contains the value http://schemas.xmlsoap.org/soap/actor/next. This value indicates that the <Acknowledgment> element must be processed by the receiving MSH.
- A <Timestamp> element – an optional element containing the time (as an XMLSchema timeInstant) that the message for which the <Acknowledgment> element is being generated was received by the MSH.
- A <From> element – an optional element containing the sender of the acknowledgment message. The construction is similar to the <From> element in the <MessageHeader>. In the sample the PartyId, ONIMAT, is defined in a domain specified with the type SAG. If the <From> element is omitted, then the party that is sending the element is identified by the <From> element in the <MessageHeader> element.
- Any number of <ds:Reference> elements – if present, these allow non-repudiation of the receipt by an MSH. It may include one or more <Reference> elements from the XMLDSIG namespace taken from, or based on, the message being acknowledged.

Here is an example of an <Acknowledgment> element:

```
<SOAP-ENV:Envelope
     xmlns:SOAP-ENV="http://schemas.xmlsoap.org/soap/envelope/"
     xmlns:eb="http://www.ebxml.org/namespaces/messageHeader">
  <SOAP-ENV:Header SOAP-ENV:mustUnderstand="1">
     <eb:MessageHeader>…</eb:MessageHeader>
     <eb:Acknowledgment SOAP-ENV:mustUnderstand="1" eb:version="1.0"
          SOAP-ENV:actor="http://schemas.xmlsoap.org/soap/actor/next">
        <eb:Timestamp>2001-03-09T12:22:30Z</eb:Timestamp>
        <eb:From>
          <eb:PartyId eb:type="SAG">ONIMAT</PartyId>
        </eb:From>
     </eb:Acknowledgment>
  </SOAP-ENV:Header>
</SOAP-ENV:Envelope>
```

### *The <DeliveryReceipt> Element*

While the <Acknowledgment> element is used as an acknowledgment mechanism between MSHs, there is a similar higher-level mechanism targeted at party-to-party, end-to-end confirmation, typically in a multi-hop scenario. This is the <DeliveryReceipt> type of acknowledgment.

The <DeliveryReceipt> element is an optional body extension block used by the To party, to let the From party know that the message was received. It is triggered when the deliveryReceiptRequested attribute of the <QualityOfServiceInfo> element has a value of either Signed or Unsigned. Its structure is shown here.

The diagrammatic representation of the <DeliveryReceipt> element is shown. The <DeliveryReceipt> element consists of the required version and optional id attributes, an optional <Timestamp> element, and any number of <ds:Reference> elements.

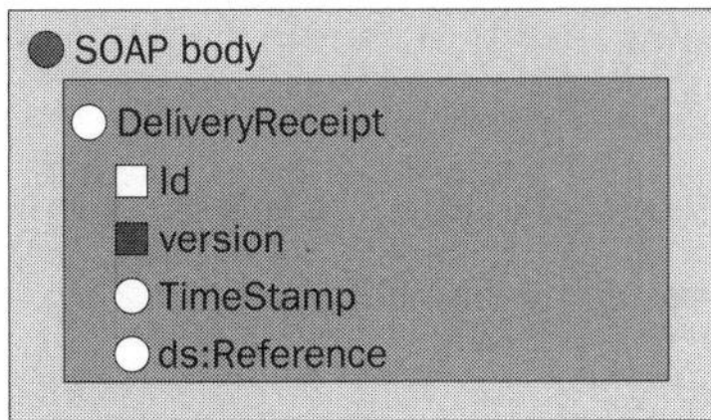


Here's an example of the `<DeliveryReceipt>` element in context:

```
<SOAP-ENV:Envelope
      xmlns:SOAP-ENV="http://schemas.xmlsoap.org/soap/envelope/"
      xmlns:eb="http://www.ebxml.org/namespaces/messageHeader">
   <SOAP-ENV:Header SOAP-ENV:mustUnderstand="1">
      <eb:MessageHeader eb:id="19650205" eb:version="1.0"
            SOAP-ENV:mustUnderstand="1">
         <eb:From>
            <eb:PartyId>urn:tamino.com:id:PartyB</eb:PartyId>
         </eb:From>
         <eb:To>
            <eb:PartyId>urn:wrox.com:id:PartyA</eb:PartyId>
         </eb:To>
         <eb:MessageData>
            <eb:MessageId>20010812.111203@wrox.com</eb:MessageId>
            <eb:Timestamp>2001-08-12T11:12:03Z</eb:Timestamp>
            <eb:RefToMessageId>20010812.11159@tamino.com</eb:RefToMessageId>
         </eb:MessageData>
      </eb:MessageHeader>
   </SOAP-ENV:Header>
   <SOAP-ENV:Body>
      <eb:DeliveryReceipt eb:version="1.0">
         <eb:Timestamp>2001-08-12T12:36:30Z</eb:Timestamp>
         <ds:Reference URI="cid:atpcheck/">
            <ds:DigestMethod
               Algorithm="http://www.w3.org/2000/09/xmldsig#dsa-sha1"/>
            <ds:DigestValue>...</ds:DigestValue>
         </ds:Reference>
      </eb:DeliveryReceipt>
   </SOAP-ENV:Body>
</SOAP-ENV:Envelope>
```

In the above sample a `DeliveryReceipt` is sent for a message received at `2001-08-12T12:36:30Z`, containing a `ds:reference` with an URI of `cid:atpcheck/`.

## ebMS Reliable Messaging Services

As we've already seen, a message is sent via a reliable delivery mechanism if *either* it has a `deliverySemantics` attribute specifying a value of `OnceAndOnlyOnce`, *or* a `reliableMessagingMethod` attribute with its default value of `ebXML`. In either case, the message must be confirmed with an acknowledgment.

MSH, supporting reliable messaging, needs to handle the delivery and acknowledgment of ebXML messages. This includes:

- Prescribed behavior for acknowledgment of messages
- A timeout and retransmission mechanism
- Persistent message storage
- An error notification mechanism

Support for reliable messaging can be implemented by using the **ebXML Reliable Messaging** protocol. Alternatively, ebXML can make use of (commercial) products providing reliable delivery of messages based on ebXML SOAP structures. Let's look at these four parts of reliable messaging.

### *Acknowledgments*

The minimum acknowledgment message contains a `<MessageData>` element, with a `<RefToMessageId>` whose value is the same as the `<MessageId>` element of the message being acknowledged. If `ackRequested` (in the `<Via>` element of the received message) is set to `Signed` or `Unsigned`, then the acknowledgment message must *also* contain an `<Acknowledgment>` element.

If the value of the `syncReply` parameter is `true`, then the responding MSH can add the `<Acknowledgment>` message to the response to the received message. This practice is known as **piggybacking** – the protocol can piggyback an `<Acknowledgment>` onto another message it just happens to be sending in that direction.

If an `<Acknowledgment>` element is being sent on its own, then the value of the `<MessageHeader>` elements must be set as follows:

- The `<Service>` element must be set to `uri:www.ebxml.org/messageService/`.
- The `<Action>` element must be set to `Acknowledgment`.
- The `<From>` element may be populated with the value extracted from the `<To>` element of the message received, or it may be set using the `<Receiver>` from the last `<TraceHeader>` in the message that has just been received. In either case, all `<PartyId>` elements from the message received should be included in this `<From>` element.
- The `<To>` element may be populated with the value extracted from the `<From>` element of the received message, or it may be set using the `<Sender>` from the last `<TraceHeader>` in the message that has just been received. In either case, all `<PartyId>` elements from the message received should be included in this `<To>` element.
- The `<RefToMessageId>` element must be set to the `<MessageId>` of the message that has just been received.

The diagram shows the reliable transfer of a message being acknowledged:

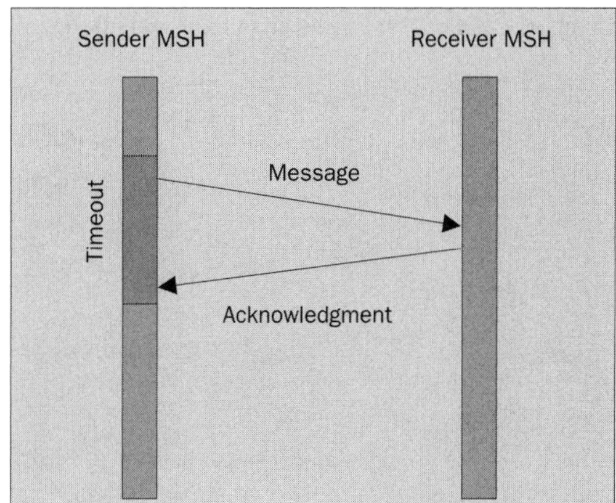


### *Retransmission and Timeout*

Suppose an MSH has sent a message. If the MSH has not received an acknowledgment message from the receiving MSH, *and* the timeout value specified in the `retryInterval` has expired, *and* the message has been resent less times than the maximum value specified in the `retries` parameter, then the sending MSH must **resend** the original message.

If the sending MSH doesn't receive an acknowledgment, we can deduce that either the message or the acknowledgment was lost. The following diagrams show both situations.

The first diagram shows a lost message, which is resent:

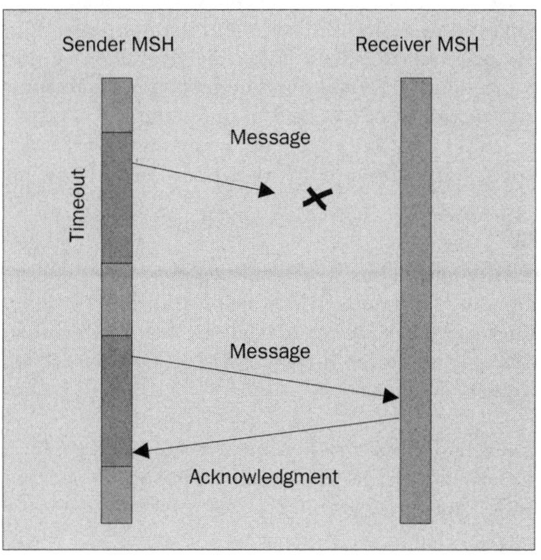

The next diagram shows the case where the acknowledgment message is lost (for example, because the timeout period has passed, or because the message really did get mislaid). The original message is resent by the sender. On receipt, the receiver will ignore the duplicate message but will resend the original acknowledgment.

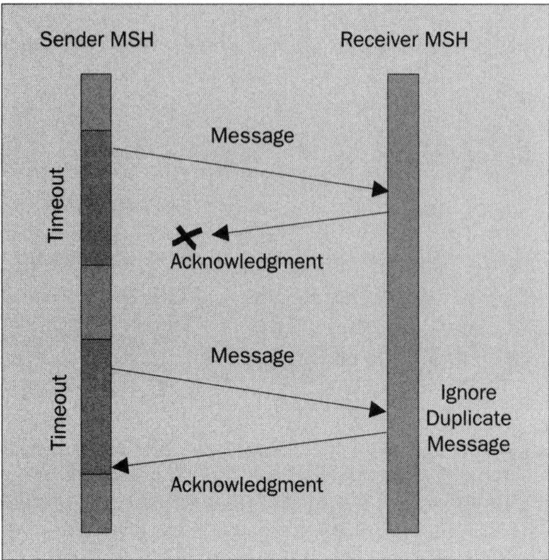


So this leaves two special cases to be handled, and the ebMS specification prescribes the following behavior:

- "If the sending MSH does not receive an acknowledgment message after the maximum number of retries is reached, the sending MSH should notify the application and/or system administrator functions of the failure to receive an acknowledgment." This is logical enough.
- "If the sending MSH detects an unrecoverable communications protocol error at the transport protocol level, the sending MSH should resend the message." This is understandable, but presumably we do not want to resend indefinitely, so there should also be some sort of fall-back or time-out mechanism here, although no such mechanism is specified. For instance, the sender may simply report (after a period of time) that it is unable to send the message; alternatively, the sender may keep retrying, while increasing the time between consecutive retries, in the expectation that the network is faulty but will eventually begin to function again.

#### *Persistent Message Storage*

An MSH that supports reliable messaging needs to keep messages persistently stored, so that it can "prevent loss of information after a system failure or interruption". Practically, this usually means hard disk storage – although alternative storage means may be used. After such a system breakdown, of course, an MSH must ensure that restored messages are processed as if nothing happened. How this is done is implementation-specific.

In order to support the filtering of duplicate messages (more on this a little later), a receiving MSH must save the `MessageId` in persistent storage. Furthermore, the ebMS specification advises that the following information is also kept in persistent storage:

- Complete messages, at least until the information in the message has been passed on to the application or other process that needs to process it.

- The time the message was received, so that the information can be used to generate the response to a Message Status Request.
- The complete response message.

### Error Notification

If a message is sent with `deliverySemantics` set to `OnceAndOnlyOnce`, and the message cannot be delivered, the delivering MSH will send a **delivery failure notification** to the `From` party. The delivery failure notification message contains:

- A `<From>` element, which identifies the party who detected the problem.
- A `<To>` element, which identifies the `From` party that created the message that could not be delivered.
- A `<Service>` element, containing the value of the reserved URI `uri:www.ebxml.org/messageService/`.
- An `<Action>` element, with the value `MessageError`.
- An `<Error>` element, with a `severity` attribute set to one of the following:
  - `Error`, if the party that detected the problem could not transmit the message (for example, the communications transport was not available).
  - `Warning`, if the message was transmitted but no acknowledgment message was received. (This means the message was probably not delivered, but that there is a small probability that it was.)
- An `errorCode` attribute with the value of `DeliveryFailure`.

Error processing and related elements are discussed later in this chapter.

## Reliable Messaging Behavior

If messages are being sent in a reliable fashion, the MSHs will behave according to certain rules – and the sending MSH and receiving MSH behave differently. We'll describe these differences in this section.

### Behavior of the Sending MSH

When the sending MSH is given data that needs to be sent reliably, it will:

- Create a message that includes a `<TraceHeader>` element, identifying `<Sender>` and `<Receiver>`.
- Set the `deliverySemantics` attribute (`<QualityOfServiceInfo>`) to the value of `OnceAndOnlyOnce`, thereby indicating reliable messaging conditions.
- Save the message in persistent storage, as described above.
- Send the message to the receiving MSH.
- Wait for the receiving MSH to return an acknowledgment message. If no acknowledgment message is received within the timeout period, then take the appropriate action, as described in the *Retransmission and Timeout* section above.

### Behavior of the Receiving MSH

The receiving MSH first needs to determine the **type** of the message received (that is, whether it is an acknowledgment or regular message). The acknowledgment is described earlier, and is distinguished by the inclusion of a `<Service>` element with the value `http://www.ebxml.org/namespaces/messageService/MessageAcknowledgment`, and an `<Action>` element with the value `Acknowledgment`. If the message *is* an acknowledgment, the MSH will look for the message in the persistent storage; if the message is found, the MSH will mark it as delivered.

If the message is a regular message, the receiving MSH needs to check whether the message is a duplicate (that is, whether there is another message in the persistent store with the same `MessageId`). If so, the receiving MSH can deduce that the sending MSH did not receive the acknowledgment (as shown in an earlier diagram).

The action taken by the receiving MSH depends on whether or not the received message is a duplicate. If the message is *not* a duplicate then the MSH will:

- Save at least the `MessageId` of the received message in persistent storage.
- Check to see whether the received message contains a `<RefToMessageId>` element, and thus refers to an earlier sent message within a conversation. If so, the MSH will then check to see whether the referenced message is stored persistently; if so, it will mark the message as having been delivered.
- Generate an acknowledgment message in response.

If the message *is* a duplicate then the MSH will:

- Respond to the sender of the message with a response identical to the one sent when the message was first received. (This response is stored in the persistent store, and can be found by matching the `<MessageId>` and `<RefToMessageId>` elements.)
- Check whether the entire message is stored persistently, or just the `MessageId`. If the `MessageId` alone is stored, then:
    - If `syncReply` is set to `true`, and if the CPA indicates an application response is included, the MSH will ignore the received message. A timeout will occur at the sending MSH that is waiting for an answer. For instance, if processing of the earlier message is not yet complete then a reply will not have been sent. This causes the sending MSH to retransmit the message.
    - If `syncReply` is set to `false` then the MSH will generate an acknowledgment message. In this case, the duplicate was sent because the sending MSH didn't get the original acknowledgment.

## Message Order

As mentioned earlier, the message ordering capability of an MSH takes care of ordered delivery of messages. We'll first describe the simple counter mechanism used in the `<SequenceNumber>` element, and then we'll describe the intended MSH behavior.

### *The <SequenceNumber> Element*

We've already met the <SequenceNumber> element earlier in the chapter. It's an optional element that forms part of the ebXML message header, and indicates the sequence in which a receiving MSH must process the messages. A <SequenceNumber> element might look like this:

```
<eb:SequenceNumber eb:status="Reset">0</eb:SequenceNumber>
```

The <SequenceNumber> is unique within the <ConversationId> and the MSH. The required status attribute is used to reset or proceed with the <SequenceNumber>. Specifying a value of Reset for the status will cause a reset to 0 of the SequenceNumber, and a value of Continue causes a sequential continuation.

> *There's clearly an element of redundancy here – if the attribute eb:status="Reset" means "reset to zero" then there should be no real need to specify the 0 value too. Our feeling is that the spec-writers are anticipating that future versions will need to allow resetting to values other than 0.*

> *Although the ebMS specification describes the status attribute for <SequenceNumber>, the ebXML schema provided doesn't define it. The specification states that the specification supersedes the examples, but in this case it's hard to determine which is an example and which is a definition. We don't recommend using the status attribute, in case the default ebXML schema is used for validation and the functionality is not necessary. But if you wish, you could adjust the schema to include a status attribute – you'll need to find the following original schema fragment:*

```
<element name="SequenceNumber" type="positiveInteger"/>
```

*...and replace it with a fragment which (we suggest) looks something like this:*

```
<element name="SequenceNumber" type="positiveInteger"/>
<complexType>
   <attribute name="status" type="tns:SequenceNumber.status"/>
</complexType>
</element>
<simpleType name="SequenceNumber.status">
   <restriction base="NMTOKEN">
      <enumeration value="Reset"/>
      <enumeration value="Continue"/>
   </restriction>
</simpleType>
```

If the messageOrderSemantics attribute of the <QualityOfServiceInfo> element is set to Guaranteed, then the <SequenceNumber> element *must* be present (this is a logical arrangement). Its value must be unique within the <ConversationId> and MSH, and (according to the specification) has a value in the range 0–99999999 (sequentially, the next value after 99999999 is 0) – otherwise, the MSH should issue an error with the errorCode="DeliveryFailure" and severity="Error".

The status attribute is required, and is used to increment the counter mechanism or to reset it to 0. To achieve these, we set the attribute value to Continue or Reset (respectively).

The <SequenceNumber> element only appears when deliverySemantics has a value of OnceAndOnlyOnce and messageOrderSemantics has a value of Guaranteed. If this is not the case, the To MSH will report an error to the From party MSH with an errorCode of Inconsistent and a severity of Error.

### MSH Message Order Behavior

The value of <SequenceNumber> is 0 in the following cases:

- It is the very first message from the sending MSH within the conversation.
- It is the first message after having received a reset.
- It is the first message after the maximum value of 99999999 is reached.

The status attribute is set to Continue, except when the sending MSH wants to reset the <SequenceNumber> to 0. This follows because of the first two situations above – it is up to the sending MSH to set the status attribute to Reset.

The From party MSH and the To party MSH each set an independent <SequenceNumber> as the sending MSH within the <ConversationID>. It is set to zero on the first message from that MSH for a conversation and then incremented by one for each subsequent message sent.

A sending MSH must wait until it has received all of the acknowledgment messages previously sent for the conversation before resetting the <SequenceNumber> of a conversation.

If messageOrderSemantics is set to Guaranteed, the To party MSH will correct an invalid order of messages. This implies that a message will not be passed on to an application until all the messages within the conversation with lower <SequenceNumber>s have been received.

## Error Reporting and Handling

Errors occur at runtime in ebMS messaging, just as in any other implementation. Errors can be caused by badly formatted messages, by security issues, or by failures, while sending messages in a reliable fashion. Therefore, ebMS offers provisions for error reporting and handling. It does so by using a standard ebXML message containing an <ErrorList> element.

Besides the ebMS-specific error handling available via this ebXML message, it's *also* possible for errors to occur at SOAP level, and standard SOAP faults generated. This means that an MSH not only needs to support ebXML error messages, but it must also be capable of dealing with standard SOAP faults.

Errors associated with the data communication protocols are detected and reported using the standard mechanisms supported by that data communication protocol, and do not use the error reporting mechanisms described here.

Below is an example of an ebXML message reporting two errors:

```
<SOAP-ENV:Envelope
      xmlns:SOAP-ENV="http://schemas.xmlsoap.org/soap/envelope/"
      xmlns:eb="http://www.ebxml.org/namespaces/messageHeader">
   <SOAP-ENV:Header SOAP-ENV:mustUnderstand="1">
      <eb:MessageHeader eb:id="19650205" eb:version="1.0"
```

```
            SOAP-ENV:mustUnderstand="1">
         <eb:From>
            <eb:PartyId>urn:tamino.com:id:PartyB</eb:PartyId>
         </eb:From>
         <eb:To>
            <eb:PartyId>urn:wrox.com:id:PartyA</eb:PartyId>
         </eb:To>
         <eb:MessageData>
            <eb:MessageId>20010812.111203@wrox.com</eb:MessageId>
            <eb:Timestamp>2001-08-12T11:12:03Z</eb:Timestamp>
            <eb:RefToMessageId>20010812.11159@tamino.com</eb:RefToMessageId>
         </eb:MessageData>
      </eb:MessageHeader>
      <eb:ErrorList eb:id='3490sdo9' eb:highestSeverity="error"
            eb:version="1.0" SOAP-ENV:mustUnderstand="1">
         <eb:Error
               eb:codeContext="http://www.ebxml.org/messageServiceErrors"
               eb:errorCode='SecurityFailure' eb:severity="Error"
               eb:location="URI ds:Signature" xml:lang="en">
            Validation of signature failed
         </eb:Error>
         <eb:Error eb:codeContext="http://www.wrox.com/ebXML/logErrors"
               eb:errorCode='LoggingFailure' eb:severity="Warning"
               eb:location="URI Logserver" xml:lang="en">
            Couldn't write logging information.
         </eb:Error>
      </eb:ErrorList>
   </SOAP-ENV:Header>
</SOAP-ENV:Envelope>
```

The message has been sent from Party A to Party B. An error has occurred, so now Party B has swapped To and From, and returned the message. The message looks very familiar until we hit the <ErrorList> element.

### The <ErrorList> and <Error> Elements

The <ErrorList> element is an optional ebXML SOAP header extension block. It indicates that the message identified by the <RefToMessageId> in the <MessageHeader> element has an error. The <ErrorList> element consists of required mustUnderstand and version attributes, an optional id attribute, and more interestingly:

- A required highestSeverity attribute, indicating the highest severity value among all the <Error> elements in the list. (There are two possible severity values – Warning and Error – of which the latter is more severe.) If any one of the <Error> elements contains a severity Error, then highestSeverity will necessarily be set to Error. In the example, two <Error> elements are present and their severity levels are Error and Warning respectively; hence the value of highestSeverity is Error.
- One or more <Error> elements, each containing the detailed information of an error message.

An <Error> element consists of an optional id attribute (an XML ID, allowing for the unique identification of the <Error> element), and the following five required attributes:

- codeContext – contains a URI to identify the namespace or schema for the errorCodes. In the example, the value is http://www.ebxml.org/messageServiceErrors – this is the default, and indicates that the error message is specified by ebMS. The codeContext attribute allows for adding application-specific errorCodes (as shown in the example's second <Error> element, which uses http://www.wrox.com/ebXML/logErrors to indicate an application-specific error).
- errorCode - indicates the nature of the error. Valid values and a description for the default codeContext are given in the table below.
- severity – indicates the severity of the error (either Warning or Error). In the case of an error of severity Error, no further error messages within the conversation will be generated by either the sending and receiving MSH. This prevents an accumulation of errors within the conversation.
- location – points to the part of the message that is in error. If an error exists in an ebXML element, and the element is well-formed, then the content of the location attribute must be an XPointer. If the error is associated with the MIME envelope, then location contains the content-id of the MIME part that is in error, so the second <Error> element in the sample above, containing location="cid: invoice232.xml@wrox.com", points to a MIME part that looks like this:

```
--MIME_boundary
Content-Type: application/xml
Content-Transfer-Encoding: utf-8
Content-ID: invoice232.xml@wrox.com

<invoice>
   <invoicedata>
      <!-- Invoice detail information -->
   </invoicedata>
</invoice>
--MIME_boundary–
```

- xml:lang – defines the language of the error content. In the sample the content is in English (as specified by xml:lang="en").

The values for the required errorCode attribute used in a message reporting an error are described in the following table:

| Error Code | Short Description |
|---|---|
| ValueNotRecognized | The value assigned to the element or attribute is not recognized by the MSH. |
| NotSupported | The specified element or attribute is not supported by the MSH. |
| Inconsistent | The specified element content or attribute value is inconsistent with other elements or attributes. |
| OtherXml | Error (other than the three specified above) in an element content or attribute value. |

| Error Code | Short Description |
|---|---|
| DeliveryFailure | Message delivery failure. |
| TimeToLiveExpired | The message's timeToLive period has expired. |
| SecurityFailure | The message's security checks failed. |
| Unknown | An unknown error occurred. |

If a receiving MSH detects an error with a highestSeverity of Warning, it will report the error via an error message back to the sending MSH. This MSH will then respond to the received error message. In case of a severity of Error, the error will be logged by the sending MSH and no further steps will be taken automatically by the sending MSH.

Error messages are only reported to the originating MSH in the case where no ErrorURI is specified in the CPA. If the CPA contains an ErrorURI, the error message is sent to this URI instead of the sending MSH. In the case of a multi-hop scenario, the originating MSH can be determined by using the <Location> element in the <Sender> of the topmost <TraceHeader>. If no <TraceHeader> is present, it automatically becomes a single-hop transmission, so the <From> element in the <MessageHeader> will be used.

In addition to those elements mentioned, the <MessageHeader>'s <Service> and <Action> elements can be used to steer the error handling. The MSH that reports the error can use these two elements to specify the process that should deal with the message. This can only be done if the reported error is a result of an earlier processed message and the highestSeverity is set to Error. An MSH is also allowed to issue error messages without relation to received messages to allow for exchange of error situations that are not connected to the processing of messages. In this special case the <MessageHeader> will contain:

```
<eb:Service>uri:www.ebxml.org/messageService/</eb:Service>
<eb:Action> MessageError </eb:Action>
```

# ebMS Security

Transfer of messages via a network presents certain security risks, such as unauthorized access, data integrity corruption, and confidentiality attacks. These risks, and the countermeasures provided by ebMS, are explained below. A global overview of e-business-related security solutions, which are partly used by ebMS, are explained in more detail in Chapter 15.

The configuration of security for the MSH is specified in the CPA, allowing a choice in how much of the message is secured: either the payload alone, or the entire ebXML message. An MSH can deliver up to 23 defined profiles, offering various countermeasures against the security risks. However, the XML security specifications are currently immature, so only the following two profiles are supported:

- Profile 0: No security services are applied to data.
- Profile 1: Sending MSH applies XML/DSIG structures to the message.

Profile 0 needs no further explanation; so we can directly move to Profile 1 and consider applying **XML Digital Signatures** to a message. Below is an example of a digitally signed ebXML SOAP message:

```
<SOAP-ENV:Envelope
      xmlns:SOAP-ENV=http://schemas.xmlsoap.org/soap/envelope/"
      xmlns:eb="http://www.ebxml.org/namespaces/messageHeader"
      xmlns:xlink="http://www.w3.org/1999/xlink">
   <SOAP-ENV:Header SOAP-ENV:mustUnderstand="1">
      <eb:MessageHeader eb:id="..." eb:version="1.0">
         ...
      </eb:MessageHeader>
      <eb:TraceHeaderList eb:id="..." eb:version="1.0">
         <!-- eb:TraceHeader elements included here as appropriate -->
      </eb:TraceHeaderList>
      <ds:Signature xmlns:ds="http://www.w3.org/2000/09/xmldsig#">
         <ds:SignedInfo>
            <ds:CanonicalizationMethod
               Algorithm="http://www.w3.org/TR/2000/CR-xml-c14n-20001026"/>
            <ds:SignatureMethod
               Algorithm="http://www.w3.org/2000/09/xmldsig#dsa-sha1"/>
            <ds:Reference URI="">
               <Transforms>
                 <ds:Transform
       ds:Algorithm="http://www.w3.org/2000/09/xmldsig#enveloped-signature">
                 </ds:Transform>
                  <ds:Transform
       ds:Algorithm="http://www.w3.org/TR/1999/REC-xpath-19991116">
                     <ds:Xpath>
                        not(ancestor-or-self::eb:TraceHeaderList or
                        ancestor-or-self::eb:Via)
                     </ds:XPath>
                  </ds:Transform>
               </ds:Transforms>
               <ds:DigestMethod
                  Algorithm="http://www.w3.org/2000/09/xmldsig#dsa-sha1"/>
               <ds:DigestValue>...</ds:DigestValue>
            </ds:Reference>
            <ds:Reference URI="cid://ATPDetail/">
               <ds:DigestMethod
                  Algorithm="http://www.w3.org/2000/09/xmldsig#dsa-sha1"/>
               <ds:DigestValue>...</ds:DigestValue>
            </ds:Reference>
         </ds:SignedInfo>
         <ds:SignatureValue>...</ds:SignatureValue>
         <ds:KeyInfo>...</ds:KeyInfo>
      </ds:Signature>
   </SOAP-ENV:Header>
   <SOAP-ENV:Body>
      <eb:Manifest eb:id="Man01" eb:version="1.0">
         <eb:Reference eb:id="ATPOrder"
            xlink:href="cid:atporder"
            xlink:role="http://www.wrox.com/ebXML/order">
            <eb:Schema eb:location="http://www.wrox.com/ebXML/order.xsd"
               eb:version="1.0"/>
```

```
            <eb:Description xml:lang="en-us">
               ATP Check for order 2389877</eb:Description>
         </eb:Reference>
      </eb:Manifest>
   </SOAP-ENV:Body>
</SOAP-ENV:Envelope>
```

The message is constructed as we've seen before, with a SOAP envelope containing the various SOAP and ebXML elements. The thing we're interested in here is the `<ds:Signature>` element.

### *The <ds:Signature> Element*

The `<ds:Signature>` element is an optional ebXML SOAP header extension block that conforms to the XML DSIG specification (http://www.w3.org/2000/09/xmldsig) for signing data associated with the message. It is used to digitally sign an ebXML message to provide security countermeasures. The `<ds:Signature>` element must be namespace-qualified, and the structure and content of the element must conform to the XML DSIG specification.

XML signatures conforming to the ebXML specification can selectively sign complete XML documents, but also portions of documents. This enables new content to be added to the documents while preserving the validity of any signatures that are already in place.

Additional information on the XML DSIG standard is provided in Chapter 15. The only elements inside the `<ds:Signature>` worth noticing at this moment are the two `<ds:Reference>` elements. For clarity reasons we will skip the `ds:` namespace information:

- The first `<Reference>` element is always present if a message is digitally signed. It includes a child `<Transforms>` element containing two `<Transform>` child elements:
  - The first has an `Algorithm` attribute with a value of `http://www.w3.org/2000/09/xmldsig#enveloped-signature` to allow for signing enveloped structures.
  - The second has a child `<XPath>` element containg a value of `not(ancestor-or-self::eb:TraceHeaderList` or `ancestor-or-self::eb:Via)`. The XPath expression is used to exclude the elements that are subject to change from the signing process. The result of the first part of the XPath statement excludes the `<Signature>` element within which it is contained, and the second XPath statement excludes the `<TraceHeaderList>` and `<Via>` elements and all their descendants.
- The second `<Reference>` element is used to digitally sign the payload, referenced by the URI `cid://ATPDetail/`.

For the sake of completeness, a general overview of the elements and attributes in the `Signature` element is presented in the following diagram:

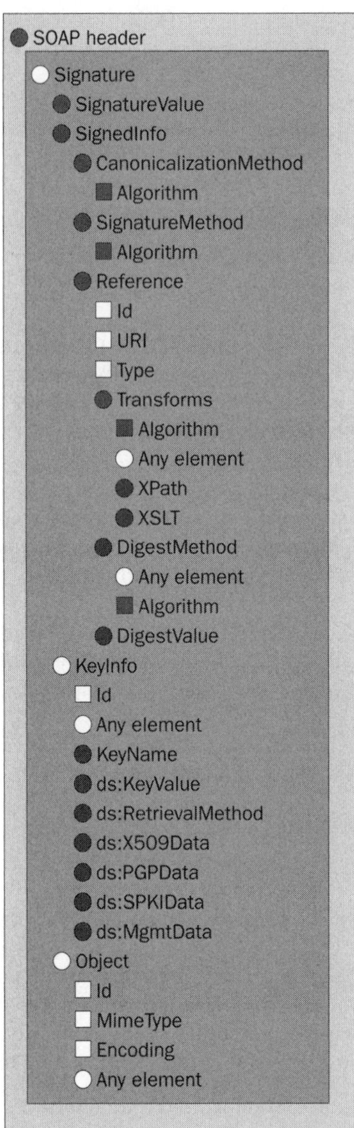


# Summary

In this chapter, we've given a fairly comprehensive treatment of the ebXML Messaging Service, ebMS:

- ebMS extends the 'standard' SOAP message structure with its own header and body extensions. The ebXML extensions support the extra levels of security and reliable messaging functionality necessary for a B2B e-business framework like ebXML.

- Often, data transmission across networks is performed in a best-effort (or unreliable) way. ebMS recognizes the need for reliable messaging, and offers a number of constructs to support that. We looked in particular at the Quality of Service (QoS) (and thus reliability) levels offered by a protocol.
- Like any TCP-IP-style protocol, reliable messaging in ebMS is based on a timeout and acknowledgment mechanism. We looked in particular at the ebMS constructs for idempotent and ordered delivery.
- ebMS provides a mechanism for secure messaging, and we looked at that with particular emphasis on digital signatures. (Digital signatures, the underlying technologies and related facilities will be covered in more detail in Chapter 15.)
- The message service handler (MSH) is the piece of software which takes care of execution of the ebMS-defined tasks at each node. We studied the MSH in some detail and presented a working example of the Ping service, which is part of the MSH interface of ebMS.

The focus of this chapter was on ebXML MSH message handling. We do encourage you to look at the advanced messaging techniques in Chapter 14 to see how Java Message Service (JMS) fits into this picture. And likewise, but possibly a bit more 'high-level', we'd like to point you to the Java API for XML Messaging (JAXM) covered in the same chapter.

ebXMLFoundationsProfessional

# 14

# Java Messaging Protocols

In Chapter 4 we introduced the Simple Object Access Protocol (SOAP). In Chapter 13 we delved further into concept of messaging, and undertook a thorough examination of the ebXML Message Service (ebMS) Specification. In this chapter we intend to build on that framework, by taking a deeper look at the ebMS specification in the context of other standards – specifically the **Java API for XML Messaging** (**JAXM**) and the **Java Message Service** (**JMS**).

This chapter will look at JAXM and JMS and investigate how they complement ebMS (and, indeed, how they complement one another). JMS offers a powerful messaging model which is based on an open standard. It provides a loosely-coupled asynchronous mode of communication, and support for synchronous and request/reply modes of communication, for both the point-to-point and publish/subscribe messaging domains. We'll explore:

- The genesis of JMS
- The purpose of JMS, and its important features and benefits
- How can JMS be used to support ebMS.

JAXM is a Java API, intended to enable access to the contents of an XML message without having to understand the format of the message itself. Thus, although JAXM is still an evolving specification, it is of interest to us as an interface to SOAP messages and ebXML messages. We'll complete the chapter with an overview of JAXM, its status, and go through some simple examples based on the reference implementation for the specification. We'll cover:

- The purpose of JAXM, and its potential
- How can JAXM be implemented with ebXML MS and JMS

# The Java Message Service

The success of an organization is often determined by its ability to handle information and exchange that information with other applications, both internally and externally. We've long been using tightly-coupled RPC-like mechanisms such as Remote Method Invocation (RMI), Common Object Request Broker Architecture (CORBA), and Enterprise JavaBeans (EJBs), to enable internal applications to exchange information with one another. While these methods are successful, they can introduce problems that stem from the dependency that the processes impose on one another. For instance, if one of the participating applications happens to go offline, it may affect other applications downstream, potentially crippling the entire process. Moreover, these methods often require applications to have an intimate knowledge of one another's interfaces, which means that changes to one application may introduce side effects to others, requiring careful orchestration of interface versioning and extension mechanisms.

As businesses began to create larger, more distributed systems between geographically-separated offices or with other businesses, the problems of tightly-coupled communication became magnified. What happens when a component goes offline without warning, or terminates unexpectedly, or responds too slowly to a request? There were various potential failings in distributed components and applications, and their increasing prevalence led to the requirement for an environment that supports a more **loosely-coupled** process-to-process infrastructure.

Several messaging systems have been developed to address this issue, and the **Java Message Service** (**JMS**) specification is one such. JMS resolves the issues of asynchronous communication in a simple yet effective manner with a well-defined, open API and set of semantics. JMS is an enterprise-capable middleware API, based on **Message Oriented Middleware** (**MOM**) fundamentals. Since it was first introduced as a Java software specification in November 1998, vendor implementations have positioned JMS as a first-class e-business messaging communications platform, capable of secure exchange of critical business data over the Internet. As we'll discuss in this section, it is now an integral part of the J2EE strategy and can be considered a foundation for electronic communications across enterprises.

> *J2EE is the **Java 2, Enterprise Edition** platform. For more information, see http://java.sun.com/j2ee/.*

While JMS is largely intended to be an asynchronous form of communication between applications, there is also a model for performing both synchronous and asynchronous request/reply invocations. The specification clearly defines what a message is composed of, and provides strict rules governing store-and-forward messaging, guaranteed delivery, message acknowledgements, transactions, and recovery from failures.

JMS is an important messaging standard and one that is likely to be around for some time, for reasons that include the following:

- **JMS is a foundation for communications across enterprises.** JMS defines the only open standard for asynchronous MOM implementations. Right now, any developer using the JMS API in his applications will find a variety of different vendor implementations (that is, JMS providers) on the market. While the JMS specification sets the API, message formatting, and delivery semantics for messaging, it does not impose a specific implementation – instead it leaves that task to JMS providers for interpretation. Thus, the robustness of the implementation varies from product to product in areas as security, load-balancing, fault-tolerance, and message routing.

- **JMS has its roots in an industry effort.** The JMS specification was an industry effort – while Sun owns the specification, they worked very closely with the messaging vendors of the time to produce that specification. The intention of that effort was to standardize a common set of APIs and message delivery semantics across all messaging products. Over the course of the work, the intention evolved into a desire to provide a specification for a first class middleware, on equal footing with RPC-like solutions such as RMI, CORBA, and EJB. The result is not a "least-common-denominator" compromise, but a powerful list of features that is a superset of the capabilities provided by the messaging vendors who participated in the effort. The importance the industry has placed on messaging is evidenced in its inclusion of emerging standards such as J2EE.
- **JMS is an integral part of the J2EE strategy.** JMS has so far been an optional part of the J2EE platform. Until recently, EJB servers and JMS servers were not explicitly related to (or tied together with) one another. With the introduction of the 1.3 version of the J2EE specification, JMS has become a required component of the J2EE strategy. Why is this so exciting? Partly, it's because of changes evident in the EJB 2.0 specification, which introduces the **MessageDrivenBean**. The `MessageDrivenBean` is a special kind of EJB that exists solely for the purpose of producing and consuming JMS messages in an EJB server environment. Details of this new model are outside the scope of this discussion, but you can find further information at http://java.sun.com/products/ejb/docs.html.

# An Overview of JMS

JMS applications use the JMS API to communicate with one another using **producers** and **consumers**. Producers *send* messages and consumers *receive* messages. It is possible for an application to be both a producer and a consumer at the same time. For instance, a manufacturer may act as producer, by broadcasting a request for price quotes to many interested suppliers (consumers). At the same time, suppliers may be responding with proposals in the form of XML documents, and the manufacturer will be the consumer of these messages.

Producers and consumers form a **loosely-coupled partnership** in the sense that they are not directly tied to each other, nor do they require any previous knowledge of one another. This is a necessary ingredient for organizations looking to become involved in business-to-business communication, where connectivity cannot be guaranteed. Instead, producers and consumers are abstractly connected to each other through two different types of **virtual channels** (called **topics** and **queues**). These virtual channels are administratively defined and can be accessed programmatically via naming and directory services (provided by a Java Naming and Directory Interface (JNDI) lookup).

## Messaging Domains

JMS defines two messaging models that support the different ways in which applications can be expected to communicate: **publish-and-subscribe (pub/sub)** and **point-to-point (p2p) queuing**. In JMS terms these are referred to as **messaging domains**.

As shown in the following diagrams, the pub/sub domain is intended for a one-to-many broadcast of information, while the point-to-point domain is intended for a one-to-one communication between two specific applications.

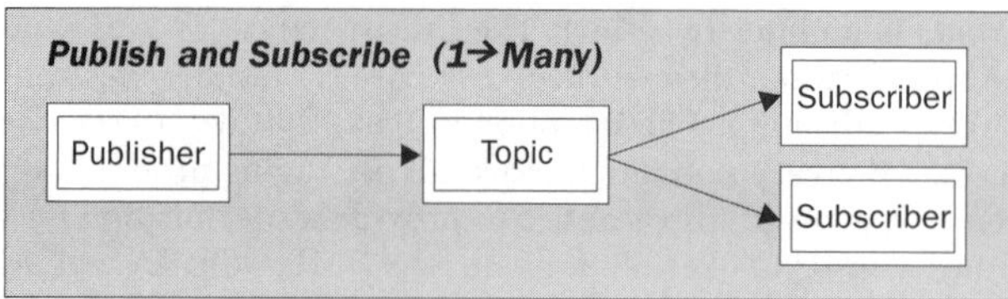


In the **pub/sub** model, multiple consumers may register an interest with, or *subscribe* to, a virtual channel called a **topic**. A producer uses the `publish()` method to send a message on that topic. Each subscriber receives a copy of that message. Some vendors also support the idea of **topic hierarchies**, where a topic can be further broken down into various levels of subtopics. For instance, a company may represent their sales data in a hierarchical structure by representing it by country, region, office, and sales representative. Clients can subscribe to the appropriate level, thereby filtering out unwanted data while supporting a flexible subject-based routing paradigm.

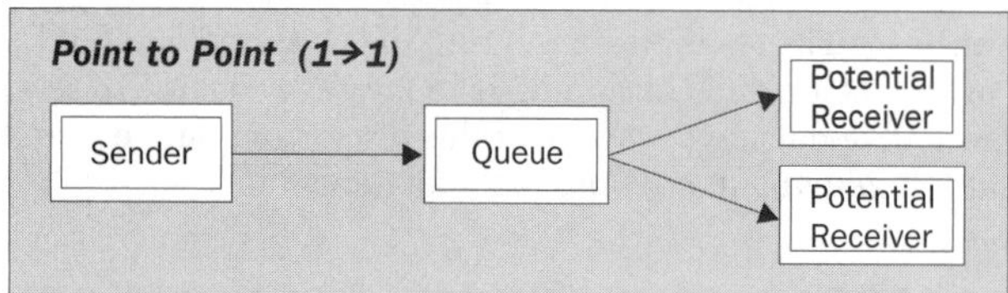


The **point-to-point** model offers a more traditional queue-based approach, where only one consumer may receive a message that is sent to a queue. Messages are sent and received in a FIFO (first in, first out) order. This means that the messaging server will store (or queue) messages and retain the order of the messages until a consumer receives them. As shown in the diagram, a point-to-point queue may have multiple consumers listening on a queue for the purposes of load balancing or "hot backup" in the event that one of the consumer processes fails; but still only one receiver may consume each individual message. JMS also provides consumers with the ability to look ahead at the messages in a queue using a "browsing" capability. When browsing a queue, the consumer is not actually *consuming* the messages in it – therefore queue-browsing can be used to programmatically control the consumption of messages based on expected messages residing in the queue. This feature could be used to search the queue for messages with a high priority, or to monitor a queue from an administration tool.

Semantically, the pub/sub and point-to-point models are extremely similar. Therefore, they afford the developer the ability to change the model being used with little effort as application requirements change and dictate a different approach.

## What's in a Message?

A **message** is the fundamental entity for which the process of messaging was created. It is self-contained and depends on the underlying messaging architecture for its safe, reliable delivery to a message consumer. A message is composed of three basic parts: the **headers**, the **properties**, and the message **payload**.

In JMS, the **header** definitions are defined by the JMS specification and are used by both the JMS provider and the application developer to provide information such as the destination, a reply-to destination, the message type, or a message expiration time. Headers are divided into two categories: those that are automatically assigned and those that are developer-assigned. Automatically assigned header values are set by the JMS provider when the message is delivered. Developer-assigned header values must be explicitly set.

The **property** section contains a set of application-defined name/value pairs that are accessible via an extensive assortment of `setXXXX()` and `getXXXX()` methods on the `Message` object. Developers will often use message properties as a means of message routing and filtering based on the value of the properties.

The message **payload** can contain any type of application data, and is accessible in a number of forms. There are five prescribed message types:

- `BytesMessage`: a stream of bytes. Intended for any arbitrary data, binary or otherwise. Typically useful for data that is opaque to the messaging system (that is, not accessible to Java), yet is structured in some native format that is known to both the sending application and the receiving application.
- `ObjectMessage`: a set of objects that is accessible by Java programs.
- `MapMessage`: a set of name/value pairs, where the values can have any Java primitive type.
- `StreamMessage`: a stream of primitive Java types, with the added value that a message may be read from and written to using a familiar file stream metaphor.
- `TextMessage`: plain text.

*Several JMS vendors have recognized the impact that XML has had and will continue to have on the industry. Therefore, many now provide an* `XMLMessage` *type by extending the* `TextMessage` *type. To date, this message type is not part of the JMS standard. Its creation is intended to help simplify processing of XML data by allowing an application to construct and deconstruct a message using a DOM tree.*

## Quality of Service (QoS)

It is up to the messaging architecture to guarantee the delivery of a message from its source to its intended target(s). The JMS specification supports this notion of guaranteed delivery by providing two different **delivery modes** and a set of rigidly-defined **acknowledgement levels**. Combining these two principles gives developers the latitude to create as strong and "bulletproof" a messaging solution as their application requires. For instance, if we are sending critical financial information to our investors for an upcoming merger, we want to make sure the information gets there, no matter what. On the other hand, if we are subscribed to stock updates and we miss a message transmission, there is no cause for concern because in all likelihood there will be another message sent in a couple of minutes.

### Delivery Modes

JMS supports two delivery modes:

- **Persistent** – also known as *once-and-only-once* delivery
- **Non-persistent** – also known as *at-most-once* delivery

In the **persistent** (once-and-only-once) delivery mode, a message is guaranteed by the JMS provider to always arrive at the intended destination and it will never be sent more than once. Even in the event of a JMS provider failure, a message will never be lost. This guarantee is made possible by utilizing a **store-and-forward mechanism**, where the message is written to permanent storage, so that in the event of a failure the message can be recovered and delivered as promised. The following figure shows how JMS providers use such a store-and-forward mechanism as part of the solution to guarantee once-and-only-once delivery of messages:

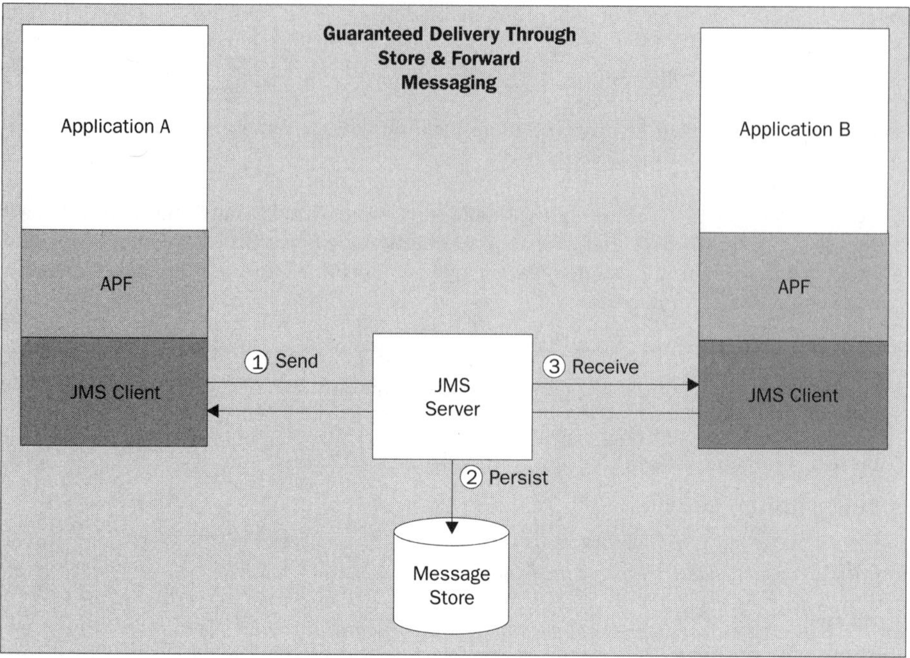


Even in the pub/sub model, where multiple receivers may consume a copy of a single broadcasted message, the rules still apply within the relative view of each consumer.

**Non-persistent** (at-most-once) delivery is a less stringent QoS setting on a message, which means that the JMS provider is occasionally allowed to lose a message. Non-persistent messages will most likely not survive a JMS provider failure.

There is often a trade-off between performance and reliability when choosing between these two modes, and your choice will be dictated by how crucial it is that the information gets to its intended destination.

JMS offers a `setDeliveryMode()` method at the producer level, so that all messages sent from that producer inherit the delivery mode set:

```
// Set the JMS delivery mode on the message producer
TopicPublisher samplePublisher = sampleSession.createPublisher(topic);
SamplePublisher.setDeliveryMode(DeliveryMode.NON_PERSISTENT);
```

### Acknowledgment Modes

A crucial part of the JMS guaranteed delivery mechanism is the concept of **acknowledgments**. As we've seen in Chapter 13, acknowledgment messages are sent between the senders, receivers, and JMS server involved, and their receipt (or otherwise) can allow us to deduce things about the safe delivery of the message, or the point at which it may have failed.

The JMS specification defines three types of acknowledgment mode: `AUTO_ACKNOWLEDGE`, `DUPS_OK_ACKNOWLEDGE`, and `CLIENT_ACKNOWLEDGE`. These modes are specified at the `SESSION` level, for example:

```
tSession = tConnect.createTopicSession(false, Session.AUTO_ACKNOWLEDGE);
```

```
qSession = qConnect.createQueueSession(false, Session.CLIENT_ACKNOWLEDGE);
```

When used in combination with the delivery modes mentioned earlier, you have a flexible and powerful messaging infrastructure at your disposal. The three acknowledgment modes differ as follows:

- `AUTO_ACKNOWLEDGE` behaves transparently to the application. It basically instructs a JMS server to acknowledge to the producer that the server has received the message and will insure that it is delivered. This mode also instructs a message consumer to acknowledge to the JMS server that a message was received and thus the JMS server has fulfilled its responsibility of insuring message delivery. What happens behind the scenes depends on the delivery mode used. With *persistent* delivery, the JMS server will write the message to permanent storage before acknowledging back to the producer that it has received the message. With *non-persistent* delivery, the JMS server could acknowledge receipt as soon as it gets the message; in this case, it's possible that the message could be lost, if a failure should occur before the message is delivered.
- `DUPS_OK_ACKNOWLEDGE` is the most loose message mode offered and operates under the premise that it is acceptable for the JMS provider to deliver duplicate messages. Developers will typically use this approach if they feel that the overhead associated with persistent delivery outweighs the chance of something happening to cause a duplicate message being sent. In this scenario, it is the developer's responsibility to handle duplicate messages programmatically.
- `CLIENT_ACKNOWLEDGE` offers the most granular acknowledgement control possible to the developer. The developer explicitly informs the JMS server that a message was received, by using the `acknowledge()` method. While extremely powerful, this approach could be problematic, as messages may tend to accumulate on the server while waiting for acknowledgment from the clients.

## Transacted Messages

JMS provides a transaction mechanism similar to the **all or nothing** notion of a distributed transaction. However, the JMS concept applies to the sending and receiving of messages, rather than the coordination of resources. The send operations are separated from the receive operations. Messages are logically grouped together and are explicitly sent (by the producer) or received (by the consumer) with a `commit()` method on the `Session` object, indicating the end of a send or receive series. In the send process, the `commit()` is between the producer and the JMS server; in the receive process, it is between the consumer and the JMS server. Likewise, messages are rejected by the issue of a `rollback()`.

This model can play a significant role in the guaranteed grouping and ordering of related information, where it is imperative that either all the messages get processed or none of them do – for example, in the case of a purchase order and its related details.

With all this said, JMS can participate in a distributed transaction if the JMS provider supports the **Java Transaction API** (**JTA**) and thus the **XA interface**. The XA interface is an X/Open specification defining the interface between a transaction manager and a resource manager. This topic is outside the scope of this chapter, but for a detailed description of how JMS supports application servers and distributed transactions, see Chapter 8 of the JMS 1.0.2 specification, *JMS Application Server Facilities* (which is available at http://java.sun.com/products/jms/).

# The JMS API

The JMS API is extremely simple to grasp conceptually. There are three simple things you need to learn: **connect**, **send**, and **receive**. Beyond that, there are a handful of interfaces, as illustrated in the following figure and explained in the following text:

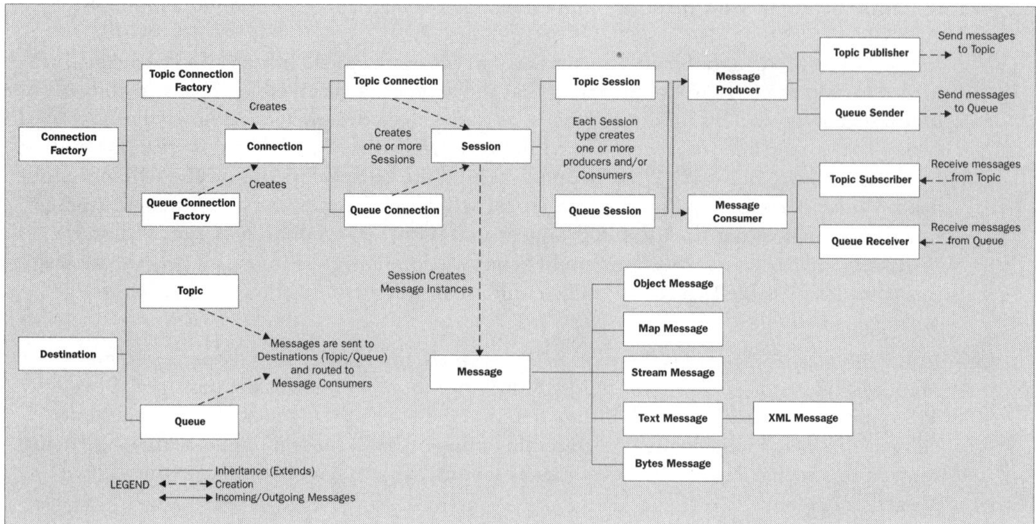


A `ConnectionFactory` begets a `Connection` object. A `Connection` object may have one or more `Session` objects. A `Session` object is responsible for managing producers and consumers (senders and receivers). As `Connections` are considered heavyweight objects, it is advisable to reuse them wherever and whenever possible.

A `ConnectionFactory` may either be a `TopicConnectionFactory` for pub/sub, or a `QueueConnectionFactory` for point-to-point. Likewise, a `Connection` may either be a `TopicConnection` or a `QueueConnection`.

The `publish()` method sends a message to a pub/sub topic. The `send()` method sends a message to a point-to-point queue. From the consumer's perspective, the message may be passively consumed via the `onMessage()` callback, or a message may be proactively received using the `receive()`, `receive(long` *`timeout`*`)`, and `receiveNoWait()` methods.

## A Code Sample

Let's step through a sample that shows the steps necessary for setting up `Connection`, `Session`, and `TopicPublisher` objects, and sending a message. This very simple example sends a message to itself.

> *The full Java source for this example contained in a file called `SimpleMsg.java`. We've included it, along with some setup notes, in the downloadable resource that supports this book (available at* http://www.wrox.com*). Of course, you'll need a JMS provider – the setup notes give directions to the SonicMQ3.5 JMS provider (available at* http://www.sonicsoftware.com*).*

We start by specifying the JNDI properties specific to the JNDI SPI that's being used:

```
Properties env = new Properties();
...
jndi = new InitialContext(env);
```

We need to obtain a connection factory, and create a connection. Once we have a connection, we can create a session for publishing, and one for subscriptions:

```
factory = (TopicConnectionFactory)jndi.lookup("TopicConnectionFactory");
connect = factory.createTopicConnection (username, password);
pubSession = connect.createTopicSession(false,Session.AUTO_ACKNOWLEDGE);
subSession = connect.createTopicSession(false,Session.AUTO_ACKNOWLEDGE);
```

Now we'll create the publisher and the subscriber. In order to do that, we need to obtain an instance of a `Topic` object:

```
myTopic = (Topic)jndi.lookup("My First Topic");
```

Next, we will associate the `onMessage()` handler with this subscriber; and then start the flow of incoming messages:

```
publisher = pubSession.createPublisher(myTopic);
subscriber = subSession.createSubscriber(myTopic);
subscriber.setMessageListener(this);
connect.start();
```

Now this application can send a message to itself:

```
TextMessage textMsg = pubSession.createTextMessage();
textMsg.setText("My first JMS message!);
publisher.publish(
   textMsg,
   javax.jms.DeliveryMode.PERSISTENT,       // delivery mode
   javax.jms.Message.DEFAULT_PRIORITY,      // message priority
   1800000);                                // Time-to-live (30 minutes)
```

This is all that's required to set up a sender and a receiver. You have to agree that it's quite simple.

The `onMessage()` handler is responsible for receiving the message. The JMS provider invokes it automatically, and it looks like this:

```
public void onMessage(javax.jms.Message message){
   TextMessage textMessage = (TextMessage) message;
   System.out.println(textMessage.getText());
}
```

The point-to-point queue version of this would be very similar – in particular, the `onMessage()` code would be identical and the structure of the rest of the code would remain the same. The only difference is that we would replace `Topic`-related objects and methods with `Queue`-related ones (thus we'd use `QueueConnectionFactory` instead of `TopicConnectionFactory`, and `createQueueConnection()` instead of `createTopicConnection()`, and so on).

# Implementing ebMS over JMS

JMS and ebMS both provide a feature-rich specification for transporting data among multiple applications in a distributed environment, and each has advantages over the other. Both support asynchronous fire-and-forget messaging and synchronous request/reply communications. Both offer the semantics of guaranteed once-and-only-once delivery of data, and explicit support for multi-message conversational context.

This is not to imply that the two messaging technologies are orthogonal. They are in fact *complementary* to one another. In this section we will describe how the overlay of an ebMS provider on top of a JMS provider is possible, and can actually give the best of both worlds. The ease of implementation can vary – it depends on the openness of the JMS provider to interoperate with non-JMS standard protocols such as HTTP and SOAP (and thus, how you do this is significantly dependent on your choice of JMS provider). However, it should be possible, with sufficient hand-coding, to do this with any JMS implementation, even if it has no such extensions.

## *Why Are JMS and ebXML So Complementary?*

The first question to ask is: "Why consider using JMS at all, when one could just build a set of message service handlers (MSHs) on top of HTTP?" The answer lies in understanding the generic benefits of JMS (see also the section *An Overview of JMS*, earlier in this chapter):

- JMS is a good standard with widespread acceptance in the Java community. It was officially introduced in November 1998, and there have been robust, proven implementations developed that have had time to mature. JMS vendor implementations can provide features such as scalability via clustering, load balancing, enhanced security, management and development tools, fail-over, etc.
- If you're looking to build an ebXML MS infrastructure, you can get two-thirds of the way there by using a JMS provider as the starting point. Chances are the JMS provider is already building the other one-third.
- One of the advantages of JMS is that the guaranteed delivery (or **reliable messaging**) mechanism is built into the underlying protocol. There are strict rules that need to be implemented by the JMS provider, yet they are not necessarily always reflected in the application layer (for example, internal acknowledgement rules and message persistence on the sending of a message). ebXML reliable messaging has the notion of acknowledgments, persistence, and redelivery of messages, yet there is much more detail that is exposed to the application code.

Not all applications across an extended enterprise will need to speak ebXML. In fact, it is more likely that only the applications at the *edge* of the network (those that need to communicate with other applications across business entities) will need to fully adopt ebXML. For the rest of the applications, a robust communications layer such as a JMS-based message-oriented middleware (MOM) is entirely appropriate.

The following two figures illustrate two implementation options for overlaying JMS and ebMS. The first illustrates the ebMS provider implemented on top of JMS:

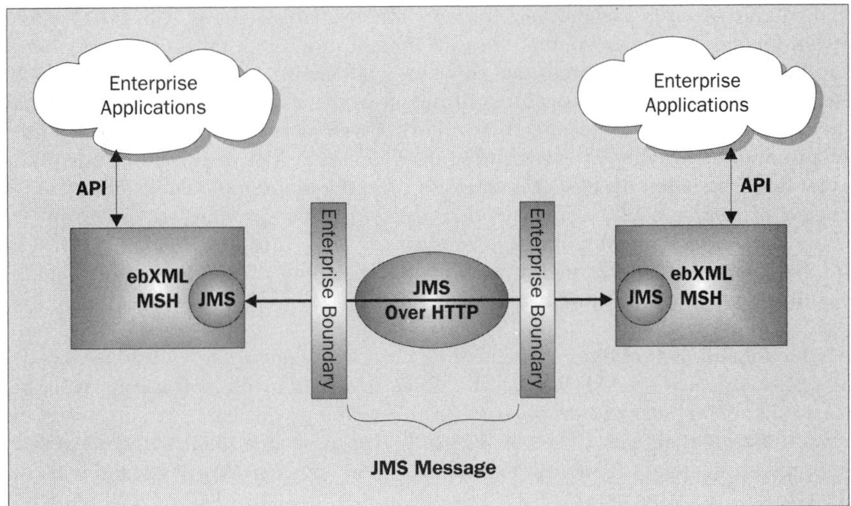


The second shows the JMS provider as an interoperable part of the solution:

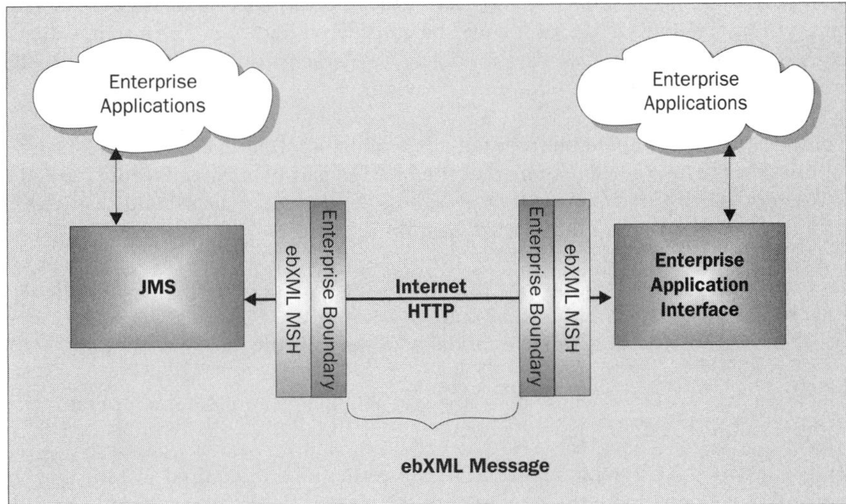


The minimum requirement for ebXML reliable messaging is that it is built on top of some other reliable protocol – either ebXML's own or some other. As we saw in Chapter 13, we use the value of the `<reliableMessagingMethod>` element to specify this:

- If its value is `ebXML`, then reliable messaging may be accomplished using the semantics of ebXML reliable messaging.
- If its value is `transport`, then it may be done by just using ebXML SOAP constructs on top of some other commercially available reliable protocol (such as JMS).

Thus, we *could* say that ebXML can be implemented over JMS simply by using ebXML SOAP constructs on top of a JMS `bytesMessage`, and thus round off this topic.

However, if you are going to use another commercially-available reliable delivery mechanism, like a JMS provider, you need to be aware that the JMS specification does not prescribe an "on-the-wire" interoperability protocol. JMS assumes that there are JMS clients at every endpoint, which communicate between each other via a provider-specific proprietary protocol. Granted, the provider may choose to implement itself over standard interoperable protocols such as HTTP, yet that still requires that a piece of the JMS provider be installed at every endpoint. The reason for this illustrates one of the key benefits of JMS – that the application developer is shielded from the underlying details of guaranteed delivery, and the associated ramifications of failure and recovery. It is the provider-specific proprietary layer just above the low-level network protocol where vendors are providing added value (not just through the masking of the details, but also through things like optimizations of network traffic, batching of messages, and aggregation of disk writes).

In addition, having full control over all of the endpoints is usually not a realistic option. That's the whole point of ebXML over SOAP over HTTP. Even if you do own all of the pieces in the foreseeable future, it is not likely that you will perpetually be able to force your business partners to install a piece of your custom code at their site. However, you still want to be able to take advantage of a JMS-based solution throughout the majority of your enterprise where you currently have (and will continue to have) full control.

At the time of writing, the OASIS ebXML Messaging Technical Committee (TC) is still trying to figure out the specific roles of the provider versus those of the application. An MSH could be considered a separate entity from the application, or it could be considered part of it. For instance, the details of the `ackRequested` attribute and the `<Acknowledgment>` element could be hidden inside the MSH, and therefore could be considered to be part of the provider.

In order for the MSH to be separated from the application, a formal API needs to be specified. For the purpose of this discussion, we will assume that the MSH is part of each application, and that each application is very aware of the semantics of ebMS – in other words the semantics of ebXML reliable message delivery is percolated up into the application logic.

Also under discussion in the TC is the idea that a message path may consist of multiple intermediaries and multiple providers, which could be a mixture of transports (MQSeries, SonicMQ, WebLogic Appserver). The goal is to create a flexible model with the following criteria in mind:

- Deploy a JMS provider, where desirable, yet still allow complete interoperability with arbitrary ebXML endpoints.
- Fully support ebXML reliable messaging semantics where required – at the edge of the network – yet don't force the semantics of the ebXML messaging system to be fully propagated to the JMS-based applications where they don't need to be.
- At some point you may deem that some aspects of ebXML reliable messaging (such as the handling of `statusRequest` and `statusResponse` messages) can't be seamlessly handled by a generic protocol converter layer, and need to be pushed up to the application layer.

The answer to this conundrum lies in the introduction of a **protocol converter**. The purpose of the protocol converter is to perform a generic mapping between the ebXML messaging service and JMS. The protocol converter may be supported natively by the JMS provider, or it may be implemented as a custom specialized JMS client that acts as an intermediary MSH. The following figure illustrates a simplistic view of where a protocol converter fits into the architecture:

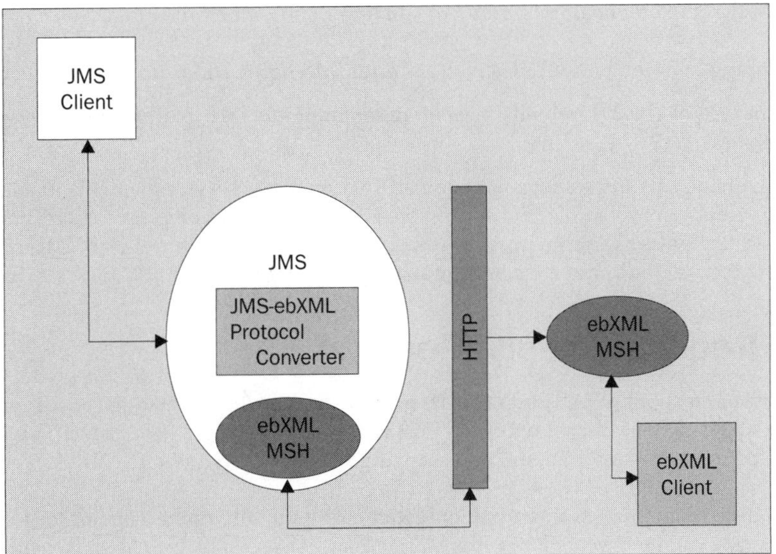


The next figure illustrates how this concept could be extended bi-directionally, to allow for JMS as the central backbone of the enterprise with ebXML communications at the edge of the enterprise:

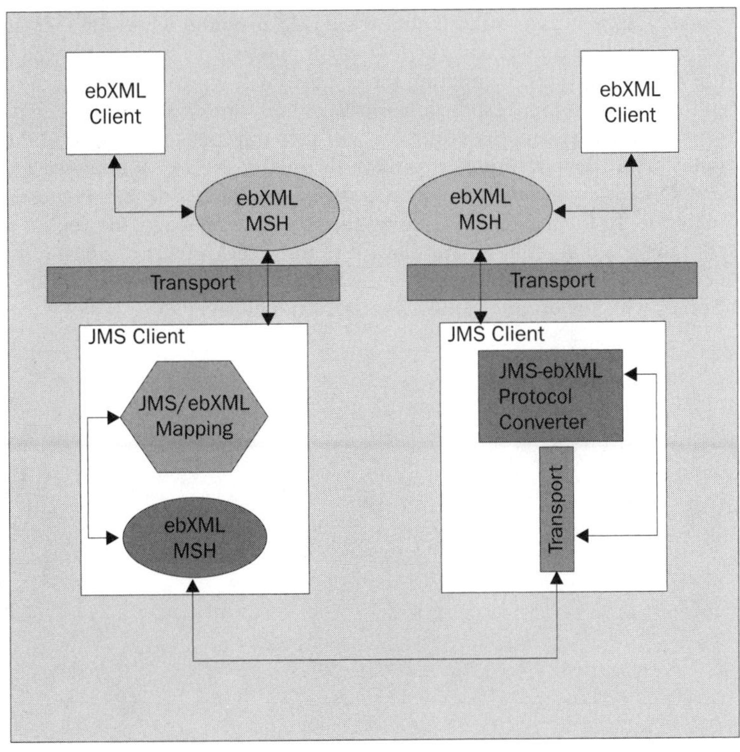

Regardless of the implementation, a protocol converter allows the following:

- Mapping between ebXML destinations onto JMS destinations (topics and queues).
- Transition of ebXML reliable messaging semantics to JMS guaranteed delivery semantics, and vice versa.
- Conversion of other transport-related ebXML message service elements to and from JMS equivalents. For example, the entire ebXML message may be placed intact into the payload of a JMS `bytesMessages` or `textMessage`. Specific things from the ebXML message, like the `refToMessageId`, can be placed into a JMS header such as `JMSCorrelationID`.

# The JMS Request/Reply Model

Since there is much about SOAP and ebXML that has to do with correlating request messages with response messages, a brief discussion of the JMS request/reply model is in order. This fundamental concept will be used later in discussing the mapping between JMS and ebXML.

The JMS request/reply model can be implemented over pub/sub topics or point-to-point queues. The request and reply can be executed as a blocking request, or it can be executed asynchronously. The model is very loosely defined in that the appropriate headers exist in the JMS message, yet there is nothing in the specification that dictates how they should be used.

There are two JMS message headers that are used in the request/reply model – `JMSMessageID` and `JMSCorrelationID`. A `JMSMessageID` is set by the JMS provider when the message is created, and is guaranteed to be unique over time across the JMS deployment. As illustrated in the following diagram, the requestor (the message producer initiating the request) will typically create a message and send it to the intended replier (the consumer responsible for receiving the message and generating a response). In the process of sending the message, the requestor will save the `JMSMessageID` of the originating request. The requestor can asynchronously `send()` or `publish()`, or it may use a synchronous blocking `request()` call. Upon receiving the message, the replier will then create a new message to be sent back as a response. In the process of creating the response message, the replier will take the `JMSMessageID` of the original request, and place it in the `JMSCorrelationID` of the response message. Upon receiving the response message, the requestor can then match up the `JMSCorrelationID` with the original `JMSMessageID` it had saved:

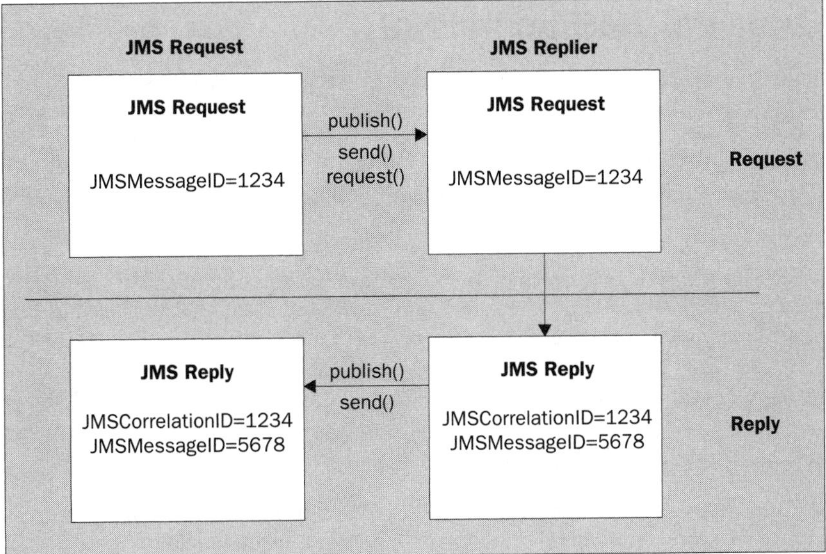


In this fashion, the requestor can be carrying out multiple request/reply conversations at once and will know how to match up response messages with requests, even when they happen asynchronously.

ebXML has very similar facilities for correlating requests with responses. If you assume there is a bi-directional mapping between an ebXML MSH and a JMS provider, then the JMS request/reply model can be used to receive an ebXML "request" and generate an appropriate "response", as illustrated in this next figure:

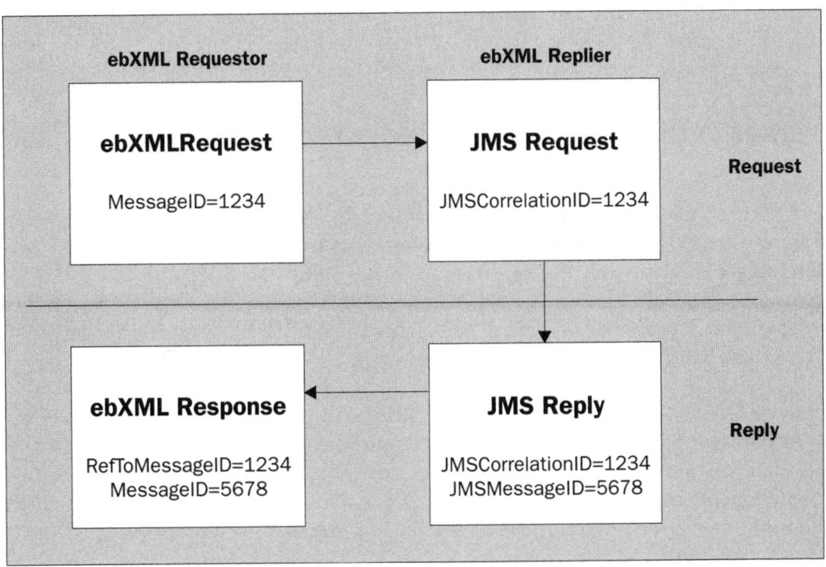

# A Comparison of JMS and ebMS

If we just scratch the surface, we can see that the relative capabilities of JMS and ebMS can be quickly summarized, and we'll show that in a table later in this section. However, when we start thinking about the details, we find there are many areas that are not a cut-and-dry mapping from one protocol to another. There are some places, like the use of the ebMS `<From>` and `<To>` elements, where there might be many ways to map into the JMS way of doing things. For those we will delve into some discussion.

There are some things in ebMS for which there just isn't a direct equivalent in JMS. Examples include the `<CPAId>` element and the `<Action>` element. For those, we can always fall back to JMS properties. JMS supports the arbitrary definition of user-defined properties in the form of name/value pairs. For example:

```
setStringProperty("ebXMLAction", "NewOrder");
```

## The <From> and <To> Elements

The `<From>` and `<To>` elements can map directly to JMS destinations. The `<To>` element can be directly mapped to a topic or queue destination. The `<From>` element can be treated as the `JMSReplyTo` destination in the JMS request/reply model (for identifying a topic or queue to send a response back). If the `JMSReplyTo` is already being used for some other purpose by the application, then the fallback position should be to use a user-definable property.

## The <MessageId> Element

An ebXML `<MessageId>` is required to be globally unique, in accordance with RFC2392 (see http://www.ietf.org/rfc/rfc2392.txt?number=2392). The JMS specification requires a `JMSMessageID` to be globally unique over time, yet the scope of "global" refers to the JMS deployment, which is all under the control of the JMS provider. The actual "globalness" may vary depending on how the JMS provider has chosen to implement the generation of the `JMSMessageID`. This is why, in the previous figure, we chose to map the `<MessageId>` to `JMSCorrelationID` instead of `JMSMessageID`.

## The <ConversationId>, <SequenceNumber>, and <RefToMessageId> Elements

`JMSCorrelationID` would seem to be a likely candidate for comparison with `<ConversationId>`, in the case of a simple single-hop request/reply conversation between the `<From>` and `<To>` parties. In a JMS request/reply conversation, `JMSCorrelationID` would typically contain the `<MessageID>` of the initiating message from the requestor. A `JMSMessageID` is guaranteed to be unique over time across the JMS deployment. The replier takes the `JMSMessageID` from the request message and places it in the `JMSCorrelationID` of the response message.

However, the ebXML `<ConversationId>` can be used in a broader scenario, where multiple messages may transpire between parties as part of the same conversation. Its mapping to `JMSGroupID` may be more appropriate when message ordering is important. The ebXML `<ConversationId>` and `<Sequence>` elements map nicely to `JMSGroupID` and `JMSGroupSeq`. JMS defines that these exist, but does not attempt to describe any rules for their use. This means they are up for grabs (provided the JMS provider hasn't taken them over for some other use).

A third piece of the puzzle involves ebXML's `<RefToMessageId>` element, which (as we saw in Chapter 13) is used in a message to indicate that it is related to a previous message. It is intended specifically for errors, acknowledgements, `<StatusRequest>`, `<StatusResponse>`, and detection of duplicates. For the error reporting case, it may be the responsibility of a JMS client on the far end to generate a fault message and send it back to the sender. In this case the protocol converter can map `JMSCorrelationID` to `<RefToMessageId>`, `JMSXGroupID` to `<ConversationId>`, and `JMSXGroupSeq` to `<SequenceNumber>`, as illustrated in the following figure:

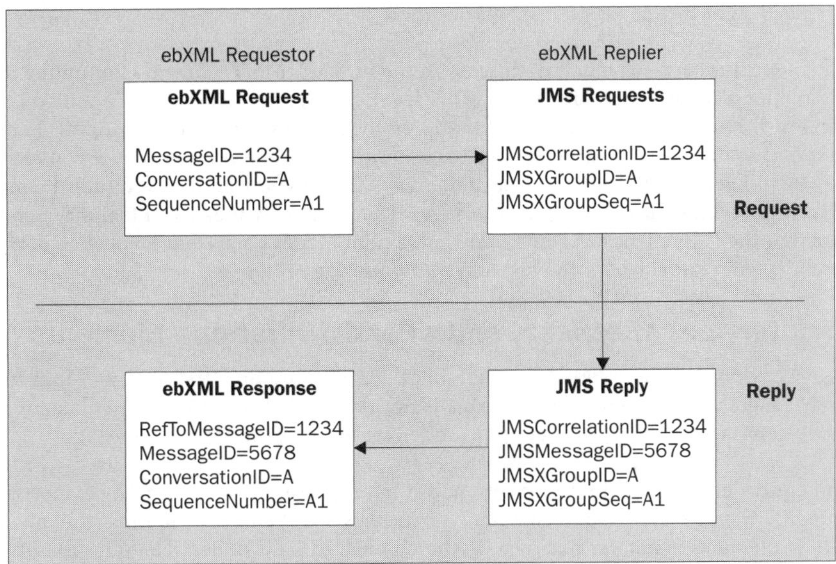


## The <TraceHeader> and <TraceHeaderList> Elements

JMS by itself does not address these concepts specifically. However, in the MOM world it is generally understood that these capabilities are provided beyond the basic functionality, sitting just above the base messaging layer. Whether they are provided by the JMS vendor directly, or through a third party add-on, these concepts map nicely to business process flow, specialized content-based routing, and auditing and tracking. In the mapping between ebXML and JMS, `<TraceHeader>`s could be mapped into JMS properties as a sort of ongoing "itinerary", which can be massaged as it traverses through the organization, through various stages of a business process.

## The reliableMessagingMethod Attribute

Reliable messaging may be accomplished using the semantics of ebXML reliable messaging, or it may be done simply by using ebXML SOAP constructs on top of some other commercially available reliable protocol (like JMS).

A third option is to combine the other two. There are current discussions taking place within the ebMS team regarding intermediary scenarios and a possible mix of solutions. For example, the first hop could use ebXML RM, the next JMS, the next ebXML RM, the next MQSeries, and so on.

### The DeliveryReceiptRequested Attribute and <DeliveryReceipt> Element

The `<DeliveryReceipt>` element indicates that the ultimate receiver represented by the `<To>` element has received the message. This is a slightly higher level of acknowledgment than the `<Acknowledgment>` element concept. The `<Acknowledgment>` element only indicates that the message has been received by another MSH – but it may only be an intermediary, and not the ultimate receiver. The `<DeliveryReceipt>` element is included within an acknowledgment message as a response to the `<DeliveryReceiptRequested>` element, and can only come from the ultimate receiver, regardless of how many intermediaries there are.

At the time of writing, there is much discussion in the ebXML MS Technical Committee as to whether this should be handled automatically at the MSH level, or whether it should be handled at a higher application level. From the point of view of mapping to JMS, it's purely a philosophical choice. Do you want to respond to the `<DeliveryReceiptRequested>` element at the protocol conversion layer, and trust that JMS will get the message the rest of the way? Or do you want to wait until the message gets to the JMS client that will be processing the message? The latter may make you feel more comfortable, but will require that the JMS client has some knowledge of ebMS. It's a system level choice, since only the systems architect can know where the last hop of the message really is.

### The <RetryInterval>, <Retries>, and <PersistDuration> Elements

The `<RetryInterval>` is a time value specifying the minimum time the sending MSH *must* wait between retries, if an acknowledgment message is not received. The `<Retries>` element indicates how many times a sending MSH should attempt to redeliver an unacknowledged message.

There is no equivalent in the JMS specification, but in any case, this functionality is most likely implemented by the provider as part of a failover strategy. At the time of writing, the interaction between these elements is not yet resolved by the ebXML MS TC either. The question of how `<RetryInterval>` and `<PersistDuration>` will work together is one question still under discussion. A current issue is that the *sender* sets the `<Retries>` and `<RetryInterval>` values based on the CPA, but the *receiver* sets `<PersistDuration>` based on the CPP. A key question is: what happens if these aren't in sync and `<PersistDuration>` expires first?

### A Summary of the ebMS To JMS Comparison

We'll complete this section with a table summarizing the mapping of ebXML MS to JMS:

| ebXML element/attribute | JMS mapping |
|---|---|
| `MessageId` | `JMSMessageID/JMSCorrelationID` |
| `Timestamp` | `JMSTimestamp` |
| `From` | `JMSReplyTo`, or user-defined property |
| `To` | `JMSDestination`, or user-defined property |
| `ConversationId` | `JMSCorrelationID`, `JMSXGroupID`, or a user-defined property |
| `SequenceNumber` | `JMSXGroupSeq`. JMS has no rules with regard to wrap around and `reset`, but that can be dealt with in the mapping rules |
| `RefToMessageId` | `JMSCorrelationID` |

| ebXML element/attribute | JMS mapping |
|---|---|
| `Service` | User-defined property |
| `Action` | User-defined property – `setStringProperty("Action", "NewOrder");` |
| `TimeToLive` | `TTL` setting on `MessageProducer` |
| `deliverySemantics.OnceAndOnlyOnce` | Inherent in the use of persistent messaging, durable subscriptions, and transactional messaging |
| `deliverySemantics.BestEffort` | At most once. Non-persistent/non-durable/non-transactional |
| `reliableMessagingMethod` | Can be a combination of both ebXML Reliable Messaging protocol and JMS Guaranteed Delivery |
| `DeliveryReceiptRequested` and `DeliveryReceipt` | Can be dealt with at the application layer or at the protocol conversion layer |
| `messageOrderSemantics` | Implied with various JMS QoS settings or persistent messages and durable subscriptions |
| `TraceHeaderList` | JMS Properties |
| `TraceHeader` | JMS Properties/Business Process Integration |
| `TraceHeader.Sender` | JMS Properties/Business Process Integration |
| `TraceHeader.Sender.PartyId` and `Location` | JMS Properties/Business Process Integration |
| `Acknowledgment` | Internal `ack` on `send()` |
| `AckRequested` | Can be automatically handled by a protocol converter |
| `Via` | Depending on the value of the `Via` element, may need to be passed on through to the receiving JMS client |
| `synchReply` | JMS `req/reply`. |
| `ErrorList` and `Error` | Application level |
| `StatusRequest` and `StatusResponse` | Not applicable with JMS, but may be treated as an application level thing in order to play nice with other non-JMS endpoints |
| Message Service Handler Ping Service | No equivalent in JMS, since JMS is by and large asynchronous decoupled communications. However it would come in mighty handy when attempting to perform a blocking `request()` call |
| `mshTimeAccuracy` | No functional equivalent in JMS. It's currently under discussion in the ebXML Messaging TC and may be removed |

*Table continued on following page*

| ebXML element/attribute | JMS mapping |
|---|---|
| `retryInterval` and `retries` | No equivalent in the JMS spec, but most likely implemented anyhow by the provider as part of a failover strategy |
| `persistDuration` | Message redelivery detection is built into the JMS protocol. For complex deployment scenarios where JMS may fall short in this area, the provider most likely has equivalent mechanisms for duplicate detection |
| `CPAId` | JMS property |
| `Manifest` | No equivalent in JMS |
| `DeliveryFailure` | Application level |

# The Java API for XML Messaging (JAXM)

The fundamental goal behind the **Java API for XML Messaging** (**JAXM**) is to provide a simple yet flexible model for enabling SOAP-based messaging with a Java application. More specifically, JAXM will provide a standard way for Java applications to send and receive SOAP and ebXML messages.

JAXM is a new API, currently under development within the Java Community Process (JCP) – an open organization, founded by Sun Microsystems, which coordinates enhancements to the Java platform. The JAXM (JSR-067) Expert Group, within JCP, is the group responsible for the development of the JAXM specifications; it includes participants from 19 organizations. At the time of this writing, the most current JAXM specification was version 0.94 – this was released for public review on September 24, 2001.

> *The anticipated release date for Version 1.0 is November, 2001. JAXM 1.0 will initially be an optional package for J2SE and J2EE, but may be mandatory in future releases. Information regarding the up-to-date status of JAXM, and ongoing releases of the Reference Implementation of the JAXM API, are available at* http://java.sun.com/xml/jaxm.

JAXM is based on the SOAP 1.1 and SOAP with Attachments specifications and is extended to work with ebXML and other higher-level messaging protocols, such as SOAP-RP. In fact, it provides a common set of APIs to be used across any number of emerging SOAP-based protocols.

In our examples in Chapters 4 and 13, we used the Apache SOAP client, but at the time of writing (October 2001), there was no established API that described how a client should access an ebXML message service handler (MSH). JAXM will provide a JCP-sanctioned standard method of supporting SOAP and ebXML communications in Java applications.

Moreover, there is currently a lot of interest in the creation of Java applications that can conduct transactions and other communications with a range of other platforms (such as Microsoft's BizTalk server) through the ebXML and SOAP protocols. The release of JAXM will greatly reduce the amount of time and effort required to develop such applications.

# Deploying JAXM in J2EE and J2SE Environments

We'll build our discussion of JAXM around two of its stated goals. One is that it should be possible to weave JAXM into (or layer it on top of) a **J2EE** deployment environment. The other is that it should provide a more *simplistic* approach that can be deployed within a **J2SE** environment. The diversity of JAXM, illustrated in the two stated goals, is manifested in the APIs, as we will see.

In understanding JAXM, a very important concept is that of the **messaging provider** – an external service that (in most cases) assumes responsibility for assigning messaging identifiers, tracking message delivery, and resending messages that didn't reach their destination the first time around. The complexities surrounding message delivery semantics – and thus the benefits of delegating that responsibility away from the client application – are fairly evident from our discussions on ebMS and JMS in this book. The advantage of using JAXM with a messaging provider is that the client using JAXM has only to make the appropriate JAXM method calls, while the messaging provider takes care of the details of actually delivering the message.

In its simplest form, JAXM messaging typically takes place within a web container, using a servlet engine such as Apache's. When a JAXM client is deployed in a web container, the SOAP 1.1 protocol is bound to HTTP:

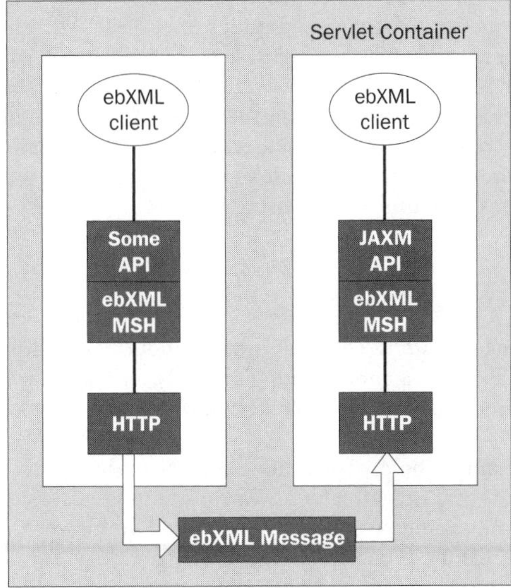


In its more complex provider-enabled form, the domain of the provider may represent the implementation of the JAXM APIs and the ebXML MSH. It could, possibly, also represent both sides of the conversation, and the wire protocol between them. While the biggest benefit of SOAP over HTTP is on-the-wire interoperability, JAXM is not dependent on HTTP, and could use other protocols in the end-to-end conversation between the two parties.

## JAXM Profiles and ProviderConnections

While SOAP defines a basic method for packaging, delivery, and correlation of messages, the majority of applications require a more sophisticated messaging protocol. That's why other higher-level protocols, such as SOAP-RP and ebXML Message Service, are evolving. JAXM has a chameleon-like capability that allows it to be adapted to support the particular characteristics of a protocol, through a concept known as a **profile.** A JAXM profile allows a JAXM client to rely on a certain set of capabilities, both in message content and communication protocol.

For example, we know from Chapter 13 that an ebXML message must contain certain elements that are specific to the ebXML Message Service – such as the `<From>`, `<To>`, and `<RefToMessageId>` elements. A JAXM provider can be taught to create an instance of such a message automatically. JAXM accomplishes this by allowing for pluggable **message factories**. A message factory contains information about how to create a particular type of message, and is contained within a profile. To create ebXML messages we use an ebXML message factory, which will be contained within a JAXM ebXML profile.

JAXM also makes use of something called a `ProviderConnection`, which fulfills a number of purposes. The JAXM client uses the `ProviderConnection` to maintain session with a known provider (such as a third-party vendor implementation of ebXML MS). One of the advantages of the `ProviderConnection` is that it allows us to relegate the requirements of the chosen messaging mechanism (ebXML MS or otherwise) to the provider level. In other words, it means we don't have to worry about the necessary message delivery semantics of ebXML MS (such as once-and-only-once delivery) at the client level, because the `ProviderConnection` takes care of it all.

The `ProviderConnection` object also contains meta data that can be queried by the JAXM client to find out what profiles are supported by the provider. In order to send an ebXML message, the client would need to check that the provider supported an `ebXML` profile. In a moment, we'll look at an example which demonstrates how this is done using the API.

## The JAXM API

Let's take a look at how JAXM's `ProviderConnectionFactory` object can be used to create a connection with a messaging provider. The code we are about to examine is excerpted from the *remote sender* example, found in `samples` section of the 0.94 Early Access release of the JAXM 1.0 reference implementation (at press time this was available at http://java.sun.com/xml/jaxm).

The first two lines in the example below show how to retrieve the appropriate `ProviderConnectionFactory` object, which we will use to create a connection to the provider. This example assumes that the messaging provider has registered an instance of its `ProviderConnection` with a Java Naming and Directory Interface (JNDI) naming service – we look up the `ProviderConnectionFactory` using the JNDI API, by passing the logical name of the messaging provider in the `lookup()` method; this method returns an instance of the `ProviderConnectionFactory` object to which the logical name is bound. Then, the connection itself is started by invoking the `createConnection()` method, which starts the `ProviderConnection` instance, `pc`:

```
ctx = new InitialContext();
pcf = (ProviderConnectionFactory)ctx.lookup("mypcf");
pc = pcf.createConnection();
```

Now that the client has established a connection with its messaging provider, it can query the messaging provider's capabilities and thus determine if it supports the appropriate profile:

```
ProviderMetaData metaData = pc.getMetaData();
String[] supportedProfiles = metaData.getSupportedProfiles();
String profile = null;

for(int i=0; i < supportedProfiles.length; i++) {
    if(supportedProfiles[i].equals("ebxml")) {
        profile = supportedProfiles[i];
        break;
    }
}
```

In the code above, we're looking in particular for a profile called `ebxml`. Having established that the provider supports the desired profile, then create a message factory using that profile name:

```
mf = pc.createMessageFactory(profile);
```

Finally, create a profile-specific message:

```
EbXMLMessageImpl ebxmlMsg = (EbXMLMessageImpl)mf.createMessage();
```

## Specifying the Destination of the Message

Destinations in JAXM are specified as `EndPoint` objects. In this case (that is, using a `ProviderConnection`), it is assumed that the `EndPoint` is contained in the SOAP message itself. It is the responsibility of the provider to extract that information and determine where to send the message.

In our example, we are using an instance of an object called `EbXMLMessageImpl`. It's assumed that this is provided by whatever is creating the profile – typically the ebXML provider. The details and capabilities of this object would tend to vary, and is dependent on how much responsibility is delegated to the provider (and how much is implemented directly in the application client). For the purposes of our discussion, let's assume that our `EbXMLMessageImpl` allows the client to set the values of the `<From>` and `<To>` elements, while it inherits everything else from the base JAXM `javax.xml.SOAPMessage`. Here is how we would specify those values:

```
private String from ="http://www.wombats.com/remote/sender";
private String to = "http://www.wombats.com/remote/sender";
...
ebxmlMsg.setFrom(new Endpoint(from));
ebxmlMsg.setTo(new Endpoint(to));
```

*In fact the source and destination are identical here, because in this simplest of examples, the application is sending a message to itself.*

We are now ready to send the message to its destination. We do this using the `send()` method of the `ProviderConnection` object:

```
pc.send(ebxmlMsg);
```

The `send()` method on the `ProviderConnection` object is responsible for placing the message in the hands of the provider. Whether the `send()` operation actually blocks and waits for the message to get all the way to its destination and wait for a response, is purely based on the profile being used, and its associated delivery semantics. If the message is intended to be asynchronously delivered, then the `send()` method may return immediately back to the caller.

### Receiving the Message

The receipt of the message is relatively simple. An `onMessage()` callback is invoked, and is passed in the `SOAPMessage`, as shown:

```
public void onMessage(SOAPMessage message) {
     System.out.println("onMessage called in receiving servlet");
     message.writeTo(System.out);
}
```

This `onMessage()` callback is implemented as an `AsynchListener`. It may be associated directly with a `ProviderConnection` and it may also extend `JAXMServlet`.

In our example so far we left out a pretty important step: populating the message with data. This we will explain in the next section.

## Adding Content To the Message

SOAP messages can include both XML content and file attachments. XML content can be delivered in the body of the message – this means that there's no need to use an attachment if the content to be delivered is expressed in XML format. As we saw in Chapter 4, the packaging model for a message *without* attachments is simple – consisting only of an envelope with a message package containing a header and body.

If any content other than XML is to be delivered, the document must have an **attachment** part, which increases the complexity of the packaging model. A message *with* attachments requires a SOAP part that contains an envelope like the one described, plus multiple attachment parts that are all contained in a MIME envelope.

For the purposes of this discussion we will step away from the specific use of the ebXML profile, and our `ebxmlMsg`, in order to illustrate that we are talking about real JAXM-supported APIs and not some theoretical extensions implemented in a profile. The following example demonstrates how to build the body of a JAXM `javax.xml.SOAPMessage`. The `SOAPMessage` contains a `SOAPPart`, which is used to obtain the `SOAPEnvelope`. The `SOAPEnvelope` itself is then used to get the body of the message:

```
SOAPMessage smsg = mf.createMessage();
SOAPPart spart = smsg.getSOAPPart();
SOAPEnvelope senvelope = spart.getEnvelope();
SOAPBody sbody = senvelope.getBody();
```

Having obtained the message body, the SOAPBody.addBodyElement() and SOAPBodyElement.addChildElement() methods can be used to create nested elements to any level within the SOAP body, as illustrated in the following code:

```
SOAPBodyElement gltp =
     sbody.addBodyElement(senvelope.createName(
                    "GetLastQuote", "zquote", "http://wombat.zquote.com"));
gltp.addChildElement(senvelope.createName(
        "symbol", "ztrade", "http://wombat.ztrade.com")).addTextNode("PRGS");
```

Next, let's create an attachment part. The content is to be a GIF image, picture.gif, whose URL is used in the initialization of the javax.activation.DataHandler object, as shown below. Then, the SOAPMessage object's createAttachmentPart() method is used to create the AttachmentPart object, which is initialized with the data handler containing the URL for the image. Finally, the AttachmentPart object is added to the message:

```
URL url = new URL(http://main/picture.gif);
DataHandler datahandler = new DataHandler(url);
AttachmentPart attachmentpart = smsg.createAttachmentPart(datahandler);
smsg.addAttachmentPart(attachmentpart);
```

## *Simplifying the Model in J2SE*

As we stated at the beginning of this section, one of the goals of JAXM is to provide a simple model that can be implemented and deployed *without* the presence of a provider. Thus, the simplest form of JAXM messaging is to perform a *direct* point-to-point request/reply interaction between two parties. In order to accomplish this, there exists an alternative mechanism for establishing a connection and creating a message. Both the SOAPConnection and MessageFactory objects contain static methods for instantiating themselves, as shown in the following example:

```
SOAPConnection connection = SOAPConnection.newInstance();
MessageFactory msgFactory = MessageFactory.newInstance();
```

To populate the message, we can use the same techniques demonstrated above – with the exception that there are no special message types allowed, since there are no special profiles supported.

The task of specifying the destination requires different usage of the API to that demonstrated in the ProviderConnection example above. In that example, we used an Endpoint object. An Endpoint takes any URI as input, and it is up to the provider to map that to a physical destination. In this simpler example we don't have a provider, so instead we use a URLEndpoint object, which represents an absolute URL address to specify the destination:

```
URLEndpoint endpoint = new URLEndpoint(someURL);
```

Finally, sending the message also requires different API usage in this simplified J2SE scenario. We use the SOAPConnection object's call() method, which takes the SOAPMessage object and a URLEndpoint as parameters. The call() method is a synchronous blocking operation that sends the message and then waits for an HTTP response:

```
// Send the message and block for a response
SOAPMessage reply = connection.call(msg, endpoint);

System.out.println("Received reply from: " + endpoint);
reply.writeTo(System.out);
```

*At the time of this writing, there is much discussion within the JAXM Expert Group relating to whether or not the `ProviderConnectionFactory` and `ProviderConnection` objects should converge or be more symmetrical with their non-provider siblings.*

## JAXM and the Future

JAXM provides an easy way for Java applications to conduct business with a wide range of different platforms and systems, and consequently it has already begun to take root in the Java developer community. JAXM should be a major force spurring the proliferation of many-to-many e-commerce relationships, because it provides a very powerful (yet relatively simple to implement) standard for conducting transactions on the Internet.

The feature that most secures the future of JAXM is its extensibility – its messaging provider and profile concepts will allow it to interoperate with new messaging and e-commerce concepts in the future.

# Summary

In this chapter, we extended the discussion of messaging to introduce the JMS and JAXM standards, and examine how they can be used with ebXML:

- JMS can enhance an ebXML MS implementation. It extends the MOM metaphor to support loosely-coupled communication for point-to-point and publish/subscribe with rich QoS semantics.
- The JMS and ebMS messaging protocols are complementary. Moreover, JMS maps well to ebXML, with just a few gaps. It is reasonable to assume that ebXML MS providers will be implemented on top of JMS providers.
- There are various vendor implementations of JMS, which provide extra value over-and-above the base specification – such as load balancing, routing capabilities, fault tolerance, and security.
- JAXM provides a great deal of potential as a common API to XML messaging protocols such as SOAP and ebXML.
- JAXM can also be layered on top of, or woven into an ebXML provider.

In short, JAXM and JMS, implemented with ebXML separately or in concert, significantly extend the value proposition of the ebMS specification. In fact, ebMS, JMS and JAXM should not be considered to be orthogonal to one another – rather, they can be seen as complementary technologies.

ebXML Foundations Professional

# 15

# e-Business Security

Within the ebXML framework (or, for that matter, within any B2B framework), one of the toughest problems in evidence is that of **security**. One reason for this is that there are (at least) two different types of security hole in any system – technical holes and organizational holes – so a security policy is needed that considers both types of security hole. Furthermore, any security mechanism can be defeated, given enough time; so there is a constant need for security policies to be updated – as new threats are detected and countermeasures to existing threats become ineffective. Any security policy provides a balance between **level of protection** (and associated outstanding risk), and **costs involved** in putting that policy in place. It's a question of choosing the policy to get the balance right.

When working with B2B frameworks such as ebXML, we could argue that there is a fundamental conflict between achieving the level of openness required to deal with a (potentially large) number of parties, and achieving the appropriate level of security. A characteristic of B2B initiatives is that they try to use the Internet – a global *communication* infrastructure – as a global *trading* infrastructure. While this is definitely a very challenging endeavor in terms of size, scope, and nature, we feel that history has shown that it is possible to successfully open up new trade routes and find acceptable ways to deal with the associated risks. We believe that ebXML will prove itself to be instrumental in opening up these new *digital* trade routes; but in doing so, it is necessary to implement a robust security strategy to protect the businesses involved.

So here's what we'll cover in this chapter:

- First, we'll identify various potential risks and counter-measures.
- Then we'll look at some of the more important security technologies – encryption, integrity checksums, digital signatures, and certification.
- Finally, we'll discuss and demonstrate some specific security initiatives important for the ebXML framework – SAML, XACML, digital signatures and XKMS.

We have already encountered some of these issues and technologies in previous chapters of this book; in this chapter, we aim to step briefly and systematically through these mentioned technologies.

# Foundations of Security

We can divide the subject of security into two parts – the **risks**, and the **countermeasures** against those risks. In this secrtion, we'll first introduce the more generic risks that can be identified in a computer environment, and then give an overview of the countermeasures available to protect against or minimize these risks.

## Risks

When looking at computer systems and data exchange in general, we can identify three security areas where risks can be identified, namely:

- **Integrity:** the assurance that data, programs, and other system resources are protected against malicious or inadvertent modification or destruction – by unauthorized persons, programs, or systems. Integrity protection involves a broad range of measures, from virus and worm control to integrity checksums used to authenticate data. We will cover the latter in more detail later.
- **Confidentiality:** the assurance that data, programs, and other system resources are protected against compromise by unauthorized persons, programs, or systems. While this is typically associated with military-style confidentiality levels ('unclassified', 'classified', 'secret', etc.) it is also applicable to business situations. For example, salary information and personnel contract details are usually confidential; information of interest to a business adversary (such as data on competitors, quotes, offers, and proposals) also needs to be protected from compromise. Encryption is an important technical measure used to protect confidentiality, as we shall see shortly.
- **Availability:** the assurance that authorized users have guaranteed access to the service infrastructure. For instance, the denial-of-service attacks we have seen in recent years are a sometimes crude (but usually effective) means to try to disrupt availability.

Within the ebXML framework, the issue of security is tackled in the *ebXML Technical Architecture Risk Assessment* document (http://www.ebxml.org/specs/secRISK.pdf). The document takes the form of a risk assessment, rather than a detailed specification of certain measures to be taken. A risk assessment typically tries to determine the susceptibility of a system to various kinds of security failure. This allows for the identification of vulnerabilities, which can then be addressed via specific countermeasures. Based on the security areas we've mentioned above, the risks are identified and classified (via the ebXML risk assessment) into the following categories:

- Unauthorized transactions and fraud
- Loss of confidentiality
- Error detection
- Potential loss of management and audit
- Potential legal liability (it is important to realize that security technologies also include a means by which a party can protect themselves by 'preventing principals from denying their actions'. This concept is called **non-repudiation**)

The main technical challenge of secure technology within an open framework like ebXML is two-fold: not only does such a framework have to demonstrate sufficient **flexibility** to evolve with new demands placed upon it, but it must meet the requirements of **interoperability**. Given these requirements, we've already learned that ebXML is based upon XML as a technology. Therefore, it will be no surprise to learn that XML is also used as the fundamental component of all security-related initiatives within ebXML. Since security initiatives and security standards in XML are not as far advanced as some of the other specifications and standards, many of the security initiatives around ebXML are still very much 'under development'. However, as we will see in this chapter, developments are very much in evidence.

# Countermeasures

Whatever security scenario you look at, three fundamental security countermeasure mechanisms can almost always be found:

- **Authentication:** the process of establishing that a requester (a person, program or system identifying themselves to a service) really *is* who they say they are.
- **Authorization:** the process of allowing a requester to access a resource based on the *identity* of the requester, and the associated authority granted to the requester in relation to that resource.
- **Error detection:** which includes intrusion detection, denial of service detection, and virus prevention.

In tandem, the first two mechanisms might be said to constitute an access control scheme. Such an access control scheme is encountered, for example, when you arrive in a new country and the authorities ask you to prove your identity (and your right to enter the country) by means of a passport. Another familiar example is the username/password protection scheme used to establish identity (and subsequently rights of access to resources) in any typical computer system. An **access control list** (**ACL**) is a common device used to allow **subjects** (or **principals** – a term commonly encountered in security literature) access to certain **objects**.

In a digital B2B setting we are likely to meet some specific technologies and practices. They can be understood more easily by realizing that, in themselves, these technologies are not extraordinary – they are merely the digital equivalents of similar mechanisms in place in 'traditional' (usually paper-based) trading practices. And chances are you have already been using technologies like Secure Sockets Layer (SSL), Pretty Good Privacy (PGP), and web site certificates, which are based on three fundamental technologies and mechanisms: **encryption**, **digital signatures** and **certification**.

We will discuss each of these in more detail in the following sections. (Of course, there's plenty more that could be written on these subjects. We've included a few resources and items of further reading at the end of the chapter, and there is a wealth of writing available on various aspects of security.)

# Encryption

**Encryption** is a science of essential importance in keeping data secret. Obviously, the need for secrecy is not exclusive to the world of espionage – we find it in everyday things too. For example, consider the need to transmit credit card information over the Internet. The basic idea of encryption is that a **sender** applies an **encryption function** to the original **plaintext** message, with the resulting **ciphertext** message being sent to the **receiver**. On receipt, the receiver subsequently decrypts the message (by applying a **decryption function**), and hence recovers the original plaintext.

The encryption/decryption process generally depends on a secret **key** (which is shared between the sender and the receiver), and a known **encryption algorithm**. When a suitable combination of a key and an encryption algorithm is used, it should be sufficiently difficult for an impostor to 'crack' the code – and thus both the legitimate sender and receiver can be confident that communication is secure.

Although not the only factor, the length of the key – typically designated in bits – has become a visible indicator of the difficulty with which a code can be 'cracked'. This is a subject surrounded with some controversy, given for instance US export restrictions on specific parts of this technology based on the need for law enforcement and for other agencies to have access to data.

Cryptography provides several services. Most notably, cryptography plays a crucial part in confidentiality, as we have just discussed; but it also provides a basis for authentication and integrity.

While cryptography is a complex field, there are three basic approaches and corresponding algorithm families of importance here: **secret key encryption**, **public key encryption**, and **cryptographic checksums**. We'll discuss them briefly in the following sections.

## Secret Key Encryption

In **secret** (or **symmetric**) **key encryption**, the same secret key is used to encode and decode the message. Symmetric key algorithms are attractive because they require relatively modest computing resources, and when used with keys of sufficient length, produce virtually uncrackable ciphertext.

However, by the nature of this method, the sender and receiver must somehow agree on the key being used for encryption and decryption – if *that* communication is compromised and the key falls into the wrong hands, then the encrypted message itself is in danger of being compromised.

The critical issue here is how to keep the key secret. So in practice, secret key encryption is usually combined with public key encryption, which we will cover shortly.

Among the better known symmetric key encryption algorithms, there are the Data Encryption Standard (DES), the International Data Encryption Algorithm (IDEA), and RC4, which is used in SSL.

You may have heard of the Advanced Encryption Standard (AES), which is the proposed successor of DES. AES has received quite a bit of media attention recently; one reason for this is that it employs an algorithm that was developed 'garage-style' by a small Belgian team, rather than by any of the established organizations. For more on AES, see http://csrc.nist.gov/encryption/aes/aesfact.html.

## Public Key Encryption

In **public** (or **asymmetric**) **key encryption**, there are two keys involved. The first key is called the **public key**: the receiving party can make this key known public. The second key is called the **private key**: this is not published, and is known only to the receiving party. The public key is used to encrypt the message, and the private key is used to decrypt it. Because the receiving party's public key is well-known, anyone can use it to encrypt a plaintext message and post the resulting ciphertext. And because the private key is known only by the receiving party, then only they can decrypt the published ciphertext and access the original plaintext message.

Significantly, the sender and receiver only need to agree the encryption key – there's no need to send the decryption key between the two parties. Therefore, there is much less risk of the decryption key falling into the wrong hands.

In general, public key encryption schemes are relatively costly in terms of computing resources – it should be computationally very difficult to deduce the private key from the public key. Because of this cost factor, public key schemes are often combined with a secret key scheme. In such a scenario, the secret key necessary for symmetric key encryption is exchanged via public key encryption techniques. This is the approach taken in SSL and the secure e-mail standard S/MIME. PGP is another popular and relatively well-known cryptosystem which also uses this approach (see (http://web.mit.edu/network/pgp.html). Some versions of PGP use RSA – a well-known public key encryption algorithm named after its inventors, Rivest, Shamir, and Adleman.

One of the fundamental problems in secret key encryption is in the secure distribution of secret message keys. As we've said, public key encryption solves this problem – it doesn't matter who accesses the public (encryption) key, provided the private key remains known only to the legitimate receiver. However, public key cryptography introduces two new problems: namely, the detection of **bogus** and **compromised keys**. How can a sender be sure that the party who issued the public key really is who they say they are? How can they tell that the key hasn't been compromised, by some impostor who has managed to acquire the corresponding private key?

A solution to these problems comes in the form of the **public key infrastructure** (**PKI**) – a system of digital certificates and certificate authorities. We'll discuss PKI shortly.

### *Cryptographic Checksums*

**Cryptographic** (or **integrity**) **checksums**, also known as **message authentication codes** (**MACs**) or **message digests**, provide a method which allows us to check the authenticity of received data. Basically, we use an algorithm to generate a value (called a **checksum**) from the data that we want to protect. Later, a party can apply the same algorithm to the data – if they get a different checksum, they know that the data has been tampered with.

The algorithms used to generate the checksum are called **hashing functions**. There are two basic approaches:

- One is based on the use of a secret key in combination with an encryption function. There are several MAC standards of this sort; ANSI X9.9 and X9.19 are two of the better-known standards. In this approach, the MAC can be stored with the data, because an impostor, not knowing the secret key, is unable to tamper with the message or the MAC without detection.
- The second approach does not require secret keys and makes use of a checksum computed through public hashing functions. The trade-off of this approach is that the checksum cannot be stored with the data. Since the algorithm is public someone could replace the data, compute a new checksum, and then replace the checksum. The Message Digest 5 (MD5) is a well-known standard of this flavor (although it has recently been considered to be no longer safe). Another well-known standard is the Secure Hash Algorithm (SHA), a US federal standard.

## Digital Signatures

Combinations of the cryptographic techniques described above are applied in the area of digital signatures. A digital signature is basically a block of data attached to a message, and its effect is to bind this data to a particular individual or entity. So it is a mechanism that can provide message integrity, authentication, and non-repudiation. It typically involves two keys: a signing key, which is private to a sender, and a signature verification key, which is made public. The binding is such that a receiver or an independent third party can verify the signature.

> *Note the similarity between public key cryptography and digital signatures. In the former, the encryption key is public and the decryption key is private. In the latter, the encryption key is private and the decryption key is public (and the private key acts as the signature).*

Two widely-used methods for computing digital signatures are RSA and the Digital Signature Standard (DSS), a US federal standard. Within the Internet and XML communities, the recent IETF and W3C proposal for XML Signature Syntax and Processing (in which XML acts as a 'wrapper' for the signature mechanism) is receiving a lot of attention. We'll discuss that later in the chapter.

## Certification

One important aspect of both public key cryptography and digital signatures is the question of **validity**: how do we know that a given public key or signature actually corresponds to a given individual? And how do we deal with fake or compromised public keys?

This issue is addressed by **certification authorities** (**CAs**). Well-known CAs include companies like VeriSign, GlobalSign, and Thawte. A certification authority will vouch for the authenticity of a public signature and supply proof of this through a **public-key certificate**. Typically, each digital certificate contains a public key, a unique identifier for the subject owning the key, and the signature of the CA. Most certificates follow the ANSI X.509 version 3 standard (X509v3), which includes fields for the public-key algorithm to be used with the key, a validity period for the key, the issuer's name and unique identifier, and other items.

The use of certificates and CAs is becoming the predominant model of attesting trustworthiness, and is relatively well known thanks to its use in web browsers. Note that CAs issue certificates in several classes – each class corresponds to the degree with which the identity has been proven. At the lowest level, the identity verification process can take place online; at higher levels, identity must be proven offline through, for example, a driver's license. It's interesting to compare the CA approach with the way things are done in PGP. PGP users sign other people's certificates, attesting that they know them personally and can vouch for the trustworthiness of that person.

A system of digital certificates and certification authorities, that verify and authenticate the validity of each party involved in (say) an Internet transaction, is called a **public key infrastructure** (**PKI**) or **trust hierarchy**. PKIs are currently very much in development but are an important component of an e-commerce infrastructure.

# XML and Security

We've already seen that security in ebXML is based on the emerging security standards around the XML technology family. The central characteristic of XML is that it provides a mechanism for wrapping data in a document made up of elements and attributes, and that we can choose a naming convention for these elements and attributes that makes the document **self-descriptive**. This is, of course, a characteristic that is in evidence through ebXML. For security, it means that as we look at specific countermeasures in the remainder of this chapter, we will meet some of the concepts and technologies we've already described – represented, usually directly, through the naming convention of the XML documents.

There are currently four important XML-based security-related initiatives. Some, such as the XML Digital Signature, have already had an impact of ebXML; others will soon have a similar impact. In the following sections, we will discuss four initiatives in more detail:

- Security Assertion Markup Language (SAML)
- XML Access Control Markup Language (XACML)
- XML Digital Signature
- XML Key Management Specification (XKMS)

# Security Assertion Markup Language (SAML)

**Security Assertion Markup Language** (**SAML**) is an initiative of the **Security Services Technical Committee** (**SSTC**) of OASIS. SAML defines an XML-based framework which facilitates exchange of authentication and authorization information. OASIS is providing information about SAML via its web site, at http://www.oasis-open.org/committees/security/.

SAML is currently in its early stages but is a very promising, and indeed ambitious, security initiative that groups and controls various other initiatives in order to come up with a uniform security architecture. The SSTC discovered that there are many initiatives each covering small pieces of the entire puzzle, and one of the strengths of the SSTC is the liaison function that they're building up with these initiatives. For instance, liaisons are managed between ebXML, XML Digital Signatures, XML Access Control Markup Language (XACML), and XML Key Management Specification (XKMS).

*We'll meet XACML and XKMS later in this section.*

SAML offers a standardized and normalized description for various security concepts, so-called **assertions**, starting off with authentication and authorization. The problem space addressed in SAML can best be explained by considering a sample process that begins with a user logon and results in a security policy describing the exact rights for this user. Such a process is shown in the following diagram:

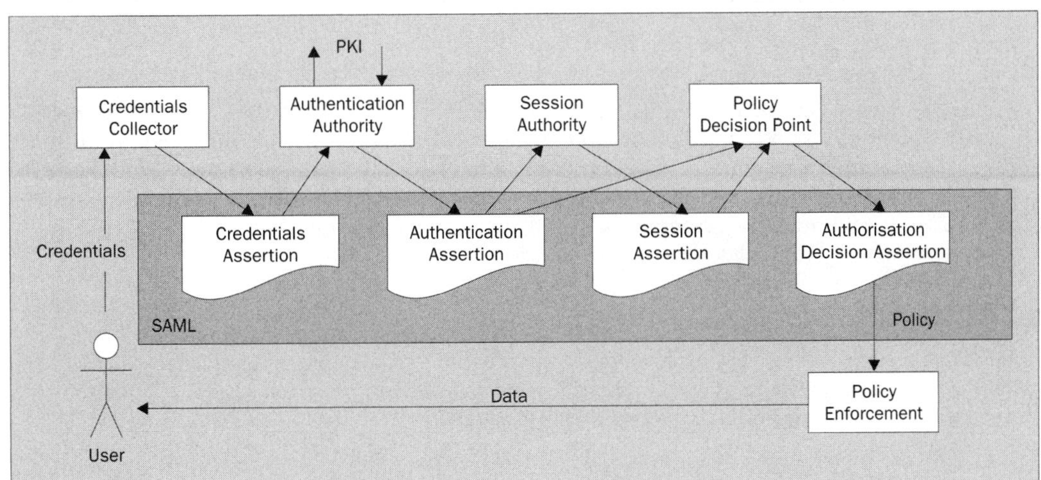

The first step in the process is the collection of the credentials (userID, password, certificates, etc.) that form the basis of the **credentials assertion**. The next step is the authentication of the user, based on the gathered credential information. The authentication might (for instance) use external PKI functionality, to come up with the **authentication assertion**. Depending on the requirements, the next step could be the definition of a `session` or a direct switch to determine and define the authorization for the user. These two steps lead to two corresponding assertions, a **session assertion** and an **authorization decision assertion**.

The SAML specification deals with the assertions and describes means of interacting with the above-mentioned authorities via a request and response mechanism.

It is beyond the scope of this book to cover SAML in any greater detail. As a final remark, we'd say that it's worth following the SAML initiative – mainly since it has a liaison with ebXML and even strives to define a binding for ebXML. Looking from an ebXML perspective, it can be seen as a potential solution for many of the outstanding security issues.

# XML Access Control Markup Language (XACML)

As its name suggests, **XML Access Control** (**XACML**) is a language for defining security measures based on access limitation via an access control list. It can be seen as the part that takes care of the policy decision point within the SAML security environment discussed above.

> *XACML is an initiative within the Security Services TC of OASIS, and is currently a work in progress. For more, see* http://www.oasis-open.org/committees/xacml/.

XACML aims at providing XML documents with a sophisticated access control model and an access control specification language. With this access control technology, access control **policies** control how an XML document appears. The policies also ensure the document is securely updated, as specified by the security programmer.

XACML is language oriented around triplets of **object**, **subject**, and **action**. The subject element allows user IDs, groups, and/or roles to be specified. The granularity of the object reference is as fine as a single element within an XML document. The action primitive consists of four kinds of action: read, write, create, and delete. Moreover, XACML provides provisional actions, in other words provisions attached to the access decision.

A valuable source of information on both XACML and XML DSIG is the **IBM alphaWorks XML Security Suite** (http://alphaworks.ibm.com/tech/xmlsecuritysuite). This suite offers an implementation of these two security mechanisms (amongst others) and a large number of examples. The solution offered by the XML Security Suite uses **XML Access Control Language** (**XACL**), an implementation of the XACML specification. It is recognized by OASIS as one of the contributions to the XACML initiative, and the examples later in this chapter are based on XACL.

## *An XACML Example*

The diagram gives an overview of the core elements in an XACML policy structure. It consists of a root element, `<policy>`, which has two child elements, `<xacl>` and `<property>`. As we'll see shortly, these two child elements embody the two parts of the policy naturally.

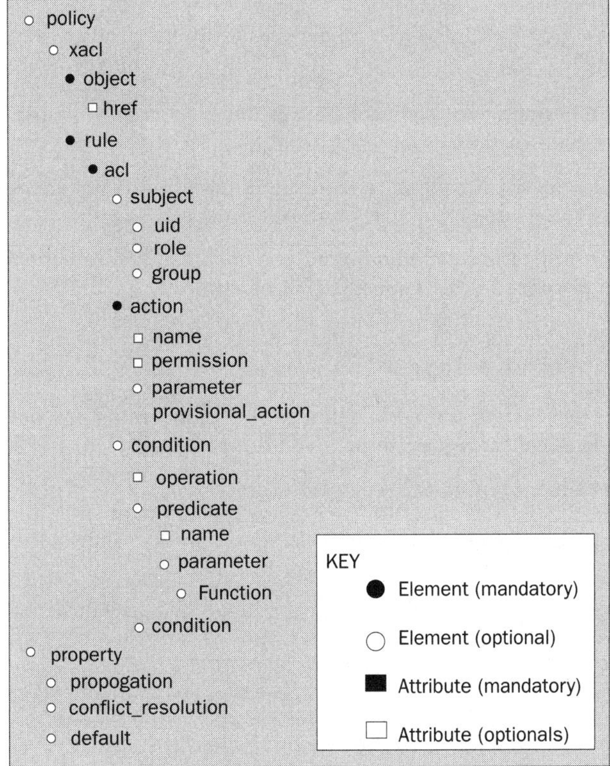


*The diagram doesn't show the complete representation of the XACML elements. Particularly at the level of the condition where the* `<parameter>` *and* `<function>` *are specified, deeper nesting of both* `<parameter>` *and* `<function>` *is defined in the actual schema.*

Rather than listing and describing all the elements in the diagram, we feel that XACML is best explained via an example. Here we will show how access to an XML document is described via a policy defined using the XACML language.

Imagine we have an XML document representing a catalog. The catalog document contains product information like this:

```
<catalog>
   <product>
      <code>TAM213</code>
      <description>Tamino XML Server</description>
      <price_sell currency="USD">50000</price_sell>
      <price_buy currency="USD">40000</price_buy>
   </product>
   <product>
      <code>TSK213</code>
      <description>Tamino XML Starterkit</description>
      <price_sell currency="USD">100</price_sell>
      <price_buy currency="USD">50</price_buy>
   </product>
</catalog>
```

The product information is self-explanatory; let's consider our access policy. In this example, let's suppose there are three groups of users who all have access to the product information, and the policy describes the following:

- Customers are permitted to read each item in the product information except for the <price_buy> information.
- Internal employees are permitted to read any information. They are also permitted to update information, if the value of <price_buy> is less than 200.
- Administrators are permitted to both read and update any information. (In this example, an administrator is defined to be a specific type of employee.)

The access control document below, written with XACML, defines these policy needs in XML format. An XACML file consists of two main parts:

- The <property> section is used to define settings concerning propagation, conflict resolution, and defaults for read, write, update, and delete
- The <xacl> element is used to specify the access.

In our example, the `policy` contains two <xacl> elements. The first controls the access for the product:

```
<policy>
   <!-- Restrictions on the /catalog/product element -->
   <xacl>
      <object href="/catalog/product"/>
      <rule>
```

Within this first <xacl> element, there are three <acl> elements. The first sets `read` access for both `employees` and `customers` for all elements within `product`:

```
         <!-- Employees and customers are allowed to read -->
         <acl>
            <subject>
               <group>customer</group>
            </subject>
            <subject>
               <group>employee</group>
            </subject>
            <action name="read" permission="grant"/>
         </acl>
```

The second <acl> is used to add `write` and `create` rights for special `employees` who have the role of `administrator`:

```
         <!-- Administrators are allowed to write and create-->
         <acl>
            <subject>
               <role>administrator</role>
               <group>employee</group>
            </subject>
            <action name="write" permission="grant"/>
            <action name="create" permission="grant"/>
            <action name="delete" permission="deny"/>
         </acl>
```

The third <acl> is more complex, and so we'll give it a little more attention. This one allows employees to write products where the <price_buy> is less than 200. The <subject> and <group> elements are used to specify that this <acl> relates to employees. The <action> describes that write permission is being granted to the specified object (which is /catalog/product – that's specified in the ancestor <xacl> element). The <condition> limits the given access by executing a standard function with the name compareInt. The parameters are the input values for the compareInt function (the equivalent logic in Java would be if (price_buy < 200) {...}):

```
      <!-- Employees are allowed to write if the price_buy < 200-->
      <acl>
         <subject>
            <group>employee</group>
         </subject>
         <action name="write" permission="grant"/>
         <condition operation="and">
            <predicate name="compareInt">
               <parameter value="lt"/>
               <parameter>
                  <function name="getValue">
                     <parameter value="./price_buy"/>
                  </function>
               </parameter>
               <parameter><parameter value="200"/></parameter>
            </predicate>
         </condition>
      </acl>
   </rule>
</xacl>
```

The second <xacl> element relates to the <price_buy> information contained within the <product> element, and is more straightforward again:

```
   <!-- Restrictions on the /catalog/product/price_buy element -->
   <xacl>
      <object href="/catalog/product/price_buy"/>
      <rule>
         <!-- Customers are not allowed to see the price_buy -->
         <acl>
            <subject>
               <group>customer</group>
            </subject>
            <action name="read" permission="deny"/>
         </acl>
      </rule>
   </xacl>
</policy>
```

### Processing with XACML

The flow from an initial request to the final result in an XACML environment consists of the following four steps:

1. An initiator submits an access request. This includes the target element (the requested element in the target XML document), the identity and roles (subject) of the initiator, and the required action (read, write, create, or delete).

2. The access request is evaluated according to the XACML policy and the status associated with the target XML document via a so-called **access evaluation module**. This module has access not only to the policies, but also to the entire target document. If necessary the group memberships are checked too. The result of the access evaluation is an access decision that contains the access information, including the provisional actions.

3. The request will now be executed in the request execution module. This module executes both the requested action and provisional actions specified in the access decision. If the requested action is a `write`, `create`, or `delete`, the target document is updated and the associated status may be updated.

4. Finally, the initiator's view is created when the requested action is `read`.

The following figure shows the architecture of an authorization model based on XACML, including the performed steps, as just outlined:

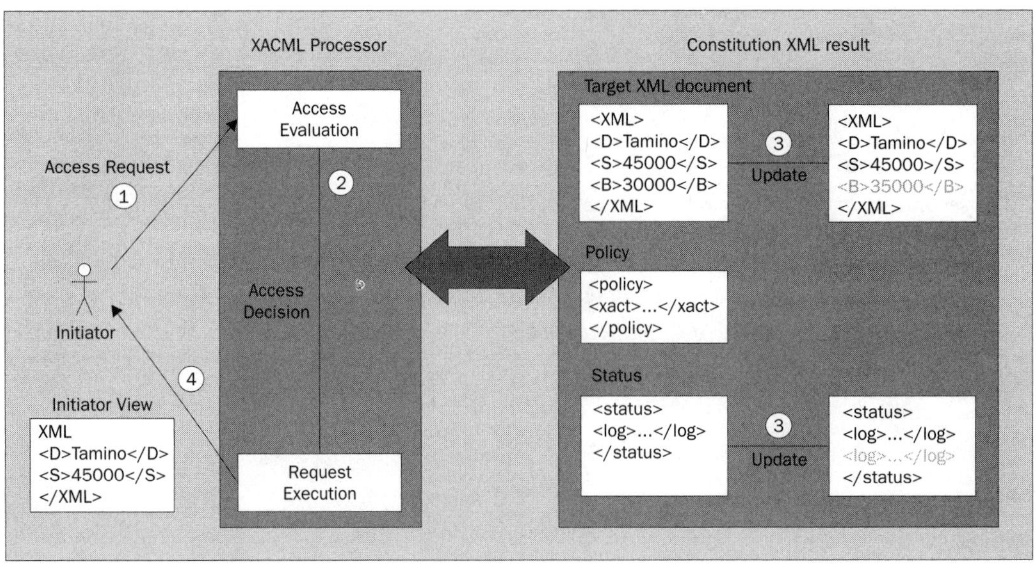


The XACML specification is currently under development and is expected to be released for initial comment in late 2001, an official adoption occurring in March of 2002. You can check for developments at http://www.oasis-open.org/committees/xacml/.

# XML Digital Signature

**XML Digital Signature**, also known as **XML DSIG**, is an initiative of the W3C and IETF. XML signatures provide integrity, message authentication, and/or signer authentication services for both XML and non-XML data.

*For more information, see the XML DSIG pages at W3C's web site – http://www.w3.org/TR/xmldsig-core/.*

We've already seen, in Chapter 4, the `ds:Signature` element that is used in ebXML messaging to sign messages. To recap, in an XML signature four main elements or groups of elements can be identified, each having a number of attributes and elements to specify the signing process:

- The `<SignatureValue>` element contains the actual value of the digital signature
- The `<SignedInfo>` element is the information that is actually signed
- The `<KeyInfo>` element is the key to be used to validate the signature
- The `<Object>` element an optional element containing application-specific information.

These can be seen in this diagram:

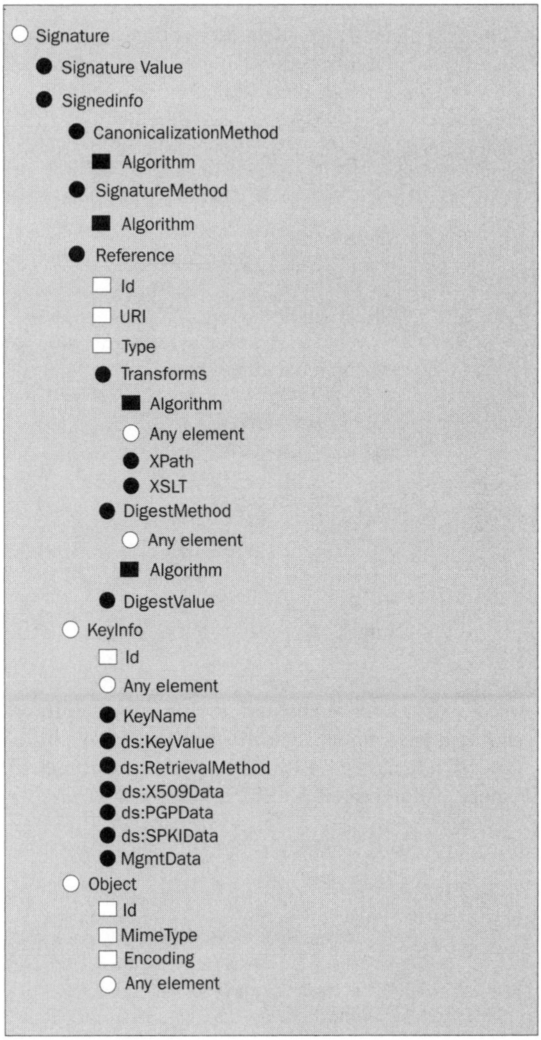

- Signature
  - Signature Value
  - Signedinfo
    - CanonicalizationMethod
      - Algorithm
    - SignatureMethod
      - Algorithm
    - Reference
      - Id
      - URI
      - Type
      - Transforms
        - Algorithm
        - Any element
        - XPath
        - XSLT
      - DigestMethod
        - Any element
        - Algorithm
      - DigestValue
  - KeyInfo
    - Id
    - Any element
    - KeyName
    - ds:KeyValue
    - ds:RetrievalMethod
    - ds:X509Data
    - ds:PGPData
    - ds:SPKIData
    - MgmtData
  - Object
    - Id
    - MimeType
    - Encoding
    - Any element

Let's look at an example of an XML signature that is used to sign order information, contained inside an `object` element.

The `<SignatureValue>` element, always encoded using base64, contains the actual value of the digital signature:

```
<Signature xmlns="http://www.w3.org/2000/09/xmldsig#" Id="signedOrder">
   <SignatureValue>er4kjlJfuoIUI79DLJHJ=</SignatureValue>
   ...
```

The required `<SignedInfo>` element is the information that is actually signed. The validation of the `<SignedInfo>` element is performed by validation of the signature and validation of each `<Reference>`. The algorithms used in calculating the `<SignatureValue>` are included in the `<SignedInfo>`; the `<SignatureValue>` itself is a separate element.

The first element we encounter is the `<CanonicalizationMethod>`. This specifies the algorithm to be used to canonicalize the `<SignedInfo>` element. The outcome is taken by the algorithm specified in the `<SignatureMethod>` (in this case, `RSA-SHA1`), and results in the `<SignatureValue>`. The final element is the `<Reference>` – this includes the digest method and resulting digest value applied to the referenced `<Object>` (in this case, `OrderInfo`):

```
   ...
   <SignedInfo>
      <CanonicalizationMethod
               Algorithm="http://www.w3.org/TR/2001/REC-xml-c14n-20010315"/>
      <SignatureMethod
               Algorithm="http://www.w3.org/2000/09/xmldsig#rsa-sha1"/>
      <Reference URI="#OrderInfo"
               Type="http://www.w3.org/2000/09/xmldsig#SignatureProperties">
         <Transforms>
            <Transform
               Algorithm="http://www.w3.org/TR/2001/REC-xml-c14n-20010315"/>
         </Transforms>
         <DigestMethod
            Algorithm="http://www.w3.org/2000/09/xmldsig#sha1"/>
         <DigestValue>jfs09wer4kjlJfuoIUI79027347=</DigestValue>
      </Reference>
   </SignedInfo>
   ...
```

The `<KeyInfo>` element contains information on the key to be used for validating the signature. It can contain keys, names, certificates, and other public key management information. In our example we specify the use of an RSA key. Other examples of supported certificates within the XML DSIG specification are DSA, X509, PGP, and SPKI:

```
   ...
   <KeyInfo>
      <RSAKeyValue>
         <Modulus>xA7SEU+e0yQH5rm9kbCDN9o3aPIo7HbPEntireXNfyxSZDU16ksL6W
            jubafOqNEpcwR3RdFsT7bCqnXPBe5EFeyenoordXRgrMvavzyBpVRgBUwUlV
            4foK5hhmbkTamino/6LpQRhDUDFE80976kjHJDFDsTvK+g9Ucj47es9AQJ3U=
        </Modulus>
```

```
        <Exponent>MNJV</Exponent>
      </RSAKeyValue>
    </KeyInfo>
    ...
```

Finally, the <Object> element contains the application-specific information, in this case a XML document expressing an order. The value of the Id attribute, OrderInfo, in the <SignatureProperty>, is used by the <Reference> element in <SignedInfo>, as we saw above:

```
    ...
    <Object>
      <SignatureProperties>
        <SignatureProperty Id="OrderInfo" Target="#signedOrder">
          <app:order xmlns:app="http://www.wrox.com/ebXML/order">
            <app:ordernumber>2389877</app:ordernumber>
            <app:item partnumber="989.546.880">
              <app:quantity>3</app:quantity>
              <app:price currency="USD">11.00</app:price>
            </app:item>
          </app:order>
        </SignatureProperty>
      </SignatureProperties>
    </Object>
  </Signature>
```

# XML Key Management Specification (XKMS)

As the name implies, XKMS is an XML-based solution for the management of public keys. It is designed to be used in conjunction with (for instance) XML DSIG. As such, it is part of a public key infrastructure. The XKMS proposal was submitted to the W3C in March 2001 by VeriSign (probably the best known commercial certification authority), together with Microsoft and Webmethods. XKMS consists of two parts:

- The **XML Key Information Service Specification** (**X-KISS**) – which is a protocol specification designed to resolve key information, from XML DSIG to other schemes which use public keys. The idea of X-KISS is to offer an API-like approach which protects a client from the complexities of the underlying PKI. In fact, one of the design goals of X-KISS is that it can be used on top of several different PKI schemes (like X.509/PKIX, SPKI or PGP). And when using XML DSIG, it allows clients to (partly) delegate processing of <ds:KeyInfo>.
- The **XML Key Registration Service Specification** (**X-KRSS**) – a protocol specification which supports the management of information related to a public key pair. Both protocols use the Simple Object Access Protocol (SOAP) and Web Services Description Language (WSDL), and are expressed using the W3C Schema language.

*There's more about XKMS at the W3C's site, at http://www.w3.org/TR/xkms/.*

## XML Key Information Service Specification (X-KISS)

X-KISS employs a **tiered service model**, since it needs to provide different levels of service to different applications. The defined tiers are:

- Tier 0 – the application processes the <ds:RetrievalMethod> element of the <ds:KeyInfo> element without assistance of a trust service. Processing is as per the XML DSIG specification.
- Tier 1, Locate Service – the application makes use of a trust service to process the <ds:KeyInfo> element. The client requests and receives <ds:KeyInfo> element public key information; however, validity of the key is not reported (see Tier 2).
- Tier 2, Validation Service – as in Tier 1, but in addition, information about the status of the validity of the key (such as its revocation or trustworthiness status) is reported.

Finally, the client must of course insure that the response from the service to a `Locate` or `Validate` operation is valid, meaning that the authenticity, integrity, and correspondence (that is, whether it's related to the request) are correct.

But before we can use any of the services we first need to register a key using X-KRSS.

## XML Key Registration Service Specification (X-KRSS)

As we already mentioned, X-KRSS is designed to provide a set of services geared towards the management of public key pair information. It consists of three main functionalities:

- Registration – used to assert a binding of information to a public key pair.
- Revocation – used to revoke previously-issued assertions.
- Key recovery – used to retrieve lost or forgotten key information.

## A Simple X-KISS Example

For completeness we will end this brief discussion of XKMS with a simple X-KISS example in which the client wants to send an encrypted XML document and requires the public key encryption parameters of the recipient. The issued request is:

```
<Locate>
   <Query>
      <ds:KeyInfo>
         <ds:KeyName>Wrox Encrypting</ds:KeyName>
      </ds:KeyInfo>
   </Query>
   <Respond>
      <string>KeyName</string>
      <string>KeyValue</string>
   </Respond>
</Locate>
```

In the above sample, the <Locate> element is a Tier 1 location request. In this <Query>, the client is looking for certain information relating to the `Wrox Encrypting` key. Specifically, the client is asking for the `KeyName` and `KeyValue` (as specified within the <Respond> element).

The trust service's response is an XML document that may look as follows:

```
<LocateResult>
   <Result>Success</Result>
   <Answer>
      <ds:KeyInfo>
         <ds:KeyName>Wrox Encrypting</ds:KeyName>

         <ds:KeyValue>
            e0yQH5rm9kbCDN9o3aPIo7HbPEntireXNfyxSZDU16ksL6W
            ubafOqNEpcwR3RdFsT7bCqnXPBe5EFeyenoordXRgrMvavz
         </ds:KeyValue>
      </ds:KeyInfo>
   </Answer>
</LocateResult>
```

In this response, the <LocateResult> element confirms that the client's query is successful, and returns the results of the query (the KeyName and KeyValue) in the <Answer> element.

Note that the <Result> element (in the response fragment, above) is used to give a first indication of the returned status of the <Query>. Valid values are:

| Result value | Meaning |
|---|---|
| Success | The operation succeeded |
| NoMatch | No match was found for the search prototype provided |
| Incomplete | Only part of the information requested could be provided |
| Failure | The operation failed for unspecified reasons |
| Refused | The operation was refused |
| Pending | The operation was queued for future processing |

# Security Within ebXML

The security threats mentioned in this chapter are all very real within the ebXML environment. By performing business via an open infrastructure such as the Internet, we're opening the door to all kinds of unwanted visits. In the current ebXML specification, there is no complete security model implemented or specified. The SAML initiative, in combination with XKMS and digital signatures, is looking very promising and should be able to form a blueprint (or even a full specification) that can be used in an ebXML environment. The progress made to date has focused on the **island (isolation) security model**, thus solving security issues within a limited scope.

The counter-measures for the security issues identified by the W3C will be explained in more detail later in this chapter. The security issues that we examine are:

- Unauthorized transaction and fraud – this combines elements of both integrity and authentication. Transactions traveling via an open network can be used for fraud by modifying them. By means of fabrication, fake transactions can be performed.

- Confidentiality – the protection of sensitive information needs special attention on an open network.
- Error detection and solving – errors in processing messages can result in transmission of incorrect messages or inaccurate reporting. It can even lead to service breakdown, causing discontinuities in a company's ability to perform business activities.
- Loss of management and audit – if the handling of messages is not implemented correctly data can get lost. In particular, audit trails and persistent storage of incoming and outgoing messages can be vital to provide evidence for legal reasons or to repair errors.
- Legal liability – this is a risk not really bound to any of the base threats. Legal liability is about the lack of legislation for the legality of electronic transactions and messages. Even though, in some countries, legal precedence has been set for the use of digital signatures, this is not universally the case. This leads to immature and even inconsistent delivery possibilities for electronic evidence between jurisdictions.

All of these issues are founded on the basic security threats (such as integrity, authenticity, and non-repudiation) that we've already met in this chapter. As we've said, these threats are solved in an ebXML environment via the isolation model. The next section will dig deeper into the means available to secure the different elements.

## Security Agreement

In an ebXML environment it is not just an individual element that needs to be secured; the whole business process defines the security needs. As we've seen, the first step in solving security problems is to analyze the risks; from this analysis, we can determine what to secure and what not to secure. This characterises the approach to security taken in ebXML. There's no attempt to secure the whole business process 100% – that simply isn't feasible – instead security is based on mutual understanding and agreements, coming up with an acceptable risk, and adjusting the security measures accordingly.

The collaboration protocol profile (CPP) contains the representation of the agreed security policy. It is created as a result of mapping the security policies and collaboration parameters onto the business process definition. This high-level result is then used as an input, together with the business process, its interfaces, and messages, and the parameters of the security environment already in place. This leads to the CPP that is stored in the ebXML repository. Thus, the CPP contains the set of possible and required security measures from your own company's point of view, after mapping to the business process. It is the first step towards a full policy-based security system.

The following diagram shows the process that we use to generate the CPP:

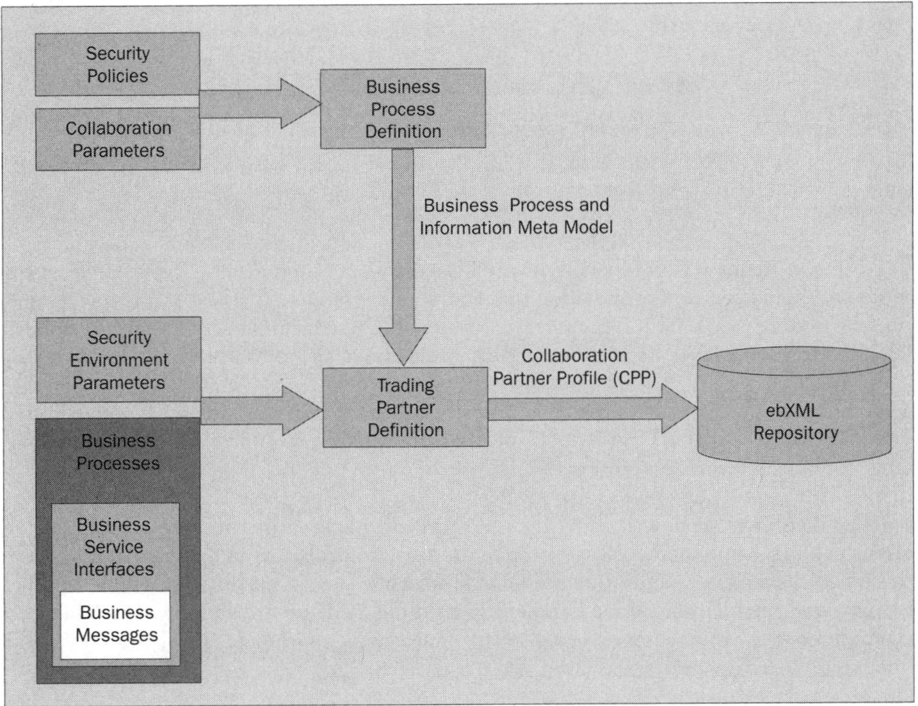


The CPP's `<Characteristics>` element contains an attribute called `secureTransport`, which defines the business requirements for providing secure transport. This is contained within the `<DeliveryChannel>` element, which we first met in Chapter 8. An example is shown below:

```
<DeliveryChannel>
   <Characteristics
      nonrepudiationOfOrigin="false"
      nonrepudiationOfReceipt="false"
      secureTransport="true"
      confidentiality="false"
      authenticated="false"
      authorized="false"/>
</DeliveryChannel>
```

The `<DeliveryChannel>` element defines the usage of countermeasures for non-repudiation, confidentiality, authentication, and authorization. Depending on the setting of the `<DeliveryChannel>`'s `Characteristics` attributes, additional elements will be introduced in the CPP. For instance, setting `secureTransport="true"` indicates that secure transport is required and implies that the CPP should contain a `<Transport>` element that contains information about the sending and receiving protocol used and certificates that the party wishes to use. If `secureTransport="false"` then the `<Transport>` element can be omitted from the CPP.

An example of a `<Transport>` element that uses SSL version 3.0 over an HTTP connection is shown overleaf. The `<Transport>` element can uniquely be identified by the `transportId`:

```
<Transport transportId="U034866">
   <SendingProtocol version="1.1">HTTP</SendingProtocol>
   <ReceivingProtocol version="1.1">HTTP</ReceivingProtocol>
   <TransportSecurity>
      <Protocol version="3.0">SSL</Protocol>
      <CertificateRef certId="WR2366"/>
   </TransportSecurity>
</Transport>
```

The CPP can also define different levels at which security may be present – for instance, the description of reliable messaging and non-repudiation that contains a reference to a <Certificate> element used to define the signing (XML DSIG) parameters for the ebXML document. But security can also be defined at the transport layer: for example, the sample above specifies use of SSL in the transport layer.

When two business partners negotiate an agreement based on the complimentary items in their respective CPPs, the resulting CPA (which specifies the collaboration profile between the two parties) inevitably contains information on security.

The negotiated security, as described by the CPA, states what security measures should be provided by the various ebXML components. However, one of the main problems in the current specification is that there is not always a clear definition of the level at which a security measure should be implemented. For instance, non-repudiation can be handled by both the MSH and the application. This forces business partners to negotiate not only the security measures, but also the level and method of implementation to be defined in the CPA.

# Specifying Security Mechanisms

As we've seen, the CPP is used to specify the available and required security mechanisms that play a role at the messaging level – the MSH, the message itself, and the process behind the message. Apart from the CPP, the <BusinessTransaction> element in the BPSS can also be used for specifying security parameters. The available elements for specifying the various security requirements will be explained in more detail below.

## *Messaging Service Security*

In Chapter 13 we covered the ebXML Messaging Service, and we saw the security measures delivered by the message service handler (MSH) and the means of specifying them. The MSH uses two elements in the CPP to figure out what type of security is required and what functionality to deliver:

- The <ReliableMessaging> element specifies the properties of reliable ebXML message exchange.
- The <NonRepudiation> element proves who sent a message and prevents later repudiation of the contents of the message.

We can also secure a message via its SOAP layer. We'll look at all three of these in the subsections opposite.

### *The <ReliableMessaging> Element*

The example below expresses the definition for a reliable message transfer, transmitted only once (`deliverySemantics="OnceAndOnlyOnce"`). It prescribes a test for duplicate messages (`idempotency="true"`). The `messageOrderSemantics` attribute specifies that the order of the messages, as passed on by the MSH to the application, must be in the same order as the sender sent them. There will be three retries if necessary, at intervals of 30 seconds. The messages are kept in persistent storage by the MSH for at least 90 seconds.

```
<ReliableMessaging deliverySemantics="OnceAndOnlyOnce"
      idempotency="true"
      messageOrderSemantics="Guaranteed">
   <Retries>3</Retries>
   <RetryInterval>30</RetryInterval>
   <PersistDuration>90S</PersistDuration>
</ReliableMessaging>
```

### *The <NonRepudiation> Element*

The `<NonRepudiation>` element is used to indicate if and how ebXML messages are digitally signed. If the element is omitted, then messages will not be digitally signed. The signature is based on the XML DSIG initiative we met earlier in the chapter, and is used to prove the authenticity of the message sender. It applies to all messages in both directions for the business transactions.

Here's an example of a `<NonRepudation>` element in the CPP:

```
<NonRepudiation>
   <Protocol version="2000/10/31">http://www.w3.org/2000/09/xmldsig#
   </Protocol>
   <HashFunction>sha1</HashFunction>
   <SignatureAlgorithm>rsa</SignatureAlgorithm>
   <CertificateRef certId="WO12"/>
</NonRepudiation>
```

Here, the required `<Protocol>` element identifies the technology that will be used to digitally sign the message – in this case, XML DSIG. The `version` attribute is obviously used to identify the version of the used `<Protocol>`. The required `<HashFunction>` sets the algorithm that is used to compute the digest of the message: in this case the value is `sha1` (see http://www.w3.org/PICS/DSig/SHA1_1_0.html). The required `<SignatureAlgorithm>` identifies the algorithm that is used to compute the value of the digital signature: in the example above an RSA algorithm is used. The required `<CertificateRef>` refers to a `<Certificate>` with a `certID` of `WO12`, specified elsewhere within the CPP.

The implementation of non-repudiation, based on the specified values in the CPP, can occur in the MSH, but this is not necessarily the case. The handling of non-repudiation can also occur in the application itself.

### *SOAP-SEC*

As we've seen, the ebXML specification itself provides mechanisms for digitally signing messages, but the story doesn't end there. An ebXML message is carried within a SOAP container, and the SOAP transport layer *also* provides such mechanisms. In fact, there's a W3C Note on signing SOAP messages posted at http://www.w3.org/TR/SOAP-dsig/.

We can sign a message using either (or both) mechanisms. While there are differences between these two mechanisms, there are also similarities – and the hope is that we will end up with a single way of applying digital signatures which combines the strengths of both mechanisms.

Currently the existence of two mechanisms means that there must be a mutual agreement regarding what mechanism of signing is applied. Perhaps it will be possible to develop an advanced and intelligent MSH, clever enough to determine what signing mechanisms are used.

We've seen some samples and explanations of digitally signed ebXML messages in Chapter 13, so we know what they look like. A digitally-signed SOAP message might look like this:

```
<SOAP-ENV:Envelope
      xmlns:SOAP-ENV="http://schemas.xmlsoap.org/soap/envelope/">
   <SOAP-ENV:Header>
      <SOAP-SEC:Signature
          xmlns:SOAP-SEC="http://schemas.xmlsoap.org/soap/security/2000-12"
          SOAP-ENV:actor="some-URI"
          SOAP-ENV:mustUnderstand="1">
         <ds:Signature xmlns:ds="http://www.w3.org/2000/09/xmldsig#">
            <ds:SignedInfo>
               ...
            </ds:SignedInfo>
            <ds:SignatureValue>
               ...
            </ds:SignatureValue>
         </ds:Signature>
      </SOAP-SEC:Signature>
   </SOAP-ENV:Header>
   <SOAP-ENV:Body
      xmlns:SOAP-SEC="http://schemas.xmlsoap.org/soap/security/2000-12"
      SOAP-SEC:id="Body">
      <app:GetAddress
          SOAP-ENV:encodingStyle="http://schemas.xmlsoap.org/soap/encoding/"
          xmlns:app="http://www.wrox.com/ebXML/customer">
          <customerID>23987987</customerID>
      </app:GetAddress>
   </SOAP-ENV:Body>
</SOAP-ENV:Envelope>
```

This is a standard SOAP messages with a SOAP `Signature` element in the `Header`. The namespace for this element is defined as `http://schemas.xmlsoap.org/soap/security/2000-12`. This SOAP `<Signature>` element contains a digital signature (`<ds:Signature>`, not fully shown) that conforms to the XML DSIG specification. The `<Body>` element contains an optional `SOAP-SEC:id` that can be used for referencing.

### *Key Management*

Key management is an important issue in the security mechanisms offered by the MSH. All digitally signed messages use keys and it is the task of the MSH to apply the appropriate keys to each message. The key management mechanism described in the ebXML specification focuses on XKMS, as proposed to the W3C and briefly described earlier in this chapter.

## CPP Security

For ebXML messages, the configuration of security for the MSH is specified in the CPP, making it possible to secure *just* the payload or the *entire* ebXML message. A MSH can deliver up to 23 profiles (as listed and defined in the ebMS Specification), offering various countermeasures against the security risks. ebMS states that it intends to support all 23 profiles. However, the immaturity of the XML security specifications means that ebMS currently supports only the following two:

- Profile 0: No security services are applied to data.
- Profile 1: Sending MSH applies XML DSIG structures to message.

The first profile is obviously trivial. In this section we'll focus on the second profile, in which XML Digital Signatures are applied to the message.

As mentioned earlier, a number of the security elements can be used at different layers in the ebXML process. A good example is the non-repudiation that can be applied at the MSH level and within the application. To specify the required security of the process and messages outside the MSH, the CPP provides the following elements:

- The `<DigitalEnvelope>` element – an encryption procedure in which the message is encrypted by symmetric encryption (shared secret key) and the secret key is sent to the message recipient encrypted with the recipient's public key.
- The `<NamespaceSupported>` element – identifies any namespace extensions supported by the messaging service implementation.
- The `<Packaging>` element – provides specific information about how the message header and payload constituent(s) are packaged for transmittal over the wire. This includes the information about what document-level security packaging is used and the way in which security features have been applied.
- The `<ds:Signature>` element – used to digitally sign the CPP itself, using technology that conforms with the XML DSIG specification.

We've already covered the `<ds:Signature>` element in some detail in this chapter. Let's briefly look at the other three.

### The <DigitalEnvelope> Element

The `<DigitalEnvelope>` element is used to define the encryption procedure in which the message is encrypted. Here's an example of a `<DigitalEnvelope>` element:

```
<DigitalEnvelope>
   <Protocol version="2.0">S/MIME</Protocol>
   <EncryptionAlgorithm>rsa</EncryptionAlgorithm>
   <CertificateRef certId="WO12"/>
</DigitalEnvelope>
```

In this sample, the required `<Protocol>` element identifies the security protocol to be used, `S/MIME`, and the `version` attribute identifies the version of the protocol to be used. The required `<EncryptionAlgorithm>` sets the encryption algorithm to be used to `rsa`, and the required `<CertificateRef>` refers to a `<Certificate>` with a `certID` of `WO12`, specified elsewhere within the CPP.

#### *The <NamespaceSupported> Element*

The `<NamespaceSupported>` element identifies any namespace extensions supported by the messaging service implementation:

```
<NamespaceSupported location = "http://www.w3.org/2000/09/xmldsig#"
                    version = "1.0">
   http://www.w3.org/2000/09/xmldsig#
</NamespaceSupported>
```

In this example, the messaging service will support `version 1.0` of the `XMLDSIG` namespace (`http://www.w3.org/2000/09/xmldsig#`).

#### *The <Packaging> Element*

The `<Packaging>` element provides specific information about how the message header and payload constituent(s) are packaged for transmission over the wire. Typically, the `<Packaging>` elements indicate the way in which the constituent parts of the message are organized. For instance, this element can describe MIME processing capabilities, providing information about MIME content types, XML namespaces, security parameters, and MIME structure of the data that is exchanged between parties. For example:

```
<Packaging id="pkg01">
   <ProcessingCapabilities parse="true" generate="true"/>
   <SimplePart id="part1" mimetype="text/xml"/>
   <NamespaceSupported location="http://www.w3.org/2000/09/xmldsig#"
                       version="1.0">
      http://www.w3.org/2000/09/xmldsig#
   </NamespaceSupported>
   <SimplePart id="part2" mimetype="application/xml"/>
   <CompositeList>
      <Composite mimetype="multipart/related" id="part3"
               mimeparameters="type=text/xml">
         <Constituent idref="part1"/>
         <Encapsulation mimetype="multipart/signed" id="part2_secure"
               mimeparameters="type=text/xml">
            <Constituent idref="part2"/>
         </Encapsulation>
      </Composite>
   </CompositeList>
</Packaging>
```

In the sample above, the required `<ProcessingCapabilities>` element is used to indicate that the packaging constructs specified in the other child elements can be both produced (`generate="true"`) and processed (`parse="true"`) at the software message service layer. The `<Packaging>` element contains two `<SimplePart>` elements, identified as `part1` and `part2`. The first has a `mimetype` of `text/xml`, the second of `application/xml`. The first `<SimplePart>` supports the `XMLDSIG` namespace. Finally, the `<Composite>` XML document (`part3`) is constituted from the two `<SimplePart>`s (`part1` and `part2`). The second part is added with additional security measures (S/MIME – `multipart/signed`) inside the `<Encapsulation>` element. The `<Encapsulation>` element is used to indicate the MIME security mechanisms, such as S/MIME or Open-PGP.

## BPSS Security

Apart from the security in the MSH and CPP (which is mainly focused on the transfer or the message itself), the business process definition allows for defining security at the process level. The focus of ebBPSS is on the following four security issues:

- **Non-repudiation** – two protocols mainly focused on gathering evidence on transactions and documents. The first protocol imposes a duty on each party to save copies of all business documents and document envelopes comprising the transaction. The second requires the responder to send a signed copy of the receipt.
- **Authorization security** – used to specify the appliance of rules that specify which interfaces or authors may be confidently relied upon as speaking for the enterprise.
- **Document security** – used to specify the required confidentiality, tamper proofing, and authentication for the business document and its attachments.
- **Reliability** – used to specify whether guaranteed delivery of the transaction's business documents is required.

Several attributes can be set for the `<BusinessTransaction>`, at the `<DocumentEnvelope>` and/or `<Attachment>` element level, to specify the required counter-measures for the above-mentioned security issues. The example below shows a single `<BusinessTransaction>` that contains both an activity to be performed when sending and one to be performed when replying to the transaction. It is an ATP check, which checks to see if the requested amount of element is in stock.

The `<RequestingBusinessActivity>` consists of a `<DocumentEnvelope>` and an `<Attachment>` – which is encrypted using S/MIME (multipart/signed) and contains the actual Order to validate:

```
<BusinessTransaction name="Stock validation">
   <Documentation>Order of 10 Tamino starterkits</Documentation>
   <RequestingBusinessActivity name="ATP check"
        isAuthorizationRequired="false"
        isIntelligibleCheckRequired="false"
        isNonRepudiationOfReceiptRequired="false"
        isNonRepudiationRequired="false"
        timeToAcknowledgeAcceptance="10s"
        timeToAcknowledgeReceipt="10s">
      <Documentation>Is the requested amount on stock</Documentation>
      <DocumentEnvelope businessDocument="ATP check"
            businessDocumentIDRef="ATP Id"
            isPositiveResponse="true"
            isAuthenticated="false"
            isConfidential="false"
            isTamperProof="false">
         <Attachment name="Order to validate"
               nameID="Order Id"
               businessDocument="ATP check"
               businessDocumentIDRef="ATP Id"
               mimeType="multipart/signed"
               specification=""
               isAuthenticated="false"
               isConfidential="false"
```

```
                isTamperProof="false">
            </Attachment>
        </DocumentEnvelope>
    < RespondingBusinessActivity name=""
            isAuthorizationRequired="false"
            isIntelligibleCheckRequired="false"
            isNonRepudiationReceiptRequired="false"
            isNonRepudiationRequired="false"
            timeToAcknowledgeReceipt="10s">
        <Documentation>Response to the ATP check</Documentation>
        <DocumentEnvelope businessDocument="ATP check result"
              businessDocumentIDRef="ATP result Id"
              isPositiveResponse="true"
              isAuthenticated="false"
              isConfidential="false"
              isTamperProof="false">
        </DocumentEnvelope>
```

For a more in-depth explanation of the non-security related elements and attributes here, see Chapter 5. The following table gives an overview of the parameters and their meanings – each of the parameters evaluates `true` or `false`:

| Parameter | Meaning |
|---|---|
| `isNonRepudiationRequired` | Indicates whether the other trading partner should save an audit trail of sent messages. |
| `isNonRepudiationOfReceiptRequired` | Indicates whether the other trading partner should digitally sign `<receiptAcknowledgement>`s. |
| `isGuaranteedDeliveryRequired` | Indicates whether the other trading partner guaranteed-deliver business documents. |
| `isConfidential` | Indicates whether the other trading partner should send the information encrypted. |
| `isTamperProof` | Indicates whether the other trading partner should use an encrypted message digest for the information entity that can be used to check if the message has been tampered with. |
| `isAuthenticated` | Indicates whether the other trading partner should associate a digital certificate with the document entity to provide proof of the signer's identity. |
| `isAuthorizationRequired` | Indicates whether the other trading partner should validate the identity of the originator against a list of authorized originators. |

## Protecting the Registry and Repository

The ebXML registry and repository are used by businesses for various activities including publishing and discovery. It is the entry point to all agreements, protocols, and other XML documents, and therefore a component requiring tight security. Security should not only be applied to the registry and repository themselves, but also to the transfer of messages to and from the registry and repository.

The security requirements of the registry and repository are derived directly from the base security issues:

- **Authentication** – is required to identify the ownership of content and to identify what "privileges" an entity can be assigned with respect to the objects in the registry. In addition, an organization might want to create private spaces for its partners – access to these private spaces requires the authentication of users.
- **Integrity** – is of course vital since the stored documents are used for mission-critical business applications. The minimum integrity expected from the registry is an assurance that content is maintained in the repository without any tampering en route or within the registry. The registry must also offer means to identify the submitting organization.
- **Confidentiality** – the repository contains information about organizations that is not public and may only be seen by their partners. Thus there needs to be a way of publishing information to only a *subset* of users – for example, partners. Confidentiality is required both "on the wire" and "in the registry".
- **Authorization** – in order to offer access to specific groups (as expresssed by the confidentiality requirement), we need an authorization mechanism to control who can access and do what with the data. The registry should provide authorization mechanisms to achieve this.

Technically these requirements will lead to a security system that should provide at least:

- Credential-based authentication, using digital certificates and signatures.
- Simple default role-based access control where:
  - The `ContentOwner` has full permission to its own documents
  - The `RegistryAdministrator` has full permission to all documents in the registry
  - The `RegistryGuest` has read-only access to all documents in the registry
- Message level confidentiality and encryption, provided by the MSH.

## Summary

In this chapter, we talked about general security concepts and specific techniques as they apply to the ebXML context. In particular, we learned that:

- Broadly speaking, in any data exchange system we can identify three security areas: integrity, confidentiality, and availability.

- Security risks are typically analysed in a risk assessment. Currently in the ebXML context, the ebXML risk assessment document is the only official ebXML document dealing with security. The ebXML risk assessment distinguished five different categories of security risks, namely: unauthorized transactions, loss of confidentiality, error detection, potential loss of management, and potential legal liability.
- Two fundamental security methods that can be found in most secured systems – authentication and authorization.
- Three related technologies make up a powerful toolset with which to secure an (ebXML) computerised system: encryption, digital signatures and certification. The public key infrastructure (PKI) brings these tools together in a comprehensive system of digital certificates and certificate authorities.
- Several XML-based initiatives making use of these underlying techniques are (or will be) important to security in the ebXML context. These technologies are SAML, XACML, XML Digital Signatures, and XKMS.

This has been a whirlwind tour of some of the relevant issues regarding security in B2B communication in general and ebXML in particular. For further reading, try *E-commerce Security: Weak Links, Best Defenses* (Wiley, 1998, ISBN 0-471192-23-6), which is a nice introductory text; *Information Warfare and Security* (Addison-Wesley, 1999, ISBN 0-201433-03-6), an excellent 'general' security book; and *Secure electronic commerce...* (Prentice-Hall, 2000, ISBN 0-130272-76-0) for good coverage of PKI.

On the web, try http://www.xmltrustcenter.org (which specialises on security and XML), http://csrc.nist.gov, and the excellent http://www.rsa.com.

# 16

# Implementing ebXML

If you've read the entire book up to this point, then you will have learned all about the different building blocks that make up ebXML. Logically, the next step is to examine how ebXML might be implemented in a production environment. At the time of writing this book, there aren't any 100% complete ebXML solutions ready to be unwrapped and installed. There is some code available on the Internet in the form of libraries, and some completed implementations of portions of the overall ebXML solution. In general, anyone implementing ebXML will have to write some code, but don't panic – it's not overly complex.

This chapter looks at a specific case study based on a real-life implementation, which illustrates some of the problems that might be encountered.

Before we delve into the specifics of this implementation, it's worth saying a few words about what it actually *means* to develop ebXML implementations at this time. ebXML is a work still in progress, and certain gaps in the ebXML specification rule out the possibility of a full implementation using the specifications. In particular, at the time of writing, the ebXML specifications still offer no guidance in the following areas:

- A party definition schema (a mechanism that defines the address and particulars of a specific party in XML format) in the CPP schema.
- A guard condition message definition for business process messages (that is, a defined message to convey an error type response back to a parent application).
- A schema for defining core components.
- A format definition for registry item query returns.
- Guidelines for CPA formation.
- A mechanism to reference meta data from document instances.

The absence of some definitive specifications means that it is impossible to achieve implementation of other mechanisms (for example, core component contextual drivers, and automatic CPA negotiation) while also following the specifications to the letter.

Moreover, there is still no full and clear definition of what it means for an implementation to be "conformant" with the ebXML Specification – this is something that will be of concern to most implementers. Ongoing work by UN/CEFACT and OASIS should provide clarification on the issue of conformance; for details of the latest developments, visit http://www.oasis-open.org and http://www.ebtwg.org. The latter is the site for UN/CEFACT's Electronic Business Transition Working Group, which will continue work on certain aspects of ebXML – many of which are detailed in this chapter.

We can expect the authors of the specifications and technical reports to work towards completeness of the specifications in the coming months. But this statement should *not* be interpreted as meaning that ebXML is currently impossible to implement. It *is* still possible to implement ebXML methodology, using some of the existing specifications to ensure some degree of interoperability. (For example, the ebXML Messaging Specification, Registry Services Specification, and Registry Information Model are needed as a common part of the infrastructure to enhance interoperability with other implementers. We'll look at some of the technical issues in greater detail during the course of this chapter.)

Programmers and implementers may be frustrated by the statements made above; but trust me, it will make sense as you read on. If you implement the half of ebXML that exists now, in the long term you will save yourself a lot of design work and you'll be halfway towards having a system which is fully compliant when the standard firms up.

A case study of an actual implementation of ebXML specifications and methodologies is a valuable study tool. In this chapter, we will examine how programmers from two organizations (**XML Global Technologies** and **Information Builders**) bridged gaps in the ebXML specifications and still managed to preserve interoperability. It is intended that this study will help other professionals to determine a course of action whenever they are presented with similar obstacles.

The case study in this chapter deals with the implementation in two parts:

- First, we'll set the scene, giving details of the context of the case study.
- Then we'll spend the rest of the chapter looking at an overview of the technical architecture used in the implementation. We'll cover:
  - The messaging system implementation.
  - The outward interfaces of the registry implementation.
  - A geographical classification mechanism.
  - The registry and repository engine.
  - Registry content (including discussion of the CPP, CPA, and BPS).
- The developers chose to code the application in Java, and so we also include some Java code fragments and discussion.

I will only show a small amount of actual code, mostly written in Java. Note that code presented in this book may deprecate as the ebXML specifications evolve over the coming months. The implementation presented in this chapter is essentially a snapshot – the work is still in progress, and so the code samples and XML files are subject to change. There is also no guarantee of stability and there may be major revisions to some of the methodologies discussed herein. As the specifications evolve, the code samples will be updated via the URL references given for each component.

I will not advocate any particular programming languages, operating systems, or platform combinations as solutions. Solutions will be presented using industry-standard object-oriented programming techniques (with apologies to all of you who were planning a Fortran or GW Basic solution). The terminology is likely to be most familiar to those readers who have programmed in Java. Where there are departures from the ebXML specifications or extensions, I will draw your attention to the fact.

*The resources discussed in this chapter include many software libraries and components, which are available from the XML Global Developer web site at* http://developer.xmlglobal.com.

# A Real World Case Study: The EPS Initiative

The case study is a description based upon a real application, involving two different levels of Canadian government. The application attempts to implement a set of common interfaces in order to streamline an electronic building permit application process. We'll refer to its solution as the **Electronic Permitting Service** (or **EPS**) application.

# Domain Specifics

The first level is a Canadian provincial government level – this level is in charge of the project. Their goal is to develop an electronic system to handle applications for building development permits in conjunction with a second, lower tier of government, which involves many different municipalities.

As an example, think of a construction company submitting an application for a permit to add an extension to commercial premises, and the subsequent processing of that application.

### *The Existing System*

In the system that was to be replaced, each municipality instance required construction companies to submit permit applications using a variety of methods – including paper, e-mail (with attachments), and fax. Some municipalities even permitted submission by telephone. Subsequently, several actors were involved in the processing of each permit application, and all of these actors needed to be able to reuse certain elements of information. While a proportion of the permit applicants were smaller parties such as homeowners, the majority of applications were submitted by construction companies.

Permit applicants were experiencing a number of different problems with these systems. For example:

- If a construction company had work in two or more different municipalities, their applications were required to satisfy (sometimes vastly different) processes and requirements.
- Applicants often found that the processing of their permit application took a long time to complete. This was because several different actors were required to interact with each permit application after it had been inserted into the municipal workflow, and because the individual steps occurred sequentially and not in parallel.
- Moreover, applicants experienced further frustration because, with each new permit application, they had to keep submitting the same information over and over, but sometimes in vastly different formats.
- Finally, applicants often experienced difficulty tracking the progress of an application during its journey through the approval system, because the municipalities were often unable to provide applicants with an *ad hoc* status report.

## The New System - EPS

The following diagram illustrates the EPS application:

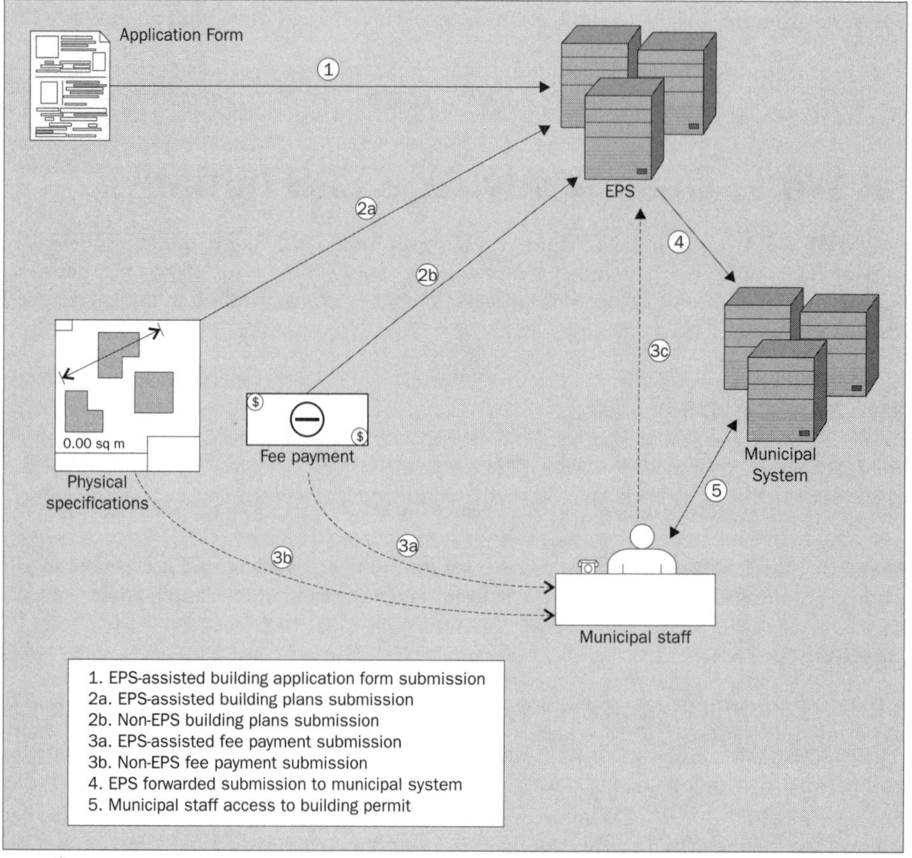


Let us consider some functions, issues, and elements of the process that the new EPS application is required to be able to deal with:

- When the municipality receives the permit application, it must first examine the permit application to ensure that the application form is filled in correctly.
- The application must then be placed into the workflow, along with several architectural drawings that detail the proposed work.
- There must be a check to ensure that any appropriate fees have been paid, or are forthcoming via conventional means.
- It is important that the system allows both for **electronic submission** of the payment and architectural drawings *and* for **legacy methods** of payment and submission (including use of the regular postal system). This is because many construction companies and smaller applicants (such as homeowners) may not have access to scanning devices, or may not wish to process payments via credit card.

*It is possible that the system may integrate other payment methods (besides credit card payment), at some point in the future. But in this first phase of implementation, we're dealing with electronic payment only via credit cards.*

- In order to avoid duplication of information during the submission process, each permit applicant will have their own profile set up in a special registry system. They'll be able to refer to this profile, via a unique identification system, whenever they intend to submit an application. Both the registry and the special applicant UID system are to be maintained by the provincial government.
- The business requirements of the system differ from one municipality to the next, and are likely to vary over time. Thus, there is a system requirement that the basic set of business information must be extensible in a truly *ad hoc* manner. Therefore, no static, global method for defining information sets (such as is found in EDI) would be acceptable as a solution. Rather, the system needs to contain an extensible architecture, such as the ebXML core components using a registry system.
- Once an electronic permit application has been created and validated on the client side, it is submitted electronically to the municipal clerk via EPS. The municipal clerk enters the application into the workflow at the municipality. Each municipality may have its own workflow associated with each permit application – therefore this system must possess the flexibility to accommodate the entire range of likely possibilities.

### *Guard Conditions*

After modeling many of the application approval processes in UML sequence diagrams, it became clear to the business analysts that each process would have several **guard conditions** that prevent the application from proceeding to the next level of workflow until the current level is completed. For example, no application should enter any external agency workflow until the payment from the permit applicant has been received and verified by the municipal clerk.

Once the payment has been received and verified, the system must execute certain run-time scenarios. For example, it might send an electronic communication to a civil engineers' office, to prompt them to examine the architectural drawings; or it might send a similar message to an external agency. Each of these steps must be driven by an **event-based model**, which uses a set of clear and concise rules to ensure that guard conditions and proper workflow sequence are followed.

### *The Actors*

The following flow diagram shows a simplified use case depicting several of the system actors. It focuses on which actors are involved in which operations:

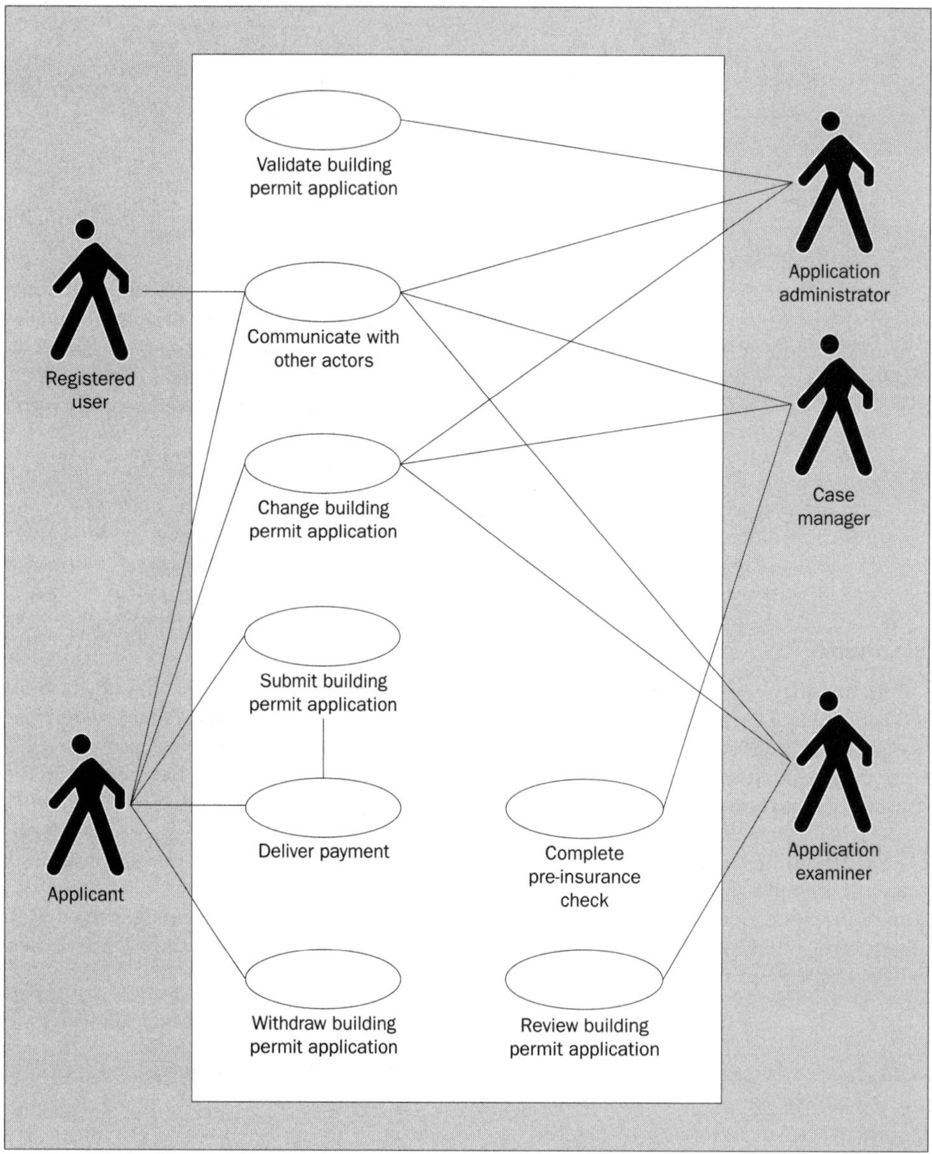


As you can deduce, the number of actors that must interact with each piece of business information demands that a solution be built using an open infrastructure. There may be several concurrent implementations, and each of them may have to discover and interoperate with others. Additionally, future layers of functionality might be built into the system, such as additional provincial actors (possibly taxation-related).

Some of the actors' requirements are not addressed in the ebXML specifications and technical reports. For example:

- ebXML does not directly prescribe methodologies for inter-enterprise role-based access to information (such as declaring roles and asserting permissions to access specific business information). The ebXML CPP may be extended to meet this requirement. Alternatively, the ebXML BPSS could be employed to describe the relationships between actors and information. Work on this front in ebXML may not take place for several years. In the meantime, developers and system integrators will have to assess whether or not the existing ebXML mechanisms will work for their specific projects. Careful modeling of processes could greatly help any analytical work in this realm.
- No ebXML specification exists for electronic payment processing (such as credit card processing). However, one could build an ebXML-based system to accomplish this.
- ebXML itself does not offer any mechanism for validation of business information. The XML 1.0 Specification and XML Schema data typing can be used, along with a programming language regular expression mechanism, to ensure information is validated.

Accordingly, we will not discuss these systems in detail. Instead, we will focus on the ebXML-centric parts of the infrastructure.

## The Key Architectural System Requirements

The EPS application's system architecture must be implemented in a **platform-independent** way, and must facilitate the need for delivery of permit application information across municipalities, provincial agencies, private organizations, and individuals.

The architecture also needs to be service-oriented, to allow programmers to add, modify or delete components as may be required from time to time. A plug-and-play approach for services (that is, the ability to insert additional services using the core infrastructure) would also be a functional improvement over static, hard-coded approaches. A transactional management-processing component, to facilitate marshaling of business messages and ensure interoperability in a secure and consistent manner, is another key point of any proposed system architecture.

The entire infrastructure must also allow users to define custom workflow rules (defined by municipal actors) that integrate seamlessly and allow information interactions within and outside of each portal site.

The entire architecture is defined by several components, each of which will have to be built using a common set of interfaces to ensure interoperability. The proposed architecture for EPS is shown in the following diagram:

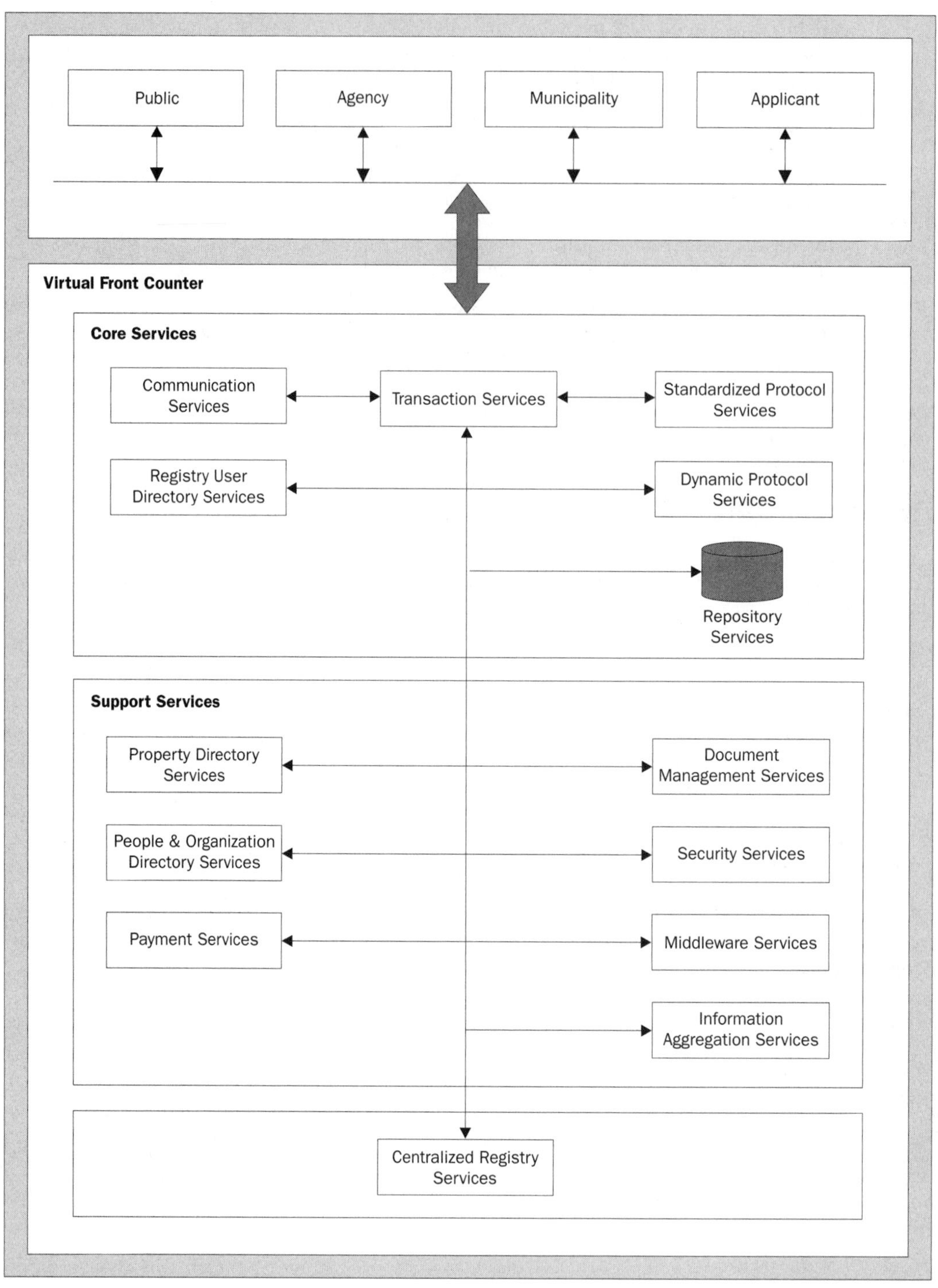

Public
Agency
Municipality
Applicant
Virtual Front Counter
Core Services
Communication Services
Transaction Services
Standardized Protocol Services
Registry User Directory Services
Dynamic Protocol Services
Repository Services
Support Services
Property Directory Services
Document Management Services
People & Organization Directory Services
Security Services
Payment Services
Middleware Services
Information Aggregation Services
Centralized Registry Services

## Future Extensibility Requirements

Assuming an alignment with ebXML to implement the system, the architecture must allow actors to extend the base set of business information by adding their own core components and making those accessible to other actors via a common and understood method.

The following paragraph, describing other future extensibility requirements, is from the EPS Technical Architecture document:

> *"The architecture of EPS allows for multiple concurrent implementations of the system. In this fashion there can be many virtual front counter (VFC) systems deployed simultaneously, each of them serving a specific client such as a municipality or a provincial agency. In addition, a private organization may deploy a VFC system to support EPS services for a number of small municipalities or provincial agencies that do not have mature or sophisticated permitting systems in place."*

The EPS application must also use technology standards wherever possible, to ensure that other users of those standards can easily integrate with it. The future requirement may be that construction companies from one jurisdiction (in this case a Canadian Province) may interoperate in other jurisdictions using the same infrastructure. It is extremely likely that other provinces will eventually adopt the system, so reliance on any single vendor's proprietary technology would be counter-productive to the long-term strategic goals.

## Alignment with ebXML Methodologies

As you may have guessed by now, the system integrators decided to implement ebXML methodologies as the basis for the infrastructure and to meet the system's requirements. While this seems like a good solution at the outset, it was important to consider the gaps that existed in the ebXML architecture at the time we wrote the EPS application. We carefully selected and used the parts of ebXML that were mature enough to ensure interoperability in critical areas, and we used and extended other ebXML specifications and technical reports in others.

> *We note again here that gaps remain in the ebXML specifications. As long as that is the case, implementers will need to bridge these gaps by using proprietary fixes. If you have different software vendors implementing different parts of your system, then this has the potential to affect the system's interoperability. You'll need to ensure that any extensions are fully documented, and the documentation shared with other software vendors who will build other key parts of the system or implement concurrent systems.*

At this point, let's look at key components of the EPS architecture and relate those components to ebXML. Each component in the EPS architecture has a key set of **requirements**. It's important to ascertain whether or not the ebXML counterparts for each component will meet the minimal set of requirements for the EPS system. Afterwards, we can also look at some of the additional benefits that ebXML provides in addition to the base set of requirements.

The following diagram shows a distributed view of the architecture:

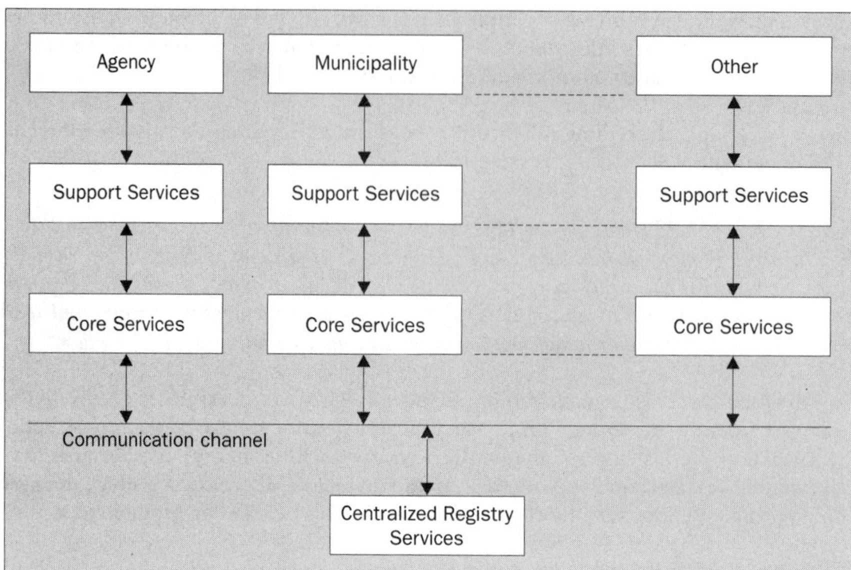


The figure includes a component labeled **communications channel**. The communications channel has its own set of strict requirements. It's reasonable to ask: "Why do we need to define a 'base' default communications protocol, when it may be overridden by other communications protocols which are more efficient for a particular party or business exchange?"

The answer is simple. If a system or actor didn't know *at least one* default communications format, then it would be *unable* to query another system to find out about the other forms of communication. By insuring that every component can use a common messaging protocol as a base, we can be sure that all the components in a distributed system can talk to one another.

### Messaging

The ebXML messaging specification works very well here. The designers of ebMS made sure that the specification is sufficiently feature-rich to handle the business functional requirements of users of ebXML-based systems. In this case study, it was necessary to implement the messaging layer for all components – including the virtual front counters (VFCs), the back-end systems, and the registry/repository communications.

> *A complete ebMS software library can be downloaded free from XML Global Technologies at http://developer.xmlglobal.com/ and it can be used free of charge for development (information correct at the time of publication). The ebMS library used in the case study is written in Java.*

### The Registry

The EPS architecture has a registry component. XML Global Technologies provided the public ebXML registry and associated repository for the EPS implementation. The EPS registry/repository functionality follows the ebXML Registry Information Model (as described in Chapter 7, and in the ebRS and ebRIM specifications, which can both be found at http://ebxml.org/specs/index.htm).

The ebXML registry specifications allow many different types of queries to the registry, each of which returns different sets of information. The EPS architecture primarily requires the registry to return links to two basic types of extrinsic objects (extrinsic means "foreign" to the registry system) – **trading partner profiles** and **core components**. System integrators decided to use the GoXML Central Registry, which supports the registry filter query as described in the ebRS specification. The filter query syntax is more than robust enough to support all the types of queries needed within EPS. The result of such queries is defined in Section 8.2.7 of the ebRS specification, expressed as a DTD. The full DTD is for a `ReturnRegistryEntry` query, which is the primary type of query most likely to be performed within the EPS architecture. Alternative queries would return only small fragments of meta data about specific managed objects. Components of the EPS system that call queries to the registry would primarily want to retrieve the entire managed object to work with.

The abstraction of how an ebXML Registry provides responses is important to understand before we start to examine actual code.

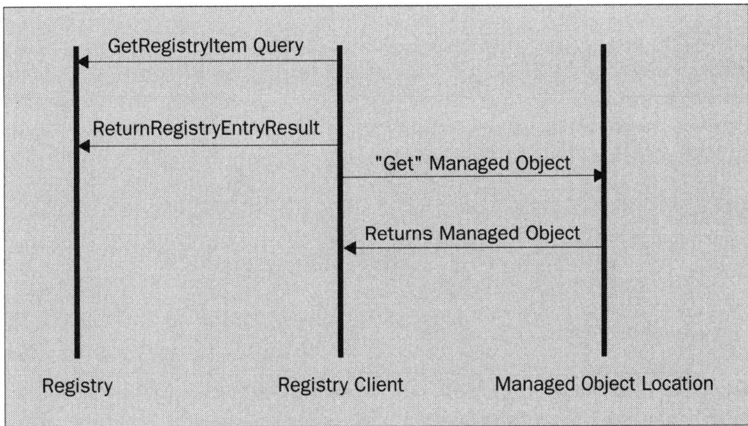


In the first step, a query is sent to the registry (using the ebMS as the transport layer) to retrieve a registry entry. A registry entry is synonymous with a managed object. Keep in mind that the registry might not actually store the managed object. Therefore, the result of this query returns the full set of meta data about the managed object being queried for. The DTD for the full set of meta data is provided below (this corresponds with the ebRIM). When the registry client receives a reply, expressed as an instance of the DTD, it can parse out a section near the bottom to get the location of the managed object. It is expressed as an `<ExternalLink>` element with an `ExternalURI` attribute.

Once this attribute value is understood, the application can issue a "get"-type request. This request, if properly formed and sent, should result in the managed object being returned. The EPS system uses HTTP requests for returning all such objects, although there is no dependency in the ebXML specifications on using HTTP.

The return DTD is as follows:

```
<!-- RIM Metadata DTD -->

<!ENTITY % ObjectAttributes "
   id          ID     #IMPLIED
```

```
   name        CDATA  #IMPLIED
   description CDATA  #IMPLIED"
>

<!ENTITY % RegistryEntryAttributes " %ObjectAttributes;
   majorVersion     CDATA  '1'
   minorVersion     CDATA  '0'
   status           CDATA  #IMPLIED
   userVersion      CDATA  #IMPLIED
   stability        CDATA  'Dynamic'
   expirationDate   CDATA  #IMPLIED"
 >
<!ENTITY % IntrinsicObjectAttributes " %RegistryEntryAttributes;">

<!ELEMENT ReturnRegistryEntryResult
   (RegistryEntryMetadata*)>

<!ELEMENT RegistryEntryMetadata
   (RegistryEntry,
    Classification*,
    SourceAssociations?,
    TargetAssociations?,
    AuditableEvent*,
    ExternalLink*)>

<!--*********RegistryEntry TREE**********-->
<!ELEMENT RegistryEntry (SlotList?)>
<!ATTLIST RegistryEntry
        %RegistryEntryAttributes; >
<!ELEMENT SlotList (Slot*)>
<!ELEMENT Slot (ValueList?)>
<!ATTLIST Slot
        name CDATA #REQUIRED
        slotType CDATA #IMPLIED
>
<!ELEMENT ValueList (Value*)>
<!ELEMENT Value (#PCDATA)>

<!--*********Classification Tree*********-->
<!ELEMENT Classification EMPTY>
<!ATTLIST Classification
        %IntrinsicObjectAttributes;
        classifiedObject IDREF #REQUIRED
        classificationNode IDREF #REQUIRED
>

<!--*******SourceAssociations AND TargetAssociations Tree*******-->
<!ELEMENT SourceAssociations ( Association* )>
<!ELEMENT TargetAssociations ( Association* )>
<!ELEMENT Association EMPTY>
<!ATTLIST Association
        %IntrinsicObjectAttributes;
        sourceRole CDATA #IMPLIED
        targetRole CDATA #IMPLIED
```

```
        associationType CDATA #REQUIRED
        bidirection (true | false) "false"
        sourceObject IDREF #REQUIRED
        targetObject IDREF #REQUIRED
>

<!--********AuditableEvent Tree**********-->
<!ELEMENT AuditableEvent EMPTY>
<!ATTLIST AuditableEvent
        %ObjectAttributes;
        eventType CDATA #REQUIRED
        registryEntry IDREF #REQUIRED
        timestamp CDATA #REQUIRED
        user IDREF #REQUIRED
>

<!--********ExternalEvent Tree***********-->
<!ELEMENT ExternalLink EMPTY>
<!ATTLIST ExternalLink
        %IntrinsicObjectAttributes;
        externalURI CDATA #IMPLIED
>
```

As you can see, the query result returns most of the meta data from the ebRIM along with the external URI for the actual managed object. This DTD is extrapolated from the DTD in Appendix A of the ebRS Specification v1.0.

The registry also had to meet the EPS requirements as described in a "Request For Proposal" document. The EPS application's requirements of the registry included (but were not limited to) the following functionality:

- **To allow users to register by setting up an account, which will be identified with a username and password.** This constitutes an extension to the ebXML specification by the addition of a user profile manager to the front end of the registry. ebXML registries are required to allow any entity to submit an object as long as the entity presents the proper credentials. Because the EPS application is not to be used horizontally across all industries, XML Global felt that the user profile manager was warranted. The EPS registry profile manager operates under the assumption that the three main roles, as described in Section 9.4.2 of the ebRS Specification, will be implemented. Those three role definitions are:

| Role | Permissions |
|---|---|
| `ContentOwner` | Access to *all* methods on registry objects that are owned by the `ContentOwner`. |
| `RegistryAdministrator` | Access to *all* methods on *all* registry objects. |
| `RegistryGuest` | Access to *all* read-only (`getXXX()`) methods on *all* registry objects (read-only access to all content). |

- **To allow the registered users to log in and be authenticated.**

- **To allow authenticated users to submit managed objects**, including party profiles (ebXML CPP-plus-extensions format), business process documents, form control documents, and additional core components.
- **To allow registered users who are content owners (COs) to modify managed objects for which they have associated rights and privileges.**
- **To allow registered users to deprecate managed objects for which they have associated rights and privileges.**
- **To allow registered users to remove managed objects for which they have associated rights and privileges.**
- **To allow unauthenticated users, defined as registry guests (RGs), to query managed objects.** Note that anyone can access anything in the system, because they will (at the very least) be granted `RegistryGuest` permissions.
- **To allow unauthenticated users to view information about the EPS system and apply to become registered users.**
- **To allow a registry client to connect to it via the ebMS Specification format.**

In the last of these, we see a tie-in between two of the ebXML specifications. The transport layer will be used for all initial communications between a registry client and the registry itself.

We'll return to consider the implementation of the registry later in this chapter. First, let's take a look at EPS's implementation of the ebMS Specification.

## The Messaging Implementation

If we are to follow the ebXML specifications, an ebXML Messaging Layer must be enabled for communications with the registry. The `ObjectManager` interface exposes a way to add content to the registry; however, the ebRS specification mandates that registries communicate using the ebXML Messaging Services in order to bootstrap registry functionality. Registries are not tightly bound to always use this messaging format; they're just required to support it as a default messaging service.

### Setting Up the Application

The following code is intended to demonstrate how easy it is to implement ebXML messaging. It makes use of XML Global's Transport, Routing and Packaging Libraries. This sample will instantiate a simple line command utility to build an ebXML message with a simple payload to query an ebXML Registry for its root-most level classification.

Before we begin to write any code, we need to import the necessary libraries to facilitate some of the lower-level functionality of the ebXML Messaging Service specification. Since the EPS system uses the XML Global Technologies libraries, and they are free for development purposes, we will use them. To download, go to http://developer.xmlglobal.com and follow the links to the Wrox book section to download the package `GoXML-TRP.zip`. The file contains:

- The jar files: `activation.jar`, `mail.jar`, `ebxmllib.jar`, `xss4j.jar`, and `xerces.jar`
- A `README.txt` file with installation instructions and notes on how to use the libraries
- The `SimpleRegistryClient.java` file, which builds a very rudimentary client, with a GUI in which a user can enter the URI for a known ebXML registry and query for a root classification node

The BuildAndRun batch file compiles the SimpleRegistryClient.java client and runs it. When the client runs, it displays a GUI on your screen. The GUI looks like this:

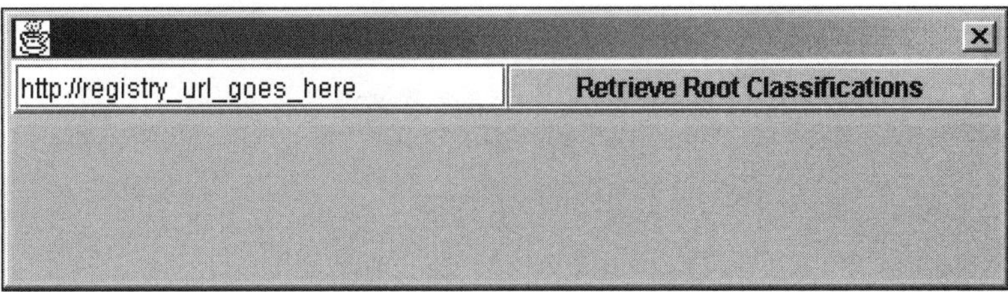


Type a URL (see next paragraph) into the textbox in the top-left of the GUI and click the Retrieve Root Classifications button, beside it. The command box should then spit out the outgoing message. The returned message should be seen in the lower portion of the GUI.

*Try the URL http://registry.xmlglobal.com. At the time the book went to press, this URL was configured to give you the expected response. However, this is subject to change, as is the software itself. To make sure you have the latest information, please check the information at http://developer.xmlglobal.com.*

Let's look at the SimpleRegistryClient.java code now and see what can be implemented.

### Importing Libraries

The first lines import the necessary libraries. Downloading the zip package will ensure you have all the necessary libraries:

```
import com.xmlglobal.ebxml.*;
import com.xmlglobal.ebxml.message.EbXMLMessage;
import com.xmlglobal.ebxml.transport.TransportException;
import javax.swing.*;
import javax.swing.border.*;
import java.awt.*;
import java.awt.event.ActionListener;
import java.awt.event.ActionEvent;
import java.awt.event.WindowAdapter;
import java.awt.event.WindowEvent;
import java.util.*;
import java.io.*;
import com.xmlglobal.xml.DOMUtils;
import org.w3c.dom.*;
```

### GUI Initialization

We need to make a class definition that extends the Java Swing JDialog component for building a GUI:

```
public class SimpleRegistryClient extends JDialog implements ActionListener {
  BusinessHome home;
  Conversation conversation;
  JButton getRootNodesButton;
  JTextArea textArea;
  JTextField addressBar;
```

All of the components are initialized above. The GoXML TRP library has several functions, as described in its Java API docs. The `SimpleRegistryClient` class contains most of the method calls:

```
public SimpleRegistryClient () {
  try {
    Properties systemProperties = initSystemProperties();
    home = new BusinessHome(systemProperties);
    conversation = null;

    initComponents();

  } catch (IOException ioe) {
    ioe.printStackTrace(System.err);
  } catch (ConfigurationException ce) {
    ce.printStackTrace(System.err);
  }
}
```

`initComponents()` builds the GUI components seen in the GUI image above. All of these are imported from the Java Swing and AWT classes. We need only four components – a text field to enter the URI of the registry we want to query, a button to create an event indicating we are ready to send the query, a text area to display the query result, and a top-level container to house those components. For the sake of simplicity, I have used the grid layout manager:

```
void initComponents () {

  JPanel topPane = new JPanel();
  topPane.setPreferredSize(new Dimension(640, 24));
  topPane.setLayout(new GridLayout(1,3));

  JPanel mainPane = new JPanel();
  mainPane.setPreferredSize(new Dimension(640, 512));

  getRootNodesButton = new JButton("Retrieve Root Classifications");
  getRootNodesButton.setActionCommand("getRootNodes");
  getRootNodesButton.addActionListener(this);

  textArea = new JTextArea();
  textArea.setPreferredSize(new Dimension(640, 400));
  textArea.setRows(1000);
  textArea.setBackground(Color.lightGray);
  textArea.setWrapStyleWord(true);
  textArea.setLineWrap(true);

  addressBar = new JTextField();
  addressBar.setPreferredSize(new Dimension(640, 24));
  addressBar.setText("http://registry_url_goes_here");

  topPane.add(addressBar);
  topPane.add(getRootNodesButton);
  topPane.setBorder(BorderFactory.createBevelBorder(BevelBorder.RAISED));
  mainPane.add(textArea, BorderLayout.SOUTH);
  getContentPane().add(topPane, BorderLayout.NORTH);
  getContentPane().add(mainPane, BorderLayout.CENTER);
}
```

Action listeners are needed to capture the events from the GUI:

```
void initListeners () {
  addWindowListener (new WindowAdapter () {
      public void WindowClosed(WindowEvent e) {
        System.exit(0);
      }
  });
}
```

### Messaging Library Properties

The `initSystemProperties` class hardcodes many of the variables that we will need in order to use the messaging library. These properties are for functions like logging, message payload handling, and setting properties for the message header, such as URIs. Most of these would normally be read dynamically or set in a static config file, but for this simple example, it is affordable to hardcode them:

```
public Properties initSystemProperties() {
  Properties systemProperties = new Properties();
  systemProperties.setProperty("home.domain", "");
  systemProperties.setProperty("home.url", "http://localhost/");
  systemProperties.setProperty("home.dir", "..");
  systemProperties.setProperty("init.services", "false");
  systemProperties.setProperty("log.file", "." + File.separator +
                                                 "SimpleClient.log");
  return systemProperties;
}

public Dimension getPreferredSize () {
  return new Dimension(640, 600);
}

public void actionPerformed (ActionEvent event) {
  String command = event.getActionCommand();
  if (command.equals("getRootNodes")) {
    textArea.append("Getting Root Classification Nodes.\n");
    getRootNodes();
  }
}
```

### Setting Up the Payload

Next we need to create a payload for our ebXML message. The payload is a registry query to retrieve the root classification node. We use `DOMUtils`, a helper class, to build the payload. The new document for the payload is called `requestDoc` and will contain only one element, `<GetRootClassificationNodesRequest>`, with one attribute, `depth`, which is set to `4`:

```
void getRootNodes () {
  try {
    Document requestDoc = DOMUtils.newDocument();
    Element root = DOMUtils.addChildElement(requestDoc,
                               "GetRootClassificationNodesRequest");
    root.setAttribute("depth", "4");
    conversation = getConversation();
```

`requestDoc` then needs to be set as the payload of our query message:

```
    EbXMLMessage request =
            conversation.createMessage("ObjectQueryManager", "",
                                "GetRootClassificationNodes");
    request.addAttachment("text/xml", requestDoc);
```

#### *Handling the Outgoing and Incoming Messages*

These next lines are included for demonstration purposes, so we can see the outgoing message in our DOS window (or Windows CMD shell as it is called now):

```
    System.out.println("EbxmlMessage Header:");
    request.writeTo(System.err);
```

The rest of the code essentially reads the incoming response and appends it to the `JtextArea` of our GUI, and deals with exceptions that are likely to occur:

```
        textArea.append("Sending message to " + addressBar.getText() + "\n");
        EbXMLMessage response = conversation.sendSynchronousMessage(request);
        Document responseDoc = response.getDefaultPayload();
        textArea.append("Response:\n");
        textArea.append(DOMUtils.makeString(responseDoc)+ "\n");
      } catch (InvalidMessageException ime) {
        StringWriter writer = new StringWriter();
        ime.printStackTrace(new PrintWriter(writer));
        textArea.append(writer.toString());
      } catch (TransportException te) {
        StringWriter writer = new StringWriter();
        te.printStackTrace(new PrintWriter(writer));
        textArea.append(writer.toString());
      } catch (IOException ioe) {
        StringWriter writer = new StringWriter();
        ioe.printStackTrace(new PrintWriter(writer));
        textArea.append(writer.toString());
      } catch (javax.mail.MessagingException jmm) {
        StringWriter writer = new StringWriter();
        jmm.printStackTrace(new PrintWriter(writer));
        textArea.append(writer.toString());
      }
    }

    Conversation getConversation () {
      Party remoteParty = new Party("TheRegistry", "");
      return home.createConversation("", remoteParty, addressBar.getText());
    }

    public static void main (String[] args) {
      SimpleRegistryClient client = new SimpleRegistryClient();
      client.pack();
      client.setVisible(true);
    }
  }
```

One more thing you may want to do if you have problems compiling the example is to compile it with the `-deprecation` flag. This way the JDK will spit out any errors related to outdated classes, etc.

## The Registry and Registry Client

It was the implementers' opinion that the ebXML messaging specification is probably too heavy-weight for all registry communications, in that the ebXML TRP may result in significantly larger messages than are always necessary. Not to worry – the ebXML teams realized this and have not mandated that *all* registry communications be done via the ebXML TRP. (It must, however, be present as a default protocol in compliant registries.) Therefore, the registry itself has its own CPP document, in which it can describe any other communications protocols that it supports. If both the registry client and the registry itself support a more efficient communications protocol, then they may engage using that protocol.

Keep in mind that the registry and the registry client must be loosely coupled, as the following diagram (of registry and registry client relationships) demonstrates. This is so that changes to the ebMS Specification over time will not render existing registries useless. Although this is largely an implementation issue, it was noted in the ebXML Technical Architecture.

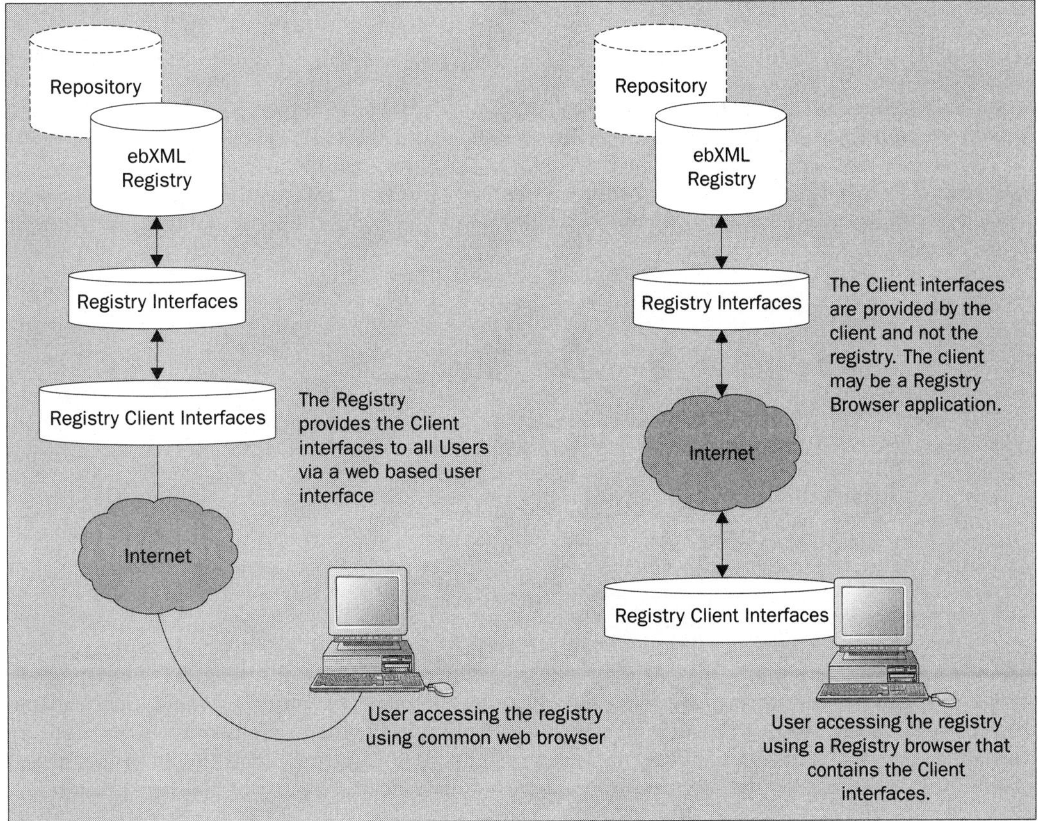


This diagram (which is based on a figure from the ebRS Specification) shows a "common web browser" being used to access a registry. The distinction to make here is that the browser may simply be accessing a web page that is written as part of a registry client. The registry client may use alternative protocols (to the ebRS and ebMS Specifications) yet the registry must support those proper protocols. In the case of the EPS architecture, most registry clients will likely use a lighter-weight protocol like SOAP for subsequent communications, and some are even contemplating CORBA.

The registry itself must support one of the various query syntaxes described in the ebRS Specification. The specification itself declares that the **filter query** is mandatory while the SQL query syntax is optional. For that reason alone, the implementers of the EPS application chose to use the ebXML filter query and its set of clauses.

> *The ebXML Registry SQL Query syntax is an alternative syntax for a registry query. The syntax for the SQLQuery of the registry is defined by a stylized use of a proper subset of the* `SELECT` *statement of entry-level SQL, defined by ISO/IEC 9075:1992, Database Language SQL, extended to include* `<sql invoked routines>` *(also known as stored procedures) as specified in ISO/IEC 9075-4 [SQL-PSM] and predefined routines defined in template form in Appendix C of the ebRS Specification. It is of interest to implementers who use an SQL-type database as the repository mechanism in the back end. The EPS implementers decided against using the SQL syntax for a query based on a number of parameters.*

## The Registry Implementation

The registry implementation used by XML Global is a generic registry server called **GoXML Central**, which uses a set of plug-in adapters to support a number of different registry syntaxes. The nice thing about this architecture is that the GoXML Registry Server can allow implementers to expose interfaces that are compliant with many different specifications, including ebXML.

For now, we'll avoid looking closely at what mechanisms are being used for the registry and repository – we'll treat them as a 'black box' (though we will return to this subject later in the chapter). We will focus on the outward interfaces only.

The preliminary architecture for the EPS registry looks like this:

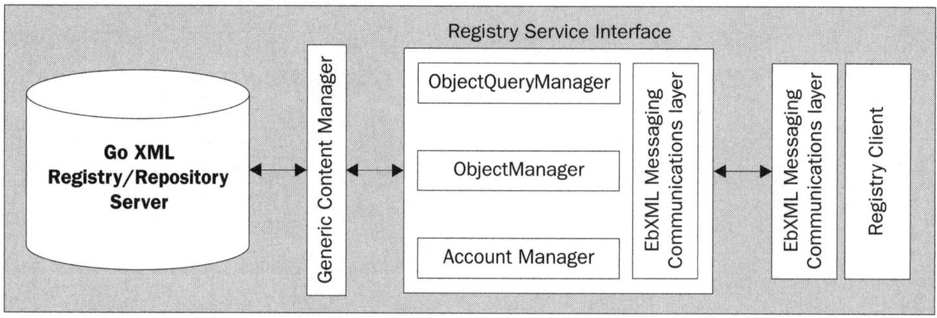


In this diagram, we can see the three main interfaces for the registry system beginning to take shape. There are two main abstract classes that programmers need to write in order to support the ebRS Specification: namely, they are the `ObjectManager` and `ObjectQueryManager` interfaces. In the EPS architecture, we extended the registry component to support a custom `AccountManager` interface.

The `RegistryService` interface is the top-level interface, and it exposes three other interfaces (`ObjectManager`, `ObjectQueryManager`, `AccountManager`) which in turn expose the methods that are used by the client to run registry-related tasks.

| Method Summary of RegistryService | |
|---|---|
| **Sub-Interface** | **Sub-interface Methods** |
| `ObjectManager` | `getObjectManager()` Returns the `ObjectManager` interface implemented by the Registry service |
| `ObjectQueryManager` | `getObjectQueryManager()` Returns the `ObjectQueryManager` interface implemented by the Registry service |
| `AccountManager` | `getAccountManager()` Returns the `AccountManager` interface implemented by the Registry service. This is an extension of the ebXML specification specific to the EPS work. |

Below is a second view of the `RegistryService` interface, as it is described in the ebRS Specification:

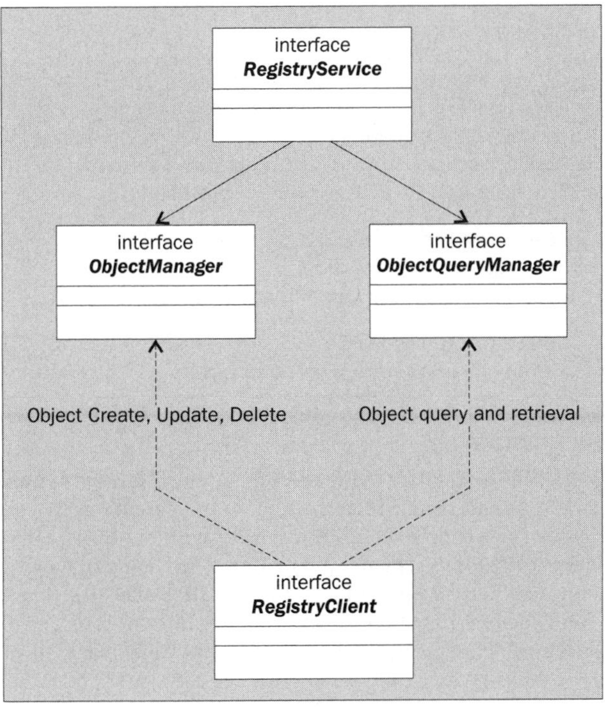

We will cover both the `ObjectManager` and `ObjectQueryManager` interfaces here, while the `AccountManager` interface will be covered later. Both the `ObjectManager` and `ObjectQueryManager` interfaces have a number of methods that can be invoked. Programmers who are looking to implement an ebXML-conformant registry will have to support all of the methods outlined in the ebRS Specification.

### *The ObjectManager Interface*

The `ObjectManager` interface provides a guideline for programmers to start coding. As it turned out, the ebXML method summary closely matched the requirements of the EPS application, and it facilitates several more methods such as `ClassifyObjects()` and `addSlots()`. We built the EPS implementation using the ebXML-defined interfaces. While the extraneous ebXML methods were not required at the time of writing, the life-cycle of the EPS project suggests that at some future stage, full ebXML functionality will be a benefit.

All of the methods listed in the this table are called by the registry client, via messages sent over the ebXML messaging service:

| **Method Summary of ObjectManager** |
|---|
| `approveObjects(ApproveObjectsRequest req)`<br>Approves one or more previously submitted objects. Returns a `RegistryResponse` object. |
| `deprecateObjects(DeprecateObjectsRequest req)`<br>Deprecates one or more previously submitted objects. Returns a `RegistryResponse` object. |
| `removeObjects(RemoveObjectsRequest req)`<br>Removes one or more previously submitted objects from the registry. Returns a `RegistryResponse` object. |
| `submitObjects(SubmitObjectsRequest req)`<br>Submits one or more objects and possibly related meta data such as `Associations` and `Classifications`. Returns a `RegistryResponse` object. |
| `addSlots(AddSlotsRequest req)`<br>Adds slots to one or more registry entries. (Slots are useful for adding attributes to registry entries. See the ebRIM specfication at http://www.ebxml.org.) Returns a `RegistryResponse` object. |
| `removeSlots(RemoveSlotsRequest req)`<br>Removes specified slots from one or more registry entries. Returns a `RegistryResponse` object. |

### *The ObjectQueryManager Interface*

A client can submit queries to the registry via the `ObjectQueryManager` interface, and expect back anything from meta data to actual content. For the EPS implementation, most of the queries are going to return either plain extrinsic objects or a classification node with multiple managed objects referenced based on a geographical classification scheme. According to the registry work done within ebXML, all managed objects may be classified by one or more **classification schemes**. There are no limits on classification schemes and each registry may employ any number of schemes. I feel that each registry would typically be loaded with classification schemes relevant to its purpose, which could include product, geographical, or industry level schemes.

Classification nodes are pinpoints within a general scheme. For instance, inside the geographical classification scheme, one may have a node for "Toronto, Ontario". Another example may be an industry level node of "Book Publishers".

Again, all of the methods listed in the two tables below are called by the registry client, via messages sent over the ebXML messaging service:

| **Method Summary of ObjectQueryManager** |
|---|
| `getClassificationTree(GetClassificationTreeRequest req)`<br>Returns the `ClassificationNode` tree under the `ClassificationNode` specified in `GetClassificationTreeRequest`. Returns a `RegistryResponse` object. |
| `getClassifiedObjects(GetClassifiedObjectsRequest req)`<br>Returns a collection of references to `RegistryEntrys` classified under a specified `ClassificationItem`.. Returns a `RegistryResponse` object. |
| `getContent()`<br>Returns the content of the specified repository item. The response includes all of the content specified in the request as additional payloads within the response message. The DTD for this response is specified in the ebRS Specification. Returns a `RegistryResponse` object. |
| `getRootClassificationNodes(GetRootClassificationNodesRequest req)`<br>Returns all root `ClassificationNodes` that match the `namePattern` attribute in the `GetRootClassificationNodesRequest` request. Returns a `RegistryResponse` object. |
| `submitAdhocQuery(AdhocQueryRequest req)`<br>Submits an *ad hoc* query request. Returns a `RegistryResponse` object. |

In the tables above, the return type of `RegistryResponse` seems a little ambiguous. No need to worry – it's clearly defined in the ebRS Specification in Appendix A – *ebXML Registry DTD Definition.*

Building code around the ebXML-defined interfaces is tedious yet relatively straightforward. There is an entire package is available from XML Global Technologies as part of GoXML Central, a set of libraries that can facilitate ebXML methodology. GoXML Central was used as the registry component in the EPS system.

### Methods of Deployment

The GoXML Central Library can be deployed in one of three ways:

- The first method of deployment is a standard `.jar` file in the classpath of a static classloader for use as a standalone library. A developer would use this option if he or she were interested in sending synchronous messages to an ebXML messaging server and nothing else. The obvious case for this method of deployment is within a client application that does not need a listening port. The only incoming messages that are processed are the response messages that are generated immediately on the open HTTP connection (as in SOAP). An application of the library in this configuration is known as the **client scenario**.
- The second method of deployment is within a J2EE-compliant web application server. The package contains a servlet and web application that can listen for incoming messages. The servlet delegates the messages to a GoXML Central homeobject that is configured to route the messages to the appropriate application connector or service. Details on how to connect applications are out of scope of this chapter, but are included within the accompanying API documentation. Application in this configuration is known as the **server scenario**.
- The last method of deployment is as a standalone server using the Jakarta Tomcat application server (or any other Java Servlet that runs Java Server Pages). Tomcat was chosen for its great abilities to serve JSPs, which provide a quick and inexpensive way to develop GUIs for system users. This is a least-effort deployment mode – it's suitable for cases where the developers are interested in deploying a server application but normally do not run a web application server at all. There is minimal support for this method of deployment, since it was used primarily by the development team for testing built-in services. These include the registry sub system. This scenario is called the **standalone scenario**.

For reasons of space, I cannot demonstrate each method within this chapter. You are welcome to download the code and accompanying API documentation from the URL noted above and experiment yourself. GoXML Central is available as a download from the http://www.xmlglobal.com web site.

## The Geographical Classification Scheme

Each municipality will enter a profile, similar to a collaboration protocol profile (CPP) document, that must be classified by the default (geographical) classification scheme. This will aid system users when they attempt to find the correct municipal authority for submitting a permit application.

This geographical classification scheme was adopted from existing regional and municipal boundaries. It's a hierarchical classification tree, and is expected to begin at the provincial level, then drill down based on sub classification nodes.

The project is for the province of Ontario, Canada, and the top-most container in the geographical classification scheme will be the entire province. The next level down will be a set of sub classifications of major regions, and within those is a series of municipal level classification nodes. Larger municipalities (such as the City of Toronto) may even contain smaller sub nodes, because their city infrastructure has more than one office.

The classification of registry-managed objects is accomplished by a set of classes that make up the **object management service**, a subset of the `ObjectManager` interface. These classes manage an object's life-cycle.

The GoXML Central registry product incorporates an additional layer of registry/repository management services (`AccountManager`) on top of the ebXML registry adapters. The registry management GUIs allow ordinary business users to interact with the registry, and a special actor called the **registry authority** (RA) can administer the entire registry/repository.

Using GoXML Central, creating the `<Classification>` node is quite straightforward. The ebXML-compliant registry in GoXML Central has an administration GUI which makes it easy for users to create and subdivide classification nodes. This is specific to GoXML Central; it's not part of the ebXML specifications, which do not actually specify any GUI components for registries. Remember that users don't need to be authorized in order to query the registry, but only the RA has privileges to add classification scheme nodes. This is an enhancement of the ebRS Specification v1.0, which states:

> "*The minimum* security policy *for an ebXML registry is to accept content from any client if the content is digitally signed by a certificate issued by a Certificate Authority recognized by the ebXML registry. Submitting organizations do not have to register prior to submitting content.*"

For illustration, a screenshot of the EPS's RegistryAuthorityGUI, built using Java Server Pages, is shown below:

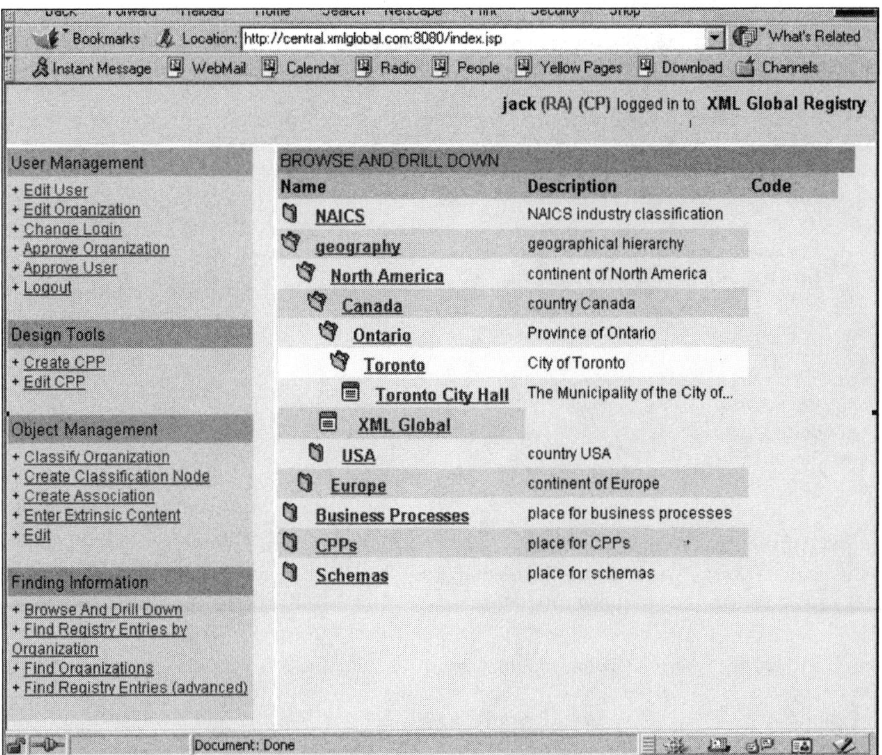


## The ClassificationNode Java Class

To see what happens under the hood, here is the `ClassificationNode` Java class. As with the other samples in this chapter, it relies on the GoXML Central libraries. The `ClassificationNode` class manages all operations connected with binding and querying on classification schemes and their associated registry items.

The first thing we have to do is write some code to import the correct libraries. This is part of the GoXML Central package (available from XML Global –http://www.xmlglobal.com). It is an illustrative guide to how XML Global implemented the classification management in their GoXML Central product. Others may choose to do it differently:

```
package com.xmlglobal.ebxml.registry;
import org.w3c.dom.Element;
import org.ebxml.registry.ClassificationNode;
import org.ebxml.registry.RegistryException;
import java.util.*;
```

Now we write the `ClassificationNodeImpl` class. This class is a collection of methods which facilitate requests directed from the JSP-based GUI pictured above. They are all part of the ebRS Specifications except where noted:

```
public class ClassificationNodeImpl
       extends IntrinsicObjectImpl implements ClassificationNode {

  public static final String PARENT = "parent";
  public static final String CODE = "code";

  public ClassificationNodeImpl (Element element) throws RegistryException {
    super(element);
    if (!element.hasAttribute(PARENT)) {
      element.setAttribute(PARENT, "");
    }
    if (!element.hasAttribute(CODE)) {
      element.setAttribute(CODE, "");
    }
  }

  public ClassificationNodeImpl (String name, String description) {
    super("ClassificationNode",null,name,description);
    setCode("");
    setParent(null);
  }
```

The next part of the class returns a collection of registry objects that are classified under the current node in the registry. `GetClassifiedObjects()` needs the `String id` of the node we're performing the `GetClassifiedObjects` query on:

```
  public Collection getClassifiedObjects () throws RegistryException {
    String id = getID();
    LinkedList results = new LinkedList();
    try {
      List classifications =
        ((Repository)associationMap).findAssociatedObjects("Classification",
                                         "classificationNode", id, false);
      ListIterator iter = classifications.listIterator();
      while (iter.hasNext()) {
        ClassificationImpl cl = (ClassificationImpl)iter.next();
        RegistryEntryImpl entry =
```

```
                                    (RegistryEntryImpl)cl.getClassifiedObject();
          if (entry == null) {
            System.err.println("ClassificationNodeImpl.getClassifiedObjects()
                                               encountered a null entry.");
          }
          results.add(entry);
        }
        return results;
      } catch (RegistryInternalException e)  {
        throw new RegistryExceptionImpl(e);
      }
    }
```

Setting the parent of a <Classification> node, in order to build a hierarchical classification scheme, is another management task. In `setParent()`, `element` comes from the `w3c.dom` package imported in the header. The class is `void` because it returns no value:

```
    public void setParent (ClassificationNode node) {
      String parentId = node == null ? "" : node.getID();
      element.setAttribute(PARENT, parentId);
    }
```

`getParent()` returns the immediate parent classification node for a given classification node. It takes the ID of the current node as an argument. IDs for classification nodes should be unique (although there is nowhere in the ebRS Specification that states this explicitly):

```
    public ClassificationNode getParent () throws RegistryException {
      String parentId = element.getAttribute(PARENT);

      try {
          ClassificationNodeImpl node =
          (ClassificationNodeImpl)associationMap.getRegistryObject(parentId);
          return node;
      } catch (RegistryInternalException e)  {
          throw new RegistryExceptionImpl(e);
      }
    }

    public String getParentID()  {
      return element.getAttribute(PARENT);
    }
```

The `getPath()` method is another method which provides essential functionality. This method returns a path to the current <Classification> node. If we were in the node of `Vancouver` and we ran a `getPath()` on the geographical classification scheme, we might get a return value of `//world/NorthAmerica/Canada/BritishColumbia`. Note that this functionality is not part of the ebXML Specification:

```
    public String getPath () throws RegistryException {
      String path = getName();
      ClassificationNode node = this;
```

```
    while ((node = node.getParent()) != null) {
      path = node.getName() + "/" + path;
    }
    return path;
  }
```

The `setCode()` method sets the code (ID) value for the current node, and `GetCode()` returns the code (ID) for the current code:

```
  public void setCode (String code) {
    element.setAttribute(CODE, code);
  }
  public String getCode () {
    return element.getAttribute(CODE);
  }
```

`getChildClassifications()` is also not part of the ebRS Specification, but is deemed essential for EPS. If we are within a given industry (such as `Construction`), we may want to find all the sub-classifications that exist within that industry. UDDI has similar functionality. `GetChildClassifications()` returns a list of all child nodes of the `<Classification>` node:

```
  public List getChildClassifications () throws RegistryException {
    String parentId = getID();
    try {
        List childClassifications =
                 ((Repository)associationMap).findAssociatedObjects(
                     "ClassificationNode", "parent", parentId,false);
        return childClassifications;
    } catch (RegistryInternalException e)  {
        throw new RegistryExceptionImpl(e);
    }
  }
}
```

## The AccountManager Interface

The `AccountManager` interface provides a relatively generic set of functionality, therefore I will not elaborate in too much detail. The requirements from EPS mandated that any registry entry request had to be made by a recognized actor; therefore, the developers followed the ebXML Registry Authority model. The table below outlines key parts of the method summary for the `AccountManager` interface for those who wish to follow a similar model of implementation. The ebRS Specification does not require the `AccountManager` interface.

| **Method Summary of AccountManager** |
|---|
| `registerUser(CreateRegisteredUserRequest req)`<br>Creates a new instance of a register user with privileges. Returns a `RegistryResponse` object. |

| Method Summary of AccountManager |
|---|
| `updateRegisteredUserProfile(UpdateRegisteredUserRequest req)`<br>Updates registered user profile. Returns a `RegistryResponse` object. |
| `getRegisteredUserProfile()`<br>Returns the content of the registered user profile from the `AccountManager`. Returns a `RegistryResponse` object. |
| `recoverLostRegisteredUserPassword(GetRegisteredUserPasswordRequest req)`<br>Returns the registered user password to the e-mail address on record for that registered user. Returns a `RegistryResponse` object. |
| `approveRegisteredUser(ApproveRegisteredUserRequest req)`<br>Reserved for administrative users to approve new user requests. Returns a `RegistryResponse` object. |

# The Registry and Repository Engine

We have talked in some detail about how to implement the registry and repository interfaces; however, I haven't said much about the back end. Earlier in this chapter, I asked you to consider the registry and repository as a black box, which we could use to call an interface and thus find the information we want. Now it's time to take a look inside that black box – how the EPS application implements the back end of the registry/repository.

Most registry/repository proponents advocate a tightly-coupled system of a data store (usually a relational database) and a data query manager. Some of these proponents are database vendors who are seeking to maintain a market for their product both as the registry *and* as the repository. Arguably, the performance gains can be noticeable; however, once you start down this road, you have to maintain a repository as well as a registry. This fact can add to the cost of implementing an ebXML infrastructure.

The query manager queries the meta data of each item managed by the registry. In ebXML-speak, these items are called **managed objects** and may include CPP documents, core components, BPSSs, and other extrinsic objects such as DTDs and even Relax/NG schemas. Design time objects could also include UML drawings.

Chapter 7 deals with registry and repository issues in greater detail; if you're considering building a conformant ebXML registry then you should use the information in that chapter. In the EPS application, we used the **GoXML Native XML database** in the back end, as the storage container for the documents.

## *Choosing a Registry Model*

There is a new notion for a lightweight registry model, which we considered for implementation within the EPS application; and this warrants a few words. Instead of maintaining both the meta data and the managed object in one location (which is a more traditional approach), a **decentralized repository model** was proposed. The idea is similar to that of a contextual XML search engine. Let me explain both implementation models in greater detail.

### The Standard ebXML Registry Model

In a standard ebXML registry, the meta data is kept in separate tables from the managed objects themselves. Each managed object is classified and described, and has associations and owners linked to the object via this meta data.

This diagram illustrates how the meta data essentially references the managed object:

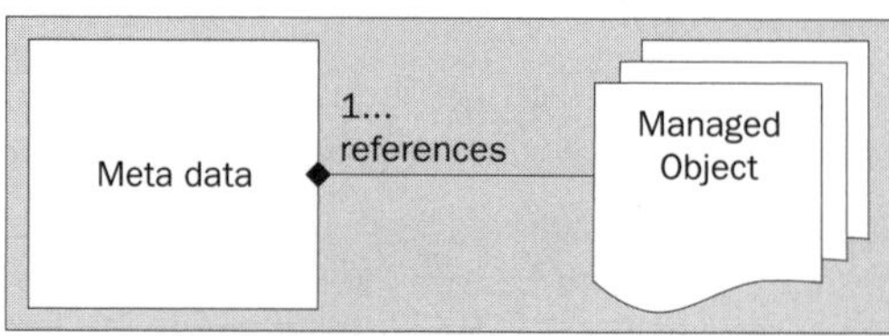


What happens when you query the registry to find and obtain a copy of a managed object and all its associated meta data? Basically, the registry has to construct the object to be returned, by first amalgamating the managed object (whether extrinsic or intrinsic) with its associated meta data into an XML syntax; then packaging it in the ebXML messaging layer; and then returning the instance back to the registry client that called it. This model is illustrated below:

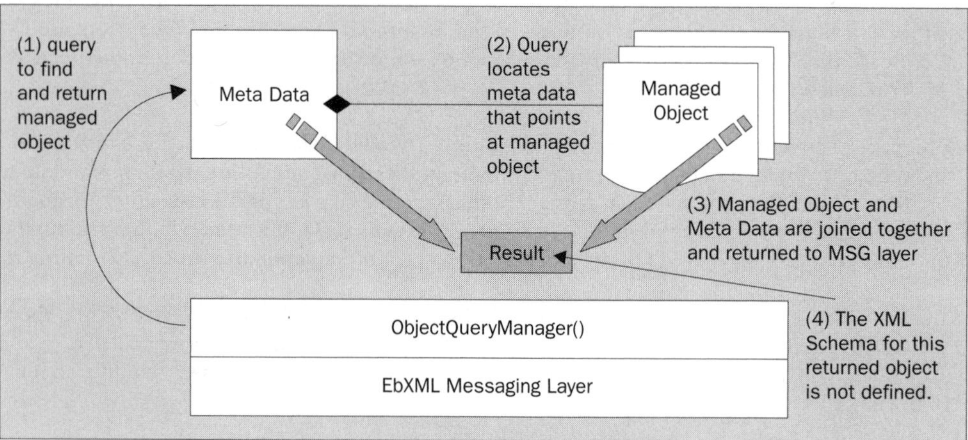


Many will argue that this model doesn't really tell the whole story. Ideally, it should only return the actual managed object itself (not a combination of managed object and meta data). However, that would lead to nightmares for those trying to manage the registry and repository systems, because any update to a managed object's meta data must be reflected by *also* updating the information contained in the intrinsic or extrinsic object itself.

### The Lightweight XML Registry Model (LiXR)

So a number of people got together, studied the ebRS Specification, and examined ways of improving the model. As a result of this study, we have a new work called the **Lightweight XML Registry** (or **LiXR**). In LiXR, the idea is to store objects as single, complete XML files. Each XML file contains the meta data folded into each managed object instance, and (of course) expressed in XML syntax. In this model, associations to other objects can then be expressed via URI links from within the instance, and classifications can be expressed within extensible branches of the XML file.

*It's expected that the work on LiXR will be continued under the auspices of a new private organization, the* ***Lobby for Internationalized Components and Freely Referenced Object Groups (LICFROG).*** *I understand that a web site,* http://www.licfrog.org, *will appear in the future.*

This approach greatly simplifies the entire registry model, and represents a move away from the relational back end model. The new model requires a query mechanism that is different from most other database query engines. The query mechanism required is essentially a contextual XML search engine, which can index instances of managed objects and provide search results containing very rudimentary meta data about each managed object (typically containing the URL, the name of the object and an object identifier that is unique to the registry itself). The LiXR model's main departure from the ebXML specification is its very limited RIM. The meta data is limited to only the object location, some basic owner information (for security and updating) and minor details about dates and revisions. Additionally, its power comes from maintaining a complete, searchable contextual index of every element, attribute and character data bit present in the original document. Documents are identified in contextual searches, their location is presented as part of the results, and any further interactions are conducted between the registry client side and the document server.

The LiXR model is not currently part of the ebXML work, but we can expect more from LICFROG in the future. At the time of writing, it *is* possible to implement ebXML methodologies using such a system; however, the system built using LiXR would not be ebXML-compliant. EPS does not use the LiXR model at the present time.

# EPS Registry Content

We've talked about the registry and repository implementation in some detail. Now let's start to examine the contents of the registry and how they relate to ebXML. The registry will contain a few different types of managed object, including a set of core components, trading partner profiles and business process documents.

## *The Electronic Party Profile*

You may recall (from our summary of the EPS application requirements, earlier in the chapter) that EPS requires a **party profile mechanism**, to create a company profile of each actor to the system. ebXML defines a similar mechanism, in the form of the **CPP**. The ebXML CPP document contains details of what a specific party's capabilities are in terms of:

- Business processes and roles supported
- Interfaces and binding points
- Transport and delivery protocols
- Security information

This type of information would be highly useful in a fully-automated system; however, they are not all necessary for the EPS.

The EPS requirements also specified that the system must be able to recognize each construction company actor, and retrieve the name of each actor. In fact, this requirement exposes a serious flaw in the ebXML CPP specification: namely, that the specification does not define an XML Schema for expressing details (for example, name, address, phone number, etc.) about a party.

The schema defined for the ebXML CPP format references a remote party file that could be anything. In order to implement the EPS application, we decided to enhance and extend the ebXML specification to include an **XML syntax party description format**. We examined the work done by two OASIS committees in this area – the XML Names Language (xNL) and XML Address Language (xAL) committees – and decided that the work of both committees was sufficiently mature to adopt. To find out more about these extensions to the ebXML CPP and CPA specifications, see http://www.oasis-open.org/committees/ciq/xnal/xnl/ and http://www.oasis-open.org/committees/ciq/xnal/xal/.

*Until such time as the ebXML CPP and CPA specifications define names and addresses in an XML meta data schema, this could be used as a 'best practice' in order to offer some degree of interoperability. It is unclear whether the definition of a party's name and address is even in scope for the Trading Partner Project Team.*

In addition to borrowing parts of the xNL and xAL DTDs, we used parts of the ebXML CPP definition to define the format of EPS's trading partner profiles. We had to incorporate a component to provide business users with the ability to build their CPP document. Now, the implementation team couldn't assume that a business user would have the knowledge needed to open server ports and add and describe electronic certificates, so we felt it necessary to hide these complexities from the user. To do this, we built a few classes into each municipality's portal site, which was tightly coupled to the municipality's EPS server. This enabled the system integrator to easily set up a pre configured box at each municipality. The actual server used was the **eBIX server** (which was built by XML Global and Information Builders). Nonetheless, the integration team were required to set up each municipality initially.

The implementation team also recognized that the construction companies represented *another* set of users who could not be assumed to have the technical expertise to build a profile. Therefore, we decided to build a scaled-down CPP creation component, which simply creates the CPP document automatically (once a business user from the construction company has answered a few questions). The component was written in Java and can be deployed as a set of JSPs or integrated into an existing system. The process of building JSPs to capture form information and build XML files is very straightforward, but not within the scope of this book. See, for example, *Professional JSP 2nd Edition* (Wrox, ISBN 1-861004-95-8).

Once the CPP is formed, it is automatically submitted to the registry, and the information collected is used to build a registry account for the construction company. The user working on behalf of the company is prompted for a password, which doubles as their registry profile password.

## Aligning Parties' Capabilities – Creating a CPA

Let's quickly revise the process in which CPPs and CPAs work together. The purpose of a CPP document is to allow an individual (or company) to express its capabilities. In ebXML, a second party who finds that company's CPP can then narrow down the list of what that company *can* do into a narrower proposal (a CPA proposal) of what the two companies *will* do. The CPA is then proposed to the first party, who subsequently either accepts the CPA, or rejects it and counter-proposes a new CPA.

### Obstacles To Progress

The process of building a CPA from two or more CPP documents is not yet sufficiently mature within the ebXML Specification to warrant an attempt to do this automatically. There is only a small and non-normative section on this at the end of the ebXML CPP/CPA Specification document, but it is hardly complete enough to begin implementation. The ebXML Specification does not include CPA formation in the scope of its work, and this has made things difficult for those trying to implement automatic CPA negotiation, for the following reasons:

- First, the specification does not specify the rules for production of a CPA in instances where **weighted preferences** don't align between two or more CPP documents. There is no 'tie-breaker' production rule; nor does a formal business process exist for negotiating a CPA. While it is possible that such a process could be written by anyone savvy enough to tackle this problem using the BPSS, there is a lot of work to be done.
- There is no documented process for proposing a CPA to another trading partner, but it is necessary to declare which pieces of information should be sent in such a proposal. It's necessary for a CPA to specify the identity of the CPP used to derive it, because the CPA examiner may have more than one CPP – and hence they need some way of telling which CPP was used in the formation of the CPA.
- Furthermore, in order to drive the contextual behavior of core components, certain business information needs to be present in both the CPP and CPA documents. The address and location of both parties needs to be defined in a consistent way, preferably in XML syntax according to a preset schema. (See Chapter 10 for more on *Core Components*.)
- We found problems with the use of ID and IDREFs throughout the entire CPP document. In particular, they make human readability of CPP documents significantly harder; moreover, it adds a burden for programmers to use the specification. The burden arises from having to write code to resolve IDREFs. Some parsers do part of the work, so implementers should carefully weigh up the consequences and benefits of using these.
- Finally, the CPP specification also does not allow for localized preferences for each business process. Instead, a CPP has a globalized preference system for items like transport, security, etc.

The ebXML team continues to work on the CPP and CPA specifications, and I am confident that these issues will be resolved in time. However, the EPS implementation team felt that, at the time of writing, it was not possible to implement the CPA from the specification in a way that was conducive to reliable system performance. We also felt that such a system was not actually *necessary* within the EPS system. Therefore, we decided to leave CPA functionality out of the system.

For readers who want to include CPAs at the current time, it is my opinion that it is simply too much bother to implement. If you are really set on implementing it, it probably *is* possible; I would recommend that anyone undertaking such a venture provides feedback to the CPP/CPA working group. Each scenario for implementation must be carefully considered within the business use cases driving the system development.

#### *Overcoming the Limitations of the CPP and CPA Draft Specifications*

Instead of implementing a CPA solution, the EPS modeling team felt that if a municipality offered to engage in an e-business process, and a construction company subsequently accepted this offer by submitting a permit application, and in consideration of the permit application fee, an *ad hoc* business relationship had been formed. There would be no further enhancements to this functionality in phase one.

The next question is: what other parts of the process must be present in the CPP document? Let's consider the construction companies first. They only really need to be able to express an identity, complete with an identification code unique to the EPS system, a physical address, and at least one form of electronic endpoint for electronic notices. A simple e-mail address will suffice for most of the construction companies, although even that is not mandatory.

For the municipalities, the requirements are larger. Each municipality must be able to derive the following functionality from CPP documents:

- The name and address of permit applicants in a consistent manner.
- A reference to a party identifier unique to the EPS system.
- A list of the processes in which they are capable of being engaged electronically. Each one of these processes must be referenced from the CPP itself via the UID of a business process.
- A localized list of preferred transport, security, and delivery protocols for each process.
- A higher-level list of all transport, security, and delivery protocols that each CPP owner is capable of.

After much careful deliberation and thought, we decided to use the full methodology described within ebXML for CPP documents, but to preserve only a small portion of the ebXML CPP document for actual use.

## The CPP Document

In the ebXML CPP specification, the CPP document is divided at a high level into four logical sections:

- The `<PartyInfo>` element, which contains the links to the details of the party, as well as the references to each role and process that the party can engage in.
- The `<Packaging>` branch, which provides specific information about how the `MessageHeader` and payload constituents are packaged for transmission over the transport route. This includes crucial information about what document-level security packaging is used, and the way in which security features have been applied. Typically, the sub tree under the `<Packaging>` element indicates the specific way in which constituent parts of the message are organized.
- The `<ds:Signature>` is an optional branch that contains information about how an exchange *may* be digitally signed according to the XML Digital Signature (XMLDSIG) specification. The content of this element (and any sub elements) is defined by the XMLDSIG specification schema, and any CPP that fails to pass validation against the XMLDSIG schema must be considered not valid pursuant to the specification.
- An additional `<Comment>` branch, which is self-explanatory.

Here's a sample CPP document:

```
<CollaborationProtocolProfile
        xmlns="http://www.ebxml.org/namespaces/tradePartner"
        xmlns:ds="http://www.w3.org/2000/09/xmldsig#"
        xmlns:xlink="http://www.w3.org/1999/xlink"
        version="1.1">
   <PartyInfo>  <!--one or more-->
     ...
   </PartyInfo>
   <Packaging id="ID"> <!--one or more-->
     ...
   <Packaging>
   <ds:Signature>  <!--zero or one-->
```

```
    ...
  </ds:Signature>
  <Comment>Comment_text</Comment> <!--zero or more-->
</CollaborationProtocolProfile>
```

The EPS implementation team decided to adopt the root and all second-level containers. Writing the code to allow users to build a CPP is relatively easy. It is even easier if you always know certain configuration parameters, such as the port number on which you implemented an ebXML listener object, and what form of security will always be present on the client side.

### The <PartyInfo> Element

Let's examine the <PartyInfo> branch in more detail. Here's what a <PartyInfo> element looks like:

```
<PartyInfo>
  <PartyId type="..."> <!--one or more-->
    ...
  </PartyId>
  <PartyRef xlink:type="..." xlink:href="..."/>
  <CollaborationRole>  <!--one or more-->
    ...
  </CollaborationRole>
  <Certificate> <!--one or more-->
    ...
  </Certificate>
  <DeliveryChannel> <!--one or more-->
    ...
  </DeliveryChannel>
  <Transport> <!--one or more-->
    ...
  </Transport>
  <DocExchange> <!--one or more-->
    ...
  </DocExchange>
</PartyInfo>
```

Here, the <PartyId> child element is generated automatically by the central registry server and is unique within the EPS system. This is a departure from the ebXML Specification, which usually advocates using another lookup to a URN type reference, such as a D-U-N-S number. (We've met D-U-N-S elsewhere in the book – it refers to a Dun and Bradstreet number that is considered to be unique for every business, and thus suitable as a unique identifier for a particular business.)

The party reference element, <PartyRef>, was intended in the ebXML Specification to point at a remote file that is defined by a URI reference or HTML web page. The EPS implementers decided to use the OASIS xAL and xNL schemas and place them inline. This constituted a departure from the CPP Specification, which declares <PartyRef> to be an empty element. Because multiple occurrences of <PartyRef> are allowed, the implementers found that if they decided to make EPS more ebXML-compliant, they could simply move the xAL and xNL to a remote location and reference them using XLink, as the specification provides. They felt that this was unnecessary, since the ebXML CPP specification does not provide a fixed schema for the party details. In addition, the ebXML CPP Specification states that the <PartyRef> element allows three attributes (xlink:type, xlink:href, and type); however, the corresponding DTD does not seem to include the type attribute. The type attribute is used to describe the document type of the external information about the party. It *must* be a URI that defines the namespace associated with the information about the party. If the type attribute is omitted, the external information about the party *must* be an HTML web page.

#### *The <CollaborationRole> Element*

The real "meat-and-potatoes" of the CPP is located under the `<CollaborationRole>` element. This element is a higher-level container for the process specification that is the actual business process. Each `<CollaborationRole>` element contains further child elements that were used in the EPS implementation. The `<ProcessSpecification>` child element is used for each occurrence of a business process that the EPS-compliant municipalities use. The following fragment exposes a `<CollaborationRole>` branch:

```
<CollaborationRole id="N11" >
   <ProcessSpecification name="PermitApplication" version="1.0">
      ...
   </ProcessSpecification>
   <Role name="buyer" xlink:href="..."/>
   <CertificateRef certId="N03"/>
   <!-- primary binding with "preferred" DeliveryChannel -->
   <ServiceBinding name="some process"
                   channelId="N02"  packageId="N06">
     <!--override "default" deliveryChannel for selected message(s)-->
     <Override action="OrderAck" channelId="N05" packageId="N09"
               xlink:type="simple"
               xlink:href="..."/>
   </ServiceBinding>
   <!-- the first alternative binding -->
   <ServiceBinding channelId="N04" packageId="N06">
      <Override action="OrderAck" channelId="N05" packageId="N09"
                xlink:type="simple"
                xlink:href="..."/>
   </ServiceBinding>
</CollaborationRole>
```

Each `<CollaborationRole>` element used in the EPS application contains a combination of business process and role assertions, plus additional elements to indicate which `<ServiceBinding>`s are preferred. The ebXML CPP specification states that the `<ServiceBinding>`s are listed in order of preference from highest to lowest. Programmers may shake their heads once they realize that there is added complexity involved in guaranteeing that this order will stay the same when you use the document in your code. A SAX parser will always read in order; however programmers will have to make sure they implement call-back routines in their code that will preserve this order in a consistent basis across all implementations.

In my opinion, it would have been much more efficient to add an attribute to each XML fragment option to indicate preference. This suggestion prevailed in our case study. As an alternative, the EPS implementers added an extra attribute, called `preferenceOrder`, to each `<ServiceBinding>` element. Each `preferenceOrder` attribute contains an integer, the lowest value indicating the preferred binding.

We extended the CPP to give each `<ProcessSpecification>` element an attribute of a unique identifier (named `UID`) that is used to locate it within the registries in the system infrastructure. Adding this attribute isn't likely to break any implementations that follow the ebXML Specification to the letter if the CPP is not validated against the ebXML-specified DTD. It is unclear how extending the CPP component may affect interoperability between disparate implementations. In my opinion, other implementations that cannot identify a BPSS with a UID from the CPP are not capable of the necessary "discovery phase" behavior, as described in the ebXML Technical Architecture specification, which would allow them to be functional. Therefore, interoperability issues will probably not arise.

We also added a localized <Description> element, which can be used to provide descriptions in many different languages – we use the xml:lang attribute to specify the language. This was necessary since the registry client is required to display relevant information in order that a human actor, operating on behalf of a construction company, could find the correct permit application process.

In the <CertificateRef> element, the certId attribute references a certificate ID located elsewhere in the CPP document.

The rest of the CPP was adopted with other minor changes. The most important piece of functionality was the requirement to drill down to find details of each process via a series of registry queries. Thus, construction companies can find out how to apply electronically for permits. The full DTD for the modified CPP document will not be shown here as it is likely to change in the months immediately after the press date of this book, and until April 2002. Instead, I describe the methodologies and discussions that led to the changes, in order to help individual implementers reach similar conclusions and 'best practices' when implementing ebXML on their own.

## The Business Process Schema

Each CPP references one or more processes. There are public processes and private processes inside the EPS system architecture. Public processes are those that are referenced from the CPP documents for others to use. Private processes are executed behind an entity's firewalls.

The diagram below represents a (very simple) sequence of events, which makes up a typical business process in the EPS application:

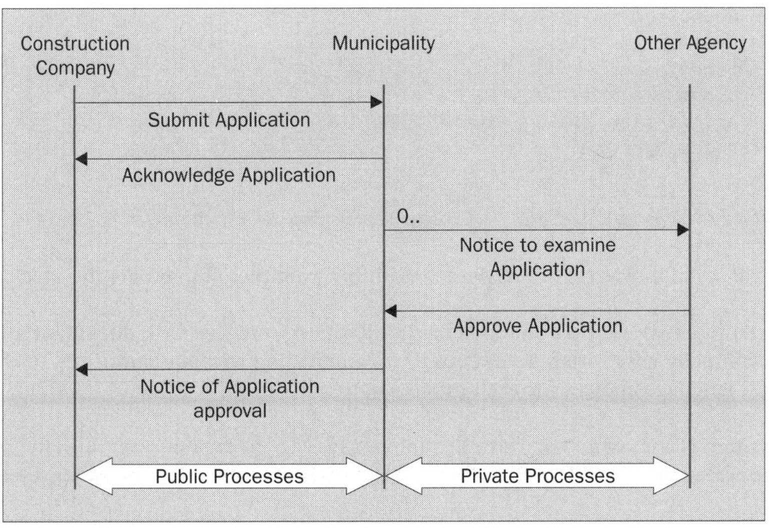


When someone finds a municipality in the registry, they can perform a query to retrieve that municipality's CPP document. To find out which business processes a given municipality is capable of performing, the users interact with an interface that grabs the contents of the <ProcessSpecification> element in the CPP document; it presents the contents to the user using the registry's *ad hoc* query interface.

Here, the EPS implementers encountered another problem. In Canada, there are two official languages – English and French. Content for all government information must be made available in *both* languages. In the official ebXML CPP Specification, we can see that there is only one `name` attribute allowed, and it is apparent that English will be used in the CPP fragment example below:

```
<ProcessSpecification
   name="Residential Addition Application - non commercial"
   version="1.0"
   xlink:type="simple"
   xlink:href="http://city.toronto.on.ca/services/application132.xml">
   ...
</ProcessSpecification>
```

In addition, there is no `UID` attribute for the business process; nor is there a registry referenced in which one can retrieve the business process. The XLink HTTP reference can suffice for some implementation scenarios. The EPS implementers decided to modify the CPP slightly further, to facilitate the business use case of dual languages. The modified CPP document fragment is written as follows:

```
<ProcessSpecification version="1.0"
   xlink:type="simple"
   UID="95002"
   registryURI=http://registry.xmlglobal.com
   xlink:href="http://city.toronto.on.ca/services/application132.xml">
   ...
</ProcessSpecification>
<ProcessName xml:lang="EN-us">
   Residential Addition Application - non commercial
</ProcessName>
<ProcessName xml:lang="FR-ca">
   Application r&#233;sidentielle d'ajout - non commerciale
</ProcessName>
```

*Note that `é` is an ISO-Latin-1 character set reference for the character é.*

The actual final solution was slightly different than this example, but you get the idea.

We can now build an application that uses the information from this CPP document to present the construction company user with a set of choices for interacting with the municipality. The user is also presented with language choices for each process option.

A few well-written classes can easily turn this into an HTML block that resembles the screenshot opposite. The screenshot was lifted directly from the early prototype for the EPS project:

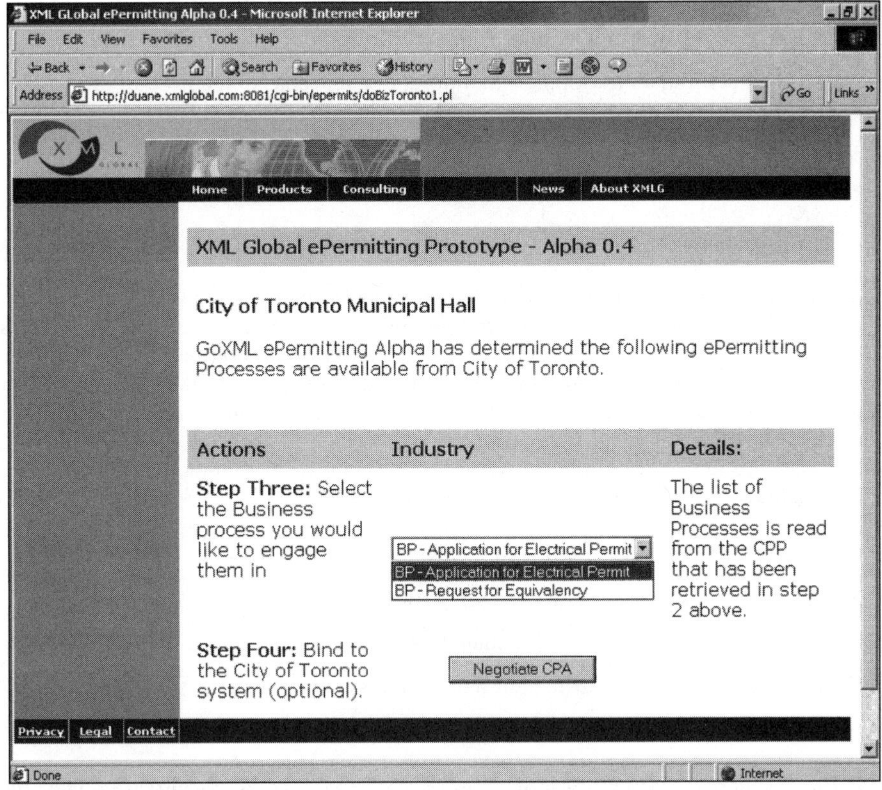


Once the user has selected the application process in which they wish to engage the municipality, a request is sent (via the ebXML TRP) to the appropriate registry, and a copy of the business process is returned. (There is an alternative flow, in which business processes that have been retrieved in the past are stored in a local cache to avoid unnecessary traffic.)

The code that drives this functionality appears to be essentially very easy. Seemingly, all one has to do is write a simple class that loads the CPP into the DOM, and then queries the document model to retrieve each branch's information about business process label and URI reference. Upon closer inspection, however, there is much more functionality needed. It may actually involve retrieving a copy of the business process, checking whether both CPPs can support the process, presenting the label in the correct local language, among other subtleties.

### Thoughts Relating To Application of the ebXML BPSS

The **ebXML Business Process Specification Schema** (**ebBPSS**) specification was proposed in Vienna in 2001, and the ebXML plenary voted on it. Personally I feel that ebBPSS is relatively immature compared to other parts of the ebXML Specification (such as ebMS). Some of the key shortcomings I see in the ebBPSS are:

- Elements like `<RequestingBusinessActivity>` and `<RespondingBusinessActivity>` should allow namespace-qualified extension elements. This can help expedite third-party vertical standards' usage of the ebBPSS framework to describe their business processes, even if these processes have not been designed to be completely compatible with UMM.

- There are no standardized guard condition error messages. Guard conditions make sure processes are executed in a manner consistent with the rules expressed in ebBPSS.
- An action level "retry" (as opposed to a process level retry) is required in the `<RequestingBusinessActivity>` and the `<RespondingBusinessActivity>` elements.
- There are some overlapping scopes between ebBPSS and other ebXML groups (like CPP/CPA and messaging – particularly with respect to message "receipts").

That said, it's worth examining the specification closely to see if it fits in with EPS's proposed architecture.

The relationship between business process and business information is tightly coupled in ebXML. The desire for the EPS infrastructure was to unbind these two entities to make the business process simpler – after all, every e-business process is essentially built using the same core block or one endpoint transmitting a message to another endpoint. There are variations, such as the endpoints themselves, the messages, the security model used, the timeouts and number of transactions that make up a process.

The ebBPSS Specification was carefully considered in the context of building the EPS business process schema. The main requirements of the business process schema used for EPS were that it must be able to:

- Reference business information within each step of an exchange.
- Support guard conditions against dropped transactions.
- Express a definitive sequence of exchanges within a specific process.
- Express the roles of each participant in a business transaction.
- Describe the business service interface for each municipality.

The last of these requires some clarification. We already have the CPP document to describe the physical interface, so why do we need to use the BPSS to further define the interface? The answer is simple – we need it to bind the business information and message (or signal) choreography to each endpoint. To implement ebXML fully (including such activities as contextual modification of core components at design - or runtime), the ebBPSS Specification will need to be beefed up considerably.

The following fragment shows the XML source for a fragment of the ebXML expression of the business process:

```
<?xml version="1.0" encoding="UTF-8"?>

<BusinessDocument
   name=" Residential Addition Application - non commercial "
   specificationLocation=
        "http://registry.xmlglobal.com/ebxml?IUD=com/xmlglobal/950002.xml"/>

<BusinessTransaction name="Submit Permit Application">
   <RequestingBusinessActivity name="">
      <DocumentEnvelope isPositiveResponse="true"
                        BusinessDocument="EPS-Permit_Application">
         <Attachment name="AccompanyingArchitecturalDrawings"
                     mimeType="Binary/jpg"
                     BusinessDocument="EPS_acknowledgement"
```

```
                    specification=""
                    isConfidential="true"
                    isTamperProof="true"
                    isAuthenticated="true">
            </Attachment>
         </DocumentEnvelope>
      </RequestingBusinessActivity>
      <RespondingBusinessActivity name="">
         <DocumentEnvelope BusinessDocument="EPS-Permit_Acknowledgement">
         </DocumentEnvelope>
         <DocumentEnvelope isPositiveResponse="false"
                    BusinessDocument="EPS-Permit_Rejection">
         </DocumentEnvelope>
      </RespondingBusinessActivity>
   </BusinessTransaction>
```

Unfortunately, the above BPSS doesn't meet the needs of the EPS system:

- First, there is no multilingual support – the Specification assumes that everyone who needs to interact with this document will speak the same language.
- Second, there is no definitive link to each message definition in the registry. Of course, you can specify the document's static location, but if you want to retrieve it from a registry, it must contain a unique identifier as well as a registry locator mechanism (remember the requirement for multiple concurrent implementations of the EPS system). It's not enough to assign a UID at runtime – for example, if the UID is not available at the time just after the CPA is formed, the parties cannot discover what information sets they need to send. Therefore, the BPSS must contain a UID for a document (or business message instance) it references. It must also have a UID for itself, which may be used to call the document from the CPP document.

There were other candidates to be considered for use as the business process component of EPS. We gave a good deal of consideration to the **Web Services Description Language** (**WSDL**). The main drawback with WSDL is that it only describes one endpoint to an exchange. Unfortunately, its eagerly-awaited and much-anticipated extension, **Web Services Flow Language** (**WSFL**), is also not sufficiently developed to be used in conjunction with EPS.

Another likely candidate was the **Business Process Markup Language** (**BPML**). BPML is the work of the BPM Initiative, a coalition of parties who are working on some joint intellectual property (IP) to address this exact problem. While it has some nice points, it is also relatively immature and likely to change, and this negates the main point for using a standards-based approach in building the EPS infrastructure.

*WSDL and WSFL can be referenced from http://www.w3.org/TR/wsdl and http://www.oasis-open.org/cover/wsfl.html. BPML is available at http://www.bpmi.org/bpml.esp.*

### The EPS Business Process Schema

The EPS implementers decided to use a proprietary business process schema. The schema uses the same meta data expression as the core component that is based on the current ebRIM (see the RIM meta data DTD, which we reproduced earlier, in the *Key Architectural System Requirements* section of this chapter). Because the proprietary schema is closely related to ebXML's BPSS and is only used for private processes, it should not affect interoperability and can be swapped out once ebBPSS meets the requirements of EPS.

The team spent time coming up with a very simplified solution to the problem. It was built as a short-term solution with the realization that this portion is likely to be replaced as the ebXML specifications mature. An instance of the simplified business process expression is shown below:

```
<?xml version="1.0" encoding="UTF-8"?>
<!DOCTYPE ebXMLProcessSpecification SYSTEM "BusinessProcess.dtd">
<ProcessSpecification xmlns:xlink = "http://www.w3.org/1999/xlink">
   <!--ELEMENT ProcessSpecification (ManagedObjectDetails,
                  BusinessTransactionDefinition,AssociativeDetails) -->
   <ManagedObjectDetails>
      <!-- some metadata here -->
   </ManagedObjectDetails>
   <BusinessTransactionDefinition>
      <Roles>
         <RoleDefinition ID="01" RoleLimit="1">
            <Role>Applicant</Role>
            <RoleDescription xml:lang="EN">
               This Role submits the application to the Receiver
            </RoleDescription>
         </RoleDefinition>
         <RoleDefinition ID = "02" RoleLimit="1">
            <Role>Municipality</Role>
            <RoleDescription xml:lang="EN">
               This Role receives the application and issues an
               acknowledgment receipt of the application.
            </RoleDescription>
         </RoleDefinition>
      </Roles>
      <Steps>
         <Step sequence="1">
            <Data Initiator="Applicant" action="transmit">
               http://developer.xmlglobal.com/registry/DateAssembler.xml
            </Data>
         </Step>
         <Step sequence="2">
            <Data Initiator="Municipality" action="transmit">
               http://developer.xmlglobal.com/registry/AckAssembler.xml
            </Data>
         </Step>
      </Steps>
   </BusinessTransactionDefinition>
   <AssociativeDetails> ... </AssociativeDetails>
</ProcessSpecification>
```

## Core Components

The core components used for the EPS system were derived from modeling the legacy paper forms used by the municipalities. The ebXML Core Components work delivered a stock set of core components in a catalog. While these generic core components are a great starter set, pieces of business information (like the identity of a contractor's liability insurance agent, needed in the municipality of Toronto) were absent. Luckily, ebXML Core Components are extensible, so any party wishing to extend the base set can do so.

The EPS consortium started by modeling each piece of business information needed for each set of processes. Acknowledging that the xNL and xAL schemas provide for a lot of the base pieces of information that are included in most permit applications, the teams specifically aimed at seeking unique pieces of business information. By placing the commonly-used core components (like 'name' and 'postal address') in the CPP, most permit applicants simply had to reference their EPS CPP document at the time the permit application is sent.

> *Note: ebXML describes that no formal modeling process is mandatory, however, if a modeling process is to be used, it shall be the United Nations Modeling Methodology (UMM) which relies heavily on UML. The modeling approach used herein is for demonstration purposes only.*

### Required Business Information

Starting with a single permit application process, the modeling teams were able to make a first pass list of the business information required for a permit application. Items on the list that are present in the EPS CPP were then subtracted and each of the remaining pieces of information was carefully analyzed. The table below shows a partial list of some of these core components:

| Element Name, datatype, occurrence | Description |
|---|---|
| `<BuildingAddress>`<br>string, required | The address that denotes the physical location of the property which is the subject of the permit application, considered to be used in conjunction with a municipality component |
| `<IsHeritage>`<br>Boolean, required | Whether or not the subject of the permit application is a designated heritage building, pursuant to local bylaws |
| `<LotNumber>`<br>string, required | The official city number used to identify the actual property on which the proposed permit application would be effective should the permit be approved |
| `<ArchitecturalMaterials>`<br>string, optional (dependent) | The location of the architectural drawings that describe the nature of the work in the permit application, as a URI |

This is very simplified; however, you can see the process taking shape. There are many more steps involved in building the entire set of business information sets associated with each process, but for the sake of simplicity I will continue the process description using the four pieces of information above and a reference to the EPS CPP document.

### Representing the Permit Application As a DTD

So, assuming (for simplicity) that these four pieces of information were the only ones needed for an application, we can begin to build a DTD to represent the actual permit application. The permit application, for the sake of demonstration, needs to have five pieces of information:

- CPP reference
- Building address
- Is it heritage?
- Lot number
- Architectural reference

Let's build a simple DTD to represent this permit application:

```
<!ELEMENT PermitApplication (CPPReference, BuildingAddress,
                                     LotNumber, ArchitecturalReference)>
<!ELEMENT CPPReference (#PCDATA)>
<!ELEMENT BuildingAddress (#PCDATA)>
<!ELEMENT IsHeritage (EMPTY)>
<!ATTLIST IsHeritage status (True | False) "False">
<!ELEMENT LotNumber (#PCDATA)>
<!ELEMENT ArchitecturalReference (#PCDATA)>
```

This is a very simple DTD for the permit application based on the legacy information requirements. Before we build the core components, I should explain why we have chosen to model the information using XML elements for each piece of information that is to be used as a core component. There is a very good reason for this, which should become clear in the next few paragraphs.

### A Sample Permit Application Document

We can now begin to build our core components. What does it mean to build the core components? After we collect all relevant information about each component in a syntax-neutral representation, we must decide on a way to express that information in XML syntax to be used during design time and runtime. The requirements for core components of the EPS system are that it must:

- Be able to provide a mechanism to link core components in instance messages to the items in the repository on a one-to-one basis via globally unique identifiers
- Provide a mechanism for a semantic description of each core component in English and French
- Provide a place to represent semantic equivalencies in different taxonomies, both XML and EDI
- Be able to build both atomic and aggregate assemblies of core components
- Be able to represent legal values for each core component in a variety of ways, including ranges, enumerated lists, datatypes and Boolean values, and so on
- Be able to leave a placeholder for future extensions of each core component including contextual modifications based on context drivers, programmatic constructs, and unknown extensions
- Be able to present the correct labels to use for each language usage

All of this is in addition to the ebXML registry information model. Without going into too much detail, the solution is presented in the following XML snippet. The important thing to keep in mind is that the DTD does not present all the information for each core component. All the meta data is kept in the registry information model, expressed in the registry meta data DTD. Combined, the two DTDs can carry all the informational requirements needed for each core component.

The immediate solution that allowed developers to move forward is expressed in the following sample XML fragment instance. Note that this reflects an atomic component only, although the DTD can also handle aggregates. I won't explain this instance here in this chapter, and I include the complete fragment just for illustration. For a discussion of core components, see Chapter 10:

```
<?xml version="1.0"?>
<CoreComponent type="noun"
               xmlns:rng="http://relaxng.org/ns/structure/0.9"
               defaultLocale="en_CA">   <!--(noun | verb | other)-->
  <MetaInformation>
    <Behaviour isExtensable="true" isRestrictable="false" />
```

```
    <!--(name | description | usage | copyright | license |
                                   commentary | note | code)-->

    <Documentation type="description">
      This is a core component for defining a monetary value.
      It is extensible to be reused globally
    </Documentation>
    <Documentation type="copyright">
      (c)2001 XML Global Technologies, Inc. All rights reserved.
    </Documentation>
    <Documentation type="license">
      Redistribution and use in source and binary forms, with or without
      modification, are permitted provided that such redistributions
      retain this copyright notice.
      This core component is provided "as is" and there are no expressed
      or implied warranties.
      In no event shall XML Global Technologies, Inc. be liable for any
      damages arising out of the use of this core component. By using this core
      component, you all assume risks
    </Documentation>

    <Identifiers>
      <Identifier type="primary" value="URN:UID:com-xmlglobal:80001"/>
    </Identifiers>

    <ExplanationOfUse>
      <Usage type="Atomic" instance="Element"/>
    </ExplanationOfUse>

  </MetaInformation>
  <DefaultAssembly>
    <Assembly>
      <BaseDetails>
        <ElementName>InvoiceAmount</ElementName>
        <Label>Invoice Amount</Label>
        <Description>
          Represents a monetary amount for the total of an Invoice
        </Description>
        <!--attributes available for this core component-->
        <Attributes>
          <Attribute name="UID" value="com-xmlglobal-registry:80010"/>
          <Attribute name="symbol" complexTypeRef="" value="$"
                     type="FIXED"/>
          <Attribute name="currency" value="USD"/>
        </Attributes>

        <PhysicalDetail>
          <Constraints minLength="1">
            <Regexp mask="" type="ORO" comment="integer"/>
          </Constraints>
          <SchemaFacet syntax="xsd" value="xsd:int"/>
          <PermittedValues/>
        </PhysicalDetail>
      </BaseDetails>

      <ExtendedDetails>
        <Context locale="en_CA"/>
        <Associations>
          <Association reference="URN;UID:org-xcbl:80112"
```

```
                        taxonomy="xCBL Library"
                        relationship="similar"
                        name=""
                        registry="http://www.goxml.com/ebXML" />
          <Dependency/>
        </Associations>
        <!--ContextGroups-->
        <!-- RELAX NG -->
        <rng:grammar ns="http://relaxng.org/ns/structure/0.9">
          <rng:start>
            <rng:ref name="invoiceAmount" />
          </rng:start>
          <rng:definition name="invoiceAmount">
            <rng:element ns="UID:com-xmlglobal-registry:80010"
                         name="InvoiceAmount">

              <rng:attribute name="UID">
                <rng:choice>
                  <rng:value>
                    UID:com-xmlglobal-registry:80010
                  </rng:value>
                </rng:choice>
              </rng:attribute>

              <rng:attribute name="symbol">
                <rng:choice>
                  <rng:value>$</rng:value>
                </rng:choice>
              </rng:attribute>

              <rng:attribute name="currency">
                <rng:choice>
                  <!--any ISO 4217 currency code can go here-->
                  <rng:value>USD</rng:value>
                  <rng:value>FRF</rng:value>
                </rng:choice>
              </rng:attribute>

            </rng:element>
          </rng:definition>
        </rng:grammar>
        <Processes/><!--any-->
      </ExtendedDetails>

    </Assembly>
  </DefaultAssembly>

  <!--Start of another Context-->
  <Assembly>
    ...
  </Assembly>
</CoreComponent>
```

#### Using the Core Component

How do we reference the core component from the actual permit application instances? We simply use a mechanism inherent to XML v1.0, called **fixed value attributes**, for each element in the instance document that is representing a core component. This is accomplished by appending the following line after each element declaration in the DTD:

```
<!ATTLIST elementname UID "uidValue" #FIXED>
```

We must also modify the DTD to point at the registry in which we wish to find the core components. There is no such mechanism for defining a registry URI in the ebXML specifications – and this is a single clinching argument for those who claim that ebXML is not implementable as written in the specifications. The ebXML team is working on a long-term solution. In the meantime, a short-term solution suggested by XML Global as a possible "best practice" is a simple attribute called `globalRegistryURI`, which provides any application with the registry location:

```
<!ELEMENT PermitApplication (CPPReference, BuildingAddress,
                             LotNumber, ArchitecturalReference)>
<!ATTLIST PermitApplication
          globalRegistryURI "http://registry.xmlglobal.com" #FIXED
          UID "com-xmlglobal:80332" FIXED>
<!ELEMENT CPPReference (#PCDATA)>
<!ATTLIST CPPReference registryURI CDATA #REQUIRED
          UID "com-xmlglobal:80034" FIXED>
<!ELEMENT BuildingAddress (#PCDATA)>
<!ATTLIST BuildingAddress
          UID "com-xmlglobal:80297" FIXED >
<!ELEMENT IsHeritage (EMPTY)>
<!ATTLIST IsHeritage status (True | False) "False"
          UID "com-xmlglobal:80943" FIXED >
<!ELEMENT LotNumber (#PCDATA)>
<!ATTLIST LotNumber
          UID "com-xmlglobal:80984" FIXED >

<!ELEMENT ArchitecturalReference (#PCDATA)>
<!ATTLIST ArchitecturalReference
          UID "com-xmlglobal:80297" FIXED >
```

We have now discussed all the mechanisms needed to build the EPS infrastructure driven by ebXML methodology.

### *The Future*

Many problems exist within ebXML, but I have no doubt that they will be solved. There are some proposed solutions contained within this chapter. If you adopt them now, please beware that the specifications may be subject to change, and that those changes may not necessarily be compatible with the workarounds proposed in this chapter.

## Piecing the Components Together

We have now described all the components in the EPS, and correlated each EPS component to its ebXML counterpart. Let's summarize the architecture and add in the last few pieces.

To implement the system, the organizations involved in implementation (Information Builders and XML Global Technologies) decided to use a **portal-based deployment model**. In addition, to facilitate manual applications by human users using a standard web browser, ONCE Corporation was brought on board to provide an automatic form generator. The automatic form generator creates user input forms based on certain information in the core components used in the application process. Initially, the form generator retrieves this information by performing callbacks to the registry. Once it has the information, it stores it in a local cache system to save future bandwidth.

The proposed technical architecture of the EPS application can be broken down into seven major components:

- The portal
- The ebXML registry with EPS API extensions
- The user profile manager
- The EPS application document repository
- The event processor
- The dynamic form generator
- The payment processing API

*We use the term* EPS application form *to refer to the user interface presented to the user at runtime. Once an instance of the form is created and placed in the workflow, it is then referred to as an* EPS application document.

These components are shown in the system overview diagram below, and described in high-level detail in the text that follows:

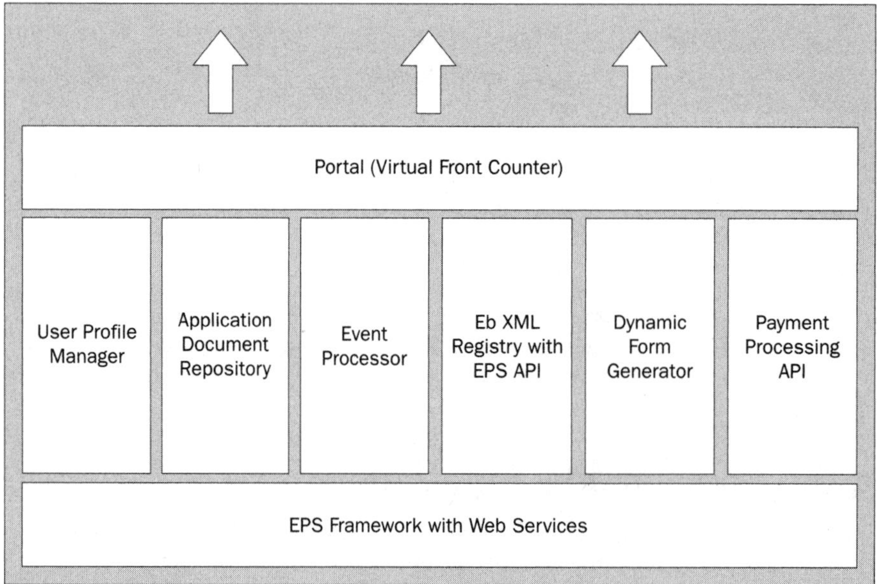


## The Portal Component

The **portal** component functions as the primary entry point to the system for a municipality, provincial government users, construction companies, and individuals applying for permits whose EPS Application Forms have been exposed via the EPS system.

A municipality is given an administrative account, with which they can define the users involved in processing or reviewing EPS application documents. Once users are set up, the administrator is able to upload form schemas, which will then be decomposed into ebXML core component definitions and placed in an ebXML registry. (XML Global provided the ability to perform this decomposition via the EPS API extension for the GoXML registry server.)

With these form definitions inserted into the system, the administrator can query the registry API for a list of core components associated with a given form, and define a form processing definition (FPD). An FPD is an XML file which defines the process flow of a form, including which users must review and approve applications, which components of a form a user has permission to view, and the procedure for review and approval of an application.

The system actor interactions are shown in the diagram:

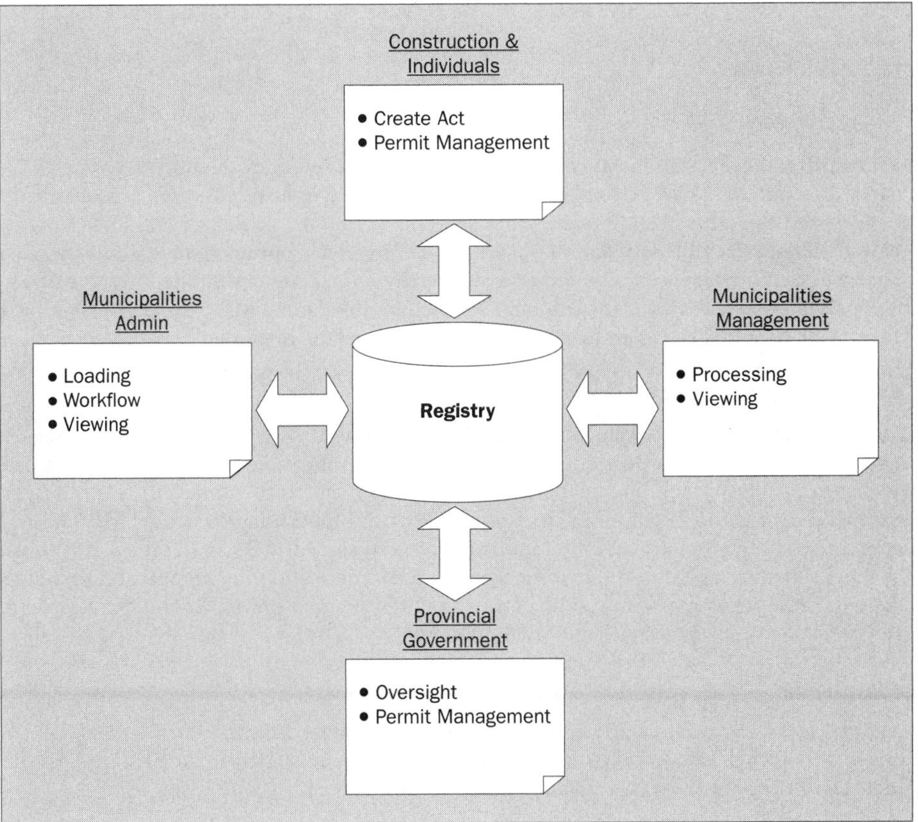


The portal provides the municipality with a simple user interface of the core component registry, where they reuse previously modeled components in their new EPS application forms.

Any construction company or individual has the ability to create an account. Subsequently it can use that account to apply for permits, to view the status of its permit applications (EPS application documents), and perform certain administrative tasks, such as printing copies of an issued permit, canceling active applications, etc.

Provincial government users are able to manage municipal accounts, and to allow broad access to the EPS system, and thereby help municipalities to manage the use and function of the EPS system. Special circumstance provincial users may also have cause to flag EPS application documents as *urgent* or *duplicate,* or with some other (as yet unidentified) status using the EPS system.

### The EPS Framework with Web Services

EPS functions exposed by the portal are also exposed as Web Services, to allow backend integration to municipalities that want to seamlessly integrate the EPS system into their own workflow. This specifically addresses the requirements of keeping the entire architecture component-based.

### The ebXML Registry with EPS API Extensions

The ebXML **registry**, with specific API extensions to support the EPS project, runs as a back-end service providing core component services to the portal and the event processor (the ebXML registry elements will be provided by XML Global). The registry server is a central aspect of the EPS architecture, as it allows role-based selection of data presented to users, and design-time services, using a standardized interface.

### The User Profile Manager

The **user profile manager** is an instance of the GoXML database (an evaluation copy can be downloaded free at http://www.xmlglobal.com/prod/db), with a lightweight, user-management-specific interface, exposed as both a Web Service and a local library on the portal server. This component relates specifically to the EPS application documents received by a municipality, which may require several users or external agencies to interact with specific information contained in the EPS application documents. Data about each user and organization will be stored in XML format as a user profile, which includes sections detailing rights and role information for specific documents.

### The EPS Application Document Repository

The EPS **application document repository** is an instance of the GoXML database that stores completed form applications. The event processor will update an EPS application document in the repository with digital signature and checksum information, as that EPS application document travels through the process flow defined in the FPD file. Each required signatory must attach a signed MD5 hash, to verify completion of the individual process. By requiring attached signed MD5 hash tables, it is possible to verify that the signature refers to the current working EPS application document, and that the EPS application document has not been modified during the inspection phase. XML Global provided software libraries to apply this checksum methodology.

### The Event Processor

The **event processor** was built using the eBIX server (provided by Information Builders). The event processor is called when the portal component receives an event related to an EPS application document. The FPD file can be dynamically translated into an eBIX control file.

### The Dynamic Form Generator

When a user wants to submit an EPS application document, the **dynamic form generator** presents the user with an interface based on business or homeowner information required by the municipality (an **EPS application form**). The information is expressed as a document, written in a form generation language, that references a set of ebXML core components. These contain information that is used by a form generator to build the EPS application form. The core components are stored in the public ebXML registry system.

The form generator is also capable of validating form input for correct values, which include (but are not limited to) the following:

- Data typing
- Enumerated lists of allowable values

#### The Payment Processing API

Payment processing is based on existing legacy procedures for each municipality brought into EPS. The **payment processing integration** was built using an API wrapper around existing payment processors, which allows us to keep interfaces consistent across all implementations.

### Software Library Downloads

The resources discussed in this chapter include many software libraries and components, which are available for use by developers. They may be downloaded from the XML Global developer web site at http://developer.xmlglobal.com. Some additional resources are located at http://java.sun.com and http://www.jdom.org.

# Summary

In this chapter, we took a detailed look at the Electronic Permit System (EPS) application, which was commissioned by a Canadian provincial government for province-wide access to municipal application processes. In particular, we focused on:

- Ways in which the EPS implementation team was able to make use of the existing ebXML specifications
- Areas in which the team found it appropriate to extend the ebXML specifications to meet the needs of the application

At the time this chapter was written, the EPS system was a closed working prototype but had not yet been implemented online. By the time this book is published, the working prototype will have been in operation for several months and it's likely that a full-blown commercial enterprise system should be well underway. Other companies and governments who are currently expressing interest in ebXML will hopefully have their pilot systems in operation too.

One of the toughest challenges facing these companies is the question of how to bridge some of the gaps that are found in the ebXML specifications at this time, while simultaneously maintaining a fair degree of interoperability. There is no easy answer to that problem; my hope is that, in 12 months time, this will no longer be a significant issue.

One last thought – be active! Get involved with the ebXML initiative and contribute to this global effort. If you are implementing ebXML, share your experiences with the community. It will help to ensure that ebXML meets the needs of all businesses, especially yours.

ebXMLFoundationsProfessional

# UML Diagram Reference

This appendix describes the different types of diagram used in UML. There are six main types of UML diagram that we will demonstrate here: **activity**, **class**, **use case**, **sequence**, **collaboration** and **state** (or **state chart**). There are two other diagram types, which are not used in this book and not demonstrated here (they are **component** diagrams and **deployment** diagrams). We'll see an example of each of the first six mentioned here, with a little commentary on how such diagrams are interpreted.

You can read more about UML in *The Unified Modelling Language User Guide* (Addison-Wesley, ISBN 0-201571-68-4) or *The Unified Modelling Language Reference Manual* (Addison-Wesley, ISBN 0-201309-98-X), or visit the UML web site, http://www.uml.org/.

## Activity Diagrams

An **activity diagram** models the behavior of a system as a flow from activity to activity, and specifies which actor is responsible for which activity. In modeling e-business systems, this diagram can be used to encode the choreography of business transactions that make up a collaboration, or of binary collaborations that make up a business process.

An activity diagram lists the performers at the top of the diagram. The activities that they perform are arranged beneath them, in chronological order – there's an implicit time line running from top-to-bottom. The arrows represent transitions between activities and states.

The following diagram, taken from Chapter 2, shows a complex activity diagram that involves two activities, three states (start, failure and success), actors, and conditions, forks and joins:

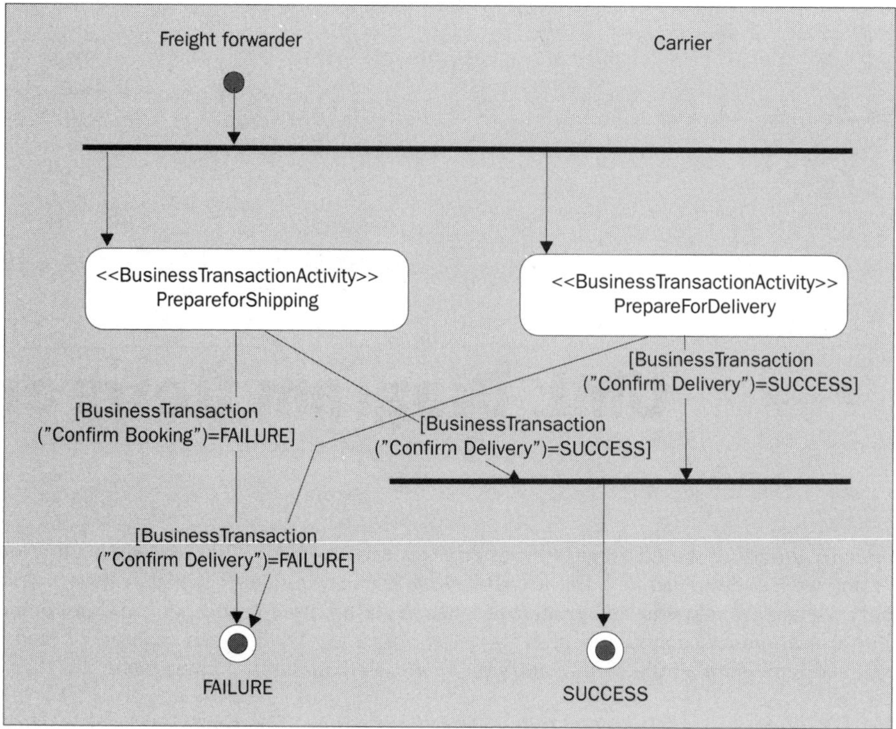


In this particular diagram, we have two actors – a 'Freight Forwarder' and a 'Carrier'. There are also two activities – 'Prepare For Shipping' and 'Prepare for Delivery'.

Apart from activity states, an activity diagram can show states that mark the start and the completion of the flow of activities (these are the filled disks and encircled disks, respectively). A completion state can be a success state or a failure state.

The horizontal bars represent parallelism in the structure. A bar with outgoing arrows is called a **fork**, and a bar with incoming arrows is a **join**. The join in this diagram, leading to the `Success` completion state, indicates that *both* activities must be completed successfully for the interaction to complete successfully.

You can add guards to transitions. A **guard** expresses a condition that must be met in order to allow the transition to be followed. You can therefore express conditional navigation among activities by having multiple guarded transitions.

# Class Diagrams

A **class diagram** is used to encode the static structure of sets of objects, and to express relationships (generalizations, aggregations, associations, and dependencies) between classes. In such a diagram, a class is represented by a box, and relationships between classes are denoted by lines between the boxes. Different types of relationship are denoted by different arrowheads (or the absence of an arrowhead).

The following diagram shows a collection of seven classes, linked via a number of relations:

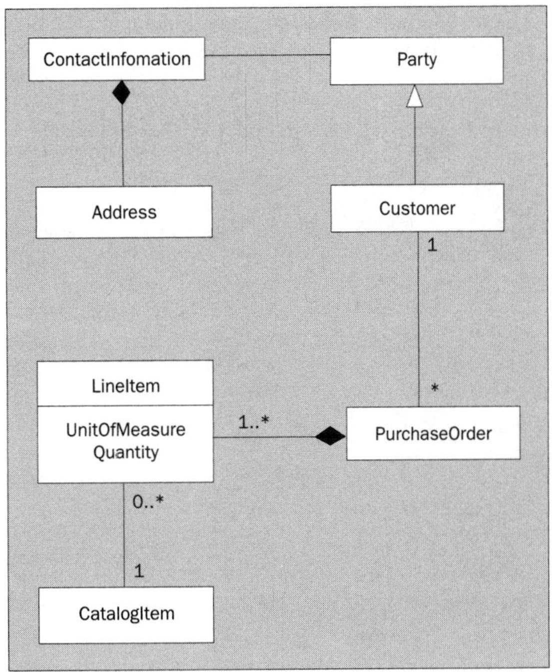


In this diagram:

- The `Party` class is a **generalization** of the `Customer` class. In other words, a `Customer` is a type of `Party`.
- The `ContactInformation` class consists of a collection of different sorts of information, including `Address` (and presumably other information, which is not displayed in the diagram). This is called an **aggregation** relationship. Similarly, the `PurchaseOrder` class is an aggregation of the `LineItem` class.
- The diagram has **cardinality** information attached to the aggregation link. It shows that there is *at least one* `LineItem` in each `PurchaseOrder` (denoted `1..*`). Similarly, each `PurchaseOrder` is issued by *exactly one* `Customer` (denoted 1) while a Customer can have issued *any number* of `PurchaseOrders` (or even none – this is denoted `*`).
- The `LineItem` class has two attributes – `UnitOfMeasure` and `Quantity`. It is also associated with the `CatalogItem` class – this association means that you can only include an item on a `PurchaseOrder` if it is a defined `CatalogItem`.

# Use Case Diagrams

A **use case diagram** associates use cases, actors, and their relationships. It focuses on "who" and "what", as opposed to "how". In an e-business context, you can use a use case diagram to express business processes and the business partners they are associated with, without looking into the internal structure of those business processes themselves.

The following diagram, taken from Chapter 2, illustrates five different types of actor, and four use cases. The arrows indicate which actors have a part to play in each use case. In this diagram, for example, the Exporter is involved in all four use cases, but the Buyer is involved in only two.

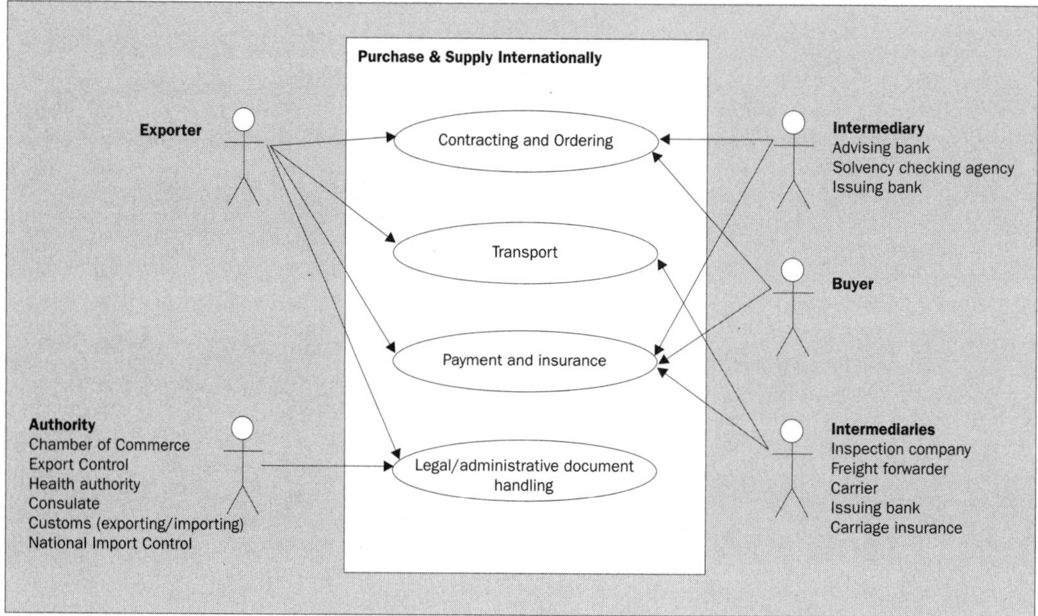

# Sequence Diagrams

A **sequence diagram** is one of two types of interaction diagram (the other is the collaboration diagram, which we'll cover in a moment). A sequence diagram shows an interaction of objects (such as business partners) with a focus on the temporal order of messages (such as business documents and business signals). The actors involved in the sequence are represented by labeled verticals, and the messages between parties are represented by horizontal arrows.

The following diagram shows a business transaction between two parties, which involves a request (for shipment insurance) and a response (which includes an electronic shipment insurance contract). There are two signals in response to the initial request: one to indicate receipt acknowledgment and one to indicate acceptance acknowledgment. There is a third signal, which confirms that the insurance contract has been received.

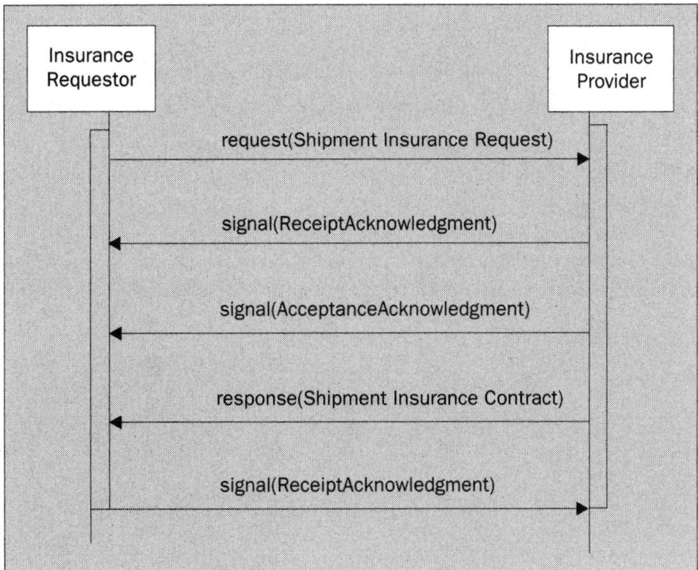


Sequence diagrams are useful when we need to express precise temporal order and synchronization. They're less useful when parallelism is involved (for example, to model the activities displayed in the activity diagram demonstration above – in that diagram, the messages that implement the two business transaction activities can occur in any order, while the sequence diagram forces us to indicate a precise order of events). In such a case, we can use a collaboration diagram.

# Collaboration Diagrams

A **collaboration diagram**, like a sequence diagram, is an interaction diagram. A collaboration diagram emphasizes the structural organization of the various objects involved.

The following example provides the same information as that shown in the sequence diagram above. Each message is labeled with a number – the numbers indicate the temporal order of the messages.

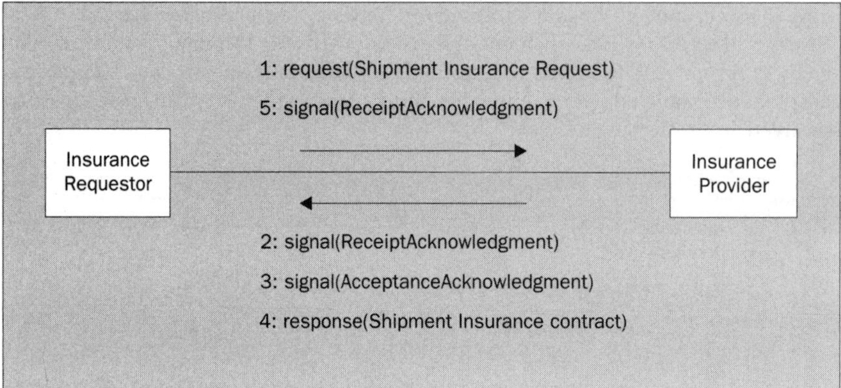


In order to express multiple parallel actions (such as two transaction activities in a collaboration), we can label the parallel activities using Dewey decimal numbers, for example 2.1, 2.2 and 2.3 for three parallel activities.

# State Chart Diagrams

A finite **state machine** is used to model the dynamics of an individual object (for instance, a business message) as the sequence of events that the object goes through in response to events.

The following diagram is a generic, and greatly simplified, state machine for receiving business activities. Note that this diagram only indicates which state the object is in and which transitions to other states it can follow. This particular diagram models the various stages of processing a request. You can easily specify loops using state charts, unlike some of the other diagrams.

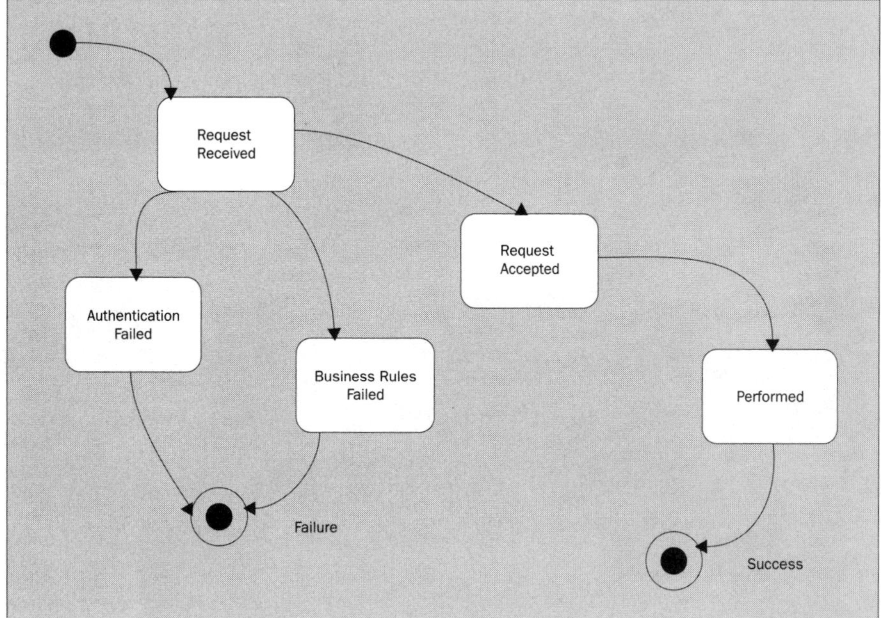

# Resources

## ebXML Deliverables

ebXML project web site: http://www.ebxml.org/

### Technical Specifications

*ebXML Requirements Specification v. 1.0.6*, ebXML Requirements Team, 8 May 2001: http://www.ebxml.org/specs/ebREQ.pdf

*ebXML Technical Architecture Specification v. 1.0.4*, ebXML Technical Architecture Project Team, 16 February 2001: http://www.ebxml.org/specs/ebTA.pdf

*ebXML Registry Services Specification*, ebXML Registry Project Team, 10 May 2001: http://www.ebxml.org/specs/ebRS.pdf

*ebXML Registry Information Model*, ebXML Registry Project Team, 8 May 2001: http://www.ebxml.org/specs/ebRIM.pdf

*ebXML Business Process Specification Schema*, 11 May 2001: http://www.ebxml.org/specs/ebBPSS.pdf

*Collaboration Protocol Profile and Agreement Specification*, ebXML Trading Partners Team, 10 May 2001: http://www.ebxml.org/specs/ebCCP.pdf

*Message Service Specification*, ebXML Transport, Routing & Packaging Team, 11 May 2001: http://www.ebxml.org/specs/ebMS.pdf

### Technical Reports

*Business Process and Information Analysis Overview*: http://www.ebxml.org/specs/bpOVER.pdf

*ebXML e-Commerce Patterns*: http://www.ebxml.org/specs/bpPATT.pdf

*ebXML Catalog of Common Business Processes*: http://www.ebxml.org/specs/bpPROC.pdf

*Business Process Analysis Worksheets and Guidelines*: http://www.ebxml.org/specs/bpWS.pdf

*Guide to the Core Components Dictionary*: http://www.ebxml.org/specs/ccCTLG.pdf

*Core Components Dictionary*: http://www.ebxml.org/specs/ccDICT.pdf

*Catalog of Context Drivers.* Version 1.04, 10 May 2001: http://www.ebxml.org/specs/ccDRIV.pdf

*Core Component Overview.* Version 1.05, 10 May 2001: http://www.ebxml.org/specs/ccOVER.pdf

*ebXML Core Components Structure*: http://www.ebxml.org/specs/ccSTRUCT.pdf

*Core Component Discovery and Analysis.* Version 1.04, 10 May 2001: http://www.ebxml.org/specs/ebCCDA.PDF

*Document Assembly and Context Rules.* Version 1.04, 10 May 2001: http://www.ebxml.org/specs/ebCCDOC.pdf

*Naming Conventions for Core Components.* Version 1.04, 10 May 2001: http://www.ebxml.org/specs/ebCCNAM.pdf

*Context and Reusability of Core Components.* Version 1.04, 10 May 2001: http://www.ebxml.org/specs/ebCNTXT.pdf

*ebXML Technical Architecture Risk Assessment.* Version 1.0: http://www.ebxml.org/specs/secRISK.pdf

### Reference Material

*ebXML Glossary.* Version 0.99: http://www.ebxml.org/specs/ebGLOSS.pdf

### White Papers

*Proposed revisions to ebXML Technical Architecture Specification* v1.0.4, 11 May 2001: http://www.ebxml.org/specs/bpTAREV.pdf

*Using UDDI to find ebXML Reg/Reps*, 8 May 2001: http://www.ebxml.org/specs/rrUDDI.pdf

*ebXML Registry Security Proposal*, 10 May 2001: http://www.ebxml.org/specs/secREG.pdf

*Risk Assessment*: http://www.ebxml.org/specs/secRISK.doc

*ebXML executive white paper:* http://www.ebxml.org/white_papers/whitepaper.htm

# Miscellaneous

***Organizations***

UN/CEFACT: http://www.uncefact.org/ and http://www.unece.org/cefact/

OASIS: http://www.oasis-open.org/

OASIS Security Services Technical Committee: http://www.oasis-open.org/committees/security/

OASIS ebXML Implementation, Interoperability and Conformance Technical Committee: http://www.oasis-open.org/committees/ebxml-iic/

OASIS ebXML Registry Technical Committee: http://www.oasis-open.org/committees/regrep/

OASIS Collaboration Protocol Profile and Agreement Technical Committee (CPPA TC): http://www.oasis-open.org/committees/ebxml-cppa/

OASIS CPPA TC public mailing list archives: http://lists.oasis-open.org/archives/ebxml-cppa/

RosettaNet: http://www.rosettanet.org/

Open Applications Group (OAG): http://www.openapplications.org/

Workflow Management Coalition (WfMC): http://www.wfmc.org/

BizTalk.org: http://www.biztalk.org

United Nations Statistical Division (UNSD): http://esa.un.org/

American National Standards Institute (ANSI): http://www.ansi.org

Uniform Code Council: http://www.uc-council.org

ACORD: http://www.acord.org

Alliance for Telecommunications Industry Solutions (ATIS): http://www.atis.org/

XML Security specialist: http://www.xmltrustcenter.org

XML Security specialist: http://csrc.nist.gov

XML Security specialist: http://www.rsa.com

UN/CEFACT Electronic Business Transition Working Group: http://www.ebtwg.org

XML Names Language Committee: http://www.oasis-open.org/committees/ciq/xnal/xnl/

XML Address Language Committee: http://www.oasis-open.org/committees/ciq/xnal/xal/

National Information Standards Organization (NISO): http://www.niso.org/

Data Interchange Standards Association (DISA): http://www.disa.org/

European Association of Aerospace Industries Standards (AECMA): http://www.aecma.org/

W3C Semantic Web Activity: http://www.w3.org/2001/sw

Metadata Subcommittee of the AAP's Metadata Information Clearinghouse (MICI): http://domino.wileynpt.com/NPT_Pilot/Metadata/mici.nsf

Korea Institute for Electronic Commerce (KIEC): http://www.ebxml.or.kr/registry/index.html

Universal Business Language (UBL) OASIS Technical Committee: http://www.oasis-open.org/committees/ubl/

UK-based Business and Accounting Software Developers Association (BASDA): http://www.basda.org

OASIS XML.org portal: http://www.xml.org/

Robin Cover's Cover Pages: http://xml.coverpages.org/

### *Standards, Initiatives, and Projects*

XML 1.0 Specification: http://www.w3.org/TR/REC-xml

Namespaces in XML Specification: http://www.w3.org/TR/1999/REC-xml-names-19990114/

XML Protocol (XMLP) a.k.a. SOAP 1.2 Working Draft: http://www.w3.org/TR/xmlp-reqs/

SOAP 1.1 note: http://www.w3.org/TR/SOAP/

XML Schema Part 2: Datatypes: http://www.w3.org/TR/xmlschema-2/

OASIS Open RELAX NG Specification: http://www.oasis-open.org/committees/relax-ng/spec-20010811.html

XML Linking Language (XLink): http://www.w3.org/TR/xlink/

Mathematical Markup Language (MathML): http://www.w3.org/TR/REC-MathML/

Resource Description Framework (RDF): http://www.w3.org/RDF/

XML Digital Signature (XML-DSIG) Specification: http://www.w3.org/TR/xmldsig-core/

XKMS: http://www.w3.org/TR/xkms/

SAML: http://www.oasis-open.org/committees/security

XACML: http://www.oasis-open.org/committees/xacml/

SHA1: http://www.w3.org/PICS/DSig/SHA1_1_0.html

Advanced Encryption Standard (AES): http://csrc.nist.gov/encryption/aes/aesfact.html

PGP cryptosystem: http://web.mit.edu/network/pgp.html

ISO 639-1 codes: http://www.oasis-open.org/cover/iso639a.html

Base 64 encoding: http://www.freesoft.org/CIE/RFC/1521/7.htm

MIME, specified in IETF RFC 1521: http://www.ietf.org/rfc.html

Dun and Bradstreet D-U-N-S (Data Universal Numbering Service) system: http://www.dnb.com

SWIFT: http://www.swift.com

EBIC (EDIRA Business Identifier Code, ISO 6523): http://www.edira.com

EAN GLNs (Global Location Numbers): http://www.ean-int.org/locations.html

SCAC (Standard Carrier Alpha Code): http://www.nmfta.org/

ABA (American Bankers Association) Routing numbers:
http://www.aba.com/Products/PS98_Routing.htm

XLANG: www.gotdotnet.com/XLANG.htm

Web Services Description Language (WSDL): http://www.w3.org/TR/wsdl

Web Service Flow Language (WSFL):
http://www-4.ibm.com/software/solutions/webservices/pdf/WSFL.pdf and http://www.oasis-open.org/cover/wsfl.html

Standards for Technology in Automotive Retail: http://www.starstandard.org/sigs/sigs_xml/default.htm

Global Commerce Initiative (GCI): http://www.globalcommerceinitiative.org/

ISO Open-edi project: http://www.iso.ch/cate/d25154.html

IBM patterns for e-business: http://www.ibm.com/developerworks/patterns/

Business Process Management Initiative (BPMI) and Business Process Markup Language (BPML):
http://www.bpmi.org/

IMS (IMS Global Learning Consortium, Inc.): http://www.imsproject.org/question/

News Markup Language (NewsML): http://www.newsml.org/

Simplified English Standard: http://www.aecma.org/Publications/SEnglish/senglish.htm

ATA (Air Transport Association) 2100 Standard: http://www.air-transport.org

Health Level 7 (HL7): http://www.hl7.org/

Open Financial Exchange (OFX): http://www.ofx.net

Interactive Financial Exchange (IFX): http://www.ifxforum.org/

Information System Agreement (ISA): http://www.isaweb.com/f_m_xml.htm

US Patent and Trademark Office XML project: http://www.uspto.gov/ebc/index.html

X12 family of standards: http://www.x12.org/

EDIFACT: http://www.edifact-wg.org/

Joint Venture Reinsurance XML Standard version 1: http://www.jvstandards.org/

Continuous Acquisition and Lifecycle Support (CALS) Standards: http://navycals.dt.navy.mil

Chemistry Markup Language (CML): http://www.xml-cml.org/

IMS Global Learning Consortium Inc: http://www.imsproject.org/metadata/index.html

Agricultural XML Metadata:
http://www.fao.org/agris/MagazineArchive/magazine/TaskForceonDCMI.htm

ISO 8601 specification: http://www.w3.org/TR/NOTE-datetime

Telematica Instituut RDS project: http://www.telin.nl/dscgi/ds.py/Get/File-17891/

UMM documentation: http://www.unece.org/cefact/docum/download/01bp_n090.zip

UMM interpretation of ITT: http://www.unece.org/cefact/docum/download/01bp015r3.doc

OMG XMI: http://www.omg.org/technology/documents/formal/xmi.htm

OMG UML: http://www.uml.org/

XML/EDI: http://www.xmledi-group.org

Zachman framework: http://www.zifa.com

BSR (Basic Semantic Register):
http://comelec.afnor.fr/servlet/ServletForum?form_name=cForumPage&file_name=TC154WG1%2FPUBLIC%2FWEB%2FENGLISH%2Fcontent.htm&login=invite&password=invite

UDEF (Universal Data Element Framework): http://www.udef.com

NIST Identifier Collaboration Service (NICS) project: http://pitch.nist.gov/nics/

Directory Services Markup Language (DSML): http://www.dsml.org

EDR (Environmental Data Registry): http://www.epa.gov/edr

UREP (Universal Repository from UNISYS): http://www.unisys.com/marketplace/urep

Ontology Markup Language (OML): http://www.ontologos.org/IFF/..%5COML/OML%200.3.htm

UN/EDIFACT D01A (First Draft of 2001) Directory: http://www.unece.org/trade/untdid/directory.htm

Component Registry: http://www.componentregistry.com

IBMs alphaWorks XML Registry/Repository (XRR): http://www.alphaworks.ibm.com/tech/xrr

xmlTree: http://www.xmlTree.com

EEMA EDI/EC Work Group Global Repository proposal: http://www.editie.nl/edifact/xml-edi.htm

ISO/IEC 11179-1 framework for the Specification and Standardization of Data Elements composition: http://www.sdct.itl.nist.gov/~ftp/l8/other/coalition/Coalition.htm

Data Interchange Standards Association (DISA) Registry Initiative (DRIve) project: http://www.disa.org/drive/

US Department of Defense (DoD) registry initiative: http://diides.ncr.disa.mil/xmlreg/index.cfm

Universal Description, Discovery, and Integration (UDDI) specification: http://www.uddi.org/specification.html

UDDI: http://www.uddi.org

IETF Electronic Data Interchange-Internet Integration page: http://www.ietf.org/html.charters/ediint-charter.html

IETF RFC 1767, MIME Encapsulation of EDI Objects: http://www.ietf.org/rfc/rfc1767.txt

UN/EDIFACT `INSREQ` message type: http://www.unece.org/trade/untdid/d01a/trmd/insreq_c.htm

XEDI approach for encoding X12: http://www.xedi.org/

European XML-EDI project: http://palvelut.tieke.fi/edi/isis-xmledi/

GoXML Central Registry: http://www.xmlglobal.com

Sun JAXR: http://www.sun.com

UNSPSC (Universal Standard Products and Services Classification): http://www.unspsc.org

NAICS (North American Industrial Classification System): http://www.naics.com/ and http://www.census.gov/epcd/www/naics.html

Standard Industrial Classification (SIC): http://www.census.gov/epcd/www/sic.html

Mappings between SIC and NAICS: http://www.census.gov/epcd/www/naicstab.htm

ISO 3166 standard: http://www.niso.org/3166.html

Microsoft GeoWeb: http://uddi.microsoft.com

Thomas register: http://www.thomasregister.com

TPAML: http://xml.coverpages.org/tpa.html

UML home page: http://www.omg.org/technology/uml/

International Standard Industrial Classification (ISIC) http://www.un.org/

UNiversal Standard Products and Services Classification (UNSPSC) http://eccma.org/unspsc/

UNSPSC Standard Industry Trade Classification (SITC): http://www.un.org/

Visa's Global XML Invoice Specification project: http://www.visa.com/

OAGI Integration Specification (OAGIS): http://www.openapplications.org/downloads/oagidownloads.htm

XML Common Business Library (xCBL): http://www.xcbl.org/

UN/EDIFACT: http://www.unece.org/trade/untdid/

ANSI Accredited Standards Committee (ANSI ASC) X12: http://www.x12.org

EJB 2.0 specification: http://java.sun.com/products/ejb/docs.html

JMS 1.0.2 specification: http://java.sun.com/products/jms/

RFC2392: http://www.ietf.org/rfc/rfc2392.txt?number=2392

JAXM: http://java.sun.com/xml/jaxm

MIME (Multipurpose Internet Mail Extensions): http://www.ietf.org/

W3C SOAP Messages with Attachments Note: http://www.w3.org/TR/SOAP-attachments

W3C SOAP Security Extensions: Digital Signature Note: http://www.w3.org/TR/SOAP-dsig

Workflow Management Coalition Workflow Standard-Operability Wf-XML Binding: http://www.wfmc.org/standards/docs/Wf-XML-1.0.pdf.

### Books

*E-commerce Security: Weak Links, Best Defenses* (Wiley, 1998, ISBN 0-471192-23-6)

*Information Warfare and Security* (Addison-Wesley, 1999, ISBN 0-201433-03-6)

*Secure electronic commerce…* (Prentice-Hall, 2000, ISBN 0-130272-76-0)

*Building B2B Applications with XML* (Wiley, 2001, ISBN 0-471404-01-2)

*B2B Application Integration. e-Business-Enable your Enterprise* (Addison-Wesley, 2001, ISBN 0-201709-36-8)

*Practical SGML* (Kluwer, 1994, ISBN 0-792394-34-8)

*Professional XML Web Services* (Wrox Press, 2001, ISBN 1-861005-09-1)

*Beginning XML 2nd Edition* (Wrox Press, 2001, ISBN 1-861005-59-8)

*Professional XML 2nd Edition* (Wrox Press, 2001, ISBN 1-861005-05-9)

*Professional XML Databases* (Wrox Press, 2000, ISBN 1-861003-58-7)

*The Unified Modelling Language Reference Manual* (Addison-Wesley, ISBN 0-201309-98-X)

*The Unified Modelling Language User Guide* (Addison-Wesley, ISBN 0-201571-68-4)

*The Unified Software Development Process* (Addison-Wesley, ISBN 0-201571-69-2)

*The Rational Unified Process: An Introduction* (Addison-Wesley, ISBN 0-201707-10-1)

*Modeling XML Applications with UML* (Addison-Wesley, ISBN 0-201709-15-5)

*Patterns for e-business: A Strategy for Reuse* (IBM Press, ISBN 1-931182-02-7)

*Communicating and Mobile Systems: the π-calculus.* (Cambridge University Press, ISBN 0-521658-69-1)

### Articles and Papers

*Using UDDI to find ebXML Registry/Repository*: http://www.ebxml.org/specs/rrUDDI.pdf

*e-BPM. The Fourth Level of IT Architecture.* J. White. http://eai.ebizq.net/bpm/white_1.html

*XML Representation of X12 EDI*: http://www.xedi.org/pdf/XEDI_Tech_Paper.pdf

*XML and EDI: Peaceful Co-Existence*: http://www.xedi.org/pdf/XEDI_Peaceful_Co-Existence.pdf

*UN/CEFACT Modelling Methodology* (CEFACT/TMWG/N090R9.1). UN/CEFACT Technology and Methodology Working Group. http://www.unece.org/cefact/docum/download/01bp_n090.zip or http://www.unece.org/cefact/docum/download/91-1.zip

*XML voor Applicatie-Integratie en Databases.* R. van der Lans. Lecture notes of a seminar delivered in Brussels, February 2001.

*XML Standards Components and Convergence. A RosettaNet Perspective.* RosettaNet presentation. http://www.rosettanet.org/dsfdf

*Standards Required to Support XML-based B2B Integration.* RosettaNet white paper. http://www.rosettanet.org/dsfdf

P&SI case: http://www.unece.org/trade/itt/itt_tip.htm and http://www.unece.org/cefact/docum/download/01bp015r3.doc

*UN-XML: The new way forward for UN/EDIFACT.* D. Raman. Presentation at the Conference Electronic Commerce Europe. Paris, 1999.

*ebXML Overview.* D. Raman. Presentation at the CEN/eBES meeting, 22/23 May 2001. http://www.cenorm.be/isss/Workshop/eBES/Documents/Document2001.htm

*ebXML Business Process.* K. Riemer. Paper presented at XML Europe 2001. http://www.gca.org/papers/xmleurope2001/papers/html/s18-1.html

*Adoption Strategies for XML Standards and the ebXML Infrastructure.* D. Nickull. Paper presented at XML Europe 2001. http://www.gca.org/papers/xmleurope2001/papers/html/s03-3.html

*A Brief History of SOAP.* D Box. http://www.develop.com/dbox/postsoap.html

*Business Modelling for UN/CEFACT.* UN/CEFACT Business Process Analysis Working Group. March 14, 2000. http://www.unece.org/cefact/docum/download/00bp024.pdf

*BPAWG Model of the International Supply Chain.* UN/CEFACT Business Process Analysis Working Group. Working Draft for the January 30, 2001 UN/CEFACT BPAWG meeting in London. http://www.unece.org/cefact/docum/download/01bp015r3.doc

*Using XML for Electronic Data Interchange.* M. Bryan. ISIS European XML/EDI Pilot Project Deliverable D9. http://palvelut.tieke.fi/edi/isis-xmledi/deliver/d9.doc

*Rules for Mapping Existing EDIFACT MIGs to XML DTDs.* M. Bryan. http://palvelut.tieke.fi/edi/isis-xmledi/d2/rules2.htm

*Conducting Business via ebXML.* S. Campbell. Paper presented at XML Europe 2001. http://www.gca.org/papers/xmleurope2001/papers/html/s03-2.html

*Comparison of deployment architectures: B2C and B2B.* B. Gold-Bernstein. Presentation at the Software Development 2000 Conference.

*Extended Enterprise Application Patterns.* IBM Patterns for E-Business Web Site: http://www-106.ibm.com/developerworks/patterns/b2bi/select-application-topology.html

*Even More Extensible. An Updated Survey of XML Business Vocabularies.* A. Kotok. August 02, 2000. http://www.xml.com/pub/a/2000/08/02/ebiz/extensible.html

*Using XML for Electronic Data Interchange: ISIS European XML/EDI Pilot Project Deliverable D9*, M. Bryan: http://palvelut.tieke.fi/edi/isis-xmledi/deliver/d9.doc

Robin Cover's discussion of modeling and XML: http://xml.coverpages.org/conceptualModeling.html

*Requirements for an XML Registry*. Logistics Management Institute (McLean, VA, USA). May 2001: http://xml.gov/lmi/registryreport.pdf

*Providing a Taxonomy for Use in UDDI Version 2*: http://www.uddi.org/bestpractices.html

UML to XML conversion: http://www.ebtwg.org

OAGI news article: http://www.openapplications.org/news/010730.htm

Open Travel Alliance (OTA) endorses ebXML: http://www.ebxml.org/news/pr_20010801.htm

Open Applications Group (OAG) endorses ebXML: http://www.openapplications.org/news/010730.htm

Covisint announces public support for ebXML: http://www.covisint.com/about/pressroom/pr/ebxml.shtml

GCI announces plans to use ebXML: http://www.ebxml.org/news/pr_20000911.htm
Namespaces FAQ: http://www.rpbourret.com/xml/NamespacesFAQ.htm

UN/CEFACT Business Process Analysis Working Group (BPAWG) working draft document on ITT as a UMM-compliant model: http://www.unece.org/cefact/docum/download/00bp024.pdf

UN/CEFACT's Technology and Methodology Working Group description of UMM: http://www.unece.org/cefact/docum/download/01bp_n090.zip

WfMC has addressed the issue of standard representations for workflow process specifications: http://www.wfmc.org/standards/docs/Wf-XML-1.0.pdf

#### *Tools/Vendors*

Omnimark: http://www.omnimark.com

Automated language translation service: http://www.FreeTranslation.com

Citrix Content management and Internet portal system: http://www.citrix.com

Datachannel Content management and Internet portal system: http://www.datachannel.com

Sterling Commerce GENTRAN: http://www.sterlingcommerce.com/solutions/products/index.asp

TIBCO Content management and Internet portal system: http://www.tibco.com

Microsoft BizTalk Server & Biztalk Mapper component: http://www.microsoft.com/biztalk/default.asp

Extensibility: http://www.tibco.com/products/extensibility/

XMLSpy: http://www.xmlspy.com/

SalCentral: http://www.salcentral.com

XMethods: http://www.xmethods.com

XMLGlobal live ebXML Registry Services implementation for testing: http://registry.xmlglobal.com

IBM UDDI operator node: http://www-3.ibm.com/services/uddi/

Microsoft UDDI operator node: http://uddi.microsoft.com

HP planned UDDI operator node: http://uddi.hp.com/

SAP planned UDDI operator node: http://www.sap.com/

Example UDDI registry designed for a private intranet: http://www.alphaworks.ibm.com/tech/UDDIreg

IBM Web Services Toolkit (WSTK): http://www.alphaworks.ibm.com/tech/webservicestoolkit

Microsoft SOAP toolkit: http://msdn.microsoft.com

Microsoft UDDI SDK: http://uddi.microsoft.com/developer/

HP Web Services Platform (HP UDDI implementation, HP SOAP, and HP Registry Composer): http://www.hp.com/go/webservices

UDDI4J: http://xml.apache.org

Idoox WASP UDDI implementation: http://www.idoox.com/products/index.html

MindElectric UDDI implementation: http://www.themindelectric.com/products/uddi/uddi.html

Bowstreet jUDDI: http://www.juddi.org

pUDDIng: http://www.opensorcerer.org

UDDI::Lite and SOAP::Lite: http://www.soaplite.com/

Xerces 1.3.1: http://xml.apache.org/xerces-j/index.html

TOMCAT: http://www.apache.org/dist/jakarta/tomcat

Apache SOAP 2.2: http://xml.apache.org/soap/index.html

Axis: http://xml.apache.org/axis/index.html

JDOM: http://www.jdom.org/

Javamail: http://java.sun.com/products/javamail

Java Activation Framework: http://java.sun.com/products/beans

J2EE (Java 2, Enterprise Edition) platform: http://java.sun.com/j2ee/

SonicMQ3.5 JMS provider: http://www.sonicsoftware.com

goXML database: http://www.xmlglobal.com/prod/db

XACML and XML DSIG: http://alphaworks.ibm.com/tech/xmlsecuritysuite

Annotated Rainbow DTD: ftp://ftp.ebt.com/nv/nv/dtd/rainbow/rbow2-5.rtf

# Index

## A Guide to the Index

The index is arranged hierarchically, in alphabetical order. Most second-level entries and many third-level entries also occur as first-level entries. This is to ensure that users will find the information they require however they choose to search for it.

## A

# B

# C

# D

# E

# H

# I

# J

# N

# O

# P

# Q

## R

# T

# U

# V



# W

# Z

Notes